WineSpeak

Entire books have been written ridiculing winespeak.
Dorothy J. Gaiter and John Brecher

That sort of winespeak *drives me personally crazy.*
It tends to make me very nervous. Too much talk
about wine is like too much talk about sex.
Jonathan Nossiter

A peculiar subgenre of the English language
...has flowered wildly in recent years, like
some pulpy jungle plant. It's called winespeak.
Frank J. Prial

The result is winespeak, *the strange artificial*
language that purports to reduce flavours to their
components, and which packages every bottle in a
fragrant envelope of metaphors.
Roger Scruton

Yet in the last few years—and I can't explain why—
winespeak *has reached a dazzling state of hyper-*
fermentation, releasing a gaseous haze of verbiage
that can be seen from Sonoma to Saint-Julien.
Bryan Miller

Talking about smell and taste is difficult, mired in
metaphor, and winespeak *all too often seems a*
private language, confusing insider talk that requires
some extended and elaborate initiation to penetrate.
Elin McCoy

:WineSpeak:

A vinous thesaurus of (*gasp!*) 36,975

bizarre, erotic, funny, outrageous, poetic, silly and ugly

wine tasting descriptors.

Who knew?

Bernard Klem

WineSpeak Press LLC
Stamford CT USA

WineSpeak

A vinous thesaurus of (*gasp!*) 36,975
bizarre, erotic, funny, outrageous, poetic, silly and ugly
wine tasting descriptors. Who knew?

Published by Wine*Speak* Press LLC,
Stamford, Connecticut.
www.winespeak.com/whineman@optonline.net

Distributed by the Wine Appreciation Guild,
South San Francisco, California.
www.wineappreciation.com

ISBN 978-0-9800648-0-3

The author acknowledges all legally
registered trademarks and trade names.

Designed by the author.

The digital typeface is *Kinesis*, designed by
Mark Jamra for Adobe Systems, San Jose, California.

All the illustrations are copyrighted;
the front cover and title page illustrations are from
New Vision Technologies, Ottawa, Canada;
all the other illustrations are from
Jupiter Images, Tucson, Arizona.

Manufactured in the United States by
Bang Printing, Brainerd, Minnesota.

This book is available at
special quantity pricing.
Please inquire for further details.

Note: No grapes were harmed
        in the making of this book.

To Rosalind,

who has lovingly shared my life,
and all the wines in it,
for over half a century.

I could not ask for more.

Great people talk about ideas,
average people talk about things, and
small people talk about wine.
Fran Lebowitz

But, Fran, what if people talk
about important wine ideas?
The author

Examine the contents, not the bottle.
The Talmud

*No man understands a deep book until he has
seen and lived at least part of its contents.*
Ezra Pound

*Road signs and indicators are the table of contents,
the index and the page numbers all at once.
If you had a book without those things,
you'd never be able to read it.*
Reyn Bowman

Contents

What we call the beginning is often
the end. And to make an end is to
make a beginning. The end is where
we start from.
T.S. Eliot

Once in the wilds of Afghanistan...I
lost my corkscrew, and we were
forced to live on nothing but food and
water for days.
W.C. Fields

I. Where It All Began

When did you first discover real table wine? Not the gaggingly sweet swill that
passed for wine during important holiday meals. And certainly not that ghastly
watery plonk we guzzled down in college, when we tried but failed to be sophisticated. Like you, my own wine epiphany probably took place in Europe, where
table wine was and still is as common a companion to meals as fresh bread. And
where both should always remain so.

Like most people, I know a lot about very few things, but little about very many
others. Wine was one of those many others I knew virtually nothing about, as
with most young Americans of my generation. It was in 1959 that I discovered the
pleasures of fermented grape juice only after being assigned to West Germany to
serve as one of Uncle Sam's unknown military counterintelligence agents.

As newlyweds living off-base in a rather moderne pie-shaped apartment in the
small Stuttgart suburb of Zuffenhausen (we could see the Porsche test track from
our tiny but high balcony), my beautiful wife, Rosalind, and I tried as many of the
European wines as we could afford, drinking mainly the cheap young local German whites hoping to find out what wine was all about. At the time, we believed
they were pretty good, but only later back in New York did we discover that the
now legendary '59s were thought to be an incredible vintage in Germany, and that
we had been washing down chicken and goulash and wursts with some of the finest Rhines and Mosels ever crafted. Like I said on the front cover, *who knew?*

During military leaves, we chugged around Western Europe in our little white
VW bug, (Max cost us US$1200 brand new), eating and drinking many of the local
specialties, most of which were cheap, filling and tasty. Once, visiting friends sta-
tioned in the storied palace town of Fontainebleau, just southeast of Paris, we real-

ly enjoyed some long, but not so cheap, memorable dinners with red wines we had never known before. Very, very fine stuff, we thought at the time. Needing something to remember that gastronomic trip, we decided to split with our friends a case of 1955 Château Cheval Blanc, for which we paid about $10 a bottle, a real extravagance at the time but still a treasured buy. Only six years old at the time, they were, of course, more than simply wonderful; to this day, we remember them and their velvety richness in our mouths. With typical American naiveté and impatience, we drank all six up before we left for home in the middle of 1961. (Today they would be worth over $1,000 a bottle. Oh, well.)

I've been drinking wine off and on ever since, trying all kinds, whatever presented itself. I claim no expertise in matters of wine's smell or taste; turns out my nose is septally challenged and therefore not up to serious wine smelling. As a consequence, I have nothing but unalloyed admiration for all the real wine experts who taste for hours every day, and write about it every night. I can only envy their zealous devotion to the grape.

When retirement finally came around within the last decade, I started reading more about wine, becoming intrigued by the florid language used to describe it. Where did this all come from and what was behind it? I asked myself the obvious question: why does wine remind so many people of so many different things? Are all these things really in the wine? How did they get there?

To find out the answers, in 2001 I started to collect these fanciful descriptors, first in a shoebox, then in a file cabinet, finally in a computerized database. Over the last few years, my collection of wine tasting descriptors grew to near unmanageable size. I simply had to do something with this evergrowing monster. But what? A book! Of course, a book, but who would read it? The casual wine drinker? The serious wine lover? The winery publicist and wine-label copywriter? The professional wine critic/writer? Except possibly the first group, all of them, I hoped. Perhaps even enthusiasts of the endlessly rich, poetic English language. Or better still, people like me who love both language *and* wine.

Moving further into the twenty-first century of wine appreciation, we know only one thing for sure: there'll be lots of changes to come, among them new vineyards and vintners, new turf fights, new and different wines, newly discovered health benefits of drinking red wine in moderation, new tastes, new styles, new labels, new containers, and of course new closures. Plus many more words to add to the vast vocabulary of the artful science of wine looking and wine smelling and wine tasting and wine drinking. Hooray for you and hooray for me!

Any pursuit filled with jargon is largely make-believe.
Thorstein Veblen

When it came to writing about wine, I did what almost everybody does—I faked it!
Art Buchwald

A good general rule is to state that the bouquet is better than the taste, and vice versa.
Stephen Potter

II. Speaking in Tongues

Wine reviews can be fun, just plain hilarious. You've only to sample the few below to find out what this collection of wine tasting language is all about:

What a year for lovers of fruity wines! Italy's 1997 Grande Scodella Frutta Mista (from Sicily, where else?) is causing a sensation. The color of blood-feud crimson with a touch of vendetta red on the rim, this curiously imprecise blend of the island's local grape varieties, Frappato Nero, Gaglioppo, Nerello Cappuccio, Nerello Mantellato, Nerello Mascalese, Nero d'Avola and Perricone, delivers a nose featuring no less than an avalanche of apples, a banquet of bananas, a barrel of berries, a cantata of cantaloupes, a chorus of cherries, a circus of citrus, a colossus of coconut, a crash of cranberries, a fiesta of figs, a pinch of pink grapefruit, odds and ends of guava skins, lemons sweet and lemons bitter, lingonberries and loganberries, mangoes manifest, nectary nectarines and, of course, the life-affirming blood oranges (again, Sicilian). Our mouth is also threatened by peaches, pears, pineapples and plums, with an occasional assault by rhubarb, strawberries, tangerines and watermelons. This aggressive much too lively fruit-forward bomba makes for very immediate drinking (yesterday would be none too soon) but will be superb as the accompaniment to any hastily eaten meal in a dimly lit local clam bar.

If fruit isn't your thing, perhaps romance is. Wine writers have been using the suggestive vocabulary of love and sensuality for a long, long time. Be forewarned, however: only those over the age of consent may read the review that follows:

Here's a sensual lust-crazed '99 Burgundian Pinot Noir from the bosom of the Côte de Nuits that erotically caresses your nose with voluptuous aromas of sultry musks and exotic spices that embrace, arouse and finally seduce you into a passionate affair with this impatient virgin ripe for the picking. The tarted-up taste of plump ripe flesh bursts upon the palate like a carefully orchestrated orgasmic crash of wave after wave of sinful flavors, ending with a satisfying afterglow of incredible length. Exhausting but deeply fulfilling. Rates a 93 after a weekend away together. O, Oh, OH...!

Still not convinced this is something you'd dare try tonight in a close romantic encounter? Then be especially brave and try the other end of the scale, where the unspeakable might lurk in your glass when you take an innocent sip:

If ever there was an alien beast of a wine, this truly disgusting Australian Shiraz from the ugly 1981 disaster of a vintage should scare the living hell out of you. This is a crazed predator whose mangled nose reeks of armpit, crushed bugs and animal gut, and attacks like Godzilla destroying all in its path. Avoid this horror at all cost, lest you fall victim to an assault of rancid cat pee, soiled diapers and raw sewage, forcing you to turn this way and that to escape. But there's more: affronts to the nose and palate also include dirty socks, old running shorts, ladies' panties, rubber boots and unwashed underwear. No one could possibly forget what this grisly swill also conjures up: a pigsty, an overheated chicken coop, a men's room in a French railway station. At least not this reviewer. Ever. On a scale of 100, a zero is far too high for this utterly ghastly plonk from Down Under. No gooday here. Shame!

Okay, okay, I confess to having concocted the reviews above using actual terms from this book. Makes you almost want to return to pure bottled spring water, doesn't it? But be assured there's much to learn and enjoy from these thousands of descriptors used by working wine tasters sampling real wines from around the world. Keep your mind wide open. Your eyes, nose and mouth, too. The more wine you try, the more knowledgeable you'll become. And when you need to find just that perfect word or phrase, however broad or nuanced, come here to the wacky wonderful world of *WineSpeak*, the most complete and authoritative assemblage of English wine tasting language anywhere.

Wine appreciation is an entirely subjective process.
Jancis Robinson

Many critics are articulate but can't taste their way out of a paper bag.
Ronn Wiegand

Experts tell us that wine is good for the body, the mind, the soul, the spirit and everything else that matters. What else do we need?
The author

III. Thank You, Thank You, Thank You

to every hard-working wine authority, critic, educator, reviewer and writer of newspaper and periodical articles, books, blogs and website materials (listed in the Bibliographic Resources starting on page 323) whose creative works form the basis of this book (and apologies to anyone I missed inadvertently).

In particular, special honors must go to three outstanding international scholars whose landmark works have both defined and refined the language of professional wine tasting: Maynard Amerine of the United States, Michael Broadbent of the United Kingdom and Émile Peynaud of France.

I must also thank the talented British satirist who created, in 1983, the hilarious artistic spoof of the wine taster's vocabulary: *The Illustrated Winespeak: Ronald Searle's Wicked World of Winetasting.* He concluded his introduction with, "The tortuous phrases that are frequently used when trying to describe music fade into insignificance beside the agonizing and often excruciating acrobatics of those whose duty it is to enlighten the baffled consumer regarding the more esoteric aspects of, say, Rotterdam rouge." Amen.

Extra thanks are also due to some very nice people who helped me at various stages along the way: Ken Anderson, Tony Aromando, Katrin Ashear, Robert Bowden, João Roque Dias, Jim Elder, Betsy Fischer, Nicholas Guild, Ronald Jackson, Mark Jamra, Adrienne Lehrer, Steve Lo, MD, Elliott Mackey, Peter Marks, Diane McKeever, Joy Nuell, Dante Ramos, Jennifer "Chotzi" Rosen, Bob Ross, Peter Ruhrberg, Emily Shiller, Ilene Strizver and Al Zuckerman.

Of course, I couldn't possibly show enough gratitude to my wonderful family for putting up with me during years of collecting and organizing terms. I hope their eye-rolling days are now over. Loving thanks to you all: especially my long-suffering yet endlessly supportive wife, Rosalind, to whom this book is dedicated; my everpatient sons and daughters-in-law, Laurence and Tina, as well as Jordan and Michelle; and my three beautiful, bright and shiny grandsons, Adam, Aaron and Kyle, who are still much too young to enjoy wine, let alone appreciate its incredible language. I hope that when they do get to wine-drinking age they'll toast the memory of their wine- and word-loving Papa. He cherished them all beyond measure.

Finally, an eerie postscript: the kind staff of Kevin Zraly (a gentleman I never met), the first cellarmaster and wine director of the Windows on the World Restaurant and also the renowned wine educator of the Windows on the World Wine School, helped to start this book off by mailing me a good long list of 500 or so wine tasting terms that he used in his classes. Ironically, I received the list by snail mail late in the morning of September 11, 2001. Watching that catastrophe unfold on live television, I was simply too stunned to connect the destruction of the world-famous twin towers with the horrific end of that renowned venue atop One World Trade Center, in the north tower. Somewhat later that ghastly week, I was very relieved to find out that Mr. Zraly himself miraculously survived the catastrophic attack, although 72 of his co-workers tragically did not. There are no words available anywhere, in any known language, to fully express the indelible horrors of that awful autumn morning now everywhere remembered as simply 9/11*, the unforgettable disaster that changed our world forever.

*How ironic that we write that ghastly date in, of all things, Arabic numerals.

There's hardly ever a "correct" answer to the question of a wine's taste.
Fred Du Bose and Evan Spingarn

Describing taste is even more complicated, because wine professionals use various words that don't necessarily have the same meaning for everyone.
Mary Ewing-Mulligan & Ed McCarthy

The closest we can come to describing flavours (which we actually perceive in aromas, whether we're tasting food or drink) is to find flavour similes.
Jancis Robinson

IV. Vino Lingo

Alone at Last If a thirsty wine lover lives alone on a desert island with enough wine to drink for a lifetime (don't ask how it got there), he or she wouldn't need any language to describe all that vino. A simple grunt of satisfaction or disgust would be sufficient. However, if two people were the sole residents of same, they would feel a need to talk; they might want to *com-mun-i-cate* about survival, maybe even about the wine. Something like, "Not bad, eh?" Perhaps, "Needs more time, you think?" Or, "Let's save this bottle to celebrate when we finish the hut."

Chat 'n Chew Just think of all the energy we'd save if we lived alone with no one to talk with, no one to dine with, party with, or compare notes with about food and wine. If you want to imagine what Hell would really be like, picture human existence without language. Fortunately, billions of us humans babble and jabber all day and long into the night because we simply must talk to each other, and very often about what we could, should and do put in our mouths.

Is...Isn't...Is...Isn't There are many excellent manuals on how to taste wine, but this isn't one of them. Nor is this instruction on how to hold a wine tasting event. In addition, it certainly isn't about either viticulture, the study and practice of growing grapes, or viniculture, the study and practice of turning grapes into wine. And finally, you won't find an exhaustive glossary here describing every one of the approximately 8,000-10,000 known varieties of grapes (depending on who's count-ing), together with their many clones, crosses and hybrids. Rather, this is a determined attempt to organize the many diverse ways wine tasters describe the unique sensations of wine in all its guises. One wine critic comfortable with aesthetics fittingly called the language of wine tasting "taste pictures." A pithy summary of how we humans deal with the more than 1,000 chemical components found in wine.

Sensational Experts tell us that we can only describe our sensory impressions in terms of stored recollections, what some call "associative memory." They also tell us that, of our five senses, smell is the strongest and most direct retriever of memories. For example, the smells of fresh-cut grass, warm bread, or any combination of vanilla, cinnamon and sugar can instantly return us to the more innocent period called *childhood*. We always seem to remember Grandma's warm blueberry pie, or fresh strawberry shortcake, or hot pancakes slathered with butter and maple syrup.

Mine, All Mine As prisoners of our sensory receptors, we're easily befuddled when experiencing a bewildering variety of impressions upon smelling and tasting both familiar and new wines. Consequently, the lexicon in the main part of this book is as open ended as human experience itself. No two people, experts included, will ever describe the exact same wine in exactly the same way. After all, not all of us have seen the color called "tile red," smelled fresh eucalyptus, tasted pie made only from genuine Key limes, or allowed our tongues to confront sandpaper. Which is exactly how there came to be so many different descriptions of wine.

Wine is Life, say the poets. If true, then the language of wine should be just as full of life. And so it is, sometimes too much by half. So what's a wine lover to do? Give up? No. Read on? Yes. The reasons are not very complicated: more people are better educated, better read, better fed, better traveled and better financed. Consequently, as more people the world over discover the pleasures of drinking wine, and talking and writing about it, they also expand the vocabularies they use to describe it. The result is a huge warehouse of descriptors that illuminates, yet sometimes confuses. Obviously, there's a need to organize all these tasting terms.

Winespeak This, then, is the result: the first major celebration of the imagery created when we articulate what we experience in this liquid, unique in all the world. For the enthusiastic oenophile this unique compendium of the wine tasting vocabulary has incorporated an always-growing tower of babble, an amazing catalogue of classic and trendy terms, metaphors of every stripe, emotional labels, romantic monikers, tiresome clichés, jarring jargon, an avalanche of adjectives, the most fanciful flights of poetry, verbal acrobatics, florid allusions, hyperbole to excess, unrestrained imagery, the whimsical, the anthropomorphic, the bizarre, the strange, the erotic, the outlandish, the mysterious, the utterly fantastic, the just plain silly and the outright funny. Nowhere else does language become so invigorated after swallowing who-knows-how-much wine. It seems that the mind gently, or not so gently, prodded by complexly flavored alcohol becomes a wondrous instrument of unrestrained creativity. Is it any wonder, therefore, why wine descriptors number in the thousands, far more than anything else we eat or drink?

A Coat of Many Colors No beverage in the known world, other than a hallucinogenic, evokes so many images as does wine. And to think that the grape vines simply pull these chemical compounds, almost all masquerading as familiar aromas and tastes, up from the soil through their roots, through the tough trunk up into the vines, and finally into the buds and flowers that mature into fruit. Utter magic. Just the briefest glance at the any of the categories shows what a great conjuring artist wine is. Drinking it allows us to truly enjoy this liquid chameleon.

Palate Loses by a Nose The adjective *organoleptic* doesn't describe a thief who steals body parts. It's just a mouthfilling mid-nineteenth-century word meaning "acting on or involving the use of the sense organs," particularly the nose (smell) and the mouth (taste). In the context of wine, all tasting is a joint effort between the two, smelling usually preceding, and absolutely dominating, tasting in the mouth. In fact, many professional wine reviewers merely take a few deep sniffs of a wine before rating it (swallowing is done only rarely when the wine is so exceptionally fine that the taster feels compelled to swallow). Yet, most professionals in the wine trade prefer to maintain the historic distinction between what *nose* (or *smell*, *aroma* or *bouquet*) tells them and what *palate* (or *taste* or *mouth*) tells them. The great British wine expert, Jancis Robinson, refers to the "palate picture." The well-known American wine teacher, Kevin Zraly, says wine *tasting* should really be called wine *smelling*. So long as we don't pour wine directly into our noses, I'm fine with that.

The Tongue Map is All Wrong One of the enduring myths in human sensory perception is that the tongue has specialized tasting regions for perceiving sweet, sour, bitter and salty. (A fifth, called *umami*, the Japanese word for *savory*, has been added recently.) Most books that touch on this topic also erroneously illustrate the classic four tongue areas of specialization. Wrong, wrong, wrong. There are no specialized taste perception regions of the tongue, as taste buds are scattered all around the mouth, especially on the tongue, but also on the soft palate, gums and even the entry to the throat. This century-old mistake resulted from a misinterpretation as well as a poor translation from German to English of a 1901 Harvard PhD dissertation by the psychologist, Dieter P. Hänig. So much for a long-standing chestnut.

Noses and Palates of Gold Renowned wine connoisseurs seem to be born with special equipment that most of us simply don't have: incredibly discriminating sensory receptors for smells and tastes that allow these gifted experts to detect every delicate shading of difference among everything they sample. Most of these supersmellers probably have a condition called *hyperosmia*, a heightened sense of smell; supertasters may have the condition of *hypergeusia*, an extrasensive sense of taste. They also have laserlike powers of concentration and legendary memories to store this vast sensory input over most of the course of their long lives. Who among us doesn't envy these sensory masters, particularly when they also have the gift of poetic language?

The Sin of Synesthesia As if *hyperosmia* and *hypergeusia* weren't heavy enough burdens, just think of the poor souls who are *synesthetes*, that is, people who suffer from, or are gifted with, *synesthesia*. This rare condition allows those affected to experience crossover sensory perceptions, such as the ability to *smell black* or *taste red*, etc. For most of us, life is complicated enough without blurring the ordinary boundaries of our five normal senses.

Wine Bards No fanciful prose has been more enjoyable and entertaining than that written by the natives of Britain, whose ancestors not only created and developed the English language, but who now use (some say *abuse*) so many of the more poetically over-the-top descriptors. Thank you, dear Brits, for contributing so much colour and flavour and humour and vigour.

Yay-Boo Wine reviewers are all over the map of wine tasting, unsurprisingly so. With just as many personal preferences as we ordinary drinkers, some critics and reviewers find fruit or oak everywhere, some detect minerals or tannins in the smallest quantity, some are overpowered by alcohol, some crave acid beyond all other components, while others have strong aversions to the minutest degree of sweetness. It's also interesting to observe how professionals agree, and disagree, tasting the very same wine. A recent example unfortunately went too public when two of the most renowned wine experts (one Brit, one Yank) strongly battled each other across the pond over a prominent Bordeaux; one called it a classic of the very highest standard, while the other characterized it as nearly undrinkable plonk. It was an out-and-out Anglo-American wine fight, and is still unresolved.

Best of the Best The 20 Special Collections are all my ways of highlighting what I personally believe are the most interesting descriptors, and are arranged in normal word order, such as *all lace and finesse*. Not everyone will agree about emphasizing the poetic, strange, erotic or mysterious qualities of wine. But I do; I selected them.

Order of Battle I've also ordered all the 27 Categories more or less in the logical sequence of wine appreciation: first, *Appearance*, then, *Smell and Taste*, and finally, *Distinctiveness*. This is how we generally evaluate wine: we look at it (winesight), swirl it, smell it, taste it, and finally spit or swallow it (I swallow, you can spit). Only then can we judge whether the wine is balanced or not, if it has varietal or other typical characteristics, how long it lasts in our mouths and throats and, perhaps more importantly, how do we want to remember it. Despite every wine taster having his or her own techniques, we all aim for the same judgment: woe or wow!

Please be aware that the entries in these 27 Categories are arranged differently, with headwords first, such as *lace and finesse, all*, a logical requirement for keyword alphabetical sort order in the full database. Sorry. (It's the software programmer's fault, not mine.)

Finally, to avoid needless repetition, many of the terms don't repeat the name of the category they're in; thus, a descriptor in the category *Fruit* can be listed simply as *juicy* rather than as *fruit, juicy*.

Oaky-Doaky With 868 entries, the sturdy oak totally dominates the entire category of *Wood*. Of the 400 or so species of oak, only a few of them are good enough to marry with wine. Therefore, by tradition and choice, oak is the king of woods in both vinifying and aging of wine, adding much of its unique creamy, smoky and, more often, vanillary qualities to the natural complexity of smells and tastes. Vintners have tried other woods, but none has ever been so successful as oak. It just seems grapes and oak are destined to walk together through enological history. *Caveat Emptor* I also didn't attempt to determine whether a wine is thought to be fairly priced or not. Price is not always a direct or fair indictor of quality, and many times there is simply no relationship whatsoever between them. Very expensive wines can disappoint; affordable ones can enthrall. So where's the formula? All you really need do is stroll around a well-stocked wine store today and compare prices of varietals and blends. Is this bottle of Château Haughty at $99.90 ten times more delicious and satisfying than the $9.99 Bounding Kangaroo down the row? Is this $30 non-vintage sparkler only a tenth as flavorful as the $300 bottle of vintage Champagne? I personally think not. In the context of this work, whether a wine is worth its cost is an area better left to the original wine review.

Food Fight! Nor have I included any suggestions for matching particular wines to particular foods, although many wine reviewers think it's essential to their work of educating the public. I don't. If I have quite a nice Pinot Noir, I don't want to be told how perfect it would be with roast duck or sautéed soft-shell crabs (both of which I love). When I don't want to eat meat one evening, I certainly don't want to be lectured as to why Zinfandel is too strong to pair with pasta or salad.

I'm also quite happy to drink wine with or without food, and enjoy food with or without wine. Wine should not be the mindless handmaiden of food; nor should food be slavishly servile to wine. Just enjoy them any way you want.

Oy! In Daniel Rogov's *Guide to Israeli Wines 2007*, he lists two kosher wines, one a Barkan and the other a Carmel, as showing hints of smoked bacon. Like I said: *Oy!*

Funny Coincidence Department There are at least six descriptors that popped up connoting smoothness (the original is probably unknowable); we simply have no clue as to whether the slippers were silk or velvet, or whether the pants or trousers were velvet or silk. No matter, the theological analogy is very clear:

> *As smooth as baby Jesus in velvet pants and silk slippers,* or
> *Baby Jesus in silk slippers sliding down your throat,* or
> *Baby Jesus in velvet pants going down your gullet,* or
> *Baby Jesus sliding down your throat in velvet slippers,* or
> *Slides down your throat like the good lord Jesus in silk trousers,* or
> *The good lord Jesus in silk slippers sliding down your throat.*

Wheels Within Wheels There are now so many descriptors of the many things one can find in wine that some wine lovers have attempted to organize them in an interesting way: wheels. So many, in fact, that I now have a whole fat folder filled with samples of them, beginning with the mother of all wine wheels, Ann Noble's 1990 *Wine Aroma Wheel* from the University of California at Davis. I have aroma wheels only and taste wheels only, combination wine aroma and taste wheels, wheels for red wine and wheels for white, a mouthfeel wheel from Australia, a wheel for barrel oak- and toast-derived wood flavors, a brandy wheel, a wine color wheel, a Canadian ice wine wheel, some wine chemistry wheels, a Zinfandel aroma wheel, red and white German wine aroma wheels, a wine education wheel, wine IQ wheels, interactive wheels about wine, a wine cellar organization wheel, wine and food match wheels, and on and on and on. What is it with wheels? Don't we have enough problems just driving? Help!

Common Ground As an aid to help future wine evaluators, I have included, on page 318, a separate long list of *Quantifiers 'n Stuff* containing such things as *a bit of*, *a little, lots of,* etc. You can use almost all of them with an abundance of abandon.

To the Wine Pro If you write about wine professionally, you need this book. Feel free to borrow any descriptors listed, as they're an essential part of your livelihood. The words are yours and those of your colleagues in the trade. So look, swirl, sniff, taste, spit and write on.

To the Wine Lover Take this book along to your next wine tasting event to help make that experience more pleasurable. Or illuminating. Or just plain hilarious.

To Everyone Else For those of you who wish to add, correct or challenge any descriptors, or simply to comment about anything in this book, please contact the appreciative author at *www.winespeak.com*. He'll probably be hard at work on the newly updated, revised, expanded and improved second edition. With an open bottle of sturdy (red, of course) old-vine Zin nearby.

May 2009
Stamford, Connecticut USA

The lexicon of smells is riddled with
descriptions of how a smell makes us feel.
Gene Wallenstein

*Scientists have identified five hundred
different wine aromas.*
Jens Priewe

*The number of words which can usefully
be made to describe or assess wine is limited.*
Auberon Waugh

*There are perhaps a couple of hundred words used
by experts to describe the qualities of wine, and
their meaning is surprisingly precise.*
Forrest Wallace and Gilbert Cross

Oh, really?
The author (is that me to the left?)

A. Author's Favorites *[A Must Read]*

If you only have time to read a single list of wine tasting descriptors, this is the
one. These dozen pages contain the best of the best, a truly amazing assortment
of my all-time favorites culled from the master *WineSpeak* database. Keep in mind
that these are all real quotes from real wine reviews; no one in any rational or
sober state of mind could possibly make them up. For the record, I don't understand a lot of them, either. So please enjoy these flights of fancy from many well-
lubricated writers, all working day and night in the service of wine appreciation.
It would be nice if you could raise a glass to honor their creative efforts.

aborigine's armpits
about as friendly as a sumo wrestler
    with diaper rash
about as subtle as the Vegas Strip
absolute nightmare
acidity acts as a sort of embalming fluid
acidity reminds you of inhaling a
    small electric eel
a health hazard
akin to drinking the blood of the grape
a levitating experience; for minutes
    I could neither see nor feel my
    surroundings—nor did I care to as
    this wine took my senses hostage
all litchi all the time

all-star linebacker who has studied years
    of ballet
all the charm of a mouthful of steel wool
all the grace of a parade of Hummers
all the subtlety of a chain saw
almost as rare as rocking-horse dung
almost Episcopalian in its predictability
almost oxymoronic freshness and
    maturity
alpine meadows inhabited by of-age
    nymphs
amped-up grassy, gooseberry, cat pee
    elements
anal
an angel peed on my tongue

angel of death is hovering overhead
angel sweat
annual convention of homemade jams
a nose so dumb it had to be dragged out
  screaming
anticipated maturity: now to doomsday
armpits of a healthy clean-living youth
  after exercise
aromas as sweet and erotic as a handbag
  full of lipsticks and scents
as comfortable as old jeans
as dark as the bruises on a cowboy's bum
as deep as a mine shaft
a sensual wine you'd want to lick off the
  one you love
as haunting as a cello solo by Yo-Yo Ma
as haunting as rose blooms trodden into
  the lawn by nighttime revelers
as if painted by Gustav Klimt:
  mysterious, gilded and unforgettable
a sleeping beauty waiting for an
  awakening kiss
as light on its feet as an elephant
as much fun as smooching with an
  unripe lemon
as oily and coagulated as axle grease
as rich as sin
as shocking and disconcerting as
  running naked in a hailstorm
as soothing and sensuous as a sumo
  wrestler in a blond wig and beauty
  mark
as spicy as a souk
as spicy as Marco Polo's baggage
as subtle as an alarm clock
as subtle as a 2-by-4 over the head
as tame as a Swede
as thick as axle grease and almost as
  difficult to shift
astonishingly dreary
astonishing marriage made in the
  heaven and hell of richness and decay
as virginal as Psyche before she met
  Cupid

as zingy and sharp as a piano wire
  dipped in lime
at its absolute best on a starry night
at least it's wet
a transvestite
attractive buxom nubile highly scented
  tart
auto exhaust fumes
autumn day in the Patagonian Andes
a wine I want to lick from cork to punt
baboon's bottom
baby fat in its nose
baby food for grownups—puréed things
  with butter and cream in them
baby Jesus in velvet pants going down
  your gullet
back of an LA school bus
badass flavor
Bangkok paddy field
barely nascent wine still frothing and
  fizzing and remembering its days as
  fruit
bathroom mold
Battlestar Galactica-style
bastard blend
beloved tractor with a gorgeous
  nude redhead on the seat
Big Mac of the wine world
bit of a cockteaser
bit of a transvestite
blushes like a white wine that's been
  embarrassed
blush is off the rosé
bog-standard
boneless, like chicken
boiled crab shells
boiled fruitcake
boiling cauldron full of herbs, black
  treacle and licorice
boneless...like chicken
bottled thunder
breakfast: a nose of applesauce, corn
  flakes and toasted bread
breakfast at grandma's house

breakfast, diner
breed in the nose
brickie's laborer in a tutu
bright umamilike definition
Bruce juice with sequins and a tiara
Brussels sprouts
bubbles clock in about halfway between
  mousse and gunshot
Bulgarian legs
burlap feedsack
burlesque of bawdy fruit and spices
burnt hair
burnt shrimp shells
buttered paper
buttered popcorn with pineapple and
  vanilla sauce
buttock-clenchingly acidic
California Chardonnay is like giving
  Pinocchio a blow job
calm sea, hot pebbles, sackcloth
camel drool
can be cellared for up to 10,000 years
can represent the planet as a wine
can light up your sensory dashboard
Carmen Miranda's headgear
carnally perfumed
cassis, cassis and more cassis
champion lady swimmer: sinewy,
  streamlined, shapely with firm
    rippling pectoral muscles
Chanel Nº5 on a gladiator's shorts
Chardonnay in the nude
Château E. coli
Château LaFeet
Château Phlegm'89
Château Two-by-Four
Château Viagra
Château Wrigley
cheap floozy
cherry pie in hell
chewed pencils
chicken fat
Chinese lollies
Chinese sweet-and-sour sauce

chocolate and schoolgirls' uniforms
chocolate-covered raisins kiss roasted
  espresso while ultraripe blackberries
  drip juice onto tar-laden spice-covered
  maidens
chromium-plated scent-impregnated
  luminous quivering giggling fruit
  flavored ice-covered heap of mother
  love
cigar box containing a Montecristo, a
  black truffle and a hot brick sitting on
  top of an old saddle
citrus as interpreted by Schubert
clean: no sweaty armpits
cleans the sinuses
closer to sunrise than sunset
clown makeup
CO (caloric orgasm)
combined fascination and repugnance:
  akin to visiting a reptile house
combo of flowers and excrement
comfort food in a bottle
commercial yuck
condom powder
confection of a chemistry set
confident sure-footed palate
confused customers with termites
confusing blue cheese
could be used as an anesthetic,
  disinfectant or antidepressant
could only have drawn its blood from
  local stones
could stand in for the lime in Thai green
  papaya salad
cracks a smile and winks at you
cream cheese and mouse droppings
creaminess of a suckling calf
creamy stones
Creature from the Black Lagoon
cross between a black cherry and Gene
  Kelly
cross between a forest fire and a war
  zone
crushed ants

crushed earthworms
crushed up with leaves and mice
cryptic conundrum
cuckoo's nest
curious mucked-out stables endtaste
Dallas airport
damn, I adore this wine
damp straw in a thoroughbred stable
dances out of the glass
Darth Vader of a wine
day of windsurfing
dead French people
decayed wombat
décolletage of juicy fruit glittered up by
    diamonds and perfumed with spice
deep-dish leather pizza
definite winegasm territory
delightfully fluent
devil farts
dentally corrosive
depraved but interesting
detonates on the palate like tiny
    grenades
digital clarity
diner breakfast
dirty nose; I do not wish to taste this
disjointed arms and legs
does a sort of slow striptease, revealing
    more each time one sniffs and sips
dollop of shit and mushrooms
Dolly Parton without her bra
don't bother pulling the cork
don't share this anyone, it's too
    wonderful
double cream smeared over pale golden
    stones
downright ugly
DPIM (Don't Put In Mouth)
dreadnoughtlike
dressed in Versace and a feather boa
drink it between now and Armageddon
    (or when the cork disintegrates,
    whichever comes first)

drink this sitting down or risk your
    knees buckling
drop-dead gorgeous, like a beautiful
    woman who walks into a room and
    causes
    immediate silence
duck fart
duck liver
dusty, musty and rusty
dusty sawdust
eau du cat piss
eggroll wrapper
elastic fruit
elephant cage at the zoo
embalmed
enormous coarse bubbles as though a
    hippo farted in the fermentation tank
enough tannin to make your tongue feel
    like the sole of your shoe
enough tannin to pucker the liver
escargot mud pie
even the nose seems chewy
evil mix of castor oil and motor oil and
    curse words
excites, intrigues and entices
exploding moonbeam
extremely naughty
feels as if it's scouring the teeth
feral stink of a sun-warmed manure pile
fermented oak juice
fire-breathing level
fir tree without too much fir
fits the taste buds like soft leather Gucci
    loafers fit the feet
flavors boogie around in the glass
flesh covering Italianate twigs and
    bushes
flourless chocolate cake and a cup of
    espresso rolled into one
flows over the tongue like apologetic
    lava: warm, smoldering and tongue-
    tingling
flyblown butcher's shop
foray into wackodom

for Hell's Angels
for men only
fragile mineral shards pierce the pillow
  of ripe   mangosteens and pineapples
Frankenstein Pinot
free-range velvet
fresh blood
frustratingly incognito
full bodied, even though your gums
  don't bleed after you've chiseled out
  a swallow
funky llama
funky nuts
gefilte fish
gerbil cage
ghastly insipid industrial swill
ghastly mixture of unknown chemicals
  turns your lips and mouth black
ghastly smelly cabbage
Ginsu blade concealed in a pineapple
gives your olfactory system an
  aromatherapeutic makeover
gnat piss, mark two
glassful of smiles
glorious tastescape
glue and bananas
Godzilla
good for cleaning false teeth
good for pickling onions
goût de terroir but not of this earth
grapey tomcat
gravlox
gravy made from the juices of roasted
  lamb
great for rinsing peanut butter off the
  roof of your mouth
great javelin-thrower
great wines are liquid geography
grotty and vile
guaranteed bodice-ripper
gumboots on the Aga
ham hocks and tar spread over
  bacon-covered marmalade
hamster cage

hardly a grape avalanche
hare's belly
has all the commercial appeal of gonorrhea with notes of dung, spare ribs,
  horse blanket, boiled cabbage and
  cardboard
has all the finesse of a horny
  hippopotamus
has balls
has meat on the bones of its fruit
has the subtlety and finesse of a Panzer
  tank brigade
Hawaiian volcanic ash-tinged notes of
  duck's breath
heady finish lasts into next week
hearty lusciousness of meaty maple-
  glazed hickory-smoked ribs
hedonists' fantasia of flavors
herb-infused jet fuel
herky-jerky
hermaphroditic
highly melodic
high thread-count wine
hits the finish line with gas left in
  the tank
Hodgepodge Lodge
hold on to your hat
holds mysteries, secrets and layers
  of promise
hot dog water
howl-at-the-moon wine
hug from the inside
ice princess
I could climb into the glass
I could wear this behind my ears
if a wine can ever be perfect, this is as
  perfect as wine can get
if I want to taste oak I'll go lick a plank
ignoble rot
impenetrable brooding River-Styx color
inane
indescribably sublime
industrial Kool-Aid
in its midlife crisis

inside of kid gloves worn by a young woman

inside of the mouth feels rasped by steel wool

inspired casserole of smoked mackerel soaked in the blood oozing from a rare sirloin steak

intense toffee-edged melonosity

intoxicating grape sweat

intriguing late-picked nose

it'll put new lead in any geriatric's pencil

its gut doesn't hang out over its belt buckle

its perfume and silky texture seduce with poetry where other wines flash credit cards and gold chains

I was immediately struck dumb and then grinned like fool for at least a half hour

James Cagney grapefruit facial

jamfest

Joseph's coat of many colors

joyous berries sing and dance on the tongue

just don't drink it, paint with it

just foreplay...no follow-through

just plain evil

just-used bathroom

kicking like new-born foals

kicks butt from first to finish

laboratory-concocted Stepford wine

Labrador on its back waiting to be scratched

ladies' underwear

lasts until the dishes are done

lavalike consistency as it coagulates in the throat

leather on the well-worn back seat of an old Jag

leathery coffee

leave it undisturbed for not less than ten years and then kill an ox

leg-spreader

legs want to climb up rather than down

lick it off your lover

like being slapped up the side of the face with a wet trout that morphs into a mermaid

like brushing your teeth with a belt sander

like chewing on a piece of red ice

like chewing the tire off a ten-year-old tractor

like drinking pills of wine

like drinking pure velvet and silk

like drinking the cold

like drinking wine through oyster shells

like finding an oak tree in your glass

like gargling with razor blades

like gazing at a Canaletto painting

like having an orgasm in the mouth

like inhaling a small electric eel

like injecting pure honey into your tongue, sending it into jolts of diabetic coma

like licking a battery

like licking out a mouse nest

like licking the sweat from the belly of a crocodile

like riding a rollercoaster: up and down with a quick finish

like rubbing Aladdin's lamp

like sex, and Thanksgiving, like sex on Thanksgiving

like sniffing and tasting toothpicks

like staring into space on a dark night

like stroking a pelt of Russian sable

like sucking on Cabernet candy

like walking through a Moroccan brothel

limp-wristed

Lincoln Logs soaked in butter

lingerie for your mouth

liqueur of lead pencils

liquid ecstasy

liquid equivalent of a night on the town with underwear models in South Beach
liquid panty remover
liquid perfection
liquid Snickers
little black dress
livelier than a sack full of ferrets
long, firm and full in the mouth like a penis
lukewarm oxidized gnat's pee
made my stomach lurch
made with artificial flavors in a jelly-bean factory
magna cum laude complexity
maiden's armpits
makes a narrow and clean beeline for your throat
makes no noise when poured into the glass; it's completely silent
makes the earth move
marches up and down on your tongue in acid-heeled stilettos
Marie Antoinette's boudoir
marijuana
masculine freight train
may be hazardous to your health
may I die drinking it
meat, sausage, blood and animal
melts away on the palate like a puff of smoke vanishing into air
men's room in a French railway station
menthol fire that would clear your sinuses on a wet Wednesday in Glasgow
merits an X-rating
metallic almost rusty notes of railway track
minerality like licking the lava off the slope of an active volcano
missing and declared dead
mongrel blend
monkey house at the zoo
monkey riding a horse bareback

monolithic dumbness
more Châteauneuf-du-Popsicle than Eskimo-Merlot pie
more going on in this wine than in a New York minute
more T'ang than Ming
more than enough wood to satisfy a beaver
most haunting and brilliant and subtle and thrilling and ancient on the planet
mouse cage
multivitamins
music of the grapes
musty, dusty and fusty
mutt of a blend
Muzak for your palate
my grandmother's attic
my palate experiences a gustatory orgasm just thinking about it
narrow-hipped
Neanderthal regional charm
Neanderthal-style
nearly melted the fillings in my teeth
neat marriage of silk and spices
nettles growing on a compost heap
never comes off as pornographic
new condom smell
newly vacated seashells
new Vaseline
nightclub bouncer of the vegetable world
night wine for a nightgown
no-fault insurance
nose pole-vaults out of the glass with Olympic precision
nose still needs to open
no splinters in your nose
not as pretty as the proprietor's wife
not especially burdened by complexity
not Technicolor-loud
not worth hating
Novocaine-like
No Wimpy Wines

nuances of bruised fenberries wreathed
   in ripe Asian moonfruit
oafish
oak bra
odd-tasting eastern European fruit soup
oh-my-God!
old drawing rooms
old fart's tipple
old hen droppings
old tarpaulin fringed with lace
one bottle tasted better than it looked
   and one bottle looked better than it
   tasted
one-hundred-year-old dirty sweat socks
one man's nectar is another man's Tidy
   Bowl
one step up from vinegar
on the way out but not on life support
   yet
oozed flavors as if it had been squeezed
   from a tube
opinionated
opulent hussy
orchard meets a candy store
organic waste
outdoorsy
outhouse
out-of-body experience
outspoken inelegant simpleton
overtones of the Great Dismal Swamp
oy!
paintball blackberries
paint stripper
paradise in a bottle
party-animal wine
Peking duck slathered in hoisin sauce
penis wine
perfect mix of Gorgonzola and lavender
perfect sipping for UFO patrols on
   summer nights
perhaps in a menopausal state
pernicious and ugly
pickled frog skin
pickle juice

pick of the litter
pigswill
Pinot envy
Pinot Grigio with a brain
Pinot on stilts
Pinot with a woody
Pinot with training wheels
plankton
plastic whiff of Eau de Mattel
plastic wrap
poi
polite cat's pee
poop
possibly the worst wine in the world
possibly xenophobic
post-rain worms
potty stuff
practically psychedelic
prehistoric granny's drink
pretty French girl with a very sly,
   yet not so innocent, smile
proto-Manischewitz concoction
Proustian
pudgy alcoholic endomorph
pulses like cicadas in a summer twilight
pure sex in a bottle
puts the Pop in Châteauneuf-du-
quintessential nonwine: no bouquet,
   no fruit, no flavors, no finish
raisins in the nose
raisin massacre
Rambo Champagne
rampant pineapplicability
rampant proportions
rancid pork
rather fishy wild goose
rat poison
refreshing from go to whoa
relentless gooseberries
resembled dill pickles more than berries
richness of chocolate mingling perilously with truffles and well-hung game
riffraff
rippling tannins of great wit

rises above bog standards
road kill
roast chicken
roast duck
roasted lobster shells
roast woodcock entrails
Robitussin or Dimetane, with skunk
    on the finish
rolling thunder
roots in the nose
roses stuffed up a goat's ass
rotten fish
rotting pineapples
rubber sealing bands stuck to the glass
    liners on metal canning tops
rubbery nose
rugged sweaty honey
rumbling thunderstorm in the distance
sacramental wine, although I wouldn't
    want to attend the church that served
    it
sackcloth
Sahara sandwich
salsa and wasabi
Sangiovese drives the boat while Merlot
    navigates
sap-laden rocks
Saran Wrap
Saturn's fifth moon after a lunar dust
    storm during an eclipse
satyrs roaming the woods looking for
    innocent young maidens
sauerkraut and toadstool sandwich
scary
scent of a woman in a bottle of wine
schizophrenic
screechy nose
secret memories of the soil
seductive come-hither creaminess
    creates a party in your mouth
seductive quality of the minute hairs on
    the back of a woman's thigh in high
    summer
sensual fruitcake

sensual? oh, yes!
sewing machine oil
sexy beast of a wine
shaggy-dog unsociability
Shanghai T'ang
shock-and-awe wine
sick and twisted
Silk Road of fruit flavors
silk stockings jumping up and down in a
    gooseberry bush
silky chocolate oral afterglow
silky feel of a lover's cheek on your
    tongue
sinus-clearing nose
sizzling, spattering volcano
skunk cabbage
skunk juice
slipcover for the tongue, ranging from
    terry cloth to suede to velvet
slow-motion waterfall of thick tears
small soaps in the guest bathroom that
    everyone's afraid to unwrap
smelled like a bad car accident on a hot
    day
smelled like a hair salon and tasted like
    light beer
smells and tastes like it's been through
    a wood chipper
smells like great sex
smoked fish
smoking clutch on an uphill grade
smoky bacon [in this kosher wine]
smoky savory deli smells
snake piss
Soave in drag
so far past its sell-by date that whoever
    stamped it is long dead
soft leather cushion on the nose
so good it gave me goosebumps
so good it's almost painful
soiled leather thong
so intense, so powerful and so complex
    as to instill fear in the taster
something between cheesy and sweaty

something carnal
something curled up and died in there
something decomposing
so normal and ordinary that I can't find
  words to describe it
so peppery you could sneeze over it
so pure, clean and serene it could enroll
  as a nun
[so sweet] it could revive the dead
so thick you can spread this on toast
soulful barnyard
sour and squalid like bad breath on a
  good goose with bad teeth
Spanish loo
splendidly buxom
spicy corned beef
spooky
squashed horseradish
stampin' stompin' stuff
stand in the presence of this wine
starts with coffee, continues with
  coffee and ends with coffee
steely nose
straight rhubarb pie without those
  strawberries
strawberries larded with furniture
  polish and caramel
strawberry jam with a little paint
  thinner
strips of burnt jam left on the rim of
  a raspberry tart
strong dill and slight pickle flavor
strumpet of a wine with tawdry cherry
  and plum flavors and a tart mouth
subterranean and extraterrestrial at the
  same time
suck-a-stone fruit
sudsy legs
suit mended, hair combed, but that's
  about it
sumo wrestler's jockstrap
sumo wrestler's thighs
sun-warmed skin
superb from good to whoa

sure-footed palate
Swedish Fish
swell swill
sweaty saddle and the horse it rode in on
sweaty underpants
sweet-and-sour doggy bed
sweet fire extinguisher
sweet odor of cow
tacky, tacky, tacky
tanginess of a thoroughbred stable
tannic bra
tannins all but take the skin off the roof
  of your mouth
tannins firm enough that you feel you
  could almost drive stakes into the
  wine
tannins grip your tongue and gums with
  the force of a wharf laborer
tannins will rip through your mouth
  like an
  18-wheeler in the fast lane
tar and shit
tarred rope
tart with a heart
taste equivalent of a Cirque du Soleil
  acrobat
tastes like blood of the vine
tastes like chicken
taste of old oak and old ladies,
  if you see what I mean
tastes so fucking good
tea and mothballs
tensile conflict
termite's fantasy dinner
terrifying chocolate
terroir or crapoir?
terrorist act
texture like the heavy hypnotic flow
  in a lava lamp
texture is like Viennese black chocolate
  melting in your palm on a hot
  summer's night
the crude oil of PX sherries
the mashed potatoes of wine

theme park of a wine
the pee in Piesporter
there's an orchestra playing right now
  in your mouth
there's no excuse for drinking muck
  like this
there's no *there* there
The Rosé Garden
thigh of a blushing nymph
thin dusty old carnival worker chewing
  gum in the sun
think hunting lodge with slain wild
  boars and you get the picture
thin shrewish acidic mess
this could start a war
this [desert island] wine is for the day
  when Friday catches a wild pig
this is the kind of wine you want to
  marry
thoroughbred horse peeing on clean
  straw
throat sandpaperer
thumping attack of violets and irises
thumping its chest and baring its teeth
  and roaring abuse
tightfisted nose
tincture of vomit
toe caresser
tomcat, gooseberries and cardboard
tongue-happy
too smooth, too round, too rotten
toothbrush red
tooth-crackingly racy
to toast with this wine is reason in
  and of itself to get married
total *dreck*
touch of death
touch of fir tree without too much fir
touch of tar and shit
toy wine that dolls might drink
trace of the cuckoo's nest
trail dust
translucent green rim like a spirit level
  from Hades

trash-can wine
trouser-opener
troweled Spackle
truffled violet silk of a Musigny
try not to inflict this on yourself
tumult of marmalade, popcorn, toast
  and mandarin oranges
tuning fork for your palate
turgid bull dust
twelve months later the chrysalis turned
  into a butterfly
*über*hip
ugliest bottle in the history of wine
ugliest wine I have ever tasted
ultraeverything
undrinkable gloppy butterball
unfolds like a Japanese fan of flavors
unmentionables
unswallowable
unusual but seductive nose of sea foam
unwinelike
uppity cherries
urine during asparagus season
uriny
use as an anesthetic, disinfectant or
  antidepressant
use it to kill rats
useless for drinking
utterly buttery
uvula cryogenics
vanilla halvah
variations on a theme by Grape
velvety and rusty nails
veritable seduction serum
very cultured plum-in-the-mouth
  elocution
very diesel-like
very soft and very round like sheep's
  eyes with square pupils
very vague: vague spice, vague apple,
  vaguely nutty and floral
vin de merde
vinous equivalent of bottle blondes
vinous equivalent of Dunkin' Donuts

vinous equivalent of Liquid Plumr

vinous equivalent of the emasculated salutation *Happy Holidays*

vinous Frappuccino

vinous lap-dance

vinous nirvana

vinous nose candy

vinous stud muffin

vinous interruptus

virile mousse

viscosity reminiscent of 10W40 motor oil

walnuts, vomit and wet dog

warp factor five

wasabi

waxy cadaver

wears the elegant tarnish of time

well-shaped buttocks

well-drilling wine

wet dog in a phone booth

wet underpants

wham-bam-thank-you-ma'am red

what angels use as an underarm deodorant

what a pity its claws were not cut

what kitty-cat leaves in her sandbox

wheelbarrow of UGLI fruit

when the rare urge to drink wine at breakfast strikes, reach for this

white Zinfandel doesn't even have the *chutzpah* to call itself rosé

white Zinfandel: training wheels for a generation of wine drinkers

white Zinfandel: what you drink when you hate wine

who wants to go to bed with a wrestler?

wild herbs and flowers pushing their way through a mountain of stones

will not frighten the horses

will potentially live longer than anyone reading this

will still be drinking spectacularly when the theory behind *The Planet of the Apes* is unraveled

will turn from frog to prince around 2005, kissing not required

will undoubtedly outlast its cork and may outlive its   bottle

Windex

winegasm

wines the color of wheat that tasted like the grapes had been brushed in your armpit after a rather enjoyable game of beach volleyball. And then splashed with custard. And squeezed with lime juice.

wins the darkest-wine-of-the-decade award

wonderful tone poem of flavors

wonderfully grouchy

won't make the Earth move

won't shrivel your tonsils

wood nymph tears

woolly, wild and woody

worst foul liquid

wow: rolling thunder

wrapped in layers of sensory delight or disgust

yak drool

yellow peaches imprisoned in diamonds

YMCA pool

you could boil this down to a thick paste and coat the one you love

you'll be tempted to eat this with your fingers

young Marco Polo's backpack on his way to China

your horse is diabetic

your tongue might be confused but it will be happy

you shouldn't feel violated, Spackled or on fire

Zen-like

zillion points from Robert Parker

The best glass of white wine is the first;
the best glass of red is the last.
Anonymous

To a real wine lover the happiest sight
is a full bottle; the saddest, an empty one.
The Author

B. The Good, the Bad, the Beautiful, the Ugly

The human tendency to qualify everything in our path seems to be hard-wired into our brains, and so is presumably normal. Our biological nature also determines our reaction to anything we put in our mouths. After the first tasting of wine, for example, we usually respond as to how we like it, somewhere in the vast spectrum between *m-m-m* and *yuck*! The abbreviated list below contains just highlights; for the full monty, jump to the category of *Quality* on page 282. *Blech? Yum?*

A1	average	blockbuster	counterfeit	distinctive	exceptional	flimsy
abhorrent	avoid	blowsy	crackerjack	distinguished	exciting	focused
abominable	awe-inspiring	boring	crass	divine	execrable	forbidding
absorbing	awesome	brash	cruddy	dog	exhausted	forget it
abysmal	awful	breathtaking	crude	dramatic	exhilarating	forgettable
acceptable	awkward	brilliant	dandy	dreadful	exotic	for the ages
aces	bad	brutal	dangerous	dreary	explosive	forthright
adequate	banal	capable	daring	drinkable	expressive	foul
admirable	bang-on	captivating	dazzling	dubious	exquisite	four-square
agreeable	bang-up	celestial	deadly	dud	extraordinary	freaky
amazing	barbaric	challenging	decadent	dull	extraspecial	friendly
ambrosial	barren	characterful	decent	dynamic	extravagant	frisky
amiable	base	charismatic	deep	dynamite	exuberant	frivolous
amateurish	beastly	charming	defective	ecstatic	fabulous	funky
A-OK	beatific	choice	definitive	electrifying	fair	funny
appalling	beautiful	class act	delectable	elegant	fantastic	gem
appealing	beguiling	classic	delicate	empty	fascinating	generous
appetizing	benchmark	classy	delicious	enchanting	faultless	genius
approachable	best	clumsy	delightful	engaging	faulty	ghastly
appropriate	best ever	clunker	delish	engrossing	feckless	gifted
arresting	best-in-show	colossal	deplorable	enjoyable	fetching	glorious
aristocratic	best-of-breed	common	desirable	enriching	fine	gnarly
aromatic	best-of-the-	compelling	despicable	enthralling	first-quality	godawful
artistic	best	competent	detestable	entrancing	first-rate	godlike
artless	bewildering	complaisant	difficult	epic	five stars	good
assertive	big	complex	disagreeable	essential	flabby	good for
astonishing	big nothing	congenial	disappointing	esteemed	flat	nothing
astounding	bilious	consistent	disastrous	ethereal	flavorful	gorgeous
atrocious	blah	consummate	disgraceful	evil	flavorless	graceful
attractive	bland	cool	disgusting	exalted	flavorsome	grand
austere	blech	cordial	dishonest	excellent	flawed	grand slam
authoritative	blissful	correct	dismal	exemplary	flawless	great

greatest
grim
grody
gross
grungy
harmless
harsh
has it all
hateful
haunting
heady
healthy
heart-
  stopping
heavenly
heaven-sent
hellish
high-class
high-ranking
ho-hum
hollow
hopeless
horrendous
horrible
horrid
horrific
icky
ideal
illustrious
imaginative
immortal
impeccable
imperfect
impressive
inadequate
inappropriate
incoherent
incomparable
inconceivable
incredible
indifferent
industrial
ineffectual
inept
inferior
innocuous
irritating
insanely good
insignificant
insidious
insipid
inspired
intense
interesting
intriguing
irresistible
joke
joyous

junk
just right
keeper
killer
kind
knockout
lackluster
laudable
laughable
lavish
legendary
letdown
life-changing
likeable
lively
loathsome
lousy
loveable
lovely
luminescent
luminous
luscious
luxurious
magical
magnetizing
magnificent
majestic
marginal
marvelous
masterful
masterpiece
matchless
mean
mediocre
medium
mellow
memorable
meritorious
meteoric
middling
mind-
  blowing
mind-
  boggling
miraculous
m-m-m
modest
monstrous
monumental
mouthfilling
mouthwateri
  ng
muddled
mysterious
naïve
nasty
natural
neat

ne plus ultra
nervous
neutral
nice
noble
no great
  shakes
nonpareil
notable
not bad
noteworthy
noticeable
nothing
nuanced
number one
obnoxious
odd
odious
off
offensive
off-putting
oh-my-God!
oh, yes!
OK
once-in-a-
  lifetime
opulent
optimal
ordinary
out-of-this-
  world
outlandish
outrageous
outstanding
over-the-top
overwhelmin
  g
palatable
paltry
pap
par excellence
passable
patrician
peachy
pedestrian
pedigreed
peerless
peeuueee!
perfect
phenomenal
phony
picture-
  perfect
piquant
pitiful
plain
pleasant
plonk

poised
polished
ponderous
poor
poorly made
potable
powerful
praiseworthy
pre-eminent
premium
prestigious
pretentious
prime
princely
prized
profound
proper
puerile
pure gold
pure poetry
putrid
puzzling
quenching
quirky
rancid
rapturous
rare
ravishing
raw
reasonable
recommend-
  able
refined
regrettable
reliable
remarkable
repellent
repugnant
repulsive
respectable
revelatory
revolting
rhapsodic
rich
right
risky
rot/rotten
round
routine
rude
run-of-the-
  mill
ruthless
sapid
saporous
satisfactory
satisfying
savory

scary
schlock
scintillating
scrumptious
seductive
select
sensational
serious
shabby
shameful
simple
sinful
singular
sinister
skillfully
  made
slop
small
smashing
smooth
solid
so-so
sophisticated
soulful
soul-
  satisfying
special
specious
spectacular
spellbinding
spiffy
splendid
spooky
spotty
staggering
standard
standout
star quality
stately
stellar
sterling
stirring
straightfor-
  ward
strange
stunning
stupefying
stupendous
stupid good
sublime
substandard
subtle
succulent
sucks
suitable
sumptuous
super
superb

super-duper
superficial
superhuman
superior
superlative
supreme
surly
surreal
suitable
sweet
swell
swill
tacky
tasteless
tasty
tedious
terrible
terrific
the pits
thrilling
tip-top
tiring
to die for
tolerable
toothsome
top-drawer
top-notch
top-of-the-
  line
tour de force
towering
transcendent
trash
travesty
treacherous
treasure
treat
tremendous
triumphant
ugly
ultradelicious
ultrafine
unacceptable
unappetizing
unattractive
unbelievable
uncanny
uncommon
uncouth
underwhelm-
  ing
undistin-
  guished
undrinkable
uneven
unexcelled
unexceptiona
  l

unexciting
unfit to drink
unforgettable
unheard of
unimportant
unimpressive
uninspiring
uninteresting
unique
unmatched
unpalatable
unparalleled
unpleasant
unprecedent-
  ed
unpretentiou
  s
unqualified
unreal
unremark-
  able
unrivaled
unsavory
unspeakable
unsurpassed
unthinkable
unusual
urggh!
useless
vapid
venerable
vile   ed
vulgar
waste of time
weak
weird
well crafted
well done
well made
wicked
wimpy
winner
winsome
wishy-washy
wonderful
wondrous
worthless
worthwhile
worst
world-class
wow
wretched
yech!
yucky
yummy
zero
zilch

Language is wine upon the lips.
Virginia Woolf

The flavor of wine is like delicate poetry.
Louis Pasteur

*Language and wine are two of the most
pleasing things we consume. They animate us
and become part of us. The English language
is as wide and deep and layered as wine is.*
Natalie MacLean

C. An Application for a Poetic License

Wine certainly has a way of loosening up soaring imaginations and facile literary dexterity. Perhaps it's the alcohol working its magic upon body and soul. Whatever the reasons, there are now so many astonishingly lyrical descriptions of wine that it's hard to choose which to showcase purely for their inventive beauty. Anyone with a love of language, whether a poet at heart or in fact, should be able to find quite a few favorites among the allusions, metaphors and similes below.

accent's on *verde* here: green herbs, green apples, green papayas
acidity almost snaps, crackles and pops
acidity burns through the wine like electricity
acidity gashes the palate like a bolt of lightning
acidity scythes through its heart like a lumberjack's saw in the dark depths of a silent forest
a concert: vibrant and complex
acrobatics on the tongue
acted like a cello in a string trio adding depth and richness
adagio of the senses
aftertaste reverberated like a singer's voice in a cathedral
airy sweetness of youthful hopes
alchemy of oak seems to clog the wine's pores like gesso on a picture frame
all lace and finesse
all the colors of the peacock's tail
all the flavors of a golden African sun in a bottle
all the flowers of the garden were present in an almost narcotically seductive bouquet
all the perfumes of the Mediterranean south
all you need is a corkscrew and a seatbelt
almost a vinous black hole in space
altogether innocent of woody vulgarity
amazing harmonica of intricate flavors
a Monet where the colors represent the complexity of the palate

ancient staircase kept carefully clean yet never quite free of dust
antirosé made in an antimodern way
a poem of a Pinot Noir
apple blossoms blown in the wind
apricots turning to peaches
apt to shake and rattle you to your socks
arboreal piquancy
Armani-slick berries
aromas are like a welcome mat
aromas bouncing all over the inside of your nose
aromatherapist on steroids
aromatherapy you can drink
aromatic welcoming committee
arpeggio of flavors
as aromatic as a breeze blowing through wildflowers
as bright as an Indian summer day
as classy as an old Bugatti automobile
as crisp, clean and vibrant as a Tasmanian spring day
as dark as a moonless midnight
as delicate as angels' tears
as dense and sleek as a sea lion
as dry as a Saharan sirocco
as edgy as a piece of ice in your mouth
as exuberant as a garden approaching full bloom
as flowery as a bride's bouquet
as fragrant as a basket overflowing with heirloom apples, Meyer lemons and wildflowers
as fresh and glancing as dappled sunlight on new grass and spring flowers

as fresh as a breeze sweeping through the lavender-scented hills of the southern Rhône
as green and grassy as a newly mown football field
as light and flighty as a spring breeze
as light as a whisper
as lively as a laugh
as ornate as a Tabriz rug
as rare and elusive as hummingbird tears
as sharp as old Granny Smith's tongue
as smoky as a brushfire racing across herb-covered hillsides
as soft as an Impressionist painting
as softly blurry as Renoir colors
as sultry as a tango
as tasty and tangy as a mango margarita
as taut as piano wire in youth
asteroid collision between a spice container and a ton of plump red and purple berries
as thick as axle grease and almost as difficult to shift
as thrilling a jolt to the senses as a bungee jump from Mount Cook
as tightly and intricately woven as any Missoni design
a successful marriage, improved with age
as unfriendly as tripping over in a patch of nettles
as uplifting as a springtime walk in a beech forest in bloom
as virginal as Psyche before she met Cupid
as zingy and sharp as a piano wire dipped in lime
Atlantic sunrise of flavors
babbling brook of berries
ballerina of a claret
balm for the tongue
barely noticeable warm kiss in its unbelievably long finish
barely out of its nappies

bark stripped from green willows

baroque end of the Sémillon spectrum
baskets of ripe nectarines strategically placed under the honeysuckle bush in the shade
basso continuo of black currants and blackberries
bawling, brawling infant
beachcombed wine
bead rises in a swirling, swaying, sensuously elegant treat
Beaune in the USA
beautiful afternoon spent outdoors under a big tree talking with old friends
beautiful tannins coat the palate like a mink coat
beauty in black: black fruit, black smoke and black bitter minerals
beeswax-rich majesty with age
Beethoven in a mellow mood
beguiling almost spiritual bouquet
berry family reunion
berry patch in a eucalyptus grove next to a coalmine
bespoke vinosity
big ripe tannins are babysitting exuberant primary blackberry-cassis fruit

blackberry bliss
blacker than the devil's heart
blessed with saucy impertinence
blew smoke rings the second the cork was pulled
bloom on peaches
blueprint for pure hedonism on the palate
blushes like a white wine that's been embarrassed
boasts the explosive power of a sprinter and the grace of a ballerina
boneless...like chicken
bottled joy
bottled poetry
bottled sex
bourbon-meets-port love child
both uplifted and downgraded by a whiff of volatile acidity
brass-knuckled punch of minerality
breeze through a cherry orchard
brings motion to your soul
bubbles as bright as stars in the sky
bubbles comport themselves with finesse and elegance
bubbles seem to trill like a nightingale
builds to a breathtaking crescendo
built like a tsunami only to die before it hits the beach
Burgundy with a suntan
buried like a pirate's treasure is a deep core of cherry fruit
burlesque of bawdy fruit and spice
burly, masculine: wine that'll take out the garbage and pull your car out of a ditch
buttoned up in an oak overcoat
buzzes with a beehive's worth of palate action
buzzing with honey
by sheer force one glass takes your palate places where you haven't been yet
California dreamin'
came on and on in waves of scented innuendo
camphor wood and loganberry jam turning to leather
can bat for the planet as the Shiraz representative
can light up your sensory dashboard
captured the rays of the sun
captures the south of France in a bottle
captures warm sunshine
caramel-coated autumn leaves
caramel-coated sunny day
caramel sun setting over a vanilla sky
cardboard box with its sweet glue

carpe diem rosé

cashmere for the tongue
cauldron of complexity
cedar and lavender fragrances waft through a river of cassis
chamomile-scented sea breeze captured in a bottle
Chardonnay in the nude
charmingly gruff elegance
charming middle-aged lady with her slip showing
charm of a frigid smile

cherries and boysenberries bounce across your palate like Ping-Pong balls

chunky wood-aged thunderbolts

cigar box containing a Montecristo, a black truffle and a hot brick sitting on top of an old saddle

citrus and minerals slice across the palate like a well-honed blade

classical music of the vineyards

cleansing explosion of lime in your mouth

clear flavors on a raft of cleansing acidity

clenched fist of high acid

closer to sunrise than sunset

cloud of the sweetest fruit imaginable

coats the palate like a plushy purple blanket

coats the taster's palate and takes it hostage for about a minute

cocooned in crisp acid

cocoon of soft vanilla oak

cold explosion of deliciousness

collision between a spice container and a ton of plump red and purple berries

color and contrast knobs seem turned down

color of polished rubies

combination candy store, fruitmonger and spice market

combined fascination and repugnance: akin to visiting a reptile house

comfort food for the thirsty

complexity and beauty of a Persian rug

complexity of petrol without all that expensive aging

complex rainbow of flavors

conquers the palate with wave after wave of sweet peaches

coolant for your tongue

cool resins of provincial herbs

coquettishly elusive flavorful extract

cornucopia of baker's shop bready-yeasty aromas

cornucopia of scents, flavors and memories

cortex-marinating strength

cosmic bath of nearly unplumbable depth

cosmic weave with wild mushrooms and minerals

Côte Rôtie on acid

cotton sheets under a clothesline on a summer day

could bring any deity to ecstasy

could have graced the cup of Bacchus himself

could inspire any musketeer to heroic deeds

crackling lemongrasslike spirit

cradled in an almost invisible web of oak

crammed with iron-steel flavors that segue into magnificent minerality

cranberry sunset

cream in the middle of an Oreo cookie

crisp hum of a good rosé

cubist pastiche of flavors

dances forth like a beautiful fairy on a misty midsummer's meadow at dawn

dances in the mouth

dancing acidity

dancing fruit

dancing in perfect step

dancing lightness

dappled shade under mighty oaks

dark and stormy…like the night

dark sun-baked cauldron-stewed fruit

daughter of blossom-infused Mediterranean breezes and sun-dried apricots

decadence of a weekday afternoon picnic beside the Seine, eating caviar with the caped d'Artagnan

decadent cold nose of the sea

decadently biscuity pong

deep brambly profundity

defies the destructive onslaught of time

delectable symphony of wild and tasty abandon like peasants at play

delicate filigree of spices and oak

delicate lacework of elegant fruit

delicious fusillade of herbs

delighted to the point of hearing angels sing

delightfully witty berries

dense fat thermonuclear Shiraz fruit bomb

destined to develop into a swan

developing like an opening flower

dewdrop limpidity

diabetic's nightmare

diamond-crusted bed of irresistible tropical and floral flavors

diaphanous in its layers

disciplined hedonism: sensuality by numbers

dissolves in the mouth into clouds of sweet fruit

dissolves into your flesh

distant hillside wildflowers when there is a nip of frost in the air

distant rumbling thunderstorm

distilled dew and honey

does not go gently into this good night

does not so much seduce you as launch a full-out perfume assault on the senses

does somersaults on your tongue

dog that's been kept on a leash all day

don't just drink it…paint with it

double cream flowing thick and unwilling from a jug

down-home fruit frivolity

draped in a diaphanous sheet of floral scents

dream-compellers

dressed in Versace and a feather boa

drifting smoke from a cowboy's campfire

drinks like a gin and tonic, easy on the lime

dripping with the apricot marmalade of noble rot

dry oriental spices as they hover in the warmth of the tropics

dull lifeless wooden interludes

dull pewter covered in dust and cobwebs

each tiny sip sent little ripples of feeling down my back

earthquake of a La Tâche that shakes the room and stains the soul

Earth's birthmark
earthy aromas burst up at you with the force of a tub
    of salad dressing opened at 21,000 feet
earthy funkiness that somehow stirs the soul
eases over the palate with creamy grace
easy-listening music for the palate
Edenic bouquet
effervescent memories
electric wine with power, polish, subtlety and grace
elegance vinified
embryonic nose of super-ripe fruit
epitome of discreet perfumed elegance
epitome of things light and summery
epitome of silk turned into wine
essence of forbidden delight
ethereal indolent effervescence

ethereal lightness of being

evanescent...the grin without the cat
every possible jagged edge, acidity, alcohol, tannin
    and wood is brilliantly intertwined in what seems
    like a diaphanous format
explosive aromatic extravagance
expresses the authentic untamed soul of the grape
extraordinary ambrosially bawdy delights
extraordinary whoosh of fragrances
extreme red gooseberry end of the Sauvignon
    spectrum
exudes elegance in a thousand different ways
exudes life
exudes oak from every pore
fabulously frothing fizz
faded beauty with twinkling eyes
faded old lady with bright twinkling eyes
faintest funky scents of a farm on the breeze
fairy-dust scented
fanfare of oak trumpets
fantastically beautiful sensual symphony was played
    for the olfactory glands
fantasy perfumed by rose water, orange blossoms and
    wild strawberries
farmer's market after a brief downpour
fat tannins coat the teeth like lacquer
feels like slipping under a fluffy down comforter
Fellini-like road of wildflowers and mad-capped
    berries
field of wildflowers on a hot spring day
fiesta in a bottle
fills every crevice of your mouth with flavors and
    extract and oomph
fine distillate of cherries and rubies transformed into
    wine
finely woven tapestry of innumerable flavors
fine marriage of fat and lean
fine mix of flesh and fresh
fire sale at the farmer's market
fireworks of finesse
fits the taste buds like soft leather Gucci loafers fit
    the feet

five pounds of melted butter churned in fresh-cut oak
flavors dance lightly to a tune
flavors echo like distant music
flavors rocket around the mouth
flavors run over the tongue like satin on skin
flavors shining like a hologram
flavors sink into the tongue and last forever
flesh covering Italianate twigs and bushes
flirtatious perfumes of youth
flits from joy to joy
floating clouds of lemons and apricots
floats and stings
flowers planted in an orchard of apricots and peaches
flowers underlaid with fresh grass
flute by still water
flutter of a nutty Edam cheese
font of sensations
forest carpeted with violets
forest underbrush after the rain
for immediate consumption before the wheels fall off
four flavors...from spring blossoms through summer
    to autumn fruit to wintry mineral austerity
fragile mineral shards pierce the pillow of ripe
    mangosteens and pineapples
fragrant cachet for your underclothes drawer
fresh come-onish juicy fruitiness
fresh linen slapping in the breeze
freshly washed sheets that have dried in the wind
fresh oranges in a bath of warm cream
frolics on the palate
frothy sighs
fruit and herbs fighting furiously for supremacy
fruit and acidity are poignantly juxtaposed
fruit and oak seamlessly welded together
fruit and wood fighting for control
fruit bowl immersed in sparkling nectar
fruit bowl inside a soulful wine with weight
fruit contests tongue space with oak...resulting in a
    drawn match

fruit driven mad with sun

fruit explosion for your taste buds
fruit gorged on sunshine
fruit poking through the thickets
fruit still locked in arm-to-arm combat with the
    tannins
fruit triumphant
fruity come-and-get-me red
full color catalog of the most attractive flavors
full of interesting and nourishing bits and bobs
full of mischief and abandon
full of sprightly twists and turns
full rising of the sap
fulsome verging on specious
gardenia petal sandwich
garden of southern Italian flavors
gentlemen's club in a bottle
gentle slightly amorphous berry fruit
gently dueling fruit essences

gets Burgundy lovers drooling into their bibs

girl of fifteen, who is already a great artist, coming on tiptoes and curtseying herself out with childish grace and laughing blue eyes

give it a little time for paradise to emerge

glint of cool sun through the ripples

glistening and sparkling like a cat's eyes

glitters like a chrome bumper

glorious ballet of honey, citrus and buttered toast

goes on and on unfolding magically on the palate

goes straight to the pleasure center of the brain

good for drinking, pouring on ice cream or dousing cakes

good mountain stream that could one day become a long peaceful river

gorgeous layers of fruit cascade over the taste buds without any sense of weight

gorgeously fruity expression of place

gossamer caress of bubbles

gossamer grace

gossamer-thin elegance

grandmother's kitchen when she was cooking fruit to make jam

grapefest in a bottle

grapes sing and touch the high notes

grass, nettles and the whole wild garden on a dewy spring morning

great extraction of fruit blossoming out across the palate

great opening stanza

green leaf aggression: green through and through… green apples, green peas, green lime zest…all sharp as knives to scrape your tongue clean

grenadine with a cool sort of leathery rusticity

gym shoes running on a hot road

hairy fruit…nicely slicked back

half-floral half-furious peppertree

halfway house between the freshness of youth and the serenity of age

handful of wildflowers picked by a cool stream

handsome slender denizen of the forest slipping quietly and gracefully through the trees

hand-to-hand combat wine hardly a lecture on balance at the university of equilibrium

hardly drinkable except on an icy night by a roaring bonfire

has all the bricks needed to build a mighty castle

has all the component parts in place poised to embark on its inexorable journey towards maturity

has gobbled up the oak like a black hole in space

has more character than most Hollywood movies

has neither the excitement of youth nor the benefit of benign maturity

has now opened its arms to the world

has relatives in Burgundy not California

has the powerful punch of a heavyweight, the opulence of a showgirl and the elegance of a dancer

has wide organoleptic bandwidth

haughty carapace of bark

haunting perfumes of wild herbs

Hawaiian volcanic ash-tinged notes of duck's breath

hay in a summer barn

hayride through a citrus orchard on a sunny day

hazelnuts and candy drowned in strawberry liqueur

heart-stopping fruit and perfume

heather in flower when the sun is on it

hedonistic opulence

hedonists' fantasia of flavors

heirloom apples found in a farmer's market

helicopters into your mouth with spinning blades of fruit

herb garden planted next to a roaring charcoal fire

high-quality mousse should assail the tongue with little irritations that are a source of undeniable enjoyment

high-quality mousse should melt in the mouth like ice and burst against the palate like a firework

history in a bottle

homogeneous voluptuosity

honey-and-nut rush

honeybee's breath

honeycomb fresh from a hive

honey from some craggy mountaintop wildflowers

honey made from a thousand flowers

honeysuckle nectar on steroids

hovering between lissome and plump ripeness

hurrah of Syrah

hypnotic perfume of smoldering frankincense

I breathe in both earth and sky

ice cave shimmering with stalactites

iconic blackstrap chunkiness

I could wear this behind my ears

if anything could drink like quicksilver looks, it's this wine

if a wine could make a person cry, it would have to be a Pinot Noir

if black has flavors this wine embodies them

I felt like I fallen into a blueberry-lined well with sweet dark violets

if fine white Burgundy is violins and violas, this is a cello

if it's possible to taste a fragrance, Moscato d'Asti manages it

if I were forced to drink just one wine, let it be this

immediate belch of fragrances

impenetrable brooding River Styx

impenetrable Stygian purple-red

improbable distillate of liquid wildflowers

incisive power of a hard stare combined with the grace of a smile

in corruptly delicious middle age

indescribable but not unbearable lightness of being

induces a dreamlike silence as its enormous almost roasted flavor envelopes the palate

inebriating perfume

infant waiting to ascend the throne

in gentle decline to fragile luminous old age
in its pretty sunset years
innumerable drops of perfume...in bursts and towers
  of scents
inside of kid gloves worn by a young woman
instills awe in the taster's heart and palate
intoxicating grape sweat
invites you to dinner
iron mountain full of rust
irresistibly appetizing whirlwind of sensations
it doesn't warble or trill, it richly roars
it doesn't just smell, it pongs
it's the singer, not the song
its voice coming out in one final absolutely strong
  perfectly pitched note
I was drinking history; I liked the taste
jewelry with beautiful delicate features
juicy grapefruit rolling languidly on lush green grass
jumble of berries black and blue
jumps around on the tongue
just goes into your pores
just hugs you
just starting to come to the boil
kind of wine you want to marry
Kool-Aid stand on a dusty road
Kublai Khan's pleasure dome in Xanadu
laced with the savor of the earth
Lafite is a tenor; Latour, a bass...Lafite is a lyric;
  Latour, an epic...Lafite is a dance; Latour, a parade
languorously sultry
landscape made tastable
late spring in a bottle
late spring or early summer evenings when flowers
  exhale their fragrances
late-summer farmstand with sun-ripened oranges
laughing boy of a wine
lavalike consistency as it coagulates in the throat
lavish tumultuous effervescence
layer upon airy layer
layer upon layer coating your tongue in explosions of
  flavors
layers of flavors that unwrap like Christmas packages
lean muscular dancer handsomely attired
leaping pearls of air
leather seats in my father's old sports car
leaves the palate vibrating and longing for more
leaves symphonic memories in the mouth
leaves with a glow like the last embers of a fire
leaves you in a state of Zen-like satisfaction
leaves your whole body feeling red
legs as impressive as the arches of Durham Cathedral
lemon juice to lemon pith spectrum
less of a shooting star, more of a damp squib
library of aromas
library of an old house scented with leather
  volumes and pipe smoke

Life is a Cabernet
life span rivaling that of a Galápagos tortoise

light melons dancing on the nose
like drinking a mousse of peach blossoms
like biting into the juicy plump flesh of a
  perfectly ripe white peach
like burying your face in a pillow stuffed with dried
  rose petals
like coming home to a suite in the Plaza

like dancing on the lawn
like drinking clouds
like drinking fruity air
like drinking history
like drinking snow
like driving through the lemon groves of Sicily with
  the car roof down
like eating your candy in liquid form (with plenty of
  alcohol)
like falling into a six-foot-thick down comforter
like falling into a strawberry patch littered with
  walnuts
like injecting pure honey into your tongue...
  sending it into jolts of diabetic coma
like licking the flesh of cool, fresh-cut apples
like opening a cedar chest filled with blackberries and
  potpourri
like picking berries on a hot summer day in the
  mountains
like pouring diamonds into a tulip
like rekindling an old love in a new body
like relaxing into a favorite chair
like running my tongue over the essence of each
  vineyard
like sitting on the back porch on a sunny autumn
  evening eating peach sorbet
like standing in the middle of a field of sweet black
  earth after a spring rain
like standing right next to a large rosebush covered
  with blooms
like stepping inside a painting by the Tahitian-period
  Gauguin
like strolling through a tropical paradise
like stumbling into wild blackberry bushes without
  any thorns
like tasting rainbows
like tasting the earth and the sun at the same time
like walking past a Body Shop on a hot summer's day
like walking through a cherry orchard in mid-July
like walking through a library and smelling the
  leather of the old books
like walking through a rose garden
like walking through the New England woods in
  October with a fresh loaf of sourdough bread under
  my arm
lilacs in the spring
lingering beauty is underpinned by real substance
lingers in the throat like nectar
lingers on the palate for an eternity
liquid brandysnaps

liquid buttered wholemeal toast smothered with lime marmalade
liquid cashmere
liquid decadence
liquid dessert

liquid distillate of the landscape

liquid ecstasy
liquid fudge
liquid nobility
little bit country, little bit Ritz-Carlton
little wild red berries gorged on sun
lively tumult of apricots, honeysuckle and fresh minerality
locomotive that crashes over the palate with a flamboyant display of blackberry and cassis fruit
loganberries firing on all cylinders
lollypop clouds
long fine eyelash-fluttering tannins
long gustatory crescendo
long seductive marmalade of a wine
long subtle symphony
long voyage through pleasure
looks as though only kings should drink it
lovely floral note growing amidst the blades of grass
lovely inner spirit
lubricates imagination and fuels conversation
Lucy in the Sky with Diamonds
luscious music in a bottle
lush green meadow in spring
lush ripeness wedded to power and complexity: the holy trinity of great winemaking
lush seductive evocation of France
luxurious honeyed supersmooth textured fruit bathes the palate
macédoine of fruit in a bottle
magic caravan of lilies and blueberries and herbs
magic carpet of strawberries and soft creamy contentment
magic reek of fruit and harvest bloom
magna cum laude complexity
magnificence piled upon magnificence
magnificent cardinal's robe
maidens dancing on grassy hillsides in colorful native costumes
majestic flavor breadth
majesty of the Royal Oak
makes the earth move
makes the soul wax embarrassingly poetic
makes the taste buds dance
makes your senses soar
manly wine with more backbone than a humpback whale
marries opulence to tannin in such a way that one almost drowns the other
marshmallow dropped for a second into the bonfire
masterpiece of sensuality
mature and sterling symphony with kettledrums and rumbling bass

may well outlive everyone reading these words
mélange of wonders
melds suave elegance with primordial hedonism
melodious bubbles
melts in the mouth like ice cream and runs down the throat like nectar
memories of perfumes from long ago
mesmerizing combination of mulberry and myrrh infused with notes of pine and frankincense
message of a Mozart quartet

metal wire bound in licorice

midlife crisis or seven-year itch
million tiny explosions of liquid fireworks
minerals and earth awash in sweet lemons
minimal bubbles burst against the palate like pellets of caviar
mining an apparently inexhaustible seam of complexity
minuscule rebellious bubbles
Mirabelle plums gorged on sunshine
mirage haze of hillside herbs
mixes a lash of pain with its pleasure
moist earth after a summer rain
moonlit color
more Andalusian gypsy than gentleman of Castile
more Emperor Augustus than Queen Elizabeth
more flush than blush
more grunt than a grizzly
more of an essence than a wine
more perched than balanced
more tannic than a gallon of trucker's tea
moseys around my mouth with the ambiguous solidity of a jellyfish
most gorge-caressing dessert on earth
most succinct expression of the metaphysical essence of rosiness
mousse rises like a chef's toque
mouthfeel is tantamount to millions of tiny puffy pillows
mouthful of voluptuous curves
moves to the pace of its own drum
multiple chains of fine compact bubbles
multiple layers like an encyclopedia of tastes
murky, muffled and moderate
murmur of foam
murmuring undertone of dusky earth juxtaposed with a charming aura
muscle of youth and the complexity of age
mushrooms among the flowers
music for the sense of taste
musty, dusty and fusty
Muzak for your palate
my palate experiences a gustatory orgasm just thinking about it
narrow bandwidth of flavors
necklace of pearls on a white neck
nectar to a bee
needs a smack on the bottom

needs space to move and spread its wings
needs till 2006 to unpick its lock
nettles violently slashed at with a stick
never-ending passion play of flavors
nerve-jangling teeth-on-edge acid overdose
newly vacated seashells
newly washed sheets that have been hung to dry
    outdoors
new sunrise
nice bass note of mulchy funk
noble triumphant bubbles
no other wine on earth better embodies the passage
    of time than golden Yquem
nostril-permeating menthol-white pepper
not a lot of fruit hiding in the basement
not a single wine made our socks roll up and down
not for romance and candlelight
notorious for (temporarily) staining one's teeth the
    color of cherry Kool-Aid
not so much as a toothpick of oak
not the brightest crayon in the box
no vanishing point…the flavors linger on forever
nugget of blackberry goodness
nut basket in green grass
oak aging with gay abandon
oak is the drum that anchors the symphony
oak-lavished landscape
oak tends to sit on top of the fruit like a floppy hat
oak travels in the back of the plane
oak winds up for a toast and a vanilla knockout punch
ocean breeze through conifers
ocean-spritz on your face
ode to spring
off you go into the wild black yonder
oil slick of black fruit and dark spice
old boathouse when the summer sun bakes its sides
one man's nectar is another man's Tidy Bowl
one sip is like a trip to Tahiti
one wonders whether some of the rot was less than
    noble
on gossamer wings of minerals
only now freeing itself from the ruddiness of youth
only wine in the world you can hear
oozes flavor as if it had been squeezed from a tube
oozy layers of expensive sweets
opened up into an unforgettable crescendo
opens like a peacock's tail
opulent marmalade on burnt brown toast
opulent unctuous stunner
orange blossom and wild strawberry fantasy
    perfumed by rose water
orchestra of flavors

organic dark wild-eyed beauties

orgy of aromas
oriental spices inhabit the dark corners
overblown ripsnorter
overwhelming sense of tedium
painted with delicate brushstrokes

painter's palette of flavors on the tongue
Parisian-brothel fragrance
Parma violet sweets with a slight plastic edge
paradise for the sweet-toothed
passionately entwined flavors
peachy enough to become Georgia's state wine
peacock's tail of aromas and flavors
peacock's tail with quite a few feathers missing
pearly train of bubbles
peppered with *poivre*
peppers sliced with a silver knife
perfect for an actress's slipper
perfectly ripe watermelon on the hottest day of
    summer
perfect sipping for UFO patrols on summer nights
perfumes born of the sun
Persian miniature painted with pigments derived
    from spices harmonized in detail and color
piccolo of floral flavors
picnic baskets full of smoked salmon
picnic in a bottle
picnic in a meadow
pineapple upside-down cake with a butterscotch
    glaze baked in a wood-burning oven
pink-cheeked bright-eyed old lady

Pinot with training wheels

pirouettes of spices
playful fawn of wine
plays sun off earth
plenty of night here…a bit of daylight might come as a
    welcome relief
plenty of poise and aplomb
plenty of Rubensesque Grenache flesh
plenty under the hood for aging
plethora of celestial aromas
plummy fruit comes rocketing through
plump, peachy and practically perfect
plum pudding in a bottle
plush texture feels like the palate is resting on a
    waterbed of over-ripe black fruit
pockets of fruit exploding in the mouth
poetry of Pinot Noir
poised perfection
polished blocks of dark fruit cemented with minerals
polyphonic counterpoint with divine melodic lines
positively swoony perfume of violets
potpourri in my grandmother's bathroom
powerful and muscular yet remarkably feminine and
    elegant
power like a burst of adrenaline
precocious child: impatiently trying to talk and walk
preserves balance like an angel
pretty child with an upturned nose
primal flavors of sun and earth
primps and tweaks the taste buds
prismatic luminescence
profound fruit bobbing up and down
profoundly expressive of its territory

proud to be pink
provides great entertainment on the tongue
puffs of wind from a raspberry patch
pure Deep Secret red rose
pure nirvana
pure passion fruit pulp
pure symmetry between its building blocks of tannin,
    acidity, alcohol and extract
purple fury of inky rich quality
purple giving off fumes of brambles and rum
purist hit of wet dog you could care to inhale
pushes the sensory circuits into overdrive
Pythagorean harmony
quiet communiqués from soil to air to nose
quite possibly one of Gladstone's boots
quivering caress of bubbles
racehorse ready to burst from the starting gate
raging rapids of dark fruit
rainbow of aromas
rainbow of flavor
rainforest nut-scented
rain-refreshed lilac
rainy-cloud density
rare auditory elegance
real bitzer: a multibreed like the proverbial junkyard
    dog
really sings on the palate
red-fruit freshness of distant youth
red painted black
red, white and blue Popsicles
red wine with serious cleavage
regal suggestions of vanilla
regional earth and tar
regular roller-coaster ride
remarkable berries and well-clotted cream
remarkable crescendo of flavor
remarkably delicate pretty lacework of flavors
resonates and lingers on the palate like a tuning fork
    does to the eardrum
retronasal resonance
reverberates at least as long as Pavarotti's high C
revitalizing sprinkling of summer dust
richest shade of shimmering ruby
rich tannins of great couth
rich unctuous liquid feast
rides in waves across the palate
ringing intense finale
ringing tones forming intricate sustained chords
riot of flavors
ripe berries struggling to squeeze between charred
    oak planks
ripe fruit baking in the sun on the ground in an
    orchard
ripe fruit easing into senescence
ripeness in restraint
ripe to the edge of opulence
robe of spicy new oak
rolling down honey, peach and candied orange peel

and swooping back up in a lemon-lime burst
rolls across the palate like a giant ocean swell
rosary of fine irrepressible bubbles
rosé in full bloom
roses scattered over the forest floor
rough suede with emery edges
round rich relaxed fruit seems to go straight to your
    heart
Rubensesque woman in her flowerbed
rub of new-cut lemons
runs up and down the scales of flavor
saltiness reminiscent of seaside vineyards
satisfies the soul in that dark cavernous interior
    where few wines dare descend
sauvage gaminess
savage almost coarse throaty roar of flavors
scatters the petals of a virtual garden of bubble flowers
scent caught through gauze
scented beeswax candles dripping on an ancient teak
    table
scented lady's handbag full of lipstick
scents of a meadow after the rain
scents of the *maquis* on a warm summer wind
schist child
scintillating shiver of acidity
scratching at the door of perfection
sea air after a summer rain
sea-breeze freshness
seamless beauty where color, tannin, acidity and fruit
    are emotionally intertwined like lucky life partners
seductive majestic wine-drinking experience
seemingly inexhaustible persistence of scents
seems to dance due to popping acidity
seems to have swallowed the summer sun
seems to wrap itself around you
sense of gathering strength as it rolls down the throat
sense of place in a bottle
sensory battle royal
sequins of amber-gold
sets every tactile and taste sensor ringing
sets sail in your mouth a raft of dried herb, licorice
    and superfine tannins
sharp dusty smells inside my great-grandfather's brass
    mantel clock
shaft of intensity lances the air
sherbet lemon tingle
shimmering minerally crystal chandelier of a wine
shines like a beacon
Shiraz with the volume turned down
shirt-collar grabbing verve
shut down like a pair of grizzlies in hibernation
Sibelius symphony: full of melancholy, happiness and
    romance
simple rosé to drink out of a woman's slipper
singing beautifully
singing with the plum-prune-tea medley
sings a pretty song
sings on the palate

skyscraper-like profile of fabulous concentration and
    length
skyscraper with multiple levels
sleepless night in a Cohiba factory
slender weak-kneed flavors
slightly corroded by the tooth of time
slightly funky earthy we're-not-in-Kansas-anymore
    nose
slightly *jejune* artifice
slightly sullen bitter undertow
slips down like greased oysters
slithers around your mouth and down your throat,
    caressing as it goes
slow-blooming flower in your mouth
smells black
smells like rain on a bitumen road
smells red
smells thick
smoke from a distant fire
smoking tarmac on a hot summer's day
smoky bonfire night snorts
smoky minerals awash in sweet peach juice
smoky toast and jammy fruit (sounds like breakfast)
smooth and eternal like the nameless flower which
    blooms every year in memory of an eternal love
smorgasbord of earthly delights
snare drum of citrus
so absolutely round and complete that it's spheric
soaring upward in a merry column
soars like a meteor shower
so bright it seemed to light up the room
so brimming with sugar they tasted like tiny bon-bons
so concentrated it tastes as though all the fruit has
    evaporated...leaving only the spirit behind
so dark and deep it's impenetrable
so dark it was like looking into space
so dark, rich, heady and fruity that it would
    attract bees from the whole neighborhood
so delicious it melts the heart
so filled (with fruit) that it's like sparklers
so fragrant it's as if fields of wildflowers must grow
    between the vines
so fresh that it was dancing like a teenager when
    opened
soft accents of sealing wax and truffles
soft couch of glycerin
so glossy and well fed...like a prize trotter
so heavily mineral the bottle should be heavy to lift
so honeyed you'd think they aged it in a beehive
so incredibly sublime and unworldly that it could
    create a stampede at auction
so intense that every taste receptor reacts as if
    electrically stimulated
so luscious it could make grown men swoon
some dirt under its fingernails
something bolted together with planks of tannins
so much depth you don't drink it so much as fall
    into it

song of Shiraz and the sea
so outrageously rich and fruity it should be a
    controlled substance
so perfect one almost cried tears of joy
sorbet for your nose
so rich it's almost its own food
so rich that it's liable to suffocate folks who prefer
    pecks on the cheek to large-scale embraces
so seductively fragrant you want to dive into it
so strong you feel it in the room when the wine is
    poured
so thick it could be spread on toast
so thick it might roll out like paste instead of pouring
    like liquid
so thick it needs to be drunk with a spoon
so thickly clotted you'd swear you could grease an axle
    with it
so wickedly delicious it's probably illegal in 25 states
so zesty it would wake the dead
speaks to your soul
spectacular as it unfolds in waves
spicy breeze laden with juniper elements
spicy juicy black plums kissed with vanilla
splash of cold water on your face on a hot day
splendored perfection of maturity
spot-on marriage of gentle sweetness and sheer zest
spreads out like a comfortable blanket on a featherbed
spring blossom of a wine
spring cherries on a bed of newly harvested hay
squishily juicily fresh
statement of humankind's creative genius
sticky and warm but not uncomfortably humid
still hides many things...like an unopened rose
    blossom
strawberries peeping through wood
strawberry kissing a melon
stream of rich coffee and sweet prunes
stroll in late fall
strumpet of a wine with tawdry cherry and plum
    flavors and a tart mouth
study in orange: orange blossoms, orange peel, light
    orange fruit
study of beauty in black: black fruit, black smoke and
    black bitter minerals
stunning mosaic of flavors
stuns the taste buds into admiring submission
sublime almost pagan Riesling fruit
subterranean and extraterrestrial at the same time
subtle whiplash of flavor
succulent luau of grilled pineapples, honeysuckle
    and herbs
such a delight to taste I was seriously tempted to
    swallow
summer cookout in a bottle
summer rain on a gravelly road
summertime on the front porch
summer walk through a botanic grove
summer wind with refreshing and cooling elements

summery feelings of strawberries and whipped cream
sumptuous quivering bubbles
sun-dappled lawns
Sunday-breakfast aromas of strong coffee, mixed
   berry jam and sizzling bacon
sunniest, most comfortingly perfect sense of
   pure fruit ripeness
sunshine in a bottle
sunshine was here
superbly vital, like a lady who has aged with grace
supermarket of complex flavors
surprise after surprise: the throat is stunned
swashbucklingly spicy
swell of fragrance and flavors
sweet conspiratorial mousse
sweetness in the background waiting to titillate
sweet tannins drowning in waves of fruit
sweet web of botrytis
sweet white thunderbolts
swell of fragrances and flavors
swimmer: sinewy, streamlined and shapely with
   rippling pectoral muscles
swirls and sashays lithely and elegantly
symbol of the flower of civilization
symphonic harmony
symphony for the palate
symphony of exotic aromas and flavors
symphony of the Pinot grape's various incarnations
   where the aftertaste reverberates like a singer's voice
   in a cathedral
tails off with a sweet kirsch kiss
tanginess of thoroughbred stables
tannic tonsil-threatening
tannins like a three-day-old beard
tannins rising up through the wine like a galloping
   herd
tannins spread like a Turkish carpet across the tongue
tannins that all but take the skin off the roof of your
   mouth
tannins tremble on the brink of dominance
tarted up like a bridesmaid
tasted like honey and stung like a wasp
taste of furious passion
taste of sunshine
tastes blue
tastes brick red
tastes deep black
tastes like it's staining my insides
tastes like sunshine
tastes pink
tastes purple
tear-jerkingly refreshing
texture feels like the palate is resting on a waterbed of
   overripe black fruit
texture is so plush that the palate gets lost in a
   dizzying smorgasbord of flavors and aromas
texture like the heavy hypnotic flow in a lava lamp
the bearable lightness of being

the Concorde: bumpy takeoff, steep climb,
   then supersonic
the elegance femininity of a ballerina and the muscle
   of a bodybuilder
the Gandhi of Pinot Noir: intense, quietly powerful
   and capable of great things
(the journey of wine) will transport you to its
   birthplace
the orchestra is playing a lovely melody, but you
   have to listen closely to hear it
the saddle without the sweat
the sea combined with strawberry jam
the stuff not just made of dreams but of legends
the thrill of wine is in its complex mercurial nature
thick and dusty like the door to Ali Baba's cave
thick brush strokes of berries
thick strawberry jam flavors waltz with your taste
   buds
think of the Earth as wine's birthmark
thin skein of sweetness
throaty roar of flavors
thumbprint of Earth's maker
thumping attack of violets and iris
thumping its chest and baring its teeth and roaring
   abuse
thumps your gums with tannic sledgehammers
thunderclap on a hot autumn evening
tickles the soul as well as the tongue
tightly wound beams of pinpoint flavors
tingle verging on a burn
toast, leather and spiced wood surf a rippling wave of
   red fruit
top-class act from go to whoa
towel snap of acidity
towering skyscraper in the mouth without being
   heavy or disjointed
transports you straight into some deep autumnal
   forest
traveling fair: popcorn, candy floss and vanilla
   ice cream
treasure chest of smoky, earthy, animal flavors
tropical fruit aromas speak of islands
tropical rainforest with all its exotic flowers
truffles made into wine
truffley tarry Gigondas typicity
tuning fork for your palate
turbulent red whirlpool of ripe damson fruit and
   chewy grainy tannins
turbulent surge of bubbles
turns on the water taps in the mouth
Tuscan elixir belongs in the papal treasury
two chalk erasers slammed against each other
unctuous tangerine-flavored fruit bomb
unfolds like a Japanese fan of flavors
unfolds on the palate without a hiccup
unkissed by the oak fairy
unmistakable surge of Bentley-like power under the
   bonnet

unrolls like a very dark red carpet across your palate
unusual bed partners of licorice, acetone and lemon
vacation on the island of sweet dreams
vanilla cookies and cocoa do an attractive little dance
vanilla ice cream melting in the mouth
vanilla pastry tucked into its slim frame
vanilla-tinged fruit slides over the palate with no
     bumps or bruises
various flavors blooming at different times
V8 engine throbbing away gently on the massive
     midpalate
veritable seduction serum
vervy acidity happily wakes up the taste buds
vibrant ruby shade en route to black
vinous arm-wrestle happening here
vinous black hole in space
vinous firework waiting to explode
vinous Lothario

vinous Viagrafication

vinous whore
violets dance
violets in a grassy lawn after a rain
virtual party in your mouth
virtuosic expression of the vineyard
volcano of flavors
voluptuous indolence
waft of sea-splashed winds
wafts you off into a red-wine reverie
walk in the woods on a crisp fall day
walks the right line down every taste
walk through the forest on a misty autumn day
wanders off with a slightly blurred finish
warm embrace for breezy beachside nights
warm spring day in the country
warms the mortal soul
water balloon filled to bursting with grape and
     cherry jam
water of green grapes
waves crashing on a sandy beach
waves of limpid crystalline laughter
wearing its cherry and raspberry fruit with a smile
weightless…like drinking clouds
wet retriever after a day on the moors
whiffs of camphor wood and loganberry jam turning
     to leather
whiffs of waffles
whisper in a courtyard
wildflowers picked alongside a babbling brook
wildflowers sprinkled amid grasses
wild horse…beautiful and untamed
wild jungle of competing but somehow perfectly
     integrated dark fruit
will hypnotize your taste buds
wine is the song of the earth
will light your primal fire
wind over the barren prairie
wine for Wagnerian Rhine maidens
wine: old men's milk

wine that dreams are made of
wine you want to dance with
winter sunset
wispy licorice veil
women with parasols playing croquet in the sunshine
     on an enormous lawn

wonderful tapestry of aromas

wood nymph tears
woven together with veils of exotic fruit
wrapped in ripeness
yellowy winter sky
yeoman-of-the-guard sturdiness
your first French kiss from a long-term unrequited
     crush
youthfully bubbling over like a calf let out to pasture
zigzags across your palate like a pinball

...the writer should never like a wine, he should be in love with it; never find a wine disappointing but identify it as a mortal enemy, an attempt to poison him; sulphuric acid should be discovered where there is the faintest hint of sharpness. Bizarre and improbable side-tastes should be proclaimed: mushrooms, rotting wood, black treacle, burned pencils, condensed milk, sewage, the smell of French railway stations or ladies' underwear—anything to get away from the accepted list of fruit and flowers. As I say, I am not sure it helps much, but it is much more amusing to read.
Auberon Waugh

D. A Bizarrerie of the Truly Strange

Here are some amazing oddities you don't always expect to find in wine terms, let alone in the wine itself. Nonetheless, very experienced professional wine tasters with a commanding grip on the English language do come up with these, day after day, month after month, year after year. Apparently, wine evokes all manner of mental phantasmagoria. While these are all real terms and expressions taken from real wine reviews, many are just plain baffling. Particularly some that seem to be more about what we call *hygiene* rather than wine. In fact, many of them are so normally repellent that we all should be very glad we aren't the ones doing the tasting. Er-r-r, try to enjoy.

2 x 4 plank
3-IN-ONE oil
'63 Chevy Nova exhaust
aborigine's armpit
about as friendly as a sumo
    wrestler with diaper rash
acetone
acidity acts as a sort of embalming
    fluid
aged grease monkey
aged raw meat
aged sausages
aged venison stew
aging sexpot
air freshener
aioli
alcohol-fortified pancake syrup
algae
all dry bones
all the charm of a mouthful of
    steel wool
almost livery

ambergris
Amarone-asphalt
anal
anchovies
ancient inner tubes
animal gut
antiseptic mouthwash
any men's room
argumentative white pepper
armpits of a healthy clean-living
    youth after exercise
aromas eerily reminiscent of a
    live lobster
artificial cough drops
artificial sweetener
asbestos
as delicate as a poised iron
    butterfly
Asian lady beetles
as long as an F-18 vapor trail
as old as dirt

asparagus and gooseberries
    dance on the nose
asparagus tart
aspergillus rot
asphalt
Aspro Clear soluble aspirin
as tight as nails
axle grease
baby food
baby poop
baby powder
baby's diaper
bacon fat
bacon-laced minerals
bacony oak
bacterially infected
badly burnt cabbage
baked pencils
baklava
ballpark franks
Band-Aids
bangers

Bangkok paddy field
barnyard filth
barnyardy asparagus
bar rag
baseball glove
battery acid
Bayer aspirin
beef blood
beef jerky
beer towel
beeswax
Beirut pastry shop
belly-button lint
Bengay
bilgewater
billy goat
bitumen
black and cloudy like water mixed
  with the contentsof an ashtray
black punk rocker
blanching water
bland McWine
bleach
Blitzkrieg on my palate
blocked drains
blood of a mythological beast
bloody note to the meaty cherries
bloody Scud missile
blue cheese
boiled crab shell
body-builder wine
bordering on liquid crack
bog-standard rosé
boiled cabbage water
boiled mutton
boiled twigs
boneless, like chicken
bongwater
bouillon and stables
boxed rosé his mother forgot
  in the garage
brace of partridges
brake fluid
Brasso
Brazilian woman
brown barnyardy swill
brown beans slightly overcooked
brush fire
bubble bath
bubblegum pop music
bug spray
bunch of dead chrysanthemums
  on the grave of a stillborn West
  Indian baby
burlap feedsacks
burning tires
burnt crust with a bit of tar
burnt horn

burnt rubber
burnt shrimp shells
buttered popcorn with pineapple
  and vanilla sauce
butterscotchy smoke
cactus pears
calf gravy
calf's foot jelly
camphor
candied eggplants
candied herbs
candied stones
candified booze
can liner
canned heat
caramelized leaves
caramelized stones
carborundum
carpentry solvents
cast-off cigarette paper
Castrol XL motor oil
cat-pee stinker
caustic
celery-iodine
charcuterie fat
charred raisins sweetened
  with boiled must
cheap children's paint
cheap mouthwash
cheese straws
cheesy feet
cheesy manure
Cheetos
cherry Chloraseptic
cherry-covered cigar box
cherry-drenched quartz
cherry fruit and cold cuts
chicken blood
chicken coop
chicken fat
chicken guts
chicken shit
children's cough syrup
chlorine
chlorophylly
chocolate and cabbages
cistern
citronella
clam chowder
clamshells
clean bandages
clove cigarettes
clown makeup
coal tar
coconut suntan oil
cod-liver oil and malt
coke oven
cold-sore ointment

coleslaw
combo of flowers and excrement
compost
confusing blue cheese
congealed blood
cooked mulberries and
  undergrowth
corrupt cherries
cotton candy
cotton sheets
cough drops
cough medicine
cowboy character
cow manure
cowpat
cow piss
cow shit
cow stall
crabmeat
crackers, black charcoal
C-rations
crawfish juice
crayfish stock
creamed minerals
Creepy Crawlers
creosote-infused blackberry
  liqueur
cricket bats
cross between a forest fire and
  a war zone
crushed bugs
crushed earthworms
crushed up with leaves and mice
curious mucked-out stables
  endtaste
curly black hair
cushion on which an incontinent
  person has been sitting
cyanide
damp basement
damp carpet
damp concrete
damp nappy
damp straw in a thoroughbred
  stable
dank
dairy-farm feed
datura
Day-Glo
dead animal
dead French people
dead leaves
dead sheep
decaying flower water
deep aftertaste of tar tablets
deep-fried nettles
defrosted refrigerator
De Gaulle-ish

Del Monte fruit cup
dentist's surgery
designer soap
detergent
Devil Dogs
devil farts
diesel exhaust
diesel fuel
dirty birdcages
dirty dishrag
dirty feet
dirty floorcloth
dirty hot tub
dirty shower
dirty socks
dishcloth
dishwashing soap

disinfectant

distinct traces of lederhosen
doesn't taste like Ben & Jerry's
   Chunky Monkey
dog breath
dog food
Dole pineapple cannery
domestic gas
donkey
doo-doo
Doritos
down mold
drains
dried seaweed
dried twigs
Driza-Bone clothing
dry porcinis that turn into
   blackberries
duck liver
dung fire
dusty cellar
dusty church
dusty old attic
dusty old carpet
dusty sawdust
dusty smells of bone-dry corrals
dusty stonewalls
dwarf bananas
eastern European fruit soup
Eggos
eggroll wrappers
electrical fire
elegant printer's ink
embalming fluid
enamel-ripping
engine oil
escargot mud pie
escargot-shell sensation
ether
even the nose seems chewy
evil mix of castor oil and

motor oil and curse words
expensive shotgun
explosive almost obnoxious
   aromas of litchi nuts and
   jasmine bathed inrose water
exposed mudflats
extraterrestrial
eye-watering
faded bouquet stolen from
   someone's grave
faintest whiff of Led Zeppelin
faint horsehair edge
fajitas
fake butter
farmyard animal richness
fascinating old smells of
   unswept floorboards
feline
feminine yet muscular
fennel-infused hot dog
   with sauerkraut
feral
fertilizer
fermented compost heap
fermented Kool-Aid

feta cheese

five pounds of melted butter
   churned in fresh-cut oak
Fig Newtons
filling-station forecourts
filthy fur
finish of English peas
finish of snail shells
finocchio fronds
fish glue and paraffin
fish oil
flaming fruit punch
flat Schlitz
flesh covering Italianate
   twigs and bushes
flies
flock of pelicans landing on the
   ocean
floor mop
floor wax
foaming toothpaste
foreign mouthwash
Formula 409 in Hawaii
fowl
Frankenstein Pinot
frankincense and myrrh
French-fry oil
French railway station
fresh-drawn blood
freshly caulked boat
Friar's Balsam
fruit rollups
frustrated honey

fuel oil in my furnace room
fungal-to-barnyard
fungal-truffle
funky earwax
fur and torrefaction
furbelows
furnace oil
furniture polish
furtive small game
fusty stink of rotting clothes
gamy
ganja
garbage
garden mercury
gasoline
gas station
gastric
gefilte fish
gelatinous veal stock
Germanic lime juice
gentle and violent
ghastly cheap pine disinfectant
ghastly strawberry soda
ghee
Ginsu blade concealed in a
   pineapple
girlfriend's damp Nike trainers
glistening fresh sweat
glue and bananas
gnat's piss mark two
Godzilla
gong-laden
gooey
grapefruit and lemon milkshake
grass cuttings steaming away
   on the compost heap
grilled oak
grilled sausages
grotty and vile
ground beef

guano

gunpowder
gunpowder tea
guts
gym bag after a win
gym shoes
Habitrail
hair gel
hair lotion
hairspray
halitosis
ham hocks and tar spread over
   bacon-covered marmalade
hamster cage
hard-smoked rubber
hare's belly
hater-aide
haunted house

Hawaiian volcanic ash-tinged
  notes of duck's breath
headache and anise
headcheese aged in oak
hencoop
hen droppings
hermaphroditic
herpes-infected prostitute
highly resinous skunk
hippy incense
Hodgepodge Lodge
honeyed crushed stone
Horlicks with dust and cobwebs
horsehide
horseshit
horse stable
horse urine
hospital smells
hot cross buns
hot dog water
hot dry concrete
hot tarmac
huge piles of dirty laundry
hulls of shelled pecans
hung game
hung game birds
if you like 'em big and a touch
  funky, get tattooed
IHOP cherry pancake syrup
immature acetone
immature celluloid
indescribable absolutely
  ravishing stink
indole
industrial Kool-Aid
infused roots
instant whiff on antiseptic
inviting salt and vinegar crisps
iodine
Italian-like creosote
its once-firm bosom is sagging
jalapeño
jam machine

Janitor in a Drum
Jekyll and Hyde characteristics
jelly babies
Jolly Rancher on steroids
Juicy Fruit
juicy grapefruit rollinglanguidly
  on lush green grass
jujubes
just corsets and bones
just-opened petrol can
just-used bathroom
K & B wine-flavored mouthwash
kerosene- and petrol-like
  maturity

kitchen sink
kitty litter box
kitty pee-pee
kneepads-needed Zin
  monstrosity
knows how to shake its booty on
  the dance floor
laboratory-concocted Stepford
  wine
Labrador breath
Labrador on its back waiting
  to be scratched
labyrinthine
lactic baby-sick notes
lactic strawberries
lamb shanks
lantana brandy spirit

lacquer thinner
lard
laser-sharp backbone
last-minute Halloween costume
latex paint
lathered horse
laundromat filled with jalapeño
  peppers
laundry soap
leather and saddle soap
leather compost
leather polish
Lemon Pledge
library paste
lichen-covered churches
lighter fluid
lightly stewed grass
like brushing your teeth
  with a belt sander
like chewing the tires off a
  ten-year-old tractor
like drinking wine through
  oyster shells
like inhaling a small electric eel
like licking a battery
like licking a piece of wine-
  impregnated wood
like licking a telephone pole
like licking the inside of a French
  oak barrel
like taking Virol, the malted
  meaty tonic for anemic girls
like urine, but not in a bad way
like walking into a sawmill
lime and linoleum
lime sports drink
linalool
Linford Christie without
  his jockstrap
linseed oil

lint, bandages and iodine
liqueur of stones
liquefied charcoal beef
liquefied Viagra
liquid Drāno
liquid granite
liquid lead pencils
liquid leather
liquid that collects in the
  toilet-brush holder
liquid voodoo magic
Listerine
little soaps you never use
locker room after a football game
  on a warm September evening
London bricks
looks like the North Atlantic
loquat jam
lots of grass and sour cream
Louisiana steamed crawdads
lovely fish scales
low-key cat's pee
lymphatic
lymph red
Mace
made in a jelly bean factory with
  artificial flavorings
male armpits
mangy
marijuana
marine creosote
Marmite
marrow
marshy nightmare
masculine exterior, feminine
  underneath
mashed digestive biscuits
Maui Blanc
McChardonnay
McDonaldized
meaty Bovril
meaty leather
medical clinic
medicated shampoo
medicine cabinet
medicinal cherry
melted stones

melting road tar
men's cologne
men's room at a baseball park
  during a game
menthol and smoked fish
mentholated butterscotch
mentholated quince
mentholated raspberries
menthol off a spoon of
  cough medicine

mercaptan
mercurochrome
merde
mesmerizingly lanolinish
mesquite
mess of prunes
metal wire bound in licorice
microbes
Mighty Mouse
Milk Duds
milking parlor
milk of magnesia
mincemeat
minestrone in its tannicity
minty alfalfa
model airplane glue
moist navel lint
moistened brioche
moldy Band-Aids
monkey house at the zoo
monkey riding a horse bareback
MoonPies
more spicy pickle barrel flavor
    than fruit
mosquito repellent
mothballs
Mott's on steroids
mouse cage
mouse piss
mousy
mouthfeel is like nails
mouthfeel resembled giblet gravy
mouthful of dirt
mouthwash with substance
mucilaginous
mucky
mucous
mummified
mushroom mold
musk stick
mustard and manure
mustard gas
my father's carpet slippers
my father's old Labrador
my grandfather
my grandmother's dye-works
my grandmother's duck-egg
    custard
nail polish
nail polish remover *au poivre*
natural gas
natural hemp rope with prickly
    loose fibers
nauseating
near narcotic
neutron bomb of fruit
new balloons
new-Barbie smells

new black rubber tires
newly ironed laundry
newly unwrapped toffee
    wrappers
newly vacated seashells
new plastic, cheap sherry and old
    apples
nightclub bouncer
nightmarish
Nivea Creme
nori
nose leaks hard cheese
noteworthy sexpot personality
    (in plain English: a slut)
No. 36 bus
not of this world
not worth a rat's ass
Novocaine-like
numbles
nut-lilac
nutty velvet
oak bra
oak sawmill
obnoxious silkiness
office products
oil of Tokay
oil shale
old ashtray
old chesterfields
old driftwood
old kitchen J Cloth
old leather boots
Old MacDonald's Farm
old mistress
old penknives
old pennies
old running shoes
old running shorts
old silk clothes
old tarred sea timbers
oleaginous
one man's nectar is another man's
    Tidy Bowl
opium
orange Jell-O
Orange Tang
Oreos
organic wastes
oscillating plums
ostrich poop
overcooked coconut flapjacks
overly fragrant bath salts
overtones of the Great
    Dismal Swamp
oysters, ozone and clams
oyster shells
Oz Clarke's post-squash game
    T-shirt

Pacific storm
packet of chicken noodle soup
paintball blackberries
paint thinner
paper mill effluent in the
    River Tame
Parisian-brothel fragrance
parsnips and rutabagas
patchouli
peanut butter
pear and apple shampoo
peat
Peking duck slathered in
    hoisin sauce
perfect mix of Gorgonzola
    and lavender
penetrating slick of fresh paint
penicillin
perhaps in a menopausal state
perm solution
Persian cat
pesticide
pet litter tray
pet sweat
petroleum and nuts together build
    a symphony
phantomlike truffles
pickle barrel
pickled frog skin
pickle juice
pickles and sauerkraut
pigsty
pineapple doughnuts
pineapple LifeSavers
pine-clad sauna
Ping-Pong balls
piss and vinegar
pizza sauce
poison
plain ol' dirt
plank of two-by-four
plastic shower curtain
plastic wrap
poached salmon
polite cat's pee
polygamous
pond water
popcorn
poopy diaper
pork and boot polish
powdered stones
powder puff
predator beast
preserved plums you get in
    Chinatown
pressed caviar
prickly pear cactus
primitive rocks

proscuitto
pseudothermic
public restroom after it's
    been cleaned
pungent snow peas
pungent wet blanket
puppy's breath
putrid
putty
PVC
quail-egg casserole
Quercus fragmentus
quince cheese
quince paste
rabbit pee
rack of southern-style smoked ribs
railroad track
railway
rain on tar-macadam
rancid corn ships
rancid peanut butter
rancid tar-and-turpentine
    mouthwash
rancid vegetable mold
ragweed
raisin massacre
randy goat
raspberry Kool-Aid
rats
rat's tail
ravishes the olfactory mucosa
rawhide
raw meat

raw sewage
refined liquid botrytis
remains of a drained car sump
renal
rennet
revving-up airplane
rheumy
rich barnyard
rich old stables
ripe meat extract
ripe savory miso soup
ripe Stilton
roasting tins
Robitussin DM
rococo caramel
root beer
ropy
roasted cherries with
    cherry tomatoes
roasted lobster shells
roasted quail
roast woodcock's entrails
Rolling Rock
roofing felt
rotmouth

Roto-Rooter
rotten onions and garlic
rotting apricots
rotting cabbage
rotting garbage
rubber bands
rubber boots
rubber cement
rubber gloves
rubbing alcohol
Russian fur
rustic meat
rusty car bodies
rusty steel
sackcloth
sack sweat
sacramental incense
saddlebags
sailor's licorice
salami
Saltines
salt-laced slate
salty seashells
Saran Wrap
sauerkraut and toadstool
    sandwich
sauna
sausage-charcuterie
sausage meat
scabrous
scented old boots
schizophrenic
Screaming Yellow Zonkers
scuppernongy
sealing-wax maturity
seashells and carpentry
seasick
sea urchin
seems to have been strained
    through a doormat
serious dog poop
sewer gas
Shanghai Tang
sharp leather
sheepskin blanket
Shetland sheepdog
shellac
shoe polish
sick and twisted
sickly spearmint
silicone
Silly Putty
singed animal hair
singed doormat
singed rubber
singed top of rice pudding
sizzling spattering volcano
skatole

Skittles
skunk cabbage
slight crushed-ant character
slightly perfumed aftershave
slight whiff of Tupperware
Slim Jims
slimy
slobbering slate
sluglike
Slurpees

smelly old people
smoked meat fat
smoked oysters
smoked rubber
smoked veggie burger
smoky backbone
smoky bacon crisps
smoky barbecue pit
smoky bonfire
smoky liverwurst
smoky Nordic berries
smoky rotting compost richness
smoldering tires
Snapple for adults
snow globe
soapsuds
so dry it sometimes seems to
    vacuum out your whole mouth
so good it's almost painful
soiled filter pads
so inky and dark it is clearly an
    octopus wine
somber mushrooms
something at Rite-Aid
something between cheesy
    and sweaty
something carnal
some very interesting dirty
    French aromas
so much oak I'm still picking
    splinters out of my teeth
[so sweet] it could revive the dead
soupy bouillabaisse
sour cream and mature
    meat pie (don't ask)
sour milk
sour weeds
soy intertwined with leather
soy sauce
Spackles right over the crack
    in the wine
spaghetti western
Spanish chorizo sausage
sparklers
spiced olives
spicy cough syrup
spicy *jalapeños*
spicy meatballs

spoiled Camembert cheese
spoiled orange juice
squirrelly
stable tack
stagnant water
stale stair carpet
steely waxy bacon fat
stewed asparagus
stewed fish
stewed green beans
sticking plasters
stinging nettles
stink bomb
stinky cheese
stir-fry
strange goaty cream cheese
strange horseradish
strawberries larded with
    furniture polish and caramel
strong pickle-barrel character
sturdy sweaty fruit
styptic
sucked peach stones
sudsy wet dog
sullen blueberries
sumo wrestler's jockstrap
sumo wrestler's thighs
sun-dried gravel
sunscreen
suntan lotion
surgical bandages
surreal cocktail of perfume,
    pomegranate and cherry
    Kool-Aid
sushi bar with everything but
    the sushi

swamp thing
sweating horse
sweaty berries
sweaty fat
sweaty feet
sweaty horse blanket
sweaty raspberries
sweaty saddle
sweaty underpants
Swedish fish
sweet anchovies
sweet milkshake oak
sweetness of well-hung game
sweet odor of cow
sweet pickles
sweet rubber
sweet-savory tomato paste
sweet slate
sweet tar
swimming-pool chlorine
swoosh of pungent fenberries
syrup of figs: the old-fashioned

medicine for those suffering from
    constipation
Tabasco sauce
table tennis balls and marker pens
tadpole effect
talcum powder-dusted
    red fruit
tanginess of thoroughbred
    stables
tang of cheesy feet
tannins like hacksaw blades
tarred rope
tart's boudoir
tastes the way old books smell
teeth-rattling
teeth-scraping
tending to tadpole in style
teriyaki sauce
texture of 10W40 motor oil
texture of axle grease
texture of chicken soup in a glass
texture of nail polish
The Gap at the Gulfport
    (Mississippi) outlet mall
the only red wine of Veedercrest
    I can swallow without
    looking for a toilet

thermonuclear
thoroughbred horse peeing on
    clean straw
thorny
throat lozenges
tidal pool
timber merchant's shed
time-bomb cherriness
tincture of vomit
tinny
tire rubber
toad's eyes
tobacco-tinged tar
toffee wrappers
tomato bushes
tomcat
too smooth, too round, too rotten
tooth-enamel ripping
tooth-enamel stripping
toothpicky
tooth powder
tooth-rattling
Tootsie-Rolls
towelettes
trading-card powder
trail dust
trail mix barbecued over an open
    fire
trampled stinging nettles
traveling fair: popcorn, candyfloss
    and vanilla ice cream

troweled Spackle
truffles verging on barnyard
Turkish delight
turpentine
turtle water
tutti-frutti
twisted violets
ultrafresh sardines splashed
    with salt

unmucked cowstall
unpicked cherries
unraveled knitting
unset jelly
unwashed sweats
urine during asparagus season
urinous
vacillating between smoke
    and musk
vaguely amniotic
vaguely reminiscent of durian
vanilla Creamsicles
vanilla dust
varietal fish oil
varnishy
Vaseline and vanilla
Vaseline gold
veal demi-glace
Velveeta cheese
venison stew
venomous
very ripe dead fruit
very soft and very round like
    sheep's eyes with square pupils
viaduct
Vicks VapoRub
vinegar-fly taint
vinous equivalent to goose
vinous whore
Virol and pungent old stables
viscera
volcanic ash
volcaniclike dust
vomit
vulcanite
wacky raspberry-flavored
    red fizz
warm piss
warped blackberry Nips
water bag
waterlogged Buick Riviera
watermelon rind mixed with
    ginger ale
waxy cadaver
WD-40
weasels
wee-wee
weightlifter
well-aged Colombian weed

well-aged Topps bubble gum
wet animal fur
wet Band-Aid
wet cat
wet cement
wet clay
wet cobnuts
wet end of a great Cohiba
wet fur
wet hair
wet horse
wet horse blanket
wet Labrador
wet leather and armpits
wet metal
wet mouse
wet newspapers
wet pooch
wet Pendleton shirt
wet rag
wet rodent
wet shellac
wet sheep dog
wet wooly jumper
wild flügelberries on the
    midpalate
wild odors of cat urine
Windex
wooden bra
woodland sprites
wool fat
wool hat
wood louse
Worcestershire sauce
world-weary courtesan's scents
wormy
yellow genet
yellowing Chinese liquid
    with a pickled lizard
    inside it
yeoman farmer's muddy boots
YMCA pool
youthful kerosene

No wine, no wisdom. Too much wine—the same.
Pascal

As humans we are surprisingly poor at imagining aromas and flavors.
Barry C. Smith

A bottle of wine contains more philosophy than all the books in the world.
Louis Pasteur

Quickly, bring me a beaker of wine, so that I may wet my mind and say something clever.
Aristophanes

E. A Mind of Its Own

One of the more curious linguistic associations in this work is between the taste of wine and the intellect. To quite a few experienced tasters, a complex and memorable wine presents an intellectual challenge to reflect upon, to analyze fully and thoughtfully. All those aromas and flavors, so many to ponder, so little time. Consequently, don't even think about wasting cerebral energy on thinking about the simple stuff. It just may not be worth it.

above rational discourse
absolutely blows your mind
adult and thoughtful
a little obtuse
almost schizophrenic
almost too rich for anything
   but meditation
analytical
appeals to the intellect rather
   than the stomach
argumentative
astute
attentive
batty
begs for contemplation
berserk rage-inducing
bit confused
blew my mind
blows your mind with the first sip
broad-minded
bypasses the brain to grab the soul
causes you to stop and think
cerebral aromas
cerebral complexity
cerebral offering
cerebral appeal
cerebral stuff

certainly knows its mind
clear thinking
clever stuff
complex and intellectually
   stimulating
comprehensible
confusing to comprehend
conjures up thoughts of a
   bygone age
constant source of thought-
   provoking conversation
constantly challenges the intellect
contemplative
conversation piece
cultured
deeper communication
deeply introspective
defies all logic
delightfully witty berries
demands the attention of the
   taster from first sip to last
demands some degree of
   introspection
deserves contemplation
difficult to analyze
dim-witted

doesn't demand or merit
   microscopic examination
doesn't require any thought
doesn't require much introspection
don't drink this unless you're
   paying attention
don't get too cerebral about it
drink with thoughtful care
dry wit
dull-witted
easily understood
elegant but cerebral
engages the intellect
excellent companion for moments
   of contemplation
fails to engage the intellect
fair-minded
fills the mouth and blows the mind
finishes wittily
fluent
for immediate quaffing without
   too much deep discussion
for inquiring minds
for parties and mind-switched-off
   drinking
for people who like to meditate
genius

gets the conversation flowing
gives one pause for thought
gives physical pleasure but not
    intellectual satisfaction
gives temporary pleasure and
    leaves you with no food for
    thought—just like an American
    comedy
goes straight to the pleasure
    center of the brain
hallucinatory
hare-brained
has willpower
has wit
hedonistically and intellectually
    stimulating
hypnotic
imaginary
imaginative
imbecilic
impossible to intellectualize away
    the greatness of this wine
initiates conversation at the table
inspires contemplation and
    wonder
intellectual charm
intellectually challenging aspect
    to its personality
intellectually engaging
intellectual rigor
intellectual turn-on
intellectual vapidness
intelligent, quite
intelligent use of oak
intelligent winemaking
intelligible
intuitive
irrational
isn't for cerebral appreciation
it's not just big…it's clever
kind of complexity that we often
    refer to as wisdom
less communicative
lesson in contemplative enjoyment

little clueless

lubricates imagination and fuels
    conversation
lucid
mad
made with a hedonist's mentality
makes no demands on the intellect
makes our palates and minds
    stretch a little
mature and adult without being
    intellectual
meditative
mind-bending in a Methuselah
mind-blowing

mind-boggling
mind-numbing
mindless swill
misunderstood
more intellectually satisfying
more muscle than brains
moronic
needs time to make up its mind

no-brainer

noncerebral
not a whole lot to remember
not for intellectual gratification
nothing cerebral or highbrow
nothing that would tax the brain
no thinking required
not one to ponder
not very eloquent
offers a lot of pleasure without
    demanding a lot of thought
of intellectual interest
open-minded
overintellectualized
pensive
philosopher of a wine
pleasing classiness and wit
positively cerebral complexity
rare integrity and intelligence
rather intellectual
rational
real mind-stretcher
richly cerebral
satiates both the hedonistic and
    intellectual senses
satiates the olfactory senses yet
    pleases the mind's intellectual
    yearnings
satiates the intellect
satisfies my cravings for both
    corporeal and intellectual
    gratification
satisfies soul and body together;
    or intellect, perhaps, rather
    than soul
scholarly
serious brains
sharpens the brain
simple-minded
slightly intellectual…slightly
    boring
scores high on both pleasure and
    cerebral meters
sharply single-minded
sharp-witted
simple-minded
smart
smarty-pants wine
sometimes an ephemeral finish
    lingers on the mind

somewhat thoughtful
so simple it's almost simple-
    minded
speaks with polish and wry soft
    vowels
statement of humankind's creative
    genius
stops conversation at the dinner
    table
strangely eloquent
strong-minded
strong-willed
stupid
supersmart
takes some thinking to appreciate
takes time to understand
talks well
tastes wise
thick honeyed musings
thinking man's claret
thoughtful
thoughtfully crafted
thought-provoking artisanal wine
thought-provoking bouquet
thought-provoking depth
to contemplate with each sip
to meditate on
to think about as you drink it
truly intellectual wine: every sip
    a challenge and a discovery
ultimate wine for contemplation
unable to speak
unbelievable intellectual appeal
understanding
unintellectual
unintelligent
very imaginative
vino da meditazione
wacked out/wacko
when you're not in the mood for
    too much serious analysis
where the intellectual meets
    the sensual

wholly obtuse

will appeal to tasters who enjoy
    thinking what's in their mouth
witty
witty idea
wine for contemplation
wine of a genius
wine of wit
wise
wonderfully cerebral
won't require a master's degree in
    wine to enjoy
woodland thoughts

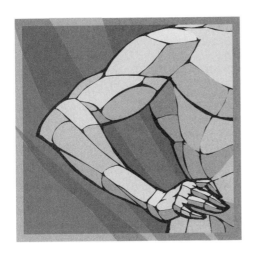

We live on the leash of our senses.
Diane Ackerman

*Beauty is only skin deep, but ugly
goes clean to the bone.*
Dorothy Parker

*Whoever named it necking was a
poor judge of anatomy.*
Groucho Marx

*No man should marry until he has studied
anatomy and dissected at least one woman.*
Honoré de Balzac

F. The Anatomy Lesson

It's hard not to notice just how many body parts and their effluvia are in your glass of vino (but not all at the same time, one hopes). Seems that wine conjures up all manner of physical similes from fists to wrists, from lips to hips, from nose to toes, from chin to skin. Plus, a whole lot of nice stuff and nasty bits in between.

anal/anus	cadaver	fart	hips	olfactory	saliva	toenails
armpits	cerebral	fat	joints	system	salivary	toes
arms	chassis	feces	knees	oral	glands	tongue
arteries	cheeks	feet	knuckles	ordure	scat	tonsils
ass	chest	figure	legs	orgasm	senses	torso
back	chin	filth	limbs	palate	sensual	underbelly
backbone	cleavage	fingernails	lips	palms	sensuous	urine
balls	cock	fingers	liver	pat	shell	**uvula**
beard	curves	fists	locks	**paunch**	shit	veins
beauty mark	dental	flab	lymph	pee	shoulders	venom
belly	digestive	flesh	marrow	pelt	sinews	viscera
belly button	system	frame	*merde*	perspiration	sinuses	vomit
bladder	doo-doo	funk	midpalate	pheromones	skatole	waist
blood	drool	gams	midriff	penis	skin	wazoo
body	droppings	girth	midsection	*pipi*	spine	wee-wee
bollocks	dung	**glands**	mouth	piss	spray	wrists
bones	ears	grease	mucus	poop	stomach	
bosom	earwax	gullet	muscles	pores	sweat	
bottom	elbows	gums	nails	pulse	tail	
booty	**entrails**	gut(s)	**navel**	pupils	tits	
bowels	excrement	hair	neck	rash	**taste buds**	
brain	eyeballs	hams	nerves	renal	tears	
breath	eyelashes	hands	nose	retronasal	teeth	
bum	eyelids	head	nostrils	rib cage	thighs	
butt	eyes	heart	oil	ribs	throat	
buttocks	face	hide		rump	thumbs	

There is no recipe for making wine and there is no formula for sensuality.
Frédéric Drouhin

There is more codswallop talked and written about wine, especially the so-called 'grand stuff,' than any subject except sex.
Malcolm Gluck

Ever wonder why wine language is rife with adjectives like sexy, seductive, smooth, velvety and lush? Because wine is one of the last legal sybaritic pursuits.
Diana Jacklich

G. An Ecstasy of Erotica

Sex sells. Oh, my, does it ever. No surprise, then, just how many wine descriptors reflect the more sensual aspects of our life experiences, particularly seductions. (Do people still seduce each other in this day and age?) In any case, wine drinkers apparently have no trouble whatsoever identifying the pleasures of wine with pleasures of the flesh. If so, this must a very good thing indeed for the continuation of our species in the best biological sense. *Come here, my darling. A bit more wine?*

absurdly rich and seductive
achieves the apotheosis of paradoxicality: dryness with sensual fruitiness
afterglow of any pleasurable activity
afternoon dalliance
air of romance
all about seduction
all foreplay
allow yourself to be seduced
all the flowers of the garden were present in the almost narcotically seductive bouquet
all the slurpy sexy mouthfeel you could want
alluring sexy personality
almost carnal meaty overtones
almost erotic
almost narcotically seductive
almost shockingly seductive personality
almost voluptuous

amply proportioned scent-bomb seductress
among the most voluptuous
amorous
amply endowed
androgynous
aphrodisiac
aphrodisiac qualities
aroused/arousing
as cerebral as it is sensual
as erotic as a handbag of lipstick and scent
as sexy as a chemise
as smooth as satin sheets
as soft as a kiss
as virginal as Psyche before she met Cupid
astonishingly virile
awesomely endowed
awesomely sexy and sensuous personality
Bacchanalia on forest floors
balanced package of wonderful seduction

barely noticeable warm kiss in its unbelievably long finish
beautiful contradiction of the seductive and the *noli-me-tangere*
best and most romantic seductive drink
better than sex
bit of a cockteaser
bit of a whore
black fruit-scented sexpot
body as soft as a pillow
bosomy
bottled sex
boudoir scents
burning love
buxom
California Chardonnay is like giving Pinocchio a blow job
caresses of spices
caresses the tongue in the most delightful way
caressing effervescence
caressing mouthfeel
caressing...silky...long

caressingly soft
caressing texture
caressing-tingly in the mouth
carnal
carnal of the world's red wines,
  merlot is the most
cashmere caress
certain seductive elegance
characteristic sensuality
chaste
climactic
clingy
come-hither palate
come-hither smokiness
complex seductive afterglow
curvaceous and sexy
dainty dish
dances seductively on the palate
dangerously voluptuous
dark seductress
decadently sexy personality
deeply sexy red
definite winegasm territory
deliciously seductive
deliciously voluptuous luxuriance
different with each sip, teasing
  the senses with ephemeral,
  heavenly tastes, and sex
disarmingly seductive
disarmingly sexy
disciplined hedonism: sensuality
  by numbers
does a sort of slow striptease,
  revealing more each time one
  sniffs and sips
doesn't so much as seduce you as
  launch a full-out perfumed
  assault on the senses
doesn't want to end
downright sexy
dreamy afterglow
easy virtues
embarrassingly sensual
embodiment of flesh and pleasure
endlessly voluptuous
enormously endowed
equivalent of liquid
  Viagra
erotically earthy
erotically multilayered
erotically perfumed
erotically subtle
erotic exotic thing
erotic mouthfeel
erotic wildness
erotic with its sea notes
erotically perfumed
excitingly sensual

exhibits a certain sexiness
extraordinary voluptuousness
extremely seductive
fabulously seductive
faintly perfumed gown of a
  sleeping Venus
fantastically beautiful sensual
  symphony was played for the
  olfactory glands
feminine charms
fiery ardor
fiery passion
final kiss
flaunts everything it has in an
  unabashedly sexy and
  voluptuous manner
fleshy sexpot of a Syrah
fleshy textural sensuality
fleshy texture
flirtatious but not slutty
flirtatious charm
flirtatious floral flavors
flirtatious perfumes of youth
flirts deliciously with the palate
  just as it does with the nose
forbidden
for instant seduction
formidably endowed
fragrant seducer
full voluptuous texture
fully armed with seductive powers
fully aroused
glancing sex
glorious seductive fruit just asks to
  be drunk
gloriously seductive
good sex by a campfire
gorgeously seductive
gorgeously sexy chassis
gossamer caress of bubbles
hard as a rock
has passion
heaps of seductive ripe fruit
heavenly caress
herpes-infected prostitute
homogeneous voluptuosity
hot-blooded
hot sex...ummm
hugely seductive
ignited the fires of lust
immensely sexy
immodest
immoral
impassioned
impressively endowed
inarguably sexy
incredibly seductive
indiscretion of youth

instant romance
intimate
irresistible determination to
  seduce, before which one is
  helpless
irresistibly seducible
irresistibly sweet and sexy finish
I was totally seduced
James Bond kind of wine: suave,
  brawny, smoky, spicy and
  seductive
just foreplay...no follow-through
kinky
kiss
kiss from a long-term unrequited
  crush, your first French
knee-melting seduction lasting for
  over a minute
knee-weakeningly sensual texture
knockout power delivered in a
  seductively smooth velvet glove
lascivious
lasts all night
leathery sexiness
leaves a nice afterglow
leg-spreader
libidinous
licentious
like having an orgasm in the
  mouth
like performing a sexual act that
  involves silk sheets, melted dark
  chocolate and black cherries
  while the mingled scents of
  cinnamon, coffee and cola waft
  through the air
like walking through a Moroccan
  brothel
liquid equivalent of French lingerie
liquid sex in a bottle
long, firm and full in the
  mouth like a penis
long seductive marmalade of a
  wine
lover who doesn't abuse you but
  the sex isn't great
lush seductive evocation of France
lustful
lusty stuff
maiden's armpit
makes you hot and bothered
makes you want to put on Barry
  White and lap (this wine) off
  someone's belly
mammothly endowed
marvelous flesh
massively sexy
masterpiece of sensuality

maximum seduction in magnum
medium of frivolous seduction
merits an x-rating
Merlot is the most carnal of the
    world's red wines
mind-boggling quasiorgasmic
    experience
mouthful of voluptuous curves
musky
my palate experiences a gustatory
    orgasm just thinking about it
naked
narcotically seductive
naughty
nearly cultlike seduction
never-ending
nubile
nuptial
odalisquelike charms
offers itself with supple open arms
oh-my-god…
oh so sexy
oily sensuality
one big sexy mouthfeel
only sexual analogies can
    do it justice
only those with an erotic bent will
    appreciate this at the moment
ooh, those lo-ong lingering
    complex sexy flavors
oozingly seductive
open virility
oral afterglow
orgasmic

orgasm in a bottle

outrageously sensual
overendowed
overly full-bodied
overwhelmingly seductive on the
    palate
overwhelms you with sensuality
palate-caressing texture
passionate
penis wine
perfect wine for romanticlate-
    summer evenings in the sunset
Pinot-envy
pleasurable
plump ripe flesh
powerfully seductive
probably illegal
profoundly velvety flesh
polygamous
promiscuous
proper wine to serve at a seduction
provides easy seduction
provocative yet caressing
pumped up

pure sex appeal
pure sex in a bottle
purr [sic] seduction
quite a torso
quite sexy
quivering caress of bubbles
racy

rakishly seductive

rapturous
rather sexy sweaty smell
raunchy
ravishing
ready to seduce any palate it
    touches
real hottie
red wine with serious cleavage
refined and virile at once
refined taste spectrum of all the
    most sensual things one can
    think of
rich dry erotically silky mouthfeel
richly seductive
risqué
romance in a glass
romantic tension
Rubensesque sensuality
salty, almost sweaty allure of a
    man's body
screamer
seamless fleshpot
seduces rather than overpowers
seduces the palate by stealth
seduces you
seduction in a bottle
seduction in a glass
seduction lasting for over a minute,
    knee-melting
seductive aftertaste
seductive as a siren
seductive baby fat
seductive candied watermelon
seductive charm
seductive complexity
seductive dark-roast espresso
seductive dark-toned beauty
seductive deep garnet
seductive elegance personified
seductive finish
seductive from the start
seductive interplay of grapefruit
    and exotic fruit
seductive majestic wine-drinking
    experience
seductive mouthfeel
seductive musk
seductive mystique
seductive offering

seductive rather than over-
    powering
seductive sexy fruit bomb
seductive sexy spices
seductive softness
seductive structure
seductive stuff
seductive style
seductive tone
seductive whiff of smoke
seductive whisper of smoke
seductive wisp of smoke
seductive with spirit and breed
seductively beautiful
seductively complex
seductively elegant
seductively gentle
seductively grilled fruit
seductively rich
seductively rounded
seductively rustic
seductively sexy
seductively styled
seductively succulent
seductively supple
seductively velvety texture

seductress

sensationally sensual tannins
sensual acacia honey
sensual and seductive lush
    smorgasbord
sensual and seductive red
sensual beyond the usual meaning
sensual citrus
sensual fruitiness
sensual fruity-sweet layer-upon-
    layer creation
sensual lightweight
sensual? oh yes
sensual perfume
sensual pillow of fruit
sensual spectrum
sensual tannins in a swelling flow
    of unrelieved pleasure
sensual texture
sensual velvetiness
sensuality in crystal
sensually immensely satisfying
sensually pleasurable
sensually seductive
sensually velvety
sensuous and sensual
sex in a bottle
sex in a glass
sexlicious
sex kitten
sex machine
sex pot

sex sweat
sexes up the nose
sexiest Bordeaux in my life
sexually charged
sexy and seductive
sexy black stallion
sexy cocktail
sexy concoction
sexy…curvaceous
sexy *demimondaine* of
    uncertain age
sexy finish
sexy funkiness
sexy layers of apricot
sexy oak
sexy pear perfume
sexy personality bastes the mouth
sexy red
sexy satin texture
sexy, sexy and more sexy
sexy, sexy, sexy
sexy spices
sexy stuff
sexy voluptuous finish
sexy wine stacked in all the right
    places
sheer sensuality
simultaneously sensual and
    cerebral
sinful
sinfully rich
sinfully sensual
sinuous as sin
siren of a wine
sizzling
slinky
slithers around your mouth and
    down your throat…caressing as
    it goes
slutty

smells like great sex
smoky, sultry and seductive
smoldering
so good it must be illegal
so rich and sensual it must be
    illegal
so seductively fragrant you want to
    dive into it
so seductive that it stops you in
    your tracks and forces a sigh
splendid bosom
stolen kiss
spontaneous generous sensuality
spontaneously sensual
steamy
still youthful but already sexy and
    seductive
stimulating

streetwalker
stud
sugar reels you in and seduces you
sultry
superseductive
supersexy appeal
supple caressing sensation in the
    mouth can only be compared to
    an angel's kiss
supple seductress
sure to seduce
surprising sexiness
T & A wine
tantalizingly sexy
tart with a heart
tarted up
taste of furious passion
temptress of a wine
texturally seductive
this wine is all about power:
    perfume, subtlety and sensuality
    don't come into it
thoroughly sexy
torrid
tremendously seductive
trés sexuel
truffley sensuality
truly a wine where the intellectual
    meets the sensual
ultraseductive
ultravoluptuous
unbelievably sensual
undeniable sexiness
undeniably seductive
undeniably sexy
unexpected but unforgettable
    element of sensuality
unforgettable encounter with
    a raven-haired ingénue
unusual levels of seduction and
    sumptuousness
up close and personal
utterly seductive
utterly seductive mouth
utterly seductively sweet
Valentine's negligee
velvet, seduction and mystery
veritable seduction serum
very mysterious and seductive
very seductive from start to finish
very seductive oak frame
very sexy and fleshy
very virile red
Viagra Cabernet
vinous orgasm
vinous Viagrafication
violet silk sheets with your initials
    monogrammed on them

virginal pink
virile tannins
virtual flavor orgy
voluptuous and sexy
voluptuous elegance
voluptuous fatness
voluptuous marriage of opposites
voluptuous structure
voluptuously rich
voluptuously textured
wants for nothing in the way
    of pure sex appeal
wants to flirt but does not really
    dare to
warm and seductive
warm, wild seduction
well-built garishly attired whore
well contoured
well endowed
well fleshed
well-shaped buttocks
well stacked
what a body!
wholly seductive glass of fun
wholly seductive harmony
wide-eyed gamin that seduces
wisps of seductive smoke
wickedly delicious
wild abandon
wild and sexy beast
wild thing
will seduce a lot of people
winegasm
wine of seduction
wine perfect for an afternoon
    dalliance
wonderful seduction
wonderfully erotic
yes…Yes…YES!

Wine wears no breeches.
French proverb

God is definitely out of the closet.
Marianne Williamson

*Every woman should have four pets in her life.
A mink in her closet, a jaguar in her garage,
a tiger in her bed, and a jackass who pays for
everything.*
Paris Hilton

H. Out of the Closet

Used as wine descriptions, fabrics and the apparel made from them make excellent textural analogies. The feel of a soft, smooth wine on the tongue should bring a smile to any clothier; well-worn, unaired footwear, however, is a totally different story. As you'll also notice, there are a lot of items here with sexy connotations, sort of leftovers from the previous *Erotica* collection. Tailors must have all the luck.

acetate	denim	lederhosen	scarf	underwear
angora	diaper	linen	shantung	unmentionables
apparel	doeskin	lingerie	sheepskin	uniform
belt	dress	loafers	shirt	velour
bikini	feathers	mackintosh	shoes	velvet
boa	felt	mittens	shorts	velveteen
boots	flannel	moleskin	shroud	waistcoat
bra	fleece	muslin	silk	whites
brocade	frock	nappy	slacks	wig
burlap	fur	neckcloth	sleeves	wool
bustier	furbelow	necklace	slippers	worsted
cap	gloves	nightgown	sneakers	
cashmere	gown	oilcloth	socks	
chamois	handbag	oilskin	soles	
chaps	hat	organza	stockings	
chemise	headgear	overcoat	straightjacket	
chenille	hessian	pajamas	suede	
chiffon	high heels	panties	suit	
cloak	homespun	pants	sweater	
clothes	insole	parasol	sweats	
coat	jacket	pearls	taffeta	
corduroy	jeans	plimsolls	terry cloth	
corset	jersey	purse	thong	
costume	jockstrap	robe	tie	
cotton	jumper	rubbers	trainers	
cotton wool	knickers	sable	trousers	
crepe	knitting	sackcloth	tweed	
damask	lace	sateen	Ultrasuede	
décolletage	leather	satin	underpants	

A throne is only a bench covered with velvet.
Napoleon Bonaparte

*With time and patience the mulberry leaf becomes
a silk gown.*
Chinese proverb

*Musigny is a wine of silk and lace…. Smell the scents
of a damp garden, the perfume of a rose, the violet
bathed in morning dew.*
Gaston Roupnel

I. As Smooth as … As Soft as …

To human fingers there are few sensations as pleasing to their touch as velvet or silk (excepting, of course, the skin of a baby or lover). Consequently, when sampling a particularly refined wine, many drinkers describe what their mouths feel with *as smooth as silk* or *as soft as velvet*. The list below shows just how many descriptors demonstrate the pleasure to be gotten from these two historically sensuous fabrics. M-m -m.

absolute silk
all silk
almost turning a sow's ear into a silk purse
almost velvety extract
as finely textured as the best silk
as languorous and silky as a guitar solo by
   Carlos Santana
as plush as crushed velvet
as silky as a Hermès scarf
as silky as they come
as sensuous as velvet
as smooth as silk oak
as smooth as velvet silk
as smooth as washable silk
as soft as brushed velvet
as tightly woven as a fine silk rug
as warming as a robe of thick velvet
at once velvet and gossamer
baby Jesus sliding down your throat in velvet slippers
beguiling sweet silk
bewitchingly silky
big rich silky and well knit
big velvety voluptuous tannins
black velvet
bottled silk
bottled velvet and satin
bright velvety gold
brings to mind silk and velvet
Burgundy silk

cherries and raspberries baked into pie with a buttery,
   flaky, smoky crust and a dusting of cinnamon and
   brown sugar, all wrapped in silk and satin
cherry fruit linked to silky tannin in a torrid love
   affair
chunky-velvety texture
chunky yet velvety
comes as close to silk as vinously possible
corn silk smoothness
corset had bones hidden in its silk
creamy-silky
crinkled velvet
crisp acidity: velvet on steel
crushed velvet tannins
crushed velvet texture
cut from pure velvet
deep complex velvety finish
deep garnet velvet
deep rich velvety robe
delicately ruffled richness with velvet
dense velveteen
develops tannins that define silkiness
diamonds on velvet
drapes of velvet
drop-dead gorgeous silken texture
dry velvet
envelopes the palate like a perfectly tailored silk shirt
epitome of silk turned into wine
fading silky pink

feels like satin
feels like velvet gliding across the palate
fine mesh of gold silk
fine solid velvety red
finely woven silk
flows like silk and velvet
formidable structure turns to velvet
free-range velvet
future flavors are stifled in a silk cocoon
Gewürztraminer in silk stockings
glides over the palate like a silk sheet
glorious silken texture
gloriously velvety
gorgeously velvety
half-robed by a veil of gossamer silk
harmonious silkiness
heavy upholstery silk
heavy velvet curtains
hidden depth in its velvet folds of flavors are a
    revelation
impression of sinking into velvet cushions as you
    drink it
ineffably silky
intensity in a velvety package
intricate weave of silky strands
iron fist in velvet glove
knockout power delivered in a seductively smooth
    velvet glove
knockout power of ripe California fruit wrapped in
    a seamless velvet glove
like drinking inky dark velvet
like drinking pure velvet
like drinking silk
limpid crushed velvet
limpid red velvet
liquid charm and silk
liquid silk
liquid velvet
lively silk and velvet weave
long velvety finale
minty-silky
noticeably velvety
nuanced weave of silk and velvet
nutty velvet
obnoxious silkiness
otherworldly silkiness of texture
peacock's tail of flavors wrapped in silk
piece of velvet that was meant to be a throw pillow
    but was never stuffed
Pinot Noir silky
plush little velvet cushion
positively silky with age
profoundly velvety flesh
pure Fortuny silk
pure plush velvet
purple velvet gliding across the tongue
raw silk
red-velvet consistency

red velvet couch
relishable silkiness
resembles silk pajamas
ripe velvet and fruit drenched
rough heavy upholstery silk
roughly silken
rough velvet
rounded silk structure
ruffled silk
sappy velvet
satin and silk texture
satin-textured
satiny tannin texture
satiny texture
sheer silk and velvet
sheer silken brilliance
sheer velvet berries
silk and velvet
silk-clad
silk cocoon
silk stockings jumping up and down in the
    gooseberry bush
silk thread of great strength
silken blend
silken delicacy
silkened by time
silken soft
silken suede
silken texture
silken thread of acidity
silken treasure
silkier-than-silk tannins
silkiest most satiny texture imaginable
silkiest smoothest tannins you ever had
silkily clad
silkily delicious
silkily powerful
silkiness is incredible
silkiness of texture, otherworldly
silkish
silklike
silk pearl
silk road of mineral flavors
silk-robed blessings
silk-smooth
silk thread of great strength
silk-velvet blend
silky all the way down
silky blackberries
silky charmer
silky corset
silky dazzler
silky elegance
silky highlights
silky leathery tannins
silky luscious bliss
silky, mineral, cherried heart
silky minerals

silk pajamas
silky perfection
silky robe of spicy red fruit
silky Rolls-Royce power
silky sheen
silky smooth
silky softness
silky soft tannic web
silky sophistication
silky, sulky, sour
silky sveltness
silky svelte texture
silky texture(d)
silky texture...just slips down
silky vanilla
silky velvety honey
silky violets
silky-violety
slides down like silk
slides down your throat like the good lord Jesus in
    silk trousers
smoky-silky
soft silk-and-satin mouthfeel
soft velvet embrace
soft velvety truffles
spicy fruit cradled in a silky texture
spun silk
supersilky tannins
supervelvety

texture evokes silk and lace
texture is like sheer silk
texture is more silk than velvet
texture is the finest cut velvet
texture like liquid velvet
texture of a piece of new velvet
texture of raw silk
texture of silk over bark
texture of velvet on the tongue
thrilling blend of silk and steel
thrillingly fine silky texture
touch of velvet
ultimate iron fist in a velvet glove
ultrasilky
ultravelvety mouthfeel
utterly silky
velvet brushed against the weave
velvet cladding
velvet cushion
velveteen
velvet fabric
velvet glassful
velvet- glove stuff
velvet leafiness
velvet-lined
velvet-lined punch
velvet on a marble staircase
velvet on iron
velvet over steel

velvet plums
velvet quilt that you just want to sink into
velvet rather than wood

velvet, seduction and mystery
velvet sliding over the tongue
velvet-smooth firework displays performed by
    the bubbles
velvet tapestry
velvet textured
velvet waistcoat
velvet with ruffled corduroy edges
velvet with satin trimmings
velvety bombshell
velvety bubbles
velvety cherries
velvety, cushiony mouthfeel
velvety elegance on the finish
velvety fruitiness
velvety monster
velvety mouthfeel
velvety opulence
velvety red
velvety refinement
velvety silk
velvety smooth
velvety spice-filled
velvety suppleness
velvety sweet
velvety texture
velvety textured personality
velvety treasure
velvety underbelly
velvety white fruit
velvety white nectar for hedonists
velvety wonder
very delicate fizziness cossets its silky texture
very soft velvet
web of silky tannins
white velvet
who tipped the spice box into this lush velvet tangle
    of bramble fruit?
you can almost eat the texture...so soft, thick
    and velvety

Taste is a mystery that best finds its voice in wine.
Jim Harrison

Ultimately, the appeal of wine lies in its mystery.
Matt Kramer

If you pay attention to it, a good wine will always have something to tell you. What exactly it says no one can ever completely understand, of course, and that is wine's charm and its mystery.
James Norwood Pratt

J. Intrigue and Mystery

Even to highly experienced wine drinkers, wine has always had the quality of mystery surrounding it, probably due to the thousands of aroma and tastes sensations that bombard human sensory receptors, only some of which we can identify. The unknown always makes us uneasy. The unexpected, also, can be good or bad, but hard-to define qualities keep us...you guessed it...guessing.

age it for ten years and let itdevelop magic
air of mystery about it
absolutely magical
alchemy of oak seems to clog the wine's pores like gesso on a picture frame
almost secret
almost syrupy elixir
arcane wine
aura of mystery about it
bewitching
bewitchingly flavorful
black magic
blood of a mythological beast
charisma in a bottle
charismatic
chimerical
completely fails to deliver the magic
complex creamy elixir
complexity that intrigues
conundrum
cryptic conundrum
dazzling alchemy
doesn't have too many tricks up its sleeve
downright charismatic
dreamlike
elixir of life
elusive Pinot mystery
enchanted
enchanting character
enigma of tight tannins

enigmatic
ethereal
exotic mysteries of angostura
faint aura of mystery about it
fairy-dust scented
fairy tale
foresty mysteries
full of intrigue
full of strange magic
goes on and on unfolding magically on the palate
good measure of mystery here
goût de terroir but not of this earth
great intrigue
hauntingly beautiful
hauntingly elusive
haunting perfume/hauntingly perfumed
haunting musk notes point to the mysteries of the earth
haunting sweetness
heady elixir
huge mythical mouthful
imperial elixir
inexplicably enigmatic
inscrutable
intriguing berryness
intriguing complexity
intriguing depth
intriguing herbal nuances
intriguing Italianate overtones
intriguing nuances

intriguing vegetal complexity
intriguingly complicated
just so puzzling
liquid magic
little short of pure magic
living everchanging mystery-in-a-bottle
living wine of mystery and surprise
lush elixir
magic caravan of lilies and blueberries and herbs
magic carpet of strawberry and soft creamy
   contentment
magic carpet ride
magic elixir
magic in a bottle
Magic Markers
magic reek of fruit and harvest bloom
magic, sheer/utter
magical aftertaste of butter and wild raspberries
magical complexity
magical complexity of aromas that defies description
magical grace and refinement
magical harmony
magical: has everything going for it
magical moment
magical quality
magical stuff
magical supersmooth texture
magically astonishing mouthful
magically rich
magically smooth
mesmerizing earthiness
midsummer night's dream
miracle
missed out on the magic
modern-day elixir
mojo
mysterious, almost ineffable completeness
mysterious charms
mysterious earthy undercurrents
mysterious inner-mouth aromatics
mysteriously addictive
mysteriously apt for aging
mysteriously complex
mysteriously feral
mysteriously rich yet shy
mysteriously savory
mysterious spice
mystery or miracle
mystical
mythic/mythical
no magic
not a lot of mystery here
nothing short of pure magic
persists almost magically on the palate
Pinot intrigue
potent elixir
power and delicacy magically combined
precious secret character

pretty big mystique
puzzling
pure wizardry
quite a conundrum
rather mysterious
scent of all things darkly and deliciously mysterious
secret
seductive mystique
seemed to unravel intriguingly
shrouded in mystery
slightly mysterious with lurking flavors that are hard
   to pin down
slight mystery
something of an enigma
spellbinding
spellbinding complexity
supernatural
tangerine dreams
totally enchanting
total magic
tree sprites
uncomfortably surreal
utterly enchanting
velvet, seduction and mystery
very mysterious and seductive
visions of sugarplum fairies
wins you over bit by bit working an interesting spell
wondrous enchantress

One barrel of wine can work more miracles than a church full of saints.
Italian proverb

I don't like to commit myself about heaven and hell—you see, I have friends in both places.
Mark Twain

K. In Heaven or Hell

Depending on your point of view, the taste of wine can move you to roll your eyes heavenward or else curse the blasted liquid in your glass as the devil's own drink. Most of the time, though, we simply sip our wine, without much thought of good or evil on a theological level. Nonetheless, wine has always been used as a blessing, a celebratory toast, or as a sacramental substitute for a deity's blood. Hallelujah!

absolutely heavenly
achieves nirvana
almost an extra dimension that evoked thoughts of religion and some sort of higher power
almost a religious experience
almost Episcopalian in its predictability
a mystery or a miracle
an angel as opposed to an Amazon
an angel peed on my tongue
an angel tinkling in your mouth
angel of death hovering overhead
angelic
angelic nose
angel sweat
as black as hell
as delicate as angels' tears
as sinuous as sin
as smooth as baby Jesus in velvet pants and silk slippers
baby Jesus in silk slippers sliding down your throat
baby Jesus in velvet pants going down your gullet
baby Jesus sliding down your throat in velvet slippers
beatific
bedeviled
belongs to the world of the divine
blacker than the devil's heart
blend of God-knows-what
brings motion to your soul
celestial black currants
celestial butterscotch
celestial marmalade
celestial perfume
cherry pie in hell
cherubic
comes close to a spiritual experience

could bring any deity to ecstasy
darkly spiritual
dark-souled
deeply spiritual
delighted to the point of hearing the angels sing
Devil Dogs
devil farts
devilish and heavenly together
devilishly delicious
devilishly fruity
devilishly good
devilishly rude
devil-may-care fruitiness
different with each sip, teasing the senses with ephemeral, heavenly tastes and sex
divine elixir
diabolical
divinely scented
divine perfume
draconian
elixir of the gods
enduring and heavenly
eternal flavors
ethereal, with flavors and delicacy beyond description
ethereal oils
fit for the wine gods
flavors of heaven and earth
gift of the gods
glorious heavenly ripe fruit
God-awful
God-given perfection
God-knows-what
godlike
good lord Jesus in silk slippers sliding down your throat

has soul
hear the angels singing
heaven in a glass
heaven is like, what
heavenly, almost scorching, acidity
heavenly, almost theatrical, Pinot fragrance
heavenly beetrootlike fruit
heavenly black cherries
heavenly caress
heavenly cassis perfume
heavenly delight
heavenly experience
heavenly honeyed botrytis
heavenly mouthful
heavenly perfume
heavenly ripe peaches
heavenly scented
heavenly scents of cigars
heavenly smokiness
heavenly texture
heavenly treacle
heavenly treat
heavenly voluptuous sensationally good wine
heaven-sent blessing
hedonistic heaven
hell-of-a/helluva
hellish
Hell's Angels tannins
honeyed heaven
how divine
incredible difference between the first heavenly
   glass and the flat sludge that finished the bottle
just this side of a heavenly caress
just this side of sinful

kind of touching-heaven experience
kiss of an angel
lacks soul
like strolling through a tropical paradise
lingers on the palate for an eternity
liquid heaven
lush ripeness wedded to power and complexity:
   the holy trinity of great winemaking
made by God not by man
made in heaven
makes the soul wax embarrassingly poetic
miracle of nature
miraculous
nectar of the gods
nirvana
no soul
of heaven and earth
omigosh!/oh-my-gosh!
oh-my-god!
one hell of a bite
oozes devilish charm
our idea of very heaven
packs one hell-of-a-punch
paradise

plethora of celestial aromas
preserves balance like an angel
pure divinity
pure heaven
pure immortality in a glass
pure nirvana
quietly soulful
realm of the celestial
real soul
religious
religious experience
resonates on your palate for one velvety eternity
scales celestial heights
sends your soul to the beach
sharply tannic soul
sinfully sensual
slides down your throat like the good lord Jesus in silk
   trousers
so heavenly with so many tiny nuances that I could
   fill an entire page
soulful
soul-less stuff
soul-quenching
soul-stirring
speaks to your soul
spiritual aromas
spiritually purifying
stuff of the gods
superb minty heaven
supple caressing sensation in the mouth can only be
   compared to an angel's kiss
sweet nectar of the gods
taste of heaven
texturally sinful
the miracle continues
theosophical
tickles the soul as well as the tongue
took me straight to paradise
touched by God
touches my soul in a very special way
translucent green rim like a spirit level from Hades
treacly heaven
truly a miracle
truly soul-satisfying
true smorgasbord of heavenly delights
ungarbled product of the earth good for the soul, an
ungodly
utter heaven/paradise
utterly divine

what angels use as underarm deodorant
vinous heaven
whole lot of soul
will take an eternity to mature
wine of heaven and earth
wine of the gods
wino's heaven
without soul
worshiped/worshipful

Terroir is a green idea sleeping furiously.
Malcolm Gluck

Wines express their source with exquisite definition.
Matt Kramer

We don't taste a place in a wine. We taste a wine from a place....
Harold McGee & Daniel Patterson

A wine's first duty is to be good. Beyond that, terroir is bullshit.
Paul Draper

Terroir is a pivotal concept for understanding wine and the places it come from.
Brian J. Sommers

L. *Terroir* or Terror?

One of the all-time longest running arguments in the world of wine is over the concept of *terroir (tear-wah)*, by which most people in the European (particularly the French) wine trade vigorously propose that where grapes are grown (Matt Kramer's often-quoted *somewhereness*) defines the unique character of the wine made from them.

Terroir, to *terroirists*, can include any or all of the following elements of the entire grape-growing environment: latitude, topography, altitude/ elevation, aspect and slope, geology, bed-rock as well as other rocks, surface soil and subsoil, rainfall, ground water, soil moisture, drainage, humus, nutrients, minerals/minerality, indigenous microbes and yeasts, climate, weather, temperature, humidity, wind, fog, daylight, sun, cloud cover, orientation of the vineyard, the surrounding area, even neighboring plant life, roads and proximity to water bodies. Whew!

However, the primacy of this "sense of place" is just as strongly opposed by those who insist that the skilled input of humans is as important as *terroir*, perhaps even more so. After all, it's people, like you and me, who choose the place to grow grapevines, who plant them, who cultivate them and who harvest the ripened grapes for fermenting into wine. Now you decide whether *terroir* is really *somewhereness*, *someoneness* or a working combination of both.

accentuates its special *terroir*
allows us to eavesdrop on the murmurings
    of the earth
barely transcends its *terroir*
brimming with a sense of place
can taste a place
captures the site
carries mighty big *terroir* talking stick
certain patch of earth
clearly transcends its *terroir*
completely transparent vehicle for its *terroir*
dazzling expression of place
definitely prime real estate effect here
definite impression of *terroir*
displays some of the region's patented *terroir*
distinctive kiss of *terroir*
does not obliterate *terroir*
dramatic vehicle for its *terroir*
ephemeral sense of place
example of technology-enhancing *terroir*
exceptional ability to communicate *terroir*
expresses its *terroir* beautifully
fabulously balanced *terroir*
farmyardy *terroir* edge
featherlight elegance meets mineral *terroir*
fine sense of the *terroir*
full of *terroir*
gentle and violent *terroir*
good representative of its *terroir*
gorgeously fruity expression of place
goût de terroir but not of this earth
greatest expression of *terroir*
great sense of class and *terroir*
great *terroir* feel
great *terroir* made liquid
hard to detect any originality or *terroir*
has the vineyard's voice
honest expression of an honored *terroir*
human touch
ideally embodies *terroir*
identifiable sense of place
intense sense of place
landscape made tastable
lets the vineyard speak
likeable *terroir*
location, location, location!
lot of French-tasting *terroir*
magnificent expression of *terroir*
manages not to distort the characteristics of its *terroir*
mystical sense of place
obscure *terroir*
oozing with *terroir* freshness
perfect expression of Bandol *terroir*
phenomenal expression of *terroir*
pinnacle of *terroir*
prime example of *terroir* speaking
real estate
real sense of place

real song of the *terroir*
real *terroir*
resonant *vin de terroir*
retains the minerality of its rocky birthplace
rich *terroir*
rigorous sense of belong to a territory
sang of its *terroir*
sense of place in a bottle
sense of place in spades
shows its *terroir* well
shows provenance
shows true *terroir*
site expressive
site-reflective
site-specific
solid sense of place
somewhereness
sophisticated reflection of the *terroir*
speaks eloquently of the place from which it comes
speaks of its origins
speaks of its place
specificity of *terroir* is overwhelming
spot-on sense of place
stony *terroir*
sunny *terroir*
telling originality and truth to place
terroir covers fruit like a slab of marble
terroir-driven
terroir-engineered
terroir-expressive
terroir or crapoir?
terroir toujours
transcends its *terroir*
translator of soil types into the glass
tremendous real estate in the nose
triumphantly expresses a specific place and time
true expression of one man and his *terroir*
true *terroir* tipicity
unmistakable *terroir*
vegetal *terroir*
vin de terroir
very *terroir*-driven
warm *terroir*
wet stone *terroir*
when you drink this wine you drink the place
wholly true to the concept of *terroir*
wonderfully expressive of its *terroir*
you feel the power of the land

This is about as dumb of a place to put a rock quarry as you could put one.
Chris Lisle

The point of drinking wine is...to taste sunlight trapped in a bottle, and to remember some stony slope in Tuscany or a village by the Gironde.
John Mortimer

M. The Rock Quarry

It's impossible to know exactly how many of us wine drinkers have licked rocks, sucked on stones, chewed on flint, or rolled gravel around in our mouths. Countless wine reviewers make a very big deal out of all the minerally stuff allegedly pulled up from the soil by thirsty grapevines. (No one knows how or even whether this really happens.) Yet, after all, minerals do contribute complex tastes that so often rounds out a wine's characteristics of place, and seem directly related to the previous *Terroir* collection. Nonetheless, those below give a good indication of granite beyond your typical kitchen countertop.

adamantly granitic
all the stones of the world find
   their unique voice with Riesling
almost palpable sense of rock dust
almost rocky in its minerality
amazingly smooth for such a
   stony wine
as dry as stone
as firm as stones
as granitelike as any mason could
   wish for
as hard as a rock
as minerally as a mouthful of rocks
assertively mineral as if you struck
   two rocks together to create a
   spark
as slick as the polished marble in
   Florence's Uffizi
avalanche of falling rocks
awash with stones
balletic balancing act of fruit and
   slate
bare rock
beach sand
bed of stones
bedrock

blackboard-chalklike stoniness
blue stone
blues stones dancing and bouncing
   around my mouth like a rock
   tumbler
boulders
candied slate
candied stones
caramelized stones
carved from a single block of
   granite
cast in stone
chalk blackboard
chalk-dry
chalk dust
chalk soil backbone
chalky-earthy
chalky lemon juice
chalky melons
chalky minerality
chalky mouthfeel
chalky potpourri
chalky richness
chalky roughness
chalky soil
chalky tannins

chalky texture
characteristic stoniness
cherry-drenched quartz
chiseled flints
chocolate-covered blackberries and
   stones
citrus flavors buried under a heavy
   layer of rock
clean wet-stone minerality
cobblestone
coliseum of fascinating stony
   flavors
complex liquid stone
complex slate
core of stone
could only have drawn its blood
   from local stones
cream poured over gravel
crisp stones
crushed limestone
crushed pumice stone
crushed rocks
crushed sandstone-mineral
crushed stones
curious slatiness
damp rocks

dampish stones
dark granite red
deepened by stone
deeply anchored in red slate
dissolved slate
distinctive undercurrent of stones
dry austere gunflint
dusting of chalk
dusty chalk
dusty rocks
dusty stone walls
earthy-gritty texture
edgy and rocky and steep and
  sparse
essence of soil and stone
exotic spices awash in stone liqueur
extraordinary slate spine
ferrous stones
fiery granite red
flagstones
flecks of chalk and slate
flint-edged vibrancy
flintily elegant
flints and minerals to the max
flint smoke
flint striking steel
flinty acidity
flinty and aromatic to the hilt
flinty citrus
flinty crispness
flinty minerality
flinty mineral streak
flinty-oaky
flinty-pebbly dryness
flinty pencil shavings
floral perfume of crushed stones
floury-chalky
fractionally gritty
fresh slate
fruit pushes through like grass
  through cracks in the stones
gold embedded in flint
gneiss
granite cliffs
granite-edged
granite-grown Syrah
granite hardness
granite-rough
granite quarry's worth of
  minerality
granite stoniness
granitic
gravel-backed
graveled
gravel-flavored
gravel-laden
gravelly and stony
gravelly stones

gravelly pears
gravelly streak
great expression of rocks in the
  mouth
grilled stones
gritty
ground stones
gunflinty
heated stones
hillside stony minerality
hint of flint
honeyed chalk
honeyed crushed stone
honey-smeared rocks
hopelessly gritty
hot gravel
hot rocks
hot stones
hot stones after summer rain
hot sun on stony soils
hot wet stones
imbued with stones
indecipherable stony note
intense heat on stones
intriguingly stony
ironstone
lava
lavalike consistency as it coagulates
  in the throat
lick of chalk
lick of flint
like a rock face, the taste does not
  offer any handholds
like chewing on rocks
like digesting smoky stones
like drinking chalk soil
like eating banana cream pie in a
  rock quarry on a hot summer's
  day
like eating cobbler in a rock quarry
like rolling liquid rocks around in
  the mouth
like standing in the Colosseum and
  picking up ancient rocks
like stumbling into a patch of
  wildflowers among the rocks
lime-chalky aftertaste
limestone
liqueur of crushed rocks
liqueur of granite liquid minerality
liqueur of wet stones
liquid chalk
liquid granite
liquid gravel
liquid slate
liquid slate-petroleum
liquid stones
liquefied rock

liquefied stony concoction
little tug of gritty tannins
lively stones
long stony finish
lovely rainwater-on-rocks
  minerality
made on mistral-swept stones
marble quarries
marble-smooth
marked stony aspect
melted stones
mineral chalkiness
mineral cobblestones
molten rock
moss on a damp rock
mouthful of rocks
much too sandy
muted stones
oaky-flinty
palate-cleansing chalkiness
palate-polishing stone
panoply of fruit in a box of oak
  studded with stones
peachy-stony
pebbly-stony
pencil slatiness
plump layers of peach-imbued
  chalk
plums left to heat up on sun-
  warmed stones
polished to the sheen of black
  marble
polished stone
powdered granite
powdered rock
powdered stone
powdery sensation of chalk dust
powerful slate takes over
primitive rocks
profoundly stony
puff of gunflint
pure expression of the stony soils
quarry's worth of stone
rainwater spilling over rocks
rain-wet gravel road
random patches of grass growing
  through piles of stones
refreshingly stone-dry
regional powdery slate
retains the minerality of its rocky
  birthplace
river rocks
river rocks in the rain
river running over stones
roasted stones
rock-crushed stones
rock dust
rock hard

rock-hard fizz
rock-hard French biscottes
rockish
rocklike
rocklike rasp
rock quarry
rocks
rocks metamorphosed into wine
rock-solid
rocky
rocky-minerally
rocky soil
rough seaside sand sort of
    rottenness
rubbed flints
rugged rocky hillsides
saline stoniness
salty rocklike minerality
sandstone
sandy
sandy textured
sap-laden rocks
schist rocks
scorched rocks
sculpted from stones
seaside rocks
seems to be built of stones
shalelike
shimmering heat of broad flat
    stones
shower of broken schist that
    explodes out of the fruit
stones baked and scorched all
    summer long
slab of pure stone
slate-driven structure
slate interest
slaty
smoky flintiness
smoky gunflint
smoldering stones
smoothly polished by abundant
    stone
smooth river stones
soapstone
sobering slate
so flinty it could start a fire
so hard it's like rock candy
solid slate foundation
so minerally as to be built of stone
so minerally you can almost smell
    the rocks
Spanish moss on a rolling stone
squeezed from sweet black rocks
steely-flinty
still a baby: spitting up acid at you
    and coughing up forbidding
    stone dust coolness

stone-dry
stone dust
stone field after a rain
stone-infused
stone-laden
stone-, lemon- and violet-lined
    path
stonelike elements
stonelike granite
stone-lined
stones baking in the sun
stone-scented
stones roll in
stonewall of minerality
stonily crisp
stony apples
stony astringency
stony cherries
stony core
stony dryness
stony flints
stony green apples
stone gunflint aspect is
    superpresent
stony keynote
stony, like granite
stony minerality
stony-peachy
stony pears
stony soil
stony *terroir*
stony zinger
struck flints
sturdy stone churches
subtle stone
succulent stoniness
summer rain on a gravelly road
sun-baked gravel
sun-baked rocks
sun-baked stones
sun-drenched gravel
sun-dried gravel
sun-warmed stones
sweet white corn mixed with wet
    rocks
syrupy slate
syrupy stones
tangy minerals and stones
tastes as if red berries were crushed
    in a mortar of stone
terroir covers fruit like a slab of
    marble
tons of stones
tremendous slatiness
tremendously strong gravel
    tannins
true rock-solid richness
underlined by stone

underlying bedrock minerality
violets growing through a bed of
    rocks
warm flintstones
warm granite
warm stones
warm stones on summer evenings
washed stones
waves crashing on a sandy beach
water running over stones in a
    mountain stream
wet gravel
wet gravel basking in the sun
wet pebble minerality
wet pebbles
wet quartz stones
wet-rock minerality
wet rocks
wet slate
wet stones after a brief hailstorm
wet stones that sprouted some
    moss
wet-stone *terroir*
wetted stones
whetstone
wickedly flinty

I must have a drink of breakfast.
W.C. Fields

Sure I eat what I advertise. Sure I eat Wheaties for breakfast. A good bowl of Wheaties with bourbon can't be beat.
Dizzy Dean

N. The Power Breakfast

Sounds crazy, but wine sure gets some people thinking about morning meals. For elevenses? Of course. A romantic picnic lunch on a lazy summer afternoon in a rowboat with someone you love? Naturally. Maybe even an indulgent little midnight snack before retiring to bed? Sure. But breakfast? Like the General-Mills-Breakfast-of-Champions-Wheaties-type breakfast? Now really, whatever will wine make us think of next? *(Pause.)* Wine with breakfast. H-m-m-m.

All-Bran	cheese	fruit cocktail	milk	rolls
apple butter	cherries	fruit nectar	mocha	salad
apple juice	cinnamon toast	fruit syrup	Mrs. Butterworth's	sausage
apples	citrus	grains	*muesli*	scones
apricots	cocoa	grapefruit	muffins	smoked fish
bacon	coffee	grapefruit juice	nectarines	smoothies
bagels	coffee cake	grape jelly	Nesquik	Splenda
baguette	conserves	Grape-Nuts	Nutella	steak
bananas	cornbread	grapes	nuts	strawberries
bangers	Corn Flakes	griddlecakes	oak cakes	strudel
berries	crackers	guavas	oatmeal	sugar
biscotti	cranberries	ham	oranges	sultanas
biscuits	cream	herring	Ovaltine	Sweet'N Low
blackberries	cream cheese	honey	*pain grillé*	SweeTart
black raspberries	Cream of Wheat	Horlicks	pancakes	tangerines
blueberries	crispbread	hotcakes	pancake syrup	tea
Bovril	croissants	jam	pastry	toast
boysenberries	crullers	jelly	peaches	tomatoes
brambles	currants	juice	peanut butter	tomato juice
bread	Danish pastry	ketchup	pears	V8
brioche	doughnuts	kiwis	pineapples	Vegemite
buns	Eggos	Land O'Lakes	plums	waffles
burrito	eggs	*latte*	potatoes	Weet-Bix
butter	*espresso*	*lox*	preserves	Wheaties
buttermilk	figs	maple syrup	pumpernickel	wheatmeal
cantaloupes	flapjacks	marmalade	Pop-Tarts	wholemeal
cappuccino	French toast	Marmite	prunes	whole wheat
cereal	Froot Loops	melba toast	raisins	yogurt
Cheerios	fruit	melons	raspberries	zwieback

All you need is love. But a little chocolate now and then doesn't hurt.
Charles M. Schulz

That I am not alone in my like for the marriage of chocolate and wine is evident by the Chocolate and Wine Festival in Seneca Lakes, New York, held every February in the weekend closest to Valentine's Day. The two-day event is dedicated to the tasting of chocolate and wine as the ultimate symbiotic, gastro-nomical fête.
George A. LaMarca

O. Days of Wine and Chocolate

Warm bittersweet chocolate sliding down your throat like a caress from heaven. If you start to salivate at this image, you simply love chocolate, so you'll understand why this brown ambrosia has been a sensuous companion to wine for centuries. Pay no attention to people who tell us that chocolate and wine are difficult to match up. We know better. We know, for example, that chocolate magically stimulates the flow of endorphins in the brain to cause pleasure. Wine may well do the same. So savor the romance but hold the roses (they belong in the *Flower* category, anyway). If you need further proof of chocolate's affinity for red wine, check out Hersey's website at *chocolateloveswine.com*. You'll see.

abundant chocolate sauce
aftertaste of white Toblerone
almost treacly fruit, dark plums and prunes awash with licorice and chocolate and cream
archetypical bitter chocolaty fruit
as dark as chocolate
as piquant, fruity, chocolaty as mole sauce
as slick as dark chocolate
as soft as a chocolate sponge pudding
as sugary as a chocolate truffle
as viscous and sweet as chocolate syrup
backbone of chocolate
baker's chocolate
bitter chocolate

bittersweet cherries robed in the finest dark chocolate
bittersweet chocolate
black chocolate
black 'n white (chocolate and vanilla)
blackberry chocolate fondue
bowl of chocolate-covered hazelnuts capped by a whiff of smoke
burnt chocolate
burnt chocolate candy
buttery chocolate frosting
candied violets on a chocolate cupcake
caramelly Mexican chocolate
caterer's chocolate
cedar-chocolate
charred chocolate

cheap chocolate éclairs
cherry compote infused with milk chocolate
chewy chocolate with a tannin coat
choc-berry
choc-mints
chocolate
chocolated
chocolate and cabbages
chocolate and roses
chocolate and schoolgirls' uniforms
chocolate bark
chocolate-berry
chocolate biscuits
chocolate box
chocolate cake with no icing
chocolate-cassis
chocolate-chip cookie dough

chocolate-chip cookies
chocolate, chocolate, chocolate
chocolate-coated cherry
  confections
chocolate-coated orange zest
chocolate-coated peanuts
chocolate-coated plums
chocolate-coated raisins
chocolate-coated strawberries
chocolate-covered berries
chocolate-covered berry fruit
chocolate-covered blackberries and
  stones
chocolate-covered butterscotch
  candy
chocolate-covered Bing cherries
chocolate-covered black cherries
chocolate-covered blueberry cassis-
  filled candy bars
chocolate-covered butterscotch
  candy
chocolate-covered cherries
chocolate-covered maraschino
  cherries
chocolate-covered oak
chocolate-covered raisins and
  raspberries
chocolate creams
chocolate *crème brûlée*
chocolate decadence
chocolate-dipped blackberries
chocolate-dipped cherries
chocolate-drenched
chocolate-edge(d)
chocolate egg-cream pie
chocolate espresso
chocolate fondue
chocolate frosting
chocolate fruit
chocolate fudge
chocolate ice
chocolate-infused
chocolate layer cake
chocolate liqueur
chocolate liqueur infused with
  brandy
chocolate makes a cameo
  appearance
chocolate-malt
chocolate malt with blackberry
  syrup
chocolate malt shake
chocolate melting into coffee
chocolate menthol
chocolate milk
chocolate-mocha ice cream
chocolate mocha oak
chocolate Necco Wafers

chocolate nuances
chocolate nuts
chocolate oak
chocolate-orange
chocolate oranges
chocolate-peppermint sweets
chocolate powder
chocolate pralines
chocolate pudding
chocolate-rich
chocolate-saturated maturity
chocolate sauce
chocolate shavings
chocolate smoothness
chocolate *soufflé*
chocolate spices
chocolate syrup
chocolate-toffee
chocolate truffles
chocolate undergrowth
chocolate-vanilla
chocolate wafers
chocolate yogurt
chocolaty
chocolaty aftertaste
chocolaty barrel
chocolaty *basso profundo*
chocolaty but not absurd
chocolaty cherries
chocolaty depths
chocolaty dressing of oak
chocolaty earthiness
chocolaty essence
chocolaty hazelnuts
chocolaty herbs
chocolaty liqueur cherries
chocolaty prunes
chocolaty richness
chocolaty ripeness
chocolaty toffee
chocolaty undertow
choc-sappy
chunky chocolate
chunky dark chocolate fruit in a
  big thick frame
cinnamon chocolate kiss
cocoa powder
coffee and chocolate powder
coffee-cream chocolate aftertaste
coffee-infused chocolate
continental chocolate
cordial-filled white chocolate
  candy
covered in rich dark chocolate
creamy chocolate
creamy hot chocolate
dark brown chocolate
dark choccie

dark chocolate
dark chocolate bonbons at a
  campfire
dark chocolate cover
dark chocolate-covered blueberries
dark chocolate espresso medley
dark chocolate heart
dark chocolate restraints
dark chocolaty mellowness
dark Swiss chocolate
dark unsweetened bitter chocolate
decadent chocolate mousse
deep bitter chocolate intensity
deep chocolaty intensity
designer chocolate
disciplined chocolate
drinks like chocolate sauce
drenched in chocolate
dry catering chocolate
Dutch chocolate
Easter bunny chocolate
elusive milk chocolate
enough chocolate to satisfy a cocoa
  hound
espresso beans lathered in melted
  chocolate
espresso-infused chocolate in the
  finish
essences of chocolate
extremely sweet aftertaste of milk
  chocolate
far too chocolaty
fine chocolate
finished with chocolate dust
freshly baked *pain au chocolate*
fruity milk chocolate
fudgy chocolate
generous coating of chocolaty oak
Ghiardelli chocolate and raspberry
  sandwich
Ghiardelli's chocolate
globalized chocolate coating
good chocolate pudding
gooey chocolate
grilled chocolate fruit
hallmark chocolate
hazelnut-filled milk chocolate
Hershey's chocolate
Hershey's chocolate Kisses
hot chocolate
hot chocolate (Cadbury's I assume)
intense chocolate-covered cherry
  candy
intense chocolate truffles
intense unsweet chocolate
intrusive cocoa-coated tannicity
kiss of chocolate mints
leather dipped in chocolate

lick of chocolate
like a box of chocolate...you never know what you're gonna get
like falling into a very tasty black hole made of blackberries and chocolate
like performing a sexual act that involves silk sheets, melted dark chocolate and black cherries while the mingled scents of cinnamon, coffee and cola waft through the air
like sipping melted chocolate infused with Crème de Cassis
like sticking your nose into a bowl of raspberries, chocolate and vanilla
liqueur chocolate
liquid chocolate
liquid chocolate *soufflé*
liquid milk chocolate poured over ripe black cherries and sprinkled with vanilla
long aftertaste of orange chocolate
luscious chocolate
lusty chocolate
malt chocolate
malted milk chocolate
melted bittersweet chocolate
melted Valrhona chocolate
melted white chocolate
melting chocolate richness
Mexican chocolate
milk chocolate
milk chocolate chips
milk chocolate pudding
milk chocolaty oak
minerals immersed in white chocolate
mint chocolate chips
mint chocolates
mint chocolate with rum liqueur
minty chocolate
mix of Ribena and chocolate
molten bittersweet chocolate
Necco Chocolate Wafers
nut-filled chocolate
oak-based milk chocolate
oodles of plain chocolate
oozing chocolate
orange chocolate
orange chocolate blanketed in honey
pan-seared reduction of red wine sweetened with chocolate and lavender
peppery mint chocolate
plain chocolate

plain chocolate heart
plenty of chocolate and grounding
plenty of dark and milk chocolate
plum compote with a couple of chocolate mints thrown in
plums and blackberries dipped in chocolate fondue
powdered chocolate
promise of chocolate
raspberry-chocolate fondue going down your throat
regional dark chocolate
rich chocolate-style core
richness of chocolate mingling perilously with truffles and well-hung game
roasted chocolate
Rubensesque chocolate
rum-and-raisin chocolate
sensual chocolaty-raisiny complexity
sensuous chocolaty oak
serious shredded dark chocolate
short and chocolaty
silky chocolate-laden finale
silky chocolate oral afterglow
slick as dark chocolate
slow-moving creamy chocolate
smoky chocolate
smoky chocolate-covered raspberries
smoldering chocolate mocha
smooth chocolate veil
soft as a chocolate sponge pudding
sour chocolate
spicy-chocolaty
spicy mocha-chocolate
Starbucks-esque chocolate *espresso*
sticky melted milk chocolate
subtle catering-chocolate undertone
superripe chocolate-covered blackberries
sweet cherry chocolate
sweet chocolate-chip cookie dough immersed in cherry syrup
sweet milk chocolate
sweet rich melted club chocolate
Swiss chocolate
Syrah as chocolate
syrup of figs and chocolate
tea and chocolate
thick chocolate cream
triple chocolate cake
twitch of regional dark chocolate
ultraregional bitter chocolate
unsweetened chocolate
unsweetened dark chocolate

Valrhona chocolate
vanilla-chocolate
vanilla and bitter chocolate
vanilla-chocolate sweetness from oak
very chocolaty...you could pour it over ice cream
virtually pure chocolate
voluptuous chocolate
walnut and bittersweet chocolate
warm chocolate
warm chocolate brownies
white chocolate-covered minerals
white chocolate-covered pears
warm chocolate pudding
warm chocolaty *fondue*
warm gooey stuff like chocolate *fondue*
white chocolate
white chocolate powder
white chocolate truffles
white chocolate with sweet pineapple chunks
white Toblerone
white Toblerone chocolate, nuts, coffee and lilies of the valley
wrapped in chocolate
Ybarra chocolate
zippy chocolate

It is difficult to enjoy a fine wine in a bad glass.
Evelyn Waugh

Wine glasses, like fine wine, have always been a symbol of civilized living. The finest glasses are large and tulip-shaped, clear and thin, without markings, the bowl the size of a large orange or an apple. When less than half filled, such a glass permits the full enjoyment of the color, bouquet, and taste of a fine wine.
Alex Lichine

P. Through a Glass Clearly

Why would anyone want to drink wine from anything other than clear crystal or glass? If the wine is decent enough, it deserves an equally good container. A thin well-made goblet without color, decoration or etching always serves nicely. Everyday wine, however, is okay in everyday glasses, even jelly or canning jars. But only someone totally indifferent to wine would drink it from plastic (except in a pool area) or, worse still, in cardboard or paper. Clear?

a glass of this is gone before you know it
alive and kicking in the glass
apple pastry in a glass
a translator of soil types in a glass
aromas leap out of the glass to meet you
aromatherapy in a glass
asleep in the glass
as smooth as glass
as smooth as syrup in a glass
Austro-Hungarian empire in a glass
autumn in a glass
balanced glass of sunny fruit and perfume
Barry Bonds in a glass
beautiful rays of summer sunshine in your glass
becomes even more Guerlain-like in the glass
billows out of the glass
Black Forest cake in a glass
bling in your glass
bliss in a glass
blossomed in the glass
bouquet leaps from the glass to the nose
brawn in a glass

bubbles formed a tight and strong pillar in the middle of the glass
builds up in the glass
by sheer force one glass takes your palate places where you haven't been before
cherries jubilee in a glass
cherry festival in a glass: fruit, blossoms, pits and all
Christmas in a glass
class in a glass
close to a glass of immortality
collapsed in the glass
colors seem to press the sides of the glass
complex enough to return to, glass after glass
complexities unravel when the wine warms in the glass
crackles and hums in the glass
crème brûlée in a glass
cut-crystal elegance
cut-glass purity of flavors
cut-glass tastes
dances out of the glass
dead in the glass
deep dark violet-red dye in the glass

delicate mousse forms beautiful pearl necklace in the glass
dessert in a glass
dies in the glass
difficult to describe the transition from grape to glass
drooped in the glass
dying in the glass
dynamite in a glass
each sip is like a glassful
enormous perfume lasts in an empty glass for hours
eruption of a garden from your glass
evolves in the glass
excitement in the glass
fascinating aromas unfold with every swirl of the glass
fire in the glass
fireworks in the glass
fizzy sparkler in the glass
flavors boogie around the glass
flavors grow in the glass
flavors lingers in the mouth with magnificent intensity...minutes after the glass has been emptied
fount of mineral oil flavors jet from glass to palate
fragrance leaps from the glass

friend in our glass
frothy like the head on a glass of Guinness
fruitcake in a glass
fruit preserve in a glass
fruit salad in a glass
glass of butterscotch
glassful of smiles
glass of liquid oak
glass of little green apples and lemon flowers
glass of papaya juice
glass-staining
glassy
glee in the glass
glistens in the glass
glorious evolution in the glass
glows purple in the glass
goes flat in the glass
gorgeous pearl necklaces in the glass
gorilla in a glass
grandeur in the glass
great fruit leaps out of the glass
grilled meat in a glass
grows with airing in the glass
has a charisma that compels you to return to your glass again and again
heaven in a glass
I could climb into the glass
immortality in a glass
improved in the glass
incredibly complex and sinuous… evolves and changes in the glass
incredible difference between the first heavenly glass and the flat sludge that finished the bottle
intensity from/in a glass
interesting glassful
Italian sunshine in a glass
jumps out of the glass
Key-lime pie in a glass
la dolce vita in a glass
late summer in a glass
lazy bubbles at the bottom of the glass
leaves lasting streaks of color in the glass
leaves thick stains of glycerin on the glass
legs take forever to run down the sides of the glass
like finding an oak tree in your glass
loses it in the glass
layered and never stops changing in the glass

liquid gold in a glass
lot going on in the glass
lusciously coats the glass
luxury in a glass
makes no noise when poured into a glass…it's completely silent
makes you sit up and notice what's in your glass
makes you want to crawl inside the glass
meal in a glass
melted honeycomb in a glass
microscopic bubbles stream around the glass like tiny pearls
minimal bubbles which never stop streaming upward out of the glass
molten licorice in a glass
most beautiful string of pearls in the glass
naughtiness in a glass of pink
nose pole-vaults out of the glass with Olympian precision
oily viscosity clinging to the glass
orchard in a glass
ought to be served on toast rather than in a glass
passion fruit in a glass
pears leap out of the glass
poetry in a glass
positively pushing the sides of the glass
positively swelling in the glass
power and spiciness surge out of the glass like a sudden eruption of Mount Etna
practically coats the glass
practically swaggers into your glass
pure hedonism in a glass
pure immortality in a glass
pure passion in a glass
pure pleasure in a glass
quite viscous when swirled in the glass
radiance in a glass
real glass-stainer
really blossoms in the glass
rich enough to cling to the glass
rises out of the glass with such force and density you might wonder how the bottle held the cork
roars from the glass like an out-of-control locomotive
rock 'n roll in a glass
rose garden in a glass
romance in a glass
rumbled uneasily in the glass

screams from the glass in a reassuring rather than frightening manner
see it change in the glass
seemed to get sweeter in the glass
seems to glow in the glass
seems to leap out of the glass
seems to sparkle in the glass
seen through the magnifying glass of the taste buds
sex in a glass
sings from the glass
sings out of the glass
smells so good you may just want to sink your nose into the glass
so appealing you want to dive into the glass
soars majestically from the glass
soars out of the glass
so dense and dark that it stains the glass
so dense and syrupy it actually paints the inside of the glass
so intense that the color seemed to pressurize the sides of the glass
so pretty on the nose you'll want to smell the glass even after it's empty
so rich as to be clinging to the glass
so thick it's unwilling to slither down the glass
speaks through the glass
splendor in the glass
spice bazaar in a glass
stains the glass as it's swirled
sugar cube in a glass of V8 juice
summer in a glass
summer pudding in a glass
sunset in a glass
sunshine in a glass
sweet warm honeycomb in a glass
texture of chicken soup in a glass
thick against the glass
typical glass-staining purple
unadorned cut-glass purity
unfolds beautifully in the glass
velvet glassful
very tempting to drain the glass
vinous equivalent of potato chips…I bet you can't drink just one glass
viscous texture stains the glass with glycerin
you don't want to take your nose out of the glass
Zen koan in a glass
zesty grapefruit-in-a-glass

A great trademark is appropriate, dynamic, distinctive, memorable and unique.
Primo Angeli

An idealist is one who, on noticing that a rose smells better than a cabbage, concludes that it will also make better soup.
H.L. Mencken

Q. At the Trademark Office

You'd think that wine tasters would run out of comparisons using every possible substance in earth to convey what they smell and taste. But no, they still plod on, reaching deep into the dark recesses of their human sensory memories to come up with novel comparisons, such as well-known trademarked products sold the world over. I can only imagine my reaction to smelling a Big Mac in my glass, or tasting Gummi Bears splashing around in it. It's just plain hard for most of us to even think about finding many of these in a glass of wine; surely, we'd just want to return the bottle. Oh, well, here goes:

3-IN-ONE	Bass-O-Matic	Burger King	Corn Flake	Dunkin' Donut
7-ELEVEN	Bassett	Buick Riviera	Count Chocula	Earl Grey
7UP	Batman	Cabbage Patch	Cracker Jack	Eggo
Absolut	Battlestar Galactica	Cadbury	Creamsicle	Edam
After Eight	Bayer	Campari	Cream of Wheat	Enron
Alka-Seltzer	Ben & Jerry	Castrol	Creepy Crawler	Eskimo Pie
All-Bran	Bengay	Certs	Crystal Light	Euthymol
Almond Joy	Bentley	Chanel N°5	Cynar	Fanta
Amaretto	Bentlin	Cheerio	Darth Vader	Farrah's
Amstel	Big League Chew	Cheeto	DayGlo	Fazer
Angostura	Big Mac	Cheracol	DEET	Fellini
Applehead	Big Red	Cherry Ripe	Del Monte	Fernet Branca
Armani	Black Tower	Chevy	Devil Dog	Ferrari
Aspro Clear	Body Shop	Chloraseptic	Dimetane	Fig Newton
Aston Martin	Bollinger	Chunky Monkey	Dimetapp	Firestone
Aunt Jemima	Bonne Maman	Cibachrome	Dodge	Formula 409
Baby Duck	Bonnington	Cinnamon Toast	Dolce and Gabbana	Fortuny
Baby Ruth	Bonox	Crunch	Dole	Fowler
Bacardi	Boone's Farm	Cirque du Soleil	Dollar Store	Frankenstein
Bailey	Bottle Cap	Coca-Cola/Coke	Dolly Mixture	Frango
Bakelite	Bovril	Cocoa Puff	Doritos	Frappuccino
Band-Aid	Brasso	Cohiba	Dr Pepper	Frazzle
Barbie	Breyers	Cointreau	Drambuie	Fresca
Barq	Bubble Yum	Cold Duck	Drāno	Friar's Balsam
Baskin-Robbins	Bugatti	Concorde	Driza-Bone	Froot Loop

Fruit Gum
Gap
Garcia y Vega
Gentleman's Relish
Ghiardelli
Ginsu
Godzilla
Goober
Good & Plenty
Grand Marnier
Grape-Nut
Green Giant
Green Mountain
Gripfix
Gucci
Guerlain
Guinness
Gummi Bear
Habitrail
Harley-Davidson
Hawaiian Punch
Heinz 57
Hell's Angel
Hershey
Hermès
Hi-C
Hit Parade
Honey 'n Nut
Horlicks
Hostess
Hulk
Hummer
Identi-Kit
IHOP
Incredible Hulk
Islay
J Cloth
Jack Daniel
Jacobs
Jägermeister
Jaguar
Janitor in a Drum
Jell-O
Jelly Baby
Jelly Tot
Jenga
Jolt
Johnson
Jolly Rancher
Juicy Juice
Juicy Fruit
JuJube
Jujyfruit
K & B
Kahlúa
Kalle
Kellogg
Kendal

Kleenex
Knott's
Kool-Aid
Kraft Caramel
Laffy Taffy
Lamborghini
Lancer's Rosé
Land O' Lake
LifeSaver
Lincoln Log
Lion King
Liquid Plumr
Listerine
Lorna Doone
Mace
Magic Marker
Malibu
Manischewitz
Marlboro
Marmite
Mars
Mattel
McDonald
Mercurochrome
Meritage
Mighty Mouse
Milk Dud
MilkyWay
Miller High Life
Missoni
Mogen David
Montecristo
MoonPie
Mott
Mound
Mr. Bubbles
Mr. Clean
Mrs. Butterworth's
Muzak
National
     Geographic
Necco Wafer
Nehi
Nesquik
Nestlé
Nike
Nilla Wafer
Nips
Nivea
Novocaine
Now and Later
Nutella
Ocean Spray
Old Bay
Old Spice
Opal Fruit
Oreo
Ovaltine

Parma
Parmigiano-
     Reggiano
Patel's
Paul Mitchell
Pendleton
Penfold's Grange
Pepperidge Farm
Pez
Phillies
Piesporter
Pilsner
Pine-Sol
Ping-Pong
PixyStix
Planet of the Apes
Plasticine
Play-Doh
Player
Plaza
Pledge
Pond
Pop Rocks
Popsicle
Pop-Tart
Porky Pig
Prada
Punt E Mes
Raid
Raisinets
Red Hot
Red Vines
Reese's Peanut
     Butter Cup
Ribena
Ricola
Ripple
Rite Aid
Ritz-Carlton
Robitussin
Roger & Gallet
Rolex
Rolling Rock
Rolls-Royce
Rose's
Roto-Rooter
Rowntree
Saltines
Saran Wrap
Schlitz
Screaming Yellow
     Zonker
Shalimar
Shrek
Silly Putty
Skittles
Slazinger
Slenderella

Slim Jim
Slurpee
Smarty
Smith Brothers
Smucker
Snapple
Snicker
Sour Patch Kids
Spackle
Spaten
Speculoo
Speyside
Splenda
Spree
Sprite
Squirt
Starbucks
Starburst
Stilton
Stove Top
Sunlight
Swedish Fish
SweeTart
Sweet'N Low
Tabasco
Tang
Tasti D-Lite
Tate & Lyle
Technicolor
Teddy Grahams
Tetra Pak
Thrill
Thunderbird
Tia Maria
Tidy Bowl
Tiffany
Tiger Balm
Toblerone
Tootsie Roll
Topp
Torrone di
     Cremona
Triple Sec
Tupperware
Turkish Delight
Twizzlers
UGLI
Ultrasuede
Valentino
Valrhona
VapoRub
Varsol
Vaseline
Vegemite
V8
Velamint
Velcro
Velveeta

Versace
Viagra
Vicks
Virol
Vogel's
WD-40
Weet-Bix
Welch
Wheaties
Wheat Thins
Whole Foods
Wiffle
Willy Wonka
Windex
Wint-O-Green
Wrigley
Ybarra
YMCA
Yoplait
York
Yumster
Zima
Zinger
Zorro

Popularity? It is glory's small change.
Victor Hugo

Glory is fleeting, but obscurity is forever.
Napoleon Bonaparte

Fame and riches are fleeting. Stupidity is eternal.
Don Williams, Jr.

R. Central Casting

Without wine, there would still be people; without people, however, there would be no wine. So when you're sipping a glass of Zin or Ries, think about all the famous (and sometimes, infamous) folks who figure in wine descriptors: every gender, type and occupation imaginable, from Achilles to Yo-Yo Ma. Even those irrelevant to wine, such as the glitterati and their eye-candy cousins, pop up quite regularly in the vinous vocabulary, whether we like it or not.

Achilles	Don Giovanni	Joseph	Queen Victoria
Agnès B.	Duke Ellington	Julia Roberts	Rabelais
Armstrong	Emperor Augustus	Kublai Khan	Rembrandt
Angelina Jolie	Fellini	Lauren Bacall	Renoir
Arnold Schwarzenegger	Ferrari	Liberace	Rita Hayworth
Armani	Fortuny	Linford Christie	Robert Parker
Audrey Hepburn	Gandhi	Mae West	Rothschild
Bach	Garibaldi	Marilyn Monroe	Rubens
Barry Bonds	Gauguin	Marco Polo	Schubert
Baryshnikov	Gene Kelly	Marie Antoinette	Sean Connery
Bee Gees	Gladstone	Matisse	Shakespeare
Beethoven	Glenn Miller	Methuselah	Sharon Stone
Benny Goodman	Gucci	Michelangelo	Sibelius
Bix Beiderbecke	Guinness	Michel Rolland	Sofia Loren
Bollinger	Gustav Klimt	Mick Jagger	Sugar Ray Leonard
Botero	Harlan	Missoni	Tiffany
Braque	Heidi Klum	Monet	Titian
Bruce Springsteen	Helen of Troy	Mozart	Tutankhamen
Brueghel	Hell's Angels	Oz Clarke	Umberto Eco
Bugatti	Henry VIII	Pat Metheny	Valentino
Canaletto	Hermès	Paul Mitchell	Van Dyke
Carlos Santana	Hippocrates	Pavarotti	Veronese
Carmen Miranda	Hitchcock	Prada	Versace
Churchill	James Bond	Prince Harry	Wagner
Clint Eastwood	James Cagney	Proust	Yo-Yo Ma
Count Basie	Jesus	Pythagoras	
De Gaulle	Johnny Cash	Queen Anne	
Dolly Parton	John Wayne	Queen Elizabeth	

It was the smell of vanilla, champagne, longing, marzipan, peaches, smiles, cream, strawberries, raspberries, roses, melting chocolate, lilac, figs, laughter, honeysuckle, kisses, lilies, enchantment, ardor itself.
Lily Prior

S. The Kitchen Sink

Ah, the kitchen sink: the enduring image we use to conjure up a messy collection of anything. Wines with busy aromas and myriad tastes qualify with their kitchen sink-blends or styles. And sometimes you can't control all the images that come to mind when sampling especially complex wines with multiple aromas and layers of flavors. Therefore, unless you're a professional, don't spout all those descriptors at dinner with your spouse, life partner, significant other, good friend, business associate or world-weary boss. You may well dine alone for a long time to come.

acacia honey, dry figs and dates, apricots, peaches, a gazillion different flavors, orange peel, tangerine and nutmeg

apple drops, orange drops, lemon drops, smoke, ginseng, vanilla, caramel, pralines, mint, roots, ashes and burning frankincense; if nothing else it's certainly complex

apples, oranges, apricots, honey, iodine, smoke, hazelnuts, macadamias, dry oloroso sherry, Calvados, toffee, brown butter and marrow

apricot, date, fig, dried fruit, tobacco, dried mushrooms, candied fruits, saffron, flint and dark chocolate

apricots, figs, pomegranates, oranges, kumquats, Cape gooseberries, peaches, grapefruit, lemon, dates, walnuts, lavender, magical liquid acacia, honey, ginger, cinnamon, salt and smoke

beef blood, animal fur, wet dog, mushrooms, tree bark, licorice, spice, black currants and cherries

beef blood, lavender, Provençale herbs, ground pepper, melted licorice, oodles of blackberry and *crème de cassis*-like-fruit

bitter almonds, toasted almonds, pecans, sweet oranges, dried red apples, more toffee than
caramel, chocolate with some ash, cherries, black pepper, sour oranges, bitter orange zest and
tobacco

blackberries, kirsch liqueur, licorice, incense, spice box, black raspberries, blueberries, smoke
and flowers

black cherries, plums, blackberries, blueberries, violets, mocha, *café au lait*, sweet oak and
Asian spices

black cherry, raspberry, blueberry, cedar, spice, coffee, chocolate, herbs, licorice, cocoa, vanilla,
toast and tangy berries

blueberries, licorice, jammy blackberries, violets, Asian spices, stones, red currants, cherries
and fresh clay

boiled vegetables, paprika, green beans, beetroot, fish, raw meat, gunpowder
smoke, cauliflower, lavender, basil, tar and duck liver

candied black currants, cherries, rose blossoms, lilies, rosemary, stones, cassis liqueur, sautéed
morels, porcini mushroom, violets and black raspberries

charcuterie, barbecued meats, long-simmered beef stock, suggestions of earth and truffles and
crushed ants

cherries, cranberries, raspberry fruit preserves, cinnamon and cardamom spice, smoke, earth,
violets and sage spice

Cherries! Dates! Figs! Black licorice! Leather! Coffee! Bittersweet chocolate! Tobacco!
Et cetera, et cetera

cherry compote, bittersweet chocolate, vanilla beans, flowers, undergrowth and freshly made
toast

cherry jam, raspberries macerated in alcohol, bitter chocolate, graphite, bay leaf, vinegar,
balsamic vinegar and herbs

cherry, roses, wet earth, truffles, candied fruit, solid spice, catnip, dognip, might as well call it
whale-bait, bread and semisweet chocolate

chocolate-covered raisins kiss roasted espresso while ultraripe blackberries drip juice onto
tar-laden, spice-covered maidens

cigar tobacco, cedar, herbs, spice, iodine, oak, French-fry fat, plums, blackberries and chocolate

creosote, tobacco leaf, roasted coffee, chocolate, smoke, earthy black currant and blackberry fruit

crushed grapes, nuts, seeds, light vanilla, plums, honey, mocha, leather, dried strawberries, minerals, tea, coffee and *tiramisu*

crushed stones, white truffle, underbrush, black plum, fig, cedar, tar and God knows what else

deep prune, violet, rubber, bacon, mustard greens, clove, cinnamon, brown sugar, licorice and coffee

dried cherry, mocha, eucalyptus and blackberry, earth, black and red fruit, supple tannins, coffee, leather, the works

dried herbs, new saddle leather, soy, roasted duck, grilled steak, cassis, blackberry and prune

eucalyptus, leather, charcoal, raspberries, fine-grained tannins, bright strawberry fruit, forest floor and cinnamon spice

faded flowers, dried tea leaf, quinine, red berry syrup, cinnamon, figs steeped in balsamic vinegar, blackberry jam, red berries macerated in alcohol, milk chocolate and cloves

field flowers, thyme, almond, hazelnut, marzipan, white chocolate, honeysuckle, butterscotch, dried apricot, orange peel, dried fig and date

gonorrhea with notes of dung, spare ribs, horse blanket, boiled cabbage and cardboard

granite, cassis, blueberry, smoky gunflint, pepper, tar, bitter chocolate, roast coffee, leather, game and animal fur

grapefruit, lychees, bananas, mango, papaya, white pepper, cinnamon, rose petals, ginger, vanilla, peach, passion fruit and acacia honey

grassy notes hover over vanilla seeds and blackberries, cedar, cassis, spearmint, warm cherries and cocoa

gravel, earth, violets, perfume, jammy blueberries, cassis, black cherries, road tar, candied cherries, stones, rosemary, spicy oak, Asian spices and chocolate honey, baked something, *crème brûlée*, grilled almonds, orange peel, orange flowers, caramel, spice and apricots

honey, marzipan, nuts, orange, tangerine, almond, cream and lots more, but I got tired of writing!

kirsch liqueur, new saddle leather, animal fur, Provençale herbs, spice box, licorice and a salty sea breeze

knockwurst (so help me), candle wax, floor polish, kiwis, tired whipped cream, sandalwood, fabric softener, peanut brittle, mustard seed and warm brioche

lead pencil shavings interwoven with coffee, new saddle leather, melted licorice, cedarwood, black currant liqueur and violets

lemon peel, tangerine, guava, apricot, buckwheat honey, mango chutney, nutmeg, clove, goose fat, clarified butter, butterscotch, almond *tuiles* and toasted hazelnuts

licorice, cookie dough, blackberry, cassis liqueur, sweet candied black fruits, freshly laid asphalt, spice, fresh herbs and toasty oak

like performing a sexual act that involves silk sheets, melted dark chocolate and black cherries, while the mingled scents of cinnamon, coffee and cola waft through the air

liqueur of rocks, honeysuckle, buttery caramelized citrus, tropical fruit, huge ripe nectarines, smoke and minerals

liquid minerals, creamed hazelnuts, candied chestnuts *(marrons glacés)*, anise, buttered toast, stones, straw, grilled bread and sweet white flowers

meat, tomato, earth, spice, mint, fig, something herbal that was dill-like, beef *satay*, peanut sauce, cedar, gravy, Worcestershire and garden

melted licorice, smoky barbecue, truffles, earth, blackberries, currants, coffee, graphite and blueberries

melted road tar, truffle, animal fur, sweet saddle leather intermixed with kirsch, dried herbs, balsam and black cherry fruit

milk chocolate, citrus fruits, caramel, almond, hazelnut, roasted coffee bean, ultradatey, dried fig, peach and traditional balsamic vinegar

minerals, stones, gooseberries, plums, seashells, toast, raspberries, peaches, pears, honeysuckle blossoms, "Champagne" currants and flint

minerally lemon ice, nectarine, quince, green fig, asparagus, gooseberries, white pear and chamomile

molasses, dark chocolate, vanillin oak, old furniture, burnt toffee, leather upholstery, spices, coffee grounds, tar and cough mixture

mulberries, damsons, cardamom, tamarind, tobacco, leather, crumbled earth, creamy oak and ruby bramble fruits

peach blossoms, honeysuckle, toasted almonds, lemons, butterscotch, smoke, oranges and marzipan

raspberries, roasted coffee beans, licorice whips, graphite, nougat, dried cherries, toasted hazelnuts and Victoria plums

raspberry, lavender, cocoa powder, smoke, underbrush, cherry pit, flowers, menthol and rose petal

rich apricot, pineapple, cigar, beeswax, lemon curd, white flower, pear and caramelized lemon rind

ripe apple, sweet pear, smoke, clove, butterscotch, Asian spice, Juicy Fruit gum, the works

roasted nuts, dried herbs, jammy curranty fruit, sweet cedar, old wood, truffles, smoke, underbrush, black currant and cherry

rose, beef, blood, iron, menthol, Worcestershire, earth, library books, animal and lightly grilled game

rose petals intertwined with charcuterie, spring flowers, blue and black fruits, raspberries, cola and mint oil

saddle leather, roasted herbs, scorched earth, sweet black currants, minerals, spice box and cedar

sandalwood, incense, spice, berries, plums, boiled beets, black cherries, smoked sausage, tar and licorice

scorched earth, liquid minerals, graphite, blackberry, black currant jam, toast, licorice and spice box

seductively beautiful, multifaceted, Count Basie, a brothel, a summer's evening and an Aston Martin

smoked meats, ground pepper, sweet kirsch, currants, blood, herbs and God knows what else

spice, woodsmoke, barbecue sauce, cedar, coconut, berries, plums, cherries, tea, espresso and chocolate

talcum powder, lipstick, black cherry, herbs, field flowers, warmed plums, cream, nuts, dark chocolate and burnt toast

tea, ginger, tangerine rind, myriad sweet flowers, cherry distillate, truffles, *fraises des bois* preserves, bloody fresh meat and implacable chalk

truffle juice, roasted meats, minerals, smoke, red and black fruits, licorice, Chinese black tea and incense

unique, handsome, textured, individual, couth, complex, caressing yet characterful

vanilla, citrus, warm toast, dried apricot, tangerine peel, peachy apricot, Golden Delicious apples, white chocolate and fresh-baked bread

walnuts, flor, nuttiness, caramel, ginger, coconut, orange toffee, cherries, cooked cherries, figs and prunes

white flowers, pineapple, candied orange peel, dried apricot, guava, mango, cinnamon, white pepper and nutmeg

white pepper, ginger, poached pears, assorted spices, yellow plums, nutmeg, buttered toast and spiced pears

wines the color of wheat that tasted like the grapes had been brushed in your armpit after a rather enjoyable game of beach volleyball. And then splashed with custard. And squeezed with lime juice

wintergreen, nut, roasted meat, cherries, pepper, anise, caramel, older red fruits, earth and mild dust

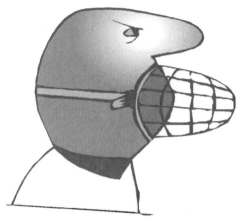

Words are such impoverished little things with which to describe wine.
Jancis Robinson

Language is inadequate really to describe the sensation of tasting a wine.
Randall Grahm

If you can't describe it in words and talk about it, like 'it reminds me of gym socks' or 'my grandmother's blackberry pie,' you can't remember it.
Karen MacNeil

T. There are No Words...

Here's the complete opposite of the previous *The Kitchen Sink,* where so many so-called experts go on and on until our eyes glaze over. Yet, sometimes even the most experienced, articulate wine pros run out of descriptive vocabularies. Many seem so stunned by the utter complexity or absolute perfection of what they're experiencing that they retreat into a never-never land where language, however evocative and soaring, is simply hopelessly inadequate. And sometimes irrelevant.

all but impossible to adequately describe
almost beyond superlatives
almost beyond words
almost defies articulation
aromas practically defy description
at a loss for words
beyond description
beyond words
challenges our vocabulary of descriptors
complexity being an utterly inadequate word to convey the layers of flavors, intensity and soaring length
complexity that almost defies description
concentration of fruit leaves me speechless
defies all attempts at verbal analysis
defies analysis
defies deconstructionist description
defies description
defies description for sheer hedonistic joy
deliciousness in it eluded analysis
description of flavors is endless
descriptors don't begin to capture the sheer breadth of aromatic expression here
difficult to analyze
difficult to describe the transition from grape to glass with this kind of wine

difficult to describe this wine without resorting to profanity
difficult to get to know
difficult to judge
difficult to pin down
difficult wine to figure
drinking this is like navigating a maze
easy-to-understand personality
elegance difficult to describe
elegance impossible to convey using the standard vocabulary of a wine taster
embryo is difficult to judge
ethereal quality that is difficult to put into words
ethereal, with flavors and delicacy beyond description
exotic flavors that are hard to describe
fantastic array of aromas and spices too numerous to even try to describe
flavor beyond words
flavors are hard to read
great wine has more than you can say in words
had this taster gasping for superlatives
hard one to peg
hard to define
hard-to-describe squeaky feel
hard to describe other than to say it lacks fruit
hard to describe the nuance and complexity

hard to find descriptors for it
hard to judge like this
hard to pin down a typical style
hard-to-pin-down flavors
hard to understand
has complexity that almost defies description
how can one describe perfection?
how can such a perfect wine be described?
how do you describe a wine of such dazzling flavors?
I'm nearly at a loss for words to describe it
impossible to describe
I'm speechless
I'm stunned and utterly speechless

I'm unable to speak

indescribable
indescribable earthiness
incredibly complex and literally indescribable
it's almost foolish to try and articulate how wines
    such as this taste, given the extraordinary number of
    nuances, layers and textures the wine has to offer
it would take a writer of Shakespeare's eloquence to
    do justice to this wine
lavish beyond description
leaves me speechless
left an entire panel of tasters speechless
left our tasting panel searching for superlatives
less than generous and difficult to get to know
like a box of chocolates, you never know what
    you're gonna get
magical complexity of aromas defy description
mysterious with lurking flavors that are hard to pin
    down
my words cannot do them justice
not a wine to describe
no words of mine can do it justice
only sexual analogies can do justice
pretty hard to read
rather diffident and evasive
really hard to describe in mere words
really too formidable to judge by normal red wine
    parameters
rich, intense, unfathomable
simply sensational, so excuse the verbose *winespeak*
so complex as to be indefinable
so complex it's impossible to give a single fruit or
    other descriptor
so heavenly with so many tiny nuances that I could
    fill an entire page
so many things going on, adjectives would do it a
    disservice
so much going on it's hard to adequately describe
[so nearly perfect] it can't be described with words
so normal and ordinary that I can't find any words to
    describe it
still a baby and easy to misunderstand
superlatives are too numerous to list
takes time to understand
tasting notes just don't do it justice

the critics are going to have to throw a thesaurus party
the purity, elegance and sheer beauty of this wine is
    frankly difficult to adequately describe as words just
    don't seem up to the task
there just aren't enough superlatives to describe it
the thesaurus has no superlatives enough to do it
    justice
this venerable wine stands outside the purview of
    mortal rating systems, and will remain so
too many complex flavors to analyze here
unknowable
unusual quality about it I simply can't pin down
unusual undertones that defy description
utterly defies comprehensive description
very difficult to describe
when it leaves an entire panel of tasters speechless,
    struggling to find words to describe a wine that
    seems to defy possibility, how can a wine score
    100 points?
when you're not in the mood for too much serious
    analysis
words are inadequate at this level
words are not the language of wine
words are simply inadequate
words cannot describe nor do this wine justice
words cannot do it justice
words remain inadequate to describe just how good
    this wine is

words simply cannot do it justice

words simply cannot express the astonishing
    aromatic complexity
writing a tasting note about such a wine is frankly
    impossible because mere words cannot possibly
    capture its greatness

She poured the thick, rubylike liquid,
and a seductive cloud of perfumes swirled
and filled the air. It reminded me of
fragrances of tropical fruit in Burma,
spices from the market in Marrakech,
cinnamon from the high valleys of the
Seychelles, the scent after a downpour
in the Marquesas, singly and together,
like banked clouds before a storm.
We drank without a word.
Ferenc Máté

He talked with more claret than clarity.
Susan Ertz

The wine of youth does not always clear with advancing years; sometimes it grows turbid.
Carl Jung

1. Clarity [Limpidity]

Wine drinkers today seem to prefer their vinous selections to be clear of anything they think they could see other than color or bubbles. To achieve this, many vintners mechanically or/or chemically filter out particulates, although some still deliberately leave their wines unfiltered to increase flavor intensity. It's sort of like cloudy unfiltered apple juice or cider that produces a fuller body and a richer taste. Nevertheless, wine should never have foreign things like glass, insects, twigs, weeds or such floating around in it (except maybe for a few bits of wandering but harmless cork.) In wine, clear may be good, but taste is definitely better.

admits no light
amazing
as bright as sunshine
as opaque as a blackbird
astonishing
beeswings
bits, crunchy
blind/blinding
blocks all light
blurred/blurry
bright it seemed to light up
   the room, so
bright, day-
bright, diamond-
bright, fall-
bright, star-
bright-edged
brightness, searchlight
brilliance, luminous
brilliance, pinpoint of
brilliant
clarified

clarified, less
clarity, rare crystal
clear as a bell, as
clear as a bright autumn day, as
clear as cool mountain spring
   water, as
clear as the purist diamond, as
clear, crystal-/diamond-
clear, impeccably
clear, near-
clear, water-
clear-cut
clogged
cloudiness is perfectly okay
cloudy like water mixed with
   the contents of an ashtray,
   black and
cloudy, little/slightly
cloudy, surprisingly
cloudy-cidery
coruscating
creased

crumpled
crystalline
dark things
dazzles/dazzling
dense
dense you need x-ray vision to see
   through it, so
deposits, healthy
deposits, no/without
deposits, some
diaphanous
diffuse
dim
dingy
dirty
disturbed
drab
dreary
dubious
dull
excellent
extrashiny

filmy
filthy
fined
flaky
flawed
flawless
fliers/flies
floaters/floating things
flocculation/flocculence/
   flocculent
foggy
free
fuzzy
gauzy
gemlike brilliance and clarity
glassy
gleaming
glimmering
glinting
glint, steely
glistening
glittering/glittery
gloomy
glows in the glass
good/goodish
gunk/gunky
haze, slightly yeasty
haze/hazy
immaculate
impure
impurities, free of
impurities, many
impurities, some
incandescent
iridescent
lackluster
laserlike
leaden
lifeless
light through, lets no
limpid as a swimming pool
   (not the municipal kind), as
limpidity and fidelity,
   photographic
limpidity, brilliant/star-bright
limpidity, dewdrop
limpidity, juicy ripe
luminescence, prismatic
luminosity/luminous
luster, sunny
lusterless
matte
medium
milky
mucky
muddied, unexpectedly
muddy
murkiness/murky

nebulous
North Atlantic, looks like the
obscure/obscured
occluded
off, distinctly
opacity, dense and dark to the
   point of
opacity, intense
opalescence, oily
opaque at the core, quite
opaque black elixir
opaque core
opaque with no tricks
opaque, almost
opaque, fearsomely
opaque, just this side of
opaque, not fashionably
opaque, totally
overclarified
pallid
particles/particulates
pearling/pearly
pellucid
permits no light
phosphorescent
pinpoint
pitted
pretty
profound
pure
radiance in the glass
radiant
reflective
reflects light like a mirror
scintillating
sediment, fine bitty
sediment, harmless
sediment, heavy/heavyish
sediment, light/lightish
sediment, prodigious
sediment-free
shallow
sheer
shimmering/shimmery
shining/shiny
so inky and dark it is clearly
   an octopus wine
somber
sparkle/sparkles/
   sparkling/sparkly
stars, bright as
stunning
swampy
translucence, shimmering
   ruby
transparency, pure
troubled
turbid

turgid
twinkling/twinkly
ultraclear
unclear
unclouded
unfiltered
unfiltered yet clean-tasting
unfined
unsettled
unusual
veil, like looking through a
veil, slight
veiled
vivid
water, spring

All roads lead to red.
Kevin Zraly

The first obligation of a wine is to be red.
Henri Murger

*The point about white Burgundies is that
I hate them myself. They so closely resemble
a blend of cold chalk soup and alum cordial
with an additive or two to bring it to the
colour of children's pee.*
Kingsley Amis

2. Color [Robe, Dress, Gown]

The British, Canadians, Australians and New Zealanders call it *colour*; the French, ever more fashion-conscious, call it *robe, dress* or *gown*. Nonetheless, all have the same meaning of wines' many hues, important keys to their grape variety, origin, age, health and quality. Wine can range from absolutely colorless to the blackest gloom of a moonless midnight. It's good to keep in mind that as red wine ages, it becomes lighter, while white wines darken with age. Yet, as the quotes above indicate, many wine connoisseurs defiantly claim that a wine's first duty is to be red. Of course, white wine drinkers would never agree, nor would those who prefer rosé. *Chacun à son goût.*

aging copper
amaranth
amber, astonishing orange-rose
amber, burnt
amber, dark
amber, deep glowing
amber, glowing/luminous
amber, light
amber, lime-shaded
amber, medium
amber, startling brilliant
amber, unhealthy
amber-gold, sequins of
amber-red
amethyst
amontillado, burnt
amoroso
apple, oxidized
apricot, bleached/pale
apricot-pink
aqua
ash, pale
atramental
aubergine, deep
auburn/auburn-hue(d)

aurora borealis
autumn/autumnal
barley, pale
beetrootlike
beige, pinky
bister/bistre
black as a miner's hankie, as
black as a moonless night, as
black as Egypt's night, as
black as hell, as
black as molasses, as
black as night, as
black as pitch, as/pitch black
black as Texas crude, as
black as the underside of a flat rock
    in a dense forest, as
black core, dark purple with a
black elixir, opaque
black has flavors this wine
    embodies them, if
black in the glass that it's like
    looking down into the back of a
    cave, so dark and
black marble, polished
black on black

black, acid
black, almost
black, boot-
black, coal-
black, jet-
black, licorice
black, midnight
black, pure dark
black, squid-ink
black leather-jacket hue, storm
black: black fruit...black minerality
    and black espresso, all
black: black fruit, black smoke and
    black bitter minerals,
    a study of beauty in
blackberry
black-blue-purple, saturated
blacker than the devil's heart
blackness, abyss of
blackness, remarkably consistent
blackness, scorched-earth
black on black
black paint, so dark and foreboding
    it looks like
black-purple, inky

black-purple/-violet
black-red, dark/deep
black, stygian
blond, straw-
blonde, dyed
blonde, sort of a blowsy
blood you'll ever see,
  darkest prettiest
blood, blue-
blood, congealed
blood, pigeon's
blood-red
bloodshot
blue, dark
blue, pinky-
blue, reddish-
blueberry
blue-black, inky
blue-black-purple, saturated
blue-black-violet, inky
blue-purple, deep
blue-purple, jazzy
blue-purple, seriously
blue-red, medium
blue-violet, dark
bluey-purple
bluish-pink
bluish-silver
blush, deep
blush, innocent
blushes like a white wine
  that's been embarrassed
blushing, definitely
bottom, baboon's
bramble, dark
brandy, apricot
brass buttons, unpolished
brass, old polished
brick, antique
brick, coppery
brick, deep
brick, faded
brick, old Tudor
brick, warm
bronze, burnished
bronze, deep
bronze-gold/bronze, golden
bronze, pale green-
brown bear
brown khaki, nut-
brown, dark chestnut-
brown, dark chocolate
brown, dark Stygian
brown, dark walnut
brown, dead/deathly
brown, deep dark
brown, deep golden
brown, deep mahogany

brown, deep marmalade
brown, deep olive-amber
brown, deep russet-
brown, deep tawny
brown, deep Van Dyke
brown, deep walnut
brown, dirty
brown, drab
brown, greenish
brown, Havana
brown, hazelnut
brown, luminous tawny-
brown, nearly coffee
brown, nut
brown, orange
brown, pale tan-
brown, pinkish
brown, reddish
brown, sandy
brown, topaz-
brown, yellowish
brown-hued, golden
brunet/brunette
burgundy
buttercup
butterscotch, pure
buttery
caramel
carbony
carmine lacquer
carmine, alizarin
carmine, deep royal
carmine-ruby, deep
carnelian
carrot
celery
cerise, deep
cerise, red
chalk/chalky
chartreuse
cherry, Bing
cherry, black/inky
cherry, brilliant
cherry, deep somber black
chestnut, golden
chili, *ancho*
chromatic
cinnabar
cinnamon
citrine
citron
claret, aged
claret, classic
coal
cochineal
coffee
cognac, aged pale
coinlike

color seemed to pressurize the
  sides of the glass, so intense
  that the
colored, day-
colored, exuberantly
colored, night-
colorful firework display
colorless, virtually
copper and brick
copper penny, new
copper, bright
copper, deep/deeply burnished
copper, orangey
copper-pink, pale
copper, reddish
copper-gold
copper-orange, pale
coppery-bronze
coppery-butterscotch,
  golden burnished
coppery-red, pretty
coral, deep
corn, soft
cranberry, deep
cranberry-garnet
crimson, bright
crimson, deep inky
crimson, full-depth
crimson, opaque bruised
crimson-purple
cyclamen-hue(d)
dahlia
dark and dangerous
dark and deep as night, as
dark and stormy
dark as blackberry juice, as
dark as chocolate, as
dark as fudge, as
dark as midnight, as
dark as the bruises on a
cowboy's bum, as
dark beauty just this side
  of opaque
dark complexion
dark fluid that spilled out of
  inkwells in older readers'
  schooldays, looks like the
dark it is clearly an octopus wine,
  so inky and
dark it looks sludgy, so
dark it turned our tongues
  black, so
dark that it was like looking
  into space, so
dark to the point of opacity,
  dense and
dark, absurdly
dark, broodingly/dark and

brooding
dark, Darth-Vader
dark, impenetrably
dark, impossibly
dark, incredibly
dark, inky
dark, wickedly
darkened with age
darker than dark
darkest of storm clouds
deathly
deep and shining like a golden
  pagoda
depth, profound
earth, baked
earth, fire-
earth, Siena
ebony, nearly
emerald, bright
fawn
flame-gold
flamingo, flaming
flaxen
fluorescent
flush than blush, more
fuchsia, vivid
full
garnet velvet, deep
garnet, blackish
garnet, Burgundy
garnet, crystalline
garnet, dark brilliant
garnet, deep raisiny
garnet, glorious
garnet, liquid
garnet, seductive deep
garnet, translucent
garnet-black, inky
garnet-brick
garnet-plum-purple, dense
garnet-purple, dark
  impenetrable
gemlike
gentian
geranium
gilded
ginger
glows in the glass
glow, splendidly shimmery
gold bar
gold button
gold leaves
gold, antique
gold, apple
gold, autumn
gold, Aztec
gold, bright velvety
gold, bright/brilliant

gold, brilliant flashing
gold, brilliant jade
gold, brown/brownish
gold, buttercup
gold, coppery
gold, dark/darkish/deep/
  deepish
gold, dense old
gold, fierce
gold, full rich
gold, gray/grayish
gold, green/greenish/greeny
gold, hazy straw
gold, light
gold, lime
gold in the glass, liquid
gold, lustrous
gold, mahogany
gold, marigold
gold, neon
gold, old
gold, orange-tinged old
gold, palest tawny
gold, pink
gold, pure nine-carat
gold, pure Tutankhamen
gold, purist glowing
gold, red/reddish
gold, shimmering
gold, shining
gold, steely
gold, sunlit
gold, sunset
gold, tarnished
gold, transparent lemony
gold, Vaseline
gold, vintage
gold, vivid pale
gold, warm
gold, white/whitish
gold, yellow
gold, young
golden, butter-
golden, fabulously/gloriously
golden, languid
golden, luminous
golden, sunny
golden-green, straw
golden-orange
golden-salmon
golden-straw, copper-tinged
gold-yellow, medium
  Grand Canyon
grape/grapish/grapey
gray wines, opposite of little
gray, ash
gray, bluish
gray, pinkish/rosy

gray-gold
gray-pink
gray-white
gray-yellow
green demon
green like a spirit level from
  Hades, translucent
green, amazing
green, apple
green, celery
green, deeply shimmering
green, extremely
green, fresh
green, glimmering
green, light lime
green, mint
green, olive
green, pale
green, salad-bar
green, silver-
green, watery
green-amber
green-gold twinkle
green-gold, great
green-gold, intense
green-gold, youthful
greenish, bright
greenish-straw
greeny, youthful
green-yellow, brilliant
greeny-white
grenadine
gris
guava juice
hazelnut, russet-tinged
healthy
heliotrope
honey, golden
honey, liquid
hyacinth
indigo dark
indigo ink
inflamed
ink, as black/dark as
ink, as dark as squid
ink, as dark as the blackest
ink, spilled bottle of India
inky abyss
inky blockbuster
inky oblivion
inky, dark to the point of
inky, fearsomely
inky-purple
iridescent
ivory
jade, iridescent
jasmine
jewel-hued/-like/-toned

jonquil
khaki, remarkably
lake
lake-mahogany
lavender
leather, wet
leaves, dead
lemon, bright
lemon, pale
lemon, very pale
lemon juice, deep
lemon, greenish-
lemon-amber
lemon-gold
lemony, rich
lemon-yellow
licorice, black
licorice, deep
lilac/lilac-hue(d)
lime, very pale
limewood
liverish
livid
lotus
lurid
luster/lustrous
lusterless
madder
maderized
magenta, bright
magenta, deep
magenta, reddish
magenta, very jolly
magenta-mahogany
magenta-purple
mahogany, burnished
mahogany, dark/deep
mahogany, gnarled
mahogany, medium reddish
mahogany, orange
mahogany, reddish
mahogany, translucent
mahogany, very deep polished
mahogany, youthful dark
mahogany-amber
mahogany-brown, very deep
maize
maple syrup
marmalade, superb golden
maroon, deep
mauve
midgarnet
midrusset
molasses, blackstrap
moonlit
moon, polar
mulberry, deepish
mulberry-purple

musk
mustard
ocher, dull
ocher, red
ocher-gold
ocher-orange, burnt
ocher-yellow
ochre and rust, somewhere
    between
oeil de lièvre (eye of the hare)
oil, engine
olive-brown, deep aged
olive-brown, impenetrable
olive-green
olive-mahogany
onionskin
opal, fire
opalescent
orange fire
orange, autumn
orange, blood
orange, bright
orange, burnt
orange, deep harvest
orange, deepest mandarin
orange, golden
orange, mature
orange, pale rosehip
orange, pale topaz-
orange, pinkish
orange, reddish
orange, rosé-
orange, rusty
orange: orange blossoms,
    orange peel, light orange
    fruit, a study in
orange-amber, warm
orange-bronze
orange-brown
orange-gold, bright
orange-gold, glowing
orange-pink
orange-red, pale
orange-tinge, pale gold
orangey-brown
orchid
oxblood, deep
oxblood, medium dark
oxblood-red, dark
pale
pansy
parchment, very pale
partridge eye, very pale
peach-rose
pearl, silk
pearlescent, beautifully
pen, you could use this to fill a
    fountain

peony, light/lightish
perse
pewter/pewtery
pink as a piglet, as
pink blush, slight
pink fluoro hue
pink gloop
pink glow
pink, antique
pink, Bermuda
pink, blazing
pink, blush
pink, bright fresh fuchsia
pink, brilliant dark
pink, brilliant violetty
pink, bubblegum
pink, Cairo
pink, candyfloss-
pink, coral
pink, dark side of
pink, dirty
pink, extremely light salmon
pink, fading silky
pink, festive
pink, fullish salmon
pink, girly-whirly
pink, golden copper
pink, gooseberry
pink, hot
pink, luminous
pink, medium deep
pink, midsunset
pink, old
pink, onionskin
pink, orangish/orangey
pink, pale orange-
pink, palest baby
pink, palest blossom
pink, palest flamingo
pink, palest powder puff-
pink, peachy
pink, proud to be
pink quaff, simple
pink, rather insipid metallic
pink, rich yellowy
pink, ruddy
pink, salmon
pink, soft
pink, startling shocking-
pink, still youthful and
pink, strawberry
pink, sunny
pink, red wine that
    doesn't know it's
pink, Tyrian
pink, very
pink, very hot purple-
pink, virginal

pink, vivid fuchsia
pink, whitish
pink-amber
pink-cheeked
pink-gold/pinkish-golden
pinkish, curiously
pinkness, fresh-faced
pink-orange
pink-purple
pinky-red
platinum, pale
plum jelly, beach
plum, black
plum, deep
plum, impenetrable black
plum, middle-to-deep Victoria
plum, opaque burnt
plum, ripe
plum, somber mid
plum, velvet
plum-black, inky
plum-carmine
plum-purple, murky
pomegranate, deep
pop, artificial pear-soda
puce
purple as it gets, as
purple blast
purple bordering on black
purple cast
purple in the glass, glows
purple ink, jolly dark
purple inkiness seems to stain
   the glass
purple like crushed
   blackberries, blackish
purple reflexes
purple spiciness

purple, ballsy deep
purple, beetroot
purple, black/blackish
purple, blue-/bluish
purple, bright
purple, brilliant blackish
purple, carmine
purple, dark inky
purple, dark/deep
purple, Day-Glo
purple, deep black
purple, deep bluish
purple, deep impenetrable
purple, deep inky nearly
   opaque
purple, deep opaque
purple, deep royal
purple, dense impenetrable   inky
purple, dense inky
purple, downright

purple, eggplant
purple, electric
purple, enchanting deep
purple, extraordinary inky
purple, fiery
purple, fluid
purple, impenetrable saturated
purple, imperial
purple, inky black
purple, intense/vivid
purple, iridescent

purple, jazzy
purple, magenta
purple, neon medium-depth
purple, opaque russet
purple, Phoenician
purple, plummy
purple, positively royal
purple, pristine flush of
purple, profound opaque
purple, pure turbo
purple, reddish
purple, royal
purple, saturated inky
purple, sprightly papal
purple, stains your tongue a deep
purple, stark
purple, typical glass-staining
purple, very
purple, vibrant black
purple, violent
purple, youthful black
purple, youthful opaque
purple-black, deep/dense
purple-black, inky
purple-black, opaque
purple-garnet, deep royal
purple-pink
purple-power jovan
purple-red, bright
purple-red, dense impenetrable
purple-red, impenetrable
   Stygian
purple-red, striking
purple-red, unbelievably dark
purple-ruby
purple-to-mauve, deep
purple-violet
purplish blast, gorgeous
purplish, vividly
purplish-blue
purplish-brown
purply-bright
purply-looking stuff, dense
pushing the sides of the glass,
   positively
radiance in a glass
raspberries, freshly crushed red

raspberry, black/blackish
raven
red as blood–you could catch flies
   with it, as thick as axle grease
   and as
red cherries, ripe
red currant
red fire
red lake, bright
red of a Tropea onion, lovely
red reflections, beautiful
red shot with ruby, tile
red terracotta tiles
red than pink, more
red tile
red velvet, limpid
red with purple-blue tinge, dark
red, aged brick-mahogany
red, aged dark brick
red, amaranth
red, angry
red, archbishop/bishop
red, autumn
red, barn
red, beet
red, bleached
red, berry
red, black-
red, black cherry
red, blood
red, blood-orange
red, blush-orange
red, Bordeaux
red, brick
red, brick-dust
red, brilliant bluish
red, brown/brownish
red, carmine-ruby
red, cheerful-looking
red, cherry Jell-O
red, churchy
red, cool transparent
red, cough-drop
red, cranberry bright
red, crimson
red, dark brooding
red, dark cherry
red, dark furniture
red, dark granite
red, dark pinkish

red, dazzling
red, deep amaranth
red, deep amethyst
red, deep dark brick
red, deep opaque
red, deep walnut-russet
red, distinct bluish
red, earthenware

red, English
red, fiery granite
red, fine solid velvety
red, fragile rose-petal
red, full glowing purple-
red, garnet
red, glowing brick-
red, golden
red, granite
red, heraldic
red, Indian
red, inky purplish
red, intense blood
red, lipstick
red, medium
red, nearly saturated blood-
red, neon
red, on the dark side of
   medium
red, orange/orangey/orangish
red, passion
red, peony
red, pinky-
red, purply light
red, rich clear
red, rich rosy-hued tile
red, ripe
red, roof-tile
red, rose
red, royal
red, ruby
red, ruby mahogany
red, rusty
red, scarlet
red, shiny black-
red, solid and bustling
red, tile
red, tomato
red, transparent
red, two shades removed from
red, Venetian
red, very dark brick
red, violet/violetish/violety
red, yellow/yellowish
red-blue
red-brown, autumnal
redder-than-red bubbly
reddish-blackberry,
   shimmering
reddish-brown
red-purple, deepish
red-purple, dense deep
   impenetrable
red-purple, dense opaque
red-purple, turbid
red-violet
rich enough to cling to the glass
rich, impressively

robe is so lasting it has no age,
   legendary
robe, deep rich velvety
robe, magnificent cardinal's
robe, ugly
rosado
roseate
rose madden/madder
rose petals
rose, antique
rose, ash
rose, blush
rose, carmine
rose, cherry
rose, dusty
rose, old
rose, orange
rose, peony
rose, purplish
rose, raspberry
rose, violet
rose, yellow
rose-gold
rosehip, rich
rose-petal, light-to-medium
rose-pink
rosé
rosé, dark/deep
rosy glow, pale
rosy peach skin
rosy-cheeked
rouge/rouged
rubellite
rubescent
rubicund
ruby gem
ruby hue, impenetrably dark
ruby shade en route to black,
   vibrant
ruby slipper
ruby suffused with violet
ruby translucence, shimmering
ruby with blue-purple
ruby, black/blackish
ruby, Brazilian
ruby, brilliant/intense/vivid
ruby, crisp
ruby, dark blackish
ruby, dark impenetrable
ruby, garnet-veined
ruby, handsome concentrated
ruby, inky dark/deep
ruby, luminous
ruby, lustrous
ruby, medium
ruby, opaque
ruby, oxblood
ruby, pale orange-shot

ruby, pink/pinkish
ruby, pure deep
ruby, richest shade of
   shimmering
ruby, shimmering midtoned
ruby, very deep purple-
ruby, wishy-washy
ruby...not garnet...not purple, not
ruby-amber, limpid
ruby-black-purple, dense
ruby-garnet
ruby-mulberry
ruby-purple, inky
ruby-purple, inky blackish
ruby-purple, youthful
ruby-red
ruby-violet
ruddiness of youth, only now
   freeing itself from the
ruddy, warm
ruddy-amber
ruddy-tawny
rufous
russet purple, opaque
russet-copper
rust
rusty, just turning
safflower
saffron
saignée
salmon, golden
salmon, light copper-tinged
salmon, silver-tinged
salmon, smoked
salmon-cherry
salmon-copper
salmon-peach
salmon-pink, ravishing
sand/sandy
sandalwood
scarlet of grenadiers
scarlet, deep dusty
scarlet, meaty
scarlet, rich dark ecclesiastical
sepia
sienna
silver-blue
silver-pink
smoky
soda, artificial pear
spinel
squirrel
straw, baled
straw, bright light green
straw, golden
straw, green
straw, medium
straw, vivid brilliant greenish

straw, warm
strawberry, vibrant
straw-bronze, very deep
straw-colored livery
straw-green, bright
straw-green, pale
straw-green, striking
straw-pink, strong
Styx, impenetrable brooding River
sun, setting
sunlight, soft
sunrise than sunset, closer to
sunset in a glass
sunset, autumn
sunset, lurid
sunset, orange-yellow
sunset, tangerine
sunset, winter
sunshine, watery winter
sun-silvered
superblack
superdark
suspicious

swarthy
tan, pale
tangerine
tawny, dark
tawny, medium orange-red-
tawny, orange-
tawny, pinkish-red
tawny, rosehip
tawny, rose-tinted
tawny, warm autumnal
tawny-amber
tawny-green, deep walnut
tawny-red
tawny-russet, deepish
tea, deep
tea, orange pekoe
terra cotta, dark reddish
terra cotta, saturated
terra cotta-mahogany, medium
thin
tiles, faded
tiles, roof
timbre, perfect
tomato
topaz, burnt
topaz, cognac
topaz, deep
topaz, pure
twilight
ugly
ultradark
ultraviolet glow
umber, deep burnt
velvet, black
velvet, limpid crushed

verde here: green herbs...
   green apples...green papayas,
   the accent's on
vermilion, dark/deep
vermilion-ruby, limpid
violacé/violaceous
violet, Bayeux
violet, bright
violet, cobalt
violet, dark
violet, Day-Glo
violet, intense youthful
violet, opaque
violet, youthful splash
violet-carmine red
violet-pink
violet-red dye in a glass, deep dark
violet-ruby, deep
walnutty
washed out
water, pale enough
   to be mistaken for
water, rusty
waterlike, pale...
watermelon, very pale
wheat, ripe
whisky, moderately diluted
white, chalky
white, greenish
white, lackluster
white, violet-flower
white, water/watery
white, yellow
wine, port
wood, blonde
wood, deep burnished
yellow, brassy
yellow, bright
yellow, bright banana-oil
yellow, bright moon
yellow, brownish
yellow, buttercup
yellow, butterfly
yellow, buttery
yellow, canary
yellow, clean pale
yellow, dark/darkish/deep
yellow, dazzling light
yellow, deep vivid linseed-oil
yellow, distinctive lime
yellow, egg
yellow, fierce
yellow, full/pure buttercup
yellow, full glowing
yellow, glowing golden
yellow, grapefruit
yellow, green/greenish/greeny
yellow, greenish buttercup

yellow, intense golden
yellow, intensely straw
yellow, lanolin
yellow, lemon/lemony
yellow, luminous straw
yellow, May
yellow, mellow
yellow, melon
yellow, Naples
yellow, nickel
yellow, Persian
yellow, pink
yellow, pure golden
yellow, rosé
yellow, developed light
yellow, soft canary
yellow, startlingly bright
yellow, sunny
yellow, topaz
yellow, unhealthy pale
yellow, waxy melon
yellow-brown, pallid
yellow-gold, bright polished
yellow-green, brilliant glowing
yellow-green, glowing
yellow-green, waxy
yellow-white
yellowy-green, brilliant
young/youthful

Champagne is a created wine.
Rémi Krug

Champagne: bottled sunlight.
Lord Thomson of Carrington

Champagne has the taste of an apple peeled with a steel knife.
Aldous Huxley

Champagne ...mysteriously manages to capture an incredible amount of festivity, elegance and sensuality in every glass.
Gérard Liger-Belair

3. Effervescence [Fizz, Sparkle]

Most wines are made to be still (no bubbles) but many aren't. If they sparkle, however, when they shouldn't or don't when they should, maintain a healthy skepticism because something is very wrong. In addition, many people think small bubble size is better, although some experts claim bubble size is more a factor of temperature and tiny imperfections in the glass bottom, and therefore has no real relation to quality. However, the longer the bubbles persist, the better the quality; few experts disagree on that. *À votre santé!*

abandon, wild
adequate
agitated
amazing, so very
auditory elegance, rare
barely any
bead column, persistent tiny
bead rises in a swirling...
   swaying...sensuously
   elegant treat
bead, aggressive
bead, creamy
bead, fine/finest/very fine
bead, good strong
bead, long-lasting
beading, good
beads, lots and lots of gas
beads, perfect
beads, persistent column of tiny
beads, terribly fine/tiny
bubble flowers, scatters the
   petals of a virtual garden of

bubble stair, beautiful
bubble train, good
bubble, seems like one big
bubbles are a thing of the past, its
bubbles are on the big size
bubbles are still fierce
bubbles as bright as the stars
   in the sky
bubbles as though a hippo farted in
   the fermentation tank,
   enormous coarse
bubbles at the bottom of the glass,
   lazy
bubbles at the rim, fine
bubbles at you, spitting its
bubbles big and aggressive
bubbles burst against the palate
   like pellets of caviar, minimal
bubbles cascade lazily to the
   surface, tiniest of
bubbles clock in about halfway
   between mousse and gunshot

bubbles comport themselves
   with finesse and elegance
bubbles constantly move
   the liquid around, tiny
bubbles continued to wind their
   way up the glass two hours after
   the wine was poured
bubbles few but fine
bubbles formed a tight and strong
   pillar in the middle
   of the glass
bubbles gambol gleefully
bubbles in long continuous chains
bubbles in loose chains
bubbles overwhelms the taste
   balance
bubbles rose constantly to the
   surface, tiny
bubbles seem to trill like a
   nightingale
bubbles sparkle on the tongue

bubbles stream around the glass like tiny pearls, microscopic
bubbles that refuse to rush to the top, languid
bubbles were precious and languid
bubbles which never stop streaming upward out of the glass, minimal
bubbles with finesse
bubbles, abundant
bubbles, aggressive/assertive
bubbles, beautiful ribbons of pinpoint
bubbles, beyond perfection
bubbles, big fast
bubbles, blanket of tightly knit
bubbles, bright nose-tickling
bubbles, bright pink foaming
bubbles, countless minuscule
bubbles, crispy
bubbles, dashing
bubbles, delicate pinhead
bubbles, elegant ribbons of tiny
bubbles, endlessly festive trail of
bubbles, enliven the mouth
bubbles, ephemeral
bubbles, evenly spaced
bubbles, explosive foaming
bubbles, faint stream of microscopic
bubbles, fairly numerous
bubbles, few venturesome
bubbles, fierce
bubbles, fierce burst of
bubbles, fine stream of
bubbles, fine tiny prolonged
bubbles, furiously fast
bubbles, galaxy of tiny pinpoint
bubbles, gossamer caress of
bubbles, graceful
bubbles, harsh
bubbles, joyous flow of fine
bubbles, lacy
bubbles, languid
bubbles, large persistent
bubbles, large ungainly
bubbles, lazy
bubbles, lazy cascade of
bubbles, leavened by
bubbles, light
bubbles, lively
bubbles, loose and unrefined
bubbles, medium
bubbles, melodious
bubbles, microscopic
bubbles, minimal perky
bubbles, minuscule rebellious
bubbles, mischievous

bubbles, most harmonious of
bubbles, most miniscule
bubbles, multiple chains of fine compact
bubbles, nice incessant stream of pinhead
bubbles, noble steadfast
bubbles, noble triumphant
bubbles, numerous
bubbles, pearl-like
bubbles, pearly train of
bubbles, perky tiny spunky
bubbles, pinhead/pinpoint/ pinprick
bubbles, playfully twirling
bubbles, pliant mousse of tiny delicate
bubbles, quivering caress of
bubbles, rich
bubbles, rosary of fine irrepressible
bubbles, rush hour of big sloppy
bubbles, shy little
bubbles, slim cordon of
bubbles, slow-beading
bubbles, slow-rising ultrafine
bubbles, sluggish flow of very fine
bubbles, small uplifting
bubbles, soothing array of fine
bubbles, sparse sedate
bubbles, spread of fine
bubbles, steady stream of
bubbles, sumptuous quivering
bubbles, tiniest of
bubbles, tiny delicate
bubbles, tiny pinhead
bubbles, tiny spirited
bubbles, tiny tumultuous
bubbles, top-notch
bubbles, tumbling
bubbles, turbulent surge of
bubbles, twinkling
bubbles, ultrafine
bubbles, uneven
bubbles, unobtrusive
bubbles, velvet-smooth firework displays performed by the
bubbles, velvety
bubbles, very aggressive
bubbles, very numerous
bubbles, very sparse
bubbles, very tiny
bubbles, vivacious beads of miniscule
bubbles? what bubbles?
bubbling apparel, fine creamy
bubbling charm and buoyancy

bubbling, continuous
bubbling, gently
bubbling, spontaneous
bubbly personality
bubbly greeting
bubbly mouthfeel
bubbly scour
bubbly, très/very
burble, only a faint
carbon dioxide is perfectly integrated
carbon dioxide, faint reservoirs of
carbonated
carbonation, natural
carbonation, pinpoint
carbonation, touch of
caressing
chimney, delicate
chimney, explosive
chimney, fine-looking
CO^2 gives it a tingle, touch of
CO^2, stuffed full of
collared, well
collerette, fine
column, soaring upward in a merry
columns, tight military
controlled
cordon de mousse
cordon, fine
cordon, stylish
crackle, nice
crackling
creaming/creamy
creamy and clingy
crémant
crown, bubbly
crown, continuous
crown, snowy
cushions to be found, one of the creamiest most delicious carbonated
cushiony
dances on the tongue, literally
demisparkling
effervescence of fine bubbles, almost perfect
effervescence, ethereal indolent
effervescence, lavish tumultuous
effervescence, miracle of elegant
effervescent fineness
effervescent, lightly
excellent
excessive
explosive
exuberant

eyes, toad
faint
fine, very
finesse, rare/uncommon
fizz on the tongue, tart
fizz that makes your heart beat
  faster, uplifting
fizz, abundant sherbety
fizz, assertive
fizz, bottle-aged
fizz, brilliantly fresh
fizz, coconutty-oaky
fizz, fabulously frothing
fizz, fine
fizz, fullish
fizz, lemony
fizz, lustrous
fizz, new-wave
fizz, nice tangy
fizz, quirkiest
fizz, rock hard
fizz, satin-textured
fizz, sherbety
fizz, sweetish
fizz, tangy
fizziness cossets its silky
  texture, very delicate
fizzing, capricious
fizzy sparkler in the glass
fizzy, only slightly
fizzy, too
flat
flat in the glass, goes
fleeting
fluffy
foam, delightful caressing
foam, murmur of
foam, uplifting wavecrest of
foaming toothpaste
fragile
fresh
frizzante
frizzante lightness
frizzantino
froth, festive
froth, fruity
froth, lively
froth, purple-tinged
frothy like the head on a glass of
  Guinness
frothy sighs
frothy type, sweet
frothy, excessively
gargle, pretty neutral sort of
gas beads, lots and lots of tiny
gas, carbonic
gas, fair bit of

gas, residual
gas, some
gas, zippy tingle of
generous
gentle
globs
good/goodish
great
gushing
heavy
impetuous
indolent
inert
jewel-like
joy, irrepressible
laughter, waves of limpid
  crystalline
legs, sudsy
light/lightish
lightness, *frizzante*
livelier than a sack full of
  ferrets
manic, less
meadow, summer
medium
melts like butter in the mouth
missile, bloody Scud
misted/misty
moderate
modest
moussant
mousse forms beautiful pearl
  necklaces in the glass, delicate
mousse is a model of buoyancy
mousse is coarse and indelicate
mousse is exaggeratedly
  intrusive
mousse is on its last legs
mousse is soft as a peach
mousse is still a bit boisterous
mousse melts in the mouth like the
  finest caviar
mousse melts like ice cream in the
  mouth
mousse of minuscule beads rise
  lazily to the surface, supersoft
mousse of tiny delicate bubbles,
  pliant
mousse of ultrafine bubbles, most
  splendid
mousse rises like a chef's toque
mousse seems indestructible
mousse should assail the tongue
  with little irritations that are the
  source of enjoyment, high-
  quality

mousse should melt in the mouth
  like ice and burst against the
  palate like a firework, high-
  quality
mousse to be found by eye or
  mouth, no
mousse was all but nonexistent
mousse, astoundingly beautiful
mousse, breezy fluffy
mousse, carpet of fine white
mousse, coarse
mousse, creamy
mousse, cushiony/fluffy
mousse, downy/feathery/gossamer
mousse, ebullient
mousse, eiderdown quilt of snow-
  white
mousse, exaggerated foaming
mousse, fantastic foaming
mousse, fantastically creamy
mousse, ferocious
mousse, fine microscopic
mousse, fluffy-frothy
mousse, gently persistent
mousse, highly active
mousse, immaculate
mousse, intense frothy
mousse, intensely whirling
mousse, irreproachably
  beautiful
mousse, irritating foaming
mousse, Meyer-lemon
mousse, pin-cushion
mousse, quiet slow-rising
mousse, slightly rough
mousse, snow-white
mousse, supersoft
mousse, sweetly conspiratorial
mousse, ultrafine
mousse, vigorous
mousse, virile
mousse, weak
mousseux
moustillant
noise, doesn't really make much
none, virtually
nonsparkling
normal
overcarbonated
pearl necklaces in the glass,
  gorgeous
pearls in the glass, most
  beautiful string of
pearls of air, leaping
pearls on a white neck,
  necklace of
pearls, necklace/string of

perfect for an actress's slipper
perlant
perlé
perles, collier de
persistent
pétillance/pétillant
petulant
pincushion
pinpricks, sparkling little
pleasant
pong, decadently biscuity
poor
pretty
prickle on the tongue, fiery
prickle on the tongue, gentle
prickle, barest
pristine
profound
prominent/pronounced
puny
rich
scintillating
seductive, powerfully
semisparkling
sharp/sharpened/sharpish
sheets, filmy
short/short-lived
slight/slightly
snap...crackle and pop
soapy
soft
sparkle, faint/slight
sparkle, light tingling
sparkle, soda-pop
sparkleless/unsparkling
sparkling, fully
sparkling, half-
sparkling, languidly
sparkling, moderately
sparkling, very slightly
spiky, somewhat
spritz, considerable
spritz, diminishing
spritz, lively
spritz, slight
spritz, youthful
spritzig-mineral
spritziness, barely discernible
spritziness, old-fashioned
spritzy fizzing texture
spurgle (sparkling Burgundy)
spumante
spumescent
starburst surface
still
strong
sudsy
superfrothy

swirls, golden
thin
tickle on your tongue, nice
tingle, slight
tingling feel
tingling, intense
tingly, pleasantly
turbulence, indolent
ultrafizzy
uncarbonated
undercarbonated
vapid
vivacious/*vivace*
volcano, sizzling spattering
weak
wonderful
zest, full of/zestful/zesty
zingy

4. Viscosity [Fluidity]

After swirling wine (in a glass with a big bowl, hopefully) we often see rivulets climbing up or sliding down the inside. This is where the famous legs and tears continue to baffle many wine drinkers. What causes them exactly, and where do they come from? The simple answer is (*drumroll, please*): *glycerol*, an alcoholic by-product of fermentation! It's all really a complicated demonstration of surface tension, evaporation, differential specific gravities and such. And it's all taking place in your glass right in front of you. Aren't you glad you asked? So wine legs and tears only indicate alcoholic strength and body weight, not quality. Tsk-tsk.

adequate
adhering/adhesive
amazing
ample
aquatic
aqueous
arches, Gothic
arches, Romanesque
clinging, palate-
clotted
clotted you'd swear you could grease an axle with it, so thickly
cloying
coats the glass, lusciously
coats the wineglass, practically
colloidal
creamy
density, unreleased
dewy
diluted, much
doughy
dribbles slowly down the sides
dribbly
drips down

drippy
droplets
eat this wine, you could
emulsive
excellent
filiform
fine
fleshy
flowing, free-
fluid, quite/very
gams, nice
gelatinous
generous
globules
gloopy/gloppy
glue/glueish/gluelike/gluey
glutinous in its fat concentrated form, almost
glycerin density
glycerin on the glass, leaves thick stains of
glycerin ripeness
glycerin stains
glycerin, abundant

glycerin...alcohol and sweet tannin, boatload of
glycerin, amazing
glycerin, boatload/truckload of
glycerin, chewy
glycerin, copious
glycerin, embarrassment of
glycerin, enticing
glycerin, gobs of
glycerin, heavy
glycerin, huge
glycerin, lines of colorless
glycerin, loads of
glycerin, lofty
glycerin, lusty levels of
glycerin, minty-
glycerin, streaky
glycerin, stuffed with
glycerin, unreal levels of
glycerin, wealth of
glycerin-imbued texture, thick
glycerin-packed/-rich
glyceriny texture, thin
glycerol heart, huge

glycerol is formidable
glycerol, good larding of
glycerol, immense
gob-stopper
good/goodish
gooey texture, wrapped in a
gooey, deliciously
grease, axle
greasy
great
gum/gumlike/gummy
gunky
harvest, late-
heavy
high, very
honey, running
icky
jellied/jellyish/jellylike
languid
legged, long-
leggy, extremely
legs as impressive as the arches of
    Durham Cathedral
legs like a thoroughbred
legs like Gothic/Romanesque
    arches
legs take forever to run down the
    sides of the glass
legs want to climb up rather down
legs wide open
legs, Bulgarian
legs, faint/slender/thin
legs, fast/rapid
legs, fat/thick/wide
legs, globular
legs, hanging
legs, long shapely
legs, massive
legs, medium
legs, noticeable/visible
legs, pronounced/strong
legs, rich
legs, Romanesque
legs, sheeting
legs, slow
legs, slow-to-form
legs/leggy
liquoreux/liquoreuse
luscious
lush
medium
melting
moderate
modest
mucilaginous
mushy
noise when poured into a glass...
    it's completely silent, makes no

normal
notable
oil slick of black fruit and dark
    spice
oil, glugs out of the bottle as thick
    as mineral
oil, heavy
oil, texture of 10W40 motor
oil-thick
oily and piney, deliciously
oily character
oily exoticism, deep
oily individuality
oily quality, deep
oily richness, superb
oily sensuality
oily-floral
oily-limy
oily-rich
oleaginous
oozes down slowly
oozes, really
paste instead of pouring like liquid,
    so thick...it might roll out like
pasty
pearling
perfect
pinquid
pleasant
poor
pretty
profound
prominent/pronounced
puny
rheumy
rich
rivulets, liquidy
rivulets, syrupy
ropy
runny, none too
runny, very
seductive
semisyrupy
sheets
slick, uncomfortably
slick, very
slimy
slipperiness, smooth
slippery, all too
slippery, none too
slippery, rather/very
slithery
sludgy, terribly
sluggish
smooth, glycerin-
smooth, not very
smooth, very
soupy

spare
spoon it right into your mouth,
    you could almost
spread thinly on toast, could be
sticking
sticky, none too
sticky, seriously
streaks
streamers
stringy
suede/suedelike/suedey
supersilky
supple
syrup and red as blood...you could
    catch flies with it, as thick as
syrupy for some, too
syrupy it actually paints the inside
    of the glass, so dense and
syrupy richness, almost
syrupy suppleness
syrupy thick
syrupy, downright
syrupy, lavishly
syrupy, mildly
syrupy, totally
syrupy-slick
syrupy-textured monster
tacky
tears of joy
tears, faint/slight/thin
tears, globular
tears, hanging
tears, heavy/thick/wide
tears, invisible/nonexistent
tears, languorous
tears, medium
tears, obvious/pronounced
tears, quick-to-form
tears, slimy
tears, slow-motion waterfall
    of thick
tears, sudsy
thick as a sauce, as
thick as axle grease and almost
    as difficult to shift, as
thick as honey, as
thick as/thickness of maple
    syrup
thick but lithe
thick it could be spread on toast, so
thick it's almost jamlike, so
thick it's unwilling to slither down
    the glass, so
thick they're almost sappy,
    flavors so
thick without being oily
thick, espresso-

thicker and sweeter than
  pure honey
thickish and oaky, too
thickness, syrupy
thin
threads, thin sinewy
trail-blazing
trails, long-lasting
treacly
tremendous
ultrasmooth
unadhesive
unctuosity, plenty of
unctuous almost jellied
  character
unctuous stunner, opulent
unctuous texture
unctuous, decadently
unctuous, incredibly
unctuous, outrageously
unctuous, perilously close to
unctuously textured
unctuousness, apricot
unviscid
usual, higher than
varietal
velvet/velvety
viscosity clinging to the glass, oily
viscosity defined
viscosity, no false
viscosity, treacly
viscous and mouthfilling
viscous and sweet as
  chocolate syrup, as
viscous compote of flavor
viscous core, slightly
viscous grape syrup
viscous in texture yet
  not extractive, almost
viscous oil, pours like
viscous richness
viscous sweets,
  homogeneous tidal wave of
viscous texture
viscous when swirled in the glass,
  quite
viscous, decadently
viscous, fairly
viscous, massively
viscous, not too
viscous, opulently
viscous, rather/very
viscous, thick and
viscous, thickly
viscously textured
watery, depressingly
watery, very
wax/waxy

weak
weeps/weepy
windows, cathedral/ church
wonderful

Wine improves with age. The older I get, the better I like it.
Anonymous

Appreciating old wine is like making love to a very old lady. It is possible. It can even be enjoyable. But it requires a bit of imagination.
André Tchelistcheff

Wine is a living liquid containing no preservatives. Its life cycle comprises youth, maturity, old age and death. When not treated with reasonable respect it will sicken and die.
Julia Child

5. Age [Development, Evolution or Maturity, Ripeness]

This most straightforward category is of the utmost importance: is the wine new-born, young, middle-aged, at its peak, over the hill, old and frail, or just plain dead? Some wines are meant to be drunk early, like simple whites; some should be enjoyed after some time in the bottle or barrel; some, like complex reds and rich, sweet dessert wines, in the fullness of maturity. Even though most wine is drunk within a few months of purchase (usually the very same day you bought it), try aging some better bottles in a dark, cool, still place for a while to appreciate just how really good some fine wines can become. And you thought we were talking about the age of the wine drinker rather than the wine. Really now!

2005…kissing not required, will turn from frog to prince around
à point, beautifully
accessible, barely
accessible, fully
adolescence to maturity, moves smoothly through
adolescence, abrasive/ aggressive
adolescence, honeyed
adolescent genius
adolescent high jinks
adolescent with an unusually complex personality, handsome
adolescent, fully fledged and fleshed
adolescent, gawky
adult and thoughtful
adulthood, finally reached
advanced than foot races, slightly more

age a remarkably long time, should
age already, teetering on the verge of old
age and youth, lovely balance of
age at a glacial pace, will
age brilliantly, will
age but full of life, showing its
age fabulously, has the stuffing to
age fast, likely to
age for a long time, could
age for a very long time… perhaps forever, will
age for centuries, might
age for decades, built/made to
age gracefully, continues to
age indefinitely, can
age into a complex blend, has the capacity to
age it
age it will sing, with bottle
age marvelously, has the capacity to
age of consent, at the

age on and on, will
age spot, not a wrinkle or
age stagnation, middle-
age starting to catch up, signs of
age supremely well, can
age whatsoever, showing no signs of
age will do much for it, unlikely
age will make it sublime
age will morph the earthy elements
age will soften the oak
age, almost unaffected by
age, amazing ability to
age, aristocratically austere with
age, assumes the properties of
age, astonishing for its
age, balanced with
age, beautifully complex with
age, becomes more and more radiant with
age, beeswax-rich majesty with
age, blossoming with

age, bouquet of
age, breathes
age, comfortable in late middle
age, could tame down with
age, darkens with
age, denies any particular
age, destined to grow wild with
age, fresh despite its
age, gradually reaching old
age, grand old
age, has amazing ability to
age, has the stuffing to
age, in advanced
age, in corruptly delicious
  middle
age, in good condition for its
age, increasingly Burgundian
  with
age, irresistible perfume of
age, leave to
age, like a successful marriage...
  it improved with
age, likely to build up weight and
  complexity with
age, may well blossom with
age, mellow meaty old
age, muscle of youth and the
  complexity of
age, needs to
age, no obvious signs of
age, no sense of
age, obvious rancio
age, patina of
age, polished with
age, positively silky with
age, remarkable vivacity for its
age, sexy *demimondaine* of
  uncertain
age, showing its
age, stooped with
age, structure designed to
age, tarry with
age, whiff of old
age, will balance with
age, will only get better with
age, wisdom of
ageability, early charm...
  complexity and good
ageable, eminently
aged appearance, middle-
aged class, shows a lot of
aged grease monkey
aged it in a beehive, so honeyed
  you'd think they
aged lady with her slip
  showing, charming middle-
aged spread at bay, flabby
  middle-

aged to a beautiful maturity
aged with grace, superbly
  vital...like a lady who has
aged, barrel-/barrique-/cask-
aged, beautifully/ fully/
  gracefully/ nicely/ perfectly/
  properly/well
aged, bottle-
aged, cellar-
aged, improperly/
  insufficiently/poorly
aged, middle-
aged, nonbarrel-
aged, oak-/wood-
aged, steel-
ageless masterpiece
ageless, absolutely
ager, graceful
ager, long
ager, not an
ages at a glacial pace
ages beautifully
ages gracefully
ages in the most ethereal way...
  spanning the centuries with ease
ages triumphantly
ages with assured composure
ages, built for the
ages, keeps for
ages, wine for the
ageworthy, not
ageworthy, quite
aging but it's a gamble, try
aging fast
aging gracefully
aging have put a half nelson on
  this wine, clear signs of
aging have sanded away all the
  rough edges, months of
aging potential fulfilled
aging potential whatsoever, no
aging potential, good
aging potential, great
aging potential, immortal
aging potential, intriguing
aging potential, serious/significant
aging potential, unlikely
aging potential, unreal
aging potential, very European
aging potential, very limited
aging potential, zero
aging sexpot
aging superbly
aging terms, idiosyncratic in
aging unhurriedly, capable of
aging very slowly
aging will be almost impossible,
  graceful

aging would be useless, further
aging, becomes ethereal with
  more
aging, built for rather lengthier
aging, capable of
aging, demands long-haul
  bottle-
aging, don't expect much more
aging, enormous capacity for
  extended
aging, excessive
aging, good backbone for
aging, great potential for
aging, high-quality blending and
aging, impressive
aging, improper
aging, needs long
aging, needs more
aging, no evidence of wood
aging, not for
aging, plenty under the hood for
aging, precocity suggests
aging, proven track record for long
aging, reluctant to budge in terms
  of
aging, strong backbone for
aging, will repay
alive, still quite
alive, very much
already building character
amortized, fully
ancient
animation, in suspended
antiquated, slightly
anywhere so drink up, not going
anywhere, could go
apex, at its consumption
apogee, approaching its
apogee, has attained its
apogee, probably at its
approachable treat
approachable, easily/very
approachable, nowhere near
approaching perfection
appropriate
arcane
archaic
arms and legs all over the place
arms and legs, still all
ASAP, drink
asleep in the glass
asleep, fast
assed, pretty tight-
augurs/portends well
autumn, in its
awake, wide-
awakens in your mouth
awkward phase, in a bit of an

babe/baby, just/still a
baby and easy to misunderstand,
    still a
baby fat in the nose
baby fat, packed with
baby fat, still showing its
baby starts out like any child:
    awkward and clumsy, this
baby, newly released
baby: spitting up acid at you and
    coughing up forbidding stone
    dust coolness, still a
baby, unevolved
backward side, on the
backward, broodingly
backward, extraordinarily
backward, ferociously hard and
backward, quite/rather
barreled, well
barrel-raised
beat, completely
become a classic, will
become more interesting, could
beginning of its long career,
    still at the very
beginning to flex its muscles
beginning to show tremendous
    form
beginning to tire
beginning to unfold, just
begrudging
best and will not improve, at its
best it will ever be, probably the
best, at its melting
better, unlikely to get any
better and better, will get
birth, constrained by its
birth, dazzling since
birth, drinks joyfully from
blockbuster in the making
blocked out
bloom in the bottle, will
bloom, in full/blooming
bloom, not yet in full
blossom and mature with
    patience in the cellar, will
blossom into a civilized
    offering, should
blossom into something
    special, could
blossomed in the glass
blossoming, majestic
blush is off the rosé
bolshie
bosom is sagging, its once firm
bottle development, fine
bottomed out
bound up, still curiously

bouquet, aging/tired
boxed in
boy grabbing what he wants
    without asking, impudent
boyish
break out, struggles to
break up, starting to
break-up, showing signs of
breath, needs to get its second
breathe, needs to
brittle, bordering on the
broaden out, beginning to
broken up, all
brown/browned/browning/
    brownish
budded, tight-/tightly
build wonderfully in the bottle,
    will
building, slow-
building, still
builds up in the glass
butterfly, beautiful
buttoned up, classically
bye-bye
callow
capricious
casked/casky
cellar candidate, solid
cellar well, will
cellar, for tucking away in the
cellar, hardly one for the
cellar, hide this beast in the
cellarability, outstanding
cellarable/cellar-worthy/
    worth cellaring
cellared, begs to be
cellared, poorly
cellared, well
cellaring for improvement,
    needs short-term
cellaring value, little
cellaring, demands prolonged
cellaring, has the requisite
    structure for
cellaring, in desperate need of
cellaring, needs more
cellaring, will become civilized
    with
cellaring, will generously repay
centuries, will keep for
century anticipated, another
century of life, for a
century…put it in a time
    capsule and give someone a
    treat, could be drunk at the
    turn of the next
chameleon
change in the glass, see it

cheeked, apple-
cherubic
child learning to speak, only a
child with an upturned nose,
    pretty
childish gaiety
childlike playfulness
children, buy for your
chrysalis had turned into a
    butterfly, twelve months
    later the
chrysalis, now emerged from the
clasped tight
claustrophobic
cloaked
clock, some time left on the
close to its vest, still playing it
closed and unyielding, quite
closed for business
closed in on itself
closed in, really
closed than not, more
closed tight as a mussel, as
closed, incredibly
coiled, tightly
collapsed in the glass
coltish
comatose
come on, will
come, only hints at what may
coming into its own now, just
coming on nicely
coming round
coming together, still
complete, fabulously
complexioned, fresh-
compressed feeling to its
    personality
concealed
condition, finally in perfect
continue to enrich and
    enchant, will
continues to flesh out
cooked, well
coquettish, charmingly
coquettish, unduly
coy
cracking up
cradle, stealing from the
cradle, truly snatched from the
creak a little, beginning to
creaking and crumbly
creaking at the joints
crisp…clean and vibrant as a
    Tasmanian spring day, as
cruising altitude, approaching
crumbly
curled up

curling like fallen leaves
cusp, at the
date, well past its sell-by
dawn/dawning
days, has seen better
dazzle, will continue to
dead as a doornail, as
dead on the spot
dead to the world
dead yet, certainly isn't
dead zone, lost in a
dead, back/returned from the
dead, brain-
dead, far from
dead, like raising the
dead, virtually
death and decay were evident
death hovering overhead,
    angel of
death, sweetness of
death, touch of
deathbed quite yet, not on its
death-defying
death's door, at
debutante
decade and it'll reward, lose it in
    the cellar for a
decade to really start strutting its
    stuff, needs a
decades to go
decades, almost indestructible
    wine that can be stored for
decades, can be stored for
decades, can last/go on for
decades, freak wine which will
    live for
decades, has the stuff to
    maintain class for
decades, will be around for
decades, will provide pleasure for
decay, no signs of
decay, subliminal
decay, sweetness of impending
decay, touch of
decline, in/declined/declining
decline, long gentle
decomposed/decomposing
decrepit but a survivor, almost
decrepit, definitely
decrepitude, at the very edge of
deepens as it breathes
degenerating
demure
descending
destined for greatness
destined for your children's
    children
destined to be a classic/legend

develop into a beauty, will
develop into a classic, will probably
develop into a swan, could
develop nicely, could
develop, needs/yet to
developed even when young
    and fresh, well
developed, fully/nicely/
    perfectly/well
developed, imperfectly/poorly
developed, not quite
developed, not terribly
developer and now fully fledged,
    slow
developer as if waiting for all the
    component parts to feel
    comfortable with each other,
    leisurely
developer but now fully fledged,
    slow
developer/developing, early
developer/developing, late-
developer/developing, fast-/
    quick-
developing like an opening flower
developing, already
developing, slow-
developing, some subtlety
developing, still-
development ahead, decade/years
    of
development at the moment, in a
    brilliantly beautiful state of
development curve, incredibly
    slow
development, good bottle
development of this wine, difficult
    to see the endpoint for the
development path, has barely
    moved down the
development potential,
    exceptional
development potential, oozes
development, at/on the cusp/
    peak of
development, disconcertingly
    rapid
development, early almost
    startlingly virile
development, going through
    an ugly phase of its
development, has all the
    requisites for
development, has potential for
development, infant in terms of
development, optimal phase of
development, unflattering
    period of

develops at glacial speed
develops without turning
    rancid
dewy
die, so much stuffing it may never
died in the bottle long before the
    mouth-searing tannins, fruit
died, wonderful for a couple of
    seconds before it rapidly
dies in the glass
diminished smells
diminishing prospect, ultimately a
dinosaur, still a
disguised
disintegrated/disintegrating
dissipated
distance, built to go the
distance, may not go/last the
DOA (Dead On Arrival)
doddering/doddery
dogs, gone to the
done, about
doomed
dormancy, about ready to settle
    down for a long period of
dormant
dotage, sweet and delicious in its
dowager, classy old
down, has no place to go but
down, needs to settle
down, on its way
downhill, already on the
    slippery slope
downward slope, definitely on the
drawn, tightly
dried out like a superannuated
    athlete
dried out, completely
dried/drying out/up
drink now
drink, ready to
drinkability, broader window of
drinkability, immediate
drinkable, instantly/readily
drink-me-now character
drink-now, perfect
drowsy
drunk right away, to be
drunk straight off the bottling
    line, to be
dry/dryish/drying out/up
dumb it had be dragged out
    screaming, nose so
dumbness, monolithic
dumb phase, in its
dusty...musty and rusty
dweller, cellar
dynamic

early charm
early consumption, for
early days, in its
early drinker
early drinking, cheerful
early drinking, designed for
early pleasure
early, drinking this wine is like getting up at dawn on a Sunday; it's too
early, insane to drink this wine this
eclipsed
edges, gawky
edges, no green
elderly gentleman in a bowler
elderly lady who has aged with grace
elderly lady, same elegance as a sophisticated
elusive
embalmed
embryo should eventually grow into something big, this
embryo that is difficult to judge
embryo, just an
embryo, very promising
embryonic rancio
emerge, just starting to/just emerging
emerge, may yet
emerge, slow to
enclosed
end of its life, at the
end of its plateau, at the very
end of the line
end, dead
ending, sad
enshrouded
ephemeral
eternal, promises to be
eternity to mature, will take an
evanescent
ever be, as good as it will
ever fully come together?, will it
evolution in store, further
evolution in the glass, glorious
evolution is cut short by premature bottling
evolution, copybook
evolution, garnet-rimmed
evolution, hoping for a beneficial
evolution, in a long positive
evolution, restless
evolution, slow
evolution, speedy
evolutionary state, in an

evolutionary track, on a fast
evolve any more, could not
evolve beautifully, will certainly
evolve bookworm's wine, slow-to-
evolve gorgeously, will
evolve into a classic, could
evolve nicely, will
evolve, needs time to
evolved bouquet, fully
evolved but not over the hill
evolved, almost too
evolved, already
evolved, barely
evolved, fully/richly/very
evolved-style
evolver, slow
evolves in the glass
evolving at an accelerating pace
evolving at glacial pace/speed, unfortunately
evolving into something grandiose, potential for
evolving magnificently
evolving simultaneously, all the component parts
evolving well
evolving, constantly
evolving, slow-
evolving, still
excellent
exhausted
experienced
express itself, still to
expressing itself, not
expressionless
extinguished
extreme
exuberant
fade, beginning to
fade, doing a slow
faded beauty with twinkling eyes
faded but clinging to life
faded charm
faded into nothing
faded...undrinkable
fading but well-mannered old lady
fading fast
fading more than growing
fading, nowhere near
fall apart, about to
fast-track
fatal
fatigue, severe/severely fatigued
fatigue, shows no signs of
fatigue, without fear of
feeble

feet, has found its
fermenting, still
fetal
fetus, still a
finished
first flush of finesse
first flush of life, still in the
flagging a little
flagging, showing no signs of
fleeting
fleetingly rich
flourishing
flower given time, guaranteed to
flower, reaching full
flower, still in full
flyer, not a
folded in on itself, still
forever, for those expecting to live
forever, ripened on the vine
forever, this is
forever, will surely keep/last/live
formative state, still in its
forward enough, not
forward side, on the
forward, really quite
forward: like a kiss on a bad date, little too
fossil character, strong
fresh and clean as a mountain stream, as
fresh and dry, piercingly
fresh and mature at the same time, paradoxically
fresh aromas
fresh as a daisy, as
fresh feel, bright
fresh mouthwatering gulpability
fresh, alpine-
fresh, bitingly/blazingly
fresh, crackling
fresh, downy
fresh, fairly
fresh, insolently
fresh, lemony
fresh, prickly/tinglingly
fresh, squishily juicily
fresh, startlingly
fresh, unbelievably
fresh-faced appeal
freshness and maturity, almost oxymoronic
freshness is almost laughable
freshness that almost crackles
freshness then goes down cool and feverless, fill's one mouth with a gushing
freshness, billowy-breezy
freshness, considerable

freshness, crunchy green
freshness, exuberant
freshness, grapey
freshness, great
freshness, gripping
freshness, leafy
freshness, lilting
freshness, lissome
freshness, nonchalant
freshness, no-nonsense
freshness, outstandingly
    incisive
freshness, pleasantly slaking
freshness, razor-sharp
freshness, sea-breeze
freshness, shameless
freshness, simple
freshness, sleek
freshness, snappy
freshness, swallow
freshness, unbelievable/
    uncanny
frisky
full-blown
funereal
future glory, reserving itself for
future in front of it, long
future predicted, elegant
future rounded maturing
future star
future this wine has, what a
future to play out, has some
future, augers well for the
future, bright/fine/glorious/
    good/great/huge/incredible
future, enormous promise for the
future, exciting promises for the
future, indefinite cellaring
future, its glories lie in the
future, looks to have a
future, no
future, promising a glorious
future, star for the
future, still has a
futuristic
gaining more complexity every
    day
gawkiness, without
gawky and unresolved, little
gawky and young
gawky edges
generation, needs a
generations of life ahead
get-go, drinkable right from the
girlish
gnarled up tight
go, hate to see you
going going gone

go, not long to
going to be a honey
going, hard to tell where it's going
    now
going, unclear where this wine is
gone forever
gone over
gone the way of all flesh, now
gone, best days are now
gone, long
graduated
grapey, still
grave now, has one foot in the
grave, already a foot in the
grave, on its way to the
grave, rising from the
green austerity
green demon
green edge, no sharp
green 'n mean
green notes
green or mean, avoids being
green streak running through it,
    slight
green stuff
green underlay, somewhat
green, fleeting touch of
green, fractionally
green, lean and
green, sappy
green, still
green, thin and
greenish elements
greenness, touch of
grow further, plenty of room to
grow in grace, will certainly
grow into itself, can
growing, not
grown up, try it when it's
grown, full-
grown-up flavors
grown-up, all/fully/very
grown-up, cunning enough to act
    like a
grown-up, not yet
grows with airing in the glass
growth spurt, experienced a
growth, good
growth, lacks
grudging
hale and hearty
hands off
hanging in there pretty well
hanging in there…just
hanging on by its toenails
hard as nails, as
hard-to-get, playing
here and now, in the

hesitant from the beginning
hidden, well
hides many things…like an
    unopened rose blossom, still
hill, undrinkably over the
history in a bottle
hoary
holding in there by the skin of its
    teeth
holding on…just, still
holds up
hole, going into a
hours of purchase, designed and
    doomed to be consumed within
humble
hurry/hurry up
hyper-ripe
immature hardness, touch of
immature, far too
immature, still totally
immediacy, glowing
immediate consumption before
    the wheels fall off, for
immediate drinking, for
immediate, stunningly fresh and
immediate, superbly
immediately forthcoming
immediately, ready to roll
immobile
immortal wonder, potential
immortal, almost
immortal, should prove to be
immortality in a glass, pure
immortality, close to a glass of
impatient
impatient, not for the
impenetrable, virtually
imperishable
imprisoned
improve, can only
improve, unlikely to
improve, will never/not
improved in the glass
improvement by cellaring, no
improvement in front of it, has
improving fitfully
inanimate
inarticulate
inchoate
incipient elegance
incommunicado, still a bit
indefatigable
indefinite life in front of it
indestructible, seems almost
indestructible, virtually
inert
inexperienced
infancy, in its absolute

infancy, still in its
infant, mere
infanticide, vinous
infantile in terms of its
   development, amazingly
infirm
ingenuous
innocent
integrated
intractable
introverted
jaded
joven, purple-power
jumpy
just showing its strength
juvenile, monster
keeper, doesn't seem like a
keeper, long
keeper, not a
keeper, real
keeping for any length, not
   worth
keeping potential, great
keeping qualities, will have
   wonderful
keeping, made for
keeping, not for
kept to fill out, should be
kicking but maturing fast, still
kid, only a
lady with bright twinkling eyes,
   faded old
last as long as you will, will
last hitting its straps, at
last legs, on its
last rose of summer
last, built to
lasting, long-
late-bottled
late-picked character, doesn't
   show any
laying away, good candidate for
laying down, for
learning to crawl
leave alone
lethargic
life ahead of it, has its whole
life ahead, good
life ahead, huge
life expectancy, medium
life in all its complex glory,
   plenty of
life is in front of it, its whole
life left, great deal/plenty of
life of decades, cellar
life predicted, long
life span rivaling that of a
   Galápagos tortoise

life span, expect a decent
life, almost infinite
life, at the cusp of
life, bags of
life, barely clinging on to
life, built for a long
life, holding on for dear
life, in the first flush of
life, just entering the prime of its
life, lively vital golden oldie at the
   apex of its
life, promise of a long
life, seemingly has an
   indefinite
lifeless, completely
lifeline, short
lifespan, promises a decent
lifetime and mine, will easily last
   your
limitless
lipped, tight-
live forever, could/may well
live in the mouth, wants to
live longer than anyone reading
   this book, will potentially
live nobly, should
live on for many years, should
lived masterpiece, long-
lived wines in the world, one of
   the longest-
lived, all too short-
lived, destined to be long-
lived wine, exceedingly long-
lived, formidably long-
lived, insanely long-
lived, not long-
lived, potentially long-
lived, short-
lived, should be exceptionally
   long-
lived, surprisingly long-
lived, unbelievably long-
lively, radiantly
living dangerously, now
locked up in itself, still
locked up tight
long distance runner
long haul, all packed in there
   for the
long haul/run/term, built/
   one for the
long stay in cellars, will have a
long way to go, still a
long-distance runner, lean
longer great, no
longest wine in the world
longevity is untested
longevity, conspicuous

longevity, excellent potential
longevity, extraordinary
longevity, mind-boggling
   potential for complexity and
longevity, no potential
longevity, not a wine of great
longevity, short
long-haul wine
long term, for the
long term, not for the
long-term cellaring wine, all the
   hallmarks of a great
long-term creature, not a
long-term improver
long-term potential
long-term proposition, not a
losing its grip on what holds the
   building blocks together,
   on the way to
lost
lumbering, bit
maderized
making, legend in the
making, real class in the
marches on
masked
matriarchal
mature and adult without being
   intellectual
mature and confident
mature at a leisurely pace,
   will undoubtedly
mature at last, finally
mature grouchiness
mature in your lifetime, will not
mature some more, could
mature than it is, tastes more
mature to old, midway from
mature with an edge
mature, beginning to
mature, fully/perfectly/very
mature, just beginning to
mature, not yet
mature, outstandingly
mature, struggling without avail to
mature, surprisingly
mature, trying to
mature, unusually
matured into something
   gentler, now
matured with an alarming speed
matured, barrel-/barrique-/cask-
matured, steel-
matured, well
matures wonderfully
mature-tasting
maturing early/early maturing
maturing too quickly

maturing, late-
maturing, quick-
maturing, slow-
maturing, still-
maturity with no loss of
 vivacity, perfect
maturity without any fuss,
 easing towards
maturity, apogee of
maturity, at optimal/perfect
 state of
maturity, beautifully
 blossomed into
maturity, blooming
maturity, chocolate-saturated
maturity, conspicuous
maturity, could be very stylish at
maturity, genius of
maturity, glorious peak of
maturity, has all the component
 parts in place   poised to
 embark on its inexorable journey
 towards
maturity, healthy peasant
maturity, just entering the
 plateau of
maturity, kerosene- and
 petrol-like
maturity, leathery raisiny
maturity, mahogany-edged
maturity, nascent
maturity, past
maturity, perfect state of
maturity, promising opulence at
maturity, rich dried-fruit
maturity, richness teased out by
maturity, sealing-wax hints of
maturity, splendored
 perfection of
maturity: now to Doomsday,
 anticipated
meander along, continues to
mellow/mellowed
memento
menopausal state, perhaps in a
metamorphosis, in
metamorphosis, legendary
middle-distance wine
midlife crisis or seven-year itch
midlife crisis, in a/its
midterm, wine for the
miles to go before it's all there, has
minute it's open, improves with
 each
minute the bottle is open, gets
 better every
missing and declared dead
moldering

moment, mercilessly hard at the
months later the chrysalis had
 turned into a butterfly, twelve
months to settle down, needs a
 few
moribund
morph easily, will
mortal, merely
mortality, shows no signs of
 impending
motoring along very nicely
muffled as if in the cold, as
muffled, slightly
mummified
mumpish
musty, dull and
musty…dusty and fusty
muted, completely/quite
naïve
nappies, barely out of its
nascent black fruit
nascent thoroughbred
nascent wine still frothing and
 fizzing and remembering its
 days as fruit, barely
nature, will stand up to the
 destructive processes of
near term, not a wine to gulp
 down over the
near- to mid-term consumption,
 requires
nearing its best
near-term drinking, for
new wine
new, all-
newborn
nothing, says
nouveau
now as it will ever get, as good
now reaching its drinking
 window, only
now, abundant presence right
now, adorable
now, as hard as a rock
now, at its height
now, drink safe…drink
now, drink/drinkable/drink-me-
now, eminently drinkable right
now, full and complete right
now, isn't going to get any
 better than it is
now, sullen and angry
obscure/obscured
obstinate
octogenarian, still holding
 together but looks like an
 odds with itself, still at
off the ground, scarcely

old age, in gentle decline to
 fragile luminous
old and tired
old aristocrats, aromas as
 dignified as
old as dirt, as
old as it will ever get, as
old before its time, getting
old bird, will develop into a tough
old bones, will make fine
old bruiser
old bush/vine
old cachet, centuries-
old chap, lively
old lady with a sharp/warpish/
 tongue, faded
old lady, gentle
old lady, not an
old lady, pink-cheeked bright-eyed
old lady, very attractive
old love, like trying to rekindle an
old man, fruity
old man, sour-natured
old now, too
old old old
old relic, remarkable
old *roué*, charm of an
old *señor*, charming
old sipper
old vines pave a path of austerity
old warhorse fights on
old wine, ropy
old wine, wise
old, already
old, creakingly
old, doesn't feel at all
old, getting/growing
old, grown
old, just plain
old, kind of
old, much too
old, not really
old, ripe without being
oldie but goodie
on and on gaining extra
 dimensions, goes
on the way out but not on life
 support just yet
on, getting
on, just holding
once great
once-fashionable dresses in a
 dowager's wardrobe,
 like expensive
one day, maybe it will integrate
open and naked, little too
open up into a cracker, will

open up nicely with brief
  cellaring, should
open, bit loath to
open, moderately
open, quite/wide-
open, slow to
opened like a flower in
  ultraslow motion
opened, like a rose which has
  completely
opened up into an
  unforgettable crescendo
opened/opening/opens up with air
opening stanza, great
opening up
opening, spirited crisp
openness, complete
opens up before you
opens up with air
optimal
out of steam, running
out, passing
out, slowly on the way
outlast/outlive us all, could/will
outlive everyone reading these
  words, may well
outlive many...including myself,
  will
outlive you, so cellarable it might
overaged/overdeveloped/
  overevolved/ overmature/
  overmatured
over-ripe, comes close to being too
over-ripe, just short/this side of
over-ripe/under-ripe thing, slightly
over-ripeness, suffers from
over-the-hill but drinkable
over-the-hill, little
over-the-hill, not at all
oxidative, too
oxidized, well
pace, still gathering
papery
passé
passed by
past glory, rediscovered
past its best, probably going
past its best/glory/peak/prime
past its peak, well
past, its bubbles are a thing of the
past, message from the
past, window into the
paternal
patience not required
patience required, infinite
patience to expose itself fully,
  needs

patience will be rewarded/should
  reward the patient
patience, demands/needs/requires
patience, will require some
  cellaring
patient, be
patina wearing thin
patriarchal
peak but will hold, at its
peak much longer, unlikely to
  remain at such a
peak of its drinkability, at the
peak of pleasure, past its
peak, a very long way from its
peak, absolutely/certainly/really/
  unequivocally at its
peak, at its sublime
peak, complete wine at its
peak, probably reached its
peak, reaching its
peak, really well beyond its
peaked
peaking now
peekaboo, plays a little
penetrate, difficult/impossible to
pent up
perennial
perfect as it will ever get, as
perfect, just
perfection, on its plateau of full
perky
peroxide wearing off
personality, tightly wound
Peter Pan, may be a
Peter Pan, veritable
petered/petering/peters out
petulant
pinched
pinched tart personality
pinnacle, at its
plateau of maturity, at its
plateau of perfection
plateaued
played out
point, à
point, at its optimal
pooped out, all
posthumous
potential for cellar storage is huge
potential is far from realized
potential is limitless
potential is not overwhelming
potential legend/superstar in the
  making
potential now realized
potential to grow
potential, abundant/glorious/
  immense/sensational/superb

potential, bags of
potential, bursts with
potential, considerable upside
potential, fantastic cellar
potential, loaded with
potential, long-term
potential, past its
potential, plenty of wow
potential, raw but with good
potential, realizing its
potential, shows full classy
potential, storage
potential, unbelievable upside
potentially drinkable
potentially live longer than
  anyone reading this book, will
potentially very generous
precocious child: impatiently
  trying to talk and walk
precocious, beyond
precocious out of the gate
precocious, uncommonly
premature
prematurely old
prepubescent
present unformed, at
present, awkward at
present, hard to assess at
present, heavy-handed at
present, only masochists will
  enjoy it at
preserved, well
pressed, looking just-
prime time
prime, in its
prime, passing/past its
prime, well past its
primordial
progress, still a study/work in
progression, sure-footed
progression, unfurls
  compelling
progression, vigorous
prolonged cellaring, demands
promise, full of/promising
promise, laden with
promise, shows great
promises much drinking pleasure
promises of things to come
promising if not over-rich
promising, distinctly/highly
promising, none too
prospect, lovely wine in
prospects, demonstrates
  excellent
pubescent
pup, just a
puppy fat

puppy fat to lose, lots of
puppy fat, will be even better when it loses its
puppy love
puppy that hasn't grown into its feet yet
puppy, one serious
put away
quaint
quick charmer
quickly, drink
raring to go
raw, bit
raw, now
raw, starkly
raw...horrid, dry...
rawness, brash
reach greatness, will
reached its full splendor, still hasn't
ready for drinking straight away
ready for prime-time drinking, not yet
ready now as it will ever be, as
ready to drink right out of the gate
ready to drink, not yet
ready to drink, will never be
ready to go, surprisingly
ready to roll right now
ready to sit at the big table, isn't yet
ready, nowhere near
ready, rough and
ready, simply not
realignment, needs
rebellious mood, in a
recalcitrant at first
reclusive
reins, trying to burst loose from its
release, drinkable on
relic, golden
reluctant to reveal is inner core
reluctant, not at all
renaissance, continuing its
reserved
reserved, far too
reserved, quite
rest, should be laid to
restrained
retarded, extraordinarily
reticence, some
reticent, maddeningly
reticent, surprisingly
reticent, very
retired/retiring
retirement community
retrospective, artistic
reveal its true face at the moment, does not

revealed/revealing, fully
reveals anything, hardly
right out of the gate, delicious
ripe and easy
ripe and fragile, so
ripe and honeyed, mind-bendingly
ripe and slurpy, lavishly
ripe as all get-out, as
ripe as berries in September, as
ripe exuberance
ripe grape, like biting into a perfectly
ripe to the edge of opulence
ripe to the point of oiliness
ripe to the point of plumminess
ripe verging on sweet
ripe without being old
ripe yet not sear
ripe, almost too
ripe, astonishingly
ripe, dead-
ripe, decadently/lavishly/ outrageously
ripe, deeply/profoundly
ripe, ethereally
ripe, explosively/exuberantly
ripe, freakishly/surreally
ripe, gorgeously
ripe, honey-
ripe, lavishly
ripe, nutty oatmealy
ripe/ripened, overly
ripe-and-ready
ripely slides down the gullet, quite
ripen out, overall beginning to
ripeness and health, oozes
ripeness barrier, struggles to reach the
ripeness in restraint
ripeness of a very hot summer
ripeness that flatters the palate, sweet
ripeness threshold, has only just struggled across the
ripeness verging on flamboyance, intense
ripeness wedded to power and complexity: the holy trinity of great winemaking, lush
ripeness with balance, impressive
ripeness, almost portlike
ripeness, amazing fruitiness and
ripeness, at the height of summer
ripeness, awe-inspiring/dazzling
ripeness, beautiful impression of warmth and
ripeness, beguiling
ripeness, beyond

ripeness, broad brushstrokes of
ripeness, chocolaty
ripeness, exceptional
ripeness, extravagant
ripeness, full physiological
ripeness, gamy
ripeness, generous
ripeness, good phenological
ripeness, hovering between lissome and plump
ripeness, insinuating
ripeness, in-your-face/over-the-top
ripeness, peak of
ripeness, pinpoint
ripeness, precocious
ripeness, purest form of
ripeness, rich
ripeness, shy of overdoing
ripeness, sits on the cusp of
ripeness, smoky
ripeness, sun-baked earthy
ripeness, sunniest most comfortingly perfect sense of pure fruit
ripeness, teasing
ripeness, true
ripeness, wrapped in
riper end of the spectrum, at the
ripey, plush and
rough stuff
runner...not marathoner, middle-distance
sagging a little
seams beginning to show
second breath, needs to get its
secretive
sedimented
sell-by date that whoever stamped it is long dead, so far past its
semideveloped, only
senescence, ripe fruit easing into
senescent
senile
senility, touch of
settle down, needs to
settled in, well
shadow of its former self
shadowy
shell, air coaxed it out of its
sherrified
shock, recovered beautifully from bottle
short term, only for the
short term, never for the
shrouded
shut down
shut down like a pair of grizzly bears in hibernation

shut/shut-in, still quite
shut-in, still solid and
shut-up, completely
shy little fella
shy that one wonders if whether
    this flower bud will ever burst
    open into full bloom, so
shy, awfully/painfully
shy, none too/not/no way
shyness, autistic
shyness, initial
silent as the grave, as
silent, tomb-
sleeper perhaps?
sleeping beauty?
sleeping giant/monster
sleeping phase, in a
sleep: patience, has soaked up the
    oak and gone to
sleepy, rather
slope, on the downward
slope, on the slippery
slow maturation, glacially
slow out of the blocks
slow to evolve/unfold
slow to open out, rather
slow to reveal itself
sly
sneaks up on you, kind of
soften, should
soldiers on
somnolent
song, has sung its swan
song, singing its swan
sooner than later, to be drunk
soonest if not yesterday, drink
speak, unable to/speechless
speedy Gonzales, no
spirit only, with you in
spoken, soft-
spontaneous
spot, dead/flat
sprightly
spring attire, still in
spring in her step, relaxed laid-
    back beautiful lady with style
    and class--but lacking a
springtime in a bottle
springy
sprinter, more of a marathoner
    than a
spry on the tongue
stage, awkward
stage, going through a rather
    embattled
stage, just isn't singing at this
stage, not exactly a charmer
    at this

stale
staleness, not a trace of
start of its life, at the very
start, off to a flying
starting to come to the boil now,
    just
starting to flex its muscles
starting to hit its straps, just
starting to sing
starting to spread its wings, just
starts off life shy and reserved
starts off promisingly
stay, built to
steam, losing
stiff and cautious, still
still crackles with joie de vivre and
    vitality
still in perfect form
still looking superb
still lovely
still on its way
stillborn
stingy and surly, little
stingy, extremely
storable, extremely
storage potential, uncommon
storage, actually craves
stored, improperly/poorly
stored, properly/well
straggling
straight away, drinkable
stride, just hitting its
stripped
striving
struggles/struggling
stubborn, frustratingly
stunning, will be
submerged
sudden
sulkiness, going through a
    period of
sulking/sulky
sullen mood, still in a
sullen, little
summit, at its
sun-ripened wealth
sunrise, new
sunset
sunset years, in its pretty
super-ripeness, raisiny
suppleness, sheer
surly now, bit
teenager when opened, so fresh
    that it was still dancing like a
teething problems/troubles,
    suffering from
teething troubles
tenacity, may surprise you with its

tender
tense and unyielding, bit
terminal
thin and green
thrive, will
tied up, still very
tight and unforgiving at present
tight and unyielding, very
tight as a drum, as
tight, hopelessly
tight-lipped
tight, nicely
tightening up, now
tightfisted nose
tight as nails, as
time be the healer?, will
time bomb
time for paradise to emerge,
    give it a little
time has siphoned off whatever
    joy was in the bottle
time has worked the kinks out,
    will be even better after
time in the bottle, will flower
    with
time in the bottle, will
    hopefully flesh out with
time in your cellar, definitely
    worth
time left, little/some
time promises smooth sailing
time should help it all come
    together nicely
time tame it a bit, let
time to balance out, needs
time to be appreciated, needing
time to become richer and
    fatter, needs more
time to come around/together,
    needs
time to come out of its shell,
    needed
time to evolve, needs
time to find its feet, needs a little
    more
time to flesh itself out, needs lots
    of
time to flower/open, needs
time to gel, will take a little
time to make up its mind, needs
time to overcome the oak, still
    needs
time to realize its potential, needs
time to relax, could use some cellar
time to reveal all its secrets, will
    take a long
time to show its best, needs
time to sort itself out, give it

time to sort itself, needs
time to spare, has
time to talk…to make contact
  with the air, needs a little
time to unfold, takes
time warp, in a
time will become stunning,
  really is amazing and in
time, almost unmarked by the
  passage of
time, begs for
time, builds steam with
time, could become tough over
time, could do with more
time, could still do with a little
  quiet
time, crying out for more crypt
time, defies the destructive
  onslaught of
time, deserves more
time, doesn't dare need
time, frozen in
time, gathers its legs with
time, gentling with
time, give it/needs
time, hasn't had the strength to
  withstand the ravages of
time, not unaffected by the
  passage of
time, resilient over
time, resists the ravages of
time, should flower with
time, should have the potential to
  withstand the test of
time, silkened by
time, slightly corroded by the
  tooth of
time, softened and smoothed by
time, will be stunning if given the
time, will become explosive with
time, will gain much charm with
time, will only get better with
timeless
timely
time's corridors, ready to gallop
  down
tire, starting to
tired and dried out
tired and faded
tired aromas
tired out
tired, dead-/dog-
tiredness, no sign of
tireless, seemingly
tiring, shows no signs of
top of its long curve of life,
  right at the
torpid

track to nowhere, on the
trails off
trajectory, long
transformed/transforming
transition stage, in an ugly
transition, in
turn from frog to prince around
  2005…kissing not required, will
turned/turned in
twists and turns, full of sprightly
ultraripe
unaerated
unapproachable
unbarreled
unbending
unborn, incredibly discreet and
undecayed
undemonstrative
underage(d)
underdeveloped
undermade, not
underperforming period,
  still going through an
under-ripe
undeveloped and miserly
undeveloped as yet, totally
undying
unevolved, extremely/painfully
unevolved, now/still
unevolved, relatively
unevolved, totally
unexpected
unexpressed/unexpressive
unexpressive, quite
unfledged as yet
unfledged, still
unfold beautifully/nicely, should
unfold beautifully over time, will
unfold nicely in the cellar, should
unfold nicely with time in the
  bottle, will
unfold with every swirl of the
  glass, fascinating aromas
unfold, just starting to
unfold, slow to
unfolding, still
unfolds beautifully in the glass
unfolds gracefully
unfolds on the palate without a
  hiccup
unfolds one element at a time,
  slowly
unfolds slowly
unforgiving
unformed and primary
unformed giant
unformed personality
unformed, slightly

unforthcoming, partly
unforthcoming, totally
unleashed, finally
unpack soon, will
unpack, beginning/starting to
unpack, still waiting to
unpredictable
unravel intriguingly, seemed to
unready, basically/quite
unready, completely/totally
unrealized
unresolved
unripe extracts
unripe monster lurking under the
  surface
unripeness, hard tight-lipped
  inarticulacy of
unripeness, lots of
unscathed, remarkably
unsettled
unveil itself, unwilling to
unwilling
unwraps slowly
unyielding no matter what
unyielding, initially
unyielding, little
up, holds
up, washed
uplift, rich tarry
upside, should have a tremendous
uptight
upwards from here, will only go
use-by date, perilously close to its
vacant, somewhat
venerable, quite
veteran
vim and vigor, full of
vinus interruptus
virginal state
vital, still
vivacious
void, total
wait up for it, don't
wait, can be drunk without a long
wait, worth the
waiting to explode like a
  time-bomb with taste, just
waiting to explode, vinous
  firework
waiting to happen, all
waiting to unfurl
waking up, just
waning
washed-out/-up
way to go, still some
weary, world-
weathered
wet behind the ears, still

when you drink it, very
  amenable as to
while to unwind, takes a
while, has to lie down for a
whispery
will become a classic
will ever get, as perfect as it
wind, seems to have regained a
  second
wings spread, has its
wings, has begun to spread its
wings, starting to spread its
withdrawn, rather
withered away
withered fruit
woken up on the right side of the
  bed, has
work in progress, a
worn out, all
worn, seems slightly
wound up, all
wound, loosely
wound, much too tightly
wrinkled/has wrinkles
wrung out, just about
year-old-with-a-temper wine,
  crazy two-
year or two to get its act together,
  needs to be forgotten about for a
year or two under the stairs,
  wouldn't mind a
years and then kill an ox, leave it
  undisturbed for not less than 10
years and then serve it with an ox
  cooked over an open pit, keep it
  for 20
years and years, will soldier on for
years are in front of it, its best
years before it begins to strut its
  stuff, needs a good 4-5
years before it mellows in a
  settled old age, still has
years for the skeleton to get some
  meat on its bones, it took
years go on, seems to get better
  as the
years in front of it, has
years left, a few
years of life ahead
years of tenderizing, almost
  impenetrable without a few
years to blossom, often needs 4 to 5
years to go, only a few
years to loosen up, takes
years to meld, needs several
years to unpack, needs
years, begs to be tucked away for a
  few

years, better in …
years, can/will last one 100 plus
years, cellar potential of up to 50
years, drinkable in…
years, good for 20 plus
years, has the stamina/stuffing
  to last for several
years, in the autumn of its
years, keep no more than …
years, needs
years, will be at its awesome best
  in 4 to 6
years, will become ambrosial
  over the
years, will live for
years, will not begin to strut its
  stuff for 5 or 6
years, will put on flesh and flavors
  for 20
yesterday, drink
yet to meld together
yet to reveal itself
young and awkward
young and elemental, very
young and gangly, bit
young and impatient like a
  sprinter in the starting blocks
young and playful
young and shut in, still very
young at heart, still
young charm, coy
young gold
young lion
young pup
young red, stroppy
young rooster let out of its cage
  too early
young thing, bright
young thing, lemony tart
young to be up so late, a little
young to even crawl…let alone
  walk, too
young to make us totally
  goggle-eyed, as yet rather too
young wine, brilliant
young, dangerously easy to drink
  when
young, extremely harsh when
young, far/much/way too
young, forever
young, gorgeous to drink
young, hollow when
young, marvelously rip-roaring
  when
young, no longer
young, obscenely
young, oh-so-
young, patently too

young, ravishing
young, showing its many virtues
young, slightly abrasive when
young, springily
young, still very
young, styled to drink
young, to be consumed
young, to be drunk very
young, you don't really want to
  drink it this
younger, with air seems to get
young-old taste, curious
youngster that needs a bit more
  schooling, raw
youngster, angular
youngster, athletic
youngster, somewhat aggro
youngster, very promising
young tasting
youth and mature aromas,
  mesmerizing mix of
youth and maturity, happy
  blending of
youth and maturity, just crossed
  the line between
youth and mushrooms in its
  maturity, cherries,
youth and the complexity of age,
  the muscle of
youth and the serenity of age,
  halfway house between the
  freshness of
youth has totally departed, bloom
  of its
youth hides many wonderful
  things, its
youth nor the benefit of benign
  maturity…like me, neither the
  excitement of
youth not gauche, beguiling
youth without showing any of the
  benefits of maturity, lost its
youth, amazing in its
youth, as mute as a
youth, as taut as piano wire in
youth, astonishing/dazzling
youth, beauty in its
youth, beguiling
youth, bit unruly in its
youth, brashness of
youth, budlike in its
youth, dull and dry in its
youth, elixir of
youth, enticing approachability
  in its
youth, exuberant
youth, fabulous in its
youth, first flush of

youth, flattering exuberance of
youth, flirtatious perfumes of
youth, for drinking in its
youth, forbidding in its
youth, fountain of
youth, gobbets of
youth, ideal candidate for
   consumption in its
youth, impatience of
youth, in its extreme
youth, in the bloom/blush of
youth, indiscretion of
youth, intriguingly drinkable
   in its
youth, lanky somewhat raw-
   boned
youth, lean and ungenerous in
youth, mean and standoffish in its
youth, monolithic
youth, movement and rapidity of
   perpetual
youth, only now freeing itself
   from the ruddiness of
youth, pays the price of
youth, polished steel in its
youth, powerhouse in its
youth, red-fruit freshness of distant
youth, self-indulgent
youth, shrieks of raw
youth, still showing some rough
   edges of
youth, surliness of
youth, tartness of
youth, undrinkable in
youth, ungiving in its
youth, virtually undrinkable in
youth, well set-up
youth, zest of
youthful and unformed, still
youthful charms, beguiled by its
youthful color
youthful cut-and-thrust
youthful dancer
youthful exuberance, has
youthful exuberance is masking
   structure
youthful hardness, touch of
youthful hopes, airy sweetness of
youthful lift
youthful liveliness
youthful looking, remarkably
youthful perfection
youthful pungency
youthful purity
youthful quaffing, for
youthful rebellious almost
   pubertal streak
youthful reflexes

youthful shell, in a
youthful spritz
youthful sweet-sour disparity
youthful to the point of
   aggression, still very
youthful vigor and *joie de vivre*,
   full of
youthful vigor and majestic
   maturity in an unsurpassed
   manner, has united
youthful, amazingly/
   astonishingly/extraordinarily/
   incredibly/unbelievably
youthful, enviously
youthful, eternally
youthful, insolently
youthful, still
youthfully bubbling over like a
   calf let out to pasture
youthfully elusive merits
youthfully harsh in the mouth
youthfully tart
youthfully tight
youthfully ungenerous
youthfully unruly, peevish and
zenith, at its honeyed nutty

Men are like wine—some turn to vinegar, but the best improve with age.
Pope John XXIII

It wasn't until (Louis) Pasteur that we knew how wine was made. Prior to that, it was like magic. In low-acid situations, you'd stick your nose in it and it would be disgusting.
Hildegarde Heymann

6. Acid

Acidity is a key element in all wine. Without its bite, wine tastes flabby, flat, even dead. It counteracts the sweetness of excessive sugar, and gives wine its immensely enjoyable refreshing quality. Wines with noticeable acid also seem to make food more companionable and better tasting. However, too much acid makes the mouth feel bitten, lashed. Another thing: many people don't like the name *acid*; it seems that some of us don't want to know we're putting such caustics into our mouths. Eek! In that case, just think of it as *crisp* or *fresh* or *racy* or *tart* and leave it at that. You and your mouth should be much happier. Much.

abrasive
abundant
accentuated
acerbic, highly
acescence/acescent
acetic/acetous
acid backbone is still there like
 stainless steel
acid balance is exemplary,
 sugar-
acid carapace
acid counterbalance, perfect
acid drops
acid level, rather stern
acid overdose, nerve-jangling
 teeth-on-edge
acid personality, low-
acid punch
acid sandwich, tannic-
acid scaffolding
acid trip
acid, clenched fist of high
acid, cocooned in crisp
acid, cuts your palate to shreds
 with untransformed malic
acid, glacial acetic
acid, malic

acid, pale purple banana-
 flavored
acid-adjusted to hell and back
acid-heeled stilettos marches up
 and down on your tongue
acidic and marvelously rich,
 paradoxically
acidic bang, good
acidic cajoling
acidic charms
acidic keel, crisp
acidic mess, thin shrewish
acidic monster
acidic package, nicely
acidic punch, noticeable
acidic sinew, elegant structure
 underpinned by
acidic structure, challenging
acidic structure, good
acidic stuff that will push up your
 dental bill, lean mean
acidic tail wagging the dog
acidic, bitingly/piercingly/
 searingly/sharply
acidic, brashly
acidic, brightly/shimmeringly
acidic, buttock-clenchingly

acidic, crisply
acidic, disappointingly
acidic, ferociously tongue-curlingly
acidic, less brazenly
acidic, mean and
acidic, mouthwateringly
acidic, piercingly
acidic, tooth-loosening/-rattlingly
acidic, viciously tannic and
acidicly challenging
acidity a bit spiky
acidity acts as a sort of embalming
 fluid
acidity almost snaps...crackles
 and pops
acidity and minerality, almost
 muscular in its
acidity burns the stomach, hard
acidity burns through the wine
 like electricity
acidity cuts through as clearly as
 sunshine on a bright winter's day
acidity drives flavors
acidity happily wakes up the taste
 buds, vervy
acidity is as raw and sharp as a
 knife

acidity is just about perfect

acidity like a shadow...it doesn't hit you over the head, earth... good fruit and

acidity needs to fold back into the wine, prickly

acidity of pure lemon juice

acidity on a rampage

acidity play, sophisticated

acidity pokes out slightly

acidity practically crackles

acidity rules

acidity scythes through the heart like a lumberjack's saw in the dark depths of a silent forest

acidity cuts like a razor blade, sharp

acidity that draws you in hook... line and sinker, breathtaking streak of

acidity that runs down your throat, electric shock of silvery

acidity to die for

acidity to invigorate the taste buds, enough

acidity to slay any hint of cloying sweetness

acidity uplift

acidity will crinkle the edges of your tongue

acidity, 1-2 punch of lemon-lime

acidity, acerbic heady

acidity, amazingly racy

acidity, appetite-encouraging

acidity, assertive penetrating

acidity, awesome/breathtaking

acidity, backbone of

acidity, bags of artificiality

acidity, beautiful beam of

acidity, bitingly robust

acidity, blazing

acidity, bootstrapped by a nice

acidity, both uplifted and down-graded by a whiff of volatile

acidity, bouncy almost raucous

acidity, bracing herbaceous grassy nettley

acidity, bracing vein of

acidity, bright burst of

acidity, bright diving

acidity, bright spangly

acidity, briny

acidity, bristling

acidity, buzzing limelike

acidity, chiselled with

acidity, civilized

acidity, clean mountain-stream

acidity, cleansing green-crabapple

acidity, clear flavors on a raft of cleansing

acidity, coherent

acidity, cooling streak of

acidity, crackling fresh

acidity, crackling green apple

acidity, cranberry

acidity, crest of

acidity, crisp backbone/ skeleton of

acidity, crisp smack of

acidity, crisp steely

acidity, crunchy

acidity, dancing

acidity, decent

acidity, delicious abrasion of

acidity, dense weave of extract and

acidity, dripping

acidity, driving edge of electric

acidity, electric/electrifying

acidity, electric-crackling

acidity, electric-sharp

acidity, enamel-dissolving

acidity, energizing

acidity, enhanced

acidity, enlivened by a thin wire of

acidity, evident spine of

acidity, excruciating level of ripe

acidity, explosive

acidity, fabulous

acidity, faint twist of

acidity, filigree

acidity, fine-bodied

acidity, fine jab of

acidity, fine linear

acidity, fine long indelible

acidity, fine thirst-quenching

acidity, flash of

acidity, fleet-footed

acidity, flighty fecundity of

acidity, flinty

acidity, frisky

acidity, good boost/cut/snap/ whack of

acidity, gooseberrylike

acidity, grabs the palate by the lapels with its green apple

acidity, grapefruit

acidity, grassy

acidity, great finishing

acidity, great layer of

acidity, green apple-peel

acidity, greengage

acidity, grippy

acidity, gum-gripping

acidity, harmonious

acidity, healthy

acidity, heaps of ripe

acidity, heavenly...almost scorching

acidity, hefty assertive lip-licking

acidity, high cleansing

acidity, high natural

acidity, high-tension/-voltage

acidity, high-wire display of ripe delicious fruit and sophisticated

acidity, honest

acidity, hot loose-end

acidity, huge searing

acidity, incisive

acidity, indelible mouth-quenching

acidity, initial fierce

acidity, inspired

acidity, jagged

acidity, jaw-stunning

acidity, jazzy

acidity, jet-propelled by

acidity, knife-sharp

acidity, laser-beam/laserlike

acidity, lashings of green perky

acidity, lemon crème

acidity, lemon squirt of

acidity, lemon-curd

acidity, lemony

acidity, less-obvious jarring

acidity, life-bearing malic

acidity, life-blood

acidity, life-preserving

acidity, lightning-bolt

acidity, lip-licking/-smacking

acidity, lively but hidden

acidity, lively mouthwatering

acidity, lofty

acidity, magnificent wall of

acidity, marvelous uplift of

acidity, metallic

acidity, middling

acidity, mordant

acidity, mountain

acidity, mouthfilling

acidity, mouth-numbing

acidity, mouth-searing

acidity, nail-polish-removerlike

acidity, natural diffuse

acidity, near-perfect tension between fruit and

acidity, nerve of good

acidity, nervous energy of its fruity

acidity, nice tang of vibrant

acidity, obtrusive

acidity, orangey

acidity, overblessed with

acidity, penetrating lemony

acidity, penetrating quartz

acidity, perfect balancing

acidity, pineappley

acidity, ping of
acidity, piquant
acidity, pleasantly piercing
  degree of
acidity, pointed
acidity, poised
acidity, prickly
acidity, pulsating/pulsing
acidity, pure natural
acidity, quicksilver seam/vein of
acidity, quivering with fresh
acidity, raft of bright
acidity, rapierlike lemon zest
acidity, raspy
acidity, rather biting orange
acidity, razor/razor-sharp
acidity, refreshing ping of
acidity, reined in by
acidity, rippling
acidity, rip-roaring
acidity, riveting
acidity, rocketing
acidity, saber-edged
acidity, scintillating shiver of
acidity, scour of/scouring
acidity, scything lime
acidity, searingly high
acidity, seems to dance due to
  popping
acidity, shaft of steely
acidity, shimmeringly fresh
acidity, shrill level of
acidity, significant undergirding of
acidity, silken thread of
acidity, sinuous
acidity, slash/slashing of
acidity, small kick from/of
acidity, smoky
acidity, snap of crisp fresh
acidity, snap of lively
acidity, snapped thread of
acidity, soaring
acidity, softish
acidity, sound framing
acidity, spark of tangy
acidity, sparkling snap of
acidity, sparks of
acidity, spike of
acidity, spiky
acidity, spine of citrusy
acidity, spine of strong laserlike
acidity, spirited
acidity, sprightly
acidity, springy
acidity, startling
acidity, steely-limy
acidity, stern
acidity, stiff spine of

acidity, stinging bite of youthful
acidity, strong backbone of
acidity, structure-building
acidity, stupendous
acidity, stylish palate-tweaking
acidity, succulent
acidity, surprisingly electric
acidity, tart but attenuated
acidity, Tasmanian
acidity, taut defining
acidity, thrillingly racy
acidity, tingle of/tingling
acidity, tingly ripe
acidity, tinny
acidity, tomatoey
acidity, tongue-tickling
acidity, tongue-tingling
acidity, tongue-wagging
acidity, tooth-meltingly high apple
acidity, trademark clean perkily
  refreshing
acidity, twang of
acidity, twist of lemony
acidity, unchallenging
acidity, underlying vein of
acidity, unobtrusive embedded
acidity, unpolished
acidity, unremitting tannin and
acidity, unrivalled tension between
  sugar and
acidity, unruly
acidity, vein of racy
acidity, very firm crunchy
acidity, vibrant vein of
acidity, vivacious tang of
acidity, wake-you-up
acidity, well-charged
acidity, well-embedded
acidity, well-structured
acidity, wheel of achingly pretty
acidity, whip of limy
acidity, whip-cracking
acidity, whistle-clean
acidity, wonderful
acidity, zingingly high refreshing
acidity, zingy bowl-o'-limes
acidity: velvet on steel, crisp
acidity?, where's the
acid-perked
acids give it buoyancy
acids know their place
acids penetrate the nerve endings,
  bright
acids, fresh complex
acids, great spritzy
acids, just-right natural
acids, shrill
acidulous vein, marked

acidulous, recklessly
acid-quickened
acid-water, flavored
acidy, hopelessly
acrid, off-puttingly
act, real live-wire
action, buzzes with a beehive's
  worth of palate
acute
adequate
adventurous ride
aggressive, incredibly
alert
alive, utterly
alkaline
amazing
amped up
ample
angry
animated
appealing
appropriate
ardent
arid
assail, can too easily
assertive tinge
attack, scintillating
attenuated
austerity runs like a dart
awkward
balanced/balancing
balsamic
billowing/billowy
bite, attractive green apple
bite, frisky
bite, shrill lemony
bite, too much
bite, toothy
bites you back
blistering
blithe
bloodless
blunt
bold
bore, full-
bounce, more
bouncy
bouncy, less
bracing, refreshingly
brash
brawny
brazen
breezy
bright/brightish
brio
brisk and taut, unnervingly
brisk, unusually
bristling

brusque
brutal/brutish
burning
buster
busy, didn't seem
busy, little too
buzzes with catty pungent green
  herbs
call, wake-up
calm
camouflaged, well
carapace
caustic
charged, well
charmless
chimes back
citric snap
cleanser/cleansing
cold
controlled
copious
correct
crackles and hums in the glass
crackles like a head of lettuce when
  you first break it open
crackling sound, has a
cranberry
crisp
crisp it almost crunches, so
crisp it shocks your system, so
crisp, borders on
crisp, electrifyingly
crisp, icy-
crisp, not too
crisp, refreshingly
crisp, stonily
crisp and vibrant as a Tasmanian
  spring day, as
crisp-looking
crispness, clean lip-smacking
crispness, high
crispness, lively
crispness, piercing
cruel
cut, fine/good
cut, indelible minerally
cut, lively
cutting
cutting-/sharp-edge(d)
daggers, piercing
deacidified/deacidulated
decent
definition, lacks
disagreeable
disappeared
dried/dried out/up
drops
dry/drying/drying out/up

dull
easy/easygoing
edge, assertive
edgy, somewhat
edgy, uncomfortably
edgy, very
edgy-jumpy
electric
electric quality
emaciated
empty
energetic
enlivened
enthusiastic
exaggerated
excellent
excessive
exuberant, wildly
eye-watering
faced, fresh-
faint
fat/fattish/fatty
fearsome
feeble
ferocious
feverish
fierce
fierce, truly
fiery
fine
firm/firmed/firming/firming up
fixed
flabby/flaccid
flaming
flat
flinty
forceful
fore, at the
fresh
fresh, refreshingly
fresh, utterly
freshness, alpine
freshness, crackling
frigid
frisky
frosted/frosty
generous
gentle
glacial
glowering
good/goodish
grapefruity
grating
great
green, terribly
grip, sinewy
hard/hardish
harmonious

harsh
hearty
heavy
hefty
high, eye-tinglingly
high, searingly
high, unapologetically
hopping
horrible
hot
impressive
inadequate
indelible
insufficient
invasive
invigorating
irritating
jagged
jangly
jaunty
jazzy
jolting
judged, well
jumps around on the tongue
keen
kick, nice
kick, real
kicky
knife, cuts like a
lacking
lactic scents
lactic, faintly
laser beam
laser-sharp
lashed/lashing
lean
lemon juice
lemon, sour
lemon-lime
lemony, far too
lemony, refreshingly
level, excruciating
level, prudent
licoricey
life, full of exhilarating
life-sustaining
lift, fairly pronounced
lifted
light/lightish
lilting
limy
lip-licking
liveliness, laser-crisp
liveliness, sweet 'n sour
liveliness, tongue-tingling
lively as a laugh, as
lively cut
lively, outrageously

lively, too
lively, wonderfully
live-wire act, real
loaded
low/lowish
lurking
malic
marked
masked
massive
mature
mean
mellow/mellowed
melting
metallic
moderate
monster/monstrous
mordant
mouthpuckering
mouth-tingling
mouthwatering gulpability, fresh
mouthwatering, obscenely
mouthwatering, succulent and
muscular
needlelike/like needles/needley
nerve underneath, stalky green
nerve, considerable
nerve/nervosity, good
nervosity, measured
nervosity, satisfying
nervous and high-toned
nervous, unsettlingly
nervousness, steely
nervy, rather too
nettley
neutral
nightmare, dental and digestive
nippy
normal
nose-wrinkling
numb/numbing
off-putting
omnipresent
optimal
orangelike
ouch!
overacidic
overadjusted
overblown
overenthusiastic/overexuberant
overloaded
overwhelming/overwhelms
pain with its pleasure, mixes a
  lash of
painful
palate-choking
palate-cleanser/-cleansing
palate-perker

palate-tickling/-tingling
peaky
peels, apple
penetrating
peppery
perfect, near-
perky
pervasive
picante/piquant
piercing
pinched/pinching
piquant, crunchy-
pitched, high-
pleasant
plucky
pointed/pointy
pokes through
ponderous
poor
potent
powerful
pretty
pricked/prickles/prickling/
  prickly/pricks
pristine
prod, good
profound
prominent/pronounced
provocative
puckering/puckery
pugnacious
pulsating/pulsing
punch/punchy
pungency, nose-prickling
pungent
puny
quantities, humongous
quenching, thirst-
quivery
raciest
raciness, driving
racy brilliance/brilliantly racy
racy charm
racy mouthwatering bite
racy, appley-
racy, incredibly
racy, nicely
racy, tooth-crackingly
ragged
rapier, cutting-edge
rapier, good
rasping/raspy
rattling, tooth-
raw
razor blades, like gargling with
razor-sharp
red-stained
refreshed, leaves your mouth

refresher" tattooed on it,
  "palate-cleansing
refreshing as a cool cucumber, as
refreshing from go to whoa
refreshing, sappily
refreshing, tear-jerkingly
refreshingness, high level of
Rembrandt on your teeth, does a
rich
ripe
ripping, enamel-
robust
rocketing
rough
round/rounded
rousing
rugged
savage/savaging
scaffolding
scintillating
scorched/scorching
scouring the teeth, feels as if it's
scraping, tooth-
scratchy
screaming
searing stuff
sensation, nasty prickly
serious
severe
shapeless
sharp as a model pupil's pencil, as
sharp as old Granny Smith's
  tongue, as
sharp nails
sharp, laser-
sharp, rapier-
sharp, razor-
sharp, searingly
sharp, severe and steely
sharp, steel-/steely
sharp, toothachingly
sharp, uncomfortably
sharp, very
sharp, wincingly sour and
sherbet, citruslike tangy
sherbetty
short, dangerously
shrill
sinew, distinct
singed/singeing
sings
sledgehammer
smarts
smooth
snappiest
snappy and refreshing, irresistibly
snappy, unpleasantly
soaring

soft/softened
sore
sour and sharp, wincingly
sour edges
sour, slightly
sour, tongue-twistingly
sourness, raw
sourness, skittery
sourness, unpleasant
spine, clean
spirited
spoiled
sprightliness, crisp
sprightliness, lemon
sprightly
sprightly, none too
springy
squeaky
stable
stark
startling
stealthy
steely
stiff
stiletto, keen
stimulating, palate-
sting, sharp
stingless
stings the teeth
streak, lean
strident, positively
stripping, tooth-enamel
strong
strung, dangerously high-
strung, high-/highly
strung, low-
sturdy
succinic
supercrisp
superfresh
super-racy
super-refreshing
supple
surface, starting to
swingeing
tame
tang/tangy
tang, zippy
tangerine
tart personality, pinched
tart spartan personality
tart twist, pleasingly
tart veneer
tart, borderline
tart, mouth-hurtingly
tart, noticeably
tart, overly
tart, penetratingly

tart, rivetingly
tartaric
tartness, clean
tartness, elastic
tartness, flaccid
tartness, penetrating
tartness, razor-sharp
tartness, signature of fresh
tartness, some
teeth-rattling
teeth-scraping
tender
terrific
terse
thin
thirst-quenching
thrust, little
thrust, real
tickling, palate-
tingling, tongue-
tinny
tolerable
toned, high-
toned, well
tongue-nipping
tonsil-grabbing
torpid, comfortably
trip
tuned, fine-/smartly/well
twangy
twitchy, slightly
ultracrisp
ultrazippy
unbalanced
uncomfortable
unharmonious
unobtrusive
unpleasant
up and raring to go
upfront
uplifting
urinous
vapid
vibrancy, exceptional/special
vibrancy, mouth-popping
vibrancy, robust
vibrancy, shimmering
vibrancy, streak of
vibrancy, wonderful
vibrating and longing for more,
  leaves the palate
vigorous
vinegar, one step up from
vinegar, sharp
violent
viperish/viperous
vital
vivacious, surprisingly

vivacity, crackling
vivacity, thrilling
volatile
wallop, packs a good
wash, crisp tart
water taps in the mouth, turns on
  the
water, makes your mouth
weak
wildfire
wire, live
wired
wobbly
wonderful
zappy
zealous
zest and zing
zest, full of/zestful/zesty
zest, juicy
zest, raw
zing and zang, lots of
zing and zap
zing, nice
zinging all over the place
zingy and sharp as a piano wire
  dipped in lime, as
zingy-nettley
zip, fantastic
zipless
zippy
zippy green tang
zippy, festively
zippy...zingy...zesty

Alcohol is a misunderstood vitamin.
P.G. Wodehouse

Wouldn't it be terrible if I quoted some reliable statistics which prove that more people are driven insane through religious hysteria than by drinking alcohol?
W.C. Fields

The most praised drink in the world is wine. Yet most think it's vile when they take their first sip. And with good reason—alcohol is a poison, and our body's immediate instinct is to reject it. It's only when we experience alcohol's ability to intoxicate that we realize how "delicious" it really is.
Stewart Lee Allen

7. Alcohol

Alcohol, the end product of the fermentation of the natural sugar in grapes, must be in harmony with other vital qualities, such as the acids and tannins. Too much alcohol, your mouth feels hot and your head get loopy pretty quickly; too little, you might as well drink pasteurized Concord grape juice from a sippy cup with the kiddies. If that's your speed, go for it. But if you want to drink real table wine, which can have an alcoholic content up to 16%, you'd best take it slow and easy, in the glass and on the road. Slow and easy means that you drink in moderation, even if you subscribe to the theory that (red) wine is good for you because it contains resveratrol, a known antioxidant and cardiac protector. So drink it because it tastes good; if it's health-enhancing, so much the better.

14% alcohol poking its nose through on the finish
14%, swooning
14.5% alcohol carried without any fuss at all
15%, freakish
16% alcohol; don't light a match near your mouth
16.5% alcohol mounts a deadly attack; best consumed near one's bedroom
17%; drink this wine in the safety of your home, a mere
17.5% is absolutely astonishing abundant

acute
adequate
adventurous
aggressive
aggressively present
alarming
alcohol and sweetness, rambunctious levels of
alcohol bothers you drink something else, if
alcohol gets in the way, high
alcohol gracefully, wears its high
alcohol headachy, not high-
alcohol in them than in a glass of Trappist beer, no more

alcohol monster, high
alcoholic percentage, unobtrusive
alcohol present, considerable
alcohol trap, avoids the high
alcohol well, handles its enormous
alcohol without heat, carries its
alcohol levels, daunting
alcohol, not sledgehammered by excessive
alcohol, plenty of lusty
alcohol, practically sends up a plume of
alcohol, sledgehammered by much too much

alcoholic block, mighty
alcoholic burn
alcoholic glow
alcoholic content, high in
alcoholic excess, soupy
alcoholic kick, slight
alcoholic mask, sometimes in an
alcoholic monster, powerful
alcoholic oaky sledgehammer, big
alcoholic power, massive wall of
alcoholic taste, hits-you-over-the-
   head
alcoholic warmth, good
alcoholic wealth
alcoholic, appropriately
alcoholic, bruisingly
alcoholic, leafy-
alcoholic, less
alcoholic, more
alcoholic, non-
alcoholic, overly/too
alcoholic, pretty
alcoholic, shade
alcoholic, surprisingly
alcohol-rich
alcoholly
alive
amazing
ample
anesthetizing effect on my palate
   (on my head more likely)
angry
animated
appealing
ardent
assertive
assertive, not overly
austere
balanced
bibulous
big but not overpowering
billowing/billowy
binding
bite, all fluff and no
bite, fair
bite, hot
bitey/biting
bland
blazing
blistering
bloodless
blunt
bold
boozy
brash
brawny
brazen
bruiser

brusque
brutal/brutish
bumpy
burn, definitely creates a
burn, hot-tasting
burn, marked
burning/burny
burningly sweet, almost
burns on your tongue
buster
chaptalized
charged/charged up
charts, off the
cockle-warming
combative
controlled
copious
correct
cruel
cutting
dealcoholized
definition, lacks
disagreeable
disappeared
discreet
disguised, well
dried/dried out/up
drops, knockout
drying as dust, as
edgy, offensively
elevated, relatively
envelope, warm
ethanol
excellent
excessive
exuberant
fatiguing
fearsome
ferocious
fierce
fiery spirit
fiery, almost
fiery/has fire
fine
fire, soft
firm/firmed/firming
flaming
forceful
fortified, heavily
fortified, lightly
free
fresh
fruity
fumy, too
fusel
generous
generous, overly
glowering

glowing/glows
good/goodish
great
grunt, plenty of
hard/hardish
harsh
head-spinning
head-swirling
heady, awesomely
heady, wildly
hearty
heat/heated
heat for tongues, deep
heat, booze
heat, fumy
heat, no
heavy
heft, way too much
hefty, far too
high, very
hollow
horrible
hot mouthful
hot sensation, burning
hot solids
hot, not the least bit
hot, unpleasantly
hot/hottie/hottish
hotness, no
hurt going down
ideal for slimmers
impressive
inadequate
incendiary, almost
indelible
inferno, towering
intoxicating
invasive
invigorating
irritating
jumpy
keen
kick, definite/pronounced
kick, has/packs a
kick, quite an ethereal
knife/knife-edge(d)/knifelike
lacking
level, dizzying
level, fire-breathing
level, head-spinning
level, knockout
level, swooningly high-
life, full of
lifted
light/lightish
liqueurish
liquorish/liquorous
lively, refreshingly

low/lowish
lusty
massive
match near here, don't light a
mature
meager
mean
medium
mellow/mellowed
moderate
modest, blushingly
monster/monstrous
mouthpuckering
muscular
needley
nippy
nonalcoholic
nonchalant, amazingly
normal
numb/numbing
octane, high-
off-putting
ouch!
overalcoholic
overblown
overenthusiastic
overloaded
overpowering
painful
penetrating
peppery
perfect
piercing
pinched
pleasant
pointed
pokey, pretty
ponderous
potent
powerful
preserving
pretty
prickly/pricks
profound
prominent/pronounced
provocative

pseudothermic

pugnacious
pulsating
punch, packs a/punchy
pungent
puny
ragged
rampant
rapier/rapier-like
rasping/raspy
raw
relentless

rich
robust
room-spinning
rough
round/rounded
rum and raisins
sauced, very
savage/savaging

scorches the palate

scorching
searing
severe
shapeless
show, starting to
silken/silky
sledgehammer/sledgehammery
slight/slightly
smarts
smoldering
smooth
snappish/snappy
sober flavor
soft
solids, hot
souped up
spiked, well
spiky
spirit fractionally intrusive
spirit somewhat jumpy
spirit, clean
spirit, slightly funky fortifying
spirit, subtle
spirited, entirely too-
spirit afterburn
spirity glow
spirity, spiky-
spirity...beery
spot, sweet
stiff
stinging/stings
straight-up
strength, good
stretched
sturdy
sufficient
swamped what fruit it had
sweet, mildly
thin
throat-burning
thunderous
tingle verging on a burn
tingling, tongue-
tipsy-inducing/-making
tongue-burner
tongue-nipping
tonic
top, just a little over-the-
torrid

treacherous
unbalanced
vibrant
vigorous
vinous
viperish/viperous
volatile
wallop, packs a
warming like a fireplace
warming, quite
warming, throat-
warms the mortal soul
warmth, marked
warmth, rich
water, made my eyes
watered down
weak
whacking
whimpish nor excessive, neither

wildfire

wonderful
zestful/zesty
zesty-toasty
zingy
zippy

8. Animal

People have a love-hate relationship with animals. If they're cute and cuddly, we luv'em; if they're big and smelly, we don't. But a touch of the barnyard can get the blood going in many of us. Red Burgundies and Rhônes, for example, are famous for their (ahem) *earthy* smells. Nonetheless, here are the smells of cats and dogs, beasts of the field and wood, fish in the sea, birds in the air, really icky creepy-crawly things, and very much worse. What a menagerie! What a zoo!

anchovies
animal aromas, superb secondary and tertiary
animal flavors, treasure chest of smoky...earthy...
animal in character, distinctly
animal kick
animal kingdom
animal manure, farm
animalist tones
animal-less
animal-like, rustic
animal-style, aggressive
animal, completely different
animal, foxy wet
animal, meat...sausage...blood and
animally fruit, rich
animal hair, singed
animal hair, wet
animal hide, tanned
animal fur/hair, wet
animal quality, un-nerving
animal. dead
animally, touch

animal-scented, musky and
animal-style, aggressive
ant character, crushed-
ants, mashed
arse, sweaty horse's
bear hug, wraps you in a great
bear of a wine, big generous
bear, brown
bears in hibernation, shut down like a pair of grizzly
bear-style, teddy
beast of a wine, sexy
beast, big beautiful
beast, big brooding
beast, black-hearted
beast, blood of a mythical
beast, classy
beast, cuddly
beast, feral
beast, predator/savage
beast, rare
beast, strange and smoky
beast!, what a
beastly

beef blood
beehives
beeline for your throat, makes a narrow and clean
bee, like nectar to a
bee-sting character
bees from the whole neighborhood, so dark...rich...heady and fruity that it would attract
beeswings
bees with its intense honeysuckle flavors, could attract
beetle
bird, odd
bird, rare
bird, will develop into a tough old
birds, hung game
boar
bovine
bugs, crushed
bull dust, turgid
bull, angry
bull, as potent as a raging
burnt/singed animal hair

butterfly brushing flower petals,
   as gentle as a
butterfly, as delicate as a poised
   iron
butterfly, emerges from its
   chrysalis like a
butterfly, extremely refined iron
butterfly, very beautiful
calf let out to pasture, youthfully
   bubbling over like a
calf, creaminess of a suckling
camel drool
canine
cat pee/piss/spray/urine
cat piss, eau de
cat urine, wild odors of
cat, civet
cat, extraordinary smells of
cat, left us grinning like a Cheshire
cat, mangy old
cat, Persian
cat, wet

cat-pee stinker
cat/catlike/cattish/catty
cat's pee on a gooseberry bush
cat's pee, low-key
cat's pee, polite
cat piss, *eau de*
cattiness, attractive
cattiness, no/without
catty-grassy aromas
chat, eau/pipi du
chicken blood
chicken fat
chicken guts
chicken yard
chicken, boneless...like
chicken/hen droppings/
   manure/shit
cicadas in a summer twilight,
   pulses like
clamshells
clams, oysters...ozone and
cobweb component
cocoon of soft vanilla oak
cocoon, could emerge from its
cocoon, silk
cocoon, tannic
cow droppings/manure/pat/shit
cow piss/urine
cow, Burgundy
cow, sweet odor of
cowhide
cows, grass is for
cows, sheep and goats in the
   summer heat, barnful of
crab shells, boiled
crawdad/crawfish/crayfish

crawfish juice
crawfish, buttery
creature from the black lagoon
crocodile, like licking the sweat
   from the belly of a
crustaceans
cuckoo's nest
deer
dinosaur of a red
dinosaur, still a
dog breath
dog charm, puppy-
dog fur, wet
dog in a phone booth, wet
dog poop, serious
dog droppings/poop/shit
dog talking, truly the
dog that's been kept on a leash all
   day
dog you could care to inhale, purist
   hit of wet
dog, a/real
dog, old wet
dog, real bitzer: a multibreed like
   the proverbial junkyard
dog, sudsy wet
dog, the big
dog, walnuts...vomit and wet
dog, well trained
dog, wet pedigree
dog, more domestic than wild
dog/doggy, damp/wet
dog/doggy/doglike
dog's breath
dogs in it, room with two
dogs, gone to the

donkey
doo-doo/droppings/dung
duckling, ugly

duck fart
duck or no-dinner-style, an all-
duck's breath, Hawaiian volcanic-
   ash-tinged notes of
dung, almost as rare as rocking-
   horse
dung fire
dunghill
dungy note, faint
earthworms, crushed
eel, acidity reminds you of inhaling
   a small electric
elephantine
elephant cage/pen at the zoo
elephant, as light on its feet as an
excrement, combo of flowers and
excrement/excremental
farmyard richness
fart/farty

fecal/feces
feline edge, more
feline reserve
feline spray
feline, fumy
feline-funky
feral beast
feral caprice
feral complexities
feral edge, interesting
feral gaminess
feral grip
feral in the vineyard, gone
feral intensity
feral muskiness
feral stink of a sun-warmed
   manure pile
feral with one foot in the funky
   camp, bit
feral, mysteriously/strangely
feral, shockingly
feral wildness
feral...feline
feral/*sauvage*/savage gaminess
ferality, most inspiring
filth/funk, barnyard
fish nor fowl, neither
fish oil, varietal
fish scales, lovely
fish skin
fish, fresh
fish, fresh sea
fish, freshwater
fish, oily/fishy-oily
fish, rotten/rotting
fish, Swedish
fishiness, strains of
fishy Pinot Noir
fishy smells, horribly
flyblown butcher's shop
fly taint, vinegar-
foal, kicking like a newborn
fowl, neither fish nor
fowl droppings/manure/shit
fox, presence of
foxy red, deep
foxy sensation
foxy wet animal
fur and torrefaction
fur, filthy
fur, Russian
furry aggression
furry friend, odd *meow* from our
fur, wet
fur/furry
game, aged
game, dead
game, furtive small

game, large
game, raw
game, rotten
game, sweetness of well hung
game, wild
game, wild feral aromas of earth...
    cured meat and
game-laden
gaminess, almost primal
gaminess, canopy-derived
gaminess, crunchily gorgeous
gaminess, distinct overlay of
gaminess, feral
gaminess, rich truffley
gaminess, silky
gaminess, sweet
gaminess, whisper of
gaminess, wild raspberry
gamy cloak, wrapped in a
gamy decadent characters,
    unusually frank
gamy flavors, overly pronounced
gamy grouse
gamy ripeness
gamy vitality, great
gamy, aggressively/pungently
gamy, distinctly
gamy, meaty-
gamy...almost funky
game-laden
gamy-oaky
game/gaminess/gamy
gazellelike
genet, yellow
gerbil
gnat's pee, lukewarm oxidized
gnat's piss mark two
goat, billy
goat, randy
goat's ass, roses stuffed up a
goats, herd of
goose, rather fishy wild
goose, vinous equivalent to
goose with bad teeth, sour and
    squalid like bad breath on a good
gorilla in a glass
greyhound, body and elegance of a
grizzly, more grunt than a
grouse
guano
hare, eye of the
hare...not the tortoise, the
    proverbial
hare's belly
hen
hippo farted in the fermentation
    tank, enormous coarse bubbles
    as though a

hippopotamus, has all the finesse
    of a horny
hog
honeybee's breath
horn, burnt
horse...beautiful and untamed,
    a wild
horse droppings/manure/
    poop/shit
horse dung, almost as rare as
    rocking-
horse is diabetic, your
horse it rode in on, sweaty saddle
    and the
horse pee/urine
horse peeing on clean straw,
    thoroughbred
horse sweat
horse, completely evolved
    purebred
horse, hot saddle after a long ride
    on a
horse, lathered
horse, old
horse, wet
horsehair edge, faint
horsehide
horses for courses
horses...through eucalyptus and
    berry fields, riding
horses, will not frighten the
horsey, slightly/vaguely
horsey undertone, sweaty
hummingbird tears, as rare and
    elusive as
jellyfish, moseys around my mouth
    with the ambiguous solidity of a
jellyfish...spineless
kill, road
kitten's tongue, as pleasingly
    prickly as a
kitty pee-pee
kitty-cat leaves in her sand box,
    what
koalas
Labrador breath
Labrador on its back waiting to be
    scratched
Labrador, my father's old
Labrador, wet
ladybugs, Asian
lamb poop
lamb, like March: in a like a
    lion...out like a
leeches
lionhearted
lion heart, full tannins make it a

Lion King, visibly proclaims its
    power and importance like the
lion of the Tuscan world
lion, young
lion...out like a lamb, like March:
    in like a
lizard in it, yellowing Chinese
    liquid with a pickled
llama, funky
lobster, aromas eerily reminiscent
    of a live
louse, wood
mammoth, uniquely
manure pile, feral stink of a
    sun-warmed
manure, cheesy
manure, farmyard
manure, mustard and
manure, ripe with
mastodon
merde, vin de
mice, crushed up with leaves and
midden
monkey riding a horse bareback
monkey, wet
mosquito repellent
mouse droppings, cream cheese
    and
mouse droppings/shit
Mouse, Mighty
mouse nest, like licking out a
mouse pee/piss/urine
mouse, wet
mouse/mice, dead
musk notes point to the mysteries
    of the earth, haunting
musk, highly perfumed
musk stick, pink
musk, seductive
musk, vacillating between
    smoke and
musk, varietal
muskiness, feral
muskiness, signature
muskiness, slight/slightly musky
muskiness, unique
musky and animal-scented
musky barnyardlike
musky nuance, complex
musky richness
mussel shell
mussel, as closed tight as a
mustang
nightingale, sung like a
octopus, angry
ordure/odorous
ostrich poop
oyster shells, crushed

oyster shells, fresh
oyster shells, like drinking wine through
oyster-shell minerality, crushed
oyster-shell tang, seabreezy
oyster-style, simply raw
oysters...ozone and clams
panther ready to spring
partridges, brace of
peacock tail feathers, long-lingering finish like
peacock's tail of aromas and flavors
peacock's tail tastes wrapped in silk
peacock's tail with quite a few feathers missing
peacock's tail. all the colors of the
peacock's tail, broadens/opens like a
peacock's tail, classic
peacock's tail, explosive
peacock's tail flare
pelicans landing on the ocean, flock of
pet, perspiring/sweating
pet, small household
pheasant, well-hung
pig blood

piglet, as pink as a

pigswill
pig, this [desert island] wine is for the day when Friday catches a wild
pigeon-blood ruby
piss, warm
plankton
pony, hardly a one-trick
pony, show
poo-poo/poop/poopy
pork and boot polish
pork fat
porky and heavy
puppy, as friendly and lovable as an excited
puppy's breath
puppy dog, eager
puppy-dog's-blend
puppy-dog's charm
puppy fat
puppy love
puppy, one tough little
quail eggs
rabbit fur
rabbit pee
racehorse in its style and elegance
racehorse muscle
racehorse ready to burst from the starting gate
racehorse, all the class of a fine

racehorse: sleek...powerful and perfectly proportioned, a
racehorse, bit of a
racehorse, real
ram, threw itself at my palate like an impetuous
rat's ass, not worth a
rat's tail
rawhide
reptile house, combined fascination and repugnance: akin to visiting a
retriever after a day on the moors, wet
retriever, damp/wet
rodent, wet
sable, like stroking the pelt of a Russian
salmon, wild King
sardines splashed with salt, ultrafresh
savage yet polished
savage, particularly
savage, quite/very
sea lion, as dense and sleek as a
seashell minerality
seashell tang
seashells, crushed
seashells, newly vacated
seashells, salty
sheep, dead
sheep, soggy
sheepdog, Shetland
sheepdog, wet
sheep's eyes with square pupils, very soft and very round like
shellfish-friendly close
shellfish, sea-saltiness of
shit and mushrooms, dollop of
shit, good old-fashion
shit, touch of tar and
skatole
skunk juices
skunk on the finish
skunk, core of

skunk, highly resinous

skunk/skunked/skunklike/skunky
sluglike
snail, leaves a trail like a
snail's pace, evolves at a
snake piss
spider web that lures you in to explore the depths of its complexity
squirrelly
stag
stallion thunders across the palate, muscle-bound

stallion, large intense
stallion, sexy black
swan, graceful
swan, regal
swan song, has sung its
sweat, pet
swinish
tadpole effect, some
tiger
toad's eyes
tomcat/piss/spray/urine
tomcat, grapey
tortoise, the proverbial hare...not the
trotter, so glossy and well bred... like a prize
trout that morphs into a mermaid, like being slapped up the side of the face with a wet

turtle water

tyrannosaurus
unicorn
urchins, sea
venison
venomous sting
viscera
vixen worth chasing, vinous
warhorse fights on, old
wasp, tasted like honey and stung like a
weasels
weevil of a wine
whale, manly wine with more backbone than a humpback
wild and wooly
wild earthy stuff
wildly exciting
wild (*sauvage*) streak in its structured personality
wild dog, more domestic than
wildfowl edge
wildness, erotic
wildness, feral
wombat, decayed
wool fat/grease
wool, rotted damp
wooly, wild and
wool/wooly, wet
workhorse red
workhorse varietal
workhorse white
worms, post-rain
wormy
yak drool

Wine is the milk of old men.
French proverb

It is well to remember that there are five reasons for drinking: the arrival of a friend, one's present or future thirst, the excellence of the wine, or any other reason.
Latin proverb

9. Beverage

This group of prepared drinks, virtually all similar to the long category of *Food* later on, contains a host of thirst-quenchers that many wine tasters seriously or sarcastically compare to wine. Beer, for example; coffee, naturally; juices of every stripe; milk; soda; of course, tea; and liqueurs galore. And why not, indeed? Who am I to argue with perception or personal taste? Or thirst, for that matter? Oh no, not I, not for a moment.

7 UP, smells horribly of
ale, ginger
ale with a twist, ginger
Amaretto, touch of
Armagnac
Bacardi chaser
Bailey's Cream gone to heaven
beer float, root
beer, Barq's root
beer, Belgian
beer, bock
beer, flat/stale
beer, fruit-flavored
beer, ginger
beer, malty Bavarian
beer, plain ol' root
beer, saltiness of Bavarian
beer, Spaten
beer, stout
beeriness, slight
beery and barleyish
Bellini cocktail
beverage, just another
beverage, tannic tonsil-threatening
Big Red
booze, candified
bourbon, double
bourbon/bourbonlike
brandy spirit, lantana
brandy, fine cherry

brandy, fine old
brandy, plum
brandy, Williamine pear
brew, brilliant toasty creamy
brew, concocted
brew, diabolical
buttermilk
café au lait
café mocha
caffè all'italiana
caffè latte with nutmeg
cappuccino foam, as lush as
cappuccino, amazing
cappuccino, cherry
cappuccino, creamy
cassis, cedar and lavender
   fragrances waft through a
   river of
*chai/chai*like
cherryade
chocolate, fancy boutique
   single-estate hot
chocolate (Cadbury's), hot
cider, bittersweet
cider, fresh apple
cider, hard
cider, mulled
cider, pear
cider, spiced apple
cider, stewed

citron pressé
citronade
cocktail, grenadine
cocktail, mojito
cocktail, sexy
cocktail, vegetable
cocoa, fresh warm
cocoa, hot
coffee bass notes, roasted
coffee cream
coffee liqueur
coffee, American roast
coffee, Arabian/arabica
coffee, bitter
coffee, black
coffee, brown sugar-laced
coffee, burnt/charred
coffee, cold
coffee, cream-filled
coffee, Dunkin' Donuts
coffee, European roast
coffee, French roast
coffee, fresh-brewed
coffee, freshly ground Arabica
coffee, fresh-roasted
coffee, Green Mountain
coffee, ground/milled
coffee, hot
coffee, Italian roast
coffee, Kona

coffee, light
coffee, mocha-
coffee, roast/roasted
coffee, robusta
coffee, smoky dark
coffee, soft vanilla-
coffee, spiced
coffee, strong
coffee, sweet/sweetened
coffee, terrific roasting
coffee, thick almost salty
coffee, Turkish
coffee, vanilla roast
coffee, Vienna/Viennese
coffee, warm roasted
coffee...continues with coffee and ends with coffee, starts with
coffee...mixed-berry jam and sizzling bacon, Sunday-breakfast aromas of strong
coffee...syrup...bergamot oil... brioche...walnuts...lime and passion fruit
coffee/-edged/-esque/-infused/ -laced/-scented/-spiked
coffee-cocoa, dark
coffee-mocha, strong
Cognac, aged/old
Cognac, fine/grand
Cognac, watered-down
Cointreau
Coke, flat
Coke/cola, cherry
cola, blackberry
cola, caramel
cola, raspberry
cola, very dry cherry
cooler, fruit
cooler, peach wine
cordial pleasure, pure cherry-
cordial, black currant
cordial, dry lime
cordial, lemon
cordial, raspberry
cordial, Rose's lime juice
cream, Irish
cream, like drinking
Crème de Cassis and Kahlúa
Crème de Cassis, real European
Crème de Framboise
Crème de Menthe
Crystal Light powder, enormous blast of
Cynar
daiquiri
delicious
Dr Pepper, vanilla
Drambuie

drink mix, powdered
drink, child's fruit
drink, lemon-lime sports
drink, perfect
drink, strawberry soft
drink/drinky, soft
drink...no more, decent
drinks, loveliest of
Earl Grey-ish
eau-de-vie, raspberry
eggnog
espresso breath
espresso medley, dark chocolate
espresso, chocolate
espresso, explosive
espresso, freshly ground
espresso, jet-black
espresso, quadruple shot of
espresso, roasted
espresso, seductive dark-roast
espresso, smoky
espresso, Starbucks-esque chocolate
espresso-thick
Fanta
foaming
Fresca
gentian
gin and tonic...easy on the lime, drinks like a
gin, cheap
Glühwein
Grand Marnier-like, orange
grape sweat, intoxicating
grapefruit wine
grapes, water of green
grappa
grappa, piquant pear
grenadine with a cool sort of leathery rusticity
grog
half-and-half
hater-ade
Hawaiian Punch, sugary
Hawaiian Punch, vinous equivalent of
hock, mild
infusion, herbal
Irish cream
Jack Daniels
Jägermeister
Joe, Burger King
juice an infant spits up, grape
juice blended with V8, grape
juice box, cranberry
juice concentrate, fruit
juice in a box, grape
juice junk, sweet
juice off a supermarket shelf, grape

juice on your tongue, drop of lime
juice seasoned with sweet spice, fresh-pressed apple
juice smothered with oak, tinned pear
juice tanginess, lemon
juice with a kick, white grape
juice with an alcoholic kick, blackberry
juice, apple-crisp tingle
juice, as dark as blackberry
juice, bad/spoiled orange
juice, black currant
juice, black plum
juice, blood orange
juice, canned pineapple
juice, chalky lemon
juice, cherry
juice, Concord grape
juice, cranberry
juice, cranberry-peach
juice, disgusting fruit
juice, extraordinary scented pear
juice, fresh lemon
juice, freshly squeezed grapefruit
juice, fresh-pressed/just-squeezed grape
juice, fruit
juice, gently sweet lime
juice, Germanic lime
juice, glass of papaya
juice, grapefruit
juice, guava
juice, happy
juice, insipid
juice, juicy squirts of lemon
juice, light cherry
juice, lime
juice, mildy grape
juice, nearly still-fermenting grape
juice, nectarine
juice, neon lime
juice, oaky tropical fruit
juice, Ocean Spray cranberry-apple
juice, Ocean Spray lemon-lime-apple
juice, old raspberry
juice, orange
juice, pear
juice, pickle
juice, prune/pruney
juice, pulpy orange
juice, ripe blackberry
juice, Rose's lime
juice, simple and undistinguished
juice, slightly sweetened grapefruit
juice, smoky minerals awash in sweet peach

juice, sugar cube in a glass of V8
juice, sweet lemon
juice, sweet pear
juice, tinned pear
juice, unfermented black grape
juice, V8
juice, vintage cranberry
juice, wimpy
juice-flavored, cherry
juice-infused, lime-
juice-scented, strawberry
julep sprinkled with nutmeg and
   clove, raspberry
julep, mint
Kahlúa
Kir Royale
kirsch, boatload of
kirsch, halfway to
kirsch, jammy
kirsch, sweet
kirsch, thick
kirsch-flavored
Kirschwasser

Kool-Aid, adult
Kool-Aid, cherry
Kool-Aid, grape
Kool-Aid, heated
Kool-Aid, notorious for
   (temporarily) staining one's
   teeth the color of cherry
Kool-Aid, peach
Kool-Aid, raspberry
lager
latte, coffee
latte, double raspberry
lemonade with the lemons
lemonade, most intense delicious
lemonade, sidewalk
lemonade, Snapple
lemonade, sweet
lime twists
limeade, fresh
liqueur infused with brandy,
   chocolate
liqueur, almond
liqueur, almost a
liqueur, apricot
liqueur, black cherry
liqueur, black currant
liqueur, black raspberry
liqueur, blackberry
liqueur, blueberry
liqueur, cassis
liqueur, cherry/kirsch
liqueur, chocolate
liqueur, coffee
liqueur, cranberry

liqueur, creosote-infused
   blackberry
liqueur, crushed cassis
liqueur, expedition
liqueur, fruit
liqueur, orange
liqueur, pear
liqueur, plum
liqueur, prune
liqueur, red berry fruit
liqueur, red currant
liqueur, rum
liqueur, spicy cherry
liqueur, super-ripe core of herbal
liqueur, Syrah
liqueur, toffeed
liqueur, very red fruit
liqueur, walnut
liqueurs, assorted herbal
liquid confection
liquid sensation, big thick
liquid, torrid
liquidity, sensational
liquor/liquorish/liquorous
marc, old
margarita, as tasty and tangy as a
mango
martini, Absolut Peppar
martinis
mash, sour
mead/meady
milk, chocolate
milk, condensed
milk, evaporated
milk, fetid/sour/stale
milk, hot
milk, malted
milk, soft

milk, stale powdered
milk, top of the
milk, vanillary malted
milk, warm
milk, wine: old men's
milkshake, cherry
milkshake, coconut-cream
milkshake, grapefruit and lemon
Miller High Life
Mott's on steroids
nectar abounding with natural
   sweetness, fabulous
nectar for hedonists, velvety white
nectar is another man's Tidy Bowl,
   one man's
nectar of old vines
nectar of the highest class, colossal
   concentrated
nectar on steroids, honeysuckle
nectar with sugar

nectar, apricot
nectar, blackberry
nectar, concentrated
nectar, exciting dark
nectar, extraordinary/magnificent/
   marvelous
nectar, fruit
nectar, jammy syrupy
nectar, lusciously sweet
nectar, marzipan-scented
nectar, orange/orange-scented
nectar, peach
nectar, pear
nectar, pineapple
nectar, sheer
nectar, smoky frothy
nectar, superspicy
nectar, sweet
nectar, syrupy
nectar, unforgettably incredible
nectar, untold layers of dense
   yellow
Nehi, grape
Nesquick, Nestlé
nostrum for blues and fatigue in
   Paris
Orangeade
Ovaltine and Horlicks
perfect
Pez, lemon
Pilsner, as refreshing as a cold
piña colada, most luxurious
piña colada, peppery
piña colada, refreshing
Poire Williams

pop, adult soda
pop, crackling
pop, fruit
pop, fruit-flavored soda
pop, sweet flat soda
port concentration
port without sugar
port, akin to a dry vintage
port, extract of a vintage
port, good officers'-mess
port, low-end
port, outstanding alternative to
port, ruby
port, this is a don't-miss if you love
port, to be savored after the meal
   just as the British sip
port, young
portlike powerhouse
portlike, indefinable dusty-
porty territory
porty thing
prunelle
punch bowl of fruit

punch fruit bomb, Hi-C
punch of fresh juices, whole-fruit
punch, citrus
Punch, Delaware
punch, flaming fruit
punch, fruit
punch, light tropical
punch, one-two-three
punch, sticky Kool-Aid
punch, tropical fruit
Punt e Mes
Ribena and chocolate, mix of
Ribena and soda pop
Rolling Rock
rosé his mother forgot in the
    garage, boxed
rum and raisin
rum pot
rum, butter/buttered
rum, dark
rum, hot/warm
rum, hot buttered
rum, intensity of dark Jamaican
rum, Jamaican
rum, vanilla-
rum-and raisin-spectrum
sangria/sangrialike
sarsaparilla
Schlitz, flat
schnapps, cherry
schnapps, peach
Scotch, Islay
Scotch, single-malt
shake, chocolate malt
shake, vanilla
sherried character
sherry, cooking
sherry, old
sherry, sweet
smoothie with a shot of *espresso*,
    blueberry-and-milk chocolate
smoothie, strawberry
smoothie, vanilla
Snapple for adults
soda with a twist, lemon-lime
soda with oaky accents, pure cream
soda, black cherry
soda, blue raspberry Jolt soda
soda, cheap
soda, cherry-cream
soda, cream/*crème*
soda, creamy vanilla
soda, dried-cherry
soda, ghastly strawberry
soda, ice cream
soda, lemon-lime cream
soda, lightly alcoholic cream
soda, lime

soda, pear
soda, raspberry
soda, real cream
soda, strawberry
soda, watermelon
Sprite, one step up from
Sprite...7UP...even Squirt
spritzer, tangerine
Squirt, lemon
Starbucks flavors
Starbucks mocha *latte*
sugar water
supercassis
sweat, grape
syrupy tea
tea (Lapsang), smoky
tea and chocolate
tea and coffee, cold
tea and coffee, stewed
tea and mocha, classic
tea and mothballs
tea and toast
tea bags, stewed
tea-esque
tea leaves left in the bottom
    of a pot, wet
tea leaves, steeped
tea with cream and sugar, cool
    Earl Grey
tea with fruit, iced
tea with mint, lemon iced
tea, aromatic
tea, Asian
tea, beef
tea, Berry Zinger
tea, black
tea, black English Breakfast
tea, Bovril beef
tea, brewed black
tea, chamomile
tea, cheese and
tea, China/Chinese
tea, cold chamomile
tea, cold green
tea, cold oversteeped
tea, cream/creamed
tea, Darjeeling
tea, Earl Grey
tea, English breakfast
tea, exotic
tea, fruit-infused black
tea, green
tea, gunpowder
tea, herbal
tea, hibiscus
tea, iced
tea, iced herbal
tea, iced orange Pekoe

tea, Lapsang Souchong
tea, lemongrass
tea, lime-blossom
tea, mint
tea, Moroccan mint
tea, old
tea, Oolong
tea, orange Pekoe
tea, orange spice
tea, oversteeped/overstrong
tea, peach
tea, pinch of smoky
tea, raw
tea, Red Zinger
tea, rich
tea, rose Pouchong
tea, sassafras
tea, scented China
tea, silver needle
tea, smoky black
tea, spiced
tea, stewed
tea, strong black
tea, sweet black Chinese
tea, sweet/sweetened herbal
tea, sweetened Earl Grey
tea, syrupy
teabag edge
teabags, sensation of sucking on 14
tealike, strangely
tequila
Tia Maria
toddy, egg
tonsil-threatening, tannic
Triple Sec
vermouth/vermouthlike
vinous potpourri
vodka
wassail
water, almost like mineral
water, black currant mineral
water, bland lemon-
water, heavy
water, lemony bubble
water, pure sugar
water, quinine
water, raspberry mineral
water, scarlet
water, short lightly refreshing taste
    like mineral
water, tastes like
water, well
whiskey sour mix
whisky, old Highland malt
whiskey, Scotch
wine, hot mulled
wine, slaking lime
Zima?, is this

I like Champagne because it always feels as though my foot is asleep.
Art Buchwald

For those of exquisite sensuality, there is nothing headier than the musky smell of a loved one moist with sweat.
Diane Ackerman

What is man, when you come to think on him, but a minutely set, ingenious machine for turning with infinite artfulness the red wine of Shiraz into urine?
Isak Dinensen

10. Body [Anatomy, Mouthfeel, Texture, Shape, Size or Weight]

A very big, important and complicated category that contains all the descriptors that wine tasters use to characterize the anatomical characteristics of wine: mass, bulk, dimension, scale, feel. The word *body* in this context is not narrowly limited to what most tasters think of as the weight of wine in the mouth; it's much broader here and hopefully more useful. Such as the many textural analogies using fabrics and the apparel made from them. And yes, you'll also find lots of those delicious erotic, sensual and sexy descriptors here, too. Chewy stuff, this.

acetate, slippery/smooth as
adequate, barely/just
agile
airy
amazing
amorous
amorphous
ample, more than
amplitude, gorgeous/outstanding
amplitude, serious
androgynous, sense of the
angel as opposed to an Amazon, an
angle-free
angles on which to hang lush fruit, offered up a few
angles, sharp
angora, as plush as
angular personality
anorexic appearance, slightly
armpit aspects, some
armpits of a healthy clean-living youth after exercise
armpits, clean: no sweaty
armpits, maiden's
armpits, male

armpits, sweaty
armpits, wet leather and
arms and legs, all
aroused/arousing, fully
asymmetrical
athlete, muscular/athletic
attenuated
awkward
back pain, has a
backed, broad-
ballast, plenty of
balls, big
balls, has
bantamweight
beautiful, satisfyingly
beefy
behemoth, charmless
behemoth, complex concentrated full-bodied
behemoth, palate-coating
behemoth, vinous/winey
bellied, big-
big and strapping
big and a touch funky, if you like
big and black

big and muscular like a purebred horse full of energy and authority
big beautiful beast
big boy/fella
big bruiser
big but not heavy-handed
big it's just about chewy, so
big mouthfiller
big strapping wine
big wine but not overpowering
big, dazzlingly
big, exceptionally
big, monstrously/whoppingly
big, numbingly
big, overly
big, proud to be
big, wall-to-wall
big...bumptious but not overdone
bigger is better
bigness, overbearing
bigness, shocking in its
big'un
bikini-size
bite into it, one can almost
bloated, slightly

blockbuster
blood like a national anthem, stiffens the
blood run hot, makes the
blood, fresh
blooded, full-
blooded, hot-
bloodless
blood-scented
blown, full-
bodice-ripper, guaranteed
bodied behemoth, complex concentrated full-
bodied explosiveness, full-
bodied monster, full-
bodied weave, full-
bodied, exceptionally full-
bodied, fully framed and
bodied, light-
bodied, limp-
bodied, meatily full-
bodied, medium-
bodied, miraculously full-
bodied, modern-
bodied, monstrously full-
bodied, overflowing full-
bodied, overly full-
bodied, ultrafull-
bodied, wide-
bodied...even though your gums don't bleed after you've chiseled out a swallow, full-
body and character, bags of
body and elegance of a greyhound
body is insulated in soft tender curves, powerful
body of a Greek god
body with ample underlying muscle, smooth soft
body you can sink your teeth into, nice
body, like rekindling an old love in a new
body, nice well-proportioned
body, plenty of fruit hung onto a firm
body, polished stylish
body, sculptured elegance of an athlete's
body, salty almost sweaty allure of a man's
body-slammer/slamming
body, thick robust legs on a hefty
body!, what a
body, youthful pumped-up muscular
bodybuilder...muscular but lean and fit, perfectly formed

bodyless
bone, more meat on the
boned, fine-
bones and little flesh, lot of
bones but not much flesh, plenty of
bones, all/nothing but skin and
bones, magnificent
bones, rounded flesh over firm
bosom, has a/bosomy
bottomed, fat-
bound, closely
bowels, irritates the
boy, big
boy, old
boyish
brain, flavor burst like stars across my palate and into my
brawn, real
brawny beast
breadth, huge/magnificent
breadth, lacks
brimming over
brocaded, richly
broad, somewhat
broad-beamed
buffed to a high sheen
build, classical
build, good assertive
build, muscular
built like a fortress/tank
built, badly
built, exceedingly well
built, lavishly
built, nicely/well
built, strongly
built, tightly
bulging out all over the place
bulky
Bunyanesque
burlap
burly bomber
burly with muscles
burly...masculine: wine that'll take out the garbage and pull your car out of a ditch
burnished
buttocks, well-shaped
buxom, splendidly
cadaver, waxy
calfskin, as supple as fine
caress, heavenly
caressing nature, extremely
carnal of the world's red wines, Merlot is the most
carnal, something
carnally perfumed, erotically/
carpet across your palate, unrolls like a very dark red

cashmere caress
cashmere softness, melted in the mouth with
cashmere scarf, threads of a
cashmere, finest
cashmere: you can wear it with jeans but it's always elegant, like
center(ed), hollow(-)
chamois-smooth
chassis, fine
chassis, gloriously sexy
chassis, tight
cheek on your tongue, silky feel of a lover's
cheeked, rosy-
chenille smooth, wraps me in
chested, hairy-
chest first, in danger of toppling over
chew it, you virtually
chew on, plenty to
chew them, so rich in aromatic essences you can almost
chew, swell/fine chewiness
chewed rather than drunk, to be
chewed to be believed, must be
chewy as coal, as
chewy fettle, fine
chewy like a grape seed
chewy, good and
chewy, so big it's just about
chewy, very
chewy-creamy
chiffon
chiseled and focused
chiseled, finely
chubby
chunky monkey
chunky yet velvety
clothed, well
clothes, fusty stink of rotting
clothes, old silk
cloudlike in the mouth, opens up
clumsy
coarse and lumbering
coarse and rough-edged, generally
coarse/coarseness, bordering/ verging on
coarseness personified
coiled, taut and spring-
colossus!, what a
compact/compacted
condensed
consistency as it coagulates in the throat, lavalike
constituted, impressively/well
constituted, poorly

constitution, enormous/
    monumental
constitution, nearly massive
constitution, robust/strong
constructed, densely/tightly
constructed, generously
constructed, overelaborately
constructed, perfectly/very well
constructed, powerfully/ruggedly
constructed, smoothly
construction, classy
contoured, softly
contoured, well
copious
corduroy, as soft as well-worn
corners, hard/sharp
corpulent
corsé
costume, last-minute Halloween
cotton sheets
cotton straightjacket
cotton, drip-dry
cotton, polished
cotton, snappy white
cotton, soft
cotton-wool, acrid
courtesan's scents, world-weary
crooked
crunchy but good
crusty
cumbersome, little
cumbersome, never
curved, gracefully
cushiony/cushy
dainty dish
defined, well
deflated
deformed
denim, patches of
density made me think I should
    reach for a spoon
dentally corrosive
denuded
desiccated impression, slightly
diaphanous
digestibility, has/digestible
digestive system, won't spoil your
dilute/diluted
dimensions, almost heroic in its
dimensions, epic/immense/vast
dimensions, grand in all its
dimensions, lacks sufficient
dimensions, lots of
dimensions, no
dimensions, Porthos-like
dimensions, really great
dimensions, unbelievable
diminutive

disembodied
disemboweled
disfigured
disintegrating
docile
down, as soft as
downy
dress, little black
driver rather than a ballerina, lorry
dwarf/dwarfish/dwarflike
earwax, funky
edge to be found, not a hard
edge(d), hard-
edge(d), soft-/soft edges
edge, dirty
edges, absolutely no sharp
edges, all sorts of
edges, challenging
edges, jagged/sharp
edges, no hard/jagged/sharp
edges, no seriously rough
edges, rough/roughish
edges, shaggy on the
edges, some interesting
edges, toasty
edges, well-rounded
edgy as a piece of ice in your
    mouth, as
edifice, magnificent
elastic
elasticity, good
elbowed, big-
elbowed, sharp-
elfin
elliptical
elongated from tip to toe
elusive
emaciated and malnourished
emasculated
emery, very fine-grained
endowed, amply/awesomely/
    enormously/formidably/
    impressively/mammothly/well
enmeshing
enormous, abnormally
enormous, quite
envelopes/enveloping
erotic as a handbag full of lipstick
    and scents, aromas as sweet and
erotic bent will appreciate this at
    the moment, only those with an
erotic exotic thing
erotic wildness
erotic with its sea notes
erotic, almost
erotic, wonderfully
erotically subtle
eviscerated

excellent
expansive, joyfully
exterior, burly/tough
exterior, crunchy
exterior, somewhat forbidding
eyes, flashing
fairy on a misty midsummer's
    meadow at dawn, dances forth
    like a beautiful
farmer with mud on his boots,
    yeoman
farts, devil
fat and happy/sassy
fat and lean, fine marriage of
fat but fit
fat fleshy flavors
fat it's almost oily, so
fat or overweight, rarely
fat, ample/considerable/really
fat, decent/good
fat, fantastically/unbelievably
fat, packed with baby
fat, running to
fat, seductive baby
fat, sweaty
fat, tannin-hiding
fat, tolerably
fat, upfront
fat-bottomed
fatness, enticing
fatness, predestined
fatness, voluptuous
fatness, wonderful
fattish, trifle
fatty, much too
featherlight
featherweight character
feathery
feet, dirty
feet, peasant's
feet, sweaty
feet, tang of cheesy
fella, big
fella, old
feminine charm(s)
feminine expression, almost
feminine frivolity
feminine intricacy and subtlety,
    wonderfully
feminine yet muscular
feminine, sublimely
femininity, restrained
femininity, supple
filiform
filigreed character
filmy
fine

fingers, you'll be tempted to eat
  this with your
firm as a rock, as
fist, carbon-crusted
flab or fat, no
flab, oily
flab, rapidly going to
flab, tendency to
flabby wetness
flaccid
flannel blanket
flannel/flannelly
flannel-soft
fleece/fleecy
fleet-footed
flesh and pleasure, embodiment of
flesh covering Italianate twigs and
  bushes
flesh in the middle, plenty of
flesh is a little loose and baggy
flesh on its bones, little/not much
flesh on its minerally bones, nice
flesh on the bones, needs a touch
  more fruit
flesh over firm bones, rounded
flesh-colored fluid, glorious
flesh, disappointingly little
flesh, gentle/soft
flesh, lacking/needs/no
flesh, lots of
flesh, marvelous
flesh, milk-fed fatty
flesh, moderate
flesh, plump ripe
flesh, profoundly velvety
flesh, slightly loose in the
flesh, still has plenty of
flesh, without much in the way of
fleshed, well
fleshier than usual
fleshiness, chewy
fleshiness, great masculine
fleshless but close, not quite
fleshless feel, dry
fleshpot, seamless
fleshy without being fat
fleshy, none too
fleshy, overly
fleshy, wondrously
flexible
flimsy
flirt but does not really dare to,
  wants to
flirtatious but definitely not slutty
flirtatious/flirty
fluffy
fluid/fluidic
foam, as light as

footed, fleet-
footed, heavy-/leaden-
footed, light-
footy
foreplay, all
foreplay...no follow-through, just
form, good/well formed
format, diaphanous
formless
fortress, built like a
fragile/frail
framed, large-
framed, small-
friable
frilly
frothy in the mouth
full and fleshy it almost needs a
  girdle to contain itself, so
full, medium/somewhat
full, on the lighter side of
full, very
fullness and drinkability, great
  combination of
fullness, big-diesel
fullness, bursting-at-the-seams
fullness, buttery
fullness, rare
fullness, sumptuous
full-on
fulsome
funk/funky
furnished, well
furry
fuzzy all over
gamin that seduces, wide-eyed
gangling/gangly
gastric
gaunt
generous
giant, big masculine
giant, brooding
giant, cocoa-textured
giant, gentle
giant, mighty
giant, nothing garish about this
  subtle yet powerful
giant, purple-hued
giant, unformed
gigantic/huge/immense
girl at school, boring
girlish/girly
girls, drunk college
girth control, never heard of
glossy
gnarly
good/goodish
gossamer/gossamerlike

gown of a sleeping Venus, faintly
  perfumed
graceful as a whippet, as
graceful serenity
grain, has
grained, close-/fine-
grained, loose-/broad-
grandfather, my
greasy
great
gristly
gritty
gullet, baby Jesus in velvet pants
  going down your
gum-caressing
gut doesn't hang out over its belt
  buckle, its
guts, all manner of
guts, atypical
guts and broad shoulders, plenty of
guts, earthy
guts, good/real
guts inside/underneath, plenty of
guts in their wine, for those who
  can't really live without
guts, lacks
guts than class/grace, more
guts than subtlety, more
gymnast/gymnastic
gymnast, muscle of a Romanian
hair, curly black
hair, singed
hair, wet
hair, wind in your
hairs on the back of a woman's
  thigh in high summer,
  seductive quality of the minute
hairy, tasted
hairy-chested
hams, fine pair of
hard and tight
hard as a rock, as
hardness, real black
hardy
harnessed, well
harsh, overly
headache and anise
hearty
heaviness, not a scintilla of
heavy/heavyish side, on the
heavy, monstrously
heavy, never/rarely
heavy, porky and
heavyweight fighter
heavyweight, blockbuster
heavyweight, full-blooded
heavyweight, luscious
heavyweight, not a

heavyweight, rich but tough
heft, beefy
heft, big-time
heft, has real
heft, mouthfilling
heft, snazzy
hefty but not overpowering
hefty swarthy bruiser
hefty to the point of carnality
hefty, seriously
height, good
he-man

hermaphrodite/
hermaphroditic

hessian, earthy
hessian, wet
hessiany-baggy
hipped, narrow-
hipped, wobbly
hips, shimmying
hollow place in the middle
hollow, virtually
horizontal than glassy, more
horrible
huge growling monster
huge it's almost bombproof, so
huge it's hard to get your tongue
    around it, so
huge mouthfiller
huge, compellingly
huge, monstrously
hulking
Hulk-sized
humongous
hung, loosely
hunk, macho
huskiness, characteristic/classic
husky drinkability
husky, nicely
hygiene, poor
immense in every way
immense in the mouth
immense, intimidatingly
immense: massive and
    gargantuan
impalpable
imposing
impressive
inflated
ingénue, unforgettable encounter
    with a raven-haired
insignificant
insubstantial, not
insubstantial, rather
intimate
itty-bitty
jagged around the edges, little
jagged, slightly

kinky
kiss, as soft as a
kiss, not a gentle
kissy
klutzy
knit to a harmonious whole
knit, beautifully/nicely/well
knit, big rich silky and well
knit, close-/closed-/tight-/tightly
knit/knitted, loose-/loosely-/open-
knitted and thick it can be worn as
    a coat, so richly
knitted out, well
knitted, very thickly
knitting, unraveled
laborer in a tutu, brickie's
lace and finesse, all
lace, as detailed...elegant...fine and
    intricate as Spanish
lace, old
laced, straight-
laced, well
lacelike finesse
lacelike personality
lacelike, delicately
laciness itself
lacking
lacy and light
lacy elegance
lacy, intricately
ladies...if you see what I mean,
    taste of old oak and old
lady, smooth and gentle
lanky

lard, hasn't a trace of

large as it gets, as
large, very
larger than life
lascivious
leaden
lean and green
lean and lithe
lean and mean
lean and pinched
lean and stringy
lean but not mean
lean edge
lean muscular dancer handsomely
    attired
lean to the point of austerity
lean and fit as East African athletes,
    as
legged, long-
leggy
legs buckle, will make your
leviathan mold, in the
libidinous
licentious

light and beautiful as a ballet
    dancer, as
light as a feather, as
light as a soufflé, as/soufflélike
    lightness
light as chiffon, as
light as foam, as
light as the air we breathe, as
light on its feet as an elephant, as
light on its feet, certainly not
light on its feet, surprisingly
light on the tongue
light/lightish side, on the
light, airily/ethereally
light, chiffon-
light, joyously
light, medium
light, not
light, rather/pretty/very
light, rich yet
light-as-a-butterfly construction
lightness of being can be more than
    just a book title, living proof that
    the incredible
lightness of being, indescribable
    but not unbearable
lightness, all
lightness, bucolic
lightness, dancing
lightness, ethereal
lightness, lovely
lightness, sensation of
lightness, unbearable
lightweight, sensual
limbed gem, slender-
limbed, clean-
limbed, fine-
limbed, long-
limber
limp
linen, rough
lingerie, liquid equivalent of
    French
lipped, full-
lissome
lithe and nimble
lithe as a ballet dancer, as
little
livered, limp and lily-
locks, long-flowing
long and thin as a supermodel, as
loose overall, little
loose, fraction
lot packed in, a
lots/tons
love in a new body, like rekindling
    an old
lumpy, bit

lush and dense
lush and lazy as a tropical holiday,
    as
lush and satisfying, uncommonly
lush personality
lush, really really
lush, surprisingly
lust, ignited the fires of
lustful/lusty
lymphatic
macho attitude
macho blockbuster
macho, robust
magnitude, blatant
maidens dancing on grassy hill-
    sides in colorful native costumes
male, alpha
malleable
malnourished
mammoth, uniquely
manly, more than
manly, not quite
masculine assertiveness, more
masculine exterior…feminine
    underneath
masculine personality, rugged
masculine side, dark
masculine vitality, irrepressible
masculinity, slightly aggressive
massage, deep
massive almost uncivilized
massive and full-bodied that you
    can stand a spoon in it, so
massive and heroic…with the
    kitchen sink thrown at it
massive in the mouth, formidably
massive, really
massively obvious
maternal
meager
meat on the bones, needs more
meatily rich
meatiness, compelling/strange
meatiness, dense
meatiness, individual muscular
meaty by nature

meaty mouthful
medium
melts in the mouth
men only, for
men, for macho
men, white-haired old
middle, luscious
middleweight
midpalate, hollow
midriff, thick
midsection, fat
midsection, layered

midsection, plush
midsection, showy
midsection, thin
midweight, supple
miniature
mistress, old
moderate
modest
moelleux
molded, well
monster Shiraz can out-sumo that
    of a Barossa

monster, sleeping
monstrous to the point of being
    grotesque
monumental
mouth and down your throat…
    caressing as it goes, slithers
    around your
mouth and sits like a lump on the
    palate, fills the
mouth as fresh as a daisy, leaves the
mouth can only be compared to an
    angel's kiss, supple caressing
    sensation in the
mouth feels coated with succulence
    for an eternity after swallowing,
    so viscous and lush your
mouth flavors, smashing
mouth has tight warp and weft
mouth like ice cream and runs
    down the throat like nectar,
    melts in the
mouth once swallowed, doesn't
    leave you with a lifeless buttery
mouth presence, lingering
mouth the wine sings, in the
mouth throbbing, sets the mouth
mouth upright, sets your
mouth with excitement, fills the
mouth with flavors and extract and
    oomph, fills every crevice of your
mouth with the ambiguous solidity
    of a jellyfish, moseys around my
mouth without offering any
    excitement, just sits there in the
mouth, angel tinkling in your
mouth, behemoth impression in
    the
mouth, bounces around in your
mouth, butters the
mouth, caresses the
mouth, caressingly tingly
mouth, clings to the side of your
mouth, curiously light entry to the
mouth, dances in the
mouth, extraordinary
mouth, firm in the

mouth, flavors rocket around the
mouth, floods every corner of the
mouth, fractionally heavy in the
mouth, fun in the
mouth, generous
mouth, grabby
mouth, hulking wine fills the
mouth, jumps around in your
mouth, launches a massive assault
    on the
mouth, luscious red fruit rolls
    around the
mouth with cashmere softness,
    melted in the
mouth, more than amply fills
    all the gaps in one's
mouth, narrows in the
mouth, nice polished wingtips
    in your
mouth, plump
mouth, quite ineffectual in the
mouth, really shines in the
mouth, rolled derby in the
mouth, seductive come-hither
    creaminess creates a party in
    your
mouth, sexy personality bastes the
mouth, simply melts in the
mouth, stacked and packed in the
mouth, sticks to the
mouth, taste explodes in the
mouth, utterly seductive
mouth, wants to live in the
mouth, you could almost spoon it
    right into your
mouth-burning
mouthcleaning
mouthcoating blast
mouthcoating gem
mouthfeel is on the fierce side
mouthfeel is tantamount to
    millions of tiny puffy pillows
mouthfeel is textured more like
    clay than oak
mouthfeel it seems almost fluffy, so
    much
mouthfeel resembled giblet gravy
mouthfeel sizzles
mouthfeel you could want, all the
    slurpy sexy
mouthfeel, abrasive/aggressive/
    hard/harsh/tough
mouthfeel, acidic
mouthfeel, adhesive/grippy
mouthfeel, almost icy
mouthfeel, approachable
mouthfeel, astringent/bitter/
    puckery

mouthfeel, awesome oily-textured
mouthfeel, beautiful/delightful
mouthfeel, big fleshy
mouthfeel, big/enormous/huge/
    large/massive/voluminous
mouthfeel, Bordeaux-like
mouthfeel, broad
mouthfeel, bubbly
mouthfeel, caressing
mouthfeel, chalky
mouthfeel, charming
mouthfeel, chewy
mouthfeel, clean racy
mouthfeel, complex/layered
mouthfeel, concentrated
mouthfeel, dry/drying/parching
mouthfeel, dynamic
mouthfeel, erotic/seductive
mouthfeel, excellent creamy
mouthfeel, exotic
mouthfeel, expansive
mouthfeel, extravagant/grand/
    sumptuous
mouthfeel, fantastic
mouthfeel, fat/fleshy
mouthfeel, flat
mouthfeel, foamy/frothy
mouthfeel, full/fullish
mouthfeel, gentle/soft/velvety
mouthfeel, good/reasonable
mouthfeel, gossamerlike
mouthfeel, great tingly
mouthfeel, green/unripe
mouthfeel, heavyweight
mouthfeel, hedonistic
mouthfeel, high-voltage piquant
mouthfeel, jammy
mouthfeel, juicy light citrus
mouthfeel, kinetic
mouthfeel, linenlike
mouthfeel, mellow
mouthfeel, molten quality to the
mouthfeel, pasty
mouthfeel, pedigreed
mouthfeel, pleasant/pleasing
mouthfeel, pleasantly soft
mouthfeel, pliant/supple
mouthfeel, plush
mouthfeel, quite burly
mouthfeel, resinous
mouthfeel, rich dry erotically silky
mouthfeel, rich/richish
mouthfeel, richly structured
mouthfeel, round custardy
mouthfeel, seamless/smooth
mouthfeel, slight grainy
mouthfeel, slightly hollow
mouthfeel, slightly jumpy

mouthfeel, squeaky
mouthfeel, stand-up
mouthfeel, starchy
mouthfeel, steely
mouthfeel, straight-line
mouthfeel, strangely powdery
mouthfeel, streamlined
mouthfeel, strong but not
    overmuscled
mouthfeel, stubborn
mouthfeel, suave
mouthfeel, suggestive leesy
mouthfeel, sumptuous
mouthfeel, supersmooth
mouthfeel, sure and focused
mouthfeel, svelte
mouthfeel, sweetish
mouthfeel, totally symmetrical
mouthfeel, ultravelvety
mouthfeel, vibrant
mouthfeel, viscous
mouthfill, good
mouthfill, poor
mouthfiller, big/huge
mouthfiller, concentrated
mouthfiller, full no-compromise
mouthfiller, good rich
mouthfiller, succulent
mouthfilling beast of complexity
    and structure, potent
mouthfilling bulldozer
mouthfilling but not clumsy
mouthfilling powerhouse
mouthfilling richness
mouthfilling yet weightless
mouthfilling, gloriously
mouthfilling, succulent fleshy
mouthfilling, viscous and
mouth-friendly as yet, not
mouthful of luxury
mouthful, almost unbeatable
mouthful, debauched
mouthful, fabulous/glorious
mouthful, fascinating
mouthful, fine/good
mouthful, great glossy
mouthful, hot
mouthful, huge mythical
mouthful, magically astonishing
mouthful, major/mighty/serious/
    sturdy
mouthful, massive extracty
mouthful, meaty
mouthful, most agreeable
mouthful, one big sexy
mouthful, passable
mouthful, polished
mouthful, quite a

mouthful, real
mouthful, staggering
mouthful, sultry
mouthful, uncivilized
mouthful, user-friendly
mouthful, wonderful
mouth-numbing
mouth-popping
mouth-spaced
mouth-staining
mouth-tingling
mouthweight, drink-now
mouthweight, terrific
multitextured
muscle power
muscle, beautiful lithe willowy
muscle, brutal
muscled-up
muscled, well-
muscles at rest, elegant and
    complex with big
muscles, big
muscles, charming bundle of
muscular elegance
muscular superhero
muscular perfection, broad-backed
muscular, gently
mushiness, some
muslin-light
naked and impersonal, touch
narrow-hipped
navel lint, moist
neck, necklace of pearls on a white
negligee, Valentine's
nerve ending, tweaks every
netted, fine-
neutered
neutral
normal
nose, aromas bounce all over the
    inside of your
nose seems chewy, even the
nose-numbing
nourished, well/nourishing
nubile
obese dimensions, almost
obese, obscenely
oblong
odalisquelike charms
olfactory system an aroma-
    therapeutic makeover, gives your
on, full-
opulent
oral afterglow, silky chocolate
orgasm in a bottle
orgasm, vinous
orgasmic
outmuscled

outsized, proud to be
overendowed/overfleshed
overmuscular
oversized
oversoft
overtoned
overweight, grossly
packed and stacked
packed, closely/densely
palate and into my brain, flavor bursts like stars across my
palate goes hither and thither
palate like a pinball, zigzags across your
palate like a puff of smoke vanishing into air, melts away on the
palate like liquid sorbet, it'll take the coating off your
palate like tiny grenades, detonates on the
palate presence, considerable/ immense/outstanding
palate presence, delightful
palate, beautifully carpets even the most fastidious
palate, challenge to the
palate, come-hither
palate, cuts a brilliant path across the
palate, cuts a gloriously large robust swath across
palate, dances seductively on the
palate, electric on the
palate, frolics on the
palate, glides really easily across
palate, highly expansive
palate, hits all the sweet spots on the
palate, languorous on the
palate, linear
palate, live-wire
palate, loaded

palate, muzzy
palate, pleases/regales/ruffles the
palate, pressureful
palate, ricochets wildly off your
palate, seems to impose on the
palate, slathers the
palate, touch lazy on the
palate, tuning fork for your
palate, very harmonious beautifully weft
palate, waddles across the
palate-busting
palate-coating/-dousing
palate-friendly, distinctly
palate-massaging

palates and minds stretch a little, makes our
palate-shocking/-stimulating
palate-tantalizing
pallid
paltry
paper-thin
passionate
passion in a glass, pure
passions being held in check, unpredictable
pasty, somewhat
people, dead French

people, smelly old
perfect
pert
petit/petite
pheromones/pheromone thing
pillow-soft/pillowy
pinch, slight
pinched, hopelessly
pipsqueaky
planed, flat-
planet-sized
pliancy, lacks
pliant, gracefully
plump around the waist
plump as a baby, as
plump as well as lean
plump, impishly
plump, snobbishly
plump, too
plump...fat...fleshy
plumped up
plumpness, grapey
plumpness, round woody
plumpness, soft
plush, out-of-this-world
plushness, layered
plushness, palate-pleasing
pointed now
polished
ponderous and boring
poop, smells like
poor
pores, just goes into your
posture, good
powdery
powerful
presence on the palate, serious
presence, real
pretty
prickly
pristine
prodigious
profound
prominent, overly

proportioned, massively/ substantially
proportioned, thrillingly
proportions made for musketeers... noblemen and rebels, of heroic
proportions, ample
proportions, gargantuan
proportions, heroic/mythic
proportions, palm-sweatingly heady
proportions, titanic
pulped/pulpy
pulsing
pumped up
puny
quasiorgasmic

Rabelaisian
ragged
rangy
rare
raunchy
ravishing
rayed, fine-
rectilinear, unnecessarily
relaxed
renal
revved up
rib cage, flavors penetrated my
ribby
rigid, bit too
ripe
risqué
robust, fatiguingly
rocker, black punk
romance, air of
ropy, lean and
ropy, old and
rotundity, excess
rough and raw, bit/little
rough and tough
rough and unpolished, somewhat
rough as old shoe leather, as
rough at the edges, pleasantly
rough edges, innocent of
rough stuff
rough, very
rough-and-ready/-tumble
round-contoured affability
rough-hewn, crudely
rough-surfaced
rough-tasting
round and supple
rounded, beautifully
rounded, seductively
rounded, well
roundness and virility, combines
roundness, extra

roundness, luscious acid-laced
roundness, middle
roundness, square
roundness, plump
ruffled
rugged and brawny, atypically
rugged, much too
ruggedness underneath
rugger player
rump, slightly heavy in the
running, free-
sackcloth, rough
sagging like the belly of a
    superannuated footballer
sailed, full-
sassy
satin sheet, as smooth as a
satin, clings like ruffled
satin, feels like
satin, like drinking
satin, as svelte as
satin, opulently sleek like
satin, well-turned
savory
scale, impressive in
scaled, big-/grand-/large-
scaled, monumentally
scaled, perfectly/well
scaled, small-
scaled, unusually large-
scary
scope, moderate in
scraggy
scrawny
scrunchy
sculpted, beautifully/nicely/well
sculpted, elegantly
sculpted, most perfectly
sculpted, subtly
seamless
seams, bursting at the
seduce any palate it touches,
    ready to
seduce, sure to
seduced, allow yourself to be
seduced, I was totally
seducer, fragrant
seduces rather than overpowers
seduces the palate by stealth
seduces, wide-eyed gamin that
seducible, irresistibly
seduction in a bottle/glass
seduction in magnum, maximum
seduction serum, veritable
seduction lasting over a minute,
    knee-melting
seduction, medium of frivolous
seduction, nearly cultlike

seduction, provides easy
seductive as a siren, as
seductive dark-toned beauty
seductive elegance, certain
seductive from start to finish, very
seductive musk
seductive rather than
    overpowering
seductive stuff
seductive tone
seductive, deliciously/richly
seductive, disarmingly
seductive, extremely/fabulously/
    hugely/incredibly/tremendously
seductive, gorgeously
seductive, narcotically
seductive, oozingly
seductive, rakishly
seductive, sensually
seductive, smoky...sultry and
seductive, texturally
seductive, undeniably/utterly
seductively gentle
seductively supple
seductress, amply-proportioned
    scent-bomb
sensation, soft
sense of taste, music for the
sensual and cerebral,
    simultaneously
sensual beyond the usual meaning
sensual perfume
sensual, embarrassingly/sinfully
sensual, excitingly
sensual, spontaneously
sensual, unbelievably
sensual? oh yes!
sensuality in crystal
sensuality, characteristic
sensuality, masterpiece of
sensuality, overwhelms you with
sensuality, sheer
sensuality, spontaneous generous
sensuality, unexpected but
    unforgettable element of
sensually seductive
sensuous and sensual
sensuous beyond belief/doubt
sensuous, excitingly/sinfully
sensuous, extraordinarily
sensuous, thoroughly
sensuousness, pure
sensuousness, undemonstrative
severe
sex by a campfire, good
sex), didn't make my wife and I
    want to (have
sex in a bottle, liquid

sex in a bottle/bottled sex
sex in a glass
sex kitten
sex machine
sex, better than
sex, glancing
sex...and Thanksgiving...like sex
    on Thanksgiving, like
sex...ummm, hot
sexes up the nose
sexier, massively
sexiness, exhibits a certain
sexiness, surprising
sexpot personality (in plain
    English: a slut), noteworthy
sexual act that involves silk
    sheets... melted dark chocolate...
    and black cherries while the
    mingled scents of cinnamon
    ...coffee and cola waft through
    the air, like performing a
sexual analogies can do justice,
    only
sexually charged
sexy and seductive
sexy and voluptuous manner,
    flaunts everything it has in an
    unabashedly
sexy aromas have crept out of the
    woodwork
sexy as a chemise, as
sexy personality, alluring
sexy personality, decadently
sexy wine is stacked in all the right
    places
sexy, disarmingly/tantalizingly
sexy, downright
sexy, gorgeously
sexy, immensely/massively
sexy, inarguably/undeniably
sexy, oh so
sexy, quite/very
sexy sweaty smell, rather
sexy, thoroughly
sexy...sexy and more sexy
sexy...curvaceous
sexy-sexy-sexy
shallow
shape, easy to
shape, nice
shape, perfect elliptical
shape, slight lack of
shaped, well/shapely
shapeless, quite
sharp edges, no
sharp in our mouths, almost
sharp/sharpened
sharpness, avoids

sharpness, no
sharp-pointed
sheepskin blanket
short
shouldered, big-/broad-
shouldered, narrow-
shoulders, has good
shoulders, substantial width
    across the
shriveled up, all
shrouded
shrunken
side, on the heavy
side, on the light
sieve, all its component parts
    have been through a
significant
silhouette, round
silk and spice, neat marriage of
silk and velvet, brings to mind
silk pajamas
silk stocking of a wine...the seam
    perfectly in place and you can
    taste it as it runs, long
silk thread of great strength
silk trousers, slides down your
    throat like the good lord Jesus in
silk, absolute
silk, as finely textured as the best
silk, as smooth as washable
silk, beguiling sweet
silk, bottled
silk, Burgundy
silk, finely woven
silk, goes/slides down like
silk, half-robed by a veil of
    gossamer
silk, heavy upholstery
silk, like drinking
silk, liquid
silk, pure Fortuny
silk, raw
silk, rough upholstery
silk, ruffled
silk, spun
silk, velvety
silken brilliance, sheer
silken delicacy
silkily clad
silkiness, harmonious
silkiness, incredible
silkiness, obnoxious
silkiness of texture, otherworldly
silkiness, relishable
silky as they come, as
silky, bewitchingly
silky, minty-

silky strands, intricate weave of
    smooth
sinew than flesh, more
sinewy, awfully
sinewy, definitely
sinuosity, has
sinuous as sin, as
size and stature, baronial
size, doesn't overwhelm with
sized, fantastically
sized, king-
skimpy
skin and bones
skin, oiled
skin, sun-warmed
skin, warm
skinned, loose-
skinny composition, somewhat
skinny stuff
slab, solid
slabby
slack
slack than tension, slightly more
sleek as well-fitting slacks, as
sleek package
sleek, excitingly
sleekness, aromatic
slender, rather
Slenderella
slight
slim jim
slimline
slinky
slip of a wine, little
slipcover for the tongue...ranging
    from terry cloth to suede to
    velvet
slippery
slithery
sludgy
slutty, flirtatious but definitely not
small/smallish
smooooooth, sooooo
smooth and polished to a satiny
    sheen
smooth as the proverbial baby's
    bottom, as
smooth as the song of an
    auctioneer, as
smooth as velvet silk, as
smooth as you please, as
smooth but monotonous
smooth, butter-/buttery
smooth, electrically
smooth, gorgeously
smooth, magically
smooth, meltingly
smooth, mirror

smooth, not very
smooth, supremely
smooth, velvet-/velvety
smooth...too round...too rotten,
    too
smoothie
smoothly enjoyable
smoothness of butter, all the
smoothness, chocolate
smoothness, cornsilk
smoothness, inviting
smoothness, oaky
smoothness, velvety
smoothness, violet-flowery
snappy
soft as chocolate sponge pudding,
    as
soft as a down pillow, as
soft as a pillow/pillow-soft
soft as an Impressionist painting,
    as
soft as brushed velvet, as
soft as can be...the smooth skin of
    a grandparent
soft decadent package, encased in a
soft slightly mushy mess
soft, caressingly
soft, flannel-
soft, headily
soft, silken/silky softness
soft, sumptuously
soft-centered
soft-edged
softness of Danish pastry
softness, cakelike/cakey
softness, cashmerelike
softness, come-hither/seductive
softness, featherbed
softness, leaves a trail of creamy
solid, very
sophisticated
sound
spare/sparse
spartan
spherical
spiky, bit
spindly
spine, flexible
spongy, fractionally
sprawling
springy
spry
spun, fine-
squarish, bit
squeaky feel, hard-to-describe
squelchy
stacked in all the right places, sexy
    wine is

stacked, well
stamina, has
starched
stark
startling
statuesque, magnificently
stature, good
steamy
stemmed, thick-
steroids, on
stiff as a board, as
stiff, quite
stomach, has
stout
strapping stuff
streamlined
streamlined, none too
stretched
stringy and rustic
stripped
strong
strung, tightly
stud
stuff, gunky granular
stuff, lusty
stuff, plenty of
stuff, sturdy
stuffed, not well
stuffed, well
stuffing in the mouth, plenty of
stuffing taken out of it, wine
  with its
stuffing, excellent/good/great
stuffing, full/lot/plenty of
stuffing, no
stuffing, not enough
stuffing, phenolic
stuffing, real
stunted
suave
substance, cushioned in
substance, dense
substantial, much more
substantial, quite
substantive
suede to velvet, slipcover for the
  tongue...ranging from terry
  cloth to
suede, silken
sufficient
sumo wrestler with a blond wig
  and beauty mark, as soothing
  and sensuous as a
suntan, Bondi Beach
supercompact
superendowed
superseductive
supersexy appeal

supersoft
superthick
supple
suppleness, extraordinary degree of
suppleness, underlying
svelte and elegant
sveltness, silky
swashbuckling
sweat, glistening fresh
sweat, new
sweat, old
sweat, sex/sexy
sweatiness, touch of
sweaty almost smelly
sweaty, earthy-
sweaty smell, rather sexy
sweaty, something between
  cheesy and
swimmer: sinewy...streamlined...
  shapely with firm rippling
  pectoral muscles, champion lady
tactile and taste sensor ringing,
  sets every
tactile delicacy, thrilling
tactile, very
taffeta/taffetalike
tailored and pressed, finely
tailored specimen, well-
tailored, brilliantly
Tanya from 8th grade
tart with a heart
tart, attractive buxom nubile
  highly scented
taste bud, prickles every
taste bud-blowing
taste buds into admiring
  submission, stuns the
taste buds like soft leather Gucci
  loafers fit the feet, fits the
taste buds, cascades over the
taste buds, perfect for charming
  your
taste buds, primps and tweaks the
taste buds, really gets hold of the
taste buds, seen through the
  magnifying glass of the
taste buds, tickles your
taste buds, wakes up the
taste buds, will hypnotize your
taut and spring-coiled
taut and springy
taut, strikingly/very
teenager, black-leather jacket
  brooding
teeny-weeny
teeth, good for cleaning false
teeth for days on end,
  will stain your

teeth-/tooth-coating
teeth-stainer, red
tempered, well
temperature, mouth
temptress, wanton black-haired
  sultry
tender, none too
tender, too
tense
tenuous
terry cloth to suede to velvet,
  slipcover for the tongue...
  ranging from
textural abrasiveness
textural interest, very little
textural sensuality, fleshy
texturally luxurious
texturally seductive/sinful
texture akin to cocoa powder
texture and structure, straight-line
texture approaching carborundum
texture as light as a feather
texture evokes silk and lace
texture feels like the palate is
  resting on a waterbed of overripe
  black fruit, plush
texture is a little loose
texture is more silk than velvet
texture is pure New Wave
texture is so plush that the palate
  gets lost in a dizzying smorgasbord of flavors and aromas
texture is the finest cut velvet
texture lacks focus, slightly furry
texture like balsam
texture like embroidery
texture like liquid velvet
texture like sheer silk
texture like the heavy hypnotic
  flow in a lava lamp
texture like the sinful strokes
  of a feather boa
texture like Viennese black
  chocolate melting in your palm
  on a hot summer's night
texture of 10W40 motor oil
texture of axle grease
texture of chicken soup in a glass
texture of custard
texture of extravirgin olive oil
texture of felt
texture of nail polish
texture of supreme class, rich
texture of sweet cream
texture of taffeta
texture in the mouth,
  extraordinary
texture of velvet on the tongue

texture that swells in the mouth
texture to take it out of the white painting category, needs more
texture, aggressive
texture, all-enveloping
texture, almost three-dimensional
texture, attractive pliant
texture, beeswax
texture, blowsy
texture, bracingly crisp
texture, broad
texture, buttercream
texture, buttery
texture, caressing
texture, chalky
texture, chunky-velvety
texture, closed
texture, coarse earth
texture, compressed
texture, crunchy
texture, crushed-velvet
texture, curious pasty
texture, custardy
texture, delicate tactile
texture, diaphanous/gauzy
texture, drop-dead gorgeous silken
texture, dusty tactile palate-coating
texture, earthy gritty
texture, easy/easygoing
texture, exquisite
texture, finely woven
texture, flattering
texture, fleshy
texture, friendly
texture, full voluptuous
texture, glorious silken
texture, gooey/sticky
texture, heavenly/terrific
texture, high-/top-class
texture, honey-thick
texture, intoxicating
texture, jazzy
texture, jellied
texture, juicy/succulent
texture, keen-edged
texture, knee-weakeningly sensual in its
texture, lightly rasping
texture, lithe
texture, lugubrious
texture, lush supple swallowable
texture, lusty/rugged
texture, magical supersmooth
texture, multilayered
texture, mushy
texture, nuanced
texture, palate-caressing
texture, pear-thick

texture, pinched compressed
texture, plump
texture, posh
texture, remarkable
texture, rich weave of its
texture, satin and silk
texture, satiny tannin
texture, seamless
texture, seductively velvety
texture, sensual
texture, sensuous fat
texture, sensuously silky
texture, sheer breed on the
texture, sheer ineffability of
texture, sheer lip-smacking
texture, signature creamy
texture, silky svelte
texture, slightly sandy
texture, slippery
texture, smooth warming
texture, soft ripe lush
texture, soothing
texture, spicy fruit cradled in a silky
texture, sultry
texture, sumptuous
texture, surface
texture, surprisingly elegant
texture, terrific ruffled
texture, thick all-enveloping
texture, thick glycerin-imbued
texture, thick puddinglike
texture, thick smokelike
texture, thickly knitted
texture, thin glyceriney
texture, thrillingly fine silky
texture, tight
texture, ultraluxuriant
texture, unduly narrow
texture, very delicate fizziness cossets its silky
texture, very dry sandpapery
texture, voluptuous tannic
texture, waxy
texture, well-padded
texture, wild chewy
texture, wrapped in the prettiest
texture…just slips down, silky
textured as a Gobelin tapestry, as detailed and
textured beauty
textured elixir, thick-
textured monster, syrupy-
textured personality, velvety
textured, chamois-
textured, chewy-
textured, chiffon-
textured, coarse-/rough-

textured, creamy-
textured, decadently
textured, densely
textured, emery
textured, fine-
textured, firm-/hard-
textured, gossamer-
textured, hedonistically
textured, lean-
textured, linen
textured, loose-
textured, mouthfillingly
textured, naturally
textured, oily-
textured, open-
textured, rich-/richly
textured, ripe-
textured, round-
textured, sandy-
textured, satin-/silky-
textured, short-
textured, slightly tough-
textured, soft-
textured, supple-
textured, thick-/thickly
textured, unctuously/viscously
textured, velour-
textured, velvet-/velvety
textured, very fine-
textured, voluptuously
textured, well
textured, wonderfully
textureless
thick a spoon could stand up in it, so
thick almost impenetrable
thick and fat
thick as fudge, as
thick as honey, as
thick as the US government's annual budget proposal, as
thick enough to eat with a fork
thick it needs to be drunk with a spoon, so
thick with taste, almost
thick you could chew it before swallowing, so
thick, espresso-
thick, incredibly/strikingly
thick, nicely
thick, ponderously
thick, smells
thick, too
thick, undrinkably
thick, very
thicken up pretty quickly, will
thick-looking
thickness, real

thickness, teeth-frightening
thighs of a rich girl depleted by
  lassitude
thighs, great
thighs, muscular
thighs, sumo wrestler's
thin but there
thin in the mouth
thin, dreadfully/painfully
thin, papery
thread of great strength, silk
threadbare
throat pain
throated, full-/throaty
throat, rolls like rough velvet down
  your
throat like the good lord Jesus in
  silk trousers, slides down your
thumbprint, maker's
tight in the mouth
tight-knit
tiny
titan/titanic
titanic proportions
toast, you can spread this on
toned, well
tongue down, doesn't weigh your
tongue in the most delightful way,
  caresses the
tongue like satin on skin, flavors
  run over the
tongue stick to the palate,
  makes the

tongue, coolant for your

tongue, dances across/on the
tongue, does a tango on my
tongue, does somersaults on your
tongue, glides across the
tongue, nice on the
tongue-coating
tongue-nipping
toothsome
top-heavy
torso, quite a
tough
toughness, leathery
transvestite, bit of a
trifle, a
trim
turned out, badly
tweed jacket, damp
twisted, bit
ugly
ultrabig
ultraseductive
ultrasilky
ultrasmooth
ultrathick

ultravoluptuous
underbelly bursting with
  glycerin…fruit and extract,
  viscous huge juicy thick
underbelly, lemony
underbelly, soft/velvety
underbelly, strange
underbelly, tarry
undernourished, appears
undertaste, slightly burnt
undertone, good
undistinguished
ungainly, never
ungainly/ungraceful
ungenerous
unidimensional
uninteresting
unknit
unmanly, nothing
unsubstantial
unwrapped
upholstered comfort, superior
upholstered, plushly
upholstered, well
urine during asparagus season
urine…but not in a bad way
uvula cryogenics
vaporous, almost
vast
vein, light
velour/velourlike
velvet and gossamer, at once
velvet and silk, like drinking pure
velvet curtains, heavy
velvet cushions as you drink it,
  impression of sinking into
velvet down your throat, rolls like
  rough
velvet embrace, soft
velvet fabric
velvet gliding across the palate,
  feels like
velvet glove stuff
velvet on a marble staircase
velvet on/over iron/steel
velvet pants going down your
  gullet, baby Jesus in
velvet rather than wood
velvet sliding over the tongue
velvet with ruffled corduroy edges
velvet with satin trimmings
velvet, as plush as crushed
velvet, blue
velvet, bottled
velvet, crinkled

velvet, free-range

velvet, like drinking inky dark
velvet, liquid

velvet, pure plush
velvet, red
velvet, rough
velvet, slipcover for the tongue…
  ranging from terry cloth to
  suede to
velvet, texture is the finest cut
velvet, very soft
velvet, white
velvet, worn
velveteen, dense
velvetiness, sensual

velvety and rusty nails

velvety monster
velvety opulence, fills the mouth
  with
velvety refinement
velvety smoothness
velvety suppleness
velvety texture, chunky-
velvety treasure
velvety, gloriously/gorgeously
velvety, noticeably
vibrant
vigorous
virginal as Psyche before
  she met Cupid, as
visceral, distinctly
viscerally pleasing
volume, extra inner-mouth
volume, good/voluminous
volume, lacks
voluptuous, almost
voluptuous, among the most
voluptuous, dangerously
voluptuousness, a matter of
voluptuousness, extraordinary
vomit from a baby fed with
  formula, baby
vomit, tincture of
vomitous/vomitlike
waist, meaty round the
waistcoat, has a
warmth, mouthfilling
washed out
watery and fruit-free
watery mess
watery, rather
weak
weave of silky strands, intricate
weave with wild mushrooms and
  minerals, cosmic
weave, cashmere-soft
weave, ornate
weave, tight dense
weave, visible
wee
weight and feel, gorgeous

weight on the tongue
weight, almost delicate in
weight, authoritative
weight, awesome/massive/
   thundering
weight, claretlike
weight, comforting chicken
   souplike
weight, decent/medium/nice
weight, dessertlike
weight, good fruit
weight, good oily
weight, great presence and
weight, grunty prunelike
weight, leanness of
weight, near-perfect/perfect
weight, oily
weight, serious
weight, undaunting
weight...only mass, has the uncanny feeling of power with no
weighted, appealingly
weightless, almost
weightless, pleasantly
weightless...like drinking clouds
weightlessness, eerie sense of
weightlifter
weighty, appropriately/satisfyingly
weighty, especially/exceptionally/
   very
welterweight
whopper/whopping
wide open
wimpy
wingtips in your mouth,
   nice polished
wiry
wishy-washy
wishy-washy about it, nothing
wisp, gossamer
wispy to really enjoy, too

woman, Brazilian

woman...not too curvaceous...
   trying...and not succeeding...
   to be swellegant, like a
womanly
women with parasols playing
   croquet in the sunshine on an
   enormous lawn
wonderful
wool, swaddled in cotton
wool, wet
woolen mittens
woolly blanket
wooly edge
wooly welcoming feel
worker chewing gum in the sun,
   thin dusty old carnival

wound, tightly
woven fruit and acids, deftly
woven, close-/closely
wrestler with diaper rash,
   about as friendly as a sumo
wrought, closely
wrought, highly
yielding
zaftig
zephyry

I know I'm not the smartest person in the world, Lord knows, but please explain to me how wine that's wet can also be dry.
Unknown

I like sweet wines. My idea has always been that when you're young, you like sweet wine; and then you get sophisticated, and you drink dry white; and then you get knowledgeable, and you drink heavy reds; and then you get old, and you drink sweet again.
Sally Raphael

11. Dryness to Sweetness

Life can be sweet; books can be dry. But wine can be everything in between, from bone-dry to the most gaggingly, cloyingly sweet. Some folks think most wines are way too dry; some, way too sweet. Whichever way they feel, they find that many of these descriptors come from tasters' comments on sparkling and dessert wines that can run the gamut from ashes to honey pot. You guess which is which.

abboccato/abocado/amabile/amado
aqueous
arid/aridity
ascuitto
ashes in the mouth as it quits the throat, almost like
balance, perfect dry-sweet
bittersweet/bittersweet-ish
brut absolu
brut de brut
brut intégral
brut natur/nature
brut nondosé
brut réserve
brut sauvage
brut zéro
brut, electrifying
brut/bruto
clotted but not cloying
cloying
cloying as candy, as
cloying attack on the palate
confected
confection, nectarously grapey
crémant
dead, [so sweet it] could revive the
demise
dental nightmare
desiccating

doce/dolce/dulce
dosé, non-
dosed
doux
drier than dry
drier than Kool-Aid
drier, speck
dry
dry a dragon must have sucked all the sugar from it, so
dry and dusty
dry and fully sweet, good halfway house between
dry and sinewy
dry as a bone, as/bone-dry
dry as a Saharan sirocco, as
dry as buggery, as
dry as dust, as
dry as stone, as
dry as the Sahara, as
dry bones, all
dry fluid, very
dry honey effect
dry it dries out our mouths, so
dry stuff underneath
dry, absorbently
dry, aggressively/blisteringly/ caustically/grippingly/intensely/ penetratingly/piercingly/

raspingly/savagely/searingly
dry, ash
dry, authentically
dry, barely
dry, blessedly
dry, chalk-
dry, challengingly
dry, confectioner's dream done
dry, crunchingly
dry, dead-
dry, elegantly
dry, fetchingly
dry, half-/medium-
dry, heavy-duty
dry, keenly
dry, much too
dry, Muscatty
dry, naturally very
dry, near-/nearly
dry, not quite
dry, not very/somewhat
dry, noticeably
dry, off-
dry, powder-
dry, powder-keg-
dry, punishingly
dry, Sahara
dry, sandpaper-
dry, shockingly

dry, skirts the edge of
dry, spry sly and very
dry, staunchly
dry, sternly
dry, stingingly
dry, stone-
dry, stylishly
dry, swingeingly
dry, technically
dry, teeth-grippingly
dry, tingly
dry, too
dry, totally
dry, truly
dry, very very
dry, wickedly
dryness of rain-washed pebbles
dryness, almost rasping
dryness, apple-skin
dryness, chalky
dryness, excellent
dryness, flinty pebbly
dryness, lacks
dryness, licorice
dryness, lovely gamy
dryness, normal
dryness, nut husk
dryness, overall masculine
dryness, raging
dryness, steely
dryness, stony
extrabrut/extradry/extrasec/
extraseco/extrotrocken
gloop, sickly sugary
goût américain
goût anglais
goût français
halbsüss/halbtrocken
herb
hypoglycemic
lieblich
liqueur, sans
liquoreux/liquoreuse
mellifluent/mellifluous
moelleux
nectary
nondosage
oily, cloyingly
overdry
oversugared
oversugary, not
oversweet/oversweetened
riche
Sahara sandwich
sec/secco/seco
sekt
semidry
semidulce/semisec/semisweet

semisweet concoction
sour and sweet
spätlese
sticky
sucre, sans
sugar bomb, flabby
sugar cane
sugar cricket bat, assaulted by a
sugar high
sugar is in retreat
sugar over waffles, breakfast
sugar reels you in and seduces you
sugar rush that goes right to your
  toes
sugar it tasted like tiny bon-bons,
  so brimming with
sugar trap, has resisted the
sugar you could blow bubbles with
sugar, bit of residual
sugar, bright residual
sugar, bursting with
sugar, cautionary example of the
  destructive power of
sugar, dollop of
sugar, excessive residual
sugar, gruesome amounts of
sugar, heaps of
sugar, nectar with
sugar, residual
sugar, rich
sugar, *soupçon* of
sugar, sprinkling of
sugar, touch of unfermented
sugar-acid balance, exemplary
sugarcanelike
sugared over
sugarphobic
sugar's coming out of its ears
sugary beam
sugary concoction
sugary disappointment
sugary wines, most insidiously
sugary, amazingly
sugary, disgustingly
sugary, excessively
sugary, much too
supersticky
supersugary
supersweet richness
süss
sweet alcopop, sickly
sweet and acid, unrivalled tension
  between
sweet and dry, walks the line
  between
sweet and fruity as all get-out, as
sweet and savory, push-pull of
sweet and shallow, revoltingly

sweet and sour, curious mixture of
sweet as chocolate syrup, as viscous
  and
sweet as its peers, not as
sweet as jam, as
sweet as molasses/molasses-sweet,
  as
sweet at the same time, sour and
sweet beast, rich
sweet botrytized honey-dripper
sweet but isn't, almost seems
sweet but not cloying
sweet end of things, tipped toward
  the
sweet for the purist, tad too
sweet glory, in all its inky
sweet it made our teeth hurt, so
sweet nectar of the gods
sweet pink stuff, syrupy
sweet sweet sweet, diabetic's
  nightmare:
sweet tart
sweet thing
sweet tooth would be happy,
  anyone with a
sweet tooth, for one's
sweet tooth's delight
sweet white thunderbolts
sweet with some food coloring
sweet without being gooey,
  attractively
sweet yet crisp
sweet yet decayed
sweet yet salty
sweet yet somewhat tangy
sweet, achingly/cloyingly/
  gaggingly/ horribly/
  ridiculously/sickly/sinfully/
  unbearably/wickedly
sweet, aggressively
sweet, almost
sweet, amazingly/incredibly
sweet, astonishingly
sweet, attractively
sweet, bloody
sweet, earthy-
sweet, explicitly
sweet, faintly/lightly
sweet, fairly/medium
sweet, frankly
sweet, fruit-
sweet, gently
sweet, gingery
sweet, implicitly
sweet, indescribably
sweet, intensely
sweet, just shy of
sweet, manages to smell

sweet, Manischewitz-
sweet, mawkishly
sweet, megawatt
sweet, molasses-
sweet, much/way too
sweet, not aggressively
sweet, not shockingly
sweet, not too
sweet, pretty
sweet, ravishingly
sweet, ripe verging on
sweet-salty
sweet, sea-
sweet, sensationally
sweet, sickly
sweet, smells
sweet, so ripe and jammy in the
   mouth it seems...painfully so
sweet, somewhat
sweet, speciously
sweet, sticky-
sweet, succulently
sweet, teeters on the edge of
sweet, teeth-jarringly lusciously
sweet, too blatantly
sweet, tooth-achingly
sweet, treacle-
sweet, unarguably
sweet, unusually
sweet, utterly seductively
sweet, velvety
sweet, very very
sweet, voluptuously
sweet, wickedly
sweet, wonderfully honeyed and
sweet...oozy and naughty
sweet...sweet and more sweet
sweet...the Achilles heel of many
   sparkling wines, mercifully not
sweet/sweetened/sweetish/
   sweetness
sweet/tart component has my
   dentist rubbing his hands with
   glee
sweet-and-sour character
sweet-centered
sweetened up
sweetened, artificially/artificial
   sweetener
sweetened, gently
sweeter in the glass, seemed to get
sweeter side of *brut*
sweeter than Amstel Light
sweeter than pure honey,
   thicker and
sweetie, amber-colored
sweetie, botrytised
sweetie, real

sweetie, rich
sweetie/sweety
sweetish center
sweetish come-on
sweetish vein
sweetly rich
sweetness and acidity, well-woven
sweetness and sheer zest, spot-on
   marriage of gentle
sweetness battling tannin
sweetness covers a multitude of
   sins
sweetness from oak, vanilla-
   chocolate
sweetness in the recesses, mild
   lingering
sweetness is a fraction distracting
sweetness of rare steak
sweetness of youthful hopes, airy
sweetness waiting in the
   background waiting to titillate
sweetness, appealing natural
sweetness, *Auslese/Spätlese*
sweetness, austere
sweetness, beautiful
sweetness, borders on outright
sweetness, breath/dash/flick/
   suggestion of
sweetness, butterscotch
sweetness, candied
sweetness, cloudlike
sweetness, confectionary-counter
sweetness, demerara
sweetness, devoid of
sweetness, edge of nutty
sweetness, electric
sweetness, explosive
sweetness, exposed
sweetness, extraordinary
   explosion of
sweetness, fabulous nectar a
   bounding with natural
sweetness, flaccid
sweetness, flirts with
sweetness, fruitcake
sweetness, graceful veil of
sweetness, haunting
sweetness, heightened sensation of
sweetness, hidden
sweetness, honey-ripe
sweetness, implied
sweetness, light kiss of
sweetness, lip-smacking residual
sweetness, liqueury
sweetness, lopsided toward
sweetness, lovely extract
sweetness, luscious
sweetness, luxurious levels of

sweetness, massive
sweetness, massively concentrated
sweetness, mere suspicion of
sweetness, mild
sweetness, Mogen David
sweetness, mulberry-toffee
sweetness, natural
sweetness, near-subliminal
sweetness, new-oak
sweetness, offers more than simple
sweetness, out-of-balance
sweetness, pleasing
sweetness, powder-puff
sweetness, pure
sweetness, rambunctious levels of
   alcohol and
sweetness, really lovely
sweetness, restrained
sweetness, reticent
sweetness, ridiculous level of
sweetness, right to the edge of good
sweetness, slightest touch of
sweetness, slippery
sweetness, soft
sweetness, soft icing sugar
sweetness, *spätlese* level of
sweetness, stingy flashes of
sweetness, subliminal
sweetness, sunshine
sweetness, sunshine-syrupy
sweetness, superintense
sweetness, tangiest most lingering
sweetness, thin skein of
sweetness, unabashed honeyed
sweetness, unbelievable
sweetness, upfront
sweetness, utter
sweetness, veil of extract
sweetness, whisper of/whispering
sweet-sour aspects, strange
sweet-sour disparity, youthful
sweet-sour interplay
sweet-sour seesaw, entrancing
sweet-sour, wonderfully
sweet-tart
sweet-tart interplay
sweet-toothed, paradise for the
sweet-woody, all-purpose
tone, coolness of
trocken
ultrabrut
ultradry
ultrasweet
uncloying
unctuous
undry
unsugared
unsweet/unsweetened

The earth speaks.
François Peyraud

Our love for wine is in part a love for the earth itself.
Andrew Jefford

Wine is grape juice. Every drop of liquid filling so many bottles has been drawn out of the ground by the roots of the vine. All these different drinks have at one time been sap in a stick. It is the first of many strange and some mysterious circumstances which go to make wine not only the most delicious, but the most fascinating drink in the world.
Hugh Johnson

12. Earth [Nature, Environment, *Terroir*, Mineral or Vegetation]

The sky above, the mud below, fields and forests, soil and dirt, fresh water and salt, rocks and stones, plus minerals of every sort. Not to mention dead grasses and live leaves, and sticks and straw and weeds and underbrush and swamps, plus climate and weather and many other elements of the natural world we inhabit. Surely you remember the still very controversial concept of *terroir* that was highlighted on page 50. Of course you do. And you also love the smell of earth, especially right after the rain. Just breathe it all in.

afternoon spent outdoors under a
  big tree talking with old friends,
  beautiful
agaric
air of Provence
air tang, salt
air, as fresh and clean as alpine
air, as light as
air, autumnal
air, blast/breath of fresh
air, clean sea
air, cold autumn
air, freshness and purity of cool
  mountain
air, ocean
air, salty sea
air, stable
airy, light and
alfalfa, cut
alfalfa, minty
amber
arboreal piquancy
artemisia
ash, cold
ash, Etna/volcanic

ash, smoky
ash, volcanic
asparagus, wild
autumn day in Piedmont
autumn day in the Patagonian
  Andes
autumn days, brisk
autumn fire
autumn flavors, time-worn
autumn fragrance, beautiful
autumn in a bottle/glass
autumn, breath of
autumn, early
autumn, essence of
autumn, taste of
avalanche of falling rocks
balmy
bamboo, green
barberries, dry
barnyard smells: sounds awful but
  it's part of the earthy soulful
  charm
barnyard, fresh
barnyard, fungal-to-
barnyard, off-

barnyard, rich
barnyard, rustic
barnyard, truffles verged on
beans, fresh/green/ unroasted,
  coffee
bindweed
birches more beautiful in bud or
  when they've just burst into
  leaf?, are
birthmark, earth's
bittersweet
black
black and rich
bluestone
bois, near-hidden touch of *sous*
bonfires, leaf
boulders
boxwood
bracken, old
bracken, singed/toasted
brackish depths, from the
brackish intensity
bramble patch
brambly-zesty

breeze blowing through wildflowers, as aromatic as a
breeze captured in a bottle, chamomile-scented sea-
breeze laden with juniper elements, spicy
breeze sweeping through the lavender-scented hills of the southern Rhône, as fresh as a
breeze through conifers, ocean
breeze, arctic sea
breeze, as fresh as a March
breeze, as light and flighty as a spring
breeze, bracing salty sea
breeze, citrus-fresh
breeze, cool sea
breeze, enchanting tropical
breeze, fresh/freshness of a sea
breeze, marine sea
breeze/breeziness, refreshing alpine
breezily scented
breeziness, vivacious
briar, lightly resinated
briary nuances
brine/briny
broom, sweet-scented
brush, aromatic
brushland, Mediterranean
brushwood
buckwheat
buds, green
burnt
bushes after the rain, rose
bushes without any thorns, like stumbling into wild blackberry
bushes, bramble
bushes, cassis/black currant
bushes, dried
bushes, thorn
bushes, tomato
brushfire
bush-flavored
bushy and restless
cacao
cactus
cactus in the afterburn
cade
calcareous
campsite, Mediterranean
campus, Stanford
canopy, green
cave shimmering with stalactites, ice
cave, damp/wet
celestial
chaffy overtone

chalk and slate, flecks of
chalk dust/dusty chalk
chalk, lick of
chalk, liquid
chalk, plump layers of peach-imbued
chalkiness, mineral
chalkiness, palate-cleansing
chalklike minerality
chalky richness
chaparral
charcoal
charcoal, mesquite
charred/scorched
chlorophyll
cinchona
cinders
clay, damp/wet
clay, dry
clay, earthy
clay, light on the
clay, rolled in red
clay-epoxy, bright
cliffs, granite
climat
clouds, lollipop
clover, essence of
clover, rose
coal dust/dusty coal/dusting of coal
coal smoke
coal that could keep miners working for years, vein of
cold, like drinking the
cold, piercingly ice-
complex
compost and barnyard
compost heap, fermented/ripe
compost, clean
compost, rich loamy
compost, vegetable
composted tropical fruit, poorly
concentrated
cool
cool, glacially
copper/coppery
copperesque, very
copse
cosmic
country, rich
country, warm spring day in the
country/rural smells
course, golf
craggy
craggy, challengingly
creek, musty
current, refreshing crisp
curry plant
damp/dampish/moist

damp, fresh-
dandelions, field of
dank
dappled wine flavors
dark and stormy wine
darkness, brooding
datura
days in Florida, bright cloudless
denizen of the forest slipping quietly and gracefully through the trees, handsome slender
dew/dewy
diamonds
diamonds into a tulip, like pouring
dirt under its fingernails, some
dirt, fine level of
dirt, fresh moist
dirt, light
dirt, mouthful of
dirt, plain ol'
dirt, sweet
dried/dry
drought-affected
dug/plowed/turned, freshly
dung fire
dust blowing through a corral, dry
dust, chalk
dust, chalky smoky cellar
dust, cherries and
dust, hot-climate
dust, powdery sensation of chalk
dust, revitalizing sprinkling of summer
dust, rock
dust, Rutherford
dust, trail
dust, volcaniclike
dustiness, tawny
dusty road, like driving down a
dusty sort of smells
dusty-watery
earth and minerals, serious underpinning of
earth and the sun at the same time, like tasting the
earth blackness, scorched
earth character, very true-to-the-
earth for its smoky minerality, reaches deep into the
earth, *goût de terroir* but not of this
Earth herself, like tasting the
earth juxtaposed with a charming aura, murmuring undertone of dusky
earth litter, rain-soaked
earth speaks, the
earth that is good for the soul, ungarbled product of the

earth tightly wound, lots of
earth under a log, wet
earth with its profound minerality, plumbs the depths of the
earth, Barossa
earth, can almost taste the
earth, certain patch of
earth, core of minerals which seems to have been mined from the bowels of the
earth, dampened
earth, flavors of heaven and
earth, from the good
Earth, Great Mother
earth, has a connection to the
earth, haunting musk notes point to the mysteries of the
earth, honest natural wine with roots in the
earth, laced with the savor of the
earth, oily layers of
earth, pictures and places waft up like the proverbial aromas of fruits and
earth, plays sun off
earth, primal flavors of sun and
earth, reward for being good to the
earth, serious underpinnings of
earth, shovelful of fresh
earth, stony
earth, substrate of varietal
earth, tang of
earth, tastes of the
earth, tobacco-
earth...cured meat and game, wild feral aromas of
earth...good fruit and acidity like a shadow...it doesn't hit you over the head
earthbound
earth-driven personality
earth-driven than fruity, more
earthiness and lightness, interesting contradiction of
earthiness and suaveness, blend of
earthiness, almondlike
earthiness, chocolaty
earthiness, complex/earthy complexity
earthiness, dusty
earthiness, elusive
earthiness, farmyard/rustic
earthiness, full of
earthiness, indescribable
earthiness, intoxicating
earthiness, leathery
earthiness, mesmerizing
earthiness, mushroomy

earthiness, peppery
earthiness, pleasing
earthiness, red clay
earthiness, robust/earthy robustness
earthiness, rugged
earthiness, savory
earthiness, soulful fruity
earthiness, soul-stirring
earthiness, sun-ripened
earthiness, sweet fleshy
earthiness, telltale
earthiness, tilled-soil
earthiness, truffle/truffley/truffle-oil/trufflelike
earthiness, unbridled
earthiness, wholesome
earthlike, fresh damp
earth-raisiny
earth-sweet
earthtone(d)(s)
earthy African twist
earthy and animal flavors, treasure chest of smoky...
earthy angle
earthy aromas bursts up at you with the force of a tub of salad dressing opened at 21,000 feet
earthy aromas, expressive
earthy aromas, hypnotic
earthy as a coalmine, as
earthy astringency
earthy austerity
earthy backbone
earthy base notes
earthy brusqueness
earthy concoction
earthy draught
earthy edge
earthy extract
earthy facets
earthy foliage, cranberry lurking beneath the
earthy forest-floor funk
earthy framework
earthy funk, pleasingly
earthy funk, touch of
earthy funkiness that somehow stirs the soul
earthy heft
earthy integrity
earthy meatiness, extra depth of
earthy notions, sweet
earthy nuances, dark
earthy oddness
earthy overlay
earthy perfume
earthy personality

earthy peaty notes as those wafting from a water-treatment plant
earthy pong
earthy rawness
earthy regional inflections, meaty-
earthy richness, almost
earthy ripeness, sun-baked
earthy robustness
earthy smells, sweet
earthy soil
earthy sort of way
earthy spiciness
earthy spicy undercurrents
earthy spirit, attractively
earthy splendor
earthy stink, fabulous
earthy streak
earthy stuff, wild
earthy substrate, faintly
earthy tang
earthy taste
earthy timbre, unmistakable
earthy truffley streak
earthy underbrush
earthy underlay, regional
earthy underpinnings
earthy undertones
earthy vein
earthy volcanic burnt flavors
earthy wallop, packs an
earthy we're-not-in-Kansas-anymore nose, slightly funky
earthy wild-ferment influence
earthy, cleanly
earthy, decidedly
earthy, erotically
earthy, musty-
earthy, notably
earthy, plummy-
earthy, surprisingly
earthy-animal density
earthy-broody
earthy-curranty
earthy-herb *mélange*
earthy-irony/-metallic/-minerally/-steely
earthy-leathery
earthy-moldy
earthy-raspberry
earthy-spicy
earthy-sweaty
earthy-sweet
earthy-truffley
earthy-volcanic
elegance, fluid
eucalyptus gum
eucalyptus, savory
evergreens, minty

extraterrestrial
fall, stroll in late
farm on the breeze, faintest funky scents of a
farm, Old MacDonald's
farm, peach
farmyard richness
farmyard stench
farmyard, delicious pongy
farmyardy-*terroir* edge
ferns, damp
ferns, dried
ferns, French
ferns, scented
ferns, singed
ferrous/ferruginous
ferrous edge, rusty
ferrous, almost
field in bloom
field of sweet black earth after a spring rain, like standing in the middle of a
field on a sunny August day, open
field, Bangkok paddy
field, like standing in a hot sunny
field, new-mown
field, open
field, soccer
field, verdant
field, warm summer
fill
fire, autumn
fire, dung
flagstones
flint striking steel
flint-edged vibrancy
flintily elegant
flintiness/flints, smoky
flints and minerals to the max
flints, chiseled
flints, lick of
flints, rubbed
flints, stony
flints, struck
flintstones, warm
flinty and aromatic to the hilt
flinty it could start a fire, so
flinty pebbly dryness
flinty, wickedly
flinty-oaky
floor, dirt cellar
forest (tree bark-earth-leaf), smells like a
forest after a spring rain/shower
forest aromas, *mélange* of
forest characteristics
forest floor with fungi

forest floor, like lying face-down on a
forest floor, mulchy
forest floor, organic
forest floor, wet
forest glade
forest in early morning, dewy pine
forest on a misty autumn day, walk through the
forest on a warm day, Jeffrey pine
forest stroll, like going on a
forest underbrush after the rain
forest with all of its moist and ripe scents, autumn
forest, autumn/autumnal
forest, clean
forest, damp/wet
forest, deep
forest, like walking through a sun-baked pine
forest, mushroom
forest, pine
forest, rain
forest, rain-wet beech
forest, rainy wet autumn
forest, spruce
forest, sweet
forest, transports you straight into some deep autumnal
forest, walk in a pine
forest, walk in/through the
forest, walk through a dry
foresty aromas, clean
foresty mysteries
foresty notes, nice
foxtail
frankincense, hypnotic perfume of smoldering
fresh, clean-
fresh, dewy
fresh, summer-
freshness, leafy
fronds, fine-snipped
frosted/frosty
frozen
fungals, funky
fungal-to-barnyard
fungal-truffle
fungal-vegetal
fungi, fresh
fungi, nasty
fungi, old
funkiness, scuppernong
ganja
garden after a rain, dry
garden of blackberries, virtual
garden, Persian
garden, spring

garden, walk in an overgrown
garden, walk through a damp
garden's worth of aromas, herb
garrique, roasted
glacial
gold embedded in flint
golf course
good/goodish
gorse baking on a parched heath
grain, rough-hewn
grain, toasted
grains, raw/uncooked
granite hardness
granite, carved from a single block of
granite, frail lilies blessed with permanence of
granite, liquid
granite, powdered
granite, stonylike
granite, warm
granite-edged
granite-rough
granitelike as any mason could wish for, as
grapevines
graphite
grass at home, green green
grass clippings/cuttings
grass cuttings steaming away on the compost heap
grass growing through piles of stone, random patches of
grass on a sunny day, fresh-mown
grass with a smattering of dandelions
grass, bales of green
grass, cut green
grass, cut/mown
grass, dried
grass, fresh sea
grass, garden-fresh
grass, just-cut/newly mown
grass, lawn
grass, lightly stewed
grass, marram (coastal)
grass, meadow
grass, sourish
grass, sun-warmed
grass, wild
grass...nettles and the whole wild garden on a dewy spring morning
grasses...leaves and other things green, handful of crushed
grassiness of the savannah
grassiness, lean
grassiness, questionable

grassiness, subtle
grassiness, varietal
grassiness, youthful
grassy antidote
grassy aromas, slightly catty-
grassy around the edges, somewhat
grassy as a newly mown football
  field, as lean and
grassy penetration
grassy pungency
grassy undercurrent, somewhat
grassy zip
grassy!, boy: talk about
grassy...green and fresh as a well-
  watered garden, as
gravel road, rain-wet
gravel, hot
gravel, liquid/wet
gravel, sun-baked/-drenched
gravel-flavored
gravel-laden
gravelly and stony
gravelly streak
gravitational force, unrivalled
green growing things
green joy
green meanies
green tang, characteristic
green tang, zippy
greenery, smells of
greenness, mistier
greens, flowershop
grit/gritty
ground cover
ground, damp
ground, from hallowed
ground it comes from, seems to
  have drawn flavors out of the
grove in full bloom, smells like a
  bergamot orange
grove of oranges, whole
grove, Florida citrus
grove, olive
grove, walnut
groves of Sicily with the car roof
  down, like driving through the
  lemon
groves on hot hillsides, pine
gumleaf/gumleafy
gunflint, puff of
gunflint, smoky
hail
hailstorm, as shocking and as
  disconcerting as running naked
  in a
hawthorn
hay bales
hay in a summer barn

hay in the haymaking season
hay on a hot summer day, bale of
hay seeds
hay spices
hay, classic apple
hay, cured meadow
hay, cut/mown
hay, damp/wet
hay, dry
hay, dusty
hay, fresh
hay, fresh-cut
hay, freshly mowed/new-mown
hay, green
hay, loft-dried
hay, moldy
hay, pale
hay, rotting
hay, sun-dried
hay, sweet
hay, warm
hay, wet moldy
hayride through a citrus orchard
  on a sunny day
haystack
hazel, witch
heather, rich scented
heather, singed
heather, wet
hedge, box
hedgerow pungency, full of
hedgerow, baked
hedgerows in spring
hedgerows, divine
hiking, like
hills, wildflower-and herb-laden
hillsides, rugged rocky
hole, vinous black
honeycomb fresh from a hive
hoplike/hoppish/hoppy/hops
hot
humid
humus/humusy
humus, decomposing
husks
ice/iced/icy
iron and minerals, complex
iron core, solid
iron nuance
iron ore
iron tonic
iron underpinned by licorice
iron, core of
iron, fragment of rusty
iron, rich in
iron-earth
ironstone
iron-tobacco

islands, tropical
ivy mixed with wild strawberries,
  ground
ivy, old
jungle/jungly
juniper, wild
jute
landscape, all the delicacy and
  refinement of a
landscape, liquid distillate of the
landscape, roasted
laurel, bay
lava, new
lava: warm...smoldering and
  tongue-tingling, flows over the
  tongue like apologetic
lavender, wild
lawn, as fresh as a dew-covered
lawn, freshly mown summer
lawn, just-mowed
lawn, like dancing on the
lawn, like mowing the
lead
lead, dried
leaf aggression: green through and
  through...green apples...green
  peas...green lime zest...all sharp
  as knives to scrape your tongue
  clean, green
leaf funk, rotting-
leaf litter
leaf, misted tobacco
leaf mold
leaf pile, autumn
leafiness, velvet
leafy floor
leafy freshness
leafy greenness, nice
leafy nuances
leafy, moist and
leafy-alcoholic
leafy-cassis
leafy-chlorophylly
leafy-figgy
leafy-fresh
leafy-mulberry
leatherwood
leaves and mice, crushed up with
leaves in autumn, pile of damp
leaves in the fall, wet
leaves just starting to turn brown
  and drop, late-autumn
leaves rotting on the forest floor
leaves turning yellow in fall, green
leaves underfoot
leaves, attractive tea
leaves, autumn/autumnal
leaves, brown

leaves, bruised/crushed
leaves, burning autumn
leaves, burnt/smoldering
leaves, caramel-coated autumn
leaves, cigar tobacco
leaves, clover
leaves, cold tea
leaves, crushed citrus
leaves, crushed geranium
leaves, crushed lemon/lime
leaves, crushed vine
leaves, currant
leaves, damp
leaves, damp autumn
leaves, dead
leaves, decaying autumn
leaves, decaying dry
leaves, dried autumn
leaves, dried/dry
leaves, elder
leaves, eucalypt
leaves, fall/turning
leaves, fallen
leaves, fresh raspberry
leaves, fresh tobacco
leaves, geranium
leaves, grape
leaves, green
leaves, gum
leaves, Havana
leaves, ivy
leaves, Kaffir lime
leaves, lime
leaves, plum tomato
leaves, raw tobacco
leaves, rotting
leaves, rubbed black currant
leaves, scented blackberry
leaves, spicy tobacco
leaves, spiky green
leaves, sweet decaying
leaves, tea
leaves, tomato plant
leaves, walnut
leaves, withered autumn
lichen
light
light, cool wet sand under
    pearly seaside
lightstruck
lime grass
lime, powdered
limestone, crushed
loam, sweet
lunar eclipse, big dark
luxuriant
mallowy, not
maquis

maquis on a warm summer wind,
    scents of the
marble quarries
marble-smooth
marijuana
marsh/marshy
marshy nightmare
matter, decaying
meadow after the rain, scents of a
meadow in spring, lush green
meadow inhabited by of-age
    nymphs, alpine
meadow, alpine
meadow, dappled
meadow, picnic in a
meadow, spring
meadow
midnight: dark…quiet…
    impenetrable
mineral ash
mineral as if you struck two rocks
together to create a spark,
    assertively
mineral austerity
mineral bath
mineral carpet under the surface,
    handsome
mineral character, ironlike
mineral character, telltale
mineral cobblestones
mineral complexities in its
    fiery core
mineral cut, indelible
mineral dust swirling about
mineral edge, fine-tuned
mineral edge, pleasantly bitter
mineral edge, unmistakable
mineral element, darker
mineral etching, nice
mineral flavors evoke earth and
    sun, profound
mineral flavors like pumping iron
mineral flavors, coal mine of
mineral flavors, silk road of
mineral foundation, robust
mineral oil flavors jet from glass to
    palate, fount of
mineral piquancy, good
mineral pit
mineral power, slow
mineral profundity
mineral salts, strong
mineral savor, deep
mineral shards pierce the pillow of
    ripe mangosteens and
    pineapples, fragile
mineral solidity
mineral spine

mineral streak, firm
mineral streak, flinty
mineral tang
mineral the bottle should be heavy
    to lift, so heavily
mineral underpinning, firm
mineral underside, ashlike
mineral underside, dark
mineral undertones
mineral varietal
mineral, flick of
mineral, limy-
mineral, malic acid edge of
mineral-charged
mineral-citrus tang, real
mineral-drenched
mineral-driven
mineral-flecked
mineral-infused
minerality, like licking the lava off
    the slope of an active volcano
minerality, almost muscular in its
    acidity and
minerality, almost salty
minerality, basso continuo of
minerality, brass-knuckled punch
    of
minerality, brassy
minerality, chalklike/chalky
minerality, clayish
minerality, cleansing
minerality, club-sodalike
minerality, crammed with iron-
    steel flavors that segue into a
    magnificent
minerality, deep/formidable/
    massive/muscular/profound
minerality, dusty
minerality, earthbound clayish
minerality, encrusted by black
    diamondlike
minerality, flourish of
minerality, fortifying
minerality, gemlike
minerality, granite quarry's
    worth of
minerality, graphite-dark
minerality, graphitelike
minerality, honeyed
minerality, intense
minerality, liquid
minerality, lively tumult of
    apricots…honeysuckle and fresh
minerality, lovely
minerality, lovely rainwater-over-
    rocks
minerality, magnificent
minerality, mountain

minerality, oyster shell
minerality, peppery
minerality, pungent lingering
minerality, quinine
minerality, salty
minerality, sea-breeze
minerality, seashell-like
minerality, smoky
minerality, spine of
minerality, steely delicate core of
minerality, stone wall of
minerality, stony
minerality, subtle
minerality, tangy
minerality, thrilling
minerality, underlying bedrock
minerality, unmistakable
minerality, Vichy-waterlike
minerality, virtually breathes
minerality, well-etched
minerality, wet-rock
minerality, zesty
mineral-laced/-laden
minerally as a mouthful of rocks, as
minerally as to be built of stone, so
minerally bones, nice flesh on its
minerally frame, lean
minerally nugget of perfection,
   tender
minerally restraint
minerally thrust, steely-
minerally underpinning, firm
minerally, vividly
minerally-fruity
mineral-propelled
minerals and a hint of cream,
   underpinning of
minerals and citrus, palate-
   whetting
minerals and earth awash in sweet
   lemons
minerals and stones, tangy
minerals as dazzling as diamonds
minerals awash in sweet peach
   juice, smoky
minerals dark as black diamonds
minerals do the talking here
minerals immersed in white
   chocolate
minerals of the sea, all the
minerals slice across the palate like
   a well-honed blade, citrus and
minerals tether it to the earth
minerals that feel like lace
minerals to build a mountain,
   enough

minerals which seems to have been
   mined from the bowels of the
   earth, core of
minerals, army of
minerals, Aussie-style
minerals, baked
minerals, balletic display of
   fruit...spice and
minerals, beautifully etched
   flowers and
minerals, beauty in black: black
   fruit...black smoke and black
   bitter
minerals, bitter
minerals, blast/jolt/punch of
minerals, body-slams of
minerals, bursting at the seams
   with spices and liquid
minerals, buttered/buttery
minerals, candied liquid
minerals, caramelized
minerals, carbonlike
minerals, charred
minerals, chiseled
minerals, chock-full of
minerals, citrus encased in
minerals, citrus juice-covered
minerals, coal-like
minerals, concentrated
minerals, creamed/creamy
minerals, crunchy
minerals, dancing on a bed of
minerals, dark
minerals. dissolved
minerals, earthy
minerals, emperor's ransom of
   gleaming
minerals, festival of
minerals, fruity
minerals, glittery
minerals, highly polished
minerals, high-octane
minerals, honeyed
minerals, impressive framework of
minerals, initial taut slash of
minerals, intense liquid
minerals, laced with salty
minerals, lemon-drenched/
   -infused/-soaked
minerals, lime-drenched
minerals, lip-smacking
minerals, liquid
minerals, luminescent
minerals, miner's depth of
minerals, mine's/quarry's worth of
minerals, notion of
minerals, nuggets of

minerals, on gossamer wings of
minerals, palate-cleansing
minerals, perfumed
minerals, polished blocks of dark
   fruit cemented with
minerals, powdered
minerals, practically dripping with
minerals, prickly
minerals, profound
minerals, rainwater-fresh
minerals, rich dried honey-laced
minerals, riveting
minerals, salty
minerals, sappy
minerals, sea of
minerals, silky
minerals, slick bed of
minerals, smoking
minerals, smoky liquid
minerals, sparked with
minerals, spoonfuls of inky
minerals, sports an armor of dark
minerals, steely spine of
minerals, stony
minerals, sugarcoated
minerals, sultry smoky
minerals, sun-baked
minerals, sweetened tea-laced
minerals, talclike
minerals, tingly
minerals, toasted
minerals, treasure chest of
minerals, undertow of
minerals, wall of
minerals, wheelbarrows of peppery
minerals, white chocolate-covered
minerals, underside of
mineral-scented
mineral-*spritzig*
mineral-starred sky
mineral-steely framework
miniearthquake
minty
moist
mold and wild fruit of the forest
molten
moon, seemed to come from the
morning, as fresh and cutting as an
   early spring
morning, as lively and fresh as a
   spring
moss on a rolling stone, Spanish
moss, cool
moss, damp oak
moss, sweet
moss, tree-
moss, wet ground-

moss, wet tree-
mossy dampness
mountain fresh
mountain, built like a/
  mountainlike
mountain stream-pure art

mud

mud flats, exposed
mulberries
mulberry and myrrh infused with
  notes of pine and frankincense,
  mesmerizing combination of
mulch that's underfoot in a wood,
  gunky
mulch, bark
mulch, composting
mulch, leaf
mulchy funk, nice bass note of
myrrh
myrtle
nard/nardine/spikenard
natural world, more than a subtle
  summary of the
natural yeast
nature gone wild
nature, little gift of
nature, miracle of
nettle aggression
nettle-fresh
nettle intensity, stinging-
nettle/bee-sting character
nettles crushed up with black
  currants
nettles growing on a compost heap
nettles violently slashed at with a
  stick
nettles, crushed
nettles, dusty
nettles, green
nettles, stinging
nettles, trampled stinging
nettles, unpleasant
nettles, white dead
nettles, young
nettley, zingy-
night, embrace of a tropical
nights, moist summer
nuggetlike
ocean air
ocean breezes
ocean floor, as deep as the
ocean spray
ocean swell, rolls across the palate
  like a giant
ocean, dip in the
ocean, gentle
oceanic
oil, hard unforgiving volcanic

orchard in mid-July, like walking
  through a cherry
orchard, breeze through a cherry
orchard, like walking through an
  apple
orchard, like walking through a
  ripe peach
orchard-fresh
organic
organically wholesome
orrisroot
otherworldly
outdoor pleasure, mature
outdoorsy
overheated
ozone tang
parched
pasture, cool
patch in a eucalyptus grove next to
  a coal mine, berry
patch, berry
patch, pumpkin
peat smoke
peat, singed
peat/peaty
peaty notes as those wafting from a
  water-treatment plant, earthy
pebbles at the bottom of a stream,
  as cool and smooth as
pebbles on a stream bottom
pebbles, dry creek
pebbles, fruity
pebbles, minerally hot
pebbles, rain-wet
pebbly-stony
perfumed
petrichor/petrichoric
pinecones, dusty
place, a sense of
place, ephemeral sense of
place, telling originality
  and truth to

planet, from another

plant material, whiff of
plantation-fresh
plants, dried
plants, forest
plants, marshy/swampy
plants, tomato
plants, water meadow
plants, wild
plenty
plowed
pondy
pools, tidal
pot
powerful
prairie, wind over the barren

prickliness, thistlelike

primordial

pristine
privet, wet
pyrogenic
quartz and tangerine flavors have
  never tasted so good together
quartz, citrus juice-covered
quartz, crystalline
quartz, fine
quartz, lemony
quartz, mineral
quartz, powdered
quartzlike flavors, crystalline
ragweed
rain on a gravelly road, summer
rain showers, fall
rain, as thirst-quenching as a spring
rainforest with all its exotic
  flowers, tropical
rainstorm, summer
rain-soaked
reediness/reedy
regional
reseda
rich
rills
river, green
roasted/roasty
rock dust
rock face...the taste does not offer
  any handholds, like a
rock quarry
rock, as firm/hard as a
rock, powdered
rocks in the rain, river
rocks, as minerally as a mouthful of
rocks, avalanche of falling
rocks, damp/wet
rocks, dusty
rocks, like stumbling into a patch
  of wildflowers among the
rocks, mouthful of
rocks, primitive
rocks, scorched
rocks, seaside
rocks, squeezed from sweet black
rocks, sun-baked
rocks, violets growing through a
  bed of
rocky-minerally
rootlike, vegetal-
roots, infused
roots, Spanish
roots/rootlike/rooty
rosemary, wild
rust
rye

sagebrush/sagebrushy
saline
salinity of breathing fresh littoral air
salt-mineral-metal
saltwater
salty tang
salty-minerally-metallic
sand, beach
sands that buried their old outside facilities, as red and dry as the southern
sand under pearly seaside light, cool wet
sandstone-mineral, crushed
sappy character, gorgeously
schist
schist that explodes out of the fruit, shower of broken
scorched
scrub, herbal/herby
scrub, piquant Mediterranean
scrub, wild herbal
scrubland, *garrique*
scrubland, Mediterranean
sea
sea and sun
sea brine/sea-briny
sea foam, unusual but seductive nose of

sea notes, erotic with its

sea scents such as seaweed...oyster shells and fishy Pinot Noir, dominated by
sea spray, fresh tangy
sea, decadent cold nose of
sea, expressive of the
sea, saline minerally scents of the
sea, tang of the
sea, wild whiff of the
sea...hot pebbles...sackcloth, calm
sea-air fresh
sea breeze, refreshing and salty
sea breeze, marine
seas, southern
sea-saltiness, shellfish
seaside
sea-splashed
seawater, cold
seawater, fresh
seaweed on the beach
seaweed, fragrant
seaweedy
secluded/seclusive
sedate
shades
shale
shoots, bracken

shoots, dry vine
shoots, pea
shrubbery, desert
silage/silagelike
silex
silica
silt/silty
silty on the tongue
singed
sky
slate foundation, solid
slate interest
slate spine, extraordinary
slate, complex
slate, deeply anchored in red
slate, dissolved
slate, fresh
slate, regional powdery
slate, sobering
slate, wet
slate-petroleum, liquid
slatiness, curious
slatiness, pencil
slatiness, tremendous
smoke wrapped in loam, hickory
smoke, barbecue
smoke, flint
smoke, peat
smoke, pure hickory
smoky beast, strange and
snow and sea
snow, as clean as fresh-fallen
snow, fresh
snowfall, as seamless as a
snowflakes
soapstone
sod farm
sod, rustic
soft
soggy
soil and stone cloak its finish
soil and stone, essence of
soil leaves some clear fingerprints
soil of the hills

soil on the nose

soil tones, distinctive
soil, arid/dry
soil, big dollop of
soil, chalky
soil, cherry
soil, damp/moist
soil, dark fertile
soil, deep moist clay
soil, fertile damp
soil, fresh dark sweet rich
soil, freshly plowed
soil, freshly tilled
soil, great deal of

soil, hot/warm
soil, layers of flavors rest on dark rich
soil, like drinking chalk
soil, loam-/loamy
soil, mineral-rich
soil, moist black
soil, pure potting
soil, red
soil, rich
soil, rocky
soil, secret memories of the
soil, smacks of the
soil, sweet
soil, tilled
soil, Tuscan
soil, underlay/underpinning of
soil, volcanic
soil, wet forest
soil-dirt
soils, pure expression of the stony
somewhereness, exhibits a sense of
sorghum
space, almost a vinous black hole in
spiky character
spring morning, as fresh as a
spring, as fresh as a mountain
spring, contains the fragrances of
spring, has a feeling of
spring, ode to
springs, hot

spring-summer fling

springtime radiance
springtime, breath of
springtime, as fresh as
sprites, tree
sprites, woodland
stalks, mulched geranium
stalky, in no way
stalky, quite
stems, berry
stems, brown
stems, fresh-picked grape
stems, green
stems, mature
stone cloak its finish, soil and
stone field after a rain
stone minerality, clean wet-
stone juice, expression of sunlight transformed into
stone, core of
stone, essence of soil and
stone, honeyed crushed
stone, like biting into a ripe peach with a pit of
stone, polished
stone, powdered
stone, quarry's worth of

stone, slab of pure
stone, underlined by
stone-dusty
stone-infused/-laden
stonelike elements
stones after a brief hailstorm/rain,
   wet
stones baked and scorched all
   summer long, shimmering heat
   of broad flat
stones baking in the sun
stones in a mountain stream,
   water running over
stones just dancing and bouncing
   around in my mouth like a rock
   tumbler, blue
stones on summer evenings, warm
stones that sprouted some moss,
   wet
stones, as firm as
stones, awash with
stones, bed of
stones, creamy
stones, crisp
stones, crushed
stones, damp/dampish/wet/wetted
stones, distinctive undercurrent of
stones, ferrous
stones, grilled/roasted
stones, ground
stones, heated
stones, hot wet
stones, intense heat on
stones, liquid
stones, lively
stones, melted
stones, muted
stones, powdered
stones, sculpted from
stones, seems to be built of
stones, smoldering
stones, sun-baked/-warmed
stones, tons of
stones, washed
stones, wet quartz
stones, wild herbs and flowers
   pushing their way through a
   mountain of
stone-scented
stoniness, blackboard-chalklike
stoniness, granite
stoniness, saline
stoniness, succulent
stony aspect, marked
stony core
stony earth
stony gunflint aspect is
   superpresent

stony keynote
stony soils, pure expression of the
stony stringency
stony *terroir*
stony wine, amazingly smooth for
   such a
stony zinger
stony, profoundly
stony-...lemon-...violet-lined path
stony...like granite
stony-peachy
storm, as intense as a tropical
storm, Pacific
stormy...like the night, dark and
storm wine, dark
straw, barley
straw, bitter
straw, clean
straw, damp/wet
straw, elegant/opulent
straw, malty
straw, medicinal old
straw, oat
straw, rich old
straw, rotten/rotting
straw, slightly cheesy damp
straw, sour
straw, sweet
straw, warm
straw-apricot
strawish, dry and
stream that could one day become
   a long peaceful river, good
   mountain
stream, as fresh and clear as a
   mountain
stream, as pure as an alpine
stream, as refreshing as a mountain
subterranean and extraterrestrial
   at the same time
subtle
sugarcane, smoky
sulfur/sulfuric/sulfurous/sulfury
sumac, bitter/sour
summer all of a sudden, feels like
summer evenings, warm stones on
summer in a glass, late
summer in the country
summer walk through a botanic
   grove
summer, early
summer, entire
summer, harbinger of
summer, recalls late
summer, smells like/summery-
   smelling
summertime in a bottle, sweet
   warm

summertime in Hungary
sun and earth, primal flavors of
sun and mellowness, radiates
sun in a bottle
sun setting over a vanilla sea,
   caramel
sun through the ripples, glint of
   cool
sun, captured the rays of the
sun, fun in the
sun, hot
sun-baked feel
sunburnt
sun-dried
sun-filled
sun-gorged
sunlight in a glass
sunlight transformed into stone
   juice, expression of
sunripe wealth
sunset
sunset, summer holiday
sunshine in a bottle/glass
sunshine in your glass, beautiful
   rays of summer
sunshine slurper
sunshine, autumn
sunshine, blessed by California
sunshine, bright
sunshine, captures warm
sunshine, full of
sunshine, golden
sunshine, Mediterranean
sunshine, reflected
sunshine, sweet
sunshine, tastes like
sunstruck
suntanned
superearthy
supersunny
swamp thing
Swamp, overtones of the Great
   Dismal
sweet, rich
sylvan
tectonic
terebinth
terra firma
terrestrial qualities, deep
territory, clear expression of its
territory, profoundly expressive of
   its
territory to perfection,
   interprets the
terroir covers fruit like a slab of
   marble
terroir-driven
terroir edge, farmyardy

terroir freshness, oozing with
terroir includes the human touch
terroir is overwhelming, specificity of
terroir made liquid, great
terroir or crapoir?
terroir speaking, prime example of
terroir *toujours*
terroir well, shows its
terroir, accentuates its special
terroir, barely transcends its
terroir, clearly transcends its
terroir, completely transparent vehicle for its
terroir, definite impression of
terroir, distinct kiss of
terroir, dramatic vehicle for its
terroir, example of technology-enhancing
terroir, exceptional ability to communicate
terroir, full of
terroir, good representative of its
terroir, *goût de*
terroir, great sense of/greatest
terroir, honest expression of an honored
terroir, magnificent/phenomenal expression of
terroir, ideally embodies
terroir, likeable
terroir, lot of French-tasting
terroir, manages not to distort the characteristics of its
terroir, pinnacle of
terroir, real

terroir, real song of the

terroir, rich
terroir, sense of class and
terroir, sophisticated reflection of the
terroir, stony
terroir, sunny
terroir, unmistakable
terroir, vegetal
terroir, warm
terroir-driven, very
terroir-engineered
terroir-expressive
territory, rigorous sense of belonging to a
thistle
thunder, completely brings the
thunderclap on a hot autumn evening
thunderclap wine
thunderstorm in the distance, rumbling

thunderstorm, comes thundering along like an imminent
thunderstorm, distant
tidal/tidal pool
tilled, freshly
tinny edges
titanium core, beguiling

toadstools

toasted-roasted/toasty-roasty
tobacco oil
tobacco road, stroll down
tobacco scents, all sorts of rich
tobacco smoke
tobacco wisps
tobacco, blond Cuban
tobacco, chewing/chewy
tobacco, cigarette
tobacco, Connecticut
tobacco, cured
tobacco, damp/moist/wet
tobacco, dried pipe
tobacco, dry
tobacco, fresh-cut
tobacco, gramp's pipe
tobacco, green
tobacco, Havana
tobacco, high-quality
tobacco, humidor-like
tobacco, leafy
tobacco, light
tobacco, nuances of
tobacco, old
tobacco, ripened
tobacco, roasted
tobacco, rustic
tobacco, singed
tobacco, slightly stewed
tobacco, stale
tobacco, sweet cigar
tobacco, sweet golden
tobacco, sweet pipe
tobacco, uncured
tobacco, unsmoked
tobacco, Virginia
tobacco, weedy
tobacco, white
tobacco, wild
tobacco-cedary polish
tobaccoey, plummy-
tobacco-tinged ferocity
topsoil
trees in tobacco field by barnyard, cherry
trees, towering evergreen
tropical-jungle
turbulence
turf, fresh
turned, freshly

twigs and bark in the mouth and nose
twigs and bushes, flesh covering Italianate
twigs, boiled
twigs, damp
twigs, dried
twigs, forest
twigs, green
twigs, snapped
underbrush after rain
underbrush, Mediterranean
underbrush, primal
underbrush, sweet
underbrush/underbrushy
undergrowth, alpine
undergrowth, autumnal
undergrowth, chocolate
undergrowth, damp
undergrowth, foresty/woodsy
undergrowth, funky organic forest
undergrowth, mossy
undergrowth, thorny
undergrowth, like walking through dense damp
unearthly
unwashed

valley smells

vegetal complexity, intriguing
vegetal richness, gorgeous
vegetal, disgustingly/unpleasantly
vegetal-bacterial
vegetality still civilized
vegetality, complex
vegetality, concentrated
vegetality, creamy
vegetality, under-ripe
vegetation, bruised
vegetation, decaying/rotting
vegetation, lake
vegetation, rain-forest
vegetation, singed
vegetation-laced
verdant as spring, as
verdant crispness
verdant, positively
verdure
verge
vine blossoms/vines in bloom
vine character, deep old
vines, ancient/old
vines, crushed tomato
vines, green
vines, tomato
vines, young
volcano of flavors
volcanic oil, hard unforgiving
volcanic spiciness

volcanic twang
volcanic soils, expressive of its
volcano, smoldering
warm
warm-crumply-rich
warmth of the Provençal summer
water and fresh seawater, fresh
water from a rusty pipe, brackish
water mist
water on your face on a hot day,
    splash/spriz of cold
water running over gray pebbles,
    clear
water with a high iron content,
    health spa
water with some wood added
water, bubbling crystal-clear spring
water, flute by still
water, fresh river
water, pond
water, running river
water, sea
water, spring
water, stagnant/stale
water, turtle
waters of the Danube, chilly
    glassine
watery
waves crashing on a sandy beach
weed ditch, Nebraska
weeds, dried
weeds, faint onion
weeds, green
weeds, roadside
weeds, sour
weeds, wet
weedy, slightly
weedy-woodsy
wet place
wheat, blown
wheat, dry
wheat, ripe
wheat, sun-roasted
wheatgrass
wild
wilderness, charming sense of
wild perfumes, movingly
wind from a raspberry patch,
    puffs of
wind in your hair
wind off the sea
wind over the barren prairie
wind with refreshing and cooling
    elements, summer
wind, autumn
winds, waft of sea-splashed
windsurfing, day of
winter, fine antidote to

witch hazel
woad
wood, deep
woodiness, rustic
woodland thoughts
woodland, damp
woods on a crisp fall day,
    walk in the
woods, autumn
woods, fungus-filled
woods, hot evergreen
woods, lumberjack in the
woods, tramps in the dry
woodsy-weedy
world with every sip, summons up
    a precise corner of the
wort, St. John's

The earth laughs in flowers.
e.e. cummings

A weed is no more than a flower in disguise.
Anonymous

Wine is the flower in the buttonhole of civilization.
Werumeus Buning

13. Flower

Is there the scent of a flower on earth that someone hasn't sniffed in wine? If so, it has eluded this listing. Apparently, wine makes many of us think of flowers, which isn't all that unusual when you realize that a vine must flower in order to produce the fruit we call grapes, and grapes must ripen in order to produce .... R-i-g-h-t.

acacia blossoms/flowers/petals
alpine
anemone
apple blossoms blown in the wind
apple blossoms, breezy
apple blossoms, ethereal
apple petals
apricot blossoms
astilbe
autumn
azalea
basket, Easter
bloom, as exuberant as a garden
    approaching full
bloom, garden in full
bloom, in full/blooming
blooms, full-blown
blossoms, all the spring
blossoms, light
blossoms, perfumed spring
blossoms, wet
blossoms, white
blossoms, wilted
blossomy fresh
blue
bouquet stolen from someone's
    grave, faded
bouquet, Edenic
bouquet-flooded
bowers
broom blossoms/flowers/petals
bunches
buttercups, dewy
camellias
carnations

chamomile, perfumed
cherries, flowering
chrysanthemums
cicely, sweet
citrus blossoms/flowers/petals
citrus grove during blossom time,
    breezy walk through a
clematis, white
columbine
cornflowers, purple
crocuses, vibrant yellow
crushed
currant blossoms/petals, black
currant buds, crushed black
currants, budding black
currants, flowering
cut, assorted freshly
cut, fresh-/freshly/new-/newly
cyclamen
daffodils, carpet of
dahlias
daisies, fresh-/freshly picked
daphne
dawn, at
daylilies, voluptuous perfume of
decaying
dried, old and
dying
echinacea
eglantines
elder blossoms/flowers/petals
elderflowers, appley
eucalyptus, midnight
eucalyptus, soothing
faded/fading

fall
field
floral arrangement, minimalist
floral as a bed of rose petals, as
floral cherry
floral depths, haunting
floral elderflowerlike
floral elegance
floral elements
floral flair, exotic
floral flavors, diamond-crusted bed
    of irresistible tropical and
floral flavors, ethereal
floral flavors, flirtatious
floral flavors, head-dizzying
floral flavors, piccolo of
floral half-furious pepper tree, half-
floral note growing amidst the
    blades of grass, lovely
floral notes, dusty
floral notes, exotic (orchids)
floral notes, showered with
floral perfume, unmistakable
floral quality, hoplike
floral scents, draped in a
    diaphanous sheet of
floral scents, lacy veil of
floral things, limy
floral tropical phenolic profile,
    overly
floral, hauntingly
floral, oily-
floral, politely
floral, uncommonly
florality, mass of

florality, sensuous
florid charm
florist's range of aromas
flower dance on the palate,
    fruit-and-
flower garden, heady
flower garden, spring
flower opening, like a
flower petals, as gentle as a
    butterfly brushing
flower water, decaying
flower which blooms every year in
    memory of an eternal love,
    smooth and eternal like the
    nameless
flower, springtime garden's every
flower-filled personality
flower-fragranced/-scented
floweriness, explosive
    indescribable
floweriness, haunting
floweriness, indescribable
floweriness, superficial
flower-infused
flowering cherries
flowering currants
flowers and excrement, combo of
flowers and fruit of the garden, all
flowers and minerals, beautifully
    etched
flowers at dawn
flowers engulf you, fruit and
flowers in bloom
flowers in the spring, bouquet of
flowers in your mouth, slow-
    blooming
flowers of the garden were present
    in the almost narcotically
    seductive bouquet, all the
flowers of the garden, all the
flowers underlaid with fresh grass
flowers, alcohol-steeped
flowers, assorted freshly cut
flowers, assorted sugarcoated white
    bastard flowers
flowers, blast-wave of white
flowers, blue
flowers, bouquet of lovely pressed
flowers, bunches of
flowers, fields of spring
flowers, garden full of
flowers, glass of little green apples
    and lemon
flowers, litany of fruit and
flowers, meadow
flowers, mushrooms among the
flowers, pronounced scents of
flowers, sea of

flowers, white hedgerow
flowers, without
flower-scented
flowery as a bride's bouquet, as
flowery charms
flowery pong
flowery undertone
flowery, dashingly
flowery, piquant-
frangipani
freesia blossoms/flowers/petals
fresh/freshly cut
fugitive
full
garden/gardenful
gardenia petal sandwich
gardenias/gardenia-scented
gardens of the Hôtel du Cap,
    smells like the
gentian
geranium blossoms/flowers/petals
geraniums, green
geraniums, peppery
geraniums, rose
geraniums, white
gillyflowers
good/goodish
grape blossoms/flowers/petals
hawthorn blossoms/flowers/petals
heartsease
heather in bloom
heather in flower when the sun is
    on it, whiffs of
hedgerow blossoms
hedgerow, white
heliotrope
hibiscus
hollyhocks
honeyed
honeysuckle and fresh minerality,
    lively tumult of apricots...
honeysuckle blossoms/flowers
honeysuckle, flickery
hyacinths
innocent
irises
jasmine, star
jonquils
lantana, quasi-
larkspur
lavender in bloom
lavender, as ethereal as
lavender, demure
lavender, garlands of
lemon blossoms/flowers/petals
ligularia
lilac, nut-
lilacs in the spring

lilacs, field of
lilacs, rain-refreshed
lilacs, roasted
lilacs, white
lilies and blueberries and herbs,
    magic caravan of
lilies blessed with the permanence
    of granite, frail
lilies of the valley
lilies, calla
lilies, damp
lilies, garden
lilies, Peruvian
lilies, regal
lilies, white
lilies, Easter
lily stems
lime blossoms/flowers/petals
linden blossoms/flowers/petals
magnolia blossoms/flowers
magnolias in bloom
mallows, marsh
maracuja
marguerites
marigolds, African
marigolds, French
marigolds, marsh
marsh
mayapple blossoms/flowers
mayflower blossoms/flowers/
    petals
meadow
megamallowy
mignonettes
mimosa
muguet
narcissus, paper white
nasturtium
neroli
oleander
orange blossoms/flowers/petals
orchids, heavy exotic collections of
orchids, nectar-dripping
orris
painting by the Tahitian-period
    Gauguin, like stepping inside a
pansy
passion fruit blossoms
peach blossoms/flowers/petals
peach tree in bloom
pear blossoms/petals
peas, sweet
pelargonium
peonies in full flower
peonies, bouquet of fresh
perfume/perfumed
pepper tree, scented blossoms of a
pervasive

petals, crushed
petunias
philadelphus, flowering
phlox
pineapple blossoms
plum blossoms/petals
plumeria lei
pollen
poppies
potpourri, chalky
potpourri, dusty
potpourri, rose-petal
potpourri, rose-lavender
prominent/pronounced
pungent
red
redolent
rhododendrons, damp
rose blooms trodden into the lawn
   by night-time revelers, as
   haunting as
rose blossoms, densely fragrant
rose blossoms, fading
rose blossoms/flowers/petals
rose, dog
rose garden in a glass
rose garden, bouquet straight
   from the
rose garden, like walking through a
rose hips
rose hips, pink-cheeked perfume of
rose oil
rose petals enveloped in smoke
rose petals laced with toasty oak
rose petals, crushed
rose petals, dried/dry
rose petals, dusty
rose petals, faded/wilted
rose petals, scented
rose petals, smoky
rose water...orange blossoms and
   wild strawberries, fantasy
   perfumed by
rose, pure Deep Secret red
rosebuds, dried
rosebuds, new
rosebush covered with blooms,
   like standing right next to a large
rosebushes
rose-infused
roses and more roses
roses stuffed up a goat's ass
roses, aggressive respiratory
   system-challenging old
roses, as fragrant as a bed of
roses, bouquet of
roses, classic damask
roses, crushed

roses, damask
roses, dark red
roses, dew-covered
roses, dog
roses, dried
roses, dusty
roses, faded antique
roses, faded hybrid
roses, freshly plucked tea
roses, grandma's
roses, hedge
roses, late-summer
roses, massive musk
roses, old tea
roses, smoky
roses, sprightly
roses, wild
rose, wilted/withered
roses, yellow
rosiness, most succinct expression
   of the metaphysical essence of
rosy perfume
scented, delicately
scents, beguiling
scents/scented
smelling, bad-
smidgen
spiced/spicy
spring
springtime, early
springtime, wild
stock
streamers
summer, early
summer, white
summer/summery
sunflowers
sweet peas
sweetbriar petals, pink
tangerine blossoms
tuberoses
tulips, faded
tulips, freshly cut Virginian
unflowery
unscented
verbena
vine blossoms/petals
vines in bloom
violet intensity
violet mustiness
violet petals
violets and iris, thumping attack of
violets dance
violets growing through a bed of
   rocks
violets in a grassy lawn after a rain
violets, achingly beautiful
violets, bitter

violets, bouquet of
violets, crushed
violets, dreamy
violets, earthy
violets, fresh
violets, infused
violets, mesmerizing
violets, Parma
violets, perfumed
violets, positively swoony
   perfume of
violets, singed
violets, spicy
violets, sweet
violets, twisted
violets, wild
violets, winter
violets, withered
violets, wonderful wet
violets, wood
violet-tar
violetty country hillside fragrance
violet-vanilla
wedding
white, assorted sugarcoated
wild
wild springtime
wildflowers among the rocks,
   like stumbling into a patch of
wildflowers growing through stone
wildflowers must grow between
   the vines, so fragrant it's as if
   fields of
wildflowers on a hot spring day,
   field of
wildflowers on a sunny summer
   day, field of
wildflowers picked alongside a
   babbling brook
wildflowers picked by a cool
   stream, handful of
wildflowers sprinkled amid the
   grasses
wildflowers, as fragrant as a basket
   overflowing with heirloom
   apples...Meyer lemons and
wildflowers, big fresh bouquet of
wildflowers, dried
wildflowers, freshly picked posy of
wildflowers, improbable distillate
   of liquid
wildflowers, white
wilting
wisteria
woodruff blossoms
yarrow
ylang-ylang
zinnias

...tantalizing hint of smoked bacon...
Daniel Rogov
[in a review of Barken Reserve Pinotage 2002,
a kosher wine from Israel.]

A flavor is simply an aroma that you can eat.
Rachel Herz

*What contemptible scoundrel has stolen the
cork from my lunch?*
W.C. Fields

14. Food

You heard it here first: next to *Quality*, the category of *Food* is the second largest
listing of similes that wine evokes; nothing else comes close. From After Eight
chocolate peppermints to zwieback (twice-toasted toast), it seems all those aromas
and flavors in wine evoke a nearly endless list of things we've eaten at one time or
another. This huge supermarket of foodie language contains everything edible
that has been prepared, processed or cooked in some way, such as *cherry jam* and
peanut butter; however, fresh *cherries* by themselves are listed under *Fruit*, while raw
peanuts by themselves are found within the category of *Herb, Spice or Nut*. Be careful
here; this could be a sticky business.

After Eights
Alaska, baked
All-Bran
almond oil
almond paste
almond powder, dusting of
almond, opulent honey-
almonds and hazelnuts, roasted
almonds, blanched
almonds, candied
almonds, deep-fried
almonds, freshly husked
almonds, grilled
almonds, ground
almonds, roasted/toasted
almonds, salted
almonds, sautéed
almonds, slivered
almonds, sugared
anchovies, sweet
Angostura Bitters
anise, creamed/creamy
anise, dried cranberry-
aniseed, crushed

apple-and-nut combo
apple, red candy
apple, slow-baked
apple, stewed
apple peels, red
apple purée, acidulated
apple wedges
apple-lemon complex
apples and cream
apples at a fair, candied like
apples with vanilla cream poured
  over them
apples, baked Russet
apples, buttered
apples, candied/candy
apples, caramel/caramelized/
  caramel-covered
apples, cinnamon-dusted
apples, cinnamon-scented baked
apples, cooked
apples, cooked cinnamon
apples, deep-baked
apples, dried
apples, fresh-/just-cut

apples, freshly cut Pacific Rose
apples, honey-coated/honeyed
apples, honey-covered baked
apples, liquefied caramel/toffee
apples, mashed
apples, my mother's baked
apples, nut-covered caramel
apples, overbaked
apples, poached
apples, pure baked
apples, sliced green
apples, sliced/apple slices
apples, smooth baked
apples, spiced/spice-coated
apples, still-warm stewed
apples, sweet baked
apples, toffee/toffeed
applesauce, cinnamoned/
  with cinnamon
applesauce, sweet
apricot dusted with spice, like
  biting into a ripe
apricot skins, dried

apricots and oranges with honey and nuts, baked
apricots, baked
apricots, candied
apricots, cooked
apricots, dried
apricots, freshly cut Otago
apricots, hickory smoke-imbued
apricots, honeyed
apricots, mocha-covered
apricots, roasted/toasted
apricots, slow-stewed
apricots, spiced
apricots, vanilla-scented candied
artichokes, canned
artichokes, cooked
asparagus, baked/cooked/steamed/stewed
asparagus, canned/tinned
aspic
bacon bone, smoky
bacon crisps, smoky
bacon fat, classic
bacon fat, meaty
bacon fat, smoky
bacon fat, steely waxy
bacon fat-scented
bacon rinds
bacon rinds, smoky
bacon, back
bacon, cooked
bacon, crackling
bacon, crispy
bacon, fried/frying
bacon, juicy
bacon, molasses-cured
bacon, old
bacon, sizzling
bacon, slabs of
bacon, smoked/smoky
bacon, smokehouse
bacon, smoky fumes of
bacon, strong smoky
bacon, Sunday-breakfast aromas of strong coffee...mixed-berry jam and sizzling
bacon, tantalizing hint of smoked
bacon/baconlike smoke/smokiness
bacony aromas, Syrah
bagel, cinnamon
bagette, fresh
baked, soft-
baklava
balls from Finland, Fazer's green jelly
balls, big thick sugar
balls, malted milk
balls, spicy malt

bamboo shoots, cooked
banana split
bananas with cream
bananas, baked
bananas, caramelized
bananas, dried
bangers
bar, caramel and nut candy
barbecue sauce
barbecued/barbequed/BBQ'd
bark, chocolate
bars, Baby Ruth candy
bars, chocolate-covered blueberry cassis-filled candy
bars, lemon
bars, Mars
bars, Snickers
bars, thick sugar of candy
bath, butter
batter, smattering of pancake
beans lathered in melted chocolate espresso
beans slightly overcooked, brown
beans, burnt
beans, buttered lima
beans, canned
beans, cooked
beans, roasted espresso
beans, roasting coffee
beans, sautéed green
beans, stewed green
beef in a soy glaze, stir-fried
beef jerky
beef jus
beef stock
beef, aged
beef, boiled
beef, braised
beef, broiled
beef, canned/tinned
beef, *carbonnade* of
beef, charred
beef, cold roast
beef, cooked/stewed
beef, grilled
beef, really nice ground
beef, roast/roasted
beef, salted
beef, spicy corned
beets, minted
beets/beetroots, boiled/cooked/stewed
beets/beetroots, roasted/toasted
berries and cherries, preserved
berries and well-clotted cream, remarkable
berries swimming in their juice, crushed red

berries that almost taste roasted, big hit of
berries, assorted honey-covered
berries, barbecued
berries, burnt
berries, candied white
berries, caramelized ripe forest
berries, chocolate-covered/-drenched
berries, crushed small
berries, finely roasted
berries, freshly crushed/squeezed
berries, gently roasted soft
berries, macerated red
berries, musky crushed
berries, poached
berries, raw crushed dark
berry and raspberry jujube confection, spicy
berry extract, filled with
betty, as tasty as a blackberry
Big League Chew, grape
birds, hung game
biscottes, rock-hard French
biscotti, almond
biscuits smeared with lime marmalade, all-butter
biscuits sprinkled with cinnamon, shortbread
biscuits straight out of the oven
biscuits, chocolate
biscuits, crumbled digestive
biscuits, fresh
biscuits, Garibaldi
biscuits, ginger
biscuits, gingery wholemeal
biscuits, honeysnap
biscuits, jam-centered
biscuits, Marietta
biscuits, mashed digestive
biscuits, nut
biscuits, oatmeal
biscuits, ships'
biscuits, sodden wholemeal
biscuits, sweet
biscuits, tea
bits, candy-sugared lemon
bitters, Angostura
blackberries and stones, chocolate-covered
blackberries, baked
blackberries, candied
blackberries, chocolate-dipped
blackberries, sugarcoated
blackberries, super-ripe chocolate-covered
blackberries...prunes and figs puréed in a blender

blackened
blackstrap chunkiness, iconic
blanched
blancmange on toast
blancmange, powdery
blancmange, vanilla
blueberries, candied
blueberries, dark chocolate-covered
blueberries, peppered
boiled
bomb of a wine, cherry
bomb, big jam
bomb, butter-and-oak
bomb, fruit
bomb, oaky butter
bomb, one-dimensional butter
bomb, overoaked butter
bomb, superficial fruit-alcohol
bomb, toasty butterscotch
bonanza, roast
bonbons at a campfire, dark
  chocolate
bonbons, cheap cherry
bonbons, raspberry
bonbons, so brimming with sugar
  they tasted like tiny
Bonox/Bonox-like
bouillabaisse, soupy
bouillon and stables
bouillon, vegetable
Bovril, meaty
boysenberries, crushed
boysenberries, lightly minted
brambles, crushed
bran, wheat
brandysnaps, liquid
brazils, buttered
bread thickly spread with butter,
  freshly toasted
bread with melted butter, freshly
  toasted
bread yeast, slightly sour cream of
bread, baked
bread, baking butter banana nut
bread, burnt
bread, butter-crusted
bread, buttered
bread, caraway
bread, cooked
bread, creamed spice
bread, crusty
bread, dark
bread, Finnish rye
bread, fresh French
bread, freshly baked
bread, freshly baked banana-nut
bread, freshly sliced grainy
bread, ghostly

bread, grilled
bread, hard
bread, hard crust of wholemeal
bread, hot white
bread, hot/warm
bread, milk
bread, muffled
bread, newly baked country
bread, pumpkin
bread, rising
bread, roasted/toasted
bread, rye
bread, spiced
bread, sweet pastry
bread, toasted yeast
bread, whole wheat
bread, yeasted/yeasty
breadcrumbs
bread crusts
breadiness, classical
breadiness, massive
breadiness, nascent
bread-in-the-oven aromas,
  intriguing
bready and bushy
bready big-house bouquet
breakfast aromas like toast…
  coffee…butter and some exotic
  fruit marmalade
breakfast at grandma's house
breakfast, celestial
breakfast, diner
breakfast/breakfasty
brioche and hazelnut flavors,
  sea of rich
brioche, baking
brioche, buttered
brioche, French
brioche, just-baked/warm
brioche, lightly toasted
brioche, spicy buttered
brittle, almond
brittle, caramelly peanut
brittle, nut
broiled
broiled, char-
broth, beef/meat
broth, chicken
broth, truffle
brownies, coffee
brownies, warm chocolate
bubblegum buoyancy
bubblegum ebullience
bubblegum overtones
bubblegum, banana Bubble Yum
bubblegum, grape
bubblegum, liquefied
bubblegum, sweet

bubblegum, well-aged Topps
bubblegummy, superpolished
  tutti-frutti
bun, hot cross
buns, Bath
buns, Chelsea
buns, cinnamon
buns, freshly baked
buns, homemade
buns, hot cross
buns, newly baked vanilla
buns, rye and sourdough wheat
buns, vanilla
burgers, smoked veggie
burning/burnt
butter churned in fresh-cut oak,
  five pounds of melted
butter drizzled over ripe tropical
  fruit, melted
butter just going rancid, aged
butter melting in the frying pan
butter melting in the sun
butter off the roof of your mouth,
  great for rinsing the peanut
butter on fresh bread, classic salted
butter straight out of the churn,
  richness of
butter, apple
butter, brown/browned
butter, burnt
butter, clarified
butter, cocoa
butter, cold
butter, complex lemon
butter, creamed
butter, enthralling almond
butter, fabulously rich creamy
butter, filbert/hazelnut
butter, fresh
butter, fresh-/newly melted
butter, hot
butter, lemon/lemony
butter, light
butter, margarine and
butter, melted salted farmhouse
butter, melted/melting
butter, mint
butter, movie-theater
butter, nut
butter, old
butter, parsley
butter, peanut
butter, plum
butter, rancid peanut
butter, rancid/turned
butter, salted
butter, slow-cooked quince
butter, smoky cocoa

butter, smoothness of
butter, sour
butter, spiced
butter, sun-heated/-melted
butter, sweet
butter, thud of a pound of
butter, vanilla
butterball, big blowsy
butterball, not a fat
buttercream
buttercream, vanilla coffee
butteriness, polished
butter-rich
butterscotch sweetness
butterscotch, bosomy peach and
butterscotch, English
butterscotch, glass of
butterscotch, mentholated
butterscotch, singed
butterscotch, stale
butterscotch, toffeed
butterscotchy, deliciously
buttery fullness
buttery taste, delicious Comtes-like
buttery, ingratiatingly
buttery, intensely
buttery, utterly
buttery, salty-
cabbage, bad
cabbage, badly burnt
cabbage, boiled
cabbage, cooked/overcooked
cabbage, ghastly/smelly stewed
cabbage, pungent
cabbage, smelled unnervingly of
  burnt
cabbages, chocolate and
cacao
cachou, delicate violet
cachou, rose-
cake and a cup of espresso rolled
  into one, flourless chocolate
cake brushed with touches of lime
  juice, hazelnut cream
cake dusted with minerals and tons
  of spices, bourbon pound
cake in a glass, Black Forest
cake mixture, raw
cake richness, soft
cake soaked in rum
cake steeped in sherry,
  Battenberg/Battenburg
cake with a butterscotch glaze
  baked in a wood-burning oven,
  pineapple upside-down
cake, almond
cake, angel food
cake, apple

cake, apple-honey
cake, Black Forest
cake, blackberry
cake, chocolate
cake, Christmas
cake, cinnamon
cake, cinnamon sprinkled on top
  of an apricot
cake, classic black licorice
  Pontefract
cake, corn
cake, crumbly
cake, dense lemon pound
cake, Dundee
cake, fairy
cake, Guinness
cake, intoxicating Christmas
cake, Kendal mint
cake, lemon cheese
cake, lemon chiffon
cake, lemon sponge
cake, liquid Christmas
cake, perfectly aged little plum
cake, plum
cake, pound
cake, raisin
cake, rice
cake, rum-soaked spice
cake, Siena
cake, sweet lemon
cake, triple chocolate
cake, vanilla
cake, warm sponge
cake, yeasty lemon-raisin
Camembert
Camembert and hazelnuts,
  delicious ripe
candy and fruit, blast of
candy awash in red cherry syrup,
  mocha
candy cane, peppermint
candy free-for-all at the
  five-and-dime store
candy in liquid form (with plenty
  of alcohol), like eating your
candy or bananas here, no
candy, acid-hard
candy, apple
candy, Appleheads
candy, as cloying as
candy, banana-watermelon
candy, black currant
candy, boiled
candy, burnt chocolate
candy, buttery
candy, cherry
candy, chocolate-covered
  butterscotch

candy, citrus
candy, coffee-flavored
candy, cordial-filled white
  chocolate
candy, cotton
candy, cream
candy, enjoyable bag of
candy, fluffy and ethereal
  like cotton
candy, fresh cotton
candy, fruit/fruit-flavored/
  hard-fruit
candy, grape
candy, green apple Jolly Rancher
candy, hard
candy, honey-flavored
candy, horehound
candy, intense chocolate-covered
  cherry
candy, jellied fruit
candy, lemon and lime
candy, lemon/lemon drop
candy, like sucking on Cabernet
candy, liquid
candy, massive buttery
candy, not liquid
candy, palate
candy, peppermint
candy, raspberry
candy, red
candy, rock
candy, shameless cinnamon
candy, smells like a bag of
candy, so hard it's like rock
candy, sour
candy, strawberry
candy, sweet hard
candy, tangerine
candy, violet
candy, watermelon-flavored
candy, watermelon Jolly Rancher
candy, wine
candy, wrapped in a cloth of the
candy-/fairy-floss
candy-coated
candyesque
candylike pungency
canes, candy
canned/tinned
cantuccini, Italian
capers
caramel, burnt/singed
caramel, buttered
caramel, Cadbury's
caramel, cooked
caramel, creamy
caramel, drizzle of
caramel, golden

caramel, lemony
caramel, liquefied/melted
caramel, milk/milky
caramel, old
caramel, strawberries larded with
   furniture polish and
caramel, vanilla
caramel-and-nut cloak
caramel-cinnamon
caramel-coated sunny day
caramel-covered
caramel-drizzled bowlful of
   cherries and raspberries
caramels, cream
caramels, Kraft
carob base
carrots, cooked
cashew nuts cut by slices of lemon
cashew smoke, grilled
cashews wrapped around the fruit,
   creamy
cashews, fresh-roasted
cassata
casserole, meat
casserole of smoked mackerel
   soaked in the blood oozing from
   a rare sirloin steak, inspired
casserole, quail-egg
caviar, pressed
celery, cooked/stewed
cereal, health Whole Foods
cereal, toasty Grape-Nuts
charbroiled edge

charcuterie fat
charcuterie stink
charcuterie, sausage-
Cheddar, mature
Cheerios, toasty
cheese and mouse droppings,
   cream
cheese and tea
cheese called Boursault, triple
   cream
cheese from Italy, soft-rind creamy
cheese meets cherries, cottage
cheese rinds
cheese rinds, Stilton
cheese topping, baked
cheese, aged
cheese, Cheddar
cheese, confusing blue
cheese, cottage
cheese, Danish
cheese, dried
cheese, feta
cheese, flutter of a nutty Edam
cheese, fresh cream
cheese, goat

cheese, good smoked Gouda
cheese, Jack/Monterey
cheese, lemon
cheese, over-ripe soft
cheese, Parmesan
cheese, quince
cheese, Romano
cheese, small side-tone of garlic
cheese, smelly/stinky
cheese, smoked
cheese, sour
cheese, spoiled Camembert
cheese, stale
cheese, Stilton
cheese, strange goaty cream
cheese, string
cheese, sweet cream
cheese, Velveeta
cheesecake, base for a
cheesecake, blueberry
cheesecake, cherry
cheesecake, perfect
cheesecake, Swedish
cheeses, Danish
cheeses, mature
cheesy and sweaty, something
   between
cheesy character here, none of the
   old
cheesy quality where milk has
   turned
cheesy, bluish-
cheesy, somewhat
cheesy, very
Cheetos
cherries and raspberries, caramel-
   drizzled bowlful of
cherries and spice, dried
cherries baked in a pie crust, ripe
cherries dusted with cocoa, black
cherries in liqueur, lingering red
cherries jubilee in a glass
cherries preserved in alcohol,
   evolved
cherries robed in finest dark
   chocolate, bittersweet
cherries soaked in brandy, black
cherries steeped in alcohol and
   black tea, Morello
cherries steeped in kirsch, essence
   of black
cherries with cherry tomatoes,
   roasted
cherries, alcohol-soaked
cherries, alcohol-steeped Morello
cherries, Amarena
cherries, baked tart
cherries, bittersweet cocoa-covered

cherries, blanched
cherries, bottled
cherries, brandied
cherries, brandied black
cherries, brandied Morello
cherries, brandy-infused black
cherries, burnt
cherries, candied Bing
cherries, candied black
cherries, chocolate-covered Bing
cherries, chocolaty
cherries, cinnamon-infused creamy
cherries, cooked
cherries, creamed
cherries, crushed
cherries, crystallized cocktail
cherries, dipped
cherries, dried black
cherries, espresso-infused
cherries, *glacé/glacéed*
cherries, jellied
cherries, just-baked
cherries, liqueur
cherries, Maraschino
cherries, mineral-infused
cherries, mocha cream-covered
cherries, mocha-covered black
cherries, mocha-tinged
cherries, molten
cherries, poached
cherries, preserved Morello
cherries, roasted
cherries, roasty red
cherries, smoked/smoky
cherries, spiced
cherries, spiced black
cherries, squashed/squished
cherries, stewed
cherries, sweet candied
cherries, sweet dried
cherries, toasted red
cherries, vivid roasted
cherries, warm baked
cherries, wrapped
cherry-cassis-cinnamon
chestnuts, grilled
chestnuts, roast/roasted
chestnuts, smoked
chestnuts, water
chèvre frais
chews, bright yellow banana
chews, raspberry and banana
chicken, tastes like
chiffon, as light as
chiffon-light
chiffon-textured
chiles, dried ancho
chili irritation

chili, ancho
Chinese
chips, cinnamon
chips, mint chocolate
chips, rancid corn
choc-berry
choccie, dark
chocolate and cabbages
chocolate and lavender, pan-seared reduction of red wine sweetened with
chocolate and schoolgirls' uniforms
chocolate blanketed in honey, orange
chocolate chocolate chocolate
chocolate cover, dark
chocolate frosting
chocolate heart, dark
chocolate heart, plain
chocolate infused with Crème de Cassis, like sipping melted
chocolate intensity, deep bitter
chocolate makes a cameo appearance
chocolate melting into coffee
chocolate mingling perilously with truffles and well-hung game, richness of
chocolate mints thrown in, plum compote with a couple of
chocolate nuances
chocolate oral afterglow, silky
chocolate restraints, dark
chocolate richness, melting
chocolate sweetness from oak, vanilla-
chocolate undertone, subtle catering-
chocolate veil, smooth
chocolate with a tannin coat, chewy
chocolate with rum liqueur, mint
chocolate with sweet pineapple chunks, white
chocolate, as slick as dark
chocolate, baker's
chocolate, bitter
chocolate, bittersweet
chocolate, black
chocolate, burnt/charred
chocolate, caramelly Mexican
chocolate, caterer's
chocolate, cedar-
chocolate, chunky
chocolate, Club
chocolate, coffee-infused
chocolate, continental
chocolate, covered in rich dark

chocolate, creamy
chocolate, dark
chocolate, dark high-cacao
chocolate, dark Swiss
chocolate, designer
chocolate, drenched in
chocolate, dry catering
chocolate, Dutch
chocolate, essences of
chocolate, like falling into a very tasty black hole made of blackberries and
chocolate, fine
chocolate, fruity milk
chocolate, Ghiardelli's
chocolate, gooey
chocolate, hallmark
chocolate, hazelnut-filled milk
chocolate, Hershey's
chocolate, hot/warm
chocolate, intense unsweet
chocolate, liqueur
chocolate, liquid
chocolate, lusty
chocolate, malted milk
chocolate, melted bittersweet
chocolate, melted Valrhona
chocolate, melted white
chocolate, Mexican
chocolate, milk
chocolate, minerals immersed in white
chocolate, mint/minty
chocolate, nut/nut-filled
chocolate, oodles of plain
chocolate, oozing
chocolate, orange
chocolate, peppery mint
chocolate, powdered
chocolate, pure
chocolate, regional dark
chocolate, roasted
chocolate, Rubensesque
chocolate, serious serious dark
chocolate, smoky
chocolate, sweet cherry
chocolate, sweet milk
chocolate, Swiss
chocolate, tea and
chocolate, ultraregional bitter
chocolate, unsweetened dark
chocolate, Valrhona
chocolate, vanilla-
chocolate, virtually pure
chocolate, voluptuous
chocolate, white
chocolate, wrapped with
chocolate, Ybarra

chocolate, zippy
chocolate...nuts...coffee and lily-of-the-valley, white Toblerone
chocolate-berry
chocolate-covered cherries
chocolate-infused
chocolate-rich
chocolates, mint
chocolates...you never know what you're gonna get, like a box of
chocolate-spice
chocolate-toffee
chocolate-vanilla
chocolaty basso profundo
chocolaty but not absurd
chocolaty depths
chocolaty essence
chocolaty intensity, deep
chocolaty mellowness, dark
chocolaty richness
chocolaty, far too
chocolaty...you could pour it over ice cream, very
choc-sappy
chops, grilled
chops, old lamb
chowder, clam
Chunky Monkey, doesn't taste like Ben & Jerry's
chutney, Indian mango
chutney, spicy mango
cinnamon and licorice
cinnamon-chocolate kiss
cinnamon, caramel-
cinnamon, cassis-tinged
cinnamon, cherry-cassis-
cinnamon, dusting of
cinnamon, ground
cinnamon, toasted
citric character, cooked
citrus peels/rinds, candied
citrus zest, dry
citrus, buttered/buttery
citrus, caramelized
citrus, chiffonlike
citrus, cooked
citrus, crystallized
citrus, grilled
citrus, honeyed
citrus, pressed/squeezed
clove oil/oil of cloves
cloves in oranges at Christmas
CO (caloric orgasm)
cobbler in a rock quarry, like eating
cobbler, apple
cobbler, blueberry
cobbler, buttery peach
cobbler, liquid cherry

cobbler, liquid peach
cobbler, peach
cobnuts, grilled
cobnuts, slightly charred
cocktail of fruits, explosive
cocktail, canned fruit
cocktail, fresh fruit
cocktail, pink grapefruit
cocktail, tropical fruit
cocktail, very fresh shrimp
cocktail, yet another fruit
cocktail, Del Monte fruit
cocoa confections
cocoa powder
cocoa, bitter
cocoa, burnt
cocoa, dry/dusty
cocoa, dusting of sweet
cocoa, fine
cocoa, ground
cocoa, minty
cocoa, rare
cocoa, shaved
cocoa, smoky roasted
cocoa, spicy
cocoa-rich depth
cocoa-textured giant
coconut oil, honeyed
coconut, burnt
coconut, roasted
coconut, sweetened
coconut, toasted/toasty
coconutty-creaminess
coffee and chocolate powder
coffee and sweet prunes, stream of
    rich
coffee beans, freshly roasted
coffee beans, just-ground
coffee beans, roasted/toasted
coffee grounds, French roast
coffee grounds, warm
coffee, dark roasted
coffee-ground tones, dark smoky
coffee-toffee
coleslaw
compote with a couple of chocolate
    mints thrown in, plum
compote, apple
compote, berry
compote, black fruit
compote, blast of dense pure
    blackberry
compote, blueberry
compote, cherry
compote, dark
compote, dark/darkish berry
compote, fruit
compote, hedonistic bowl of fruit

compote, over-ripe pear and apple
compote, plum
compote, white fruit
compotelike, black
compotelike, superdense almost fat
cones, sugar
confection overhang, slight
confection topped by a scoop of
    lime sorbet, very flavorful apple
confection trap
confection, lemony
confection, slightly jammy
confection, spicy berry and
    raspberry jujube
confectionery aromas, almost
    contrived
confectioner proud, would make a
confectionery, lolly-shop
confectionery, milk-bottle
confectionery, verges on the
confections, cocoa
confit flavors, *mélange* of fruit
confit of Indian-summer fruit,
    warm
confit with a sprinkling of nuts,
    lemon
confit, black
confit, blackberry
confit, blueberry
confit, citrus
confit, dark cherry
confit, fruit
confit, jammy tomato
confit, lemon
confit, orange
confit, pear
confit, pineapple
confit, raspberry
confit, ripe
confit, stubbier
confiture, black raspberry and
    blackberry
conserve, black currant
conserve, rich plum
conserve, strawberry
consommé, meaty
consommé, sweet
cooked
cookie, vanilla
cookies and cocoa do an attractive
    little dance, vanilla
cookies drenched in rosewater,
    mouthwatering almond
cookies, baking
cookies, butter
cookies, chocolate-chip
cookies, Christmas
cookies, sweet almond

cookies, vanilla butter
cooking in grandma's kitchen
cooking smells
Corn Flakes, Kellogg's
corn nuttiness, toasted-
corn, buttery sweet
corn, candy
corn, canned
corn, caramel
corn, cooked/overcooked
corn, creamed
corn, grilled
corn, honeyed
corn, roasted sweet
corn, spiced
cornbread
coulis of red fruit
coulis, cassis
coulis, loganberry
coulis, raspberry
crab claws
crabmeat
cracker, honey and graham
cracker crust, graham
Cracker Jacks
cracker richness, sweet wheat-
crackers, black charcoal
crackers, ginger
crackers, honey graham
crackery flavors, nice
crackle, nut
crawdads, Louisiana steamed
crawfish, buttery
cream and mature meat pie
    (don't ask), sour
cream cooked with a vanilla bean
Cream of Wheat
cream flowing thick and unwilling
    from a jug, double
cream in the middle of an Oreo
    cookie
cream on grilled grapefruit
cream puffs, lovable
cream richness, clotted
cream smeared over pale golden
    stones, double
cream sprinkled with brown sugar
    and cinnamon
cream, almond
cream, apricot
cream, banana
cream, blackberry
cream, boysenberry
cream, burnt
cream, butter
cream, caramel
cream, chestnut
cream, cinnamon

cream, clotted
cream, coconut
cream, confectioner's
cream, custard
cream, fresh
cream, full
cream, hazelnut
cream, irresistible veneer of
cream, light
cream, mushroom
cream, orange
cream, slightly sour
cream, sour/soured
cream, strawberry
cream, sweet
cream, sweet-and-sour
cream, sweet vanilla
cream, thick chocolate
cream, underlying
cream, vanilla
cream, warm
cream, whipped
creaminess of a suckling calf
creaminess, fluffy
creaminess, nice
creaminess, round
creams, chocolate
creams, custard
creams, sweet violet

Creamsicle, orange
Creamsicle, vanilla
creamy experience
creamy gentleness
creamy, extraordinarily
creamy-biscuity
creamy-buttery
creamy-silky
creation from a pastry chef at a
  five-star French restaurant
Creepy-Crawlers
crème acidity, lemon
crème and far less *brûlée*, far more
crème anglaise, biscuity
crème brûlée in a glass
crème brûlée, caramelized top of
crème brûlée, chocolate
crème brûlée, cream of
crème brûlée, dark
crème brûlée, toasted hazelnut-
  covered
crème brûlée, torched
crème brûlée, vanilla
crème brûlée, very light
crème fraîche
crème fraîche, sour
crème, sweet lemon
crisp, as juicy as a baked berry
crisp, blueberry-apple

crisp, green apple
crispbread
crispbread served with Swedish
  Kalle's caviar
crisps
crisps, smoky bacon
croissants straight from the oven
croissants, French
croissants, fresh
croissants, hot buttered
crumble with custard, blackberry
crumble, grandmother's peach
crumble, violet
crumble, warm apple
crunch, almond-vanilla
crust on newly baked white bread,
  hard
crust that's been a little burnt, pie
crust with a bit of tar, burnt
crust, bread
crust, butter-rich
crust, curious Brie
crust, pastry
crust, pie
crust, sourdough bread
cubes, stock
cucumber, cut
cumin, toasted
cumquat peels, candied
cup with an attitude, fruit
cup, Del Monte fruit
cup, pear fruit
cupcakes, lemon
curds, ambrosial lemon
curds, warm lemon
currant sandwich, black
currants spiked with vanilla, red
currants, candied black
currants, cooked/stewed black
currants, creamy-toffee red
currants, macerated
currants, roasted black
currants, spiced black
currants, stewed black
currants...plums and spices
curry powder
custard cream softness
custard grill-burnt at the edges
custard like something out of Willy
  Wonka's factory, waterfall of
custard, as rich as a fruity
custard, baked
custard, coconut
custard, coconut-orange
custard, creamy English
custard, egg
custard, lemon

custard, my grandmother's
  duck-egg
custard, slightly fudge-rich creamy
custard, smoky
custard, texture of
custard, toasted egg
custard, warm vanilla
custard-filled wafers
custardy richness
cuts, cherry fruit and cold
dairy products
dates and raisins floating in
  suspension
dates, Medjool
dates, sugared
dehydrated
demi-glace, thick caramel
dessert in a glass
dessert in itself, almost a
dessert on earth, most gorge-
  caressing
dessert trolley, best
dessert unto itself, sweet
dessert, could almost pass as
dessert, deep penetrating
dessert, liquid
dessert, not just for
dessert, perfect after-theater
dessert, quintessential
dessert, so luscious it could be
dessert, so much fruit it smelled
  like
desserts, aromas encountered in
  many Arab
Devil Dogs
digestives, biscuity notes of
  crumbled
dill and meat stew
dinner, Christmas
dinner, everynight
dinner, good old-fashioned roast
Doritos
dough immersed in cherry syrup,
  sweet chocolate chip cookie
dough supported by juniper wood,
  gingerbread
dough, almond cookie
dough, bagel
dough, bread
dough, chocolate-chip cookie
dough, fragrant bread
dough, rising bread
dough, saliva-inducing cookie
dough, sweet
dough, warm
dough, yeasted/yeasty
doughnut shape, slightly
doughnuts, blackberry-filled

doughnuts, sugared jelly
dressing, salad
drops, cherry
drops, explosion of cherry fruit-
drops, lemon fruit
drops, pear
drops, raspberry
drops, Smith Brothers cough
drops, sour
drops, wild-cherry cough
duck liver
duck skins, Peking
duck, cooked wild

duck, smoked Peking
Dunkin' Donuts
eat as much as drink, to
eat it, you don't taste this...you
eat this with your fingers, you'll be
    tempted to
éclairs, cheap chocolate
Edam cheese, nutty
Edam, flutter of nutty
edible, almost
egg shell
egg whites, fluffy/whipped
Eggos
eggplant, roasted
eggs and lemon muffins fighting it
    out, boiled
eggs Benedict
eggs, bad/rotten
eggs, buttery/well-buttered
    scrambled
eggs, hard-/soft-boiled
eggs, quail
eggy, damp and
entrails, roast woodcock
espresso beans lathered in melted
    chocolate
espresso beans, roasted
essences, concentrated meat
extract, malt
extract, orange peel
extract, ripe meat
extract, singed meat
extract, tinny meat
fajitas
fat, charcuterie
fat, chicken
fat, classic bacon
fat, meat
fat, meaty bacon
fat, pork
fat, smoked meat
fat, smoky
fat, smoky bacon
fat-scented, bacon
fennel, boiled

fennel, grilled
Fig Newtons
figs and dates rolled in bread flour
figs and prunes, cocoa powder-
    dusted
figs, ambrosial syrup of
figs, caramel-coated/caramelized
figs, dried/dry
figs, honeyed
figs, jammy
figs, syrup of
filet mignon, fresh-cut rare
filling, blueberry pie
filling, cherry pie
fish, smoked
fish, stewed
flambé, banana
flan, fruit
flan, luscious
flapjacks, overcooked coconut
flapjacks, treacle
floss, candy/fairy
flour, bread
flour, dusted with pastry
flour, fluffy pillow of biscuit
floury notes, unfortunate
flowers, sugar-glazed
focaccia, herbed
fois gras
fondant, nut
fondue going down your throat,
    raspberry-chocolate
fondue, blackberry chocolate
fondue, cheese
fondue, chocolate
fondue, fruit
fondue, veggie
fondue, warm chocolaty
fondue, warm gooey stuff like
    chocolate
food for the thirsty, comfort
food than wine, practically more
food, baby
food, dog
food; it is food, doesn't need
frangipane
Frazzles, passing whiff of
fried, deep-

Froot Loops
frosting, buttery chocolate
fruit and flowers, alcohol-steeped
fruit and nuts rolled together
fruit and nuts, dried
fruit and nuts, festive bowl of
fruit and spice, dizzying blend of
fruit and spice, high-octane blast
    of supercharged

fruit and spice, screaming with
    dark
fruit and vegetables, Del Monte
fruit and wax, crystallized
fruit boiled down to its essence,
    great
fruit bowl folded into a slightly
    toasted egg custard, whole
fruit bowl immersed in sparkling
    nectar
fruit cocktail, exotic
fruit dusted with talcum powder,
    sweet red-black
fruit in syrup
fruit infused with glycerin, jammy
fruit jellied black

fruit leather, raspberry
fruit paste
fruit poached with vanilla, dried
fruit preserved in rum
fruit slides over the palate with no
    bumps or bruises, vanilla-tinged
fruit spectrum, canned
fruit, apple crumble
fruit, archetypical bitter chocolaty
fruit, baked luscious
fruit, big licoricey
fruit, black compotelike
fruit, boiled
fruit, brandied
fruit, bruising roasted
fruit, burnt
fruit, buttered
fruit, candied
fruit, candied citrus
fruit, candied dark ripe
fruit, candied pear-laced
fruit, candied white
fruit, canned/tinned
fruit, chewy
fruit, chocolate
fruit, chocolate-covered berry
fruit, compote of cherry
fruit, compote of white
fruit, concentrated burnt dried
fruit, concentrated crushed
fruit, confiture of black
fruit, cooked
fruit, cooked warm red
fruit, cooked white
fruit, coulis of red
fruit, cream of
fruit, creamy crumbly biscuity
    honeyed
fruit, crunchy crushed
fruit, crushed
fruit, crushed-to-death
fruit, crystallized black

fruit, crystallized summer
fruit, dark sun-baked cauldron-stewed
fruit, dried Mediterranean
fruit, dried/dry
fruit, espresso-infused blackberry and cassis
fruit, fermented dark ripe
fruit, fluffy lemon pie
fruit, fresh pastilley
fruit, freshly chopped orchard
fruit, gingersnap
fruit, glacé/glazed
fruit, goodish baked cooked
fruit, grilled
fruit, grilled chocolate
fruit, half-stewed exotic
fruit, honey-dripping
fruit, honeyed peach
fruit, honey-wrapped crystallized
fruit, hot baked
fruit, incessant waves of candied
fruit, jellied black
fruit, jellied red
fruit, layers of luxurious jellied
fruit, licorice-laced dark
fruit, lightly baked
fruit, loads of jellied
fruit, magnificent burnt
fruit, mélange of
fruit, mocha cream-covered red
fruit, mocha-tinged
fruit, nutty baked
fruit, preserved
fruit, purée of red
fruit, really stuffed
fruit, rich crushed
fruit, ripe confit
fruit, roast/roasted/roasty
fruit, rum-soaked
fruit, salvo of dried tropical
fruit, seductive grilled
fruit, singed Italianate
fruit, smoked/smoky
fruit, soft-baked
fruit, stewed
fruit, stuffed
fruit, sweet candied red
fruit, sweet crushed
fruit, talcum powder-dusted red
fruit, tropical candied

fruit, typhoon of roasted

fruit, untold quantities of jellied red and black
fruit, vanilla-dusted red
fruit, very ripe dried
fruit, warm baked
fruit, well-burnt

fruit, yellow crystallized
fruitcake made from crystallized fruit
fruitcake studded with figs and cherries, molasses

fruitcake, alcoholic

fruitcake, boiled
fruitcake, cherry
fruitcake, cherry syrup-drenched
fruitcake, Christmas
fruitcake, delicious piece of
fruitcake, gorgeous apricot
fruitcake, homemade
fruitcake, honeyed
fruitcake, hot
fruitcake, just-baked
fruitcake, layered
fruitcake, like savoring the essence of liquid
fruitcake, liquid
fruitcake, masses of fierce
fruitcake, rich and chewy old-fashioned
fruitcake, singed
fruitcake, soft
fruitcake, spicy
fruitcake, warm
fruit-drop explosion, cherry
fruit-filled core, fat roasted
fruitiness, heavy baked
fruitiness, toffeelike
fruits and spices, cornucopia of candied
fruits rolled with nuts, dried
fruits, chocolate-coated liqueur
fudge, ambrosial
fudge, as dark as
fudge, as thick as
fudge, Caramac
fudge, chocolate
fudge, Christmas
fudge, Devon
fudge, honey
fudge, liquid/melted
fudge, mocha
fudge, toffee
fudge, vanilla
fudginess, delicious brown sugar
game, aged
game, hung
game, richness of chocolate mingling perilously with truffles and well-hung
game, smoked
game, sweetness of well-hung
gâteau/kuchen, Black Forest/Schwarzwalder
gelato, strawberry

gherkins
gherkins and dill, peppered
ginger and cream
ginger, candied
ginger, caramelized
ginger, dried
ginger, freshly cut/ground
ginger, pickled
ginger, powdered
gingerbread and licorice, nice spicy
gingerbread house
gingerbread man
gingerbread with a dollop of apricot jam
gingerbread, evolves into
gingerbread, smoky
ginger-nuts
gingersnaps
Goobers

Good & Plenty

goodies, baker's full range of
goodies, Christmas
goods, baked
goods, egg-based baked
gooseberries coated in icing, Cape
gooseberries marinated in lime juice, cape
gooseberries, baked
gooseberries, crushed
gooseberries, purée of
Gorgonzola
Gorgonzola and lavender, perfect mix of
goulash, as spicy as a pot of
grains meet apples
grains, cereal
grains, roasted
grapefruit zest
grapefruit, broiled
grapefruit, candied
grapefruit, dried
grapefruit, fresh-/freshly cut
grapefruit, fresh-squeezed
grapefruit, grilled
grapefruit, honey-dripping/honeyed
grapefruit, spiced
grapefruit, stewed
grapefruit, sugared
grapes covered in icing-sugar
grapes, candied
grapes, candied white
grapes, cold freshly squeezed green
grapes, freshly squeezed
gravy made from the juices of roasted lamb
gravy, beef
gravy, good flavorsome

gravy, mouthwatering Sunday
  lunch mutton
gravy, sweet warm
gremolata
grilled
griottes in Armagnac
groundnuts, grilled
groundnuts, roasted
Gruyère, indecent taste of
gum tang, fruit-
gum, banana
gum, black wine
gum, cherry mint
gum, chewing
gum, cinnamon
gum, raspberry mint
gum, spearmint chewing
gumballs
gumdrops, licorice
gumdrops, mint
Gummi Bears, citrus
Gummi Bears, white
Gummi Bears emptied into the
  fermentation tank, truckload of
gums, black fruit
gums, cinnamon
gums, red fruit
gums, rich wine
Gums: the Red Ones, Rowntrees
  Fruit
ham hocks
ham, baked

ham, cured Serrano
ham, grandmother's Christmas
ham, Parma
ham, smoked
ham, sugar-cured
hamburger meat, stale
hammy, something
hazelnut oil
hazelnut paste
hazelnut *purée*
hazelnuts and candy drowned
  in strawberry liqueur
hazelnuts capped by a whiff of
  smoke, bowl of chocolate-
  covered
hazelnuts, buttered
hazelnuts, candied
hazelnuts, caramel-covered
hazelnuts, chopped
hazelnuts, creamed
hazelnuts, dried
hazelnuts, ground
hazelnuts, roasted/toasted
hazelnuts, salted
hazelnuts, sautéed
headcheese aged in oak

healthful/healthy
herb oil rasp
herbage, fermented
herbal stuff, dried
herb-kissed limes and lemons
herbs and barbecue spices, smoked
herbs fighting furiously for
  supremacy, fruit and
herbs, blanched
herbs, burnt/charred
herbs, candied
herbs, charred
herbs, chocolaty
herbs, creamed
herbs, crushed
herbs, crushed green
herbs, dried kitchen
herbs, dried Provençale
herbs, dried/dry
herbs, dusting of green
herbs, fresh/fresh-cut/fresh-
  snipped
herbs, grilled
herbs, just-crushed dried
herbs, roasted
herbs, singed dry
herbs, smoked
herbs...black treacle and licorice,
  boiling cauldron full of
herby-fennel aromas, limy with
honey and caramel, hot
honey and flowers (sounds like a
  gentleman's hair dressing)
honey and nut rush
honey and stung like a wasp, tasted
  like
honey cut by lemon
honey dripped over fresh apples,
  light
honey from every pore, oozing
honey from mixed flowers
honey from some craggy
  mountaintop wildflowers
honey into your tongue...sending
  it into jolts of diabetic coma, like
  injecting pure
honey made from a thousand
  flowers
honey on buttered toast
honey over a bowl of peaches and
  pineapples, like dripping
honey touched by anise
honey, acacia
honey, alfalfa
honey, apple blossom
honey, apricot
honey, Argentine
honey, balsam and

honey, blond
honey, bloom
honey, box
honey, buckwheat
honey, buttery
honey, buzzing with
honey, chemically musty
honey, chestnut
honey, clover
honey, comb
honey, deep
honey, distilled dew and
honey, dried acacia blossom
honey, extroverted dried
honey, golden
honey, Greek
honey, hard
honey, heather
honey, herb
honey, ladling of clove
honey, lavender
honey, leatherwood
honey, lemon
honey, light
honey, lightly drizzled with
honey, Marsanne
honey, melting
honey, mountain
honey, orange-blossom
honey, overflowing with dribbly
honey, polyfloral
honey, pungent lanolin and
honey, pure
honey, pure clover
honey, raw
honey, rich heather
honey, rugged sweaty
honey, runny
honey, scrape of
honey, sensual acacia
honey, sigh of
honey, silk velvety
honey, spiced lemon
honey, structured
honey, sublimated
honey, sugar and sour
honey, thick as
honey, thicker and sweeter than
  pure
honey, tupelo
honey, unexpected streaks of
honey, wafts of
honey, white clover
honey, wild
honey, wild pine
honey, wildflower
honey...honey and more honey

honey...peach and candied orange peel and swooping back up in a lemon-lime burst, like rolling down a coaster of
honey/honeyed/honeyish/ honeylike
honey...nuts and caramel...yum, liquid
honey richness, lime-
honey-almond, opulent
honeybread
honeycomb in a glass, melted
honeycomb in a glass, sweet warm
honeycomb on toast
honeycomb, seem carved from a chunk of
honeycomb/honeycomblike
honeycomblike, creamy
honey-dripper, sweet botrytized
honey-dusted
honeyesque
honeyed and sweet, wonderfully
honeyed fullness, delicious
honeyed nutty zenith
honeyed richness
honeyed sheen
honeyed, ferociously
honeyed, mind-bendingly ripe and
honeyed, richly
honeyed, wonderfully
honey-hearted
honey-nutty
honey-peachy
honey-rich
honey-scented nugget
honey-tinged
honey-toffee
hors d'oeuvres, Thanksgiving
horseradish, squashed
hot dog with sauerkraut, fennel-infused
hummus
hummus, dried out
ice cream and runs down the throat like nectar, melts in the mouth like
ice cream melting in the mouth, vanilla
ice cream with fudge sauce, vanilla
ice cream, apple pie and
ice cream, banana
ice cream, blackberry
ice cream, Breyers vanilla
ice cream, coffee/coffee-flavored
ice cream, Italian vanilla
ice cream, most delicious *tutti-frutti*
ice cream, orange

ice cream, raspberry
ice cream, raspberry and vanilla
ice cream, soft melon
ice cream, strawberry
ice cream, supercharged vanilla
ice pop
ice, lemon Italian
ice, like chewing on a piece of red
ice, pink shaved
icing on the cake
icing, almond
icing, swaddled in
icing, vanilla
jam and sizzling bacon, Sunday-breakfast aromas of strong coffee...mixed-berry
jam cooking
jam flavors waltz with your taste buds, thick strawberry
jam in a bottle, jar of blackberry
jam in your nose, pot of
jam machine
jam on brioche toast, fresh quince
jam on hot buttered scones, sweet apricot
jam turning to leather, whiffs of camphorwood and loganberry
jam with the added bonus of alcohol, pot of
jam, alpine strawberry
jam, apple
jam, apricot
jam, as rich as pineapple
jam, berry
jam, black cherry
jam, black currant
jam, black raspberry
jam, blackberry
jam, blueberry
jam, bramble
jam, burnt
jam, candied grapey plum
jam, cassis
jam, cherry
jam, chewy
jam, cinnamon-laced red cherry
jam, citron
jam, Concord grape
jam, cooked
jam, crabapple
jam, dark fruit
jam, essence of blackberry
jam, fig and melon
jam, fire-laced berry
jam, fruit
jam, gooey blackberry
jam, grandma's homemade
jam, grandmother's

jam, grape
jam, heady apricot
jam, homemade
jam, light fruit
jam, loganberry
jam, loquat
jam, mango
jam, melted
jam, Mirabelle plum
jam, Mr. Bubbles meets Smucker's
jam, orange
jam, peach
jam, plum
jam, prune
jam, pure ripe
jam, quince
jam, raspberry
jam, rich warm blackberry
jam, ripe Morello cherry
jam, ripe plum
jam, slow-bubbling strawberry
jam, smoked blackberry
jam, spoonful of fresh raspberry
jam, stewed
jam, strawberry-vanilla
jam, sweet spicy quince
jam, sweet strawberry
jam, tangy pear and apple
jam, tart black currant
jam, tomato
jam, twice-boiled vegetable
jam, warm simmering
jam, wild berry
jam, wild black berry fruit
jam, yellow plum
jam...but classy jam
jam/jamlike, strawberry
jam-cigar tobacco, plum
jam-juice, typical Australian
jamlike, much too
jamlike, so thick it's almost
jammiest wines around, one of the
jammy aromas and flavors, in-your-face
jammy, assertively
jammy, characteristically
jammy, hedonistically
jammy you could almost feel tempted to spread it on your breakfast toast, so
jammy, pop-
jampot, dip into a
jams, annual convention of homemade
jawbreakers, strawberry
jellies, Christmas
jellies, orange
Jell-O mold, ambrosia

Jell-O, cherry
Jell-O, green
Jell-O, melted black cherry
Jell-O, orange
Jell-O, raspberry
jelly and marmalade, ripe quince
jelly babies, blueberry
jelly bean factory with artificial
  flavorings, made in a
jelly, apricot
jelly, black cherry
jelly, black currant
jelly, blackberry
jelly, blueberry
jelly, bramble
jelly, calf's foot
jelly, Chardonnay
jelly, cherry
jelly, concord grape
jelly, crabapple
jelly, crystallized quince
jelly, extra tart quince
jelly, gooseberry
jelly, grape
jelly, plum
jelly, quince
jelly, red
jelly, strawberry
jelly, unset
jelly, Welch's grape
jerky, beef
jerky, dried
Jolly Rancher
jubilee in a glass, cherries
jubilee, citrus
juice, pickle
juice, plum
juice, simple lemon
juices, pan
juices, red meat/*jus de viande*
juices, roasted meat
Juicy-Fruit
jujubes
ketchup, Heinz
ketchup, sweet
ketchup, tomato
ketchup-slow
Kisses, cherry-filled Hershey's
Kisses, Hershey's chocolate
Knott's Berry Farm, smells of
korma
kraut
kumquats, candied
kumquats...mandarins...
  tangerines, jellied
ladyfingers, fresh warm
ladyfingers, tangy sweet
lamb, mum's roast

lamb, roast/roasted
Land O'Lakes, tub of
lavender, perfect mix of
  Gorgonzola and
Lebkuchen
lemon peels, boiled/cooked
lemon peels, caramelized
lemon peels, dried
lemon peels, squeeze of
lemon peels/zest, crystallized
lemon peels/skins, dried
lemon rinds
lemon rinds, preserved
lemon zest
lemon zest, candied
lemon-marmalade tartness
lemons awash in spicy cream,
  candied
lemons, baked
lemons, buttered
lemons, candied
lemons, caramelized
lemons, cured
lemons, dried
lemons, honeyed
lemons, preserved
lemons, rub of new-cut
lemons, sherbet-
lemons, spiced
lemons, stewed
lemons, sugarcoated
lentils, cooked
licorice saltiness
licorice in a glass, molten
licorice sticks, black
licorice sticks, sweet red
licorice veil, wispy
licorice whips
licorice, candied
licorice, chewy
licorice, classic British
licorice, cinnamon and
licorice, distilled essence of
licorice, dried
licorice, Dutch
licorice, flash of
licorice, good whack of
licorice, high-octane
licorice, honeyed
licorice, intense bitter
licorice, iron
  underpinned by
licorice, layers of
licorice, lemon
licorice, lemon streaked with
licorice, lick or two of
licorice, lovely laces of
licorice, medicinal

licorice, melted
licorice, old
licorice, pinned down by
licorice, red
licorice, rich
licorice, sailor's
licorice, sassy
licorice, sinewy
licorice, smoked/smoky
licorice, smoky blackstrap
licorice, squashed
licorice, sweet black
licorice, sweet candied
licorice, toasty
licorice, whip of
licorice-bottomed
licorice-hearted monster, dark
licorice-infused
licorice-scented
licorice/licoricey
LifeSavers fruit flavors
LifeSavers, cherry
LifeSavers, pineapple
LifeSavers, Wint-O-Green
lime on a Thai green papaya salad,
  could stand in for the
limes, candied
lime zest
linguiça, dried
links, smoky
linzertorte
Liquorice Allsorts, Bassett's
Liquorice Allsorts, the coconut
  wheels in Bassett's
litchis, canned/tinned
litchis, clove-spiked
litchis, jellied
liver, fried duck
liver, oily concentrated goose-
liverwurst, smoky
loaves, spiced
loaves, sweetish spice
loaves, Viennese
lobster shells, roasted
jerky, beef
lollies, boiled
lollies, ice
lollies, strawberry ice
lollypop clouds
lollipops, cherry
lollipops, lemon
lollipops, lime
lollipops, red
lolly fruit, simple
lozenges, cassis-to-black raspberry
  fruit
lozenges, intense berry fruit
lozenges, peach fruit

lozenges, throat
luau of grilled pineapples...
    honeysuckle and herbs, succulent
macaroons, almond
macaroons, toasted
macédoine of fruit in a bottle
macédoine of ripe fruit
mâche and ripe tannins, bags of
malt echo, delicate sweet
malt extract
malt with blackberry syrup,
    chocolate
malt, blackberry
malt, honeyed
Malt, Radio
malt-toffee
malty-medicinal
malty-rich
mandarin, obnoxious with
    marmalade and
mandarin peels, dried
mandarins, tinned
mango, crystallized
mango, dried
mango, syrup of apricot blended
    with nectar of
mangoes sprinkled with cinnamon
mangoes, dried
mangoes, sliced
maple flavors, smoky
maple-flavored
margarine and butter
marmalade and mandarin,
    obnoxious with
marmalade on burnt brown toast,
    opulent
marmalade on hot buttered toast
marmalade, apricot
marmalade, bitter lemon/orange
marmalade, burnt
marmalade, buttery orange and
    spice
marmalade, celestial
marmalade, citrus/citrusy
marmalade, dark orange
marmalade, finest
marmalade, golden
marmalade, herbal orange
marmalade, kumquat
marmalade, lemon/lime/orange
marmalade, liquid Olde English
marmalade, marrow
marmalade, oozing rich lime
marmalade, Oxford
marmalade, quince
marmalade, rich concentrated yet
    dry
marmalade, Seville orange

marmalade, tangerine-peel
marmalade, tawny
marmalade...popcorn...toast and
    mandarin oranges, tumult of
marmaladey, exotically
marmaladey, sinfully
Marmite
marron glace
marshmallow, burnt
marshmallows dropped for a
    second into the bonfire
marshmallows, compelling notes
    of
marshmallows, roasted/toasted
marshmallows, sweet
marshmallow-vanilla fluffiness
marzipan depth, full of
marzipan, cherry
marzipan, dull
marzipan, honeyed
marzipan, orange
marzipan...dry yet somehow
    confectionary, liquid
marzipan-scented nectar
mascarpone
meal in a bottle, three-course
meal in a glass
meal in itself, almost a whole
mealy/mealiness
meat and game, wild feral aromas
    of earth...cured
meal, savory roasted
meat blood
meat cooked in beer
meat essences, concentrated
meat fat
meat grilled over a wood fire
meat in a blender, Buffal-O-Matic:
    like gamy buffalo
meat in a glass, grilled
meat marinated in wine
meat or game, smoked
meat, aged raw
meat, bitter charred
meat, burnt/charred
meat, cooked/stewed
meat, cured
meat, deli
meat, dill-flavored
meat, dried
meat, fresh
meat, fried
meat, gamy
meat, grilled spiced
meat, ground
meat, lamblike
meat, melt-in-your-mouth smoked
meat, pan-singed

meat, raw
meat, ripe
meat, sausage
meat, seared
meat, seasoned
meat, slow-roasted
meat, smoked/smoky
meat, spiced
meat, stale hamburger
meat, unctuous
meat, virtual overdose of savory
    sausage
meat, well-hung
meat...sausage...blood and animal
meatballs, spicy
meatily rich
meatiness, compelling
meatiness, extra depth of earthy
meatiness, individual muscular
meatiness, savory
meatiness, smoky leathery
meatiness, strange
meats, barbecued
meat-sweet
meaty flavors, reduced
meaty funk
meaty growl
meaty it's like drinking steak, so
meaty number
meaty pong
meaty rusticity
meaty slab of a wine
meaty snap, savory
meaty underbelly
meaty, decently
meaty, smoky-
meaty, vaguely
meaty, very
meaty...big and bouncy
meaty-cherry, high-pitched
meaty-earthy regional inflections
meaty-gamy
meaty-saltiness
meaty-sweet
Melba, hoo-ya...peach
Melba/Melba-like, peach
melon meets sugar cubes and
    candy cane
melon, ripe honeydew
melonosity, intense toffee-edged
melons, baked
melons, baked-cream
melons, crushed
melons, grilled
melons, honeyed
melons, sliced
meringue, lemon
mignonette

milk powder
milk products
Milky Way and a Reese's Peanut
  Butter Cup, hypothetical blend
  of a
mint leaves, freshly crushed
mints, after-dinner
mints, kiss of chocolate
miso paste
miso soup, ripe savory
mocha and spice, heady
mocha fudgelike
mocha, bitter
mocha, classic tea and
mocha, coffee-
mocha, creamed/creamy
mocha, glorious
mocha, raspberry
mocha, rich singed
mocha, roasted
mocha, singed oaky
mocha, strong
mocha, sweet
mocha, thick creamed
mocha, toasted smoky
mocha-caramel
mocha-chocolate, spicy
moist
molasses, baked
molasses, blackstrap
molasses, espresso-thick blackstrap
mole sauce, as piquant...fruity and
  chocolaty as
MoonPies
mousse, dark berry
mousse, decadent chocolate
Mrs. Butterworth's, beyond
muesli, toasted
muffins, freshly cut peach
muffins, rum-raisin
mulberries, burnt
mulberries, candied
mulberries, crushed
mulligatawny
muscatels, dried
Muscats, raisined
mushroom sandwich, portobello
mushrooms browned in butter,
  fine
mushrooms in honey, freshly
  peeled
mushrooms served over toast,
  butter-sautéed
mushrooms, broiled
mushrooms, butter-fried
  chanterelle
mushrooms, creamed
mushrooms, dried

mushrooms, dried Chinese
mushrooms, dried morel
mushrooms, freshly peeled
mushrooms, freshly sautéed wild
mushrooms, sautéed
mushrooms, sautéed porcini
mushrooms, smoked
mushrooms, stale dried
mushrooms, truffled
mustard and manure
mustard powder
mustard, mild yellow
mutton, boiled
Necco Wafers, chocolate
nectarines, cooked
nectarines, freshly cut
nectarines, roasted
nettles, deep-fried
Nips, warped blackberry
nori
nougat brick
nougat, almond/almond-flavored
nougat, caramel
nougat, cherry
nougat, creamy
nougat, dessert
nougat, malty
nougat, warm
nougatine, salted
nourishing
numbles
nut combo, apple-and-
nut oil, intense
nut-and-butter mold, old-
  fashioned
nutcake
Nutella
nutritious/nutritive
nuts and jasmine bathed in rose
  water, explosive almost
  obnoxious aromas of litchi
nuts baked in a brioche
nuts bathed/immersed in rose
  water, litchi
nuts rolled together, fruit and
nuts, burnt
nuts, buttered Brazil
nuts, candied
nuts, cooked
nuts, creamed
nuts, dried
nuts, dried fruit and
nuts, dry-fried
nuts, festive bowl of fruit and
nuts, freshly grilled and salted
  cashew
nuts, grilled
nuts, honeyed

nuts, honey-roasted
nuts, intense chopped
nuts, lightly caramelized dried
nuts, roasted macadamia
nuts, roasted mixed
nuts, roasted/toasted
nuts, salted/salty
nuts, seasoned
nuts, spiced
nuts, spice-laced litchi
nuts, sugarcoated
nuttiness, fruitcake
nuttiness, sherrylike
nuttiness, toasted-corn
nuttiness, very full marzipan
  almond
nutty-honey
oatcakes
oatmeal, creamy
oats, toasted
oil meets *espresso* and lemon peel
  along with a coiled-up garden
  hose, extravirgin olive
oil, burnt cooking
oil, extravirgin olive
oil, fish
oil, grapeseed
oil, no fish
oil, peach
oil, peanut
oil, rancid cooking
oil, sesame
oil, sunflower
oil, texture of extravirgin olive
oil, vegetable
oil, white truffle
oils, exotic
olive brine
olive meets Parmigiano-Reggiano,
  green
olives, burnt cooked
olives, canned
olives, cured French
olives in brine, green
olives, cured green
olives, spiced
olives, sweet cured
onions, freshly chopped spring
onions, good for pickling
onions, sweetish caramelized
orange peel extract
orange peels/rinds/zest,
  crystallized
orange peels, burnt
orange peels, dried
orange peels/rinds, candied
orange rinds, caramelized
orange wedges, candied

orange zest
orange zest, chocolate-coated
orange zest, crystallized
orange, chocolate-
oranges, burnt
oranges, burnt caramelized
oranges, butterscotch-scented
oranges, candied blood
oranges, caramelized
oranges, chocolate
oranges, creamed
oranges, crystallized
oranges, fat jellied
oranges, jellied mandarin
oranges, lacquered
oranges, smoked Seville
oranges, stewed
oranges, sugarcoated
Oreos
oysters, smoked
oysters...ozone...and clams
pain grillé
pancakes, buttermilk
pancakes, walnut-wheat
pancetta, cooked
pancetta, pan-fried
panforte
papaya, dried
papaya, spoiled

Parmesan, mature
parsley, crushed
parsnips, cooked
parsnips, roast
paste and coat the one you love,
   you could boil this down to a
   thick
paste in fig rolls, fig
paste, mushroom
paste, quince
paste, sweet-savory tomato
pastilles, anisette
pastilles, black currant
pastilles, blackberry
pastilles, Finnish tar
pastilles, fruit
pastilles, lime
pastilles, red fruit
pastilles, violet
pastries, Danish
pastry and meat
pastry edge, little lactic
pastry softness
pastry tucked into its slim frame,
   vanilla
pastry, almond
pastry, almond-cheese
pastry, apple
pastry, biscuit

pastry, buttery cream
pastry, fresh warm Danish
pastry, hazelnut cream
pastry, iced
pastry, sweet

pastry, warm sweet
pastry-rich
pâté, duck
pâté, liver
pâté, meat
patties, York peppermint
peach-apricot-fig, honeyed
peaches and cream
peaches and plums, lightly grilled
peaches and plums, stewed
peaches poached in apple cider
peaches with honey drizzled on
   them, ripe
peaches, baked/roasted
peaches, broiled/grilled
peaches, candied
peaches, canned
peaches, caramelized
peaches, cooked/stewed
peaches, cut
peaches, freshly cut Golden Queen
peaches, peeled dried
peaches, poached
peaches, sliced
peaches, sugarcoated
peaches, syrup-drenched white
peaches, tinned clingstone
peanut butter and jelly sandwich,
   fun like a
peanut oil
peanuts, awful orange
   marshmallow circus
peanuts, chocolate-coated/covered
peanuts/groundnuts, grilled
peanuts/groundnuts, roasted
pear and apple compote, over-ripe
pear, honeyed Bartlett
peardrops/peardroppy
pears dripping with honey
pears drizzled with caramel, fresh
pears drizzled with cream and
   sprinkled with spiced toasted
   nuts, baked
pears drizzled with light honey
pears immersed in minerals and
   liquid smoke, poached
pears in cinnamon
pears in syrup
pears pulled from the oven,
   as luscious as baked
pears, ample cardamom-infused
pears, baked
pears, brassy baked

pears, broiled/grilled
pears, buttered
pears, candied
pears, caramelized
pears, cooked/stewed
pears, creamed
pears, dried
pears, freshly cut Doyenné de
   Comice
pears, fresh-peeled
pears, gently spiced
pears, honeyed
pears, poached Bosc
pears, poached spiced
pears, roasted/toasted/toasty
pears, sautéed caramelized
pears, slightly stewed Bosc
pears, smoked/smoke-laden/
   smoky
pears, spiced
pears, sugar-glazed grilled
pears, tinned
pears, white chocolate-covered
peas, black pepper on
peas, canned/tinned
peas, cooked/stewed
peas, fresh-shelled
peas, puréed
peas, smushed
pecans, buttered
peel, candied

pepper dust, white
pepper in the mouth, amazing
   little explosions of black
pepper, cracked black
pepper, cracked/crushed/
   ground/milled
pepper, fermented black
pepper, fermented white
pepper, fresh-ground/freshly
   cracked black
pepper, freshly milled
pepper, freshly sliced green
pepper, grind/shake/sprinkle of
pepper, milled black
pepper, milled white
pepper, penetrating cracked
pepper, vigorous shake of white
peppers sliced with a silver knife
peppers, dry-roasted
peppers, grilled red
peppers, roasted green bell
peppers, sweet roasted red
pesto
petals, crystallized rose
petals, preserved violet
petit fours
pickle juice

pickle under the flowery
  cherry aroma
pickled, mildly
pickles more than berries,
  resembled dill
pickles, dill
pickles, fruit
pickles, ghastly
pickles, sweet
pie and vanilla ice cream,
  blackberry
pie baked in a wood-burning oven,
  quince and apple
pie crust, freshly baked cherry
pie filling, blackberry
pie fresh from the oven, blackberry
pie in a glass, Key-lime
pie in a rock quarry on a hot
  summer's day, like eating a
  banana cream
pie in hell, cherry
pie on a summer's eve, as tasty as
  cherry
pie on the windowsill, warm
pie with a slightly burnt crust,
  blackberry
pie with dark crust, black cherry
pie with melted cheddar, apple
pie with melting vanilla ice cream,
  warm blackberry
pie, airy lemon chiffon
pie, baked berry
pie, baked pecan
pie, banana cream
pie, bears more than a passing
  resemblance to cherry
pie, black cherry
pie, black currant
pie, blackberry
pie, blackberry cobbler
pie, blackberry cream
pie, blueberry
pie, boysenberry
pie, boysenberry cream
pie, caramelized cherry-apple
pie, caramel-tinged apple
pie, cherry
pie, cherry cream
pie, chewy cherry
pie, chocolate egg-cream
pie, coconut cream
pie, coconut meringue
pie, damson
pie, elderberry
pie, escargot mud
pie, explode-in-your-mouth fruit
pie, fresh rhubarb
pie, fresh warm cherry

pie, freshly baked apple
pie, fruit
pie, good old-fashioned Americana
  and cherry
pie, gooey black cherry
pie, gooseberry
pie, hot sweet blackberry
pie, just-baked
pie, just-baked cherry
pie, Key-lime
pie, lemon
pie, lemon chiffon
pie, lemon coconut meringue
pie, lemon cream
pie, lemon meringue
pie, liquid apple
pie, meat
pie, mince/mincemeat
pie, overcooked
pie, peach
pie, plum
pie, raspberry cream
pie, rhubarb
pie, spiced apple
pie, spicy fruit
pie, strawberry-rhubarb
pie, sweet peach
pie, sweet wild blackberry
pie, warm sweet cherry
pielike, apple
pimentoey
pineapple chunks, tinned
pineapple, crystallized
pineapple, extremely sweet canned
pineapple, lemon-covered
pineapples in syrup
pineapples, baked
pineapples, *brûléed*
pineapples, candied
pineapples, canned
pineapples, caramelized
pineapples, cooked/stewed
pineapples, crushed dried
pineapples, crushed fresh
pineapples, crystallized
pineapples, dried/dry
pineapples, grilled
pineapples, honeyed
pineapples, roasted/toasted
pineapples, smoky honeyed
pineapples...honeysuckle and
  herbs, succulent *luau* of grilled
pizza
pizza crust, fruit-filled
pizza, caramel corn
plumcake-style
plums and blackberries dipped
  in chocolate fondue

plums and prunes awash with
  licorice and chocolate and
  cream, almost treacly
  fruit-dark
plums going up and down,
  roasted roller-coaster
plums kissed with vanilla, spicy
  juicy black
plums preserved in alcohol
plums wrapped in prosciutto
plums, baked
plums, boiled-down black
plums, burnt
plums, candied
plums, caramelized
plums, chocolate-coated
plums, clotted
plums, cooked
plums, crushed
plums, dried Italian
plums, grilled
plums, macerated
plums, roasted
plums, rum 'n
plums, spiced
plums, stewed
plums, sweet candied
poached/poachy
poi
pomegranates with cream
popcorn with pineapple and
  vanilla sauce, buttered
popcorn, air-popped
popcorn, buttered/buttery
popcorn, caramel/caramel-dipped/
  caramelized
popcorn, fresh buttered caramel
popcorn, hot buttered
popcorn, loads of butter-dripping
popcorn, movie-theater
popcorn, toffee
popcorn, unbuttered
Popsicles, deluxe
Popsicles, buttery
Popsicles, red...white and blue
Pop-Tarts, apple
Pop-Tarts, frosted
Pop-Tarts, raspberry/strawberry
porcini, sautéed
porcinis, sweet dried
pork rinds
pork, barbecued
pork, rancid
pork, smoked
pork, spicy air-dried
Porky Pig's snout in an iron skillet,
  smoking
potato, dirty boiled

potatoes and cabbage
potatoes, boiled/cooked
potatoes, mashed
potpourri, really good cinnamon-
based meat
powder, chocolate/cocoa
powder, dusting of almond
powder, milk
pralines, chocolate
pralines, grilled/roasted/toasted
pralines, pecan
preserves, apricot and quince
preserves, berry
preserves, essence of raspberry
preserves, fruit
preserves, peach
preserves, plum
preserves, raspberry spice
preserves, strawberry
preserves, tangy strawberry
prosciutto
prosciutto, plums wrapped in
prunes and plums macerating in
brandy
prunes stewed in syrup
prunes, baked
prunes, chocolaty
prunes, cooked/stewed
prunes, dried

prunes, fermented
prunes, roasted
prunes, smoked
prunes, stream of rich coffee and
sweet
pud/pudding, plum
pudding (without the sugar),
lemon
pudding in a bottle, plum
pudding in liquid form, bread and
butter
pudding, allspice plum
pudding, Ambrosia creamed rice
pudding, as soft as a chocolate
sponge
pudding, baked lemon
pudding, British plum
pudding, Christmas
pudding, creamed rice
pudding, good chocolate
pudding, Indian
pudding, liquid Christmas
pudding, luscious rasiny plum
pudding, mum's really good rice
pudding, pineapple-butterscotch
pudding, pure fresh summer
pudding, singed top of rice
pudding, slightly burnt rice
pudding, spiced plum

pudding, spicy pineapple-
butterscotch
pudding, spicy summer
pudding, summer
pudding, sumptuous
pudding, very crunchy summer-
fruit
pudding, warm chocolate
puffs, cream
pumpkins and spice, nutty baked
pumpkins in syrup
pumpkins, baked
pungent
purée of fruit-flavored syrup
purée of red fruit
purée, acidulated apple
purée, almond
purée, dried apricot
purée, goldengage
purée, hazelnut
purée, intense Bramley apple
purée, tease of pineapple
purée, tomato
quail, roasted
quiche Lorraine
quince paste
quinces, baked
quinces, candied
quinces, mentholated
quinces, poached
quinces, puréed
quinces, stewed
quinces, sweet spiced baked
ragout of
raisin and honey softness, gentle
Raisinets
raisin massacre
raisins and raspberries, chocolate-
covered
raisins de Corinthe
raisins in brandy, sweet
raisins in rum
raisins in the nose
raisins sweetened with boiled
must, charred
raisins, ambrosial
raisins, like chewing on
explosively rich
raisins, attractively delicate notes
of
raisins, bag/box of
raisins, black

raisins, brandy-soaked
raisins, burnt
raisins, candied white
raisins, fermented
raisins, flattened/squashed
raisins, glorious celestial

raisins, golden
raisins, gooey
raisins, honey-soaked
raisins, liquidized
raisins, meaty-malted
raisins, Muscat
raisins, old old
raisins, rum and
raisins, singed
raisins, sugarcoated/sugared
raisins, white
raisiny bouquet
raisiny lusciousness
raisiny-figgy
raspberries and blackberries,
confiture of black
raspberries and vanilla cream, hot
raspberries, baked
raspberries, candied black
raspberries, caramel-drizzled
bowlful of cherries and
raspberries, cooked/stewed
raspberries, crushed
raspberries, dehydrated/dried
raspberries, jammy

raspberries, mentholated
raspberries, puréed
raspberries, smoky chocolate-
covered
raspberries, spiced
raspberries, squashed ripe
raspberry-mocha
rations, C-
Red Hots
Red Vines
Relish, Gentleman's
relish, pickled
resiny-olive oil
rhubarb, baked
rhubarb, canned
rhubarb, confectionary
rhubarb, cooked/stewed
rhubarb, freshly cut
ribs, grill sizzling with sizzling
smoked
ribs, hearty lusciousness of meaty
maple-glazed hickory-smoked
rice/ricey
richness, honeyed
richness, savory sour-creamy
richness, soupy
ricotta
ripple, raspberry
roast substances
roast, spicy nut
roast, spicy rump
rolls, warm vanilla
rollups, fruit

rosemary, roasted
rumtopf
rusks
sabayon
sage, crushed
salad bar spectrum
salad character, indeterminate fruit-
salad in a glass, fruit
salad with a refreshing squirt of lemon, fruit
salad with lime...honey and mint, summer melon
salad, black cherry
salad, burst of fruit
salad, buttered fruit
salad, canned/tinned fruit
salad, chilled asparagus
salad, citrus drizzled over fruit
salad, exotic fruit
salad, fermenting fruit
salad, festive fruit
salad, fresh fruit
salad, fresh Italian
salad, full dish of fruit
salad, green
salad, green papaya
salad, likable jumble of fruit
salad, lively citrus-toned fruit
salad, mesclun
salad, oak-chipped fruit
salad, over-ripe tropical fruit
salad, peachy fruit
salad, plain old fruit
salad, spicy fruit
salad, squashed fruit
salad, tropical fruit
salad, vegetable
salad-in-a-glass, fruit
salami, spicy
salmon, boiled/poached
salmon, broiled/grilled
salsalike
salt, sprinkling of
Saltines
sandwich, black currant
sandwich, Ghirardelli chocolate and raspberry
sandwich, sauerkraut and toadstool
sandwich, vanilla wafer-and-oak
sardines splashed with salt, ultrafresh
sardines, fresh
sardines, tinned
sauce glaze, port
sauce, abundant chocolate
sauce, almost sweet-sour like a Cantonese

sauce, as piquant...fruity... chocolaty as *mole*
sauce, as rich as blackberry
sauce, black cherry
sauce, cherry tomato
sauce, Chinese sweet-and-sour
sauce, cranberry cream
sauce, creamy egginess of *carbonara*
sauce, dark soy
sauce, drinks like chocolate
sauce, fish
sauce, Japanese soy
sauce, nutty cream
sauce, oyster
sauce, plum
sauce, raspberry
sauce, reduced raspberry
sauce, rich black plum
sauce, smoky tomato
sauce, strawberry
sauce, Tabasco
sauce, taco
sauce, teriyaki
sauce, tomato
sauce, Worcestershire
sauce: ketchup-molasses-liquid smoke, pleasing aromas of barbecue
sauerkraut
sausage, blood
sausage, dried Portuguese
sausage, grilled
sausages intermixed with dry herbs, Italian
sausages, charcuterie
sausages, dried
sausages, frying spicy
sausages, grilled Italian
sausages, spicy Italian
scones, buttered
scones, doughy
scones, raspberry
seasoning, Old Bay
seediness, grilled
seeds, cooked strawberry
seeds, roasted/toasted
sesame seeds, lightly grilled
sesame seeds, roasted/toasted
shanks, lamb
sherbet lemon tingle
sherbet without the sugar, lemon
sherbet, apple
sherbet, crisp
sherbet, fruit
sherbet, honeyed
sherbet, lemon
sherbet, luscious lime

sherbet, orange
sherbet, rich zippy
sherbet, zingy zippy
shoots, bamboo
shortbread, buttery Scottish
shortbread, savory
shortbread, uncooked buttery
Skittles along with a smorgasbord of jam
Slim Jims
Slurpees, black cherry
smoked/smoky
sorbet for your nose
sorbet garnished with Honey n' Nut bars, peach-pear
sorbet, as refreshing as lemon
sorbet, blueberry
sorbet, bubbly
sorbet, earthy lemon
sorbet, green apple
sorbet, if this were frozen it would make a really good
sorbet, like sitting on the back porch on a sunny autumn evening eating peach
sorbet, orange
sorbet, peach
sorbet, pineapple
sorbet, raspberry
sorbet, sleek
sorbet, spritzy liquid
sorbetlike freshness
sorrel, freshly chopped
soufflé lightness, surprising
soufflé, as light as a
soufflé, chocolate
soufflé, fluffy like a
soufflé, lemon
soufflé, liquid chocolate
soufflé, white coco
soup, asparagus
soup, barley
soup, black currant
soup, chicken
soup, cold cherry
soup, cream of mushroom
soup, eastern European fruit
soup, French onion
soup, mushroom
soup, odd-tasting Eastern fruit
soup, onion
soup, packet of chicken-noodle
soup, ripe *miso*
soup, sweet
soup, tomato
soup, wine
sour-creamy richness, savory
sourdough

sourness, cheesy
soy intertwined with leather
soy sauce
soy, Asian
soybeans, fermented
soy-fruit
speck, touch of
spice and minerals, balletic display
  of fruit...
spice powder, Chinese five-
spices immersed in rose water
spices, Christmas pudding
spices, cornucopia of candied fruits
  and
spices, crash of mashed Asian
spices, creamed sweet
spices, dried
spices, dusting of Spanish
spices, dusting of sundry
spices, high-octane blast of
  supercharged fruit and
spices, oil slick of black fruit and
  dark
spices, roasted Indian
spices, roasted/toasted
spices, toasted sweet
sprouts, Brussels
spuds, buttery mashed
Starbursts, cherry
steak covered with freshly ground
  pepper, grilled
steak tartare
steak, charred
steak, grilled
steak, herb-lathered grilled
steak, pepper
steak, really good rare
steak, savory
steak, so meaty it's like drinking
steak, sweetness of rare
steak, well-hung bloody sirloin
steamed
stew, aged venison
stew, beef
stew, dill and meat
stew, game
stew, hearty
stew, hung game
stew, Irish
stew, meat
stew, mushroom
stew, old-fashioned (mum's) beef
stewy and soupy
sticks, bread
Stilton, ripe
stir-fry
stock complexity, meat-
stock cubes

stock, beef
stock, crayfish
stock, gelatinous veal
stock, heavily reduced
stock, strongly reduced chicken or
  vegetable
stock, veal
stock, vegetable
strawberries and cream, fresh
strawberries and whipped cream,
  summer feelings of
strawberries drowning in Aunt
  Jemima Pancake syrup
strawberries larded with furniture
  polish and caramel
strawberries, candied
strawberries, caramelized
strawberries, chocolate
  -coated/-dipped
strawberries, crushed
strawberries, jellied
strawberries, pulped wild
strawberries, sugarcoated
strawberries, tinned
strawberry-saturated
strudel, baked apple
strudel, cream-topped apple
stuffing
stuffing, Stove Top
suckers, all-day white plum
sugar cube in a glass of V8 juice
sugar of a candy bar, thick
sugar on a chunk of Turkish
  Delight, icing
sugar over waffles, breakfast
sugar, bergamot-flavored barley
sugar, brown
sugar, burnt
sugar, cane
sugar, caramelized
sugar, cassis brown
sugar, Chelsea bun
sugar, cinnamon
sugar, confectioner's
sugar, dark brown
sugar, demerara
sugar, flower petals dipped in
sugar, hefty boiled
sugar, hot burnt
sugar, icing
sugar, lemon-flavored barley
sugar, liquid barley
sugar, liquid cane
sugar, little shot of
sugar, maple
sugar, minty barley
sugar, moist brown
sugar, muscovado

sugar, old barley
sugar, opulent Barbados
sugar, powdered
sugar, sculpted
sugar, singed barley
sugar, singed brown
sugar, smoky burnt brown
sugar, soft brown
sugar, spun
sugar, syrupy sweet Splenda-fake
sugar, totally burnt
sugarcomb
sugarplums and puréed mulberries
sugarplums, mellow scent of
sultanas and clementines, dry
sultanas and raisins and dates,
  gooey dark brown flavors of
sultanas, big fat
sultanas, peeled
sultanas, singed
sultanas, smoky old
sultanas, squashed
sundae, caramel
sundae, pineapple
sundae, rich ice cream
Sweet 'n Low
SweeTart
sweetmeats, diverse
sweetmeats, luscious
sweets with a slight plastic edge,
  Parma violet
sweets, boiled/cooked
sweets, chocolate-peppermint
sweets, fizzing boiled
sweets, homogeneous tidal wave of
  viscous
sweets, oozy layers of expensive
sweets, orange
sweets, Parma violet
sweets, red car
sweets, smorgasbord of
sweets, tinned travel
sweets, unripe strawberry boiled
syrup blended with mango nectar,
  apricot
syrup by the bucket, blackberry
syrup of Cabernet
syrup of figs and chocolate
syrup of figs, ambrosial
syrup of figs...the old-fashioned
  medicine for those suffering from
  constipation
syrup of Shiraz
syrup of smoky spicy fruit, golden
syrup of wine, chewy-textured
syrup than wine, more like fruit
syrup, almost a
syrup, as thick as maple

syrup, as viscous and sweet as chocolate
syrup, blackberry
syrup, boysenberry
syrup, canned fruit-cocktail
syrup, cassis
syrup, chocolate
syrup, dark sensuous cassis
syrup, deep pineapple
syrup, essentially a
syrup, French toast soaked in
syrup, fruit in
syrup, golden
syrup, IHOP cherry pancake
syrup, IHOP raspberry pancake
syrup, lime
syrup, luscious peach
syrup, maple
syrup, mocha
syrup, mocha candy awash in red cherry
syrup, nectarine
syrup, nectary
syrup, peaches in
syrup, pineapple in
syrup, pink
syrup, plum
syrup, purée of fruit-flavored
syrup, red and black fruit
syrup, red cherry
syrup, red fruit
syrup, rich strawberry
syrup, rose hip
syrup, sour cherry
syrup, strawberries drowning in Aunt Jemima's pancake
syrup, strawberry
syrup, sugar cane
syrup, sultana
syrup, sweet blackberry concentrated
Syrup, Tate & Lyle Golden
syrup, toffee
syrup, treacle
syrup, viscous grape
syrup, warm maple
syrup-drenched white peaches
syrup-textured
syrupy, mildly
syrupy-textured, almost
tablets, violet

Taffy, banana Laffy
taffy, massive strawberry
taffy, mint
taffy, saltwater
taffy-caramel
taffy-toffee thing
tahini paste

tamarind
tangerine peels, dried
tangerine peels, sugared
tangerine zest
tangerine zest, candied/ crystallized/preserved
tangerines and marmalade, caramelized
tangerines, candied
tangerines, dried
tangerines, honey-covered/ honeyed
tangerines, squeeze of
tapenade
tapenade-scented perfume

tapioca
tart just out of the oven, blackberry
tart sprinkled with cinnamon and vanilla wrapped in smoky-sweet buttery pie crust, cherry and cassis
tart, apple
tart, asparagus
tart, baked cherry
tart, bramble
tart, frangipane-pear
tart, French
tart, French pear
tart, fruit
tart, hot Bakewell
tart, just-made red currant
tart, lemon
tart, orange
tart, pear
tart, pecan
tart, pie
tart, sour cherry
tart, strips of burnt jam left on the rim of a raspberry
tart, succulent raspberry
tart, tasty red berry
tart, treacle
tarte tatin with a nutty pastry crust
tarte tatin, burnt
tartine, pear
teriyaki
thyme and rosemary, roasted
thyme, dried
toast and jammy fruit (sounds like breakfast, right?), smoky
toast dripping with butter and honey, hot
toast dripping with honey and spices, buttered
toast made from full-grain bread
toast smothered with lime marmalade, liquid buttered wholemeal

toast soaked in syrup, French
toast with a smear of honey, buttered
toast, bacony

toast, burnt buttered
toast, buttered cinnamon
toast, cinnamon- and vanilla-dusted French
toast, dark
toast, French
toast, grainy
toast, grilled buttered
toast, honey on
toast, hot buttered
toast, jelly
toast, judicious
toast, lightly browned
toast, limes and
toast, makes you want to spread it on breakfast
toast, Melba
toast, really crunchy
toast, shrouded in
toast, slight twang of burnt
toast, smoky oak
toast, so jammy you could almost feel tempted to spread it your breakfast
toast, sweet
toast, tea and
toast, ultraclassic
toast, unctuous buttered
toast, wall of
toast, whack of bacony
toast, whole wheat
toast, without flashy
toast...leather and spiced wood surf a rippling wave of red fruit
toasted-roasted
toastiness, mouthwatering
toasty edge, framed with a
toasty going to coffee
toasty, appley-
toasty, lemony-
toffee burnt in the pan, Farrah's Harrogate
toffee crunch
toffee lover's dream
toffee sweetness, mulberry-
toffee, brown
toffee, burnt
toffee, butter
toffee, butterscotch
toffee, caramelized
toffee, chocolaty
toffee, coffee
toffee, creamy
toffee, Devon

toffee, dried/dry
toffee, English
toffee, fat oily
toffee, homemade coconut
toffee, honeyed
toffee, licorice
toffee, lightly burnt
toffee, melted/melting
toffee, milk
toffee, mint
toffee, Mum's
toffee, nut
toffee, old
toffee, raspberry
toffee, smoky
toffee, soft
toffee, sweet
toffee, tawny
toffee, thicket of Harrogate
toffee, vanilla
toffee-apple, glorious
toffee-caramel, corpulent touch of
toffeelike fruitiness
toffee-mocha
toffees, veritable bag of
tomatillos, stewed
tomato purée
tomato sauce
tomato, dried
tomato, roasted
tomato skins, dried
tomatoes, baked
tomatoes, canned
tomatoes, chopped/diced
tomatoes, cooked
tomatoes, fried
tomatoes, rich stewed
Tootsie-Roll pop
topping at IHOP, blueberry
   pancake
topping, baked cheese
topping, ice cream
tortillas, burnt
tortillas, fresh corn
treacle, alcoholized
treacle, brown
treacle, decadent
treacle, dried black
Treacle, Fowler's Black
treacle, heavenly
treacle, melted
treacle, orange
treacle, oxidized
treacle, peachy
treacle, singed black
treaclelike raisined richness
treacly lusciousness
truffle oil

truffles, fresh-cut black
truffles, honey-coated
truffles, intense chocolate
truffles, melted black
truffles, raspberry mint
Turkish delight in a bottle, savory
Turkish delight, almond
Turkish delight, intensely
   perfumed
turnovers with mascarpone, apple
tutti-fruitiness, thoroughly
   rounded
tutti-frutti, strawberry
twists, raspberry
Twizzlers
vanilla and honeyed fruit, bags of
vanilla beans, crushed
vanilla pods macerated in
   blackberry liqueur
vanilla pods, newly cut
vanilla sheen, toasty
vanilla, burnt/singed
vanilla, custardy
vanilla, honey-toned
vanilla, luscious overlay of creamy
vanilla, lush cherry-
vanilla, roasted
vanilla, slightly stewed
vanilla, truffled with
vanilla-and-toast flavors, whack of
   upfront
vanilla-cherry
vanilla-chocolate sweetness from
   oak
vanilla-chocolate/vanillary-
   chocolaty
vanilla-coffee, soft
vanilla-cream
vanilla-licorice
vanilla-peach
vanilla-rum
vanilla-toffee
Vegemite
Vegemitey touch, light
vegetables sautéed in sweet butter,
   spiced
vegetables, canned/tinned
vegetables, grilled
vegetables, roasted summer
vegetables, steamed
vegetables/veggies, cooked/stewed
veggies, buttered
Vela-Mints
venison, roast
vinegar sifted through a dirty sock
vinegar, pure old balsamic
vinegar, raspberry
vinegar, wine

violets from the top of a party cake,
   crystallized
violets on a chocolate cupcake,
   candied
violets, candied Parma
violets, candied/crystallized
Vogel's, toasted
wafers, chocolate
wafers, vanilla
waffle piled with strawberry jam
   and whipped cream, Swedish
waffles, Eggo
waffles, whiffs of
walnuts dipped in icing
walnuts, blanched
walnuts, caramelized old
walnuts, chopped
walnuts, cooked
walnuts, pickled
walnuts, roasted/toasted
wasabi
water, boiled cabbage
water, candy
water, hot dog
water, spinach
watermelon, seductive candied
Weet-Bix
Wheat Thins
wheat, cracked
wheat, gamy puffed-
wheatmeal
wholemeal/wholewheat
wildfowl, butter-fried
wine sweetened with chocolate
   and lavender, pan-seared
   reduction of red
wrapper, eggroll
yams with lots of marshmallows
   on top, liquid equivalent of
yogurt, frozen
yogurt, lemon
yogurt, raspberry
yogurt, sourness of natural
yogurt, spicy lemon
yogurt, strawberry
yogurt, vanilla
yogurt-scented
yogurty-creamy
zabaglione, Marsala
peels, burnt orange
zest, dried
Zonkers, Screaming Yellow
zucchini, grilled
zwieback

After melon, wine is a felon.
Italian proverb

*Watermelon—it's a good fruit.
You eat, you drink, you wash
your face.*
Enrico Caruso

15. Fruit

Ripe fruit is good; almost everybody likes it, almost nobody doesn't. Given the choice, most of us (people and animals alike) probably prefer fruit to vegetables ten to one. Must be the natural sweetness that appeals so much to our palates. In fact, wine reminds people of fruit nearly as much as prepared foods in general. From apples to youngberries (whatever they are), fruit is one of the most evocative group of wine descriptors. Nothing shocking here, as wine is made from (ta-da!) the fruit of the vine. Of course, being wine-smart, you knew that already.

abrasive, pleasingly
abundant
acid, high-
adequate, just
aggressive, youthfully
alluring
almond-edged/almondy
amalgamation, delicious
amazing, really
anise-laden
any, you have to search for
apple bite, attractive green
apple cores
apple crumble
apple, unripe
apple peels, Cox's
apple peels, fresh
apple peels, yellow
apple peels/skins, green
apple richness, golden
apple seeds
apple tones, unpolished
apple underpinnings
apple-citrus
apple-core greenness, sharp
apple-flavored
apple-infused
applelike crispness

apple-pear
apple-quince
apples and lemon flowers, glass of
    little green
apples found in a farmers' market,
    heirloom
apples in a hayloft, old
apples in the fall, as hard as green
apples warmed by the sun
apples, as fresh and crisp as good
apples, autumn/fall
apples, Avize
apples, barrowloads of
apples, bell-clear
apples, botrytis-dusted
apples, Bramley
apples, bright green
apples, bright red
apples, bruised
apples, buttery
apples, Calvados-like
apples, Christmas
apples, cider
apples, clean bright green
apples, cold snap of green
apples, cooking
apples, Cox's Orange Pippin
apples, crisp green

apples, crisp Worcester
apples, crisp/crunchy
apples, culinary
apples, custard/cherimoyas
apples, dried-out old
apples, earthy
apples, eating
apples, exaggerated
apples, fall
apples, fresh
apples, Gala
apples, gentle kiss of
apples, golden
apples, golden Delicious
apples, granary
apples, Granny Smith
apples, heirloom
apples, juicy Cox's orange
apples, lean
apples, light green
apples, loft
apples, McIntosh
apples, minty green
apples, musky
apples, old
apples, over-ripe
apples, Pippin
apples, raw cooking

apples, really rotten
apples, red
apples, rennet
apples, ripe Bramley
apples, ripe Cox's
apples, ripe Fuji
apples, ripe Goudreinet
apples, ripe Pippin
apples, ripe red Katy
apples, Russet
apples, sappy yellow
apples, smoky tart
apples, snap of green
apples, soft
apples, sour crab
apples, sour-sweet
apples, stale
apples, stony green
apples, sun-drenched
apples, superripe red delicious
apples, sweet pink
apples, tart Granny Smith
apples, tart green
apples, under-ripe/unripe
apples, vague inert
apples, vanilla/vanillary
apples, viscous sour
apples, white
apples, windfall
apples, winter
apples, yellow
apples, zingy green
apples...Meyer lemons and
  wildflowers, basket overflowing
  with heirloom
apple-spice
appley aromas
appley, intensely
appley-elderflower
appley-pineappley
appley-racy
appley-strawlike
appley-toasty
apricot medley
apricot pits/stones
apricot skins
apricot, deep blushed
apricot-quince
apricots turning to peaches
apricots, ancient/old
apricots, creamy
apricots, good old
apricots, high-toned
apricots, intense ripe
apricots, leafy
apricots, mineralized
apricots, oily
apricots, ripe gourmet-grocery

apricots, rotting
apricots, sexy layers of
apricots, smoky
apricots, sun-dried
apricots, sun-ripened
apricots, *sur-maturité*-laced
apricots, unripe
apricots, vague
apricots, waxy
apricots...honeysuckle and fresh
  minerality, lively tumult of
assertive, nicely
autumn/autumnal
avalanche
avocados
awash
bags/bagfuls
baked, sun-
banana oil
banana, dried
banana peels/skins
banana skins, old/over-ripe
banana-estery
banana-like-flowery
banana-nut
bananas here, no candy or
bananas, cooking
bananas, creamy
bananas, dwarf
bananas, glue and
bananas, green/unripe
bananas, intense vanilla-mellowed
bananas, over-ripe
bananas, rich
bananas, ripe
bananas, sun-ripened dwarf
bananas, sweet
bandwidth, narrow
base, rich
basket/basketful
bawdy
Beaujolais-type
bereft
berried delight, pure
berried, savorily
berried, strikingly
berries black and blue, jumble of
berries gorged on sun, little wild
berries in hedgerows
berries just picked, sun-warmed
berries lurking, some red
berries on a hot summer day
  in the mountains, like picking
berries sing and dance on the
  tongue, joyous
berries straight off the bush,
  ripe red

berries struggling to squeeze
  between the charred oak planks
berries with charred edges
berries, Armani-slick
berries, authentic earthy
berries, babbling brook of
berries, background of
berries, basket/bowl of
berries, bodacious
berries, brambly bushes laden with
berries, brash
berries, briarwood
berries, brooding intense
  all-enveloping dark
berries, bustling
berries, California monster
berries, charcoal-edged
berries, cheerful
berries, cherry-red
berries, creamy wild red
berries, crunchy red and black
berries, cushiony dark
berries, dark/darkish/darkest
berries, delightfully witty
berries, dense deep
berries, earthy tart
berries, essence of
berries, field
berries, generic
berries, gentle
berries, gently pressed very fresh
berries, *goji*
berries, handful of
berries, crunching
berries, lipsmackin'
berries, little black
berries, little wild
berries, mature
berries, meaty
berries, medley of focused wild
berries, minty
berries, mixed ripe
berries, myrtle
berries, ocean of
berries, opulent
berries, pert
berries, polished
berries, punchy
berries, rare
berries, red summer
berries, reticent red
berries, ripe woodland
berries, ripe-to-bursting
berries, rowdy
berries, sappy red
berries, sea of wild
berries, sheer velvet
berries, shriveled

berries, sloe
berries, spicy
berries, squashy red
berries, squashy ripe
berries, sticky
berries, sultry
berries, summer
berries, sun-baked
berries, sun-dried/dry
berries, sun-fattened
berries, sunny
berries, tart wild
berries, tenacious
berries, thick brush strokes of
berries, thorn bush
berries, throaty
berries, tight little wild
berries, ultramellow
berries, ultraripe
berries, whole ripened
berries, wild pungent jam
berries, wild sun-warmed
berries, woodland
berry ball, real/true
berry bomb, jammy Australian
berry bouquet, huge
berry cornucopia
berry family reunion
berry kiss, juicy
berry patch in a eucalyptus grove
  next to a coalmine
berry patch, like walking through a
berry qualities, rife with
berry sappiness, intense wild
berry scents, thrusting
berry spectrum, dark
berry-driven
berry-filled
berryish bliss
berryishness, just touching
berry-laced
berrylike richness, sweet
berrylike undercurrent,
  unforgettable
berrylike, vaguely
berryness, intriguing
berry-picking time!, it's
berry-rhubarb, dusty
berry-smoky
bilberries
billowy
bite, distinct
bitter
black as night, as
black brick-scented
black is beautiful here
black, blackest of
black, brick-scented

black, bruising
black, crushed
black, crystalline
black, ethereal
black, explosive
black, inky-
black, nascent
black, night-
black, oak-empowered
black, saucy
black, steely
black, voluptuous
blackberries and black currants
  pulling in different directions
blackberries and chocolate, like
  falling into a very tasty black
  hole made of
blackberries and tar, olive-scented
blackberries picked in the
  hedgerows
blackberries with seeds, ripe
blackberries, aggressive
blackberries, brambly wild
blackberries, briary
blackberries, burly
blackberries, bushels of
blackberries, cedar-scented
blackberries, dead ripe
blackberries, dry porcinis that
  turn to
blackberries, fistful of late summer
blackberries, fleshy
blackberries, hedgerow-ripe
blackberries, just-ripe
blackberries, like drinking
blackberries, like eating
blackberries, long
blackberries, mint-tinged
blackberries, paintball
blackberries, peppery
blackberries, schnappslike
blackberries, silky
blackberries, sullen
blackberries, sun-baked
blackberries, sun-drenched
blackberries, sun-roasted
blackberries, sun-warmed
blackberries, sweet-tart
blackberries, tobacco-flecked
blackberries, varietal
blackberries, virtual garden of
blackberry bliss
blackberry goodness, nugget of
blackberry-cassis
blackberry-plum
blackberry-raisin-date-raspberry
blackberry-spice
blackberry-themed charms

blackthorns
blast
blatant
blessed
blessed by the sun
blocky
blue
blue, deep dark
blueberries and blackberries,
  humongous quantities of jammy
blueberries and raspberries, silky
blueberries, juicy
blueberries, just-picked
blueberries, mountain/wild
blueberries, nutty
blueberries, tart
blueberries, virtual garden of
blueberry-stuffed
bodacious
bonanza
bosomy
bounce, more/bouncy
bountiful/bounty
bouquet, Edenic
bouquet, fresh
bowl
boysenberries, hot
boysenberries, ripe wild
boysenberry-spice
brambles, black
brambles, blackberry
brambles, dark/darkish
brambles, seedless
brambles, sweet
brambly, relishably
brambly, zesty-
brambly-sorrel
brash
breadfruit
breezy
bright approachable
bright as an Indian summer day, as
brightish
brooding, dark
Bual-like
bumbleberries
bumper
burnt, well
bursting at the seams
buttery
California, untamed
candylike
cantaloupe, just-ripe
cantaloupes, musky
carambola
caramel-like, creamy
cascade

cassis and black figs, rolling
  flavors of
cassis showing through tobacco
  overlay
cassis, cedary-
cassis, chocolate
cassis, cinnamon-scented
cassis, *crème de*
cassis, crunchy
cassis, dusty
cassis, earthy
cassis, fist of
cassis, gamy
cassis, initially pure
cassis, jammy
cassis, lavish vivid
cassis, licorice-infused
cassis, spicy
cassis, syrup-laden
cassis, violet-laced
cassis, weedy
cassis...cassis and more cassis
cedar-tinged
cedary
Chablis-like
changing, endlessly
character, laid-back
characterless
characters here, no upfront
Chardonnay, succulent
Chardonnay, unadorned
charm, has oleaginous
charred
cheery
cheesy
cherimoya
cherries and blackberries, jammy
  black
cherries and boysenberries bounce
  across your palate like Ping-Pong
  balls
cherries and dust
cherries on a bed of newly
  harvested hay, spring
cherries, barrels of
cherries, Bigarreau
cherries, Bing
cherries, biting black
cherries, bitter/bitterish
cherries, bittersweet black
cherries, bloody note to the meaty
cherries, breezy black
cherries, bright
cherries, brooding black
cherries, Burlat
cherries, cedary
cherries, corrupt/corrupted
cherries, creamy

cherries, crescendo of lively
cherries, crisp
cherries, dark/darkish
cherries, decent black
cherries, deceptively innocent
cherries, deep
cherries, dry
cherries, dusty
cherries, earthy black
cherries, elegant
cherries, essence of
cherries, fistful of
cherries, flood of
cherries, flower-imbued
cherries, fortifying
cherries, fully corrupted
cherries, Gean
cherries, glossy
cherries, Griotte
cherries, heart
cherries, heavenly black
cherries, light sour
cherries, masses of fierce
cherries, meaty
cherries, Montmorency
cherries, Morello
cherries, mouthwatering mix of
  red and black
cherries, musty
cherries, Nanking
cherries, oak-covered
cherries, oozing ripe black
cherries, perky
cherries, pie
cherries, Queen/Royal Anne
cherries, Rainier
cherries, red
cherries, refreshing bitter
cherries, ripe Bing
cherries, ripe black
cherries, sappy
cherries, sharp
cherries, softish kirsch
cherries, sour/sourish
cherries, still-simple
cherries, stony
cherries, stony Griotte
cherries, sun-baked black
cherries, sunburnt
cherries, sun-dried
cherries, super-ripe
cherries, supple black
cherries, sweet
cherries, sweet-and-sour/
  sweet-sour
cherries, sweet black
cherries, sweet wild
cherries, tangy

cherries, tart black
cherries, tart red
cherries, telltale
cherries, undeveloped/unripe
cherries, unpicked
cherries, uppity
cherries, varietal
cherries, velvety
cherries, very ripe
cherries, waxy
cherries, waxy red
cherries, Whiteheart
cherries, wild
cherries, woodsy red
cherries, youthfully tart
cherries...cherries and more
  cherries
cherry accents beneath the hard
  veneer
cherry and plum flavors and a tart
  mouth, strumpet of a wine with
  tawdry
cherry aroma, little pickle under
  the flowery
cherry centers, black
cherry cherry cherry
cherry concentrate
cherry concentrate, black
cherry cores, whopping Bing
cherry exposition
cherry festival in a glass:
  fruit...blossoms...pits and all
cherry fruit linked to silky tannin
  in a torrid love affair
cherry kernels
cherry orchard in mid-July,
  like walking through a
cherry orchard, breeze through a
cherry pips/pits/stones
Cherry Ripe
cherry skins
cherry tartness
cherry tartness, herby sour-
cherry, creamy-
cherry, flecks of
cherry, like biting a
cherry-berry, ripe
cherry-blackberry-plum, black
cherry-cheeked
cherry-cranberry
cherry-earth-cedar
cherry-inflected, red
cherry-laced wallop
cherry-laden treasure
cherry-meets-plum, sour-
cherrylike vibrancy
cherrylike, tangy black
cherry-scented

cherry-strawberry
cherry-vanilla, lush
chewy
chocolate
chocolate, dark
chocolate/chocolaty-menthol
chokeberries
chunky
citric backbone
citric nippiness
citric snap
citric, refreshingly
citric, seriously
citric, vaguely
citrons
citrus and minerals slice across the
  palate like a well-honed blade
citrus as interpreted by Schubert
citrus brilliance
citrus character, rounded
citrus delight
citrus encased in minerals
citrus flavors buried under a heavy
  layer of rock
citrus flavors, whole bowl of
citrus is the name of the game here
citrus oils
citrus peels/rinds/skins
citrus pith
citrus sensations, vibrant
citrus squeeze, refreshing
citrus zing
citrus, all sorts of
citrus, atypical
citrus, bright
citrus, buttery
citrus, cornucopia of
citrus, crunchy
citrus, epic
citrus, flinty
citrus, fresh
citrus, honey-
citrus, just-picked
citrus, minerally
citrus, pithy seedy
citrus, puckery
citrus, quasi-
citrus, rapier-sharp
citrus, seething cloud of
citrus, sensual
citrus, sings with fresh
citrus, slinky arrows of
citrus, smoldering with smoke and
citrus, snare drum of
citrus, spicy
citrus, striking buttery
citrus, subtle tannic
citrus, sweet-and-sour

citrus, tailored-patchwork
citrus, tart
citrus, tight
citrus, treeful of good
citrus, very dry
citrus, whistle-clean lick of
citrus, whole bowl of
citrus, zippy
citrus-flavored pleasure
citrus-laced
citrus-petrol
citrus-to-apple
citrusy oomph
citrusy freshness, fabulous
citrusy rich, elegant
citrusy verve, full of
citrusy, thrillingly
citrusy-rich, elegant
class, world-
clean-cut
clear, bell-
clear, crystal-
clementines, dry sultanas and
cloddish
cloudberries
clumsy, slightly
coagulated
coats your mouth
cohesive
collage, gorgeous
compact
complex
complexed, yeast-
compressed it's almost like essence,
  so
concentrated, highly/really/very
concentrated, intense
concentration, fabulous
concoction, lovely
confit
copious
coquettish
core, sweet inner
core, vibrating
cornucopia, summer
cornucopia, veritable
corseted, firmly/tightly
covered, well
cowberries
crabapples, sour
crammed
crammed, absolutely
cranberries, fresh
cranberries, sweet
cranberries, tart
cranberries, white
cranberry lurking beneath
  the earthy foliage

cranberry tartness, slight
cranberry, cherry-
cranberry-anise, dried
cranberry-orange
creamiest
creamy-cedary
creamy-malo
crisp, nicely
crosscut, tangy
crunchy
currant concentrate, black
currant power of blistering
  intensity black
currant richness, irresistible black
currant skins, dry black
currants and berries, juicy
currants and blackberries,
  basso continuo of black
currants and blackberries,
  beautifully etched
currants and raspberries, piercing
  scents of black
currants veering into ripe cassis,
  black
currants, boisterous black
currants, cedary
currants, celestial black
currants, chewy
currants, chunky
currants, dark
currants, deep black
currants, earthy
currants, earthy black
currants, elderly
currants, fennel-like black
currants, leafy black
currants, leathery
currants, loamy-tinged black
currants, nutty
currants, old leathery
currants, pink
currants, plums and spices, effuses
currants, plush
currants, raisined
currants, raw black
currants, red
currants spiked with vanilla, red
currants, reticent black
currants, sleek with heaps of spicy
  brambly black
currants, sumptuous cushion of
  black
currants, tangy
currants, weedy black
currants, white
currants, wild
curtain, opulent
damson skins

damsons, black
damsons, classy
damsons, dark
damsons, drenched
damsons, leafy
damsons, sharp
damsons, white
dancing
dark, inky
dark, zesty
dead, borders on
dead, good and
decayed/decaying
deep/deeper
define, hard to
definition, good
delicacy yet incisive
delicious
demure
dense, massively
density, impressive
density, no
depth, awesome
depth, majestic
desiccated, slightly
devoid, almost completely
dewberries
dexterity
discreet
display, firework
downside, on the
drenched
drunken
dry
durian
dusty
dynamite
earthy
easy-to-like
edible
effect, crisp punchy
effusive
elastic
elderberries, black
elderberries, prodigiously ripe
elderberries, red
elderberries, wild
electric/electrifying
elegant
elevated, highly
elevated, less
eloquent
elusive, coquettishly
emblematic
eminent
enough to cover the oak, not
enough, more than
enough, nowhere near

escaping from the black hole
essence/essential
essences, gently dueling
etched, finely
ethereal, almost
evolved
excellent
exotic
expansive
explosive/explosion
expression, beautiful/
   grand/marvelous
expressive
expressive, not terribly
extract, clean and lively
extract, lacking
exuberant
fabulous
fade, beginning to
faded
fair
farmy
fashion, in a somewhat linear
fat/fatty
fat and sassy
feisty
fenberries wreathed in ripe Asian
   moonfruit, nuances of bruised
fiesta
figgy, gloriously
figgy, leafy-
figgy, raisiny-
fights bravely
figs and dates, soft
figs, season's first
figs, black
figs, decadent
figs, essence of
figs, focused layers of
figs, fresh
figs, fresh fuzzy
figs, green
figs, lush
figs, meltingly ripe
figs, ripe/ripest
figs, season's first
figs, soft
figs, sun-ripened
figs, sun-warmed
filled that it's like sparkles, so
fine, very
firework display
firm/firmed/firming
flabby
flashy
flavored/flavorful/flavorsome
flavors wrapped in truffle-scented
   smoke

flavors, hedgerow-
flavors, lacks serious
flavors, there's more going on here
   than simply
fleshy, heavily
fleshy, very sexy and
flinty
flooded
floral, gently/politely
flourish, swashbuckling
flowery
fluffy
flügelberries on the midpalate,
   nuances of wild
focused, beautifully/nicely/well
forceful
forest, austere
forward, vivid and
foxy
fragrant
fraise des bois
framboise, joyous blast of
framboise-scented
fresh, pineappley
fresh, tinglingly
freshness, billowy-breezy
freshness, juicy
freshness, limelike/limy
friendly
frightening
front, up-
fruit abound, black
fruit all the time, all
fruit and acidity like a shadow...
   it doesn't hit you over the head,
   earth...good
fruit and acidity, near-perfect
   tension between
fruit and chewy grainy tannins,
   turbulent red whirlpool of ripe
   damson
fruit and class, oozing with
fruit and cold cuts, cherry
fruit and conviction, lacks both
fruit and dark spice, oil slick of
   black
fruit and flowers engulf you
fruit and flowers, litany of
fruit and harvest bloom, magic
   reek of
fruit and herbs fighting furiously
   or supremacy
fruit and leaves, appealingly wild
   edge of brambly
fruit and minerals, *mélange* of
   light
fruit and minerals, symphony of
fruit and oak dressing

fruit and oak, nice presentation of
fruit and oak, perfect marriage of
fruit and oak, subtle interplay of
fruit and perfume, heart-stopping
fruit and perfume, sublime appley
fruit and plenty of it, all
fruit and ripe tannins fight the
  good fight, ripe cassis/berry
fruit and spice, bounty of
fruit and spice, burlesque of bawdy
fruit and torrefaction, mixed
fruit and wood fighting for control
fruit and wood is almost garish,
  display of
fruit aromas speak of islands,
  tropical
fruit at the sweet end of the varietal
  spectrum, flooded with
fruit baking in the sun on the
  ground in an orchard, ripe
fruit ball
fruit basket, whole
fruit bathes the palate, luxurious
  honeyed supersmooth textured
fruit below the surface, powerful
fruit bobbing up and down,
  profound
fruit bomb deluxe
fruit bomb with flesh on its bones
fruit bomb, citrus-
fruit bomb, dense fat
  thermonuclear Shiraz
fruit bomb, expansive
fruit bomb, explosive/
  thermonuclear
fruit bomb, fat slurpy
fruit bomb, headspinning
fruit bomb, hedonistic
fruit bomb, huge viscous
fruit bomb, majestic
fruit bomb, massively destructive
fruit bomb, oaky
fruit bomb, quintessential
  hedonistic
fruit bomb, seductive sexy
fruit bomb, spice/spicy
fruit bomb, tropical
fruit bomb, unctuous tangerine-
  flavored
fruit bound tightly into a focused
  complex whole, awesome
fruit bowl inside a soulful wine
  with weight
fruit bowl, Algerian
fruit bowls you over
fruit brought out by fine wine
  making, all the

fruit cascade over the taste buds
  without any sense of weight,
  gorgeous layers of
fruit cemented with minerals,
  polished blocks of dark
fruit characters here, no upfront
fruit classic, summer-
fruit coats your mouth
fruit colliding with Firestone tires
  and oil
fruit coma, almost dizzying:
  I might go into a
fruit comes rocketing through,
  plummy
fruit concentration, fantastic
fruit conquers the taster's palate,
  layer upon layer of sultry
fruit contests tongue space with
  oak...resulting in a drawn match
fruit dashed across in painterly
  fury
fruit dialed in like a sniper's rifle
  on your palate
fruit does the talking
fruit doesn't really evolve,
  bright basic unreconstructed
fruit drive, lovely
fruit driven mad with sun
fruit driven, tropical
fruit essences, gently dueling
fruit evident beneath the oak
  veneer, generous
fruit exploding in the mouth,
  pockets of
fruit explosion for your taste buds
fruit expression, wonderful
fruit extract, sappy
fruit fighting for independence
fruit flavor in the bottle, loses all its
fruit flavors wrapped in truffle-
  scented smoke
fruit flavors, doesn't slip into
  tinned
fruit flavors, hedgerow-
fruit flavors, lacks serious
fruit flavors, Silk Road of
fruit flavors, there's more going on
  here than simply
fruit flesh on the bones, needs a
  touch more
fruit forward
fruit galore, scenario of black
fruit gluggability, wonderful juicy-
fruit gorged on sunshine
fruit has blotted up the oak
fruit has dropped off, any
fruit has dropped out...but just
  hanging in

fruit has gobbled up the oak
fruit health, black
fruit here seems as light as a
  feather, concentrated
fruit here, no lollipop-candy
fruit hiding in the basement,
  not a lot of
fruit hung onto a firm body,
  plenty of
fruit imaginable, cloud of the
  sweetest
fruit in a bottle, concentrated
fruit in a box of oak studded with
  stones, panoply of
fruit in a dusty vineyard
fruit in buds, very ripe
fruit in the backseat, considerable
fruit in the mouth, mashed
fruit intensity, succulent sweet-
fruit is all you could ask for,
  simplicity and clarity of
fruit is mostly suppressed beneath
  a youthful tannic crust
fruit it crushes your palate, so
  much
fruit it isn't, juicy
fruit it smelled like dessert, so
  much
fruit it's like sparkles, so filled with
fruit jousting with raw tannin,
  good crisp
fruit just asks to be drunk, glorious
  seductive
fruit largely suppressed beneath
  tannic texture and the heat of
  alcohol
fruit leaps out of the glass, great
fruit leaves me speechless,
  concentration of
fruit lover's friend
fruit lurking, some red berry
fruit mush, unrelenting
fruit obscures blemishes, sweet
fruit of the forest/forest fruit
fruit of the garden, all the flowers
  and
fruit of the summer, all the
fruit on attack, fat and fleshy
fruit on its head
fruit orchard, English
fruit peeking through, tons of fresh
fruit peels/skins
fruit peering through the planks
fruit-picking, high summer
fruit pill, hard-to-swallow
fruit pits/stones
fruit poking through the thickets
fruit potency

fruit power, tremendous
fruit purity
fruit push, little
fruit pushes through like grass
through cracks in the stones
fruit quality, pinnacle of
fruit required for greatness, lacks
the depth of
fruit richness, unbelievable
crunchy
fruit ripeness, sunniest most
comfortingly perfect sense of
fruit rouges, very petit
fruit sat there without budging
further, muffled
fruit seems to go straight to your
heart, round rich relaxed
fruit shackled in tannin,
concentrated
fruit shines through, exotic
fruit spectrum, tropical
fruit still locked in arm-to-arm
combat with the tannins
fruit stones
fruit struggles to carry its oak
burden, delicate
fruit sweetness, runnel of
fruit sweetness, skerrick of
fruit they're almost like essence,
so compressed with
fruit to cover the oak, not enough
fruit to the max
fruit underneath, real old-vine
fruit weight, good
fruit well packed
fruit with a smile, wearing its
cherry and raspberry
fruit with finesse and complexity,
potpourri of red and black
fruit with Old World backbone,
New World
fruit without pride,
smirking beauty of
fruit, absence of forceful
fruit, all flash and
fruit, almost Porty sweet
fruit, almost thick with
fruit, avalanche of red
fruit, awesome core of ripe
fruit, awesome in the depth of its
fruit, bazaars...sultans and exotic
fruit, Beaujolais-like light
fruit, beautifully clear creamy-
cherry Pinot Noir
fruit, big fat
fruit, big figgy
fruit, big mouthful of
fruit, big overloaded

fruit, big smack of fresh
fruit, big tannin mashing the
fruit, blast of high-quality
fruit, boggles the mind with its
never-ending layers of pure
fruit, bolero of zingy red and
orange
fruit, bowl filled with exotic
fruit, breath of tropical
fruit, bright shock of
fruit, buried like a pirate's treasure
is a deep core of cherry
fruit, bursting with ripe
fruit, buzz of juicy
fruit, cacophony of mixed
fruit, callow juicy berry
fruit, clarity of
fruit, clean and lively extract of
fruit, clearly expressed varietal
fruit, cocktails of exotic
fruit, complex red
fruit, cornucopia of ripe tropical
fruit, covered in loads of lush
fruit, crisp almondy
fruit, curious *mélange* of ripe and
green
fruit, dark satiny
fruit, delicate lacework of elegant
fruit, delicious core of
fruit, deliciously fresh bowl of
fruit, delightful dance of summer
fruit, demure spiced
fruit, densely packed black
fruit, disjointed stewy
fruit, dissolves in the mouth into
clouds of sweet
fruit, drenched in
fruit, dripping with rich
fruit, dull
fruit, easygoing red berry
fruit, elegantly focused spicy and
floral
fruit, elusive tropical puckerish
fruit, embryonic nose of superripe
fruit, essencey raisiny
fruit, every kind of wild
fruit, explosion of sweet
fruit, explosive black
fruit, expressive Black Forest
fruit, extracty old-vine
fruit, extremely elegant pineapple
fruit, fabulously rich mind-
bogglingly complex
fruit, fairly bulging with wads of
fruit, fiesta of
fruit, fills your mouth with a
basket of dark
fruit, firework display of

fruit, firm bittersweet cherrystone
fruit, flooded with
fruit, focused layers of other
fruit, French finesse with robust
California
fruit, fresh red
fruit, fresh summertime
fruit, full canopy of dark black
fruit, full of
fruit, full-bodied serious
fruit, full-frontal
fruit, generic red
fruit, gentle slightly amorphous
berry
fruit, Germanic persistence of
fruit, glorious heavenly ripe
fruit, gloriously young
fruit, gobs of complex black
fruit, good earthy black curranty
fruit, good gutsy
fruit, gorgeous cushion of
fruit, green pea
fruit, gush of wild black
fruit, gushes with gorgeously ripe
fruit, gushing easy tender
fruit, gushing ripe Pinot
fruit, gushing with
fruit, heaps of seductive ripe
fruit, heaps of strapping
fruit, heaps of vanilla-rich spicy-
cassis
fruit, heavenly beetrootlike
fruit, heavily pumped up with
fruit, hedgerow
fruit, helicopters into your mouth
with spinning blades of
fruit, herb-tinged berry
fruit, here the driver is red cherry
fruit, high-octane Pinot
fruit, hot bramble
fruit, huge gutsy dark
fruit, hyper-ripe red and black
fruit, indecently packed with
fruit, innumerable tropical
fruit, intense drenched inky
fruit, intensely vivid brambly
fruit, intoxication of
fruit, in-your-face sweet
fruit, irresistibly pure
fruit, Italianate brambly
fruit, jet-black
fruit, juicy deep
fruit, just oozes
fruit, just-picked jammy
fruit, kinky red-black
fruit, knot of
fruit, kumquat botrytis
fruit, laden with everything except

fruit, languorous black
fruit, lashings of plum-berry
fruit, lashings of sweet
fruit, last embers of sweet
fruit, lavishly rich
fruit, layered with decadent
fruit, layers and layers of fine
  tannins and
fruit, leathery black
fruit, little sign of primary
fruit, loads of unbridled delicious
fruit, lot of wacky
fruit, lovely bright singing ringing
fruit, lovely flowery
fruit, lovely racy
fruit, lovely waxy Chardonnay
fruit, luscious exotic rose- and
  orange-peel
fruit, marvelous long
fruit, meaty black
fruit, megaripe black
fruit, *mélange* of summer
fruit, melt-in-the-mouth
fruit, middle core of
fruit, mineral-laced black
fruit, mountain built of
fruit, mouthfilling/mouthful of
fruit, mute red
fruit, neutron bomb of
fruit, nice collection of extracted
fruit, nice core of ripe
fruit, nice skein of red berry
fruit, nice uplift of crisp
fruit, no errant
fruit, no frills…just
fruit, no hint of raisined dead
fruit, no obvious sense of
fruit, nutty orange
fruit, oak destroys the
fruit, oak underpinning crisp
fruit, oak used as a crutch to hide a
  lack of
fruit, oak-empowered black
fruit, oaky enough to bury the

fruit, odd rotting

fruit, offered up a few angles on
  which to hang their lush
fruit, old-vine
fruit, oodles of fresh crisp
fruit, optimally ripe pink
fruit, opulent cigary
fruit, opulent curtain of
fruit, overblown jammy dollop of
fruit, packed with
fruit, panoply of
fruit, pepper-laced white and
  yellow
fruit, perfect peachily

fruit, pit
fruit, plenty of black
fruit, plethora of
fruit, plumped-up
fruit, poorly composted tropical
fruit, powerful densely packed
fruit, powerful thrust of rich spicy
  black currant
fruit, power-packed ripe
fruit, promising young
fruit, prototypical stone
fruit, *puissant* black
fruit, pulsating red
fruit, pulverized strawberry
fruit, pure blast of sweet
fruit, pure grapey
fruit, pure primary
fruit, pure summer/summery
fruit, pure summery Muscat
  explosion of
fruit, raging rapids of dark
fruit, rare exotic
fruit, rather fleeting neutral
fruit, really uncanny retention of
  youthful
fruit, red forest
fruit, resplendent with lush
fruit, reverberating red

fruit, rich animally

fruit, rich bittersweet cherryish
fruit, rich cockle-warming
fruit, rich creamy
fruit, riot of chewy
fruit, riotous
fruit, ripe Cabernet
fruit, ripe hedgerow
fruit, ripe succulent yellow
fruit, ripe tannins are buried in
  sweet
fruit, rock
fruit, rush of green
fruit, salty citrus
fruit, sappy dark core of explosive
  Shiraz
fruit, satiny white
fruit, Scandinavian autumn
fruit, sea of dark berry
fruit, sheer fury of its
fruit!, show me the
fruit, shower of broken schist
that explodes out of the
fruit, silky robe of spicy red
fruit, simple lolly
fruit, sings with
fruit, smoke-scented bramble
fruit, smooth weave of dark
fruit, smorgasbord of black
fruit, snappy cheerful red

fruit, soft autumn
fruit, soft slightly amorphous dark
fruit, softly explosive exotic
fruit, solid structure buried in fat
fruit, spiced autumn
fruit, spiky nettle
fruit, splendid excess of
fruit, splendid opulent
fruit, star
fruit, staunch red
fruit, steel core is wrapped in a core
  of fleshy
fruit, sticky black
fruit, stone
fruit, structure overwhelms
fruit, stuffed full of youthful
fruit, stuffed with
fruit, stuns the taster with its
  unbridled
fruit, sturdy sweaty
fruit, suave black
fruit, subjugated to the
fruit, sublime almost pagan
  Riesling
fruit, succulent core of rich
  honeyed

fruit, suck-a-stone

fruit, sultry depth of
fruit, summer
fruit, summer tree-
fruit, summer-pudding
fruit, sun-baked autumn
fruit, superelegant stone
fruit, superextraction of
fruit, sweet moscato
fruit, sweet-sour plummy
fruit, sweet-tasting
fruit, syrupy black-currant
fruit, syrupy fatty
fruit, tangy white
fruit, tannins grapple with
fruit, taut red
fruit, teeming with summer
fruit, telltale topical
fruit, texture is so plush that it feels
  like the palate is resting on a
  waterbed of over-ripe black
fruit, thick pot-of-jam
fruit, titan of black
fruit, toast…leather and spiced
  wood surf a rippling wave of red
fruit, tons of fresh
fruit, tons of superb
fruit, totally powered by
fruit, tower of vanillin
fruit, tropical two-
fruit, truckloads of jammy
fruit, ultrafresh melon

fruit, ultratropical honeyed
fruit, unbelievable concentration of ripe
fruit, unbelievably intense ripe
fruit, undercurrent of good
fruit, under-ripe hedgerow
fruit, upfront lively
fruit, uplifted dark stone
fruit, utterly voluptuous black
fruit, velvety white
fruit, veneer of sweet
fruit, very concentrated urgent
fruit, very dark bush and tree
fruit, very old vine
fruit, very pleasing soft
fruit, very ripe dead
fruit, very ripe quasitropical
fruit, very sophisticated nettley
fruit, very sweet ripe thick-tasting
fruit, vibrates with
fruit, vibrating core of
fruit, violet-imbued
fruit, violetlike refreshing
fruit, virtual cascade of
fruit, virtual full palate of tropical
fruit, viscous waves of black
fruit, volleys of ripe
fruit, wallop of ripe
fruit, wanton wild black
fruit, waves of
fruit, waxy black
fruit, wealth of
fruit, welcome lift of
fruit, whack of
fruit, wheelbarrow of UGLI
fruit, whisper of
fruit, wild brawny
fruit, wild jungle of competing but somehow perfectly integrated
fruit, whole panoply of
fruit, wonderful concentration of pure
fruit, wonderful warm
fruit, wood gets the better of the
fruit, wood-laced white
fruit, woven together with veils of exotic
fruit, wrapped up in plush
fruit, yeast-complexed
fruit, youthful magisterial
fruit, zesty dark
fruit, zippy orchard
fruit...black smoke and black bitter minerals, beauty in black: black
fruit...fruit...fruit
fruit...nicely slicked back, hairy
fruit...not oak, driven by

fruit...spice and minerals, balletic display of
fruit?, where's the
fruit?, who tipped the spice box into this lush velvet tangle of bramble
fruit-alcohol bomb, superficial
fruit-and-flower dance on the palate
fruit-bomb, far-flung
fruit-bush, soft smoky
fruit-centered
fruit-closed
fruit-dominated, tropical
fruit-drenched
fruit-drive, lovely
fruit-driven bouquet
fruit-driven, blindly
fruit-driven, tropical
fruited power, black-
fruited profile, charming
fruited, bright-
fruited, crisply
fruited, deeply
fruited, directly
fruited, explosively
fruited, grippy firm-
fruited, lushly
fruited, richly
fruited, rustic-
fruited, smartly
fruited, very clearly
fruit-filled
fruit-flooded
fruit-focused
fruit-forward
fruit-free dross, red
fruit-free, watery and
fruitiness and ripeness, amazing
fruitiness explodes in your mouth
fruitiness is explosive
fruitiness, almost American exotic
fruitiness, autumn
fruitiness, avoids the sticky
fruitiness, boatload of kirsch
fruitiness, dancing
fruitiness, darkly wild
fruitiness, devil-may-care
fruitiness, direct/straightforward/ upfront
fruitiness, excessive
fruitiness, explosive
fruitiness, exuberant
fruitiness, fleshy
fruitiness, fresh come-onish juicy
fruitiness, heavy dark
fruitiness, in-your-face
fruitiness, light tangerine

fruitiness, oaky
fruitiness, palate-cleansing
fruitiness, red-brick dusty
fruitiness, relaxed
fruitiness, reticent
fruitiness, shimmering
fruitiness, short-lived
fruitiness, slightly fragile
fruitiness, slim
fruitiness, sprightly
fruitiness, sweet easy
fruitiness, uninhibited fresh
fruitiness, velvety
fruitiness, wet
fruitiness, whispery sweet melony
fruit-infested bouquet
fruit-inflected, red
fruit-laden
fruitless
fruit-loopy
fruit-packed
fruit-packed, red-
fruit-rich
fruits and earth, pictures and places waft up like the proverbial aromas of
fruits with inner fire, dark
fruits, black jelly
fruits, clove- and coffee-flavored black
fruits, elegant gently undulating
fruits, orchard
fruits, smooth basket of red
fruits, wild forest
fruit-shrivel characters
fruit-smoky, much beyond pure
fruit-spangled
fruit-sweet
fruit-sweetness, bucketloads of
fruit-sweetness, lost its robe of
fruity air, like drinking
fruity approachability
fruity as all get-out, as sweet and
fruity bouquet
fruity character, full
fruity concoction, massively
fruity dimension
fruity façade, exotic
fruity freshness, little overwhelmed by the
fruity frivolity, down-home
fruity goodness, bushel basket of
fruity goodness, full of
fruity it isn't, juicy-
fruity monster
fruity oomph
fruity personality
fruity scents, ever-so-slight

fruity zing
fruity, blatantly/brazenly/
  ebulliently/extravagantly/
  exuberantly/fantastically/
  flamboyantly/lavishly/opulently
fruity, confidently
fruity, decidedly
fruity, deeply
fruity, devilishly
fruity, effusively
fruity, explosively
fruity, forwardly
fruity, gloriously
fruity, intensely
fruity, marvelously
fruity, obnoxiously
fruity, openly/overtly
fruity, rampantly
fruity, ridiculously
fruity, ripely
fruity, shamelessly red-
fruity, stunningly
fruity, thumpingly
fruity, transparently
fruity, tropically
fruity, wildly
fruity-acid, nervous
fruity-fragrant
fruity-minerally
fruity-peppermint
fruity-woody
full, chock-
full-on
fulsome
fusillade, delicious
gages, ripe
gamy
garish
gaudy
generosity, lacking in/lacks
generous
gentle
Germanic
gingersnap
glazed
glycerin-imbued
gnarled
gobs
goji berries
golden
goldengages
goodish, rather quite
gooseberries lined with nettles and
  thyme, deep basket of
gooseberries, aromatic
gooseberries, Cape
gooseberries, Chinese
gooseberries, crisp tart green

gooseberries, freshly picked
gooseberries, lovely crunchy
gooseberries, newly picked
gooseberries, plump
gooseberries, potent
gooseberries, purple
gooseberries, racy
gooseberries, red
gooseberries, relentless
gooseberries, squashed
gooseberries, tart
gooseberries, unknit
gooseberries, unripe
gooseberries, youthful
gooseberry freshness, ripe
gooseberry intensity
gooseberry skins
gooseberry smack, unripe
gooseberry-infused
gooseberryish, tantalizingly
gooseberry-packed
goosegogs
gorgeous
grainy-textured
Granny Smiths, divine
Granny Smiths, sackfuls of
grape avalanche, hardly a
grape extract
grape flavors, pure
grape pips, sunburnt
grape pips/seeds
grape pulp, dissolved
grape skins, Muscat
grape skins, real
grape skins, steeped
grapefest in a bottle
grapefruit all the time, all
grapefruit and exotic fruit,
  seductive interplay of
grapefruit and orange, perfumy
grapefruit citrus
grapefruit element stops just short
  of sour
grapefruit peels/rinds
grapefruit pith
grapefruit richness, exciting
grapefruit rinds, dry
grapefruit rolling languidly on lush
  green grass, juicy
grapefruit, crisp
grapefruit, electric
grapefruit, explosive pink
grapefruit, fresh
grapefruit, frisky
grapefruit, mild-mannered
grapefruit, nutty
grapefruit, pinkest of pink
grapefruit, pure brittle flavors of

grapefruit, ripe
grapefruit, ruby red
grapefruit, slightly sour weak
grapefruit, smoky
grapefruit, sweet ruby
grapefruit, ultrafragrant
grapefruit, unripe
grapefruit, white
grapefruit, zippy
grapefruit-edged
grapefruit-facial, James Cagney
grapefruit-in-a-glass, zesty
grapefruit-melon
grapefruit-petrol, rich
grapefruits, bracing white
grapelike, Concord
grapes into your mouth, like
  stuffing handfuls of sweet
grapes sing and touch the high
  notes
grapes, desiccated
grapes, Erbaluce
grapes, flatland
grapes, fresh
grapes, fresh green
grapes, freshly/just-picked
grapes, hothouse
grapes, over-ripe
grapes, raisinated/raisined
grapes, rotten
grapes, singed
grapes, sooty taste of scorched
grapes, table
grapes, tart green
grapes not wood, tastes like
grapes, unripe
grapes, very green
grapes...forsooth, tastes of
grapey, deeply
grapey, explosively/exuberantly
grapey, joyously exultant
grapey-minty
grapiness, crunchy
grapiness, explosive
grapiness, grassy
grapiness, kerosene
great
green, early picked
green, verdant
greengages, newly picked
grenadine
guava richness
guava, garbage over-ripe
  sweet smell of
guavas, bone-dry
guavas, green
guavas, mouthwatering
guavas, tropical

guavas, white
gummy
gutsy
happy
hard/hardish
harmonious
headgear, smells like Carmen
  Miranda's
heaps
heavenly
hedgerow
Herculean
hesitant
hidden, well
hide and seek, plays
hits like a hammer
hollow
honest
honeydew-cantaloupe-mango
hot
hothouse, concentrated
huckleberries, wild
humongous
hunky
immaculate
impudent
inadequate
indelible
indigenous
infusion, good
inky
insufficient
intense, dazzlingly
intensely flavored
intensity, piercing
intensity, sun-broiled
intoxicating
intriguing
in-your-face
jackfruit
jammy, full
jammy, real
jasmine-touched
jostaberries
joyful, insanely
juicy jollity
juicy, totally
jumpy
juneberries
keen-edged
kernels/kernelly
keyed and subdued, low-
kiwifruit, golden
kiwis-melons
kumquat zest
kumquats
lack is a big letdown
lacking

laid-back
laser beam, icy
laser-guided
laserlike
lavendery
lavish
layered
layers cascade over the taste buds
  without any sense of weight
layers, fleshy
layers, unbelievable
leads the charge
leafier
lean and mean
leather-infused
leftover
lemon and lime, extraordinary
  waves of
lemon and lime, sweet-tart wakeup
  call of fresh
lemon and lime, tongue-wagging
lemon bomb
lemon in beer
lemon mousse, Meyer
lemon oil
lemon peels, squeeze/twist of
lemon peels/rinds/skins
lemon pith plus
lemon pith, fresh
lemon segments
lemon sprightliness
lemon squeeze of a wine, clean
  scintillating
lemon streaked with licorice
lemon, as much fun as smooching
  with an unripe
lemon-anise
lemon-citrus
lemon-lime flat taste
lemon-lime verve, crisp
lemon-orange peels
lemon-peel twist
lemon-pineapple
lemons and apricots, floating
  clouds of
lemons and limes, jumping with
lemons and wildflowers, as
  fragrant as a basket overflowing
  with heirloom apples...Meyer
lemons, bitter
lemons, crisp
lemons, enticing drift of
lemons, Lisbon
lemons, lively/racy/snappy/zesty
lemons, long-lasting
lemons, Meyer
lemons, over-ripe/rotting
lemons, perfumed Sicilian

lemons, pleasantly pithy
lemons, ripe
lemons, smoky
lemons, soapy
lemons, sweet
lemons, under-ripe/unripe
lemons, waxed
lemony edge, sprightly
lemony scowl, light
lemony spikiness
lemony tang
lemony tartness
lemony, impishly
lemony-fresh
lemony-mango, bright
lemony-oaky
lemony-pear, spicy
lemony-toasty
level, copious
level, glorious
lifted
light
like, easy to
lime and linoleum
lime attack, needle-sharp
lime-drenched
lime edge, refreshingly bitter
lime in your mouth, cleansing
  explosion of
lime juice, freshly squeezed
lime kick
lime notes, high-frequency
lime peels/rinds/skins
lime pith
lime segments
lime tanginess, zingy
lime tartness, edgy
lime zest aggression, serious
lime zip
lime, squeeze/twist of
lime, ultrafragrant
lime-citrus backbone
lime-drenched
limelike freshness
lime-ridden
limes and lemons, herb-kissed
limes, blast of intensive
limes, cool composed
limes, creamy
limes, floral
limes, glorious smoky
limes, harmony of
limes, hot
limes, Kaffir
limes, Key
limes, margaritalike
limes, oily
limes, Persian

limes, ripe
limes, sweet
limes, tangy/tart
lime-splashed
lime-stuffed
limy freshness
limy lift
limy with herbal-fennel aromas
limy, blimey...this is
limy-floral things
limy-mineral
linear/linearity
lingering
lingonberries
lingonberry-scented, loose and
lipsmacking
litchis, fresh
litchis, spicy
litchis...papaya and their ilk
loaded
loads, bucket
loganberries firing on all cylinders
loganberries, cascading
loganberries, very ripe
long, as complex as it is
loquats
lump, huge unwooded spirity
lurking in the background
lusty
malic
mandarin peels
mandarins, jammy
mandarins, pure
mangoes, Alfonso
mangoes, stale
mangoes, sweet
mangosteens
marionberries
massive
mature, exuberantly
mayapples
meager
medium
medlars
meek than forceful, more
mélange
mellow/mellowed
melon balls, green
melon meets sugar cubes and
   candy cane
melon quality, rich
melon rinds/skins
melon, rock
melons dancing on the nose, light
melons of the summer, first
melons, billowing
melons, Cavaillon
melons, chalky

melons, Charentais
melons, Crenshaw
melons, demure hay-edged
melons, dirty
melons, discrete
melons, green
melons, honeydew
melons, meaty
melons, mineralized
melons, musky/muskmelons
melons, Prince
melons, racy
melons, rock
melons, soft sweet
melons, under-ripe Ogen
melons, vegetal-edged Ogen
melons, wacky very ripe
melted
merciless in its intensity
midcitrus
midfruit, good
milky
mineral-tinge(d)
minty/mintish
Mirabelles
missing
mocha
moderate
modern
modest
molten
moonfruit, gobs of Asian
moonfruit, nuances of ripe Asian
Morellos, sweet
moscato, succulently sweet
mountain/mountain-grown
mouthfilling/mouthful of
mouth-flooding
mouthful, big/great/huge/massive
mouthful, whopping
much left, not
muddle, delicious
muffled
mulberries, brooding
mulberries, muffled
mulberries, ripe
mulberries, smoky
mulberries, sweet
mulberry-toffee sweetness
mûre
Muscat/Muscatty
muscatels, fleshy
muscatels, hothouse
muscatels, singed
muscular
mushy
musky
muted

nectarberries
nectarine skins
nectarines strategically placed
   under the honeysuckle bush in
   the shade, baskets of ripe
nectarines, white
nectarines, zippy
neutral
new
nirvana
nondescript
normal
nose, just about bites your
notes, everchanging
oaked, mildly
obvious and overt, very
oils, ethereal
oily
olallieberries
olivaceous, ripely
olives, black
olives, green
olives, Kalamata
olives, martini
olives, Provençal
olives, ripe
oodles
open/opened/opening
optimum
opulent, dense
orange bitterness, Seville
orange oil
orange peel bitterness
orange peel, old
orange peels, deep
orange peels/rinds/skins
orange-peel attack, late
orange zest
oranges, aged
oranges, bergamot
oranges, bitter
oranges, blood/blood-red
oranges, demure mandarin
oranges, explosion of
oranges, fresh
oranges, juicy blood
oranges, late summer farmstand
   with sun-ripened
oranges, light
oranges, mandarin
oranges, peppery
oranges, pungent
oranges, ripe/over-ripe
oranges, Satsuma
oranges, Seville
oranges, sour
oranges, sun-ripened
oranges, sweet Florida

oranges, unpeeled
orange-sated
orchard in a glass
orchard meets a candy store
orchard, delicious
orchard, English
ostentatious as to be gaudy, so
out, dipping
out, has fallen
outrageous
outspoken
overdone
overfruited, wildly
overfruity
over-ripe quality, faint
over-ripe, on the edge of being
overtly
overtones, baggy
overweight
packed to the brim
packed, tightly/well
palate-awakener/-awakening
palpable
pampelmousse, sweet
panoply, extraordinary
papaya pulp
papayas, tree-ripened
papayas/pawpaws
parade, luscious
paradise, strolling through a
    tropical
passion fruit and kiwis with lime
    zest
passion fruit in a glass
passion fruit, blimey...talk about
passion fruit, ebullient
patina of age, has already attained
    the
peach and butterscotch, bosomy
peach essence
peach fuzz
peach kernels
peach-meets-white pepper, white-
peach peels
peach pits, tangy
peach pits/stones
peach skins, fresh
peach skins, odd
peach stones, sucked
peach with a pit of stone, like
    biting into a ripe
peach you ever had, as delicious
    as the best
peach, as fresh as a late summer
peach, like biting into the juicy-
    plump flesh of a perfectly ripe
    white
peach, like chewing on a sweet

peach, steely
peach-and-tangerine bomb,
    startlingly ripe
peach-apricot-fig
peach-cranberry
peach-drenched
peach-driven
peaches and apricots, sultry
peaches and pears, untold
    quantities of
peaches and pears, *zaftig*
peaches imprisoned in diamonds,
    yellow
peaches jump out at you, basketful
    of white
peaches, barely ripened
peaches, billowing
peaches, bitter
peaches, bloom on
peaches, bruised
peaches, clingstone
peaches, conquers the palate with
    wave after wave of sweet
peaches, creamy
peaches, crunchy
peaches, doughnut
peaches, dry
peaches, explosive
peaches, green
peaches, heavenly ripe
peaches, midsummer
peaches, musky
peaches, old blowzy
peaches, orange-scented
peaches, pale
peaches, Pavie
peaches, puppy-fat
peaches, red-fleshed
peaches, red-skinned
peaches, ripe/over-ripe
peaches, skins of still-green
peaches, slightly unripe white
peaches, smoke-covered/smoky
peaches, sweet
peaches, tobacco smoke-infused
peaches, under-ripe/under-ripened
peaches, unripened
peaches, vineyard
peaches, vividly ripe
peaches, white
peaches, zesty
peachfuzz, aggressive form of
peachily perfect
peachiness, fuzzy-skinned
peachiness, lush
peach-pear
peach-plum-apricot, oodles of
    upfront

peach-spice, positive
peach-vanilla
peachy and practically perfect,
    plump...
peachy enough to become
    Georgia's state wine
peachy madness
peachy, buttery-
peachy, crispy-
peachy, delicately
peachy, fullish-dryish-
peachy, honey-
peachy, sweety-
peachy-coconutty
peachy-stony
pear juiciness, green
pear perfume, sexy
pear skins, ripe-yet-unripe
pear underpinnings
pear, essence of
pear-apple
pear-infused
pears and apples, hyper-ripe
pears and citrus, light
pears, acid-charged Bartlett
pears, Alexander
pears, Asian/Nashi
pears, Bartlett/Williams
pears, bell-clear
pears, Beurré Bosc
pears, butter/buttery
pears, cactus
pears, chiffonlike
pears, Comice
pears, crisp white
pears, crispy Asian
pears, crunchy
pears, deeply ripe
pears, dry
pears, earthy
pears, exotic
pears, explosive
pears, fall
pears, gravelly
pears, Hardy Beurré
pears, hyper-ripe spicy
pears, juicy drippingly ripe
pears, light
pears, long-lasting
pears, musky
pears, nutty
pears, oily
pears, old
pears, Passé Crassane
pears, perfectly ripe Bosc
pears, petrol-infused
pears, plump
pears, prickly

pears, raw Anjou
pears, ripe
pears, Sekel
pears, soft
pears, soft over-ripe Rocha
pears, spicy old
pears, stony
pears, sun-drenched
pears, super-ripe
pears, tart
pears, tropical
pears, unripe
pears, winter
pears, wonderfully rich young
pear-thick texture
peels/peely/peely character
pellets, intense
penetration, lacks
perfect
perfume/perfumed
perfumed, gorgeously
persimmons, ripe
picked, freshly/just-
piercing
pineapple chunks
pineapple, field-ripened
pineapple husks/rinds
pineapple party
pineapple rinds, intense
pineapples, acetone
pineapples, buttery
pineapples, creamy
pineapples, lemon-
pineapples, luscious sweet
pineapples, perfumy
pineapples, pure
pineapples, ripe
pineapples, rotting
pineapples, sinuous
pineapples, super-ripe
pineapples, sweet rich buttery
pineapples, tangy
pineapples, tart
pineapples, tropical, sun-ripe
pineapples, youthful captured
pine-toned
pink
piquant
pit tartness
pit, assorted
pit, black
pitched, high-
piths/pithy
pits/seeds/stones
platform, juicy
pleasant
plentiful
plum crazy

plum pits
plum skins, black
plum skins, red
plum, biting into a tart red
plum-blueberry-style
plumminess, dense
plummy-earthy
plummy-tobaccoey
plum-nectarine
plump, irresistibly
plum-prune-tea medley,
    singing with the
plums and berries, deftly woven
plums and blackberries, focused
plums and cherries, clearly
    expressed
plums *en branche*
plums gorged on sunshine,
    Mirabelle
plums on the branch
plums, black
plums, Black Doris
plums, blood
plums, blue
plums, bright
plums, bruised
plums, buried
plums, burnt/charred
plums, cinnamon-scented
plums, Damson
plums, deep purple
plums, deep-set
plums, doesn't follow the usual
    trail of
plums, Dorset
plums, dusty
plums, earthy
plums, fleshy
plums, flood of
plums, fresh
plums, genteel spicy
plums, golden
plums, Greengage
plums, Italian
plums, jammy
plums, juicy green
plums, juicy Greengage
plums, juicy Victoria
plums, lifted
plums, lovely rubbery
plums, mature
plums, mess of ripe
plums, Mirabelle
plums, mouthwatering
plums, opulent
plums, overripe
plums, pillow
plums, purple

plums, red
plums, ripe
plums, sour
plums, spicy
plums, squashy
plums, streaky
plums, succulent green
plums, supple
plums, sweaty
plums, sweet
plums, tart
plums, uncluttered
plums, Victoria
plums, vivid
plums, waxy
plums, wild
plums, wild sour
plums, yellow
plum-tomato aromas, typical
plushy, generously
polished, beautifully
pomace/pomacy
pomegranate, peppery
pomegranate, rhubarb-
pomegranate-like tartness
pomegranates, ripe
pomelos
poor
porty
powerful, monstrously
presented, lovingly
pretty
pristine
produce, fresh
profound
profuse/profusion
prominent/pronounced
proportions, gargantuan
prunelle
prunes, Agen
prunes, mess of
prunes, smoky
pruney, sweetly
pruney...grunty and deep
pulp/pulpy
pumped up
pumpkins
punches you in the face
puny
pure
purebred
purity, unadorned cut-glass
purple, telltale
push, needs a little
pushes through like grass through
    cracks in the stones
quince-edged
quinces, apricotty

quinces, perfectly ripened
quinces/quincey
quincey, spicy-
raisin seeds
raisin spectrum, rum-and-
raisiny roughness
rambutans
raspberries right off the bush, fresh
raspberries with the thorns
   included
raspberries, circus of spicy black
raspberries, creamy black
raspberries, essence of
raspberries, explosive black
raspberries, hybrid black cherries-
raspberries, leathery black
raspberries, mouthwatering
raspberries, old
raspberries, piercing scents of
   black currants and
raspberries, pure heady
raspberries, purple
raspberries, rich feminine
raspberries, seedy red
raspberries, silky blueberries and
raspberries, soft
raspberries, sour
raspberries, sun-baked
raspberries, sweet
raspberries, tart wild
raspberries, unfettered ripe
   sun-warmed
raspberries, unripe
raspberries, varietal
raspberries, virtual garden of
raspberries, wild
raspberries, yellow
raspberries...chocolate and vanilla,
   like sticking your nose into a
   bowl of
raspberries...cranberries...tar
   and spices on horseback
raspberry piquancy, unusual
raspberry, earthy-
raspberry-cherry
raunchy
ravishing, utterly
raw
razor-sharp
red and black, syrupy
red, avalanche of
red, electric
red, pulsating
red, small
red-brown
redolent
repressed, fractionally
restrained but ripe

retreating
rhubarb intensity
rhubarb tartness
rhubarb, deep strawberry-
rhubarb, dusty berry-
rhubarb, sweet
rhubarb-pomegranate
rich and elegant,
   incomprehensibly
rich that it's liable to suffocate folks
   who prefer pecks on the cheek to
   large-scale embraces, so
rich, awesomely/fabulously/
   outrageously/ridiculously
rich, lusciously
rich, toasty
richness, immense
richness, spiced with liquid
richness, sumptuous
riot/riotous
ripe skin character
ripe, confit
ripe, dead-/very
ripe, deep brooding
ripe, deeply rooted
ripe, flamboyantly
ripe, only-/just-
ripe, piercingly
ripe, sensuously
ripe, tangily
ripe/ripened, overly
ripened, insufficiently
rotten/rotting
rough-hewn
rugged
rustic, exaggerated
salmonberries
sappy
sappy-plummy
satsumas, ripe
saturated
saturated, sun-
savory
scents/scented
scrumptious
sedate
seductive, warm and
sensational
sensuous
serious, dark and very
serious, really
set, deep-/deeply
sexy, quite/very
shadowy
sherbetlike, elegant
short
shy
signature

silky
simmering
simple/simply
singed
sinks into the plate
sits in the driving seat
skins
sloe
slurpable/slurpy
smile-inducing
smoked/smoky/smoke-tinge(d)
smooth...roselike...rich
snappy
soft and suave
soft yellow, soft
soft, very pleasing
soggy
so-so
soulful
sound
sour/soured/sourish/soury
specious
spiceberries
spicy
spicy-chocolaty
sprightly
sprung, tightly
squashy
squishy
stage, puppy-
staggering
stalky
starfruit
steely
sticky and warm but not
   uncomfortably humid
stifling
stone
strawberries and fresh raspberries,
   frozen
strawberries peeping through
   wood
strawberries, alpine
strawberries, autosuggestion of
   more
strawberries, basket of fresh-picked
strawberries, bitter
strawberries, creamy
strawberries, faded
strawberries, fresh wild
strawberries, freshly picked
strawberries, ground ivy mixed
   with wild
strawberries, moreish
strawberries, musk
strawberries, over-ripe
strawberries, pithy
strawberries, pure wild

strawberries, rather light dilute
strawberries, ripe sun-kissed
strawberries, rough-hewn
strawberries, smashed
strawberries, smoky
strawberries, Spanish
strawberries, stalky
strawberries, svelte
strawberries, sweet
strawberries, tiniest of alpine
strawberries, trombone of
strawberries, warm
strawberries, wild
strawberries, wood
strawberries-raspberries, slinky
strawberry and soft creamy
  contentment, magic carpet of
strawberry fantasy perfumed by
  rose water, orange blossom and
  wild
strawberry patch littered with
  walnuts, like falling into a
strawberry saturated
strawberry succor
strawberry tang, mild
strawberry-rhubarb, deep
strawberry-watermelon
strolling through a tropical
  paradise, like
struggles to express itself
stuffed, really
stunner/stunning
stupendous
suave
subdued, slightly
subjugated
submerged
subtleties, genial
sugar, enjoyable patina of
sugary
summer, late/ripe
summer, warm/warmth of
sun-baked
sunburnt
sun-dried
sun-filled
sun-kissed
sunlit
sunny/sunshiny
sun-ripened
sunshine on the beach when I was
  a child, as bright as
sunshine-filled/-drenched
superabundance/superabundant
supercharged
superclean
superconcentrated
superfruity

superplummy
super-rich
super-ripe
supersweet
supple easygoing
suppressed to taste, too
supreme
sustained
sweet prunes, stream of rich
  coffee and
sweet, almost porty-
sweet, broken
sweet, diminished
sweet, softly
sweet, succulently
sweetness, confectionery
sweetness, runnel/skerrick of
sweet-tasting
swell, great
talking, does all the
tamarillos
tamarind
tamed, beautifully
tangelos
tangerine citrus
tangerine dreams
tangerine peels/rinds
tangerine peels/skins, barely
  heated
tangerines, buttery
tangerines, fusillade of
tangerines, green
tangerines, honey-sweet
tangerines, luscious
tanginess, mouthwatering
tangy-citrusy
tangy-toasty
tart, deliciously
tart, overly
taut
tawny-brick
tayberries
tearaway
teasing
tenuous
terrific
textured, diaphanous-
thick, almost
thinness, disappointing
thrilling
throttle(d), full-
tight
tinny
tobacco-tinge(d)
topical, telltale
tranquil
transparent
tree, summer

tree, temperate
tree, tropical
tropical wealth
tropical, flamboyant
tropical, impossibly
tropical, verging into the
truckload
true
truffle-infused/truffley
twist, exotic
*über*fruit
ultra-aristocratic
ultrafresh
ultrafruity
ultragenerous
unbridled
unconscious
uncowed
underfruited
underpowered, little
under-ripe
understated
uneasy
unfruited/unfruitful/unfruity
ungenerous
unintegrated
unripe
upfront
uplifting
vanilla, spicy
vanilla-kissed
vanilla-laced
vanillary
vanilla-veined
varietal, incisive
velvety
vestiges
vibrant
vigorous, overly
viney
vine, very old
violet-imbued
violetlike
vivacious
vivid
voltage, masculine high-
voluminous
voluptuous and sexy
waiting to emerge
warm
wash, crisp tart
watered/watery
watermelon on the hottest day
  of summer, perfectly ripe
watermelon peel
watermelons, seedless
waves, continuing to build in
weak

wealth
weedy
weight, massive
weighted, good
welded together, fruit and oak
   totally
whatnot
whimsical
whispery
white, assorted
white, buttery
white, lemony
whole
whortleberries
wild
windfall
wineberries, Japanese
wineberries, tangy
withered
wonderful
woodberries
work, does all the
wrought, finely
yellow, soft
youngberries
youthful
yummiest
yummy-creamy
zippy-zingy

It's the entrancing perfume of the wine, spices that keep you inhaling to the end, a Syrah so lush and dark and rich that the brooding flavors go straight to the soul.
Ferenc Máté

It was almost spiced, so sweetly aromatic it was. It caressed the gullet; it spread its greeting over all the mouth, until the impatient throat accused the tongue of unfair delay.
Maurice Healy

16. Herb, Spice or Nut

Nearly all the herbs and spices lurking in the typical household cabinet or drawer have been linked, one way or another, to the taste of wine, together with nuts of nearly every kind. Whether ordinary snippets from the kitchen garden or exotica from the East, herbs, spices and nuts resonate in most all the world's wines. Mint, pepper and vanilla seem to be the most popular in this relatively short but flavorful category. If you're a grape nut, you'll feel right at home here.

acorns
allspice
allspice and nutmeg, tumble and jumble of
almond crunchiness
almond kernels
almond lines, smooth
almond pits/stones
almond shells
almond skins
almond, peach-
almonds, bitter
almonds, delicate
almonds, fresh
almonds, green/raw
almonds, sweet
almond-vanilla extract
almondy, strangely
angelica/angelica root
angostura, exotic mysteries of
angostura, medicinal fumes of
anise, Chinese
anise, flecked with
anise, focused layers of
anise, headache and

anise, nearly indiscernible
anise, restrained
anise, star
aniseed, stale
anise-lemon
applemint
arrowroot
artemisia
balsamic
basil, purple
basil, sweet
basil, Thai
bay leaf/leafy
bay leaves, fresh
bay leaves, dried
bergamot oil
bergamot, creamy
bergamot, dried
bergamot, smoky
borage
bouquet garni
butternuts
cacao, afterthought of
cacao, dry
caraway seeds
cardamom, Malabar
cashews, creamy

cashews, deeper
cashews, French
cashews, salty
catnip
cayenne
celery seeds
chamomile, breezy
chamomile, perfumed
chervil, sweet
chervil, wild
chestnuts, distant
chives
cilantro/coriander
cinnamon mint
cinnamon spice veneer, warm
cinnamon spice, unmistakable touch of
cinnamon stick, like sticking my tongue inside a
cinnamon sticks, fresh
cinnamon, Mexican
cinnamon, soft
cinnamon, spicy
cloves and cardamom, good dose of
cloves of uncertain origin

cloves, dash of
cloves, oaky
cobnuts, wet
cobnuts/filberts/ hazelnuts
coconut, mellow
coconut, sprinkle of
coconut/coconutty
coconut-dill
coconut-oak
concentrated
coriander, fresh
coriander, intense
coriander-paprika edging, subtle
cumin, warm
cumin/cuminlike
cumin-laced
dill, coconut-
dill, peppered gherkins and
dill/dill seed/dill weed
echinacea
epazote, as exotic as
extraherby
fennel, smoky
fennel, wild
fenugreek

filberts, warm
filberts/hazelnuts, dried
filberts/hazelnuts, roasted/toasted
filberts/hazelnuts/cobnuts
filé
frankincense and myrrh
garlic, crisp wild
generous
gentian
ginger and elderflower-like, unusual
ginger behind petroleum
ginger spice
ginger, fresh
ginger, green
ginger, lifted
ginger, stem
ginger, sweet
ginger-pepper, sweet
gingery warmth
hazelnut extract
hazelnut husks
hazelnuts and walnuts, wet
hazelnuts, bitter skin of
hazelnuts, smoky
hazelnuts, sweet-smelling
herb flavors sing
herb garden planted next to a roaring charcoal fire
herb garden, dry
herb shadings
herbaceous, coarsely
herbaceous, oddly
herbaceousness, forward
herbaceousness, green
herbaceousness, peppery
herbaceousness, racy
herbaceousness, weedy tobacco
herbage, fermented
herbal ambrosia
herbal aromas, English
herbal bite, nice
herbal bitterness, interesting
herbal complexity
herbal edges
herbal flavors, complex
herbal gatekeeper
herbal greenness
herbal infusion
herbal nuances, intriguing
herbal perfume

herbal scrub
herbal sidenotes
herbal stuff underneath, little
herbal underbelly
herbal wildness
herbal, aggressively
herbal, funky-
herbal, piney-
herbal, strangely
herbal-mineral perfume
herbalness, touch of
herbal-smelling, dusty
herbes de Provence/herbs of Provence/Provençale herbs
herbes, fines
herbiness, clear streak of
herb-kissed
herb-laced/-laden
herbs and anise, subtle markings of
herbs and spices, Provençale
herbs lurking in the background
herbs of Provence, wild
herbs parched by drought
herbs, alpine/mountain
herbs, aromatic riot of
herbs, as aromatic as mountain
herbs, bitter
herbs, buzzes with catty pungent green
herbs, complex
herbs, cool resins of provincial
herbs, Corsican wild
herbs, delicious fusillade of
herbs, dynamite
herbs, exotic
herbs, garden/kitchen
herbs, garland of
herbs, green
herbs, haunting perfumes of wild
herbs, heart-rushing fresh
herbs, Italian
herbs, light green
herbs, magic caravan of lilies and blueberries and
herbs, magnetic
herbs, medicinal
herbs, Mediterranean

herbs, mirage haze of hillside
herbs, picante
herbs, pinch of
herbs, precious
herbs, punch of
herbs, pungent bitter
herbs, rasping hillside
herbs, resinous
herbs, rough brush of
herbs, roughed up with hillside
herbs, savory
herbs, scrubby wild
herbs, southern
herbs, spicy mountain
herbs, stale
herbs, steeped in
herbs, superlush
herbs, sweep of
herbs, sweet deeply pitched
herbs, Tuscan
herbs, unbridled wild
herbs, waxy
herbs, wild hillside/mountain
herbs, wild Provençale
herbs, wispy
herb-scented bath
herb-scented beauty
herb-strewn
herby and tailored, quite
herby richness, thrilling
herby roughness
herby scrub
herby twist
horehound
hyperspicy
juniper berries/junipers
laurel, bay
laurel, pepper
lemon balm
lemongrass zing
lemongrass, fresh green
lemongrass-like spirit, crackling
lemony-grassy
licorice root
lime leaves, Kaffir
linseed oil
lovage, posy of
mace
marjoram
menthol and smoked fish
mentholated
mignonette

mint, blows notes of ripe sweet
mint, butter
mint, earthy
mint, eucalyptus-
mint, garden
mint, julep
mint, spikes of green
mint, sprigs of
mint, topped with sprigs of
mint, wallop of
mint, wild
mintiness, eucalyptus
mintiness, huge
mintiness, piquant
minty heaven, superb
minty, decidedly
minty, grapey-
minty-bay leaf
minty-glycerin
minty-herbal
minty-silky
mustard seeds
myrtle, lemon
nut husks
nut skins, classic
nut spectrum
nut, banana-
nut, kola
nut-laden
nutlike tang
nutlike, tart
nutmeg, grated
nutmeg, understated
nutmeg-cinnamon
nut-oiliness
nuts, basket filled with assorted
nuts, bitter creamy Brazil
nuts, chocolate
nuts, cola
nuts, crisp
nuts, desiccated
nuts, fresh Brazil
nuts, funky
nuts, green
nuts, liquid
nuts, macadamia
nuts, oriental
nuts, pine
nuts, red-hot
nuts, sweet
nuts, Swiss
nut-scented, rain forest
nutshells, slightly aged
nuttier slightly deeper flavors

nuttiness, nut-kernel
nuttiness, oxidative
nuttiness, rich
nuttiness, subtle
nutty barrel
nutty cherry kernels
nutty oak-vanillin
nutty savoriness
nutty zenith, honeyed
nutty, marginally
nutty, startlingly
nutty-curranty
nutty-smoky
nutty-spongy
oregano, fresh
oregano, wild
origanum
orrisroot
paprika
paprika pods, fresh
parsley and cilantro,
  halfway between
patchouli
patchouli exotic and
  green
peanuts
pecans
pecans, hulls of shelled
pepper astringency, keen
  white
pepper bomb, beautiful
pepper to taste like a
  pepper mill, enough
  black
pepper up your nose,
  black
pepper, argumentative
  white
pepper/peppercorns,
  black
pepper, cayenne
pepper, Malabar
pepper, nostril-
  permeating
  menthol-white
pepper, parsimonious
pepper, Penja
pepper, pink
pepper, red
pepper, Sichuan
pepper, snappy black
pepper, Tellicherry
pepper, tingle of
pepper, white-peach-
  meets-white
pepper/peppercorns,
  white
pepper/peppery

peppercorns,
  characteristic dusty
peppercorns, green
peppercorns, pink
peppercorns, rebellious
  flash of
pepper-laden
peppermint/
  pepperminty
pepper-pot's worth
peppers, rich hot
pepper-scented
pepper-strewn
peppery backnotes
peppery glory
peppery grace notes
peppery spirit, whack of
peppery tang
peppery, deliciously
peppery!, oh so
peppery, outrageously
perfumed
picante/piquant
pignoli
pimpernel
pistachios
poppy seeds
potpourri in my
  grandmother's
  bathroom
potpourri, liquid
pralines, vanilla
pungent
pure
quinine, inky
redolent
rosehips
rosemary sprigs
rosemary, arresting
rosemary, boisterous
rosemary, resiny
rue
saffron
saffron-saturated
sage leaves
sage, earthy
sage, pineapple
sage, rustic
sage, wild
salt and pepper, wild
salt and smoke
salt, celery
salt, sea
saltiness, iodine-like
saltiness, seaside vineyard
sarsaparilla
sassafras root
savory

seasonings
sesame seeds
spearmint freshness
spearmint, sickly
spice augmented
spice bazaar in a glass
spice bazaar, glorious
spice bomb, concentrated
  earthy full-bodied
spice box into this lush
  velvet tangle of
  bramble fruit?, who
  tipped the
spice box/cabinet/
  chest/rack
spice chest full of flavors,
  whole
spice garden
spice girl than sumo
  wrestler, more
spice notes, broad
spice notes, local riff of
spice package, real
spice quarter of the
  casbah, like getting lost
  in the
spice rack, Grandma's
spice toast, cedar-
spice, bitter oaky
spice, black
spice, blackberry-
spice, boysenberry-
spice, Germanic
spice, Merlot cake
spice, Moroccan
spice, mulberry
spice, oak is a
spice, souk's worth of
spice, subtle liqueur
spice, tenderly oaky
spice, vermouth
spice, warm
spice/spiciness,
  mysterious
spice-infused
spiceless/unspiced
spices and herbs,
  breath of
spices and liquid
  minerals, bursting at
  the seams with
spices and oak, delicate
  filigree of
spices as they hover in the
  warmth of the tropics,
  dry oriental
spices awash in perfume
  and blackberry liqueur

spices inhabit the dark
  corners, oriental
spices is almost
  introverted, extract of
spices of the Levant/
  Middle East
spices, all kinds/sorts of
  interesting
spices, apple pie
spices, Asian/Eastern/
  Far Eastern/oriental
spices, bags of
spices, bakery/baking
spices, barbecue
spices, bewitching
spices, bitter
spices, bland
spices, blast of
spices, boiled-down
spices, boisterous Asian
spices, botrytis
spices, Bourbon-like
spices, bright
spices, brown
spices, burlesque of
  bawdy fruit and
spices, burnished
spices, burst of
spices, caresses of
spices, cedary
spices, chililike
spices, chocolate
spices, Christmas
spices, cinnamon-type
spices, complex
spices, complex South
  Asian
spices, cool-climate twist
  of
spices, copious
spices, curry
spices, dark
spices, deep dive-into-me
  aromas and serious
spices, deep oak
spices, demure/subdued
spices, dizzying blend of
  fruit and
spices, dry
spices, dusty
spices, dusty baking
spices, dusty brown
spices, dusty brown
  oriental
spices, ethereal
spices, excellent woody
spices, exotic
spices, fabulous

spices, faint tickle of
spices, flashes of tar and
spices, garrique
spices, German
spices, hard
spices, haunting
spices, hickory barbecue
spices, barrel-ferment
spices, hot
spices, Indian
spices, kernel of
spices, kiss of oak
spices, kitchen
spices, kitchen-rack full of
spices, lick of
spices, lift of
spices, little wisps of
spices, loads of botrytis
spices, lush
spices, measured
spices, mixed
spices, Moroccan
spices, mulled/mulling
spices, myriad (of)
spices, mysterious
spices, neat marriage of
   silk and
spices, oak/oaklike/oaky
spices, oak-induced
spices, on fire with
spices, oozes
spices, peppery
spices, Persian
spices, pickling
spices, pie
spices, piquant
spices, pirouettes of
spices, plush creamy
spices, positive peach
spices, precious
spices, prickly
spices, profusion of
spices, Provençal pines
   and
spices, pungent
spices, Rhône-like
spices, ripples of
spices, sassy
spices, scratches of
spices, screaming with
   dark fruit and
spices, seductive sexy
spices, sexy
spices, simmering
spices, simmering
   afternoon
spices, sinews of
spices, smoky

spices, smoky-briary
spices, smorgasbord of
   Asian
spices, soft Indonesian
spices, soft South Asian
spices, specks of
spices, sprinkled with
   sweet
spices, sultry
spices, sundry dry
spices, superlush
spices, sweet and piquant
spices, sweet cake
spices, sweet oak
spices, swirl of/swirling
spices, tea chest of
spices, Thai
spices, tingling
spices, toasted Indonesian
spices, toasty apple pie
spices, tobacco
spices, tons of
spices, very fine
spices, virtual cascade of
spices, voluptuous
   bouquet of
spices, warm baking
spices, warm
   Mediterranean
spices, weak
spices, well-articulated
spices, whisper of
spices, wild and crazy
spices, wintry
spices, wood
spiciness, black-plum
spiciness, cuminlike
spiciness, earthy
spiciness, mysterious
spiciness, piquant/
   pungent
spiciness, pithy oak
spiciness, purple
spiciness, sinful
spiciness, telltale
spiciness, typical botrytis-
   derived
spiciness, volcanic
spiciness, wild charged
spiciness, wintry
spicy as a souk, as
spicy as Marco Polo's
   baggage, as
spicy backnotes
spicy come-hither wine
   to die for
spicy depths
spicy heat, little bit of

spicy kick, good/nice
spicy promise of
   something more
spicy, aggressively
spicy, almost painfully
spicy, bit intrusively
spicy, earthy-
spicy, lavishly
spicy, not assertively
spicy, resinous-
spicy, robustly
spicy, strikingly
spicy, swashbucklingly
spicy, unbelievably
spicy-peppery, somnolent
stick, licorice
superspicy
tarragon
thyme
thyme, wild
tisane
turmeric
ultraherbaceous
ultraspicy
vanilla bean, Madagascan
vanilla bean, Tahitian
vanilla beans, fragrant
vanilla beans, smoky
vanilla, delicate
vanilla essence
vanilla extract
vanilla finesse
vanilla notes to distract
   the drinker, no
vanilla pod
vanilla, breath of
vanilla, cherry
vanilla, chewy
vanilla, creamy
vanilla, ethereal
vanilla, great swoosh of
vanilla, light misting of
vanilla, plain
vanilla, rather speciously
   fragrant
vanilla, regal suggestions
   of
vanilla, silky
vanilla, slightly sickly
vanilla, smoky
vanilla, soft
vanilla, sour lavender and
vanilla, spicy
vanilla, sticky almost
   sickly
vanilla, sweet
vanilla, Swiss
vanilla, tangerine-

vanilla, trademark
vanilla, understated
vanilla, Vaseline and
vanilla, violet-/violet-
   tinged-
vanilla, waxy
vanilla, well-disguised
   sweet
vanilla-laden
vanilla-propelled
vanilla-rich fusion
vanilla-scented
vanilla-scented gloss,
   luxurious
verbena, lemon
walnut husks, green
walnut peels, unripe
walnut shells
walnut skins
walnuts, crescendo of
   lively
walnuts, English
walnuts, fresh
walnuts, green
walnuts, papery skins of
walnuts, pelted with
walnuts...vomit and
   wet dog
walnutty
wintergreen, fresh
wintergreen, wild
woodruff
wormwood
wort, St. John's

Wine is a chemical symphony.
Maynard A. Amerine

We are now familiar with television presenters on food programmes sipping a cheap supermarket white and immediately reeling out lush lists of descriptors. Some of them may be faking it, but the game is not as ridiculous as it looks—only it takes some training. What makes the wine business interesting is not so much the result, pleasant though it is, but the requirement that the chemical cornucopia be achieved using grapes alone.
Luca Turin

17. Miscellaneous [Artificial, Manufactured or Biological, Chemical]

Quite a few serious wine drinkers claim to detect weird whatchamacallits in their wine, many of which appear on the list below. Other than animals, which are covered elsewhere, there are lots of thingies that lurk in nature, could be cooked up in laboratories or produced in factories, that are here for your (ahem) vinous experiences. While barrels, leather and smoke are the big guns in this catch-all category, there are a very odd host of peculiar items not normally associated with wine. Battery acid! Of course. Boxes of every kind! Oh, yes. Insecticide! Sure. Paper and pencils enough to stock a school! Bet on it. Even those naughty little blue Viagra tablets! Yup. Quite a few people would find it hard to accept the unexpected in what they smell or taste in wine. Even though many of the sensations are as comfortable as old shoes, others are just plain disgusting and repellent. At least to most of us who try to be careful about what we put in our mouths. Tread carefully here.

accident on a hot day, bad car
acetaldehyde
acetate, ethyl
acetone, immature
acid than wine, more like battery
acid, butyric
acid, sulfuric
aftershave, slightly perfumed
airplane, highly complex...intense
  and excellent
airplane, revving-up
airport, Dallas
alchemy
alcohol, rubbing
aldehyde characteristics, sherrylike

Alka-Seltzer start
ammoniac vagaries
ammoniated
amyl acetate, whiff of
anesthetic...disinfectant or antidepressant, could be used as an
antiseptic, instant whiff of
aquarium-esque
armchair, big old comfy leather
armchairs, old leather
artificial
asbestos
ash, cigar/cigarette/tobacco
ashtray
asphalt, Amarone-

asphalt, burning
asphalt, freshly laid
asphalt, melted
asphalt-laden
aspirin, Aspro Clear soluble
aspirin, baby
aspirin, Bayer
attic, dusty old-fashioned
attic, my grandmother's
attic, old
backpack on his way to China,
  young Marco Polo's
bacterial-vegetal
bag after a win, gym
bag, oak tea

bag, water
Bakelite
bakery can produce, barrage of the most wonderful aromas a
bakery full of pastries, entire
bakery in the morning
bakery smells, French
bakery, all the treasures of the
bakery, croissant
bakery, insides of a
Bakery, like walking past the Sullivan Street
bakery, smell of a good
ball, melted Wiffle
ball, pink rubber bouncer
balloons, new latex/rubber
balls, freshly popped can of Slazinger tennis
balls, new tennis
balls, Ping-Pong/table tennis
balm, lemon
bandage, adhesive/plastic strip
bandages, clean
band, huge red rubber
Band-Aids, moldy
Band-Aids, wet
bands stuck to the glass liners of metal canning tops, rubber sealing
bands, rubber
bar with everything but the sushi, sushi
bar, smoky
barn/pen/shed/stall
barnful of cows and sheep and goats in the summer heat
barrel and wiping your tongue off with an old leather belt, like licking an
barrel character, old
barrel character, powder-dry
barrel character, strong pickle-
barrel ferment, smoky-
barrel flavor than fruit, more spicy pickle-
barrel regimen, aggressive powerful
barrel scents, new-
barrel, essence of
barrel, hello-goodbye encounter with an oak
barrel, nutty-
barrel, unsullied by the heavy thud of the oak
barrel-/barrique-aged
barrel-/barrique-fermented
barrel-driven
barrel-fermented

barrel-flavored
barrel-marked
barrels the wine was aged in, can almost taste the
barrels, acaciawood
barrels, American
barrels, ash
barrels, burnt
barrels, cherry
barrels, chocolaty
barrels, creamy caress of oak
barrels, dirty old
barrels, exhausted/tired
barrels, insides of many oak
barrels, lesson in oak
barrels, moldy
barrels, musty
barrels, New World
barrels, Old World
barrels, overgenerous exposure to oak
barrels, spanking new oak
barrels, steers clear of costly
barrels/casks, large acacia
barrels/casks, oak
baseballs
basement, damp/wet
bass humming soulfully down deep, bug upright
bat, aluminum
bath, *crème de menthe* bubble
bath, very hot cherry-scented bubble
bathroom, just-used
bath-scented, bubble
bats, cricket
batteries, old
battery, like licking a
beans, oak
bed, sweet-and-sour doggy
bedroom with the windows and door shut tight
beeswax from a honeycomb
beeswax, warm
Ben-Gay
benzene
bilge/bilgy
bilgewater
biological/*biologico*
biologically neutral
blackboard, chalk
blackstrap
blades of fruit, helicopters into your mouth with spinning
blanket, beach
blanket, pungent wet
blanket, sheepskin
blanket, sweaty horse

blanket, warm
blanket, wet horse
blanket, woolly
bleach/bleachy
blunderbuss, chunky
boat, freshly caulked
boathouse on days when the summer sun bakes its sides, old
Body Shop on a hot summer's day, like walking past a
bomb, sulphery chemical stink bomb
bomber but a precision one, a
bonfire night snorts, smoky
bonfire, dying
bonfire, leaf
bonfire, smoky
bonfire, summery
bongwater
bookbindings/books, old
books, old leather/library
boot polish, pork and
boots, as tannic as a pair of old work
boots, dusty
boots, farmer's muddy
boots, new
boots, old leather
boots, quite possibly one of Gladstone's
boots, rubber
boots, scented old
boots, worn
boots, yeoman farmer with mud on his
botrytis rampant
botrytis, dusted with
botrytis, full-on/very strong
botrytis, heavenly honeyed
botrytis, intense raisiny
botrytis, phantom effects of
botrytis, refined liquid
botrytis, shrieks of
botrytis, sweet web of
botrytised, intensely
bottle stink, fungi
bottle, rubber hot water
boudoir, Marie Antoinette's
boudoir, tart's
bouquet, extraordinary Cohiba
bouquet, fermentative
bouquet, musty
box full of tobacco, cedar
box into this lush velvet tangle of bramble fruit?, who tipped the spice
box with its sweet glue, cardboard
box, candy

box, cedar
box, cherry-covered cigar
box, chocolate
box, coffee
box, flower
box, fresh spice
box, grandpa's cigar
box, muted cigar
box, old cedar cigar
box, pungent cigar
box, shoe
box, youthful tobacco
box/tray, kitty/pet litter
bra, oak
bra, wooden
brass/brassy
Brasso
breadbasket, light
breadboard/breadboardy
brett police, might excite the
    attention of the
brett police, not for the
brett, sure to raise argument about
brick, as hard as a
bricks needed to build a mighty
    castle, has all the
bricks, baked
bricks, hot/warm
bricks, London
bricks, red
bricks, smells and almost the
    weight of a pile of
Bubbles meets Smucker's jam, Mr.
Buick Riviera, waterlogged
bulldozer, mouthfilling
bullets, oak
burlap
burnt
bus, back of an LA school
butane, grape-infused
butter, coconut
butter, fake/imitation
butter, rancid artificial
butts, cigar
butyric
Cabbage Patch kid
cabinet, old wooden
cabinet, spice
cage at the zoo, elephant
cage, dirty bird
cage, gerbil
cage, hamster
cage, mouse
campfire, extinguished
campfire, smoldering
camphor, gum
can of Slazinger tennis balls,
    freshly popped

can, just-opened petrol
candles, ordinary
candles, scented
candle wax, burnt-out
cannery, Dole pineapple
car, muscle
car, nitro-burning funny
carbolic
carbon
carborundum
cardboard, damp/wet
cardboard, musty
carnival: popcorn...cotton candy
    and vanilla ice cream, scents of a
    traveling
carpentry, great
carpet, as rich and complex
    as an Isfahan
carpet, damp
carpet, dusty old
carpet, stale stair
case, cigar
casein
casings, old tire
caskiness, unpleasant
casks, chestnut
casks, evidence of exposure to new
    oak
casks, patinated
cellar dust
cellar, bad
cellar, barrel
cellar, Champagne
cellar, damp/dank old
cellar, deep dark
cellar, earth
cellar, unclean
cellar, underground
cellar, wet
cellar, wine-soaked earthen
celluloid, immature
cellulose
cement, rubber
cement, wet
Certs
chains, oak
chair at your computer,
    your leather swivel
chair, favorite cozy old leather
chair, like smoking a pipe in a
    leather
Chanel N°5-ish powdery rosy
    aromas and flavors
Chanel N°5 on a gladiator's shorts
chaps, rawhide leather
char, barrel
char, smoky
charcoal, burning

charcoal, wood
charcoal-graphite
charred, heavily
charred, lightly
charred, medium
chemical, something vaguely
Cheracol, cherry
chest filled with blackberries and
    potpourri, like opening a cedar
chest full of flavors, whole spice
chest of smoky...earthy...animal
    flavors, treasure
chest with wool mittens, cedar
chest, camphorwood
chest, medicine
chest, old cedar
chest, treasure
chips, big tea bags full of oak
Chloraseptic, cherry
chlorine, swimming-pool
churches, lichen-covered
churches, sturdy stone
cigarettes, clove
cigarettes, oak tree addicted to
cigar bar filled with men in musty
    colognes, like walking into a
cigars, as smoky as lit
cigars, good/great Havana
cigars, heavenly scents of
cigars, old
cigars, unlit
ciggie nuances, trademark herbal-
cistern
citronella, annoying
clay, baked
clean, very high-tech
cleaner, cream leather
clinic, medical
clock, sharp dusty smells inside my
    great-grandfather's brass mantel
closet, back of a
closet, cedar
closet, overstuffed
closet, your grandmother's oak
    armoire
cloth, Louviers wool
cloth, oil
cloth, old kitchen J-
cloth, wet
clothes, fusty stink of rotting
clothes, old silk
club in a bottle, gentlemen's
club, comforting congenial men's
Club, Tame Valley Tennis
clubhouse, wooden
clutch on an uphill grade, smoking
coat, oiled waterproof
coat, old fur

cod-liver oil and malt
Cohiba, wet end of a great
cologne, lot of sweet
color, artificial
comforter, buried under a down
comforter, feels like slipping
  under a fluffy down
compost, leather
Concorde: bumpy takeoff...steep
  climb...then supersonic, like the
concrete, damp/wet
concrete, hot dry
condom powder
condoms, new
confessional at St. Joseph's church
congestion-free
constructions, soul-less assembly-
  line
contaminated
contamination, metal
cookers, old tire
coop/shed, chicken
cooperage, touch of French oak
cork, contaminated by a tainted
cork, moldy/musty
cork, tainted beyond a bad
corked, badly/disastrously/
  horribly
corrals, dusty smells of bone-dry
corrupt
corsets and bones, just
cosmetic characters, strange
cottage, country
couch, overstuffed
cough-drop character
coumarin
counter, confectionary
courts, dusty hard
courtyard, whisper in a
courtyards
cowbarn, urine and straw
cowshed rather than fresh country
  air
cowstall, unmucked
crayons, melted
cream, cold/face
cream, hand
Cream, Pond's Cold
creams and skin potions,
  entire battery of face
Crème, Nivea
creosote, Italian-like
creosote, marine
crystals, tartrate
crystals/diamonds, wine
cubes, oak
cupboards, ancient
cupboards, apothecary

cupboards, unaired
curtain, heavy velvet
curtain, plastic shower
cushion on which an incontinent
  person has been sitting
cyanide
dank
darkroom
deadly
décolletage of juicy fruit glittered
  up by diamonds and perfumed
  with spice
decomposed
decomposing, something
deli, Italian
deodorant, what angels use as an
  underarm
detergent
diamond sparkles and glints,
  gives itself the way a
diamond, brilliant
diaper, baby's
diaper, poopy
diesel exhaust/fumes
dirty, rather/very
diseased
disgusting
dishcloth/dishrag, dirty/soiled
dishwater
disinfectant, ghastly cheap pine
door to Ali Baba's cave, thick and
  dusty like the
door, old metallic screen
doormat, seems to have been
  strained through a
doormat, singed
down mold
drainpipe, stench from a
drains, blocked
Drāno, Liquid
drawer in grandma's bedroom
  where she kept her big scary bras
drawerness, dusty
dress and a string of pearls, vinous
  equivalent of a little black
Driza-Bone
drops, Ricola cough
dust from old floorboards
dust on rubber bands
dust, brick
dust, carpenter's
dust, chalky smoky cellar
dyeworks, my grandmother's
eau de Cologne
ebonite/vulcanite
effluent in the Tame River,
  paper mill
electric

elixir of the gods/divine elixir
elixir, almost syrupy
elixir, complex creamy
elixir, heady
elixir, imperial
elixir, lush
elixir, magic/magical
embers in a dying fire
emery paper, very fine
empyreumatic
engine, gasoline
enriched, artificially
Enron because it didn't deliver
  what it promised, like
epoxy, bright clay-
erasers slammed against each
  other, two chalk
erasers, pencil
ester, rising
esterification, acetone
estery, banana-
estery, unpleasantly
ether/etheric/etherized/etherlike
ethyl acetate
exhaust fumes, auto
exhaust, '63 Chevy Nova
exhaust, diesel
extinguisher, sweet fire
factory, inside a Pepperidge Farm
factory, rubber tire
factory, sleepless night in a Cohiba
factory, yeast
fag ends
fair: popcorn...candy floss and
  vanilla ice cream, traveling
feed, dairy-farm
feed-sacks, burlap
ferment, fusty
fermented/fermentative/fermenty
ferments, wild
fertilizer
fetid
filtered, charcoal
filtered, too tightly
filth/filthy
filtration or fining, without
filtration, flattened by
fire and a war zone, cross between a
  forest
fire in a grate, old
fire in the fireplace
fire that would clear your sinuses
  on a wet Wednesday in Glasgow,
  menthol
fire, brush
fire, burning charcoal/wood
fire, damped-down wood
fire, electrical

fire, remains of a burnt-out
fireplace
fireworks
flavorings in a jelly bean factory, made with artificial
flavors unfold endlessly, oriental spice box
floor, damp/wet cellar
floorboards, fascinating old smells of unswept
floorcloth, dirty
flooring, hardwood
flor
fluid, brake
fluid, lighter
flutelike and pure
formaldehyde, faint suggestion of

Formula 409 in Hawaii

fort, builds a
foul
frame, wood
freshener, air/room
freshener, vanilla car
fruit of wild strawberries, artificial
fruit, lozenge
fuel, diesel
fuel, herb-infused jet
fuel, motorbike/motorcycle
funk than fruit, more
funk, *à la mode*
funk, barnyard
funk, brawny
funk, Burgundian
funk, French
funk, friendly
funk, nice bass note of mulchy
funk, none of the
funky but not unattractive
funky character, charred
funky yet polished
funky, pleasantly
funky, unattractively
furbelows
furniture of the wine world, antique
furniture, cherry/cherrywood
furniture, mahogany
furniture, old
fusty
Gap at the Gulfport (Mississippi) outlet mall, The
garage-oriented
garbage, rotten/rotting
gas leak
gas, bottled/propane
gas, mustard
gas, natural
gas, sewer

gasoline engine
gasoline/gasoliney
gassy, dry-
gel, hair
gentian
Geographics, pile of old National
glassy
globe, snow
gloss, lip
gloves worn by a young woman, inside of kid
gloves, new baseball
gloves, rubber

glue and bananas

glue and paraffin, fish
glue, aero-/airplane-
glue, children's white
glue, clear yellow paper
glue, marzipan-smelling
glue, model
glue, paper
goudron
grapes, plastic
graphite, smoky
grease, axle
greenhouse/hothouse
grill loaded with sizzling smoked ribs
grinder, coffee
Gripfix
grocery, feels as if you stumbled into a Mediterranean
grubby
Guerlain-like in the glass, becomes even more
gumboots on the Aga
gummy
gunpowder-stained
guns and roses
gunshot
gunsmoke
gym bag after a win
hairspray
handbag full of lipstick, scented lady's
handbag with a wooden handle, my grandmother's cloth
hat, wool
Havana
hazel, witch
hearth, empty
heat, summer
heater fires up for the first time in the fall, scent similar to when a baseboard
heaters, old-fashioned paraffin
helicopters into your mouth with spinning blades of fruit

hencoop
hide, tanned animal
horsebarn/horse stall
hospital smells
house at the zoo, monkey
house, brick
house, entire coffee-roasting
house, haunted
humidor, as heady as a
humidor, Churchill's personal
humidor, cigar
hydrocarbons
hygiene, poor
hygienic, not terribly
IHOPy
immaculate, consistently
immaculate, utterly
impure
incense, eastern/exotic
incense, ephemeral
incense, hippie
incense, sacramental
incense, smoking
indole
infected, bacterially/bacterial infection
ink and oak overlay
ink, black
ink, elegant printer's

ink, fountain pen

ink, India
ink, lemony
ink, red
ink-rich
inky elixir
inky oblivion
inky potion, rich
insecticide
inserts, oak barrel
insoles, leather
iodine twang, pleasing
iodine, celery-
iron vitamin-like
iron, tannate of
iron, wrought
item, manufactured
jacket, damp tweed
jacket, favorite leather
Janitor-in-a-Drum
jelly, petroleum
jewelry with beautiful delicate features
jockstrap, sumo wrestler's
joint, smoky barbecue
jumper, damp/wet wooly
kennel, dog
kerosene, classic/hallmark
kerosene, old-fashioned

kerosene, youthful
kitchen when she was making
  jam, grandmother's
kitchen, nana's
knickers/panties/underwear,
  ladies'
knickers/underpants, wet
knife, steel
Kool-Aid mix
lace, old
lacquer, high-toned
lactic scents
lamp with a new wick, flickering
  oil
lanolin and honey, pungent
lanolin, soft
lanolin, underplayed
lanolin…Vaseline…lemon curd
lanolinish, mesmerizingly
latex
laundromat filled with
  jalapeño pepper
laundry, huge piles of dirty
laundry, newly ironed
laundry, three-day-old
lead, covered in pencil
lead-pencilly oak
leather and spiced wood surf
  a rippling wave of red fruit,
  toast…
leather and tobacco, lick of
leather dipped in chocolate
leather notes of a (new) fine shoe,
  beautiful
leather on the well-worn back seat
  of an old Jag
leather smoothness, chamois
leather splashed with lime juice
leather underneath, bit of
leather, as rough as old shoe
leather, Australian
leather, black
leather, bookbinder's
leather, boot
leather, burnished
leather, buttery Italian glove
leather, cedary sweet
leather, charred/singed
leather, chesterfield
leather, complex
leather, decidedly rakish dash of
leather, dressed in
leather, exotic Russian
leather, faded
leather, fine old
leather, fresh
leather, genteel
leather, great

leather, hot
leather, Italian
leather, jauntily craggy
leather, like chewing on
leather, Moroccan
leather, new
leather, new glove
leather, newly tanned saddle
leather, newly/recently polished
leather, oiled
leather, oil-polished
leather, old saddle
leather, polished
leather, regional
leather, Russian
leather, scented sweet
leather, shiny
leather, slap of
leather, smoky new saddle
leather, soft Morocco
leather, soft shoe
leather, soy intertwined with
leather, spicy saddle
leather, squeaky
leather, sweaty saddle
leather, sweet saddle
leather, tanned
leather, tired and old
leather, typical sweet shoe
leather, upholstery
leather, very expensive
leather, warm saddle
leather, well-weathered
leather, well-worn
leather, wet
leather-clad personality
leatheriness, smooth
leatherlike, smooth and
leathery aromas, expressive
leathery complexities
leathery roughness/toughness
leathery rusticity
leathery, earthy-
leathery, tarry-
leaven/leavening/leaveny
lederhosen, distinct traces of
lees/leesy
Lemon Pledge
lethal
library, dusty/old
library, venerable old paneled
light-damaged
linalool
Lincoln Logs soaked in butter
linctus, Benylin cough
linctus, cherry cough
linen dried in the sun and wind,
  newly washed

linen slapping in the breeze, fresh
liner, can
linoleum, lime and
linoleum, refined
linseed oil, volatile
lint…bandages and iodine
Liquid Plumr, vinous equivalent of
liquid that collects in the toilet-
  brush holder
Listerine/Listerine-like
loafers with ruffled velvet
  stitching, vinified Gucci leather
loo, Spanish
lotion, aftershave
lotion, calamine
lotion, hair
lotion, hand
lotion, suntan
lumber, fresh-sawn
lumberyards of new oak
mac, black plastic
Mace
machine, lean green grass-cutting
maderization, corroded by
  excessive
Magic Markers
magnesia, milk of
makeup, clown
malignant
malodorous
manufactured, poorly
manufactured, well
marble in Florence's Uffizi,
  as slick as the polished
marble, polished to the sheen of
  black
marbles, oak
marijuana
mark of hot rubber and asphalt,
  skid
market after a brief downpour,
  farmers'
market in midsummer, farmers'
market, fire sale at the farmers'
market, Southeast Asian fruit
market's worth of flavors, spice
Marlboroughs, black-market
mash, sour
mastic
match, burnt French
match, flaring
match/matchstick, burnt/burning
matchstick, like sucking a
matchbook's striking surface
matches, just-lit
matchhead
matter, foreign
matting, coconut

mechanic and petrol nose, wild
medical element
medicinal, malty-
medicinal, slightly strange and
medicinal-piney
medicine/mediciney, cough
medicine, plum-flavored cough
menthol lift
menthol off a spoon of cough
    mixture
menthol, distinct counterpoint of
menthol, minty
menthol/camphor greenness
mentholated, slightly
menthol-like streak, green
menthols, pack of
merbromin
mercaptan
Mercurochrome
mercury, garden
metal contamination
metal, expansive
metal, green
metal, rusted/rusty
metal, wet
metallic overtones, canned
metallic shavings
metallic, faintly
metals, precise
microbes/microbiological
mildew/mildewed/mildewy
miniature painted with pigments
    derived from spices harmonized
    in detail and color, Persian
mittens, woolen/woolly
mixture and Punt e Mes, cross
    between cough
mixture, children's cough
mixture, flabby cough
MLF (MaloLatic Fermentation),
    textural
mold, bathroom
mold, mushroomy
mold, rancid vegetable
mold, wet
Montecristo…more like Phillies
    or Garcia y Vega, no
mop, floor
mothballs, tea and
mothballs-naphthalene
motorcycles, images of
mottled
mouth rinse, good
mouthwash, antiseptic
mouthwash, dentists' pink
mouthwash, foreign
mouthwash, I feel like I just had
mouthwash, K&B wine-flavored

mouthwash, rancid tar-and-
    turpentine
mouthwash, your basic crisp
Mr. Clean
nail, rusty
naphtha/naphthalene
nappy, damp
narcotic
narcotically seductive, almost
nard/nardine
nasty
nauseating/nauseous
neoprene
nest, like licking out a
    mouse's/rat's
newspapers, moldy/musty
newspapers, old
newspapers, wet
nonmalolactic
noxious
nuclear
nursery, redolent of the
oak, artificial flavors of
oak, cigar-box
odor, oxidation
odor, reduction
office products
office, smelled like a dentist's
oil, 3-IN-ONE
oil, as dense as/density of motor
oil, as rich as motor
oil, as viscous as motor
oil, cade
oil, Castro XL motor
oil, coconut suntan
oil, fusil
oil, hair
oil, juniper-tar
oil, linseed
oil, mineral
oil, sewing-machine
oil, sump
oiled, well
oilskin, wet
oily and coagulated as axle grease,
    as
ointment, cold sore
ointment, wart
Old Spice
opium
outhouse
oven, coke
overcoat, buttoned up in an oak
overcoat, raspberry cinnamon
oversulfured
oxidation odors
oxidation, slightly squalid notes of
oxidative cracks

oxidative nuttiness
oxide, iron
oxides, exaggerated
oxidized, horribly
oxygenated, micro-
packet, Player's Navy Cut cigarette
padish/padlike/paddy
pads, asbestos filter
pads, soiled filter
paint, added coat of
paint, cheap children's
paint, gloss
paint, latex
paint, penetrating slick of fresh
paint, purple
paint, so dark and foreboding
    it looks like black
paint, wet
pajamas, resembles silk
paneling, oak
pantry, well-stocked
paper, blotting
paper, burnt/singed brown
paper, buttered
paper, cast-off cigarette
paper, moldy wet
paper, old book
paper, rice
paper, sweet brown
paraffin
parchment used in bookbinding
parchment, old
parlor, milking
paste, library
paste, shoe
pasteurized
Patel's Cash and Carry in
    Iselin New Jersey
pâtisserie on a summer morning,
    French
pavement, hot summery
pavement, wet
pen, chewed end of a wooden
pen/shed/stall, animal
pencil shavings, blast of
pencil shavings, flinty
pencil shavings, lead
pencil shavings, new
pencil shavings, wet
pencilly oak
pencilly, little
pencils, baked
pencils, burnt
pencils, cedar/cedary lead
pencils, freshly sharpened lead
penicillin
penny, copper
pens, marker

perfume section of a department
  store, like walking into the
perfume, cheap artificial
perfume, cosmetic
perfume, heavenly cassis
perfume, old lady
perfumes from long ago, memories
  of
perm solution
pesticide
petrol without all that expensive
  aging, complexity of
petrol, lead-free
petrol, rich grapefruit-
pétrole, goût de
petroleum, ginger behind
petroleum, liquid slate-
petroleum, oily
petrolly complexity
petrol-resin
pewter covered in dust and
  cobwebs, dull
pharmaceuticals
pharmacy, pinch of a good
phenolic firmness
phenolic heaviness, avoids
phenolic profile, overly floral
  tropical
phenolic stuffing
phenolic trap, avoids
phenolic, not excessively
phenolics, no hard
pigeons, clay
pigpen/pigsty
pill, hard-to-swallow fruit
pillow, as soft as a down
pillowy
Pine-Sol
pipe in a leather chair, like
  smoking a
pipes, passed through water
pitch/pitchy
pizza, deep-dish leather
plank, like licking a
plank, woody taste of a
planks, juicy fruit peering through
  the
planks, oak
planks, ripe berries struggling to
  squeeze between the charred oak
planks, tank
plant, earthy peaty notes as those
  wafting from a water-treatment
plaster/plastery
plastic-esque
plastic whiff of Eau de Mattel
plastic wrap, new
plastic, good dose of

plastic, heated
Plasticine
Play-Doh
plimsolls, wet
plywood
poison, rat
polish and caramel, strawberries
  larded with furniture
polish, cheap furniture
polish, French
polish, leather
polish, nail
polish, old beeswax
polish, silver
polish, violet-scented furniture
polish, waxy furniture
polish, wood
polish/paste, boot/shoe
polyphenolic structure, solid
pool, indoor swimming
pool, public swimming
pool, vinyl swimming
pool, YMCA
porcelain, light-piercing
port, Greek
potions, entire battery of
  face creams and skin
potpourri, Dollar Store
potty
pouch, tobacco
powder, concocted from a
powder, fine bath
powder, finest hand-ground
powder, fresh talcum
powder, honeyed face
powder, household cleaning
powder, sweet baby
powder, trading-card/-gum
powder, washing
preservation-free
prints, Cibachrome color
processing
project, bit of a science
puff, powder
pump, petrol
punnets, iron
punnets, juicy-fruity black currant
purse, the inside of your
  grandmother's
putrid, mildly
putty, strange mineral taste like
pyrogenic
quicksilver/quicksilvery
quinine, youthful refreshing bitter
  kick of
rack, spice
radiators, central-heating
rag, bar/wet

rag, oily
Raid
railway
rancid, borders on the
rancid, disgustingly
rancid, just plain
rancio, autumnal
rancio, extreme
rancio, piercing strand of
rancio, smoky
rank
rawhide
reduction ferment
reduction odors
reductive pong
reduction, burnt match
reduction, complex trace of funky
reduction, distinct matchstick
reduction, trembles on the brink of
reductive elements, slightly blurry
refinery
refrigerator, defrosted
remover, nail polish
rennet
restaurant, Asian
restroom after it's been cleaned,
  public
ride, magic carpet
Rite-Aid, something at
road of wildflowers and mad-
  capped berries, Fellini-like
road repairs
road, newly paved
road, smells like rain on a bitumen
roasted, massively
robe of thick velvet, as warming
  as a
Robitussin DM
Robitussin or Dimetane...with
  skunk flavor on the finish
room after a football game on a
  warm September evening, locker
room at a baseball park during a
  game, men's
room in a French railway station,
  men's
room odor, unpleasant laundry-
room where they never open the
  windows
room, any men's
room, freshly painted
room, leather-furnished drawing
room, locker
room, made in a laundry
room, medicinal
room, musty vacant
rope with prickly loose fibers,
  natural hemp

rope, sisal
rope, tarred
rose water and perfume, concentrated
rot character, plenty of noble-
rot was less than noble, one wonders whether some of the
rot, aspergillus
rot, dripping with the apricot marmalade of noble
rot, has undergone noble
rot, ignoble
rot, noble/nobly rotten
rot-infested
Roto-Rooter
rottenness, rough seaside sand sort of
rubber, artificial
rubber, burning
rubber, burnt/singed
rubber, gum
rubber, hot/warm
rubber, obligatory
rubber, sweet
rubber, tire
rubbers, wet
rubbers in a wallet, old
rubbery component, curious damp
rug, as tightly woven as a fine silk
rug, complexity and beauty of a Persian
run, hen
rusty, rustic and
sachet for your underclothes drawer, fragrant
saddle after a long ride on a horse, hot
saddle and the horse it rode in on, sweaty
saddle without the sweat
saddle, mouthful of
saddle, sweaty
saddle, warm/warmed
saddlebags
salon and tasted like light beer, smelled like a hair
salts, overly fragrant bath
sander, like brushing your teeth with a belt-
sanitized
Saran Wrap
sauna, pine-clad
sawmill, like walking into a
sawmill, oak
scents twelve-year olds spray on their valentine cards, cheap
scents, boudoir
skuzzy

seat, sweaty bicycle
seats in my father's old sports car, leather
semiputrid
sewage, raw
shampoo, medicated
shampoo, Paul Mitchell
shampoo, pear and apple
shavings, metallic
shavings, oak
shed, gardener's
shed, timber merchant's
sheets that have been hung to dry outdoors, newly washed
sheets that have dried in the wind, freshly washed
sheets under a clothesline on a summer day, cotton
sheets with your initials mono-grammed on them, violet silk
sheets, clean sun-dried
sheets, sun-dried newly laundered
shellac, wet
sherrified/sherrylike
shirt, wet Pendleton
shock, bottle
shoes running on a hot road, gym
shoes, degenerated training
shoes, dirty
shoes, five-year-old jogging
shoes, new
shoes, tennis
shoeshine
shop aromas, metal
shop at Hammersmith Station, the shoe repair
shop dispensing aromatherapy oils
shop smells, coffee
shop, baker's/pastry
shop, Beirut pastry
shop, cabinet
shop, carpenter
shop, florist's
shop, fresh flower
shop, old-fashioned butcher's
shop, sweet
shop, tire
shorts, old running
shotgun, expensive
shower, dirty
sickly, rather
sickly, slightly
sickness, bottle
sickness, travel
sidewalk, cracked
silicone
silk, liquid
silos

singed and sooty
sink, kitchen
skyscraper in the mouth without being heavy or disjointed, towering
skyscraper, massive
slats, oak
slick across the palate, spreads like a delicious oil
slippers, my father's carpet
sludge/sludgy
smelling, vile-
smells, new-Barbie
smelly, just plain
smoke and black bitter minerals, beauty in black: black fruit...black
smoke and citrus, smoldering with
smoke and musk, vacillating between
smoke bomb
smoke from a distant fire
smoke from a struck match
smoke from its pores, seems to ooze
smoke of a cowboy's campfire, drifting
smoke rings the second the cork was pulled, blew
smoke when you pop the cork, exhales
smoke, acacia-perfumed
smoke, ashy
smoke, autosuggestion of
smoke, balsamic
smoke, barbecue
smoke, beechwood
smoke, black/blacker/blackish
smoke, blatant dosage of toasty
smoke, bonfire
smoke, campfire/campfire smokiness
smoke, Cape coal dust
smoke, cigar
smoke, coal
smoke, coiled in
smoke, cool
smoke, fireplace
smoke, fueled by oak-induced
smoke, haunting
smoke, hickory
smoke, laden with
smoke, liquid
smoke, pistol
smoke, powerful
smoke, puff of
smoke, rich hickory
smoke, scrim of

smoke, sealed by a kiss of
smoke, seductive
smoke, sultriest
smoke, sweet
smoke, sweet cigar
smoke, tangy
smoke, thick
smoke, white
smoke, wisp of
smoke, wrapped in
smoke-charred
smoke-crammed character
smokehouse and a spice shop,
  somewhere between a
smokiness, come-hither
smokiness, heavenly
smokiness, mouthwatering
  baconlike
smokiness, steely
smoky aromatics
smoky as a brushfire racing across
  herb-covered hillsides, as
smoky as a chimney, as
smoky as Mount Vesuvius, as
smoky aspects, some
smoky like the embers of a wood
  fire
smoky qualities, mystical
smoky, sweet-sour-
smoky...earthy...animal flavors,
  treasure chest of
smoky-berry
smoky-meaty
smoky-spicy, intense
smoky-stinky
smoldering
sneakers, nasty
snuff
soap, creamy saddle
soap, dishwashing
soap, leather and saddle
soap, lemon
soap, lily of the valley
soap, perfumed/scented
soap, Sunlight
soap, violet-scented Roger & Gallet
soaps in the guest bathroom that
  everyone's afraid to unwrap,
  small
soaps you never use, little
soapsuds
sock, vinegar sifted through a dirty
sockiness, old
socks, 100-year-old dirty sweat
socks, clean old
socks, dirty gym/sweat
socks, dirty/stinky old
socks, gendarme's

socks, moldy
socks, muddy football
socks, old/vintage
socks, Pierre's old
socks, smelly
socks, sweaty
socks, unwashed
sofa, dusty
sofa, fusty old leather
softball into the pine trees,
  like hitting a
soiled
soles, rubber
solvent
solvents, carpentry
something that doesn't belong
  there
soot, warm
sorbate
souk, as spicy as a
souk, like walking through a
Spackle, troweled
Spackles right over the crack
  in wine
sparklers
spinach water, old
spoilage, bacterial
spoiled, completely
sponges
spores
spotless
spray, bug
spray, fly
squares, oak
stable yard
stable, damp straw in a
  thoroughbred
stables, horse
stables, mucky
stables, bouillon and
stables, rich old
stables, spicy old
stables, tanginess of thoroughbred
stables, Virol and pungent old
stables, well-patronized
stably old flavors
stagnant
staircase kept carefully clean yet
  never quite free of dust, ancient
stand in the Ozarks, fruit
stand on a dusty road, Kool-Aid
stand, whole market fruit
staircase, velvet on a marble
station, gas
staves, curtains of oak
staves, oak inner
staves, oakwood barrel
steel core is wrapped in a coat of

fleshy fruit
steel, backbone of
steel, cold
steel, flint striking
steel, rusty
steel, stainless
steeliness, unmissable
steely attack
steely austerity
steely mouthfeel
steely nervousness
steely sharp, severe and
steely smokiness
steely spine of minerals
steely streak, cold
steely, tangy-
stick, faint joss
stick, musty joss
sticks, oak
stink that drives men to drink,
  exotic
stink, characteristic
stink, complex
stink, fungi bottle
stink, indescribable absolutely
  ravishing
stink, thick exquisite
stinky, pleasantly
stinky, somewhat
stockings jumping up and down in
  the gooseberry bush, silk
stogies
store, antique
store, candy
store...fruitmonger and spice
  market, combination candy
storeroom, undertone of
  subterranean
stove, solid-fuel
strap, leather
stringy
stripper, paint
strips, oak
stuffiness, closed-window
stuffiness, touch of
styrene
suite in the Plaza, like coming
  home to a
sulfide, hydrogen
sulfited
sulfur dioxide
sulfur, bottling
sulfur, cardboardy
sulfur, free
sulfur, good belt of
sulfur, reeks repulsively of
sulfury fumes, blows off its
sulfury stench

sullied
sump, remains of a drained car
sumpy
superclean
superglue
superphosphate
superpure
supertarry
surgery, dentist's
sweater after being caught in the rain
sweater, cardigan
sweats, old
sweats, unwashed
sweetener, artificial
synthesis of lemon and sugar, laboratory
syrup, black currant cough
syrup, children's cough
syrup, prescription cough
syrup, simple cough
syrup, spicy cough
syrup, sticky cough
syrup, terrific cherry cough
table, old walnut
table, sturdily crafted oak
tack room

taint, vinegar-fly

tainted, hopelessly
talc, peach
talcum across your palate, trail of
talcum powder, pink
tallow/tallow
tank character, just topped-off-my-tanky
tar and shit, touch of
tar and spice, flashes of
tar reduction, noble
tar, as dense as
tar, coal
tar, deep taste of hot
tar, dusty
tar, freshly laid road
tar, juniper
tar, melted/melting driveway/road
tar, olive-scented blackberries and
tar, subtle
tar, sweet
tarlike undercurrent
tarlike, strangely
tarmac, hot
tarmac, newly spread
tarmac, strip of
tar-macadam, rain on
tarpaulin fringed with lace, old
tar-resin
tarriness, extreme
tarry center/edge

tarry heart, dark
tarry stuff, glorious
tarry uplift, rich
tarry-leathery
tar-violet
TCA-tainted
technotasting
Terminal, like walking through Grand Central
terpenes
terra cotta
thiamin
thinner, lacquer/paint
tiles baked by the evening sun, terra cotta
tiles, hot Provençale
tiles, roof
timber, freshly cut/hewn

timbers, old tarred sea

tin, just-opened biscuit
tincture
tinfoil
tins, roasting
tires off a ten-year-old tractor, like chewing the
tires and oil, fruit colliding with Firestone
tires, burning/burnt/smoldering
tires, new
tires, old automobile/rubber
tobacco, classic pipe
toothpaste/toothpowder
toothpicks, like chewing
towel, beer
towel, damp/wet
towelettes
track, railway
tracks, creosote-soaked railroad
tracks, metallic almost rusty notes of railway
tractor with a gorgeous nude redhead on the seat, beloved
trainers, girlfriend's damp Nike
trolley, pastry
trouser-opener
trumpets, fanfare of oak
tub, dirty hot-
tubes, ancient inner
Tupperware, slight whiff of
turpentine
two-by-four thwack, good
Two-by-Four, Château
two-by-four, like chewing into a length of
two-by-four, oak
two-by-four, plank of
unclean
unguent, marvelous

unhealthy
uniforms, chocolate and schoolgirls'
unmanufactured
unmentionables
unspoiled
untainted
upholstery, finest chamois
upholstery, new-car
vanillins, sappy-sweet
VapoRub, Vicks
varnish of highly polished new casks
varnish, musty
varnish, wood/varnishy-woody
Varsol
Vaseline
Vaseline and vanilla
Velvet, deep purple
velvet, drapes of
venomous
viaduct

Viagra for flaccid reds

Viagra, Chateau
Viagra, liquefied
Vicks Formula 44D
Vicks VapoRub
vinyl
Virol and pungent old stables
Virol, strange
Virol...the malted meaty tonic for anemic girls, like taking
virulent
vitamins
vulcanization barrier
walls, dusty stone
washer, clothes
wastes, organic
water, bilge
water, cough syrupy goopy sugar
water, soapy rose
wax and honey
wax and truffles, soft accents of ceiling
wax of beeswax candles dripping onto an ancient teak table, scented
wax, auto
wax, burnt sealing
wax, floor
wax, furniture
wax, melting candle
wax, shoe
wax, sweet candle
wax-and-lanolin character, fat
WD-40
well-drilling
wheel, sparks like a Catherine

whetstone
whey
window syndrome, closed-
winery, like walking into a
wire bound in licorice, metal
witch hazel
wood and cream, artificial tastes of
woodwork, often creeps out of the
workroom/workshop, carpenter's
works, my grandmother's dye
wrap, plastic
wrapper, cheap cigar
wrappers, newly unwrapped
  toffee-
wrappers, sweet
xanthophyll
yard, timber
yeast softening in warm water
yeast, balsamic wild
yeast, complex funky wild
yeast, creamy
yeast, cultured
yeast, flor
yeast, fresh
yeast, hot
yeast, peppery
yeast, pure
yeast, wet baker's
yeast, wild
yeastiness, vitamin B-tablet
yeast-influenced
yeasty depths
yeasty primal smells
yeasty richness
yeasty waftings from start to finish
yeasty, subtly

I have to have wines that sing, that shout, that roar their personalities.
Oz Clarke

The way we drink wine is changing fast and consumers of today want smooth, powerful, high-alcohol wines, often to be enjoyed without food.
Peter Sommer

18. Power [Strength, Concentration, Extract, Intensity]

You know when you meet a powerful wine; it doesn't caress your nose and palate, it confronts them. It tells you to sit up and take notice because it has something important to say. *Extract*, for example, is the sum total of all the solids in the wine after fermentation and filtration, if any; a good amount helps to provide you with a memorable mouthful. In the cause of power, no company has coined a better motto than Sonoma's Ravenswood Winery: *No Wimpy Wines*. Amen.

aggression, has no
aggression, packed with
aims for the bleachers
amped-up grassy-gooseberry-
   cat-pee elements
amps, extra
anemic, sadly
assault on the sense, less of an
assertive take-no-prisoners
assertive yet languorous
assertive yet refined
assertive, explosively
assertive, never
assertiveness, agreeable
assertiveness, avoids extremes of
assertiveness, lacks
authority, like someone speaking
   in a low voice imbued with
awe, sense of shock and
balls back into the wine, puts
balls, big
ballsy
balls to the wall
barn-burner
bashful
bashful, never
big dog it is, comes on like the
big-ass
bite, lacks a certain amount of
bland
blast, full-

blast, mouthcoating
blaster, ghetto
blasts your palate off
blazing, all guns
Blitzkrieg on my palate
Blitzkrieg, comes on like a
blockbuster, huge sun-soaked
blockbuster, inky
blockbuster, macho
blockbuster, not a
blockbuster, ostentatious
blockbuster, profound
blockbuster, refined
blockbuster, sensational
blockbuster, unruly
blockbuster, young
blockbusting
blooded, full-
bludgeons you with flavor
blunt instrument, more of a
blushing violet, no
blustery or overaggressive, not too
body press, full-
bold
bomb waiting to go off, fully
   primed
bomb, unexploded
bomber, burly
bombshell, velvety
bore, comes out of the gate full-
bounce to the ounce, more

bravado, characteristic
bruiser of a red
bruiser with a full tank of fuel
   behind it, real
bruiser with a soft side
bruiser, big masculine
bruiser, old
bruiser, opulent
bruiser, real
bruiser, saturated
brutal stuff, aggressive savage
brute it could well be, far removed
   from the
brute, big
brute, gorgeous dark classic
brutish, rather
bull, a
bulldozer way, merciless in its
   insensitive
bulldozer, mouthfilling
bursting at the seams
car, nitro-burning funny
charges out of the blocks
chops, has the
clout, has
coiled, tightly
collision between a spice container
   and a ton of plump red and
   purple berries, asteroid
compressed
concentrate of wine

concentrate, atomic bomb
concentrate, Châteauneuf
concentrated and dense, insanely
concentrated and essential,
  incredibly
concentrated and powerful as they
  come, as
concentrated as it gets, as
concentrated but not
  overextractive, immensely
concentrated dimension, total
concentrated essence
concentrated essence that is always
  thick and saturated with nectar
concentrated flavors
concentrated form, in its most
concentrated fruit
concentrated full-bodied
  behemoth, complex
concentrated imperious mix
concentrated it tastes as if all the
  fruit has evaporated...leaving
  only the spirit behind, so
concentrated monster, not a
concentrated mouthfiller
concentrated opulent heart, lovely
concentrated style, prodigiously
concentrated that it takes one's
  breath away, so unbelievably
  rich and
concentrated wallop, intense
  headily
concentrated wine, big staggeringly
concentrated wines we've ever
  tasted, one of the most
concentrated, 100%
concentrated, almost too
concentrated, astonishingly/
  enormously/fabulously/
  highly/incredibly/immensely/
  intensely/phenomenally/
  spectacularly/staggeringly/
  stunningly/stupendously/
  unbelievably
concentrated, atypically
concentrated, beautifully
concentrated, decadently
concentrated, impassively
concentrated, magically
concentrated, not especially
concentrated, richly
concentrated, sensationally
concentrated, splendidly
concentrated, unbeatably
concentrated, uncompromisingly
concentrated, very
concentrated...almost
  undrinkable, massively

concentration and depth,
  monstrous levels of
concentration and extract, majestic
concentration and extract,
  phenomenal
concentration and focus,
  impressive combination of
concentration and length,
  skyscraperlike profile of
  fabulous
concentration of fruit leaves me
  speechless
concentration of pure fruit,
  wonderful
concentration or extract, without
  bone-crushing
concentration, almost impossible
concentration, almost sorbetlike
concentration, almost too much
concentration, awesome/dazzling/
  enormous/exceptional/extreme/
  fabulous/fantastic/incredible/
  lavish/marvelous/phenomenal/
  sensational/sheer/terrific
concentration, balanced
concentration, beautifully tuned
concentration, beef bloodlike
concentration, boiled-down
  kind of
concentration, brilliant
concentration, crunchy
concentration, demiglazelike
concentration, enrapturing
concentration, epitome of richness
  and
concentration, eye-watering
  density and
concentration, freakish
concentration, goodish
concentration, heady
concentration, heaps of
concentration, hefty
concentration, lacks focus and
concentration, laserlike
concentration, legendary
concentration, majestic
concentration, never loses
concentration, on another plane
  of power and
concentration, over-the-top
concentration, real fruit
concentration, startlingly deep
  dark
concentration, sumptuous
concentration, superb
concentration, thrilling levels of
concentration, uncommon/
  unusual

concentration, unreal levels of
concentration, wild heady
concentration, you can smell the
condensed
condensed, less
confrontational
considerable
constructed, ruggedly
construction, rigorous
crusher, sandshoe
cryoextracted
dainty
daunting, almost
daunting, less
defanged
delicacy from start to finish
delicacy magically combined,
  power and
delicacy, almost gossamerlike
delicacy, much
delicacy, ravishing
delicate as a butterfly, as
delicate as angels' tears, as
delicate brushstrokes, painted with
delicate jewel
delicate little thing
delicate nuances
delicate, ethereally/hauntingly
dense and sleek as a sea lion, as
dense as motor oil, as
dense stuff
dense you almost eat it, so
dense, extraordinarily/
  fabulously/gloriously/
  gorgeously/unbelievably
dense, massively
denser constitution
density of flavor, fantastic
density, admirable/goodish/
  impressive
density, awesome/super/
  unbelievable
density, earthy-animal
density, excessive
density, ineffable
density, no
density, off-the-chart
density, old-vine
depth of pure fruit, extreme
depth, unbelievable
dilute confection
dilute it by half and still receive its
  message, you could
diluted, highly/much/very
direct, surprisingly
disintegrating
docile
dominant, overpoweringly

dominating
dreadnoughtlike
drink it...paint with it, don't just
drink this sitting down or risk
  your knees buckling
drive to it, really good
driven/driving
dynamite in a glass
dynamite, gold-hunter's
dynamite, pure
dynamo
earth-shattering
effortless
electricity, few volts of
electrifying
emaciated
emasculated
empty
enamel off your teeth, will take the
enamel-ripping, tooth
enamel-rotting stuff, tooth
energetic yet demure
energy shoots through
energy to fulfill, the nose promises
  more than the palate has the
energy well under control, adult
energy, bags/plenty of high-
energy, has inner
energy, irrepressible
energy, sense of pent-up
engine raring to go, look under
  the hood to find an
enormous
essence, boiled down
essence, reduced to intense
eviscerated
excellent
explode at any moment, could
explode, waiting to
explodes on the palate/tongue
explosion in the mouth, incredible
explosion, controlled
explosion, delicious
explosive aromatics/explosively
  aromatic
explosive impact
explosive, highly/richly
extract and acidity, dense weave of
extract and balance, marvelous
extract and density, mind-blowing
  levels of
extract and richness, surreal levels
  of
extract behind the wall of tannin,
  good
extract is mind-boggling, level of
  fruit
extract is so thick it's almost visible

extract levels, teeth-staining
extract of a vintage port
extract sweetness on the length
extract sweetness, lovely
extract, almost chewable in its
  wealth of
extract, almost velvety
extract, amazing/extraordinary/
  phenomenal/sensational
extract, austere sumptuous
extract, bitter
extract, brimming with
extract, candylike
extract, chockablock-full of
extract, concentrated/monster/
  strong/thick/weighty
extract, coquettishly elusive
  flavorful
extract, could have more
extract, crammed with
extract, drop-dead levels of
extract, dry
extract, earthy
extract, excellent/good control of
extract, excellent/great/lovely/
  wonderful
extract, filled with berry
extract, flaunts elegant
extract, fleeting bitterness of
  undeveloped
extract, fruit
extract, generous/high
extract, gobs/masses/oodles/
  truckloads of
extract, good
extract, high/huge
extract, lacking fruit
extract, lacks meaty
extract, layers of
extract, major-league richness and
extract, masses of concentrated
extract, mind-boggling level of
  fruit
extract, muscular
extract, pure
extract, real leather and meat
extract, rich and thick with
extract, sappy fruit
extract, slightly sour
extract, supercharged with
extract, thrilling levels of
extract, undeveloped/unripe
extract...concentration, perfectly
  packed
extract-crazy world, rare exercise in
  restraint in an
extracted inky macho red wine I
  have ever encountered, the most

extracted style, seriously
extracted to the nth degree
extracted, decadently
extracted, deeply/enormously/
  highly/hugely/massively/
  seriously/terribly/well
extracted, highly fruit-
extracted, not crudely
extracted, too highly
extraction of fruit blossoming out
  across the palate, great
extraction, almost obscene
extraction, avoids excessive
extraction, exceptional/
  marvelous/tremendous/
  very good/wonderful
extraction, hard-bodyish
extraction, monster
extraction, prodigious fruit
extraction, terrific fruit
extraction, very good
extractive weight, good
extractive, almost viscous in
  texture yet not
extractive, incredibly
extract-rich
extracts, bountiful
extracts, unripe
extracty mouthful, massive
extracty, very
extrahorsepower
eye-watering stuff, lean
face and needs to back away,
  in your
fading
faint of heart, isn't for the
fearsome challenge for the unwary
feeble
feisty character
feisty, rather too
ferocious
fierce juice
fierce, just short of
fierce, mighty
fighter, heavyweight
fine
firecracker
firepower, has serious
fireworks
firm
fist in a velvet glove, ultimate iron
fisted, ham-
fisted, two-
fistfight, as if it took a tumble in a
fist-in-the-face
flimsy
flimsy palate
floppy

flowing
force experience, full-
force of its spirit
force one glass takes your palate places where you haven't been before, by sheer
force ride, full-
force, brute
force, void of
forceful personality, appealingly
forceful, extraordinarily
forceful, fairly
forceful, threateningly
forcefully, opens
fortified, heavily
fortified, lightly
forward, rugby
fragile to drink, almost too
frail
frighten the horses, will not
Frankenstein Pinot
front, up-
frontal, full-
full/full-tilt
full-on, fairly/pretty
gangbusters, coming on like
gas in its tank, has
gas, both feet on the
gas, never steps off the
gentle and violent
gentle as a butterfly brushing flower petals, as
gentle giant
gentle line, toes a
gentle, totally
gentleness, creamy
gentler, kinder-
gentlest palates in the dessert wine kingdom, one of the
gently into this good night, does not go
get up and go, has
giant/gigantic
glaring
glass-staining
Godzilla
good/goodish
gorilla in a glass
great
grunt than a monster truck, more
grunt, rustic
gum-numbing
gun, big
guns blazing, all
gushy, too
gutless wonder
guts and broad shoulders, plenty of

guts in their wine, for those who really can't live without
guts inside/underneath, plenty of
guts, atypical
guts, good/real
guts, lots/plenty of/no lack of
guts, more than enough
guts, no real
gutsy personality
gutsy, very
hair on its chest, has
hair on your chest, will put
hard
hard-nosed
harsh
headstrong
hearted, faint-/light-/soft-
hearted, not for the faint-
hearty
heavy-duty
heavy-handed
heavy-handed, not at all
hefty
Herculean
high
hits you between the eyes
hitting, heavy-
hollow
hood for aging, plenty under the
hopped up
horrible
huge
Hummer, all the grace of a
hyper
hyperconcentrated
hyperdense
hyperextracted
immense
impact, quiet
impotent
impoverished
impressive, powerfully
improving
infirm
inflated
infused, well
insipid
insubstantial
intense and ephemeral, both
intense as a tropical storm, as
intense as the night sky over Manchester during a blackout, as
intense as you can imagine, as
intense deep-set, very
intense entry
intense experience, very
intense it seems to have a kick, so

intense that every taste receptor reacts as if electrically stimulated, so
intense that I was moved to tears, so
intense, almost shockingly
intense, almost troublingly
intense, amazingly/exquisitely/ extraordinary/incredibly/ indescribably/phenomenally/ piercingly/searingly/smashingly
intense, hauntingly
intense, quite/really/very
intensity and power, untold
intensity and subtlety at the same time, unmistakable combination of
intensity in a glass
intensity in a velvety package
intensity in spades
intensity meets finesse, textbook example of
intensity that lances the air, shaft of
intensity, awesome/boggling/ colossal/daunting/ extraordinary/fabulous/massive/ phenomenal/unimaginable
intensity, blistering/scorching
intensity, dark coffee-ground
intensity, deep
intensity, essencelike
intensity, extraordinary sappy
intensity, feral
intensity, fiery
intensity, freakishly high levels of
intensity, laserlike
intensity, licoricelike
intensity, mind-boggling
intensity, molar-crunching
intensity, old-vine
intensity, provocative
intensity, rare
intensity, riveting
intensity, startling
intensity, stinging nettle
intensity, striking
intensity, succulent sweet-fruit
intensity, tightly wound
intensity, turns up the
intensity, unbridled
intensity, unheard-of
intensity, unique
intensity, youthful inky
intensity...drive, excellent
intensity...structure and style
intrinsic

iron, pumps
jacked up
jolt to the senses, electric
jolting
juiced up
kick in the teeth
kick-ass
kickback, tarry
kicks butt from first to finish
knock on the door and wait
politely, does not
knock you flat, will never
knockout punch
knocks you off your chair
knocks you out
knocks your socks off
lacking
lackluster
laid-back
lame
languid/languorous
lapels, grabs your
larger than life
light
limp
limp-wristed
linebacker who has studied years
of ballet, all-star
lion...out like a lamb, like March:
in like a
little goes a long way
low
lustily, drinks
lusty drinking, appropriate for
massive
mawkish
maximal
medium
meek, disappointingly
meek, not for the
megaconcentrated
megaintense
mighty

Mighty Mouse

mild as a summer breeze, as
mild thing
mild-mannered
moderate
modest
monster from the cellar
monster, black
monster, chucky
monster, dark licorice-hearted
monster, far from a hedonistic
monster, immense/massive
monster, juicy
monster, temperamental
monster, velvet/velvety

monster, veritable
monster, vinous
monsters, not one of your fat
hedonistic
muscle and refinement,
compelling juxtaposition of
muscle of a Romanian gymnast
muscle of youth and the
complexity of age
muscle than brains, more
muscle than fat, more
muscle with crystalline grace,
combines
muscle without finesse
muscle, abundant/considerable/
enormous/major/plenty of
muscle, admirable
muscle, brutal
muscle, iron-fisted
muscle, less obvious
muscle, not a little
muscle-bound, not

muscle-bound, very

muscled, well
muscles, beginning to flex its
muscles, really flexing its taut
muscular crescendo in the
midpalate, builds to a
muscular stuff, pretty
muscular yet graceful
muscular, remarkably
muscularity, disdains ostentatious
neutral
no-holds-barred
normal
nuclear
octane stuff, high-
octane, ultrahigh-
oomph to get by, just enough
oomph, more
oomph, needs much more
oomph, plenty of
oomph, real
overblown
overconcentrated
overdrive, all olfactory senses on
overdrive, maximum
overextracted
overextraction, does not stray into
overloads tasters' olfactory
receptors
overloads the olfactory senses
overpowering
overpowering facets, no
overpowers, seduces rather than
over-the-top
overwhelming, trifle

packed enough to go the extra
mile, not
painful to drink, not
Parkerized
penetrating and elegant at the
same time
penetrating, very
peppery
perfect
personality, extravagant
piss and vinegar, full of

pistol-packing

pithy
point
poor
Pop in Châteauneuf-du-, puts the
potency with delicacy, combines
potency with elegance
potency, old-vine
potent as a raging bull, as
potent delicacy
potent mouthfilling beasts of
complexity and structure
potent palate takes no prisoners,
massively
potent, absurdly
potent, enjoyably
potently built
pounding nose
pow...right in the kisser
power allied to elegance, classic
example of
power and brawn, sheer
power and complexity, masterpiece
of
power and complexity: the holy
trinity of great winemaking, lush
ripeness wedded to
power and concentration are
masterly
power and definition, extravagant
wine that marvelously marries
power and delicacy magically
combined
power and elegance, abundant
power and elegance, admirably
balances
power and elegance, combines
natural
power and elegance, rare
power and finesse, brilliant
marriage of
power and finesse, rare
power and generosity, rules with
grace...
power and grace, flavor-laden
explosion of

power and importance like the Lion King, visibly proclaims its
power and majesty
power and spiciness surge out of the glass like a sudden eruption of Mount Etna
power is well harnessed
power like a burst of adrenaline
power of a sprinter and the grace of a ballerina, boasts the explosive
power of blistering intensity, black-currant

power of our closest star
power of ripe California fruit wrapped in a seamless velvet glove, knockout
power of the wine lies partially in wait, huge
power over finesse, displaying
power ready to be unleashed
power that can often take the breath away, has finesse yet with a
power to burn
power to refresh
power to spare, has
power under the bonnet, unmistakable surge of Bentley-like
power with great elegance, struts its
power with no weight...only mass, has the uncanny feeling of
power with subtlety, combines
power, atypical
power, awesome/enormous/ great/massive/monumental/ tremendous
power, bewitching
power, black weight of its
power, black-fruited
power, blockbuster
power, brooding
power, brute/monster/raw
power, collected inner
power, considerable
power, explosive wave of momentous
power, for those who expect their palates to be assaulted by the pungent spice-shocking
power, great aromatic
power, great staying
power, great underlying
power, hidden
power, high-octane
power, intractable

power, like lightning this wine hits you with a bolt of
power, manly/masculine
power, measured/subdued
power, more finesse than
power!, my...what dense mighty

power, oozes
power, opulence lurks behind the
power, outright
power, pop and
power, reined-in
power, rugged honesty and
power, shows real
power, silky Rolls-Royce
power, small marvel of class and
power, stifled underlying
power, surprising inner
power, swoon at its
power, thick churning
power, tons of
power, unbelievable/unbridled/ unrestrained/untold
power, unbridled naked
power, without overweening
power, wonderful inner
power, wonderful unreleased intrinsic
power, world-class
power!, wow...what dense mighty
power...wildness and grace all at once, has
power: perfume...subtlety and sensuality don't come into it, this wine is all about
power-dressed
power-packed
powered, high-
powered, ultrahigh-
powerful (whew)
powerful and complex it very nearly imprisons the senses, so
powerful and hyperexpressive
powerful and muscular yet remarkably feminine and elegant
powerful attack
powerful complexity
powerful enough to fuel a musketeer and graceful enough to win the heart of a lady
powerful giant, nothing garish about this subtle yet
powerful in all respects
powerful it startles, so
powerful like a desert, colossally
powerful mode, in fully
powerful monster, massive
powerful of noble wines, one of the most

powerful personality, massively
powerful punch of a heavy-weight...the opulence of a show-girl and the elegance of a dancer, has the
powerful punchy style
powerful stuff
powerful welterweight
powerful, astonishingly/extremely
powerful, broodingly
powerful, dangerously
powerful, dense and
powerful, doggoned
powerful, openly
powerful, perhaps too
powerful, silkily
powerful, subtly
powerfully charged
powerhouse
powerhouse in its youth
powerhouse red
powerhouse, concentrated
powerhouse, creamy citrus-kissed
powerhouse, fully packed energetic
powerhouse, glorious
powerhouse, minor
powerhouse, monstrous
powerhouse, mouthfilling
powerhouse, muscular full-throttle
powerhouse, not a
powerhouse, portlike
powerhouse, real/true

powerhouse, revved-up
power-laden/-packed
powerless/unpowerful
prisoners end of the spectrum, in the take-no-
prisoners, takes no
prissy, not
prodigious
prominent/pronounced
pronounced they practically knocked me off my chair, aromas so
provocative
puffed-up
pugilistic
puissance/puissant
pump up and thump its chest, doesn't
pumped/pumped up
pumps iron
pumps up the volume
punch and stuffing, more
punch, good
punch, lacks
punch, packin'/packs a
punch, packing half a

punch, packs a K.O.
punch, packs a meaty
punch, packs one hell of a
punch, signature one-two
punch, velvet-lined
punches, pulls no/spares few
punching above its class
punching well above its weight
punchy, quite
pungency, youthful
pungent and forceful
pungent, gosh...talk about
puny
pure
push, has
pushover
pushover...this, no
pushy, little too
quasiblockbuster
racehorse, true-blooded muscular
raging
rare
raw
restrained, paradoxically
revved-up Harley of white wine
rip-and-tear, fine
rip-roaring
rip-snorter
Robert Parker here we come
robust constitution
robust, extremely
robustness, good
rocket, takes off like a
rocking
rolling
rough-and-tumble
rough, wildly
ruggedness, robust
ruthless
sauvage, the strange sexy sweaty
   thing the French daintily call
screamer
seatbelt when you consume
   this wine, wear a
sedentary
semiweak
shake and rattle you to your socks,
   apt to
sheer

shock and awe, sense of
shouts
shouts but whispers persuasively,
   never
shy wine by an means, not a
sinuses, clears the
sirenlike
sissies, not for
sit-around-sip wine, isn't a

slammer/slamming, body-
slap upside the head
slap you silly but creeps up
   sideways, doesn't
sledgehammer, undrinkable
snorting
soft
soft-centered
souped up, not very
souped up
spindly
spring, highly coiled
spring-coiled, taut and
squeamish, not for the
stain, liquid
stained the bottle black
stain your teeth for days on end,
   will
stainer, real glass-
staining my insides, tastes like it's
staining one's teeth the color of
   cherry Kool-Aid, notorious for
   (temporarily)
staining, mouth-/palate-
stains the glass as it is swirled
stains the glass, so dense it
stains your tongue a deep purple
stamina, has
stentorian
steroids, aromatherapist on
steroids, German Riesling on
steroids, on
stops pulled/out, all the
storming/stormy
straight-to-the-point
strength as it rolls down the throat,
   sense of gathering
strength, astonishing
strength, deeply vibrating
strength, glowing
strength, great thrust of
strength, industrial-
strength, intractable
strength, lacking in
strength, quiet underlying
strength, real explosion of
strength, silk thread of great
strength, unbridled
strength, underlying sinewy
strengthless/unstrengthened
stretched
strong aromas
strong juice
strong punch, delivers a very
strong you feel it in the room when
   the wine is poured, so
strong-minded/-willed
strong-tasting

strong-voiced
stud but a solid performer, not a
stud muffin, vinous
stud wine
stuff, dense
stuff, not kid
stunning
sturdiness, yeoman-of-the-guard
sturdy, unexpectedly
subdued
subtle it ain't
subtlety as a Louis XIV chandelier,
   as much
supercharged/superconcentrated/
   superdense/superextracted/
   superintense/superpowered/
   superpowerful/superpungent
supercompact
superdense...fat...almost
   compotelike
superpowerful and concentrated
   palate almost takes one's breath
   away
supersappy
superwrought
suppressed
swaggers into your glass, practically
swingeing
swings for the fences
tame as a Swede, as
tamed character, darker less-
taming it, no
tangle with for long, not a wine to
tearaway, full-throttle
tender on the palate, turning
tensile conflict
tension to great effect
tension, high-
tension, thrilling
thermonuclear
thimblefuls, best drunk in
throat, goes for the
throat, makes a narrow and clean
   beeline for your
throttle job, extrafull-
throttle/throttled, full-
thrust, good/real/superb
thruster, not a
thrusting
thudder
thump its chest and overwhelm
   you, doesn't
thumping its chest and baring its
   teeth and roaring abuse
thunder, completely brings the
thunder, rolling
thunderbolt, big meaty
thunderbolt, big rich buttery

thunderclap wine
thundering/thunderous
tiger
tiger by the tail, like catching a
tilt boogie, full-
timid/timorous
tired, trifle
titan over the tongue, rumbles
  like a
titanic
tough as nails, as
tough little puppy
tough nut
tough, rough and
toughness, bit of attractive
train, masculine freight
turbocharged/turbodriven
turbodriven blend
turbowine that knocks all your
  senses for a loop, real
twee, tad
tyrannosaurus
ultraconcentrated
ultradense
ultrapotent/ultrapowerful/
  ultrastrong
unbelievable
unbridled
uncle, it'll make you cry
unconquerable
unconstrained
uncontrolled, almost
underextracted/unextracted
underlying
underpowered
unforgiving
ungentle to a degree
uninitiated, not for the
unrestrained, marvelously
untamed
unusual
unyielding
V8 engine throbbing away gently
  on the massive midpalate
vapid
va-va-voom
vibrant
vigor and character, quiet
vigor and joie de vivre, full of
youthful
vigor, beneficial/healthy
vigor, rustic
vigorous, overly
violent, gentle and
virile at once, refined and
virile, very
virility, combines roundness and
vitality is awesome

volcanic
volcano in a making
voltage, high-/ultrahigh
voltage, low-
volume turned up
waker-upper
wallflower, not a delicate
warp factor five
watered down
watery, bit
wattage, high-/ultrahigh-
wattage, low-
waves, keeps coming in
weak although it's all there
  somewhere, everything is
weak at/of heart, not meant for the
weak in the middle
weak, somewhat
weak-bladdered
weak-hearted
weak-kneed
weakling, no
weaklings, not for
weighty
whisper, classy
wild and woolly
wild one
wimp, no
wimpish, not/nothing
wimpish...subtle...innocuous
wimps, not a red for
wimps, not for
wimpy juice
Wimpy Wines, No
wine that smokes
wishy-washy about it, nothing
wonderful
wow: rolling thunder
wrestler?, who wants to go to bed
  with a
zesty it would wake the dead, so

Deep colour and big shaggy nose. Rather a jumbly, untidy sort of wine, with fruitiness shooting off one way, firmness another, and body pushing about underneath. It will be as comfortable and comforting as the 1961 Nuits-St-Georges once it has pulled its ends in and settled down.
Gerald Asher

19. Structure [Frame, Core or Backbone, Spine]

What actually hold us humans up are exactly the same things that metaphorically hold wines up to prevent them from falling apart (or down): good, stable frameworks, such as acidic and tannic backbones and spines, necessities for wines to live long enough to get from the barrel to the bottle to the glass to the lips. Our lips, yours and mine. Neat, eh?

adequate
amazing
amorphous, strangely
ample
angular, bit too
appropriate
architecture, enduring internal
architected, well
architecturally perfect
architecture, fine
armature, strong
articulated, clearly
asymmetrical
attenuated
awesome
awkward
backbone for aging, good/strong
backbone is still there like stainless steel, acid
backbone of absolute dryness
backbone of acidity, crisp
backbone of acidity, strong
backbone of oak, smoke and toast
backbone of steel/steel backbone
backbone of steely acidity, crisp
backbone than a humpback whale, manly wine with more
backbone that sucks the life out of your palate, tannic

backbone, acid/acidic
backbone, brick wall of mineral
backbone, cast-iron
backbone, chalk soil
backbone, citric
backbone, crisp
backbone, decent/good
backbone, dry
backbone, earthy
backbone, elegant
backbone, firm/powerful/rigid/ stiff/strong
backbone, good acidic
backbone, hard-thrusting tannic
backbone, hidden
backbone, intriguing acid
backbone, lacks real
backbone, lime-citrus
backbone, limp
backbone, little
backbone, lovely mineral and steel
backbone, metallic
backbone, New World fruit with Old World
backbone, not a great deal of
backbone, pleasant tar
backbone, real earthy
backbone, sleek
backbone, smoky

backbone, sound
backbone, spicy
backbone, superb
backbone, tannic
backbone, tart
backbone, tinder-dry
backbone, uncommon
backed, well
bare
based, solidly/well
baseline, earthy
beam, steel
beamed, broad-
behemoth
big
blown, full-
bones and little flesh, lot of
bones but not much flesh, plenty of
bones, all/nothing but skin and
bones, needs a touch more fruit flesh on the
bones, not much flesh on its
boned and structured, finely
boned, big-/large-/larger-
boned, clumsily big-
boned, feminine-
boned, fine-
boned, medium-
boned, raw-

boned, small-
boneless...like chicken
bone, more meat on the
bones are good
bones, all dry
bones, angular
bones, good
bones, heavy/thick
bones, no/without
bones, rack of
bones, rounded flesh over firm
bones, showing
bones, shows good
bone structure, impressive
bony, bit/somewhat/slightly
bony, quite
Bordeaux-like
breathtaking
brittle and gone
built and balanced, regally
built, aristocratically
built, badly
built, finely/well-
CBS: complexity...backbone and
   structure, has got
cheekbones, fine
coil, steel
colossal/colossus
compact
complete
complex, thrillingly
composed, well
compressed
concentrated
condensed
considerable
consistent
core lurking below, powerful
core supported by ripe acidity,
   bright creamy
core, balanced
core, boiled down to its
core, compact
core, fabulously oily-textured
core, fine-tuned
core, firm fruit
core, focused
core, hugely pleasurable
core, lacks a certain
core, reluctant to reveal its inner
core, solid inner
core, steel
core, strong central
core, superexpressive
core, tightly wound inner
corseted, tightly
covered, well
crooked

crystalline
dainty
delicate
delicious, bewitchingly
delineated, well
designed, poorly
designed, well
dilute/diluted
diminutive
disintegrating
disjointed
elegant
elongated
enviable
excellent
exemplary
falling apart
fearsome
fine
firm
flabby
flexible
flimsy
fluidic
formed, well
formless
fortresslike
foundation, has solid
fragile
fragmented
frail
frame, balanced
frame, big/gigantic/massive
frame, broad/bulky/muscular/
   stout
frame, buoyant balanced
frame, chunky dark chocolate fruit
   in a big thick
frame, dry
frame, easygoing/loose
frame, elaborate/ornate
frame, elegant
frame, fabulous
frame, flabby
frame, forbidding
frame, healthy/robust
frame, high-wattage
frame, lanky/lithe/trim/skinny
frame, lean minerally
frame, light
frame, lithe sleek
frame, meaty
frame, refined
frame, seamless
frame, sharp-cornered
frame, slight/small/tiny
frame, somewhat spare
frame, spry/wiry

frame, streamlined
frame, surprisingly refined
frame, tight/tightish
frame, woodsy-tannin
framed and bodied, fully
framed gutsy wine, broad-
framed, big-
framed, broad-
framed, heavy-
framed, small-
framed, tightly
framed, well
frameless/unframed
framework, aggressive
framework, diaphanous
framework, earthy
framework, good/solid
framework, lively
framework, mineral-steely
framework, pleasing citrus
framework, sinewy
framework, smooth-edged
generous
giant/gigantic
good/goodish
Gothic
graceful
grand
great
hard as a rock, as
hardy
harsh
heavy
heavy, top-
hefty
hollow
horrible
house, built like a
house, built like the proverbial
   shit-
huge
immense in every way
impeccable
imposing
impressive
inflated
insubstantial
international
intricate
joint, out of
lacking
large
league, major
lean
light
limber
limp
linear axis

linear feel
linear, very
lithe
little
lofty
loose
lovely
magnificent
majestic
malleable
mammoth
massive
meager
medium
mighty
moderate
modest
molded, well
monolithic
monster/monstrous-sized
monumental
multitiered
muscular
narrow
normal
oblong
open
ornate
overendowed, not
paltry
perfect
planed, flat-
platform, dependable
platform, good
pliable
polyphenolic, solid
ponderous
poor
portlike, big
powerful
pretty
prodigious
profound
prominent/pronounced
pumped up
puny
ragged
rare
rectilinear
relaxed
rickety
rigid
robust
rock, as hard as a
Romanesque
rough/rough-hewn
round
rugged

scaffolding, acid
scaffolding, good
scaled, big-/grand-/large-
scaled, small-
scaled, well
seamless
severe
shaky
shallow
shaped, well
shapeless
shelterlike, bomb-
shriveled
shrunken
significant
simplicity, certain
size/sizable
sized, king-
skeletal, somewhat
skeletal...hardly a wine now, very
skeleton, fine
skeleton, heavy
skeleton, lacks that vital
skimpy
sleek
slight
small
snuff, well up to
solid, rock-
sophisticated
sound
spare
spine of minerality
spine of minerals, steely
spine, attractive
spine, extraordinary slate
spine, finely refreshing citrus-clad
spine, firm tannic
spine, flexible
spine, good acidic
spine, plenty of
spine, shows
spine, solid
spine, stable harmonious
spineless
spine-stiffening
sprawling and hollow
statuesque
steel, filigreed
stiff
stocky
stout
straightjacket, in a
structural elegance
structural framework, solid
structural heft
structurally disjointed
structurally perfect

structurally weak
structure and balance, perfect
structure and muscle, plenty of
structure and style, intensity...
structure buried in fat fruit, solid
structure department, bull's-eye
  in the
structure designed to age
structure is messy, entire
structure is that of a fortress, tannic
structure overwhelms fruit
structure seems absent, underlying
structure still locked up
structure underpinned by acidic
  sinew, elegant
structure, almost monumental
structure, ample
structure, biggish/huge/strapping
structure, classic
structure, classic Burgundy
structure, cold-steel
structure, compact
structure, corpulent
structure, correctly lean
structure, crisp
structure, curiously short on
structure, dapper elegant
structure, dense and impressive
structure, does not have overmuch
structure, enveloping
structure, enviable
structure, faultless balance and
structure, filigreed
structure, fine cohesive
structure, fine-grained
structure, firm gutsy
structure, fluid in
structure, formidable polyphenolic
structure, good bone
structure, good internal
structure, grandiose
structure, heady
structure, heroic
structure, impressive
structure, impressive bone
structure, lacelike/lacy
structure, lacks
structure, lean/slender
structure, linear
structure, little floppy in
structure, little light in
structure, lithe yet flavor-packed
structure, lively/racy
structure, majestic
structure, massive
structure, meaty
structure, minimalist tannin
structure, more personality than

structure, muscular tannic
structure, narrow rigid
structure, near-perfect
structure, needs a touch more
    authority in the
structure, never a hard
structure, nice angular
structure, no real
structure, no shortage of
structure, not a great deal of
structure, potent mouthfilling
    beast of complexity and
structure, promising
structure, pronounced iron tannin
structure, real
structure, remarkable
structure, rich muscular
structure, right-on
structure, rippling in
structure, robust/strong tannic
structure, rounded silky
structure, seamless
structure, seductive
structure, sense of outer beauty
    and inner
structure, sinewy
structure, slate-driven
structure, soaring
structure, somewhat angular
structure, soothing ripe tannin
structure, splendid
structure, sprightly
structure, straight-line texture and
structure, superlative
structure, tannins not fully
    amalgamated into the
structure, taut
structure, vivid
structure, voluptuous
structure, youthful exuberance is
    masking
structured and undemanding,
    simply
structured base
structured by a steel frame
structured honey
structured leathery character
structured mouthfeel
structured personality, with a wild
    (*sauvage*) streak in its
structured sparkler, hugely
structured that it polarizes opinion,
    so massively
structured, beautifully/finely/
    richly
structured, classically
structured, densely/firmly/
    highly/solidly/strongly

structured, fairly stiff-
structured, finely boned and
structured, formidably
structured, impeccably/perfectly
structured, less
structured, massively
structured, opulently
structured, poorly
structured, really well
structured, seriously
structured, supremely
structured, tautly/tightly
structureless/unstructured
stunted
sturdy
substantial
substructure, sound
sufficient
supple
support, good
supported, well
symmetrical
tart
thick
thin
tight
tiny
tired
top-heavy
tough
tremendous
trim
twisted
uncomposed
underlying
underpinning, lacks
underpinnings, solid/strong
unforgiving, most
ungainly
unidimensional
uninteresting
unstructured, depressingly
unsubstantial
vivid
voluminous
wall-to-wall
weak
weighty
wide
wimpy
wispy
wonderful
wrapped, not well
wrapped, well
Yquem-like

Sour, sweet, bitter, pungent, all must be tasted.
Chinese proverb

*Wine such as young Bordeaux or Barolo need
protein and fat to counteract their puckeriness.*
George A. LaMarca

20. Tannin [Astringency, Bitterness]

Here's the bite, the pucker, the styptic sensations that dance around in a mouthful of wine. No good red wine, no great red wine, is without a healthy dose of astringent tannins to give it lift and longevity. Almost all reds have much more tannin than whites, so if you love that grippy feel in your mouth, drink the red stuff; but if you aren't thrilled with some pucker, drink white. Easy, peasy.

abrasive, not
abrasive, pretty/quite
abrasive, shockingly
abundant, more than
adequate
aerial-style, graceful
aggressive, bumptiously
aggressive, not
aggressive, savagely/very
aggressive, unnecessarily
amalgamated into the structure,
    not fully
amalgamated, perfectly
amazing but not unpleasant
ameliorated
ample enough, quite
angry and nasty
animated
appealing
approachable
ardent
arid
armed
art, work of
asperity, biting
asperity, harsh
asperous
assertive edge
assertive yet tolerable
assimilated, perfectly
astringence leaves your palate
    puckered
astringence, abrasive core of

astringency rubs the palate all the
    way down
astringency, becoming modest
astringency, dusty
astringency, earthy
astringency, fruity
astringency, hard/stern
astringency, mouthwatering
astringency, pleasant
astringency, puckering
astringency, satisfying
astringency, savory
astringency, stemmy
astringent monster, woody
    dried-out
astringent snap, pleasantly
astringent, noticeably
astringent, overly
attenuated
austere
austerity, steely
awkward
background, in the
balanced
band, seamless
banished
battering, palate-
bay, at
bedding down
beefy
belt, fair
big but negotiable, pretty
billowing/billowy

biscuity
bite, one hell of a
bite, perhaps too much
bite, plenty of
bite, rasping
biting, downright
biting, often
bitter edge, appealing/pleasing
bitter twist, mouthwatering
bitter, barely/mildly
bitter, half-
bitter, highly/strongly/very
bitter, pleasantly/pleasingly
bitter-metallic
bitterness, arugulalike
bitterness, burnt sugar
bitterness, Campari-like
bitterness, espressolike
bitterness, nicotine
bitterness, quinine
bitterness, raw
bitterness, tart
bitterness, tealike
bittersweet
blast, drying
blatant, beautifully
blistering
bloodless
blunt
blurry as Renoir colors, as softly
boards, emery
boatload
bold, rather

bouncer of the vegetable world, nightclub
brash
brawny
brazen
brisk
bristling, pronounced
brittle
brusque
brutal/brutish
buried in deep layers of fruit
burning
burnt
burnt, excellent thick...toasty and almost
buster
butter, as soft and melted as warm
calm, very
capsule
caressing
cassis undertone, obscuring
caustic
caution, approach with
cedary
chain, long
chalky
challenging
cheek-grabbing
cheesy
chew on but not be blasted by, enough to
chewy
chocolate, bitter
chocolate, disciplined
chocolate, terrifying
chocolate-edge(d)
chunky
citrus/citruslike/citrusy
civilized
clad, silk-
clad, well
clamps down on your tongue like a vise

clanging
clangy on the teeth and gums, not too
clawing
claws were not cut, what a pity its
clench and length, more
clenched personality
clenches softly rather than bites
clogs the throat
clotted
coarse
coffee grounds
comforting
commanding
complex

control, under perfect
controlled
copious
correct
craggy
crisp
cruel
crumbly
crunchy
crushed
cutting

daggers, piercing
daring
definition, lacks
dense and chalky
desert-dry
dirty, downright
disagreeable
disappeared
disciplined
discreet
disintegrating
distributed, evenly/well
dominates
dried out/up
dry your tongue right out, may
dry, searingly
drying, noticeably
dryness, aggressive
dusty
dynamic
earthy
edge, assertive
edge(d), surly
edgy
elbows, some sharp
elegant, very
emphatic
empty
encroaching
endowed, liberally
energetic, wildly
enormous and problematic
enough in it to pucker up the liver
envelopes/enveloping
etched, finely
excellent
excessive
explosive
extracted, dexterously
extracted, well
faded/fading
faint
fatigue, no fear of
fatiguing
fearsome
feeble
ferocious and unrelenting

fierce
fine
fine...long...slinky
firm, lip-smackingly
fisted, iron-
flaming
flat
fleeting
flick
floury-chalky
forbidding
force, out in
forceful
formidable
fortress, strong
framing
frisky
fruit-coated
fruit-drenched, ripe velvet and
full
furriness on the tongue
furry
fuzzy
gauged, nicely
generous
gentle
glossy
glowering
gnarly
good/goodish
gorgeous
grabs you, reaches out and
grainy/granular
grapple with, hard to

gravelly
gravylike
great
green, harsh
green nerve, rawish
green, pronounced...almost
green, very
grilled/grilled-edge(d)
grip, awesome/outstanding
grip, fine
grip, lively
grip, mineral
grip, packing good
grip, viselike
gripping but lithe
gripping, tongue-
grips but never bruises
grips the palate, really
grips your tongue and gums with the force of a wharf laborer
gritty, fractionally
gritty, hopelessly
gruff
guard, standing surly

gummy
gum-puckering/-withering
gums, easy on the
gum-thwacking
hair-raising
hammerlike
handed, little heavy-
hard to grapple with
hard, rock-/hard-as-a-rock
hard, unapologetically
hardness at center
harsh, overly
harsh, unrelentingly
heaps
hearty
heavy
hefty
hefty but negotiable
hewn, nicely
high, brutally
high, gum-numbingly
hollow
horrible
hulking
hulls of shelled pecans
imaginable, softest
imaginative, very
impenetrable
inadequate
indelible
inky
insistent
insufficient
integrated
intelligent
intense
intensity, piercing
interesting
intrusive, touch
invasive
iron, jaw-locking
iron-fist-in-velvet-glove
irritating
jackhammer type, not the
jagged
jagged with an edge of greenness
jagged, extremely
judged, judiciously
judged, poorly
judged, well
judicious
juicy
keen
kick in the stomach
kick, packs a
killer, palate-
knifelike
knit, tight-

lacking
larger with each passing minute,
    getting
lashing
lean
leathery
level is bothersome
level to the limit, pushes
level will be enjoyed only by
    masochists, mouth-searing
level, blistering/excruciating/
    ferocious
level, mouth-blasting
level, uncivilized
level, unfashionably high
lies resplendently on the memory
life, full of
life-supporting
linger!, boy do they
lip-licking
lip-stripping
lithe
little
lively, little too
liver, enough to pucker the
long, uncommonly
lurking
luxurious
make your tongue feel like the sole
    of your shoe, enough to
malleable
mammoth
managed, well
management, excellent
marked
masked
massive
mature
meager
mean streets
meaty-tarry
medium
meek, anything but
mellow/mellowed
melt away, will never fully
melted the fillings in my teeth,
    nearly
melted, completely
melting away, in the process of
melting into delicate oak
metallic
milky
moderate, manageably
modulated, beautifully
monstrous, almost
mountain
mouth cotton-dry, leaves the
mouth-coating, substantial

mouth-drying
mouth-numbing
mouth-puckering, awfully
mouth-searing levels
much for its own good, much too
much, little too
muffled
muscular
nails/nail-like
naked, now
nap, fine
needlelike/like needles/needley
needley and prickly
nervy
neutral
nippy
noble
nonabrasive
nonexistent, nearly
none whatsoever, absolutely/
    virtually
nonintrusive
normal
numb, makes the gums
numbing
nutty
obscuring cassis undertone
obvious
off-putting
off the charts, level absolutely
oily
omnipresent
on, full-
oozing
ouch!
overabundance
overassertive
overblown
overblown, not
overenthusiastic
overloaded
overplayed
overtannic
overtart
overvatted
overwhelming
paced, well
painful
palate down and cause your taste
    buds to shrink away, can simply
    close your
palate, not too brutal on the
palate-choking
palate-clinging
palate-killing
palate-puckering
palpable
parching, severely

222 | Tannin

pencil-like
penetrating
peppery
perceptible, hardly
perfect
pervasive
pesky
phenolic
piercing
pillars
pinched
Pinot-esque, distinctly
pips/pippy
piquant
pixilated but lacy
pleasant
pliant
pointed
polished
poor
potent
pound away, don't
powdery
powerful but digestible
preservative, fabulous
preservative, good
pressed
pretty
prickly sensation, nasty
pristine
problematic, may be
profile, high-
prominent/pronounced
provocative
pucker, long on
pucker-fix
puckeriness, citrusy
puckering, palate-
puckery, ominously
pugnacious
punchy
pungent
punishing
puny
pushy
ragged
rapier/rapier-like
rasp, characteristic
rasp, rocklike
rasp, slightly resinous
rasps on the tongue
raunchy, very
raw
reeling, sends you
regulated, well
relaxed
relentless
residual

resinous/resiny
resolved
rich
rigid, still a bit
rigid, too
ripe
ripe yet copious
ripened, prodigiously
rippling
robust
rock, as hard as a/rock-hard
rope-a-dope, plays
rough on the gums early in its life,
    little
rough, noticeably
rough-hewn
roughing-up
round/rounded
rubbery
rugged
rustic
rusty, almost unyieldingly
sandblaster
sandpapery throat torture, no
sandpapery-textured
sandy
sappish/sappy
satin/satiny
saturated
savage/savaging/*sauvage*
savory
scabrous
scary
scattered, finely
scintilla remaining, only a
scouring
scratchy
scrumptious
sculpted
seamless
searing
secret, almost
seductive
semibitter
separating out, on the verge of
severe levels
shaped, deliciously
shapeless
sharp as a dagger, as
shocking
significant
silk, lovely gossamer
silty
sinewy
sings
sipper, no soft
sledgehammer
slick

slinky, superbly
slippery
slithery
smarts
smooth, not very
smooth, silk-
smooth, tongue-coatingly
snappy
soapy, slightly
soda, yummy red-wine
soft, baby-
soft...fleshy...masked
softness, powdery
solid
some, needs to lose
soupy
sour/soured/sourish/soury
spicy
spreads like a Turkish carpet across
    the tongue
stalky
starchy
stealthy
stemmy
stick in the eye
stiff/stiffish
sting with toughness
stinging/stings
stout
strident
stringy
strong
strong and numbing
stroppy, not too
structure is that of a fortress
structure, lacy
structure, rich multipixilated
structure, soothing ripe
structured, well
structures are still sublime
stuff, sterner
sturdy
styptic
suave
subdued
subtlety of a chain saw, all the
suedelike
suede-smooth
superfine
supersilky
supersweet
supervelvety
supple, pleasingly
surges
surly edge
svelte
sweaty...leathery
sweet

sweet, silty
sympathetic, touchingly
taffeta, as soft as
take over, tends to
talcy
tame/tamed
tangy
tannic and acidic, viciously
tannic and astringent, painfully
tannic and tough wine that numbs
  the palate, extremely
tannic as a pair of old work boots,
  as
tannic backbone, hard-thrusting
tannic bang
tannic beast

tannic bra
tannic brutality/brute
tannic cape
tannic charge and depth of
  character cal almost suck you
  over the event horizon
tannic clout, finishes with a
tannic corset, firm dry
tannic death-grip
tannic distraction, little
tannic envelope, dry
tannic grip runs the full length of
  the palate
tannic juice, savagely
tannic mantle
tannic monster, amazingly
  backward
tannic pillars
tannic precision
tannic presence, full-throttle
tannic richness
tannic shell, thick
tannic shroud, great
tannic sleep, beginning to emerge
  from a
tannic soul, sharply
tannic that this wine is getting
  medieval on you, so
tannic towel, smothered by a
tannic structure, strong
tannic surliness
tannic texture, voluptuous
tannic than a gallon of trucker's
  tea, more
tannic underpinning, firm
tannic vise, your mouth is locked
  in a
tannic weave, dense
tannic, adamantly
tannic, bitterly

tannic, brutally/colossally/
  extremely/ferociously/
  forbiddingly/profoundly/
  rampantly/severely/terribly
tannic, cheek-grippingly
tannic, distinctly sweaty and
tannic, distressingly
tannic, excruciatingly
tannic, far too/overly
tannic, feverishly
tannic, frighteningly/frightfully
tannic, gratingly
tannic, grippingly
tannic, impenetrably tough and
tannic, impossibly
tannic, less
tannic, mean and
tannic, mercilessly/torturously/
  unrelentingly
tannic, mind-numbingly
tannic, not especially
tannic, optimally
tannic, profoundly
tannic, ruggedly
tannic, seemingly less oppressively
tannic, smells
tannic, swingeingly
tannic, urgently
tannic, vaguely inconsequentially
tannic-acid sandwich
tannic-grippy
tannicity with finesse
tannicity, freshness of
tannicity, intrusive cocoa-coated
tannicity, lithe
tannicity, refined
tannicly classy

tannicly teasing
tannin and acidity, unremitting
tannin biting at your gums
tannins brocade the wine,
  light graceful
tannin for the amount of fruit,
  possesses entirely too much
tannin galore
tannin management exemplary
tannin mashing the fruit, big
tannin sledgehammers,
  thumping your gums in with
tannin slick, belt of
tannin to arouse their taste buds,
  definitely not for those who
  require the shock of excessive
tannin water
tannin, chestnut
tannin, monolith of fruitless
tannined, tough-

tannin-filled
tannin-free zone
tannin-generated abrasiveness
tannin-heavy, little
tannin-hiding fat
tannin-related stiffness
tannins all but take the skin off the
  roof of your mouth
tannins are buried in sweet fruit,
  ripe
tannins coat the palate like a mink
  coat, beautiful
tannins coat the teeth like lacquer,
  fat
tannins dovetail in perfectly,
  fine-grained
tannins drowning in waves of fruit,
  sweet
tannins fight the good fight,
  ripe cassis/berry fruit and ripe

tannins give it gravitas
tannins grapple with fruit
tannins have real presence
tannins here, no killer
tannins immersed in jellied fruit,
  abundant superripe
tannins know their place in the
  scheme of things
tannins like a three-day-old beard
tannins like old socks, sweaty
tannins obtrude
tannins of depth and *chutzpah*,
  gripping
tannins of great couth, rich
tannins of great wit, rippling
tannins tethered by plenty of
  luscious fruit, rugged
tannins that are not for the faint
  of heart, formidable
tannins that define silkiness,
  develops
tannins that make your tongue
  stick to the gums, very strong
tannins to heel, still to bring its
  lively
tannins tremble on the brink of
  dominance
tannins you ever had, silkiest
  smoothest
tannins, aggressive furry
tannins, all strapped in by a battery
  of strong
tannins, bags of *mâche* and ripe
tannins, battery of
tannins, big velvety voluptuous
tannins, black pepper
tannins, boatload of

tannins, bristling
tannins, brutally high
tannins, burnt
tannins, butch
tannins, cast-iron
tannins, chains of
tannins, clanging
tannins, cocoa-powder
tannins, copious quantities of mouthsearing
tannins, cradle of evenly distributed
tannins, cradled by soft
tannins, crowned by miraculous well-integrated subtle
tannins, crushed-velvet
tannins, darkly brooding
tannins, decade's worth of
tannins, dense fine fruit-drenched
tannins, dry mouthwatering
tannins, elegant
tannins, emasculated of
tannins, encased in dryish
tannins, enological
tannins, envelope of ripish
tannins, fine fruit-drenched rusty
tannins, fine lingering squeaky
tannins, fine pippy
tannins, finest possible
tannins, firm probing
tannins, firm web of woody
tannins, flimsier
tannins, flush of oak
tannins, freshly woven basket of supporting fruit
tannins, fruit still locked in arm-to-arm combat with the
tannins, furious blast of
tannins, girdled by soft
tannins, good extract behind the wall of
tannins, good irony minerally
tannins, gossamer-fine
tannins, hardly tickled by the
tannins, healthy
tannins, heavy coating of concrete
tannins, high-tensile green
tannins, huge handshake of
tannins, iron clasp of austere
tannins, layers and layers of fine and fruit
tannins, leathery old
tannins, little tug of gritty
tannins, lovely milky
tannins, marred by an excess of
tannins, masses of quite hard
tannins, melted/melting
tannins, milky

tannins, mineral quarry
tannins, minimal
tannins, monolith of fruitless
tannins, monster/monstrous
tannins, mouth-searing levels of
tannins, nicely dry tingly
tannins, no desperately clanging
tannins, no hard vulgar
tannins, not-too-shy
tannins, obstinately grounded by its
tannins, overtaken by
tannins, persistent rubbery textured
tannins, pervasive dry
tannins, pillow-feather
tannins, pounding
tannins, powdered
tannins, prodigiously ripened
tannins, pronounced almost bristling
tannins, ragged
tannins, rolling soft
tannins, ruffled with voluptuous
tannins, sandy
tannins, satiny
tannins, scour of grapeskin
tannins, silkier-than-silk
tannins, silky leathery
tannins, silty
tannins, slightly nippy
tannins, slippery
tannins, snug particulate
tannins, soft fluffy
tannins, something bolted together with planks of
tannins, soupy highly pixilated
tannins, stewed tea
tannins, stubborn hard mountain
tannins, suave
tannins, superbly glossy
tannins, supersilky
tannins, sweetness battling
tannins, tart dry
tannins, teeth-gritting
tannins, tight envelope of ripe
tannins, tingling/tingly
tannins, toasted iron
tannins, tremendously strong gravel
tannins, treasure chest of
tannins, turbulent red whirlpool of ripe damson fruit and chewy grainy
tannins, ultrasoft
tannins, unapproachable thickets of
tannins, uncomplicated by oak or

tannins, undemanding soft
tannins, unsparing of
tannins, urgent grilled
tannins, very fine pixilated
tannins, web of silky
tannins, welcome scrape of
tannins, well-polymerized
tannins, white pepper
tannins, will tackle your taste buds to the ground with
tannins, youthfully rigid
tannin-touched
tannin-wracked little wench
tealike, black
teases and tugs at the same time
teeth dark purple, guaranteed to turn your
teeth together, glues the
teeth/tooth-staining
teeth-coating/coats the teeth
teeth-grinding
teeth-gripping
template, muscular sinewy
tenacious to the point of rudeness
texture, satiny
textured, richly
textured, velvet-/velvety
textured, well
thick and soupy
thick but manageable
thick...soft and complex, wonderfully
thin
throat sand-paperer
throat, bludgeons the
throbbing
throttle(d), full-
tidy
time, big-
tobacco/tobacco-edge(d)
toffee, sticky
toned
tongue, won't exfoliate your
tongue-coating/-dusting
tongue-gripping sensation
tongue-nippin/gripping
tongue-tingling
tons
tonsils, won't shrivel your
top, over-the-
tough
tough, undrinkably
towel, mouth felt like it had been wiped dry by a
toughness, gum-drying
transparent, almost
treacherous
trembling on the brink

tug, good/nice
tug, puckery
tuned, fine-
tweak, cautionary
ultrafine
ultrarich
ultraripe
unaggressive
unassertive
unbalanced
unbridled
ungenerous
unintegrated
unnoticeable, almost
unobtrusive, relatively
unrelenting
unresolved
unripe, bluntly
untamed, like a wild
  horse...beautiful and
unyielding
upfront
urgent
vapid
vatted/vatting
vegetal
velveteen
veneer, hard
vicelike
vicious
vigorous
violent
viperish/viperous
viscous
viselike
volatile
vulgar
wall, iron
wall, solid
wallop, has some
wallop, nasty
walloping
weedy
whack, fair
whoa
wildfire
wily
withered, totally
wonder, a/wonderful
wooded, excessively
woodsy
woody
wool, all the charm of a mouthful
  of steel
youthful

Vegetables are interesting but lack a sense of purpose when unaccompanied by a good cut of meat.
Fran Lebowitz

A fruit is a vegetable with looks and money. Plus, if you let fruit rot, it turns into wine, something Brussels sprouts never do.
P.J. O'Rourke

21. Vegetable

Ooh, veggies! The kid in all of us, with some exceptions (you know who you are), hated eating most vegetables. Squash, peas, cauliflower, broccoli. Gross! However, we're grown up now, and we not only drink wine but also eat veggies, lots and lots and lots of veggies. No big deal, then, when vegetables in all their guises pop up in our noses and mouths. Such as those cute miniature cabbages, Brussels sprouts, for heaven's sake. (Parboil 'em first, then sauté in butter, add a splash of balsamic vinegar and a sprinkle of slivered almonds. Yum.) Surprise yourself!

adzuki
artichokes, Jerusalem
arugula
arugulalike bitterness
asparagus
asparagus at the bottom of this greengrocery basket
asparagus juice
asparagus spears
asparagus tips
asparagus, barnyardy
asparagus, faintest *soupçon* of
asparagus, garden-fresh
asparagus, white
asparagus-scented and -flavored, appallingly
barley
barleyish, beery and
bean sprouts, mung
beans, broad
beans, *fava*
beans, *garbanzo*
beans, green
beans, roasted Brazilian coffee
beans, runner
beans, wax
beetrootlike, old
beetroots, ambrosial
beetroots/beetrootlike/beetrooty

beets, red
beets, sugar
beets/beetroots, earthy
beets/beetroots, fresh
beets/beetroots, old
beets/beetroots, refined
boiled
borage
brassica
broccoli
bulby
cabbage
capsicums, green
capsicums, red
capsicummy
carrots, sweet
cauliflower
celery sticks, fresh
celery, snappiness of fresh
celery, vegetal
celery-iodine
cèpes, fresh
chantarelle-scented
chicory
chilies, green
corn
corn, creamy sweet Connecticut white
corn, sweet

corn, white
corn-on-the-cob
cress, pure
cress...tar...smoke...marigolds... smoked meat and tobacco, garden
cucumbers, seedless
dandelions/dandelion greens
eggplant
endive, Belgian
feijão
fennochio fronds
flageolets, French
freshness, gardenlike
fungi, wild
garlic, delicate
garlic, rotten
garlic, wild
green essences
greens, beet
greens, bitter
greens, dandelion
greens, field
greens, leafy
greens, salad
greens, spring
greens, summery field
jalapeños, piquant/spicy
kale

kernels
leeks
lentils/lentilly
lettuce, fresh
lettuce freshness, Romaine
lettuce, iceberg
lettuce, like breaking open a very
  crisp head of
lettuce, perfectly fresh
lettuce, wilted
mâche
mange-toute
morel-fruit
mushroom forest
mushroom peels
mushroom stalks
mushrooms among the flowers
mushrooms, agaric
mushrooms, boletus
mushrooms, champignon
mushrooms, chanterelle
mushrooms, decaying

mushrooms, dirt-laden

mushrooms, dollop of shit and
mushrooms, earthy
mushrooms, field
mushrooms, forest
mushrooms, freshly picked
mushrooms, freshly picked
  chantarelle
mushrooms, morel
mushrooms, musky porcini
mushrooms, penny-bun
mushrooms, porcini
mushrooms, raw
mushrooms, shiitake
mushrooms, sweet
mushrooms, wild
mushrooms, woody
mushroomy monotone
mushy
mustard and cress
olives, smattering of green
onion skin, dry
onions and garlic, rotten
onions, garlic
onions, green/spring
onions, half-rotten/rotten
onions, intense brown
onions, sweet spring
parsnips
pea pods, Asian
pea pods, grassy
pea pods, green
pea pods, like biting on just-picked
peas, freshly picked
peas, green
peas, shelled

peas, snap
peas, snow
peels/skins
pepper kick, bell
peppers of every color
peppers, bell
peppers, characteristic Bien Nacido
  black
peppers, chili
peppers, fiery sweet jalapeño
peppers, green
peppers, green bell
peppers, green chili
peppers, hot
peppers, mint-green
peppers, pecks of
peppers, rawish green
peppers, sweet
peppers, yellow
peppers, yellow-green sweet
picante/piquant
potato peels/skins
potatoes, raw
potatoes, sweet
produce, fresh
produce, organic
pungent
radicchio
radishes, red

radishy middle

root, angelica
root, orris
roots, slightly smoky Spanish
rotten/rotting
scallions
shallots, garden-fresh
sorrel
sorrel, brambly-
spinach
spinachlike, greenness that's
  slightly
sprouts, Brussels
squash flavors, very distinct
starchy
sugarcane
tatsoi
tired
tomatillos
tomato aromas, typical plum-
tomatoes, cherry
tomatoes, fresh beef
tomatoes, green
tomatoes, over-ripe
tomatoes, ripe Italian
tomatoes, sun-dried
tomatoes, sweet heirloom
tomatoes, tart
tomatoey savoriness

tomato-like leanness
truffle, fungal-
truffled, almost
trufflelike earthiness
truffles and well-hung game,
  richness of chocolate mingling
  perilously with
truffles made into wine
truffles verging on barnyard
truffles, deeply scented
truffles, earthy
truffles, glorious raw black
truffles, newly shaved white

truffles, phantomlike

truffles, pure dark black
truffles, soft velvety
truffles, unctuous black
truffles, Vaucluse
truffles, white
truffle-scented masterpiece,
  grandiose magically
truffley sensuality
truffley, sweet-
truffleness, slight
vegetable peels/skins
vegetable roots
vegetables, earthy root
vegetables, garden
vegetables, tender spring
veggies, whole
watercressy edge, wet
whole
yams
zucchini

*Old wood best to burn, old wine to drink,
old friends to trust, and old authors to read.*
Sir Francis Bacon

*It doesn't mean the most expensive wines get
wood chips, but some very competitive wines
do. It does a marvelous job and cuts the price.
Hence, Yellow Tail.*
Richard Steltzner

22. Wood

Ah, wood. Particularly oak, which has proven for centuries to have the very best natural qualities for storing and maturing wine. Yet, hardly any taste characteristic of wine is so controversial as oak. Wine drinkers either love it or hate it, whether there's a lot, a little or none. Whatever the amount, oak usually plays a critical role in fermentation and aging, particularly in red wines. Oak bombs or oak bras: who would have suspected an innocent tree of such naughty things?

acacia
adequate
aggressive and ugly
amalgamated, well
arboreal
ash
background, stays in the
balanced, sanely
balsa, bit of
balsam and honey
balsam, elegant
balsam, Friar's
balsam, resiny
balsam, texture like
balsamic intensity
balsamic shades, pleasant
balsamic tones, overlay of
balsamic-textured richness,
    gorgeous
bark in the mouth and nose,
    twigs and
bark, damp moldy
bark, haughty carapace of
bark, old
bark, Peruvian
bark, wet tree-
beech
beech, magnificence of purple
birch bark
blatant

boisé
box tree/boxwood
briarwood
brushwood
burning/burnt
burnished
buttery
buttery-toasty
camphorwood
caramel/caramelized/caramelly
cedar essence
cedar, boiled-down
cedar, chunky
cedar, dark
cedar, dusty
cedar, echo of
cedar, fresh-cut
cedar, freshly split
cedar, gnarled
cedar, muffled
cedar, old
cedar, polished
cedar, savory
cedar, slightly singed
cedar, stocky
cedar-cassis
cedar-chocolate
cedars of Lebanon
cedar-spice toast
cedarwood perfume

cedarwood, Spanish
cedary nuance
cedary polish, tobacco-
cedary, tight and
cedary, toasty-
charred, heavily
charred, lightly
charred, medium
charred, much too heavily
cherrywood
chestnut/chestnutty
chips
chunks
cindery
controlled
copious
cordwood, piled on like so much
cream/creamy
damp
dark
dinner, termite's fantasy
discreet
dreamin', California
dried/dry/drying out/up
elderwood
eucalyptus wood
evergreens
excellent
excessive
faint

fine
fir
fir cones
firewood, burnt
floors, like walking into a house
  with newly sanded
full
generous
gnarled/gnarly
good/goodish
great
green/greenish
gum, sweet
hard
hawthorn
hickory
hickory smoke
honeyed
judged, well
juice
juniper
lacking
laurel/bay laurel
lemon trees
light/lightish
lime tree
linden
linden, dried
lumberjack in the woods
lumberlike
managed, perfectly
maple and spice, waves of
maple, charred
maple, rustic
maple, smoky
medium
megaoaky
mesquite
milled, freshly
moderate
modest
natural
neutral
new, sweet
noble
nonoaked
normal
noticeable, barely
oak a bit jagged, new
oak a little too strongly at the fore
oak a sideline player
oak adjuncts
oak aging with gay abandon
oak aging, light/modest
oak aging, neutral
oak an impeccably behaved
  observer
oak and butter, mouthful of

oak and fruit, lashings of
oak and old ladies...if you see
  what I mean, taste of old
oak and Riesling don't get on, new
oak as seasoning
oak at all, sees no
oak at the fore
oak background, rich
oak bags
oak balls
oak barrel and wiping your tongue
  off with an old leather belt,
  like licking an
oak barrels, insides of many
oak be damned
oak beam or two in their wine, for
  those who love an
oak blend
oak bomb
oak bomb, butter-and-
oak bomb, California
oak bra
oak bringing up the rear
oak bruiser, big American
oak burden, delicate fruit struggles
  to carry its
oak chains
oak char, heavy
oak character is massive
oak character, veil of
oak chips
oak chips/chunks, tea bags of
oak church pews, carved
oak clobbers the original style of
  wine
oak clogging up the finish a little,
  touch of
oak component, shockingly high
oak contact, subdued by extended
oak contribution negligible
oak contribution throughout,
  strong French
oak cossetting, lavish
oak cubes
oak definition, grilled bacon-
oak destroys the fruit
oak distracts, slightly raspy
oak does the talking
oak doesn't get in the way of the
  nice fruit
oak doesn't overwhelm
oak dominoes
oak dressing, fruit and
oak dust
oak enhanced
oak entirely absorbed
oak essences
oak evident but subservient

oak evident, no
oak extract, liquid
oak fairy, unkissed by the
oak fits like a glove, overlay of
  smoky
oak flavoring
oak flavors do not flatter the wine
oak flexes its muscles
oak floating on top, drop of
oak floors, freshly sanded
oak forcing, no
oak for oak's sake
oak framing, classy
oak from every pore, exudes
oak garnish, dry
oak gently honing the acidity
oak Goliath
oak granules/granulates
oak handling, deft/impeccable
oak handling, sensuous
oak has drenched this wine, lots of
oak has not been overplayed
oak have been seamlessly/totally
  welded together, fruit and
oak held nicely in restraint
oak here, didn't get carried away
  with too much
oak hits you between the eyes
oak impression, slight
oak impute, minimal
oak in diminuendo
oak in pure support role
oak in/takes the back seat
oak in which it was matured,
  demolished the French
oak incidental
oak inflected
oak influence, admirable lack of
oak influence, classy
oak influence, perfect
oak infusion, subtle
oak input is minimal
oak input, moderate
oak inserts
oak intimidates the fruit on the
  finish, charry barrel-ferment
oak is a bit intrusive
oak is a spice
oak is a touch too prominent
oak is complementary rather than
  blatant
oak is folded in seamlessly as a
  subtle seasoning
oak is incidental, any
oak is merely a prop
oak is moderated, use of
oak is nicely underplayed
oak is not overbearing

oak is over the top, pungent bacony
oak is practically invisible
oak is prominent but proportional
oak is the drum that anchors the
  symphony
oak judged to perfection
oak juice, fermented
oak just a whisker assertive
oak keeps a respectful measure of
  quiet throughout
oak knows its place in the scheme
  of things
oak largely invisible
oak length, sweet
oak like a black hole in space,
  the wine has gobbled up the
oak like a special seasoning, new
oak liquid
oak lurking in the background
oak makes a major statement
  throughout
oak makes a minimal impact
oak makes the wine cumbersome
oak management exemplary
oak marbles
oak maturation
oak merely an observer
oak monster
oak moss, damp
oak moss, nasty
oak not overplayed
oak nuances, stunning savory
oak once again imperceptible
oak or tannins, uncomplicated by
oak overlay, ink and
oak over-rides the natural flavors
oak phenolics do loom large on the
  finish
oak playing second fiddle
oak plays a good citizen role
oak plays a pure support role
oak plays only a junior/minor role
oak powder
oak present but trailing behind
oak push, some
oak pushes the envelope
oak reeks class, upfront
oak richness rather like Ovaltine
  or Nesquick, nice
oak rush, toasty
oak sawdust
oak seamlessly interwoven,
  fruit and
oak seasoning
oak seems to have all but
  disappeared
oak selection, slightly dubious
oak severely overdone

oak sheen, new-
oak should be a silent partner
oak should be a spice not a sauce
oak shroud, vanillary
oak slightly over the top
oak slightly persistent
oak smoke
oak *sotto voce*
oak spice
oak spices, deep
oak spices, kiss of
oak spices, sweet
oak spiciness, marked veneer of
oak spiciness, pithy
oak spirals
oak staves
oak sticking out
oak sticks
oak stringbeans
oak studded with stones, panoply
  of fruit in a box of
oak style, big walloping
oak subordinate/subservient
oak support, discreet
oak sweetening, some
oak sweetness, new-
oak tannins, flush of
oak tends to sit on top of the fruit
  like a floppy hat
oak that fits like a glove, little
  touch of
oak to its limits, pushes the
oak to make its point, doesn't need
oak to obliterate its profile, no
oak toast, smoky
oak tones, deep
oak trailing neatly behind...
  precisely where it should be
oak travels in the back of the plane
oak treatment, excessive/
  heavy-handed/overbearing
oak treatment, no
oak treatment, prolonged
oak tree addicted to cigarettes
oak tree in your glass, like finding
  an
oak tree, old
oak (tree not cask), old
oak type is not convincing
oak underpinning crisp fruit
oak underpins everything
oak use, controlled
oak use, judicious
oak use, sensitive
oak used as a crutch to hide a lack
  of fruit
oak utterly overwhelms the fruit

oak veneer, generous fruit evident
  beneath the
oak winds up for a toast and vanilla
  knockout punch
oak wrapped around the fruit,
  lots of American
oak zigzags
oak, 200% new
oak, accented
oak, Adygey
oak, age will soften the
oak, aged in
oak, aggressive overlay of
oak, airbrush of/delicate/
  dollop of/dusting of/gentle/
  faint/jab of/kiss of/minimal/
  negligible/polite/restrained/
  sensitive/splash of/subtle/
  twist of/waft of/whisper of
oak, Alabama
oak, Allier
oak, American
oak, Appalachian
oak, appetizing
oak, appropriate jab of American
oak, Argonne
oak, Arkansas
oak, aromatic ashy
oak, artificial flavors of
oak, assertive/in-your-face/
  overinsistent
oak, background wash of
oak, bacon-smoke
oak, bacony
oak, Balkan
oak, Baltic
oak, barely restrained
oak, barest suggestion of vanillary
oak, barest suggestion/touch/
  twist/ whiff/whisper of
oak, baseline of sweet
oak, bathed in gentle
oak, beautifully integrated
oak, beautifully judged
oak, beautifully modulated
oak, beautifully seasoned
oak, Bellème
oak, Bercé
oak, Bertrange
oak, big
oak, bit overweighted toward the
oak, bitter
oak, bitter new
oak, black-as-night
oak, blatant/brazen
oak, blitzed with
oak, boatload of toasty new
oak, Boisé

oak, Bosnian
oak, Bosnian-Herzegovinian
oak, Bouconne
oak, Bourgogne/Burgundy
oak, brushed with
oak, bubblegum
oak, Bulgarian
oak, buried
oak, burnt
oak, butter...menthol...tropical...
oak, buttery
oak, buttressed by
oak, Cadoux
oak, camouflaging
oak, camphory
oak, Canadian
oak, caramel/caramelly
oak, carefully judged
oak, Caucasian
oak, cedar oil
oak, cedarish/cedary
oak, Centre
oak, chained by slightly sticky
  oppressive
oak, charred American
oak, charry barrel-fermented
oak, charry chestnut warmth of
  good
oak, Cher
oak, chewy
oak, Chinese
oak, chippy touch of
oak, chippy-stavey
oak, chocolate mocha
oak, chocolate/chocolaty
oak, chocolate-covered
oak, chocolaty dressing of
oak, Citeaux
oak, clever smattering of new
oak, cleverly accented
oak, clove spice
oak, Cluny
oak, coarse-grained
oak, coconut-/coconutty
oak, coconut-caramel
oak, cocoon of soft vanilla
oak, coffee-tinged
oak, complex toasty-cedarwood
oak, controlled
oak, copious maple-tinged
oak, core of mocha-laced
oak, covered up by some very
  heavy
oak, cradled in an almost invisible
  web of
oak, creamy
oak, creamy coffee-
oak, creamy vanillary spicy-

oak, creamy-spicy
oak, Croatian
oak, crying out for
oak, curiously ill-fitting
oak, cushioned by
oak, Czech
oak, deft
oak, deft touch/use of new
oak, deliberately underplayed
oak, delicate filigree of spices and
oak, devoid of any
oak, devoid of new
oak, disappointing
oak, discernible touch of
oak, discreet use of
oak, divine
oak, does battle with heaps of
  American
oak, doesn't overdo the
oak, does not see
oak, Dordogne
oak, downplayed
oak, dried
oak, drowning in
oak, dumbed down with a lot of
oak, dusty
oak, Eastern European
oak, easy on the
oak, elegantly framed by
oak, elevated
oak, evident but not oppressive
oak, exaggerated
oak, exemplary
oak, exotically spicy
oak, extremely subtle use of
oak, exuberant use of
oak, faint web of smoky
oak, faintly dusty
oak, fancy
oak, far too much
oak, fatty
oak, fine-grained
oak, finely tuned
oak, finessed the
oak, finishing kiss of sweet
oak, fired
oak, five pounds of melted butter
  churned in fresh-cut
oak, flashy new
oak, flick of
oak, floral
oak, Fontainebleau
oak, for fans of
oak, for those eager to taste
oak, forest load of cedary coconutty
oak, forest of
oak, fractionally assertive
oak, fractionally oily

oak, French
oak, freshly sawn green
oak, freshly sawn white
oak, fruit has bottled up the
oak, fruit has gobbled up the
oak, fruit popping up through
  the smoky-vanilla
oak, full malolactic new-
oak, garish display of toasty
oak, Gascogne
oak, generous coating of chocolaty
oak, generous slather of new
oak, gentle custardy
oak, gentle flick of
oak, gentle substrate of
oak, Georgia
oak, German
oak, gets nowhere near
oak, gingery sweet
oak, given only the briefest contact
  with
oak, glass of liquid
oak, gnarled
oak, going down with the old
oak, good slug/smack of
oak, grace note of
oak, granular
oak, graphitelike
oak, great deal of refined new
oak, great integration of fruit and
oak, great prominence of
oak, green
oak, grilled
oak, grotesque
oak, gussied up in new
oak, Haguenau
oak, hard slightly planky but spicy
oak, hardly recognizable
oak, has quite certainly seen no
oak, Haute Futaie
oak, healthy amount/dose of
oak, heaps of charry
oak, heavily charred
oak, heavily larded with new
oak, heavy/lavish/loud/massive/
  opulent/ pronounced/robust/
  strong/supercharged
oak, heavy-handed use of
oak, hefty dose of
oak, hello
oak, hemmed in with tannin
  and new
oak, herbal-
oak, Herzegovinian
oak, hidden
oak, high-class French
oak, high-class toasty
oak, high-fired

oak, high-toned
oak, high-toned vanilla
oak, Hungarian
oak, impeccably handled French
oak, imperceptible
oak, Indiana
oak, indifferent
oak, indifferent choice of
oak, intelligent use of
oak, invasive
oak, Iowa
oak, irrelevant
oak, judicious new
oak, Jupilles
oak, Jura
oak, just a whiff of
oak, just the right amount of
oak, just-right veneer of
oak, Kentucky
oak, kiss of sweet
oak, ladles of vanilla/vanilla-
   scented
oak, landslide of new
oak, lashings of expensive
oak, lashings of new malty
   cashew nut
oak, lavish coat of new
oak, lavish dollop of American
oak, lavished with substantial
oak, lavishly smoked
oak, lemon-vanilla
oak, lengthy stay in
oak, less-obvious larding of
oak, less-obvious new
oak, less-overt
oak, lick of toasty
oak, light hand with the
oak, light lick of vanilla
oak, light veil of
oak, light veneer of bitter
oak, lilting perfume of new French
oak, Limousin
oak, lingering aftertaste of
oak, Lithuanian
oak, little new
oak, little overpowered by the
oak, loads/lots of
oak, Loches
oak, lots and lots of
oak, loud
oak, low-fired
oak, low-keyed
oak, lumbered with
oak, magical touch with
Oak, majesty of the Royal
oak, malty
oak, malty smoky
oak, malty-bran

oak, masses of
oak, massive
oak, matchstick
oak, matty
oak, mercifully it's not
oak, mercifully subtle French
oak, milk chocolaty
oak, Minnesota
oak, Mississippi
oak, Missouri
oak, mocha/mocha-laced
oak, moldy old
oak, Mormal
oak, musty
oak, nary a splinter of
oak, neat
oak, neatly managed
oak, needs to throttle back on the
oak, Nevers
oak, new
oak, new US
oak, new-sawn
oak, nice click of
oak, nice presentation of fruit and
oak, nicely handled
oak, nicely integrated
oak, Nièvre
oak, no
oak, no designer
oak, no detectable
oak, no pounding
oak, no-holds-barred
oak, no-new-
oak, not so much as a toothpick of
oak, nonmalolatic new-
oak, North Carolina
oak, not cluttered up with
oak, not contaminated by
oak, not enough fruit to cover the
oak, not mucked up by
oak, not overwhelmed/
   swamped by
oak, not swamped by French
oak, not too much
oak, not yet fully absorbed
oak, nutlike/nutty
oak, obnoxious
oak, obvious
oak, Ohio
oak, oily
oak, old
oak, one-dimensional
oak, only the briefest contact with
oak, Ontario
oak, oodles of high-quality
   American
oak, open-grained
oak, opulent

oak, Oregon
oak, Orient
oak, ostentatious new
oak, outspoken American
oak, overbearing
oak, overburdened by
oak, overenthusiastic use of
oak, overlay of
oak, overly charred
oak, over-the-top
oak, overtoasted
oak, Ozark
oak, Paimpol
oak, peck of
oak, Pennsylvania
oak, perfect marriage of fruit and
oak, perfect whisper of new
oak, perfectly managed
oak, perfectly pitched spicy malty
oak, perfectly seasoned
oak, perfumed
oak, perhaps too much new
oak, pleasant veneer of
oak, plenty of sweet fruit to be
   found once you peel back the
oak, plumped up with French
oak, plush American
oak, Polish
oak, polished
oak, ponderous
oak, Portuguese
oak, positive
oak, powdered
oak, preponderant
oak, pronounced
oak, pumped up with
oak, pungent
oak, pushy
oak, raisiny
oak, Rambouillet
oak, raw
oak, raw splintery
oak, raw unintegrated
oak, red
oak, robe of spicy new
oak, Romanian
oak, rose petals laced with toasty
oak, rough
oak, Russian
oak, sappy
oak, Sarthe
oak, savory mocha
oak, savory older French
oak, sawdusty
oak, sawn green
oak, screeching
oak, scrub
oak, sea of

oak, sees no
oak, sensible level of
oak, Serbian
oak, Sessile
oak, sexy
oak, sheen of French
oak, sheen of new
oak, sherried
oak, sherry-cask
oak, shipload of toasty
oak, short rest in
oak, shot of
oak, skillfully administered
oak, slabs of vanilla
oak, Slavonian
oak, slight surplus of
oak, slightly charred
oak, slightly fuzzy vanilla
oak, slightly intrusive
oak, slightly raw bitter
oak, slightly sawdusty vanilla
oak, slightly singed with
oak, Slovakian
oak, Slovenian
oak, smidgen of
oak, smoke and toast backbone of
oak, smoky
oak, smoky bacon
oak, smoky coffee/espresso
oak, smoky French
oak, smoldering
oak, smoothly integrated
oak, smothered by American

oak, smothered with

oak, soaks up
oak, sometimes clumsy overt
oak, somewhat strident
oak, soupçon of
oak, South African
oak, South Carolina
oak, spared
oak, specious spicy
oak, spicy
oak, spicy cedary
oak, spicy clove
oak, spicy nutmeg
oak, spicy-smoky
oak, splintery
oak, stifled by new
oak, still needs time to overcome the
oak, still shackled by an abundance of
oak, stops short of going overboard on the
oak, stranglehold of
oak, strong
oak, strong dose of

oak, strong spicy clove
oak, sturdy
oak, subliminal
oak, subliminal touch of vanilla
oak, subtle frame of
oak, subtle interplay between fruit and
oak, supercharged
oak, supple
oak, surface-sitting
oak, surfeit of new
oak, suspicion of

oak, swamped by

oak, swamped with smoky bacon
oak, swathed in toasty
oak, sweet
oak, sweet kiss of
oak, sweet milkshake
oak, sweet new
oak, sweet vanilla
oak, sweetening effects of good
oak, tannins melting into delicate
oak, tarry old
oak, taut cedar-French
oak, Tennessee
oak, thick slathering of
oak, tinned pear juice smothered with
oak, toasted/toasty
oak, toasty mocha
oak, toasty new
oak, toffee
oak, Tronçais
oak, tropical coconut nuances derived from
oak, Ukrainian
oak, unadorned by
oak, undercurrent of
oak, underlying
oak, underplayed
oak, unencumbered by
oak, unencumbered by excessive/ too much
oak, unfettered by
oak, uninhibited use of
oak, unintegrated
oak, unnecessary clothing of
oak, unobscured by new
oak, unsullied by
oak, untrammeled by
oak, vanilla/vanillary
oak, vanilla-chocolate sweetness from
oak, vanilla-imbued/-infused/ -laden
oak, vanillin
oak, violety-vanilla
oak, very surreptitious

oak, virgin
oak, Virginia
oak, virtually imperceptible
oak, Vosges
oak, wall of
oak, wallops of
oak, well-charred new
oak, well-handled
oak, well-handled background
oak, well-integrated creamy
oak, West Virginia
oak, western Loire
oak, wet kiss of
oak, whisk of American
oak, whisper of
oak, white
oak, Wisconsin
oak, without the distracting influence of American
oak, wrapped in spicy
oak, yellow
oak, young unintegrated smoky
oak, Yugoslavian
oak, yummy new
oak, Zemplen
oak...resulting in a drawn match, fruit contests tongue space with
oak...unlikely to ever integrate, too much
oak/oaklike/oaky spices
oak-aged
oak-chipped

oak-chipped fruit salad

oak-clobbered
oak-coconut
oak-conditioned
oak-covered cherries
oak-dominated finish, slightly rough
oak-driven
oaked format, judiciously
oaked red, revival
oaked smoothie, obviously
oaked subtly/subtly oaked
oaked, barely/gently/lightly/ mildly
oaked, cleverly
oaked, heavily/lavishly/ substantially
oaked, judiciously/moderately/ well
oaked, pleasantly
oaked, richly
oaked, somewhat extravagantly
oaked-up
oak-coated
oak-empowered black fruit
oak-free

oak-free blend
oak-free frame, ultralight
oak-free, blissfully
oak-free-style, vegetal
oak-fruit balance spot on
oak-imbued finish, tannic
oak-induced smoke, fueled by
oak-induced spices
oakiness, charred
oakiness, coconutty
oakiness, emerging
oakiness, grotesque
oakiness, intimidating and
  ill-poised
oakiness, lush sweet vanillin
oakiness, resinous
oakiness, trufflelike
oakiness, warm
oakiness, well-dosed
oakiness, without ponderous
oak-influenced, unabashedly
oak-infused
oaking, deft
oaking, judicious
oaking, tactful
oaking, well-managed
oak-inundated
oak-kissed
oak-lavished landscape
oaklike, silver
oak-phobic
oak-pumped
oak-pushed
oak's influence to smooth
  harmony, time will sand the
oaks, dappled shade under mighty
oak-slathered
oak-soaked
oak-style, big walloping
oak-tinge(d)/-tone(d)
oak-tolerant, for the
oak-tweaked, spanky
oak-vanillin, nutty
oakville
oak-weary, huge relief for the
oakwood
oaky accents, pure cream soda with
oaky afterbirth
oaky but not oppressively so
oaky cloves
oaky clunker, overbearingly
oaky dimension
oaky distractions, no
oaky enough to bury the fruit
oaky fizz, coconutty-
oaky for some, probably too
oaky for some, too
oaky fruitbomb

oaky fruitiness
oaky garnish, light
oaky mocha, singed
oaky monster
oaky needles
oaky nuances
oaky shimmer, opulent
oaky sledgehammer, big alcoholic
oaky smoothness
oaky spice, tenderly
oaky tropical fruit juice
oaky vanillins
oaky veneer, beautiful
oaky veneer, slight
oaky, Cabernet-
oaky, clumsily
oaky, dauntingly
oaky, far too
oaky, flinty-
oaky, gamy-
oaky, gently
oaky, lemony-
oaky, not too dreadfully
oaky, overwhelmingly
oaky, speciously
oaky, strongly
oaky, too thickish and
oaky, wildly
oaky-berry
oaky-citrusy-creamy
oaky-cokey
oaky-flinty
oak--yummy-tasting French oak --
  but oak nevertheless, swept away
  by a tidal wave of
oaky-vanilla
obvious
off-putting
oil
old
omnipresent, too
overdone
overenthusiastic
overlay, heavy
overoaked butter bomb
overoaked monster
overoaked plonk
overoaked, blatantly/wildly
overoaked, no way
overoaked, not underfruited
  and/or
overt
overwhelming, not
overwooded
pepperwood
perfect
perfume
pine and spice, Provençal

pine boughs
pine chips
pine dust
pine forest
pine gum
pine needles, forest bed of
pine needles, moldy
pine needles, wintery
pine oil
pine pitch/resin/sap
pine resins, discreet
pine shavings
pine trees
pine trees, like hitting a softball
  into the
pine, Canarian
pine, forest
pine, fresh-cut
pine, mountain
pine, pitch
pine, pleasant ribbon of
pine, resiny
pinecones, dusty
pine-fresh
piney, deliciously oily and
piney, medicinal-
pitch
planks
pleasant
plumwood
plywood/plywoody
polished, well
ponderous
poplars, balsam
precious
present and accounted for, all
pretty
profound
prominent/pronounced
pulpy
pungent
puny
quercine
quercus fragmentus
quinine bark
rancid
rancio
raw
redolent
redwood shavings
redwood/redwood bark
resin, cool
resin, tarry
resinous, lightly
resin-petrol
rich
roasted, very
rosewood

rotted/rotten/rotting/rotty
rough
sandalwood, freshly polished oriental
sap, aromatic
sap, full rising of the
sap, green
sap, sweet
sappiness, nice touch of
sappy, light-
sassafras
saturated
sawdust, damp/wet
sawdust, fresh
sawdust, mouthful of
sawdust, peppery
sawdust, pile of
sawdust, pure
sawdusty
sawed/sawn, freshly/newly seasoned
serious
shavings
smoke/smoked/smoky
smoothness, well-married
soft
spades, laid on in
spalded
spicy
splinters
splinters in your nose, no
splintery taste
spruce forest, freshly cut
stick, as dry as a
stiff
strong
style, old-
subtle
superoaky
supersappy
support
sweet
sweetwood
tanky
teak oil
teak...mahogany and cedarwood, all
termites, confused customers with
three by four, bit of
tight
timber club, member of the no-
timber to get in the way, no
timber, American
timber, brand-new
timber, charred
timber, fair whack of
timber, gentle
timber, pretty solid

timber, seasoned
timbery
toasted, slightly
toasty-roasty
toothpicks, like sniffing and tasting
topping, vanilla-cream
touch, knowing
treatment, little
tree bark, lick of
tree bark, maple tree
tree bark, wet
tree oil
tree sap
tree, bird cherry
tree, Christmas
tree, something from a
trees, lot of
tropical
twig, green
twig, snapped
twig/twiggy
two-by-four, splintered
ultraoaky
underoaked
underwood
unforced
unoaked
unoaked Chardonnays, one of the most complex
unoaked version, laser-clean
unoaked, blissfully
unoaked-style, pleasant
unpleasant
unsullied
unwooded/nonwooded
upfront
used sparingly and well
vanilla from American barrels, telltale
vanilla sheen, woody
vanilla, intrusive
vanilla, jolt of
vanilla, oaky
vanilla, tide of
vanilla-drenched, sawdusty
vanilla-oak
vanillin, nutty oak-
vanillin, slightly stewed
vanillin, smoky
vinewood
walnut oil
wet
willow bark, peeled
willow switch
willow, slender
willows, bark stripped from green
wisp/wispy
witch hazel

wonderful
wood added, water with some
wood aging, no evidence of
wood and loganberry jam turning to leather, whiffs of camphor
wood at this stage of its life, powered by
wood bark roughness
wood chips, entire room seemed to be filled with
wood chippy
wood does the talking
wood dryness
wood effects are pretty well modulated
wood evident, some
wood fighting for control, fruit and
wood fire
wood fire, meat grilled over a
wood frame
wood focus, excellent
wood gets the better of the fruit
wood in the mouth, lot of
wood influence (thankfully), no
wood is almost garish, display of fruit and
wood juice
wood notes, wild
wood notes, without intrusive
wood nymph tears
wood sap
wood smoothness, well-married
wood support
wood surf a rippling wave of red fruit, toast...leather and spiced
wood treatment, little
wood underpins everything
wood used sparingly and well
wood, all-purpose sweet
wood, aromas aren't lost in the
wood, augmentation with
wood, background
wood, better balance with the
wood, blatant new
wood, can't get past the
wood, clean ancient dry
wood, cluttered by
wood, doesn't exaggerate the
wood, doesn't hit you over the head with too much
wood, fruit is hiding behind the
wood, gingerbread dough supported by juniper
wood, good dose of
wood, had help of a little
wood, heavy overlay of
wood, honeyed mature
wood, knowing touch of

wood, like licking a piece of wine-
   impregnated
wood, marked presence of new
wood, never sees so much as a
   splinter of
wood, object lesson in how to use
wood, old marine
wood, old warm
wood, overt taste of
wood, pleasant
wood, precious very roasted
wood, resiny balsam
wood, sawing
wood, screams new
wood, steer clear if you're adverse
   to
wood, sweet-smelling musty
wood, tastes like grapes not
wood, too marked by the
wood, too much creamy
wood, unencumbered by
wood, wacky with
wood-aged thunderbolts, chunky
wooded, lavishly
wooded, sweetly
wooded, well
wooden interludes, dull lifeless
wood-fruit
woodiness, vanillary
woodless
wood-lightened
woodpile, dry
woods, exotic
woods, various
wood-scented
woodsmoke/woodsmoky
wood-smooth without wood taste
woody Chianti can't, can go places
woody crystalline
woody edge, mild
woody onslaught
woody plumpness, round

woody taste of a plank

woody vanilla sheen
woody vulgarity, altogether
   innocent of
woody, bitter-
woody, green-
woody, too
woody-pitchy
worked, well
wormwood
yew/yew bark

*Life is like riding a bicycle. To keep your balance
you must keep moving.*
Albert Einstein

*Okay, so it has sophisticated assertiveness, pre-
sumptuous breeding, crisp authority, complex
balance, elegant power, and respected fitness.
What's it taste like?*
Anonymous

23. Balance [Harmony, Proportion]

Another very critical component of quality wine: are all the key elements of acid,
alcohol, fruit, sugar and tannin in balance with one another, nothing dominating?
If so, you have a winner in your glass. Few properties of a well-made wine are as
important as long-lasting harmonious relationships. Sort of like good marriages.

act together, seems to have
   gotten its
act, high-wire
adequate
admirable/admired
alignment, everything is in
all-of-a-piece
amazing
ascendancy, flower...fruit and
   honey fight for
assembled, extremely well
asymmetrical
atonal
awe-inspiring/awesome
awful
awkward
balance and equilibrium, virtually
   perfect
balance and finesse, perfect
balance and structure, faultless
balance and subtlety over
   flamboyance, recognizes
balance and symmetry, uncanny
balance and symmetry, virtually
   perfect
balance at the university of
   equilibrium, hardly a lecture on
balance between cool and warm,
   nice
balance between sweetness and
   prickle, nice

balance front to back, superb
balance in diminuendo, length and
balance is a bit patchy, overall
balance is exemplary, sugar-acid
balance like an angel, preserves
balance of acid to fruit, pinpoint
balance of elements, lovely
balance of sugar and acidity,
   knife-edge
balance out, needs time to
balance perfectly, yin and yang
balance spot on, oak-fruit
balance with age, will
balance with the wood, better
balance, all the component parts in
balance, complete jewel with
   perfect
balance, excellent fruit-acid
balance, extraordinary
balance, fabulous
balance, gorgeous
balance, impressive ripeness with
balance, lost any sense of
balance, marvelous extract and
balance, master class in wood-fruit
balance, masterpiece of
balance, narrow feminine
balance, never loses its sense of
balance, nice oak-to-fruit
balance, nigh-on perfect
balance, nothing is out of

balance, off-/out of
balance, peerless
balance, perfect structure and
balance, racy
balance, remarkable acid-sugar
balance, seamless mix of flavors in
   perfect
balance, searching for
balance, signature
balance, stunning acidity-fruit-
   tannin
balance, toes the line of
balance, totally in
balance, uncanny
balanced and composed,
   beautifully
balanced and harmonious whole
balanced behemoth, well-
balanced brilliance, keenly
balanced bundle of energy, well-
balanced concentration
balanced glass of sunny fruit and
   perfume
balanced harmonious whole
balanced on a dime
balanced package of wonderful
   seduction
balanced palate is prodigal with
   chewy pulp, intense
balanced to a tee
balanced way, elastic in a perfect

balanced, 100%
balanced, astonishingly/
  impressively
balanced, badly
balanced, beautifully/exquisitely/
  immaculately/impeccably/
  perfectly/properly
balanced, deftly/dexterously
balanced, finely/well
balanced, harmonically
balanced, imperfectly
balanced, more perched than
balanced, most perfectly
balanced, not entirely
balanced, poised and
balanced, precariously
balanced, properly
balanced, regally built and
balanced, sumptuously
balanced, supremely well
balances spice and fruit so
  flirtatiously
balancing act between sheer
  pleasure and sensory overload
balancing act of fruit and slate,
  balletic beautiful
breathtaking
brilliant
calibrated acidity and tannins,
  perfectly
calibrated, nicely/perfectly
center of the flavors, no real
center stripe of the highway,
  down the
center(ed), soft(-)
center, hollow
center, lacks a real/true
center, loses a little steam in the
center, somewhat off-
center, totally off-
centered, well
chaos, complete brouhaha of
check, in

classical
coherence/coherent
cohesion, complete
cohesion, lacking/lacks
compartments, still in
compatibly together, berry flavors
  and mineral aromas nestle
component part is out of place, no
component parts excessively
  represented, all the
components in all the right places,
  all the right
composed nicely
composed, perfectly
condition, out of

confident
consistency, red-velvet
consistent, completely
consistent, more
consistent, uncannily
control, wildly out of
controlled
correct
deft
delicate, exquisitely
disarray, in
discordant edge
discordant note to it, without a
discretion, harmonious
disharmonious
disjointed arms and legs
disjointed components, very
disjointed, hopelessly/seriously/
  very

disjointed, subtly
disjointedness, ever-so-slight
disjunctive, somewhat
distant
distorted
disunified
easy
edge(d), knife-
edge, discordant
edge, poised on the razor's
effortless
elegant
envelope, marred by a green tannic
equilibrated, perfectly
equilibric masterpiece of the very
  top drawer
equilibrium, admirable/fine
equilibrium, exceptional/
  extraordinary/fabulous/
  impeccable/impressive/
  perfect/superb/terrific
equipoised
Euclidean proportions, of
even
even-handed
excellent
exceptional
exemplary
exquisite
extraordinary
fabulous
faulted, cannot be
fine
flawless
flowing/flows
fluid
folds together nicely
formed, well
fuse nicely with alcohol, tannins

good/goodish
gorgeous
great
hangs together impressively

harmonic choir
harmonious acids
harmonious complexity: nothing
  overdone...everything in its
  place
harmonious continuum,
  satisfyingly
harmonious jewel, elegant
harmonious lemony smoky bliss
harmonious package that keeps
  echoing and changing with
  every sip
harmonious silkiness
harmonious structure
harmonious wine imaginable,
  most
harmonious, 100%
harmonious, entirely/utterly
harmonious, gorgeously/
  majestically/wonderfully
harmonious, naturally
harmonious, not
harmonious, outstandingly
harmoniously, bound together
harmonize, struggling to
harmonized, well
harmony and class, defines
harmony and finesse, all
harmony is simply perfect
harmony, all the component parts
  working in
harmony, astonishing/impressive/
  miraculous/seamless
harmony, beautiful
harmony, closely woven
harmony, complex/symphonic
harmony, everything in total
harmony, magical
harmony, model of
harmony, natural
harmony, overall sense of perfect
harmony, Pythagorean
harmony, understated
harmony, wholly seductive
holistic
horrible
humble
imbalanced/unbalanced
immaculate
impeccable, simply
impeccable, virtually
inconsistent
incorrect
inharmonic/inharmonious

integrated into a classy seamless whole, beautifully
integrated, beautifully/perfectly/smartly/well
integration of fruit...acid...alcohol...tannins and other phenolics, near-perfect
integration, impeccable
intertwined in what seems like a diaphanous format, every possible jagged edge of acidity...alcohol...tannin and wood is brilliantly
interwoven so that nothing stands out, everything is
intriguing
judged, well
just
juxtaposed, fruit and acidity are poignantly

kilter, out of

knife-edged
lacking
lovely
marriage of opposites, voluptuous
married and mellowed, all individual parts
married, fully/perfectly/well
married, not well/poorly
marvelous
masterful
masterpiece
masterwork
matched, ill-
measured doses, everything hitting the olfactory senses and palate is in
modulated, beautifully
modulated, unusually well
neutral
normal
off, distinctly
off-center
on the money, right
ordered, well
orderly
orderly opulence
over the map, all
overbalanced with dry tannins
overbalanced, somewhat
paragon
perfect, near-
perfect, nigh on/well-nigh
perfect, virtually
pieces at present, in
place, all key elements squarely in
place, everything is in its proper
place, not a hair out of

place, nothing seems out of
pleasant
poised
poor
present, all the necessary goodies are
pretty
profound
proportion, all the wine's elements are in
proportion, like a Michelangelo...everything is in perfect
proportion, nothing is out of
proportion, right tastes are in lovely
proportioned, all the components beautifully
proportioned, beautifully/evenly/gorgeously/perfectly/well-stunningly/wonderfully
proportioned, classically
proportioned, eloquently
proportioned, not too well-
proportioned, sensitively
proportions, wine of Euclidian
rare
refined
rigid
rigorous
scintillating
seamless personality
seamless, amazingly
seamless, utterly
show-stopping
signature
silken/silky
skewed
smooth
stabilized, well
stable
staggering
stands out, no one element in its makeup
step, dancing in perfect
suave
super
superb
supple

symbiosis, lovely

symmetrical effort, pure
symmetrical wine, complete
symmetrical wine, the most perfect
symmetrical, gorgeously
symmetrical, hauntingly
symmetrical, highly/perfectly
symmetry between its building blocks of tannin...acidity...alcohol and extract, pure

symmetry, no discernable
symmetry, beautiful/gorgeous/outstanding/perfect
symmetry, fabulous sense of
symmetry, overall
symmetry, uncanny
sync, in/synchronized
sync, out of
syncopated, properly
synergistic
synergy between fruit...oak and acidity, perfect
tender
tense
tension never eases
tension of a coiled spring
tension, good
tension, really nice
tension, under
tensioned, highly
terrific

tightrope walker

together well, comes
together, all-
together, coming
together, hasn't come
together, not
together, seems to have gotten its act
together, well put
tremendous
tuned, finely
unbalanced feeling
unbalanced, demonstrably
unbalanced, slightly
uncanny
uncomposed
uncompromising
uncoordinated
undefined
underbalanced
uneven
ungainly
unharmonious
unified/unity, has
unintegrated
united, well
unmarried
unresolved
unsettled
unstable
unsteady
unsyncopated
whack, almost out of
whack, nothing too out of
whack, out of
wonderful

Wine is a complicated soup, the nature of which scientists are only just beginning to understand.
Jamie Goode

For all its wonder, wine is complex and unstable, and we human beings are little different. That is why the language of wine is spoken in so many tongues.
Andrew Caillard

Any wine, young or old, is more than an amalgam of smells and tastes and organic components waiting to be picked apart, labeled, numbered, and nailed to the wall
Gerald Asher

24. Complexity [Depth or Focus]

One unchallenged characteristic of wine that absolutely defines quality is complexity: how many layers of aroma are there, how many levels of taste are there? One dimension and little depth do not a fine wine make. However, if there are many dimensions, accompanied by sharp focus and a serious depth of flavor, then you are most likely holding a glass of very good wine indeed. Now sip and savor it.

accuracy, pinpoint
acrobatics on the tongue
act song, one-
all-of-a-piece
amalgam, delicate
amalgamated, deftly
amalgamated, perfectly
amalgamated, well
amalgamation, delicious
ambiguous
analysis, defies
analyze, difficult to
arpeggio of flavors
array of flavors, amazing
assembles itself into more than the sum of its parts
backpack on his way to China, young Marco Polo's
ballet of honey...citrus and buttered toast, glorious
bandwidth of flavors, narrow
bandwidth, lots of
bandwidth, wide organoleptic
basket of aromas and flavors, veritable
bed partners of licorice...acetone and lemon, unusual
bells and whistles, all the
bits and pieces are in the right place, all the

bouquet of fruit and sugar
box of flavors all in marvelous harmony, Pandora's
braided composition, wonderfully beautifully
breadth, enormous/huge
breadth, excellent/magnificent
brocade, rich
brouhaha of chaos, complete
cacophony of flavors
caravan of lilies and blueberries and herbs, magic
carnival of flavors
carpet across the tongue, tannins spread like a Turkish
cascades of aromas
catalog of the most attractive flavors, full-color
CBS: complexity...backbone and structure, has got
chameleon/chameleon-like
changing with every sip, harmonious package that keeps echoing and
chaotic
chorus, sings with a
cloud of tastes
coalmine of mineral flavors
coat of flavors, Joseph's
coat rainbow of aromas, alluring Joseph's-
cocktail of perfume...pomegranate and cherry

Kool-Aid, surreal
coherent
coliseum of fascinating stony flavors
colors of the rainbow, all the
combo of freshness...grace and lively fruit, addictive
commingled
communication, deeper
complex and elemental...a paradox, very
complex and intellectually stimulating
complex and layered
complex and strangely perfumed
complex and well interwoven, fantastically
complex aromas, wealth of
complex array
complex as a Fellini flick, as
complex as an Isfahan carpet, as rich and
complex as a Renoir, as rich and
complex as it is long, as
complex as to be indefinable, so
complex berry and barrel flavors, sensuous
    combination of
complex bouquet
complex burst of flavors
complex but awkward
complex but seamless amalgam
complex concentrated full-bodied behemoth
complex core
complex creamy elixir
complex earthiness
complex fruit, layer after layer of
complex harmony
complex herbal flavors
complex interplay
complex intertwined subtle spectrum of aromas
complex it very nearly imprisons the senses,
    so powerful and
complex it's impossible to give a single fruit or
    other descriptor, so
complex it's like a meal, so
complex matrix
complex musky nuance
complex nuances, tons of
complex personality
complex personality, handsome adolescent with an
    unusually
complex rainbow of flavors
complex slate
complex that their flavors change in your mouth
    like the light through a prism, so amazingly
complex through very delicate experience
complex trace of funky reduction
complex unoaked Chardonnays, one of the most
complex web
complex whole, awesome fruit bound tightly into a
complex wine, extraordinarily opulent
complex wine, lively
complex with big muscles at rest, elegant and
complex world tucked away inside

complex yet immensely subtle
complex, 100%
complex, astonishingly/awesomely/extremely/
    fabulousy/highly/hugely/immensely/profoundly/
    remarkably/stupendouly/thrillingly/unbelievably
complex, broodingly
complex, classically
complex, deep and
complex, elegantly
complex, endlessly
complex, enticingly
complex, exceedingly
complex, extraordinarily
complex, giddily
complex, intriguingly
complex, like a concert: vibrant and
complex, mathematically
complex, mind-blowingly
complex, most
complex, mysteriously
complex, nascently
complex, not
complex, not overly
complex, not particularly
complex, obnoxiously
complex, seductively/seductive complexity
complex, singularly
complex, spellbindingly
complex, tortuously
complex, unusually
complex, voluptuously
complex...complete and cultured
complexities in its fiery core, mineral
complexities singe themselves into an almost
    physical memory
complexities, feral
complexities, full of mature oily paraffin-touched
complexities, leathery
complexities, unseen
complexities, Vegemite-yeast autolysis
complexity achieves grandiose parameters
complexity and beauty of a Persian rug
complexity and longevity, mind-boggling potential
    for
complexity and richness, staggering
complexity and structure, potent mouthfilling beasts
    of
complexity and style, nascent
complexity as it comes out of its hole, gaining more
complexity coupled with elegance, piercing
complexity every day, gaining more
complexity everywhere you turn
complexity like a symphony, developing
complexity not obtrusive, extra level of
complexity of age, muscle of youth and the
complexity of aromas which defies description,
    magical
complexity of petrol without all that expensive aging

complexity of the noble rot
complexity of the palate, a Monet where the colors represent the
complexity that never seems to end, intense concentrated
complexity that screams France, yeasty
complexity we often refer to as wisdom, has the kind of
complexity, admirable
complexity, almost amontillado
complexity, aromatic
complexity, astonishing
complexity, beautifully botrytized
complexity, beguiling/engaging
complexity, boatload/tons of
complexity, building
complexity, burgeoning
complexity, buttery
complexity, candied-peel
complexity, cauldron of
complexity, cedary-minty
complexity, cherry liqueur earthy
complexity, chocolaty
complexity, Christmas cake
complexity, clovelike
complexity, coffee-caramel
complexity, compelling skein of
complexity, considerable degree of
complexity, creamy
complexity, creamy-spicy cedarwood
complexity, decent
complexity, deep
complexity, delicate
complexity, does not aspire to
complexity, don't look for
complexity, drama and
complexity, dreamy layers of
complexity, earthy
complexity, enormous
complexity, every facet of elegance and
complexity, fantastic/magnificent/wonderful
complexity, fine roasted-toasted herbal
complexity, full-on
complexity, gamy
complexity, gentle
complexity, good inner-mouth
complexity, great deal of
complexity, great hazelnut-walnut
complexity, hedonistic
complexity, herbal
complexity, herby-cedary
complexity, honest
complexity, honeyed mineral
complexity, impressive
complexity, incredible
complexity, intriguing vegetal
complexity, iodine-seaweedy

complexity, lacks the ineffable sublimity of richness and
complexity, lanolin
complexity, layers of briary and nettley
complexity, leesy
complexity, like a painting by Monet with its summery mild colorful
complexity, little foresty
complexity, loaded with
complexity, lovely warm cedary
complexity, magical
complexity, magna cum laude
complexity, magnificent
complexity, masterpiece of power and
complexity, matchless
complexity, meat-stocky
complexity, meaty
complexity, meaty mocha
complexity, mellow gingerbread
complexity, mind-boggling crossword-puzzlelike
complexity, mining an apparently inexhaustible seam of
complexity, modest
complexity, modicum of
complexity, multitiered/polyphonic
complexity, no lack of depth and
complexity, no monster of
complexity, no particular
complexity, no semblance of
complexity, nougatlike barrel ferment
complexity, nutty
complexity, oak-driven
complexity, only just beginning to show its
complexity, perfect
complexity, petrolly
complexity, positively cerebral
complexity, potential
complexity, powerful
complexity, remarkable
complexity, riveting
complexity, roasted nut
complexity, savory
complexity, sensual chocolaty-raisiny
complexity, shortbreadlike developed
complexity, shy on
complexity, slight bottle-age
complexity, slow-building
complexity, smoky
complexity, smoky sultry
complexity, smoky-buttery-spicy richness and
complexity, smoky-toasty
complexity, some botrytis
complexity, special sweet
complexity, spicy
complexity, spicy-raisiny
complexity, spider web lures you in to explore the depths of its
complexity, straw bale

complexity, stunning sensory
complexity, subtle
complexity, surprising
complexity, surprising amount of
complexity, tantalizing
complexity, toasty-oaky
complexity, touch of gamy
complexity, tremendous
complexity, uncommon
complexity, unencumbered by
complexity, unfolding
complexity, unsurpassed
complexity, untold
complexity, vegetal
complexity, you can peel layers of fruit and tannins
    away and still never get to the end of the wine's
complexity, zero
complexity: nothing overdone...everything in its
    place, harmonious
complexity: the holy trinity of great winemaking,
    lush ripeness wedded to power and
complexity...it's just about fun, it isn't about serious
complexly constructed
complexly transforming
complicated and/or complex, every bit the opposite
    of
complicated, intriguingly
complicated, not too
component parts, fully loaded with all the
components, subtle tropical
components, tastes too much like its
composed, well
composition, near-perfect
comprehensiveness quite out of the ordinary
concentrated form, almost glutinous in its fat
confused, bit
connected, well
consistent
constituted, impressively
constituted, poorly
constituted, well
construct, dizzily delicious
constructed in every dimension, brilliantly
constructed, impressively
constructed, not well/poorly
constructed, well
contours, layered
contradicting/contradictory
contradictions, mass of
contradictory feel
contradictory, pleasantly
contrasts, a wine of
convergence, has
cornucopia, berry
cornucopia of baker's shop bready/yeasty aromas
cornucopia of candied fruits and spices
cornucopia of citrus fruits
cornucopia of ripe tropical fruit

cornucopia of scents...flavors and memories
cornucopia, summer
cornucopia, veritable
cornucopian darts here...there and everywhere
dashboard, can light up your sensory
deconstructionist descriptions, defies
deep and dark
deep as a mine shaft, as
deep as a well, as
deep as the ocean floor, as
deep dive-into-me aromas with serious spice
deep you feel you can get lost in it, so
deep, digs
deep, fathoms
deep, incredibly/profoundly
deep, marvelously
deep, rapturously
deepest
deeply flavored
deep-set
deep-set, immensely
defined, beautifully/clearly/perfectly/superbly/well
defined, ill-/poorly
definition and delineation, outstanding
definition, could use more flavor
definition, lacks any real
definition, laser
definition, perfect/superb
definition, very precise
delineated, beautifully/fabulously
delineated, extraordinarily well
delineated, nicely/well
delineated, poorly
delineated, precise and clearly
delineated/delineation
delineation, amazing/exceptional/remarkable
delineation, brilliant/superb
dense mighty power, my...what
depth and complexity, fabulous
depth and richness, acted like a cello in a string trio
    adding
depth in its velvet folds of flavors are a revelation,
    hidden
depth is not its strong point
depth isn't its calling card
depth just lurking around the corner, magnificent
depth of flavor was comparable to the Mariana
    Trench
depth of flavor, bottomless
depth of flavors that never goes away, enormous
    exotic
depth of flavors, interesting
depth of flavors, without the exciting
depth of this wine, you can lose yourself in the
depth required for greatness, lacks the
depth with delicacy
depth you could dive into, solidity and
depth you don't drink it so much as fall into it,

so much

depth, awesome/colossal/exceptional/great/huge/
    incredible/stunning/thrilling

depth, black

depth, brooding

depth, certain

depth, cocoa-rich

depth, cosmic bath of nearly unplumbable

depth, crystalline

depth, decent/fine/good/magnificent/real

depth, full of dark

depth, great potential

depth, has a certain

depth, infinite

depth, intriguing

depth, lacks great

depth, mellowed

depth, monstrous levels of concentration and

depth, nascent

depth, not a lot of/not much

depth, penetrating

depth, practically infinite

depth, primal in its

depth, sheer flashy

depth, spellbinding

depth, super-Tuscan

depth, thought-provoking

depth, uncommon/unusual/very special

depth, uncommonly profound

depth, unmistakable

depth, unmplumbable/unplumbed

depthless/undeep

descriptors to it, hard to fit

detail, lovely

detailed and textured as a Gobelin tapestry, as

detailed, beautifully

detailed, highly

detail-oriented

diffuse, awfully/totally

diffuse, disappointingly

diffuse, elusively

dimension, another/whole other

dimension, lifts you to another

dimensional, one-

dimensional, two-

dimensionality, has a certain one-

dimensionally dysfunctional

dimensions give it some depth, extra

dimensions of flavors, multiple

dimensions unfold on the palate, multiple

dimensions, extra

dimensions, extra flavor

dimensions, manifold/multiple

dimensions, multiple flavor

dimensions, reveals pleasantly varied

dimensions, terrific aromatic

dimensions, will take you to other

discombobulated

disunified

diverse flavors and smells

drawing together opposing elements of raw force and
    gentle persuasion, adept at

dual personality

elegant

elemental and brutish, still

elemental, still quite

endless, description of flavors is

entropic

entwined flavors, passionately

even

everchanging taste tour

everything, has too much of

exact

excellent

exceptional

explore, much to offer and

faceted, many/well

fan of flavors and finesse

fan of flavors, unfolds like a Japanese

fans out in the mouth

fantasia of flavors, hedonists'

feature, no exceptional

featureless

fine

firework display, colorful

fireworks, aromatic

flavor breadth, majestic

florid

focus and concentration, lacks

focus, accurate

focus, chiseled

focus, clarity of/clean/clear

focus, could use more

focus, curious lack of definition and

focus, doesn't quite come into

focus, excellent wood

focus, fantastic

focus, ferocious

focus, fine

focus, firm/tight

focus, in sharp

focus, lacks a keen

focus, laserlike

focus, mind-boggling

focus, no

focus, out of

focus, precisely

focus, reticent

focus, rich without losing

focus, sleek

focus, slightly furry texture lacks

focus, smooth

focus, stellar

focus, tasty

focused leanness, honed to a

focused personality, more

focused, beautifully/brilliantly/gorgeously/
  magnificently/perfectly/sharply/superbly
focused, cleanly/immaculately
focused, elegant awesomely
focused, nicely/well
focused, not particularly
focused, pin-
focused, searingly
forest of flavors, veritable
fragmented
frankness...solidity...bouquet and body
fuzzy, slightly
good/goodish
great
harmonica of intricate flavors, amazing
harmonious
hold, on
holistic
homogeneous/homogenized
horn of plenty
horrible
hypercomplex
impenetrable
imprecise, totally
inaccurate
inexact
innumerable aromas
integrated, none too/not very/poorly
integrated, well
integration of fruit and oak, great
interlocked flavors, intricately
intricacy, has marvelous
intricate as an oriental carpet, as
intricate, lacily
intricately woven as any Missoni design, as tightly
  and
jumble, strange though intense
kaleidoscope of beauty
kaleidoscope of tastes
kaleidoscope, shifting
kaleidoscopic
kaleidoscopic array of fruit aromas and flavors
kaleidoscopic, explosively
labyrinth of fruit...floral...herb and mineral flavors
  is no conundrum; it's simply delicious, this
lacking
lamp, like rubbing Aladdin's
layer after layer of shimmering flavors
layer at a time, can be peeled one
layer upon layer coating your tongue in explosions of
  flavors
layer upon layer of flavors
layer upon layer of quality
layered as baklava, as
layered contours
layered flavors, many-
layered flavors, rich long
layered mouthfeel

layered palate impression
layered personality
layered textures, many-
layered with decadent fruit
layered, amazingly/spectacularly
layered, deeply/richly/well
layered, elegantly
layered, gorgeously
layered, many-
layers and layers
layers are missing, a few taste
layers of dense yellow fruit nectars, untold
layers of flavors rest on dark rich soil
layers of flavors that unwrap like Christmas packages
layers of flavors, many
layers of flavors, many many many
layers of indescribable grapiness and ultrasophisticated luxuriousness caress the tongue like a
  velvety carpet of music delivered by Pat Metheny
layers of interest, multiple
layers of jammy compotelike fruit, unending
layers of melted tannin
layers of onion skin, flavors peeling off like
layers of sensory delight or disgust, wrapped in
layers of taste
layers of taste, unlimited
layers, all sorts of
layers, chameleonlike
layers, deeply ensconced
layers, diaphanous in its
layers, gracious subtle
layers, lots of/many/multiple
layers, unending
layer-upon-layer concoction of goodies
layer-upon-layer creation, sensual fruity-sweet
level, nice and
levels, multiple
library of aromas
linear
lopsidedly flavor-packed
many wines in one
megadimensional
mélange of aromas
mélange of berries
mélange of flavors and character
mélange of forest aromas
mélange of fruit
mélange of fruit confit flavors
mélange of grace...vigor...power and finesse,
  admirable
mélange of light fruit and minerals
mélange of memories, heady
mélange of ripe and green fruit
mélange of summer fruit
mélange of wonders
mélange, curious
mélange, earthy-herby
meld, doesn't entirely

melded, well
melded/meshed, beautifully
meshed together, not yet
meshed, exquisitely
meshed, well
misses the mark
modulating flavors
monochromatic
monodimensional
monodimensional, still
monolithic, boringly
monothematic
monotone, linear powerful
monotonous
mosaic of flavors, stunning
mosaic, stunning aromatic
multidimensional allure
multidimensional drinking experience, fine
multifaceted
multifaceted, fantastically
multifacited richness
multiflavored
multilayered
multilayered as strudel, as
multilayered richness
multilayered richness, real glimpses of
multilayered texture
multilayered, erotically
multilayered, hauntingly
multiple collections of smells
multiple flavor dimensions
multiple flavor levels
multiple levels, skyscraper with
multiplicity of flavors envelopes the tongue
multitasking
multitextured
multitiered
multitoned
multitracked
multitude of tastes
myriad flavors and aromas
nooks and crannies to explore, plenty of
normal
nuance, each sip offers a different
nuances, endless
nuances, rich in
numerous impressions
one-note, pretty/tad
one-track
orchestra is playing a lovely melody but you have to
   listen closely to hear it, the
orchestra of string instruments in the background
orchestra playing right now in your mouth, there's
   an
orchestral, rich and
orchestrated, expertly/well
orchestra, glorious/gloriously orchestrated
orchestrated, not particularly well

orchestration of flavors
ornate
ornate as a Tabriz rug, as
over the place, all
palette of aromas and tastes, broad
palette of flavors, painter's
panoply of aromas, flaunts a
panoply of flavors, rich
panoply of fruit
panoply of fruit in a box of oak studded with stones
panoply of scents
panoply of sweet flavors
panoply, extraordinary
parts seem nicely assembled, all the
pastiche of smells
pastiche of flavors, cubist
pastiche, California winemaking
pastiche, evocative
pastiche, Near Eastern
patchwork of flavors
peacock's tail of aromas and flavors
peacock's tail of tastes wrapped in silk
peacock's tail with quite a few feathers missing
peacock's tail, all the colors of the
peacock's tail, broadens like a
peacock's tail, classic
peacock's tail, explosive
peacock's tail, opens/opens out like a
plain, just
plenty going on in this wine
plenty happening
poem of flavors, wonderful tone
polyphonic counterpoint with divine melodic lines
ponderous
poor
precise, gorgeously/magnificently
precise, mind-numbingly
precise, not very
precise, totally
precision of flavors, terrific
precision yet *élan*, meticulous
precision...elegance and definition, trademark
prodigious
profound
prominent/pronounced
rainbow of aromas/flavors/tastes
rainbow of aromas, alluring Joseph's-Coat
rainbow, all the colors of the
rainbow of flavors, complex
rainbow, right side of the
rare
riot of aromas/tastes
riot of chewy fruit
riot of flavors
riot of herbs, aromatic
riotous array of fruit
riotous fruit
satisfying as a Mozart piano concerto: effortless...

fluent...tuneful...silky...seemingly a doodle to play
but really bewilderingly complex, every bit as
seam, without a noticeable
seamless appearance
seamless as a snowfall, as
seamless beauty where color...tannin...acidity and
fruit are emotionally intertwined like life partners
lucky in love
seamless in every respect
seamless personality
seamless, utterly
seamlessly interwoven/welded, fruit and oak
seamlessly stitched together
seamlessly welded together, aromas-flavors-texture
are
seamlessly welded together, fruit and oak have been
secrets, deep and dark
seductively beautiful...multifaceted...
   Count Basie...a brothel...a summer's evening
   and an Aston Martin
self, expresses its inner
shaded beyond the obvious
shallow
simple in the best sense of the word
simple it's almost simple-minded, so
simple modern pleasure
simple sipper by any means, not your
simple tune
simple, relatively
simple, surprisingly
simple-jammy, bit
simpleton
simpleton, outspoken inelegant
simplex and complex, straddles the border between
simplicity itself
simplicity, flirts with
simplicity, perfect/wonderful
simplicity, stunning study in
simplistic
simplistic, not
single-minded, sharply
singular
singular expressions that is a riveting wine in its own
right, undeniably
singularity, admirable
smorgasbord of aromas
smorgasbord of Asian spices
smorgasbord of black fruit
smorgasbord of earthly delights
smorgasbord of sweets
smorgasbord, sensual and seductive lush
smorgasbord of flavors and aromas, texture is like
getting lost in a dizzying
smorgasbord: it contains everything and is unlike
anything else
sneaks up on you
sorts of fruity flowery things, all
sorts of promising perfumes, all

souk of aromas, a
souk, as spicy as a
souk, like walking through a
souk's worth of flavors
souk's worth of spice
spectrum of all the most sensual things one can think
of, refined taste
spectrum of aromas, Belle Époque
spectrum of aromas, broad
spectrum of aromas, complex intertwined subtle
spectrum of flavors, unique
spectrum of tones, complete
spectrum, at the big end of the style
spectrum, at the ripe end of the
spectrum, baroque end of the
spectrum, canned fruit
spectrum, salad bar
spectrum, savory
spectrum, sensual
spectrum, tropical fruit
spectrum, weird distorted
splendored, many-
stacked, delicately
stacks of flavors
starburst of flavors
straight as an arrow, as
straightforward, quite
striptease...revealing more each time one sniffs and
sips, does a sort of slow
stupendous
sum of its parts, more than the
sunrise of flavors, Atlantic
supercomplex
superficial, little
surprise after surprise: the throat is stunned
symphonic harmony, complex
symphonic masterpiece
symphonic memories in the mouth, leaves
symphony by Mozart/Mozart symphony
symphony by Sibelius: full of sadness...joy...nature
and romance, grand
symphony for the palate
symphony of aromas
symphony of fruit and flowers
symphony of fruit and minerals
symphony of full complex aromas, unmistakable
symphony of scents and flavors, beguiling
symphony of sensations
symphony of the Pinot grape's various incarnations
where the aftertaste reverberated like a singer's
voice in a cathedral
symphony of wild and tasty abandon like peasants at
play, delectable
symphony was played for the olfactory glands,
fantastically beautiful sensual
symphony, developing complexity like a
symphony: full of melancholy...happiness and
romance, Sibelius

symphony, long subtle
symphony, oak is the drum that anchors the
symphony, petroleum and nuts together build a
symphony with kettledrums and rumbling bass,
    mature and sterling
tapestry of aromas, wonderful
tapestry of flavors
tapestry of fruit, marvelous
tapestry of innumerable flavors, finely woven
tapestry, as detailed and textured as a Gobelin
tapestry, beautiful
tapestry, tropical
tapestry, woven
tastes, thousands of
theme park of a wine
tidy, not entirely
together brilliantly, hangs
together, all-
tones forming intricate sustained chords, ringing
track, one-
tune, simple
twisted
two-note samba
ultracomplex
ultracomplex blend
unambiguous
uncluttered
uncomplex
uncomplicated
uncomplicated by oak or tannins
uncomplicated joys
uncomplicated, attractively
uncomplicated, happily
uncomplicated, perhaps too
uncomplicated, refreshingly
uncomposed
uncoordinated
undefined
undertones that escape description, unusual
unusual
undifferentiated
uneven
unfaceted
unfathomable
unfocused, seriously
unfocused, slightly
unidimensional
unified, well
unified/unity, has
unintegrated
uninteresting
unknowable/unknown
variations on a theme by Grape
variety and cohesion of the whole lot into something
    wonderful
waves across the palate, rides in
waves of flavors
wealth of flavors, fantastic

whack, bit/little out of
whirlwind of flavors
whirlwind of sensations, irresistibly appetizing
whole of rare finesse
whole was better than the individual parts
whole, fantastic
wildness and grace all at once, has power...
woven as any Missoni design, as tightly and
    intricately
woven together, nicely
woven, well

When I lived in California, I found that the innocent pleasures of wine were too often diminished by prodigies real or self-imagined—bent on deep-reading a glass of grape juice. There is no such blundering here [in Tuscany]. These farmers make their wine in the vineyard rather than in the laboratory the way commercial wine-makers do. The fruit—undisguised, unmanipulated, and just as the gods send it—is the stuff of their wine.... Rough, lean wines, wines to chew, thick rubescent elixirs that transfuse a tired, thirsty body like blood are these. No fragrance of violets or vanilla, not a single jammy whiff nor one of English leather, these wines are the crushed juices of the grape, enchanted in a barrel.
Marlene de Blasi

25. Typicality/Typicity [Origin, Style or Type]

This long, interesting, complicated and diverse category [in which the word *wine* is often implied] includes the characteristic, the representative, the huge variety of wine, where the grapes originate, as well as all the varied styles produced by countless vintners in over 70 countries worldwide and in all of the 50 of the United States. Even in Sarah Palin's Alaska, of all places!

ABC (Anything But
  Cabernet/Chardonnay)
aberrations, dense
adult pleasure, pure
African sun in a bottle, all the
  flavors of a golden
African twist, earthy
afternoon in the backyard,
  perfect for a balmy
alcopop
Algerian bowl
Algerian fizz
Algerian red
Alsatian character, pronounced
Alsatian charm, disarming
Alsatian fizz, authentic
Alsatian Gewurtz
Alsatian in style, fat
Alsatian snapshot
Alsatian wine, Burgundian-style
Alsatian-style, textbook
Amarone in character/Amarone-
  like
Amarone, A-1
Amarone-asphalt

Américaine, very good *à l'*
Americana and cherry pie,
  good old
American and very proud, very
American and proud of it,
  brash and
American guts, real
American oak bruiser, big
American Parkerized monsters are
  striking, similarities with fruit-
  propelled
American spirit
American taste?
American West Coast rock album,
  clean and attractive like a well-
  produced
American wrestling version of a
  smack-down wine
American, so/uniquely/very
America's Yquem
Amerique bottling
ancestral aromas
Andalusian gypsy than gentleman
  of Castile, more
animal, completely different

animal/beast, rare
antimodern way, antirosé made
  in an
anything, could be
anytime, good pour for
apéritif for all seasons
apéritif of exception
apéritif tipple, wonderful
apéritif whistle-wetter, superb
apéritif, brilliant warm-weather
apéritif, excellent terrace
apéritif, sublime summer
aperitivo, perfect
appellation, definite impression of
appellation, far exceeds its
approach, back-to-basics
Arab desserts, aromas encountered
  in many
Armani of a wine...elegant and
  sober
Armstrong at the Sunset Café:
  virtuoso...perverse and glorious
arranged, a touch too carefully
artifice, free of/without
artifice, full of winemaker's

artifice, worked with all the
vintner's
artisanal
atypical of its appellation/region
Aus-Ital blend
Auslese/Auslese-like
Aussie Chardie
Aussie Shiraz-style powerhouse
Aussie, easygoing
Aussie-style minerals
Aussie-style, no-holds-barred
Australia but nowhere else in the
world, type of wine made in
Australia, classically western
Australia, oozes
Australian bush
Australian character, traditional
Australian jam-juice, typical
Australian wine wizardry, definite
Australian, daringly un-
Australian-style, archetypical
Austria, nice chunk of
Austro-Hungarian empire in a
glass
authentic taste
authentic untamed soul of the
grape, expresses the
Baby Duck
backdrop to a quiet evening,
beautiful
backyard, perfect for a balmy
afternoon in the
banquets as it is for modern
barbecues, as appropriate for
ancient
Barberry flavors from the Barberry
coast
baroque end of the spectrum
baroque splendor
Barossa earth
Barossa red, manly hairy
Barossa, monster Shiraz can
out-sumo that of an
barrel regimen, most perfect
Barsac, big busty
bastard child
Bauhaus-lean
Beaujolais, bog-standard
Beaujolais, sovereign among all the
wines of
Beaujolais, square-jawed
Beaujolais-like light fruit
Beaujolais-like/-style
Beaune in the USA
Bee Gees of wine
Beerenauslese
Beethoven wine

Benny Goodman is surely a
Riesling
Big Mac of the wine world
biodynamic
birthplace, (the journey of wine)
will transport you to its
bitzer: a multibreed like the
proverbial junkyard dog, real
Bix Beiderbecke, subtle harmonies
and lilting vitality of
bladder-pack
blanc de blancs
blanc de noirs
blazing a trail
blend for the wine library, luxury
blend of God knows what
blend of old-vine Syrah and
Barbera, raucous
blend of practically everything but
the kitchen sink, nonvintage
blend of younger and older
material, excellent
blend, avant-garde
blend, big-boned
blend, blinding
blend, bog-standard
blend, bogus
blend, bracing
blend, bright berried
blend, bucket-shop
blend, clever/cunning
blend, drink-tonight
blend, field
blend, fun
blend, funky
blend, good/nice
blend, gorgeous
blend, high-end interregional
blend, humble
blend, jumpy
blend, low-key
blend, meaty
blend, mongrel
blend, multivintage
blend, mutt of a
blend, oak-free
blend, one-of-a-kind
blend, polished
blend, puppy-dog's
blend, quixotic
blend, rambunctious southern
French
blend, rich multiregional red
blend, Right Bank-styled Bordeaux
blend, rule-bending
blend, silken
blend, split-identity
blend, superb macho red

blend, superpremium
blend, synergistic
blend, tangy
blend, tradition-busting
blend, turbo-driven
blend, ultracomplex
blend, unconventional
blend, unsuitable
blend, untraditional
blend, wacky one-of-a-kind
blend, weird
blend, whimsical
blended with the highest degree of
winemaking artistry
blending and aging, high-quality
blending material, good
blending, great example of
blending, masterful
blending, micromanaged
blending, shows the benefit of
multiregional
blondes, vinous equivalent
of bottle
blues, will cure any afternoon
Bollinger-style, would-be
Boone's Farm
boots-and-all-style
booze, candified
Bordeaux berries in a bottle, five
sorts of
Bordeaux but tastes of Hawaii,
made in
Bordeaux in my life, sexiest
Bordeaux look-a-like
Bordeaux mold, very much in the
Bordeaux taking the local
Bordeaux, aged
Bordeaux, baby
Bordeaux, classic
Bordeaux, eerily like a moderately
mature high-quality
Bordeaux, kinder gentler side of
Bordeaux, picnic
Bordeaux, rosélike
Bordeaux, *trés petit*
Bordeaux/Bordeaux-esque/
Bordeaux-fashion/Bordeaux-ish/
Bordeaux-like/Bordeaux-style
Bordeaux-like finesse
Bordeaux-like mouthfeel
Bordeaux-like, disconcertingly
Bordeaux-style elegance
Bordeaux-style, Merlot-heavy
Bordelaise in character
Bourbon-meets-port love child
Bourgogne blanc...heart of
breakfast Champagne,
completely wonderful

Bruce juice with sequins and a tiara
Brunello, bawdy
Brunello, Big Daddy
Brunello, country gentleman
Brunello, true-blue
bubbly, big mouthful of
bubbly, dessert
bubbly, fabulous
bubbly, fun consumer-friendly
bubbly, high-class connoisseur
bubbly, house
bubbly, kosher
bubbly, not a kick-up-your-heels
bubbly, plump
bubbly, redder-than-red
bubbly, seems halfway between
    a still wine and a
bubbly, top-notch
bubbly, wedding
bumpkin, rustic country
Burgundian character, very potent
Burgundian funk
Burgundian in its inflection, quite
Burgundian lushness
Burgundian mold, in the
Burgundian personality, decisive
Burgundian rapture, glorious
Burgundian stink
Burgundian tang
Burgundian, distinctly/quite/very
Burgundian-style Alsatian wine
Burgundian-style, quasi-
Burgundy character
Burgundy imposter
Burgundy is all about, what great
    white
Burgundy lovers drooling into
    their bibs, gets
Burgundy moment, a
Burgundy not California, has
    relatives in
Burgundy on steroids
Burgundy silk
Burgundy structure, classic
Burgundy with a suntan
Burgundy, map of
butterballs, undrinkable gloppy
bygone age, conjures up thoughts
    of a
bygone winemaking era, like
    taking a trip back to a
by-the-glass pour, good
Cab, high-elevation desert
Cabernet blend, baronial
Cabernet look-a-like, plummy
Cabernet on steroids
Cabernet profile, almost
Cabernet retrospective

Cabernet rules with haughty
    disdain
Cabernet Sauvignon should be,
    paradigm of everything
Cabernet spectrum, quasi-
Cabernet, benchmark Napa Valley
Cabernet, exuberant fountain of
    full rich
Cabernet, faceless international
Cabernet, kick-butt mountain
Cabernet, new-style
Cabernet, syrup of
Cabernet, un-Cabernet
Cabernet: the red king
Cabernet-oaky
Cabernet's iron
Cabs in the world, one of the finest
Cahors, black wine of
California combo, wild
California cult/cult California
California in style, unmistakable
California Kool-Aid, no
California sunshine, kissed with
California super-Cab
California winemaking pastiche
California" personality,
    unmistakable "made in
California, almost a whiff of
California, mistaken for a
Californian than Bordeaux, more
Californian, pure
Californian, very
Californian-style, plummy jammy
California-style, restrained
Cal-Ital/Italian-esque
call, evening wake-up
candy, vinous nose
cannon, loose
caricature, descending into
Carlos Santana, as languorous and
    silky as a guitar solo by
casual occasions, terrific pour for
Catalan accent
category, notable in its
Chablis, boiled
Chablis, show-stopping
Chablis, textbook
Chablis, trying to out-Chablis
Chablis-character
Chablisien, almost
Chablis-style, traditional
chairman's, railroad
Champagne I have ever drunk,
    the mightiest
Champagne look-a-like, real
Champagne should taste like,
    almost a primer on what
Champagne without the bubbles

Champagne, Coca-Cola
Champagne, conveyor-belt
Champagne, garden-wedding
Champagne, marc de
Champagne, old
Champagne, Rambo
Champagne, tarts'
Champagne, woody
character, cold-growing-season
character, cowboy
character, expressive of each
    vintage's
character, in/characteristic
character, shining example of grape
Chard, anti-
Chard, house
Chardonnay at its most perfect
Chardonnay blend, unusually
    combative
Chardonnay character
Chardonnay cut from Chablis cloth
Chardonnay fatigue
Chardonnay fruit, lovely waxy
Chardonnay impersonator
Chardonnay in the nude
Chardonnay is a little like the
    Kleenex of white wine
Chardonnay is the vanilla pudding
    of wine
Chardonnay mania
Chardonnay on steroids,
    unwooded
Chardonnay on the planet Jupiter
Chardonnay trying-to-be/wannabe
Chardonnay, big-time
Chardonnay, blanketed in a
    eiderdown quilt of mature oily
Chardonnay, Burgundian
Chardonnay, charred
Chardonnay, crackerjack
Chardonnay, flashy showpiece
Chardonnay, florid California
Chardonnay, full-blown style of
Chardonnay, full-frontal
Chardonnay, hits-you-over-the-
    head
Chardonnay, Identi-Kit
Chardonnay, intriguing suggestion
    of
Chardonnay, life-changing
Chardonnay, low-fat
Chardonnay, pure unalloyed
Chardonnay, same-ish oaky New
    World
Chardonnay, straight-on
Chardonnay, trademark
Chardonnay: the white queen
Chardonnay-flavored apple juice

Chardonnay-like, too
Chardonnays, fighter pilot of
Chardonnays, one of the most complex unoaked
Chardonnay-style, blockbuster
Chardonnay is the equivalent of the ice cream sundae
Château Latour-like, vaguely
Château Wrigley
Châteauneuf concentrate
Châteauneuf, dead-ringer for
Châteauneuf-du-Popsicle than Eskimo-Merlot pie, more
Châteauneuf-style junior cheese course, for the after-dinner
Chenin Blanc-like
Chenin does the cha-cha-cha
Chenin's acrobatic abilities
Chianti, killer
Chianti-style, old
chic as Agnès B., as
chic, paradoxically chunky-
Chilean
Chinon-style
Christmas in a glass
Churchill of a wine…meaning larger than life
churned out like candy bars
clairet
claret classicism
claret dancing around my palate
claret defined
claret ever, most complete
claret flavors, positive
claret in composition
claret, ballerina of a
claret, bathtub
claret, claretty
claret, dependable club
claret, house
claret, no wimpy
claret, thinking man's
claretlike weight
claretty flavors, positive
class apart, a
class experience, world-
class juice, cutting-edge world-
class red, on the verge of world-
class wine of self-evident style and individuality, toweringly brilliant world-
class wine, unsurpassable world-
class, aggressively middleclass, blares
class, definitely upper-
class, excellent/nice/very good for its

class, scrumptiously robustly world-
class, working-
class, world-/world classic
classic and idiosyncratic at the same time, both
classic brute, gorgeous dark
classic build
classic incarnate
classic line, toes the
classic of its kind
classic rendition, beautifully
classic that never seems dated
classic waiting in the wings
classic wine from a classic region made in a classic vintage
classic, absolute/great
classic, copybook
classic, destined to become a
classic, ethereal
classic, gentlemanly
classic, majestic
classic, minor
classic, monumental
classic, quirky
classic, seamless
classic, true
classical character
classical restraint
classical, quite/very
classically constructed
classically flavored
classically proportioned
classicism, claret
classicism, pure
cliché
cliché nor artifice, resorts neither to
cliché, miles away from the fruit-and-flowers
climatish, cool-
Clint Eastwood scowl
coastal-climate feel
Cold Duck
cold-growing-season character
collector's item now
comer, real
commercial appeal of gonorrhea with notes of dung…spare ribs… horse blanket…boiled cabbage and cardboard, has all the
commercial mode, unthreatening
commercial offering, rather dull
committee to offend no one, crafted as if by a
committee, designed by a
common as dirt, as
concentrate, grape

concoction, pure
concoction, rich heady
confection, curious
confectionary, verging on
contrived and neutral, too
contrived corporate-looking
contrived, cleverly
convenience store
conventional
conventional about this wine, nothing
conversation piece, real
cooking
cookout, summer
copybook
corporate-looking, contrived
correct for its own good, too
correct, not completely politically
correct, politically
correct, technically
cosmetic
cosmopolitan
Côte-Rôtie look-a-like, near/almost
Côte-Rôtie on acid
couch potato
counterfeit
countrified
countrified charm, real
country
country bumpkin, rustic
country, cool-
country, heart is in the
country, hot-
country…little bit Ritz-Carlton, little bit
country-fair
courant, au
course, after-dinner cheese
couture version
crafted, hand-
cross between a black cherry and Gene Kelly
crossed
crossover
crowd, one of the
cru, grand/premier
crude
crust, upper
cuckoo's nest, trace of the
cult/cultlike/cultish
curio, extraordinary
curio, historical
curiosity, delicious
curiosity, interesting
curiosity, rare
curiosity, uninspiring
curious but delicious

curious, altogether
current
custom/customary/
  custom-built/customized
cutting-edge
cuvées, deluxe/prestige
dalliance, afternoon
dark and stormy expression
darling, media

Darth Vader of a wine

day, of the
day/daytime
day-in and day-out use, for
dealcoholized
deck and patio
decks...docks...parties and picnics,
  great for
decoration, tasting-room
decorative, disappointingly
default
definitive
De Gaulle-ish
deluxe
demand, much in
demanding
democratic
designer
detail, product of fanatical
  attention to
different animal, completely
different ball game, totally
different, radically/very
different, thrillingly
different, wonderfully

disco, pink

disguised
dishonest, totally
distinct to this growing area
distinctive expression of its climate
distinctive richness
distinctive, truly
Dolly Parton with a lot up front
Dolly Parton without her bra
Dolly Parton-style: alluring,
  ultimate
Dolomitic charm
domestic
domesticated, little too
downscale
down-to-earth
downtown
dresser, cross-
drink, fine predinner
drink, perfect midmorning
  weekend summer
drink-at-home
drinker, solid day-in day-out
Duck, Baby

Duck, Cold
duckling, ugly
Duke Ellington numbers: massed
  talent in full cry
dumbed down to please the masses
early wine, good
Earth as wine's birthmark, think
  of the
East Coast
East Side socialite, poise and polish
  you'd expect from an
eastern
easy to drink, scarily
easygoing
eccentric in a lovable way, little
eccentric, marvelously
echoing
eclectic
edge(d), cutting-
edition, limited
edition, upmarket
efficient
effortless, seemingly
Eiswein
elbow-bender
elevenses, would certainly do for
elite
Emperor Augustus than Queen
  Elizabeth, more
emblematic
end of town, at/from the big
end stuff, high-
end, lower-
engineered
English (not French) Golden
  Delicious apples
English fizz, serious
English taste/English-y
English, herbaceously

English, quintessentially

Englishman's claret
English-style, old
enriched
entry point, beginner's
entry-level
environment, derives from its
ephemeral
equal of fine sweet wines across the
  world, easily the
era, suggests a bygone
eraser, warm-weather heat
erratic
ersatz
estate/estate-bottled
Etna ash
eucalyptus-glycerin
EU table
Euro blend, dull

Euro elegance
European feel
European in character, almost
European mold, elegant
European, earthy
European, looking quite
European-style finish, long
European-style red
European-style, classic
Euro-styled delicacy

Eurotrash

evening wake-up call
evening, very good way to
  spend an
evenings by the fireside, made
  for cold
evenings, ideal for summer
event
everyday consumption, for
everyday enjoyment, for
everyday pour
everyday, marvelously simple
  glugging
everyday, not your
everyday, quaffable
everyday, unthinking
everyone, not for
exclusive
exotic, positively
exotic, sensuously
exotic, sweetly
exotic, wickedly
exotic, wildly
exoticism, over-the-top
expert
experts, defeats even the
explosion
expression of its vineyard, virtuosic
expression of the grape, truly
  evocative
expression, true
expressive of its volcanic soils
extraterrestrial
extreme
faithful to its vineyard, very
fake, tawdry
false
famed/famous
familiar
familiar and unfamiliar
  at the same time
family connections, excellent
fancy, not/nothing
fancy-shmancy
fashion as monocles, as out of
fashion, classic no-frills
fashion, unforced
fashionable, currently/quite

fashionable, utterly fantastically
fashionable, wildly
fashionable, world's most
fashioned, new-
fashioned, old-
fault...like car insurance, no-
faux
favorite, anyday
femme fatale
fermented, cool-
Ferrari of the wine world
festival-special
festive
feudal
fictitious
fiddle, second-
field, right out of left
fightin'
fireplace
fish nor fowl, neither
fish, quintessential
fizz, classic-style
fizz, crude hyperbubbly
  quick-and-dirty
fizz, everyday easy-drinking pink
fizz, first-class
fizz, low-end tank-fermented
fizz, new-wave
fizz, party
fizz, pink
fizz, red
fizz, soft harmonious summer
fizz, spice
fizz, wacky raspberry-flavored red
flag in a really nice way, shows the
flagship
flag-waving, very
flamboyant personality
flashy
flavored, artificially
floozy, cheap
floozy, pleasantly
Florentine arrogance
fly-by-night
folksy character, very nice
food in a bottle, comfort
food, fast-
food, fine
food, good everyday
forced
forced to be something it isn't, not
foreign mouthwash
foreign, tastes
form, right up to
formal, much too
formal, somewhat
formulaic, rather
fortified, heavily

fortified, lightly
foxy
France in a bottle, captures the
  south of
France, lush seductive evocation of
France, yeasty complexity that
  screams
Frankenstein red
fraudulent
freak of nature
freakish
freebooter, elegant
French aromas, some very
  interesting dirty
French characters, dirty
French finesse with robust
  California fruit
French in character, quite
French poodle of a wine:
  prissy...fussy and
  downright snotty
French roast-like
French Sauternes, in the style of
  the best
French wannabe, not a
French, happy-go-lucky
French, haughty and very
French, rather/very
French thing, stinky
French, unmistakably southern
Frenchified smells
French-inspired
French-like burnt match
friends easily, makes
frills or pretensions, no
functional
funny/strange
futuristic
Gallic accent, has a
game, totally different ball
gangbuster
garage, quasi-
garage, ultimate
garargiste
Gatsby
gauche
gauchos and city slickers alike,
  perfect drinking for
gaudy
gender-bender
gender-challenged
Gene Kelly of a wine
generation, next-
generic, awesome
genius
gentleman of pleasure
gentlemanly
genuine item

German dessert wine
German masterpiece
Germanic characters, some
Germanic fruit
Germanic in style, quite
Germanic rosé, very
Germanic, distinctly
Germanic, recognizably
Germanic, very
German-style white
Germany, evokes the sweet stars of
get-together, impromptu
Gewürz character, real
Gewürz, tense
Gewürz, textbook
Gewürztraminer can be,
  spectacular display of all
Gewürztraminer in silk stockings
Giaconda, poor man's
Gigondas typicity, truffley tarry
gimmicky
girl-next-door
girl of fifteen...who is already a
  great artist...coming on tiptoes
  and curtseying herself out with
  childish grace and laughing blue
  eyes
Glenn Miller, charm and good
  manners of
glitzy
global
global taste
globally brilliant
glop, soda-pop
glug, good
gluggable, seriously
glugger, brambly
glugger, sweetish winey
glugger, young
goods, factory
go-to, excellent
goût de lumière
grand cru
Grange, poor man's
Graves moderne
Graves-like
Grecian melodies, earthy
Greco, textbook
Green Giant, wine for the jolly
Grenache flesh, plenty of
  Rubensesque
grotesque
grown-ups, for
growth, classed/classified
growth, first-
growth, second-
gulp, satisfying
gulpability, sheer refreshing

gulpable, very
gusher
gutsy, real in-your-face
guzzler/guzzley
hamburger, fine
handcrafted, fantastically
handed, high-
handmade, painstakingly
handy
hanger-on
happy-go-lucky
harvest, early-
harvest/harvested, dangerously
    late-
harvested, well
harvesty
hat, old
haul wine, long-
Hawaiian shirt of a wine
Hawke's Bay Sauvie, good
headache-inducing/gives
    headaches
headaches, gives me
headachy now, bit
healthy, surprisingly
hear, only wine in the world you
    can
heated, flash-
heavy-duty
Heinz 57 of the wine world
heirloom
Helen of Troy...more like Sharon
    Stone, hardly
Hell's Angels, wine for
helpful
hemisphere, northern-
hemisphere, southern-
Henry VIII red wine-style
heritage, faithful to its
heritage, good
Hessian, virile
high-end
hip as Gucci, as
historical reputation, of
history, like drinking
history, piece of
Hit Parade, not on the
Hitchcock movie, as thrilling as a
hock

Hodgepodge Lodge
holiday table in a bottle
holistic
homegrown/homemade/
    homespun/homey
homely but knowing
homogeneous/homogenized
hopped up
horses for courses

house pour, excellent juicy
house, beach
house, hot-
house, perfect everyday
Hulk Hogan vs. Iron Sheik
Hungarian white, thick brown
Hunter, splendid no-compromise
    old
hussy, brazen
hybrid/hybridized
hyper
Iberian flair
ice, perfect for that big tub of
icebox/refrigerator
icewine, brash side of
icewine, fake
icewine, rare red
icewine, sparkling
icewine, true benchmark
icon/iconic
identifiable
identifiable, not
idiom, in its own
idiosyncratic and fascinating
idiosyncratic but fabulous
idiosyncratic, deliciously
idiosyncratic, distinctly/highly/
    totally/vividly
idiosyncratic, fantastically
imbecilic
imitation
imitator, poor
implausible
important
imported
imported, not
improper
inappropriate
inauthentic
inbred
incognito, frustratingly
incorrect
Incredible Hulk of a wine
independent
indigenous
individual, darkly
individual, quite an
individual, strikingly/very
individual, wondrously
individualistic, highly
individuality personified
individuality, brimming with
individuality, handcrafted
individuality, possesses some
individuality, real
individuality, tremendous
individuality, unclassifiable
individuality, unmatched for

industrial swill
industrial, light and
informal personality, scandalously
informal yet good
inimitable, utterly
innovative
institutional
intergalactic
international blend, innocuous
international flair
international tastes, hasn't sold
    out to
international/internationalized
internationally styled, soulless
intimate
introductory
invalid
inventive
inveterate
in-your-face, quintessential
island, desert
Israeli red
Italian café vibe
Italian fizz, upmarket
Italian flavors, garden of southern
Italian of French wine-styles, one
    of the most
Italian red, Beaujolais-styled
Italian red, gamy robust southern
Italian red, old-style
Italian red, quintessentially
    southern
Italian red, very polished
Italian twist, characteristic
Italian, northern
Italian, quite
Italianate brambly fruit
Italianate nose
Italianate overtones, intriguing
Italianate twigs and bushes,
    flesh covering
Italianate twist
Italianate, unnervingly
Italian-ness, unmistakable
Italian-style oxidation
It-Girl
James Bond kind of wine:
    suave...brawny...smoky... spicy
    and seductive
Janus-headed
jejune
jellied
John Wayne kind of wine
Johnny Cash man-in-black
joker in the pack
Jolly Rancher on steroids
jug, chug-a-lug
jug, mass-produced

jug, old-fashioned
jug, pinkish
juice for adults, happy
Julia Roberts of a Merlot
Kabinett
keyed, low-
key, major
kind, cooing
kind, good of its
kinky
kitschy
kooky
kosher, boiled/cooked
kosher, not bad
lab, made in a/lab-made
label, second-
laced, straight-
ladylike
Lafite Rothschild, classic textbook
Lafite-style, quintessentially
  elegant
laid-back
lakeside sipping, good for
landmark
Landwein
Languedoc, epitomizes the
  wind...sun and herbs of the
laserlike
late-bottled vintage
Latour-like, vaguely Château
Lauren Bacall kind of wine
league, major/minor
left field, way out in
legend/legendary
Levant in a bottle, captures the
  essence of the
Levant-like flavors
lightweight
line confection, assembly-
line, little out of
line, way out of
Linford Christie without his
  jockstrap
liqueur than a wine, more a
local
local oddity
location location location
Loire Valley legend
Loire, taste of the
Loire/Loire-like/Loire-style
loner
love it or hate it, you either
luncheon, perfect light
luncheon, quintessential
lunchtime, agreeable
lunchtime, perfect all-around
luxurious/luxuriousness/luxury
macho

Macon-style
Madeira/Madeira-like
madeover
Maderized
"made", too
mailing-list/mail-order
mainstream, definitely out of the
mainstream, in the
mainstream, well removed
  from the
major
Malbec, full fruit-style of
Malbec, Italianate
manipulation, excessive
manipulation, obsessive flavor
Manischewitz
manufactured not crafted
manufactured, poorly
manufactured, well
Margaux-like
marginal
Marilyn Monroe voluptuousness
market, perfect for the mass
Marlborough Sauvie on steroids
Marlborough Sauvie, classic
Marlborough sunshine, simply
  screams of
marque, grande
marriage of convenience, perhaps a
Marsanne honey
Maui Blanc
maverick, burly
maverick, true
McChardonnay
McCoy, Real
McDonaldized
McPinot
McWine, bland
meal, for a casual midweek
mean, kinda
meaty blend
mediator, perfect
medieval
Mediterranean blend, East meets
  West in this unique
Mediterranean breeze, as
  refreshing as a
Mediterranean breezes and
  sun-dried apricots, daughter of
  blossom-infused
Mediterranean campsite
Mediterranean overtones,
  distinctly
Mediterranean savor, warm juicy
Mediterranean scrubland
Mediterranean south, all the
  perfumes of the
Mediterranean tang

Mediterranean underbrush
Mediterranean winds
Mediterranean, earthy
Mediterranean, trans-
Mediterranean-scented
Mediterranean-style
medley, cleaner...drier...
megared, no
Mendoza fruit ball, your typical
Meritage, puts the merit in
Meritage-blend
Merlot exuberance
Merlot for the faint-hearted, not a
Merlot mania
Merlot on steroids
Merlot varietal character, strong
Merlot, monster
Merlot, muscled
Merlot, off-centered
Merlot, storming southern French
Merlot-style, monumental
Merlowering of standards
Meursault
Meursault in character, very
microchâteau
micromanaged
Middle Eastern flavors
middle of the road, solid
middle-of-the-road red for every
  day affairs, good
Midi, warmth of the
Midi spice, touch of
midmorning, perfect
midnight, very after-
midsummer night's dream
midweek meal, for a casual
midwinter flavors, deep
minibar
minimalism, exercise in
mix, concentrated imperious
mix, coruscating
mobile, definitely upwardly
mock
modern sheen
modern spin
modern, unabashedly
modern-day elixir
modern-day smash-mouth
modernity, essence of smooth if
  somewhat soul-less
modernity, model of enlightened
modern-style red
modish
Mogdigliani than Rubens, more
Mogen David
monovarietal
Montepulciano fruit, dark
mood-lifter, instant

moon, howl-at-the-
Moorish feel
Moscato d'Asti manages it, if it's
    possible to taste a fragrance…
Moselle-like
mountain grown
mountain origins, showcases
mouth and fork
mouthwash, cheap
Mouton, poor man's
mulled
multivineyard
mundane
Muscadelle-like grapiness
"Muscat" at the top of its lungs,
    screams
Muscat, Mr. Skoda's
Muscat, old Australian
Muscat, slightly powdery
muscatel-like grapiness
Muscat-like, almost obscenely
Muscat-scented
Muscatty treacle
museum piece, real
music, bubblegum pop
mysterious
mythical
Napa babes, for
Napa-like, un-
native
natural and unadulterated, very
natural at the table
natural, little too
natural, rigorously righteously all-
Near Eastern pastiche
Nebbiolo on steroids
nebulous
nelly
neophytes, not for
new aesthetic
new generation
New Wave, texture is pure
new wine
New World character
New World cult
New World flashy
New World juice
New World masterpiece
New World smoothies, soft ripe
    fruity
New World standards, big wine
    even by
New World, big red
New World, unabashedly
New Zealand relative, racy
New Zealand, screams
New Zealandy aroma and taste,
    hyperstrong

newcomers, good starting point for
newfangled
Niagara…the other in Burgundy,
    got one foot in
niche
night, for a cold rainy
nightcap, fortified
night-harvested
nights, for autumn
nights, for lazy
nights, for sultry
nights, for wintery
nights, warm embrace for breezy
    beachside
nineteenth-century tastes, for
    those with
nocturnal
nonalcoholic
nonchalant
nonclassic
nonconformist
nondescript
nonentity
nonpareil
nonsipper, defiant
nonsparkling
nonvintage
nonwine, quintessential
nonwinelike, strangely
northern climate
northern hemisphere
notorious
nouveau, yet another
novel
novelty than a great wine,
    more of a
nuanced
nullities, slightly sour
numbers, made by the
nuptial
obscure
obvious, winemaker's fingerprints
    a little too
occasion pour/wine, special-
occasion, for the right
occasion, joyous
occasion, luxurious wine for a
    special
occasion, not only for the right
occasion, terrific pour for a casual
odd notes, some unresolved
odd, bit
odd, very
oddball, total
oddities, parade of
oddity, interesting
odd-man out, something of an
off the wall

offbeat
off-the-beaten-path thrill
off-the-wall
old country, evokes the
old manner, in the
old school
old-fashioned Americana and
    cherry pie, good
old-fashioned but a good 'un, touch
old-fashioned, very
old-fashioned, wonderfully
old-time
old-vine cuvée, irresistible
Old World/Old-World-style
Old-World charm, classic
one-of-a-kind marvel
one-of-a-kind personality, strong
Oregon accent
Oregonian, definitively
organic feel to it, rather an
organic, good-hearted
organically produced
oriental, almost
orientalist fantasy
origin, of noble
origin, robust
original, certainly/highly/
    hugely/truly/utterly/very
original, superbly
originality or terroir, hard to
    detect any
originality, goes beyond mere
originality, unmistakable
origins, proclaims its cool-grown
origins, screams its
origins, wild mountain
orthodox
otherworldly
out from the crowd, stands
out of favor, totally
outdoorsy
outlaw beauty, rugged with
outside the square, falls
outside-the-box
overdressed
overfashionable
overhyped
overmanipulated
overstylized
own drum, moves to the pace of its
oxidative
pace, change of
package, sophisticated
painting-by-numbers feel, slight
paradoxical character
Paris bistro standard
Paris Hilton-esque
park, good for sipping in the

Parkerized
parochial indomitability, exudes a
parody
parties and mind-switched-off
   drinking, for
party animal
party, casual
party, failsafe
party, garden tea
party, great
party, respectable
party, will liven up a cocktail
pasteurized
pastiche, evocative
pastoral
patio
Pauillac defined
Pauillac fruit bomb, hedonistic
Pauillac-style
peasant patriarch, dignified
peasant stock, hardy
peasant, rosy-cheeked
peasants are drinking in that happy
   Breughel, what the
peasanty something
peculiar
pedestrian, boringly
pedigree, ritzy
peers, tastes of its
Peloponnesus in a bottle
pepper pot of a wine
period piece, real
Perlwein
pickling onions, good for
picnic, just right for an Indian-
   summer
picnic, roadside
picnic, summer
picnic, tart
picnic, ultimate
picnic, year-round
Piedmontese typicity, plenty of
Piedmont's juice bomb
Piesporter, not a cheap sugar-and-
   water
piña colada
pink quaff, simple
pink, naughtiness in a glass of
pink, sweetened-up pale
Pinot, Frankenstein
Pinocity, has
Pinot Blah, anything but
Pinot envy
Pinot fragrance, heavenly almost
   theatrical
Pinot Grigio with a brain
Pinot Grigio, Lamborghini of a
Pinot Gris, rococo variation on

Pinot Gris's homely Eliza Doolittle
   personality into My Fair Lady
   with some success, tries like
   Henry Higgins to boost
Pinot intrigue
Pinot is all about, this is what
Pinot Noir fruit, dark brooding
Pinot Noir in character, somewhat
Pinot Noir silky
Pinot Noir sounds like an
   oxymoron, full-bodied
Pinot Noir that isn't ashamed
   to be itself
Pinot Noir, card-carrying
Pinot Noir, if a wine could make a
   person cry it would have to be a
Pinot Noir, nice old red rather than
   a nice old
Pinot Noir-like, almost
Pinot perfection
Pinot to a T, cool-climate
Pinot to write home about
Pinot with a woody
Pinot with attitude
Pinot with training wheels
Pinot, caricature of
Pinot, fishy
Pinot, Frankenstein
Pinot, none of the wildness of great
Pinot, rooty
Pinot, stewed old
Pinot, sweet rich roasted old
Pinotage
Pinot-esque, tannins are distinctly
Pinot in-old-socks, warm
Pinot Noir-esque, downright
Pinotphiles, will satisfy
Pinots, does not sing like the best
pizza, perfect
place from which it comes,
   speaks eloquently of the
place in a bottle, sense of
place in spades, sense of
place, brimming with a sense of
place, can taste a
place, dazzling expression of
place, gorgeously fruity expression
   of
place, intense/strong sense of
place, mystical sense of
place, real sense of
place, speaks of its
plain, pretty
plain, tending
plain/plain vanilla
plate, cheese
please wine lovers…not wine
   writers, made to

plebian
Pomerol bliss, pure
Pomerol, internationally styled
Pomerol, picnic
Pommard, echoing
poncy
poolside sipping, thirst-quenching
pop, everyday
popular for good reason
popular, gruesomely
porch
portlike structure, big
port on toast
Portuguese personality,
   unmistakable
pour, everyday
pour, house
pour, restaurant
practical
prehistoric granny's drink
preordained
presence, real
preservative-free
prevalent
primeur
primitive
Priorat, epitome of backyard
private
private reserve
processed
processed, overly
product, fruit-flavored
proper
proprietary, textbook
prototype/prototypical
provenance, geographical
provenance, submerged
Provençal aspect, warm
Provençal dryness and herbiness,
   expensive ineffably
Provençal, distinctly
Provence in a bottle
Provence, air of
Provence, liqueur of
provincial
psychedelic, practically
pudding, not a
puddle
pungency, little streak of
purebred
purist, for the
purpose, all-
pushy
quaff, buy-and-
quaff, coarse unsophisticated
quaff, juicy
quaff, simple pink
quaffability, thirst-quenching

quaffable, pleasantly
quaffer, pleasant critter
quaffer, summer
quaffer, very moreish
quaffing, light fruity
quaffing, perfectly suited to
  uncritical
quaffing, youthful
quaint
queen Champagne, snow-
quencher/quenching
quickie, light
quintessential
quirkiness
quirks, full of/quirky
Rabelaisian occasions, for
radar, under the
radical
ragtag
Rambo Champagne
rancio
razor range, not at all in the
  cut-throat
ready-to-wear bottling
real
real-world
recognizable
red biddy
red for wimps, not a
red giant, jolly
red ink
Red Ned
red on the scale of Mount
  Rushmore
red painted black
red rather than a nice old Pinot
  Noir, nice old
red that pulls no punches
red to drink with enthusiasm,
  succulent outdoorsy
red wine, workman's
red wine can do, does everything a
red wine lover's nose on a
  white wine, big
red with everything, sturdy
  suggestive
red, amazingly delicious
red, animated
red, attractive commercial
red, balls-out
red, big beefy palate-coating
red, big bold
red, big butch
red, big winter
red, big-on-fruit...soft-on-tannin
red, bistro-styled
red, black-as-night
red, blockbuster blended

red, blue-chip
red, blunt
red, brooding
red, bruiser of a
red, burly southern
red, bushy-tail
red, charred berry-laden
red, cheap holiday
red, cherry-berry cocktail
red, chewy
red, classic/classy
red, concept
red, cracking
red, decadent
red, delicious everyday
red, don't-worry-be-happy
red, durable
red, everyday/everynight
red, expressive
red, feasting
red, flagship
red, flavor-packed
red, fresh keen flashy
red, fruit-driven/fruit-rich/fruity
red, fruit-to-the-max
red, fruity come-and-get-me
red, full
red, full-blast country
red, funky
red, gamey robust southern Italian
red, gentlemanly
red, good choice for house
red, good dark rasping
red, good wine-bar
red, great wintertime
red, gut-rot/rot-gut
red, heady raging
red, hedonistic
red, high-octane
red, holistic lie-back-and-pour-it -
  down-my-throat-
red, honest no-nonsense
red, hot-country
red, house
red, huge/monster/
  powerhouse/turbocharged
red, ideal spaghetti
red, ideal trattoria
red, idiosyncratic
red, inky
red, in-your-face
red, juicy
red, keenly edged dark fruit
red, light mountain
red, lip-smacking
red, lodestar Australian
red, lunch/lunchtime
red, macho

red, marquee
red, memorable
red, middleclass
red, model
red, modern-style
red, new-combination
red, new-direction
red, new-fashioned
red, new-millennium
red, new-wave
red, nightmare
red, no-nonsense
red, *nouveau*-style
red, on the verge of being a
  world-class
red, palatial
red, perfect everyday
red, plain ol'
red, pleasant commercial
red, plush
red, polished
red, possibly the greatest
red, potent winter
red, powerhouse
red, rather old-style
red, raucous
red, revival oaked
red, rich fully oaked corpulent
red, richly structured
red, ripe juicy
red, roasted
red, sensual and seductive
red, serious
red, sexy
red, simply gluggable sweetish
red, soft smooth
red, soulful
red, southern-smelling
red, spaghetti
red, stick-to-your-ribs
red, student-friendly
red, super-duper
red, superendowed
red, supermarket
red, supple and fruity by-the-case
red, thumping good plummy
red, top-end/-shelf
red, unabashedly drink-now
red, unpretentious
red, vegan-friendly
red, very virile
red, warming
red, wham-bam-thank-you-ma'am
red, wintery
red, workhorse
red, workmanlike
refreshment, casual
refreshment, lip-smacking

regime, traditional
region well, serves its
regional character, strong
regional charm, Neanderthal
regional dark chocolate, twitch of
regional definition, excellent/
    superb
regional distinctiveness
regional earth and tar
regional earthy underlay
regional elements
regional inflections, meaty-earthy
regional provenance, shows all the
    hallmarks of
regional provenance, strong
regional wine, commonness of a
regional, wonderfully
regionally authentic
regionally representative
regular
regular, not your
release, early-
release, late-
release, library
release, reserve
relic of the (WWII) war, real
renaissance
renegade appeal
representative, regionally
resemblance, family
reserve, lean
reserve, private
reserve, single-barrel
restaurant
retsina
revolutionary
Rhenish, reduced
Rhine maidens, wine for
    Wagnerian
Rhine or Rhône...whatever
Rhône in flavors
Rhône in style, very northern
Rhône look-a-like, blockbuster
    New World
Rhône Ranger special
Rhône Ranger-ish
Rhône typicity, undeniable
    southern
Rhône Valley characters, strong
Rhône Valley red, northern
Rhône, as fresh as a breeze
    sweeping through the lavender-
    scented hills of this southern
Rhône-ish slant
Rhône-ish, distinctly/quite
Rhône-like beef blood
Rhône-like leather component,
    northern

Rhône-like spices
Rhônish charm, warm spicy
Rhônish, distinctly
rice
Riesling [in Australia] is the
    Barbie doll
Riesling icewine, paint-by-
    numbers
Riesling just feels health, drinking
    this
Riesling kerosene-type aromas,
    some quasi-
Riesling on steroids, German
Riesling regular or unleaded
Riesling, all the stones of the world
    find their unique voice with
Riesling, electric
Riesling, Sauvignon Blanc-like
Riesling, upstate variety...mostly
Riesling, well-honed
Riesling-heavy blend
Riesling-like delicacy
Right Bank
Rioja defined, traditional
Rioja in brash form, big-time
    modern
Rioja is all about, what
Ripple
Rita Hayworth, the 1940s' red-
    headed pin-up girl...the slim yet
    curvaceous
ritzy
road, middle-of-the-
roadhouse
rock music, vinous equivalent of
rock 'n roll in a glass
rococo
Rolls-Royce of a wine
romance and candlelight, not for
Romanée-Conti of Barolo
roots, reveling in its
rosado, one delicious
rosé de saignée
rosé in full bloom
rosé to drink out of a woman's
    slipper, simple
rosé with attitude
rosé, barely
rosé, bog-standard
rosé, boilerplate
rosé, cherry-stuffed
rosé, crisp hum of a good
rosé, high-octane
rosé, one-night
rosé, serious
rotgut, flawed
rotgut, real
rotmouth

rough and ready
rough-hewn, somewhat
routine
rubbish
Rubens heroine
Rubens sur la Loire
Rubens, more Mogdigliani than
Rubensesque woman in her
    flower bed
Rubens-like vivacity
run-of-the-mill, boring
rural smells
rustic and proud of it
rustic and rusty
rustic and stringy
rustic breed
rustic country bumpkin
rustic edge, sharp
rustic grunt
rustic heritage
rustic maplelike-edge
rustic masterpiece
rustic perfection
rustic pleasure
rustic richness with some modern
    touches
rustic romp, real
rustic vigor
rustic wild edge
rustic yet elegant
rustic, coarsely
rustic, not at all
rustic, seductively
rustic, supremely
rustic, verging on the
rusticana, pure
rustic-barnyard
rusticity, down-home
rusticity, elegant
rusticity, leathery
rusticity, meaty
Saar austerity
sacramental wine...although I
    wouldn't want to attend the
    church that served it
safari
safe
saignée
salad, ambrosial
samey, rather
sample, barrel
Sancerre, almost like
Sancerre, glistening
Sancerre, pungency of a
Sangiovese drives the boat while
    Merlot navigates
sangria material
sanitized

sardine
Sassicaia-esque nobility
Sassicaia-style, in the
Sauternes, cousin of
Sauternes, essence of
Sauternes-like
sauvage spark, just misses out on that
sauvage, touch of wild
Sauvignon Blanc, dessert-style
Sauvignon Blanc, easy style of
Sauvignon Blanc, stereotypical
Sauvignon spectrum, extreme red gooseberry end of the
savage, bit of a
savage/*sauvage*
savagery, potential for
savor on its own, to
scamp
scary
schlock, low-end
scholastic
school, old-
scoring, high-
Scotch, looks like
Scotsman, character of a dour
screwtop
scuppernong funkiness
scuppernongy
Sean Connery in the making
Sean Connery kind of wine
seasonal
seasonal rotation, interesting foil for a
second
second, super
second-fiddle-/-label-/-tier
seduction, proper wine to serve at a
seductress, dark
Sekt
select/selective
sélection des grains nobles
Sémillon spectrum, baroque end of the
Sémillon with attitude
serious
serious, not too/very
serviceable
sexy red, deeply
sham

Shanghai T'ang
shape-shifter
sherried, slightly
sherrylike nuttiness
Shiraz and the sea, song of a
Shiraz can out-sumo that of a Barossa, monster
Shiraz for masochists, old-style

Shiraz representative, can bat for the planet as the
Shiraz with the volume turned down
Shiraz, big-framed
Shiraz, cool-climate
Shiraz, flexible
Shiraz, not benchmark
Shiraz, surreal otherworldly styled
Shiraz, syrup of
Shiraz, yardstick

Shirazes, the Merlot of
Shiraz-style
show-off, bit of a
show-off, good
showy, extremely
Shrek of a wine
Sicilian dessert in a bottle, exotic
sickly
signature aromas
signature stink
signature, clean satisfying
sipper, basically a simple fruit-cocktaily
sipper, best winter
sipper, dandy/fine/pleasing
sipper, delicious/tasty after-dinner
sipper, ethereal after-dinner
sipper, everynight
sipper, grapefruit-flavored summer
sipper, in no sense a cute little
sipper, lean
sipper, nice 'n' easy
sipper, nice summertime
sipper, no casual
sipper, not a bad
sipper, old
sipper, perfect brunch
sipper, routine
sipper, serious
sipping at the end of a meal, ideal for
sipping for UFO patrols on summer nights, perfect
sipping, afterdinner
sipping, casual/easy
sipping, for poolside
sipping, ideal for sofa
sipping, perfect for midmorning
site-specific
sleeve, quickly evolving heart-on-
slick
slinky
slippers, certainly not the stuff for chorus girls'
snob
Soave universe, master of the
Soave, not your grandmother's

soil, fine expression of the
soil, quintessence of this great
soil, secret memories of the
soil, true to its
solo mode, slam-it-down-fast
something it isn't, not forced to be
sophisticated
sound-treated
South Sea flavors, zany
south, sunny ripeness of the
southerly feel, distinctly
southerly juice
southern climate
southern hemisphere
southern sensation, supple spicy
southern swill
southern twang
spaghetti western, quintessential
spaghetti, Italian-style
Spain, taste of old-world

Spanish bebop
Spanish holiday red
Spanish mold
Spanish roots
Spanish, authentically/very
sparkler to fall in love with
sparkler, appley
sparkler, big delicious
sparkler, bigger-style
sparkler, cheerless
sparkler, classy
sparkler, full-throttled
sparkler, hugely structured
sparkler, red
sparkler, reliable
Spätlese-style, almost a rich
special, punter's
special, rather
Spice Islands flavors
splashy
spoofalated/spoofulated
sporty
spring in a bottle, late
springtime charmer, lovely
springy
St.-Émilion fruit bomb, hedonistic
St.-Émilion, textbook
standard, torrid
standards, meets international
standby for a quality dry white, cast-iron
standby, good home consumption
standby, good old
starting point for newcomers, good
statesmanlike
steel-conditioned
Stepford wine, laboratory-concocted

sticky school, from the thick-and-
sticky, clean
sticky, full-throttle
sticky, heavy-duty
sticky, one-of-a-kind
sticky, stunningly original
still
stink, signature
stop, pit-
stop, truck-
store, convenience-
storied
straightforward
strained
strange and strained
strange, quite/rather
strange, stranger than
straw-wrapped
street, high
stressed/stressful
stretching the bounds a bit
stuff, archetypal copybook
stuff, frat-boy
stuff, love-it-or-leave-it
stuff, lovely glugging
stuff, low-end
stuff, syrupy sweet pink
style and dash, plenty of
style built for the long haul
style claret, picnic-
style down, hard to pin a typical
style evolved-
style feel, old-
style for the modern palate, old-
style gyrations, seems to go
    through extreme
style here, guile and
style honed to perfection
style mainstream, in the
style one is dumbfounded,
    so pure in
style red, modern-
style red, *nouveau*-
style slot, right in the
style spectrum, at the big bold end
    of the
style to highlight fruit, made in a
style with finesse, ultraripe
style with humor
style you either love or hate
style, aberrational-
style, abrasive-
style, acme of
style, aggressive animal-
style, all-
style, almost a rich Spätlese-
style, altogether austere-
style, an all-duck or no-dinner-

style, ancient-/archaic-/old-/old-
    fashioned-/retro-/traditional-
style, animal-
style, apéritif-
style, approaching a sec in
style, archetypal Tasmanian-
style, archetype of the modern-
style, artisanal-
style, attention-getting-
style, austere classic-
style, average unwooded-
style, baroque-
style, Battlestar Galactica-
style, beguiling flavorsome-
style, big chunky full-on-
style, big modern-
style, big ultraripe
style, big walloping oak-
style, big-hitting
style, big-is-beautiful-
style, bistro-
style, bittersweet-
style, blatant-
style, blender-
style, blowsy-
style, bold-
style, bone-dry-
style, boots-and-all-
style, brash-
style, brasserie summer-
style, broodingly backward-
style, burly old-
style, busty fruity-
style, buttery-
style, café-
style, challenging-
style, citric grapefruity-
style, claret-
style, classic-
style, classic ageworthy-
style, classic show-
style, classic *sotto-voce* Tasmanian-
style, classical regional
style, cold-climate-
style, complex-
style, complex worked-
style, compressed-
style, confrontational
style, confronting-
style, confronting drier-
style, conservative-
style, contemporary-/modern-/
    new-
style, cool-grown
style, corpulent fat-
style, country-/rustic-
style, craftsmanlike-
style, crisp apéritif-

style, crunchy-
style, cut-and-thrust-
style, dazzling-
style, dead-set cellar-door-
style, decadent extracted-
style, determinedly alternative-
style, disarming-
style, distinctive-
style, drink-me-up-
style, drop-dead cellar-door-
style, drop-dead easy-drinking-
style, dry-
style, dry ultralight-
style, dyed-in-the-wool early
    drinking-
style, dying-
style, earlier-harvested-
style, early drinking-
style, easily enjoyed-
style, easy-to-drink classic-
style, eerily Germanic-
style, effortless-
style, emphatic drink-now
style, English-
style, epic
style, especially saturated
    aggressive-
style, estate-
style, evolved-
style, exceedingly long-lived-
style, excellent cellaring-
style, excellent lunch-
style, exceptional expression of the
style, explosive flamboyant-
style, extraordinarily plush-
style, extravagant overwhelming-
style, extreme-
style, fantastic flair and
style, far less fat-
style, fast-developing-
style, feminine-
style, finesse-
style, fino sherrylike-
style, firm adroit-
style, fist-in-the-face-
style, flamboyant-
style, flavor-packed-
style, fleshy-
style, free-flowing-
style, fresh yet intense-
style, freshest crispest fruity-
style, fruit-driven-
style, fruit-saturated-
style, full serious-
style, full-blooded show-
style, full-blown international-
style, full-bodied peaches and
    cream

style, full-frontal-
style, garish ostentatious-
style, gaudy-
style, gentle-
style, gentle low-acid-
style, good attempt at
style, gorgeous-
style, graceful-
style, grand-
style, hard to pin down a typical
style, hauntingly beautiful-
style, heartland-
style, heavy-handed-
style, hedonistic-
style, hefty warm-area-
style, heroic-
style, high-cheekbone-
style, highly extracted barrique-
 aged-
style, high-pitched-
style, hock-
style, house-
style, hyperconcentrated-
style, incredibly acidic apple cider-
style, intensity...structure and
style, international-
style, in-your-face-
style, irresistible show-
style, juicy fruit lip-smacking-
style, lacelike-
style, lean-
style, least imitable wine-
style, left field-
style, less coarse modern-
style, leviathan-
style, light apéritif-
style, light...easy-to-enjoy-
style, light-/lightish-
style, lighter easy pleasant drink-
 now-
style, long-lasting cellaring-
style, love-it-or-hate-it-
style, low PH
style, lushly textured-
style, macho-
style, made with dash and
style, mainstream-
style, marked baroque
style, massively powerful in-your-
 face
style, maturation-
style, medieval-
style, meditation-
style, milkshake-
style, minimalist-
style, modern-
style, modern Napa-esque-
style, modicum of

style, monumental-/very big-
style, more elegant than brash in
style, mountain-
style, nearly over-the-top-
style, neat-
style, new organic-
style, nice seafood-
style, no-
style, no-frills-
style, no-holds-barred-
style, no-nonsense-
style, northern-
style, not-too-heavy-
style, *nouveau*-
style, oak-kissed-
style, old-fashioned moribund-
style, opposite of more-is-better-
style, opulent richly oaked Cal-
style, ostentatious-
style, out of the mainstream-
style, outdoor-
style, outstanding-/superior-
style, overblown-
style, over-the-top-
style, overworked buttery-
style, pedestrian-
style, Peter Pan-
style, pleasant unoaked-
style, plumcake-
style, pop-
style, positively hedonistic-
style, powerful punchy-
style, precocious-
style, precocious flattering-
style, preserved-
style, pretty pretty-
style, protectively made-
style, public fruity-
style, puppyishly friendly
 California-
style, purist-/purity of
style, quasimodern-
style, quasitraditional-
style, quicker-developing-
style, quite a worked-
style, quite distinctive-
style, quite dramatic and
 rambunctious-
style, razorlike-
style, real sunny-holiday-
style, relatively light-bodied
 luncheon-café-
style, restrained-
style, Rhône Ranger-
style, rich-
style, rich drink-now-
style, rich round regional-
style, right out of

style, *ripasso*-
style, riper drink-now-
style, ripe sun-drenched-
style, roasted-
style, Rothschild-
style, rough-hewn-
style, rumbustious riproaring-
style, *sauvage*-
style, savory flesh upfront-
style, seductive-
style, serious-
style, seriously extracted-
style, shallow washed-out-
style, shellfish-
style, shimmering steel-fermented-
style, show-stopper-
style, signature-
style, singing in
style, simple raw oyster-
style, somewhat unpolished
style, southern-
style, spaghetti-
style, spread-out-
style, streamlined-
style, strong thumbprint of house-
style, successful drink-now-
style, superbly eccentric-
style, super*cuvée*-
style, superendowed-
style, supersweet-
style, superwrought Alsatian-
style, take-no-prisoners-
style, tannic brightly acidic-
style, teddy bear-
style, tender-/*tendre*-
style, tending tadpole in
style, thick milkshake-
style, tougher adult-
style, traditional fruity-
style, truly over-the-top-
style, underpowered-
style, understated-
style, unforced-
style, unforgettable-
style, unimpeachable
style, unorthodox savory-
style, up-front precocious-
style, user-friendly-
style, usual extremity of
style, utterly seductive
style, utterly unique
style, vaguely round-but-crisp-
style, vegetal oak-free-
style, very big-
style, very corporate in
style, very indelicate-
style, very ripe fat-
style, welcoming-

style, well-muscled-
style, wild and naughty-
style, wishy-washy-
style, worked-
style, youthful drinking-
styled claret, picnic-
styled to drink young
styled, massively
styled, soul-less internationally
styleless
styles, most sumptuous of
styles, threads the needle between the traditional and modern
stylish and boring
stylish personality
stylish to be decadent, too
stylish, altogether/ever-so-
stylish, ever-so-
stylish, less than
stylish, supremely
stylish, very emphatically
stylish--*sotto voce*
stylistic groove, still to find its
stylistic, very
stylistically in the right ballpark
stylized, overly
sugar daddy
Sugar Ray of a wine
sugar water, dismal
sui generis, entirely
summer afternoon, perfect for a
summer cookout in a bottle
summer drink, appealing
summer drinking, great
summer evenings, ideal/just right for
summer fling, anything but a simple
summer floral flavors, late-
summer gulper, ideal
summer heat away, chases the
summer house
summer nights, made for pleasurable
summer picnic
summer refresher, fabulous
summer standard, perfect
summer staple
summer supper
summer wine, compelling
summer wine, utterly thirst-quenching
summer, cheerful
summer, great for
summer, great house wine for
summer, hot
summer, ideal
summer, Indian

summer, light-hearted
summer, screams
summer, will keep you cool in deepest
summer, will refresh even the doggiest days of
summery charm, straightforward
summery intermezzo, perfect
summery than wintry, more
summery-smelling
sun
superbubbly
supercontemporary
superexclusive
superexotic
superinternational
supermarket
supermarket fantasy
superpremium
supersecond
supertraditional
super-Tuscan(ville)
sup-me-quick
supper, after-theater
swan, graceful
swan, regal
swashbuckling
Swedish fish
sweetie, crystal-clear little lime
swigable
swillable
swiller, Sunday afternoon
swimming pool
Swiss chocolate
Swiss precision in a bottle
Sylvaner, indescribable something one gets from good
Sylvaner, sly
symbiotic, truly
synthetic berrylike fruitiness, almost
synthetic, awfully
synthetic, nice but
synthetically fruity
synthetic-fruity
Syrah as chocolate
Syrah bacony aroma
Syrah bliss, pure
Syrah for a Sunday, spicy
Syrah fruit, bursting with
Syrah liqueur
Syrah masterpiece
Syrah, granite-grown
Syrah, textbook
Syrah, very un-
Syrah, wild-eyed
table, generic
table, poorly vinified

table, sturdy
table, well-vinified
Tafelwein
Tahiti, one sip is like a trip to
tango, evoking the music and dance of the
tanker
tankerful, probably made by the
Tasmanian acidity
Tasmanian-style, true
Tassie, typical
taste, nine-to-five
taste, something of an acquired
tastes, main street
tastes, nineteenth-century
tastes, popular
teaching, could be used for
tears, without
teatime, perfect spring-summer midmorning-late morning
tech, high-
technical
temperate
Tempranillo-ish
terrace
Teutonic accent, slight
Teutonic heaviness, normal
Teutonic, significantly less
textbook drinkability
textbook example/stuff
textbook rendition
theater, after-
thing, happy little
thing, lovely old
thing, the real
things light and summery, epitome of
things-to-all-men, all-
thinking required, no
throwaway
throwback to times past
throwback, quite a
thumbprint of earth's maker
Thunderbird
tie, black-
Tiffany of wines
tin-shack, obscure
tipple, exotic
tipple, old fart's
Tokaji-like
Tokay, maltlike
Tokay, oil of
Toscana-/Toscano-like
tourist/touristy
town, comes from the bad side of
tradesmanlike
traditional, hopelessly
transitional

trap, tourist
traveled, well
trends, immune to
trendsetters, must-have for
trendy
trick, hat-
tricked up, not
trickster, bit of a
tricky
Trocken
Trockenbeerenauslese
troika, lush
trollop
trophy
tropical richness
tropical, mildly
truck stop
true
true-to-form
tsunami only to die before it hits
   the beach, built like a
tub, hot-
Tuscan elixir belongs in the papal
   treasury
Tuscan red ever, perhaps the
   greatest
Tuscan red, good down-home
Tuscan red, inky coastal
Tuscan soil
Tuscan titan
Tuscan wine world, lion of the
Tuscan-style, unique
Tuscanville, Super
Tuscany, evokes visions of
Tuscany, monument to
type, appropriate/correct/true to
type, extrovert
type, fun-and-games
type, sweet frothy
typical plum-tomato aromas
typical, not your
typical, utterly
typical, village-
typicity in a bottle
typicity, extreme
typicity, good regional
typicity, great raisiny
typicity, has both varietal and
   regional
typicity, little varietal
typicity, plenty of Piedmontese
typicity, striking in its
typicity, textbook
typicity, very pronounced
überhip
ubiquitous
ultraconservative
ultrafashionable

ultramodern
ultrasoft
ultratraditional
ultratypical
ultrauser-friendly
Umbrian
unacceptable, commercially
unauthentic
unblended
uncharacteristic
uncharacteristically hollow
uncivilized mouthful
uncivilized, almost
unclassic
uncommon
uncommon treat
unconventional
unconventionally appealing
uncultured
underrated
undistinctive
unfamiliar
unfamiliar grapes, made from all
   sorts of
unfancy, utterly
unfashionable, all but completely
unfashionable, deeply/resolutely/
   totally
unfashionable, fantastically
unfashionable, well beyond
unfiltered
unfined
unflashy
unforced
unfortified
unfussy
ungrapey
unidentified
uniform and boring
uniform, perfectly
unique, absolutely/
   unquestionably/
   utterly/wonderfully
unique, big pull on palates eager
   for the
universal
unknowable/unknown
unmanipulated as possible, as
unmanipulated, clearly
unmanufactured
unmatchable/unmatched
unmistakable
un-natural
unoriginal
unorthodox
unponcy
unpretentious
unrefined

unrepresentative
unserious, delightfully
unshowy
unstylish
unsuitable
untamed flavors
untraditional
untrendy, deliberately
untrendy, incredibly
untrue
untypical rusticity
untypically baked
untypically sweet and fruity
unusual and not to everyone's taste
unusual but compelling
unusual, far from
unusual...unique, not just
unvarietal
unwiney
unworked, relatively
up-and-coming
up-and-down
upmarket
upper class/crust
uppermost
upscale
uptown
upwardly mobile, definitely
urban
urbane
useful, more than
useful, terribly
useless for drinking
user-friendly mouthful
user-friendly personality
user-friendly, least
usual feckless charmer, not the
usual
usual, not your
usual, well away from the
utilitarian
vampish
varietal acacia blossoms
varietal almonds
varietal appeal, accurate
varietal aromas, excellent
varietal aromas, richish
varietal authenticity, unexpected
varietal blackberries
varietal breed, true
varietal but enjoyable, not terribly
varietal character is spot-on
varietal character par excellence
varietal character somewhat
   blurred
varietal character, bell-clear
varietal character, bit shy on/lacks
varietal character, excellent/great

varietal character, expressive
varietal character, impeccable
varietal character, losing
varietal character, overt
varietal character, strong Merlot
varietal character, unforced
varietal characteristic gaudiness
varietal cherries
varietal correctness, hits the spot
   perfectly for
varietal curiosity
varietal definition
varietal delineation, excellent
varietal dry leaves
varietal earth, substrate of
varietal expectation, falls within
varietal expression/personality,
   good
varietal fish oil
varietal focus, no
varietal fruit, delicate
varietal fruit, incisive
varietal grassiness
varietal intensity, great
varietal markers, no
varietal musk
varietal nose, positive
varietal punch, lacks
varietal purity, exquisite
varietal purity, intense
varietal purity, revelatory
varietal raspberries
varietal spectrum, flooded with
   fruit at the sweet end of the
varietal spicy edge, pronounced
varietal tang and cut, good
varietal taste, no
varietal taste, real out-there
varietal tendencies, classic
varietal unripe cherries
varietal viscosity
varietal voyeurs, for
varietal zestiness
varietal, character
varietal, dull staple
varietal, fighting
varietal, funky
varietal, if nothing else is certainly
varietal, less direct
varietal, mineral
varietal, not overtly/particularly
varietal, off-putting
varietal, partially
varietal, quintessentially
varietal, quite
varietal, regional
varietal, relatively unfashionable
varietal, stand-alone

varietal, strongly
varietal, tooth-smacking
varietal, unashamedly
varietal, workhorse
varietally correct
varietally distinct/distinctive
varietally expressive
varietally incorrect
varietally precise
varietally pure
varietally true
varietally, nonspecific
varietal's characteristic gaudiness
varietals, kitchen-sink assemblage
   of seven
varieties, blend of
variety, 100% pure expression of
   the
variety, almost a paradigm of its
variety, common/garden
variety, love-it-or-leave-it
variety, named
variety, near-perfect rendition of
   the
vendage tardive
Veneto in perfect pitch, sings the
   praises of the
Verdelho with attitude
Verdicchio dressed by Valentino
village character
vin biologique
vin blanc
vin de café
vin de coupage
vin de garage
vin de garde
vin de glace
vin de l'année
vin de liqueur
vin de merde
vin de messe
vin de paille
vin de pays
vin de plaisir
vin de table
vin de voile
vin demisec
vin d'honneur
vin doux naturel
vin fou
vin grand
vin gris
vin jaune
vin mousseux
vin moustillant
vin naturel
vin noir
vin nouveau

vin ordinaire
vin rosé
vin rouge
vin santo
vin sauvage
vin sec
vin terroité
vin, grand
vin, ouvert
vin, petit
vina typica
vine/viney, old
viney, old-
vineyard, essence of the
vineyard, liquefied expression of its
vineyard, redolent of the
vinho de mesa
vinho regional
vino bianco/blanco
vino clarete
vino corriente
vino crudo
vino da dessert
vino da meditazione
vino da tavola
vino de aguja
vino de la tierra
vino de la/della casa
vino de mesa
vino de pasto
vino del país
vino dolce/dulce
vino espumante/espumoso
vino frizzante
vino jovens
vino locale
vino nero
vino novello
vino peleón
vino rosado/rosato/rosé/rosso
vino rustico
vino santo
vino secco/seco
vino tinto
vino, local
vino, serious
vinous equivalent of the
   emasculated salutation
   "Happy Holidays"
vintage character in spades,
   reflects the
vintage smells and tastes, hot-
vintage variation, seemingly
   unaffected
vintage-typical buttery fruit
Viognier, restrained
VIW (Very Important Wine)
warm-weather winner

weather pour, refreshing warm-
whistle-wetter, great preprandial
white wine jewel
white, amiable everyday
white, classic transitional
white, coastal
white, easy-drinking
white, elevenses
white, fancy
white, flavorful island
white, flighty
white, fruit-pump
white, fun
white, happiest
white, high-altitude dry
white, ideal nonthreatening
  cocktail
white, lip-smacking
white, mushy aimless
white, no-nonsense
white, old sweet
white, revved-up Harley of
white, richly structured
white, seafood
white, simple cocktail
white, wild
white, workhorse
white, world-class
wild side, walking on the
wine appropriate for any sort of
  simple occasion
wine as if painted by Gustav Klimt:
  mysterious...gilded and
  unforgettable
wine beyond the pale
wine candy
wine cooler
wine fills the mouth, hulking
wine for a nightgown, night
wine for a special occasion, special
wine for brunches and hot tubs,
  perfect
wine for Christmas Day at the
  whaling station
wine for collectors only
wine for everyone to love
wine for hard-core bikers
wine for lazy summer days, nifty
  hammock
wine for macho men
wine for neophytes, not a
wine for polar explorers
wine for romantic late-summer
  evenings in the sunset, perfect
wine for that special occasion, epic
wine for the cocktail hour
wine for the curmudgeonly, not a

wine for the mass palate,
  cookie-cutter
wine for Wagnerian Rhine
  maidens
wine for well-to-do gypsies
wine in our plastic cup at the
  beach, we want this
wine in the world, most idiot-proof
wine in vogue/voguish
wine lite
wine not for beginners
wine of a genius
wine of heaven and earth
wine of individuality
wine of little character...no matter
  how well made, homogenized
  indistinct
wine of no pretension
wine of the day
wine of yore, blackstrap
wine par excellence, pizza-party-
  picnic
wine perfect for an afternoon
  dalliance
wine pour, natural summerhouse
wine product, tasted like a
wine sea change
wine that dolls might drink, toy
wine that sings, white dessert
wine to contemplate with each sip
wine to defeat experts
wine version, new-wave
wine with all the winemaker's
  artifice, developed worked
wine with everything
wine with perfect pitch, musical
wine without character,
  commercial
wine you could use to fill a
  fountain pen, sort of
wine you want to marry, kind of
wine, "Juicy Lucy" easy-come-easy-
  go kind of
wine, "wow"
wine, aberrant/aberrational
wine, abnormal
wine, absolutely/utterly atypical
wine, academic
wine, adulterated
wine, adventurous
wine, affected
wine, afterdinner sipping
wine, airline/airplane
wine, alien
wine, all-things-to-all-men sort of
wine, altar
wine, altered
wine, ambidextrous

wine, ambiguous
wine, American wrestling version
  of a smack-down
wine, amphora
wine, ancient vine
wine, anonymous
wine, any-day favorite
wine, aphrodisiac
wine, apocryphal
wine, appropriate/apropos
wine, apt
wine, arbor
wine, arcane
wine, archaic
wine, archetypical
wine, archetypical bitter chocolate
  fruit
wine, Arnold Schwarzenegger-like
wine, aromatized
wine, artful/artistic/arty
wine, artifact
wine, artisan/artisanal/artisanal-
  tasting
wine, art-opening
wine, assembly-line
wine, avant-garde
wine, Bach-like
wine, backcountry
wine, backseat
wine, back-to-basics
wine, bag-in-a-box
wine, barbaric/barbarous
wine, barbecue/barbeque/BBQ
wine, barrel-worked
wine, base
wine, batty
wine, beach
wine, beach-blanket
wine, beachcombed
wine, beginner's
wine, belly-button
wine, best-foot-forward
wine, better than basic
wine, big floozy in-your-face
wine, big hairy
wine, big red wine lover's nose
  on a white
wine, bimbo
wine, biodynamic/*biodynamie/
  biologique/biologico/biologisch*
wine, bit wacky
wine, bit weird
wine, blackberry or raspberry fruit
wine, black-tie
wine, bladderbox/bladder pack
wine, blanc de blancs
wine, blanc de noir
wine, bling

wine, blokey
wine, blush
wine, bog-standard
wine, bogus
wine, boilerplate
wine, bourgeois
wine, boutique
wine, box/boxed/carton/cartoned
wine, branded
wine, brasserie bulls-eye
wine, British
wine, brave little
wine, bubblegum
wine, bulk
wine, bull-in-a-china-shop
wine, burlesque of a
wine, bush vine
wine, business, all-/businesslike
wine, butch
wine, buttered fruit-salad
wine, buy-and-quaff
wine, BYO (Bring Your Own)
wine, Byzantine
wine, California cult
wine, canned/tinned
wine, canoe

wine, caricature
wine, carnivore's
wine, casual
wine, casual celebration
wine, casual porch-sippin'
wine, casual refreshment
wine, ceremonial
wine, chancy
wine, changeable
wine, chaptalized
wine, chillable
wine, clean scintillating lemon
   squeeze of a
wine, clinical
wine, Coca-Cola
wine, cocktail-party
wine, coda
wine, cold/cool climate
wine, collector
wine, commercially acceptable
wine, commodity
wine, commonplace
wine, communal
wine, communion
wine, complete everything
wine, completely whacked out
wine, complex suggestive baroque
wine, concept
wine, confected
wine, conservative
wine, consumer-friendly
wine, contemporary

wine, contrarian
wine, contrasting
wine, contrived/contrived-tasting
wine, cookie-cutter
wine, cooking
wine, cool Victorian ideal
wine, cornucopia
wine, country-specific everyday
wine, crass...slutty and drink-now
wine, crazy two-year-old-
   with-a-temper
wine, crossword-puzzle
wine, cult
wine, decent boating
wine, decent weekend
wine, delicate antique
wine, delicious warm-weather
   drinking
wine, designer

wine, dial-a-flavor
wine, difficult to describe the
   transition from grape to glass
   with this kind of
wine, dot-com
wine, doughy waxy monster of a
   dessert
wine, downright weird
wine, down-the-hatch jug
wine, easy-quaffing mass-market
wine, epitome of a pick--crush it--
   tank it white
wine, everyman
wine, everynight kind of
wine, extremely artisanal
wine, fabulously celebratory
wine, farmer's daughter sort of
wine, fireplace
wine, flagship
wine, flashy show
wine, fruit
wine, fruity simple bistro
wine, fun breezy
wine, gastronomic
wine, gaucho
wine, good evening
wine, good everyday drinking
wine, good peasant
wine, good-time
wine, grapefruit
wine, great bistro
wine, great carafe
wine, green
wine, hard-working
wine, head and shoulders
wine, headache
wine, head-banging
wine, hideously bastardized
wine, hot/warm climate

wine, hot-weather
wine, house brand
wine, ideal all-purpose
wine, ideal brasserie
wine, ideal summer terrace
wine, indifferent bag
wine, isn't a sit-around-and-sip
wine, Jackie Onassis
wine, killer barbecue
wine, laughing-boy of
wine, lazy afternoon
wine, less than basic
wine, library
wine, light-footed feminine
wine, little left of center
wine, little/slightly Wagnerian
wine, love-it-or-hate-it
wine, low-calorie
wine, lunch-meeting
wine, makes-you-smile
wine, manly man's
wine, master-and-commander
   kind of
wine, megawatt dessert
wine, millionaire
wine, model
wine, most backwardly made
wine, Nantucket
wine, new
wine, new-wave
wine, nice whore's
wine, no also-ran
wine, no BS-sort of
wine, no bumpkin
wine, no kindergarten
wine, no-frills
wine, not a beginner's
wine, not a caricature
wine, not a food wine...not an
   aging wine...not a varietal
wine, not a pudding
wine, not a Technicolor loud
wine, not your basic
wine, odd bird of a
wine, odd honey
wine, offbeat/oddball
wine, off-road
wine, off-vintage
wine, old-school
wine, out-of-the-box
wine, pain-free red

wine, paint-by-numbers
wine, paper bag-covered/-encased
wine, Parker
wine, party animal
wine, penny
wine, people's
wine, perfect aperitif

wine, perfect fin-de-siècle
wine, perfect springtime sipping
wine, perfect wedding cake
wine, picnic-in-the-park
wine, piñata
wine, pleasing café
wine, pleasing powder puff of a
wine, pouch
wine, pretechnology
wine, pretty-boy
wine, proprietary
wine, pudding
wine, quite vulgar
wine, railroad chairman's
wine, rather agricultural
wine, raw yet gorgeous throwback
wine, real fat cat of a
wine, real-world
wine, rockin'
wine, sacramental
wine, safety-blanket
wine, second
wine, Seder
wine, seemingly effortless
wine, September
wine, serious bling-bling
wine, shellfish
wine, shimmering minerally
  crystal chandelier of a
wine, shorts-and-sandals
wine, show
wine, show-off
wine, showpiece
wine, signature
wine, simple direct no-foolin'
wine, simple quasi-dessert
wine, single vineyard
wine, singular artisanal
wine, sit-by-the-pool
wine, skeletal essence of bad
wine, skillfully artisanal
wine, slightly out-of-the-ordinary
wine, slow-to-evolve bookworm's
wine, smart new can
wine, social
wine, soft cuddly sort of
wine, sophisticated little
wine, sought-after cult
wine, soul
wine, soul-warming red
wine, Southern Hemisphere
wine, spaghetti-western
wine, special natural
wine, spring blossom of a
wine, springtime luncheon
wine, starched beeswaxed
  Old-World society
wine, stealth

wine, stick-to-your-ribs
wine, straw-flask supermarket
wine, strictly for adults
wine, strident loudmouth of a
wine, strong man of a
wine, stud
wine, sturdy curmudgeonly
wine, stylishly chic
wine, syrupy sweet cult
wine, take-no-prisoners
wine, temperate climate
wine, Tetra Pak
wine, textbook proprietary
wine, the mashed potatoes of
wine, thick honey of a
wine, thinking person's
wine, thought-provoking artisanal
wine, throwback
wine, total porch
wine, totally aberrational
wine, totally civilized
wine, trash-can
wine, treasure-chest
wine, trickster's
wine, trophy
wine, ultimate picnic
wine, uncommonly chic
wine, upbeat cherry-cranberry
  sun-splash of a
wine, useful all-purpose
wine, vegetarian
wine, Venetian
wine, vermouthlike
wine, Veronese
wine, versatile
wine, very Wagnerian
wine, village
wine, vineyard-driven
wine, vinous
wine, wacko/wacky
wine, warm-weather
wine, weaning
wine, weird/weirdo
wine, well to the left of center
wine, West Coast
wine, western
wine, whey-based
wine, whimsical
wine, wild
wine, wimpy
wine, wine warrior's
wine, winemaker's
wine, winning
wine, winter/wintry
wine, wintertime celebration
wine, witty
wine, wonderfully vulgar
wine, workaday

wine, workman's red
wine, world-beating
wine, worldly
wine, yeomanlike
wine, your basic
wine, zip-code
wine: a nose of applesauce...
  cornflakes and toasted bread,
  breakfast
wine?, you call this
wine-in-a-box/can
winey
winter drinking, delicious
winter drinking, well suited for
winter warmer
winter, better in
workmanlike at best
world apart, a
xenophobic, possibly
yeomanry, sturdy
Yquem copy
Yquem-like structure
Yquem of all time, perhaps the
  most staggeringly rich
Yquem, shades of
yuck, commercial
Zen/Zen-like
Zin front...Cab back
Zin in every sense of the word,
  macho
Zin monstrosity, kneepads-needed
Zin, country-style mountain
Zin, high-alcohol
Zin, in-your-face
Zin, sinfully good
Zin, wacky
Zin, wild
Zin, zinfully great
Zin, zinfully zesty
Zinergy, full of
Zinfandel doesn't even have the
  chutzpah to call itself rosé, white
Zinfandel is red...wine wimps to
  the contrary, the only real
Zinfandel to the max
Zinfandel, high-class
Zinfandel, weedy white
Zinfandel: the fool's gold of wine,
  white
Zinfandel: the worst possible
  beginner's wine, white
Zinfandel: training wheels for a
  generation of wine drinkers,
  white
Zinfandel: what you drink when
  you hate wine, white
Zinfandel: yech, white
Zinfandel-like

Great is the art of beginning, but greater is the art of ending.
Henry Wadsworth Longfellow

The fine wine leaves you with something pleasant; the ordinary wine just leaves.
Maynard A. Amerine

26. Finish [Aftertaste, Endtaste, Finale, Length, Persistence, Tail]

Persistence in wine is a very big deal. When you swallow a wine, how long you sense it in your mouth and throat tells a great deal about its quality. The finish is what separates the everyday wine from the particularly fine one. What does it for wine drinkers is how long the taste lasts after swallowing or spitting: nada, a few seconds, minutes, hours, the rest of the night, into next week? Like so many pleasurable sensory experiences, the longer it lasts the better. Much better. And since you ask: yes, it's just the same as *that*.

abbreviated
abrupt
absent
acerbic
acid, good oaky
acid, good whack of
acid, gooseberrylike
acid, hard
acid, harsh
acid, sharpish
acid-driven
acidic kick, snappy
acidic, long vibrant nicely
acidic, pinpoint accurate
acidic, quite
acidic, screwed-up/twisted
acidic, slightly hollow
acidic, sweet-/sweetly
acidic, tinglingly
acidic, upturned
acidity, crunchy
acidity, pungent
acidity, scintillating
acidity, slightly congested
acidity, taut
acidity, tingly-tangy
acidity, vivid
acrid
adagio

adequate
adequate, less than
admirable but not wonderful
admirable/admired
afteraromas, good
afteraromas, seemingly endless
  capacity for complex
afterburn of Grenache power
afterburn, cactus in the
afterburn, spirity
afterglow of any pleasurable
  activity
afterglow, dreamy
afterglow, leaves a nice
aftergrip, somewhat astringent
afternote of honey, soft
aftersmells, good/lovely
aftertaste as pure as mountain air
aftertaste has a desiccating
  bitterness
aftertaste is phenomenally long
aftertaste is the longest I've ever
  experienced
aftertaste kicked me in the rear
aftertaste lasted for an entire three
  minutes
aftertaste lasted for a full three
  minutes, dry Cognac-like
aftertaste lingers for many minutes

aftertaste of butter and wild
  raspberries, magical
aftertaste of butterscotch, ultralong
aftertaste of *crème caramel*,
  wonderfully long
aftertaste of gunpowder
aftertaste of licorice, interwound
aftertaste of milk chocolate,
  extremely sweet
aftertaste of newly picked
  Mediterranean lemons
aftertaste of oak, lingering
aftertaste of orange chocolate, long
aftertaste of out-of-this-world
  vanilla sauce
aftertaste of pure acacia honey
aftertaste of saffron
aftertaste of tar tablets, deep
aftertaste of the juiciest apples
aftertaste of veal fond, long
aftertaste of walnuts, long
aftertaste of white Toblerone
aftertaste oppression
aftertaste reverberated like a
  singer's voice in a cathedral
aftertaste sticks around for ages
aftertaste that spreads out over the
  whole tongue, everlastingly
  sweet

aftertaste truly lasts minutes
aftertaste, accelerating fat
aftertaste, almost indelible
aftertaste, amiable
aftertaste, awesomely long
aftertaste, bit thin and bony in the
aftertaste, bitter caramelized
  orange
aftertaste, blueberry(ish)
aftertaste, caramelly
aftertaste, chocolaty
aftertaste, coffee-cream chocolate
aftertaste, complex seductive

aftertaste, curt

aftertaste, deliciously honeyed
aftertaste, distinctly biscuity
aftertaste, endless
aftertaste, equilibristic restrained
aftertaste, ethereal
aftertaste, extraordinary black
  currant
aftertaste, extraordinary mint leaf
aftertaste, extremely long ringing
aftertaste, fancy
aftertaste, flavors continue to
  unfold in the long
aftertaste, grubby
aftertaste, honeyed
aftertaste, ignominiously short
aftertaste, incredibly long
  butterscotch
aftertaste, inelegant
aftertaste, kernelly
aftertaste, lime-chalky
aftertaste, lingering haunting
aftertaste, lingering lime-
  pastillelike
aftertaste, long gushing fruity
aftertaste, majestic
aftertaste, much too short
aftertaste, never-ending iodine
  and balsamic
aftertaste, nutty-sweet
aftertaste, powerful
aftertaste, rather sophisticated
  rosehip
aftertaste, reedy
aftertaste, seductive
aftertaste, sharp nettle
aftertaste, slight caramelly
aftertaste, stunning
aftertaste, sweet tarry
aftertaste, syrupy fat
aftertaste, vanilla
aftertaste, vegetal
aftertaste, warm creamy
aftertaste, woody resiny
aftertastes, most fragrant of

aftertastes, one of the most
  prolonged
afterthought of cocoa
aggressive, bit
aggressive, quite
aimed, well
alcohol bitterness
alcohol burn
alcohol nip, pronounced
alcohol, hot blast of
alcoholic
almond pit
almond, roasted bitter
almond, trademark bitter
amazing, totally
anise, star
appealing
appetizing
apple blossoms
apple crisp
apple, bitter
apple, Granny Smith
apple, oaked
apple, spicy green
applelike, green
apples and seltzer
apricot, sun-baked
apricot…raisin…vanilla
apricots, candied
arid, somewhat
ash, bit of
asphalt-flavored, melted
assertive, fractionally
astounding
astringency, stark
astringent
attenuated, becomes
attractive
austere
authoritative
average
average, above-
backtaste, negative
backtaste, smoky
backtaste, strange
balsamic
banana and vanilla custard, ripe
banana, honeyed
basil, dried

bass gets turned up

beautiful, endlessly
beauty, pure
beefy
beery
beguiling, long and
berry cream
berry, juicy
berry, minty-

big
biting
bitter twist, classic
bitter-edged, refreshingly
bitterish tang
bitterish, gently
bitterish, pleasantly
bitterness, cocoa
bitterness, refreshing

bitterness, shaft of

bitterness, spicy juniper-berry
bittersweet
blackberry
bland and cardboardy
blockbuster this, no
Bloody Mary, lingering
blossom, lovely apple
blossoming
blueberry-like
blurred
bon-bons, sweet
Bordeaux-ish
bore, full-
bounce, big
bouncy
bracing
brambly
brandy, apple
brandylike, almost
breezy
briary
brief, all-too-
bright
brilliant
brisk tangy
brooding
bubbly
buffed, well
building, great
builds in the mouth
built, supremely
burning, slightly
burnt
butter, fresh
butter, oaky
butterscotch, light shot of
café au lait note, fine
café crème
cake, intense honeyed fruit
candied…almost confectionary
candy flowing across the palate
candy, hard
candylike, cotton
captivating
caramel/caramelly
carbon dioxide, prickle of
cardboard/cardboardy
caressing

carries on and on
carry, long and satisfying
carry, long fruit
carry, nice
carry, very long
cassis syrup
cat, wet
cedar-inflected
celerylike
chalky-earthy
character, lasting
characterful
cheese, touch of
chemical, odd
cherry, chocolate-dipped
cherry, slightly bitter
cherry, sweet
chewy...muscular...robust
chililike, unusual...almost
chocolate and roses
chocolate, bitter/bittersweet
chocolate, burnt
chocolate, dark unsweetened bitter
chocolate, elusive milk
chocolate, luscious
chocolate, slow-moving creamy
chocolate-malt
chocolate-orange
choppy
chunky
cigar smoke
citrus, sweet
clay, splash of
clean and bracing
clean...earthy
clean-cutting
clean, squeaky
cleansing but persistent dry
clear, crystal-
clear-cut, not so
clementines
clipped by the presence of copious
    tannins
clipped through
clipped, short
clipped, somewhat
clipped-compressed
close, characteristic spicy
clove/clovelike/clove-flavored
cloys fractionally
clunky
coal-like
coarse
coats the taster's palate and takes it
    hostage for about a minute
cocoa bitterness
cocoa, soft
cocoa-stained

coffee and hot chocolate, Starbucks
coffee and woodsmoke
coffee grounds
coffee, ground
coffee-flavored
coffee-spiked
comes back up and gets you
complete
complex
compote, rich prune
compressed
concentrated, very
conclusion peters out
concrete
congested, slightly/somewhat
consistent
controlled
convincing, particularly
corpulent
correct
correctness, gentlemanly
cottony
crafted, beautifully
cream, berry
cream, lemon
creamy fresh
creamy...flowery...sherbety
creditable, most
crescendo without becoming
    cloying, builds to a voluptuous
crescendo, booming
crescendo, long gustatory
crescendoing, almost
crisp and vital
crisp it tickles the mouth, so
crispness, flinty
crispness, zippy
crispy
crumbles a bit
crystalline, long
cucumberesque
cuddly
cumbersome
currantlike, stunning lingering
cushiony
custard/custardy
cutting
cymbal-crashing
damson
dances
dead/died in the glass
decadent
deceptive
deft
delicate
delicious
delineated, well
departing twitch of alcohol

die for, to
dilute/diluted
dim
diminish, starting to
direct
dirty, rather
disappeared abruptly
disappears
disappointing
discordant, slightly
disintegrating
disjointed, slightly
distance, never fails to go the
dough, bread
doughy note, delicious
downhill run, on the
drab
dramatic
drawn-out, long...pure and
drive, full of
droopy
droppings, hen
dry as dust, as
dry twist
dry, bone-/chalk-/dead-/searingly/
    tinder-/totally/truly
dry, longish
dry, nicely trimmed
dry, off-
dry, refreshingly stone-
dry, stick-
dry, tingling
dry, unapologetically
dry, warming off-
dry...quick
dry-as-a-bone
dryish, longish and
dryness, Sahara-desert
durable
dusty, lightly
dusty-dry
dynamite
earth and mushrooms, black
earth, lick of
earth, sweet
earth, very pleasant sweet-
earthiness rebounds, deep
earthiness, rough
earthy, slightly
easygoing, rather
echoing
edgy, little
eggnoggy
elaborate
elderflower-like
elegant and blossoming
elongated, surprisingly
elusive

emphatic
empty
end
end acidity, grapefruitlike
end bite, quite an
end point, without a foreseeable
end, bit of a burn at the
end, bite at the
end, doesn't seem/want to
end, ethereal at the
end, exquisite crystallized violet
end, fades toward the
end, falls flat at the
end, fielders' glove on the back
end, lingers nicely to the
end, nails at the very back
end, pepper at the
end, pleasant creamy
end, pure toast at the
end, spearmint and walnuts at the
end, tang at the
end, upturned
end, without
end-bite, noticeable
ended, blunt-
ended, open-
ending, ample
ending, never-/endless
endless for all intents and purposes
endless, seemingly
endlessly satisfying
endnote of earth, mushroom
   and truffle
ends stylishly
ends with satisfying vibrancy
endtaste of violets and black
   currants
endtaste, bracken on
   the/brackenlike
endtaste, curious mucked-out
   stables

enduring and heavenly
engaging
engrossing
enticing
ephemeral
escargot, mushroomy
espresso, shot of
espresso-tinged, firm
etching, nice mineral
eternity lingers on the palate for an
eternity, resonates on your palate
   for one velvety
ethereal
evading/evasive
evanescent, strangely
evasive
everlasting

evocative
excellent
exceptional
exciting
exemplary, highly
exit, forceful
exit, majestically dignified and
   distinguished
exit, quick to
exit, quiet in its
exotic
exploded then faded
explosive, prodigious
expressive, extremely/highly/
   immensely/massively
expressive, quite
exquisite
extended/extensive
extract-rich
extraordinary
exuberant yet rustic
fades in the blink of an eye
faint
fair, only
falls away markedly
fans out
fantastic
farewell kiss, totally tropical
farewell, fond
farewell, lingering

farewell, long delicious
fatigued
fearsome
feminine
fenberries, swoosh of pungent
fennel/fennel-flavored
fiery
fig baked in the sun, Italian
fig-accented
figgy
filigreed
final absolutely strong perfectly
   pitched note, its voice coming
   out in one
final kiss
final taste impression, quite
   memorable
finale infused with almonds
finale, endless
finale, fruit-driven
finale, harmonious
finale, long velvety
finale, lovely endless full-fruited
finale, masterful
finale, powered
finale, rich
finale, ringingly intense
finale, silky chocolate-laden

finale, smooth forceful
finale, sweet
finale, teeth-gripping tannic
finale, world-class
fine
finish a little, touch of oak clogging
   up the
finish and aftertaste, flavors build
   and intensify to a long
finish is in no hurry to fade away,
   lengthy
finish is the *coup de grâce*, creamy
finish keeps you company for most
   of the evening, suave
finish line with gas left in the tank,
   hits the
finish lingers on your mind,
   sometimes an ephemeral
finish of pinpoint accuracy,
   blackberry-chocolate
finish on the tongue, Velcro
finish sails on, dry lithe
finish stains the palate, brisk
finish that lasts into next week,
   heady
finish, 14% alcohol poking its nose
   through on the
finish, 15.5% really does burn the
finish, acidity tidies up the
finish, barely noticeable warm kiss
   in its unbelievably long
finish, brisk tangy
finish, chops off fractionally on the
finish, clean succulent fleshy
   large-scaled
finish, coriander on the
finish, creams caps the
finish, deep complex velvety
finish, easy fruity
finish, grapefruit keeps humming
   on the long
finish, haunting on the long
finish, large-framed muscular
finish, like riding a rollercoaster…
   up and down with a quick
finish, long butterscotchy
finish, long carry and
finish, long steely
finish, long stony

finish, long sultry
finish, mild coffee-oak on the
finish, mind-numbingly long pure
finish, monstrous concentrated
   intense
finish, more up front than on the
finish, much of the taste is in the
finish, oak phenolics do loom
   large on the

finish, omnipresent and very
    necessary acidity on the
finish, phenomenal thrust of its
finish, piquant peppery
finish, positive from start to
finish, practically phosphorescent
    in its Key-lime
finish, protracted rosehips and
    pink grapefruit
finish, rich dimensional
finish, slightly rough oak-
    dominated
finish, slightly twitchy
finish, snaps to a quick
finish, snaps to an abrupt
finish, soft spicy peppery
finish, struggles towards the
finish, tannin attack on the
finish, unending syrupy
finish, unfurls a very classy
finish, very long suave
finish, wanders off with a slightly
    blurred
finish, young abrasive peppery
finish…it just went on and on, did
    not have a
finished the glass and the lights
    have gone out, creaminess keeps
    you company long after you
finished the bottle, incredible
    difference between the first
    heavenly glass and the flat
    sludge that
finishes honorably
finishes ignominiously
finishes on a note of margarita,
    surprisingly
finishes with a bang
finishes with a gleam
finishes with a maraschino cherry
    on top
finishes wittily
finishes, longest of
finishes, unfurls the longest of
    elegant
finishing acidity, great
finishing bitterness
finishing finesse, characterfully
    deep
finishing flavors, sneaky
finishing fruit clings to the palate
finishing fruit goes on and on,
    powerful
finishing kick
finishing kiss of sweet oak
finishing like apple pie with an
    extra touch of cinnamon
fire, gentle

fireplaces, smoky
firm/firmed/firming
fishy-oily
flag, checkered
flamethrower
flavor, long mulberry smoky
flavor, remarkable crescendo of
fleeting, disappointingly
fleeting, somewhat
fleshed-out/fleshy
flimsy
floral
flounces
flourish, honeyed
flourish, ripe-fruit
flowerlike/flowery
fluffy
foamy
focused, softer less-
focused, well
follow-through is textbook stuff
follow-through, good
follow-through, incredibly long
follow-through, no/lacks
follow-through, seriously fine
forever, flavors sink into the
    tongue and last
forever, lingers in your mouth
forever, seemingly lasts/lingers
forever, seems to continue/linger/
    go on/last
fragrant
Frango Mint
fresh
fresh-faced
friendly, food-
frisky
frothy, gently
fruit is in no hurry to disappear,
    fleshy
fruit, big sweet
fruit, buoyant
fruit, glazed citrus
fruit, glimmer of
fruit, good smack of sweet
fruit, green
fruit, heroically structured
fruit, hot
fruit, lemon
fruit, lovely classy roasted
fruit, peppery
fruit, pleasant belt of sweet
fruit, reverberates with
fruit, sneaky black
fruit, sugar-dusted red
fruit, tart
fruit, toffee
fruit, tropical

fruit, waves of
fruitcake, intense honeyed
fruitcake…citrus and vanilla, rich
fruit-drenched
fruit-driven barely brushed with
    tannins
fruit-driven, slinky soft
fruit-filled, long…baked…dark and
fruit-filled, rich endless
fruit-forward, rousing
fruity flourish, ripe
fruity, explosively
fudge, cream-
fugitive
fun
fungus and rot, touch of
fungus, old
furry, slightly
fuzzy and blurred
gamy
generosity, some unexpected
generous
gentle
gingerbread
ginger-cinnamon
gingery, brisk and
girth and substance, some
gloss, cherry lip
glossy, long and
glycerin-alcoholic, heady
go over the edge, starting to
goes on and on unfolding
    magically on the palate
goes on for miles
goes on for minutes
goes on forever
going and going, keeps
gone
good, lipsmackingly
gorgeous, unexpectedly
graceful
grained, long fine-
grand
granitic, adamantly
grapefruit peel
grapefruit, bitter
grapefruity
grassy
gravy, calf
great
grip, appealing spicy
grip, slightly phenolic
grippy
gritty
grubby
guillotined
gummy
gunflint, dry austere

gushes with fruit
gutsy
halt, abrupt
hang on and on, flavors
hangs about for an age
hangs out
happy
hard, faintest bit
hard, surprisingly
harmonious
harsh…throaty, unmistakably
haunting, nicely
hay and minerals
hazelnut, lovely
hazy
hedonistic, plush layered
headachy
heady
hearty
heat, burst of
heat, little alcohol
heat, sweet
heavy
hedonism, pure
herbaceous
herbal tea-laden
herbal-mineral
hollow
honey comb, endless
honey, Cretan
honey-lemon-packed
honeysuckle, beguiling
honey-sweet
hopeless
horrible
hot
hot with alcohol, turns
hot, pretty
hot, very
hours long, seems
huge
hurry to sign off, in a
hurry, in a bit of a
hypoglycemic
ice cream, coffee
ice cream, strawberry-vanilla
imperceptible
impersistent/nonpersistent
incredible
indifferent
infinite
inspired
intense, extraordinary
interminable, almost/nearly
intricate, maddeningly
invisible
invites you back for another glass
inviting

irksome
iron and blood
iron filings, dry
iron, bitter
iron, tannate of
iron, terrible
irresistible
jagged
jam, black cherry
jam, concentrated
jam, freshly made raspberry
joyous
juice, tangy jumpy lemon
juicy
Juicy Fruit
kaleidoscopic
keen-edged
kero, Aussie-style
key, low-
kick like a mule, has a
kick, alcoholic
kick, peppery
kickback, real alcoholic leathery
kirsch, sweet
kirschwasser
kiss from a long-term unrequited
    crush, like your first French
knit, nicely
knockout
languorous
last forever, seems to
last in your mouth well into
    next year, seems to
lasting impression
lasting, long-
lasts a minute
lasts all night
lasts and lasts and lasts in the
    mouth
lasts beyond a minute
lasts forever on the palate
lasts for minutes
lasts in an empty glass for hours,
    enormous perfume
lasts until the dishes are done
lavender, nice
lavish beyond description
layer upon airy layer
layered
leafiness, green
lean/lean-edge(d)
leaps up gracefully
leather, Cheval Blanc
leaves a lasting mark
leaves you in a state of Zen-like
    satisfaction
leaves your whole body feeling red
lemon and cayenne pepper

lemon cream
lemon peel, kiss of concentrated
lemon zest
lemon, bitter
lemon, crystallized
lemon, delicate kiss of
lemon, zesty
lemon/lemony
lemon-cream
lemons, green
lemony bite, appealing
length almost to infinity,
    pushes the
length and balance in *diminuendo*
length and persistence, scores a
    bull's-eye
length is insufficient
length one could wish for, all the
length runs a couple of minutes
length, amazing/astonishing/
    dazzling/enormous/
    exceptional/exemplary/
    fabulous/fantastic/great/
    interminable/perfect/superb
length, effortless
length, endless warmth and
length, excellent
length, extract sweetness on the
length, fair
length, flavors plus
length, goodish
length, impression of great
length, indeterminable
length, more than decent
length, nonstop
length, plenty of flavor
length, sheer
length, skyscraper-like profile of
    fabulous concentration and
length, sneaky
length, some
length, structural
length, surprising
length, sweet oak
length, uncommon
length, unforgettable
lengthy, very
letdown
licorice, tangy
life, friend for
life, full of
life, short
light and effusive
light, rather
likable/easy to like
lime cream topped with nutmeg
lime marmalade
lime, snappy

lime-laced
limited
linearity, impressive
lingering beauty is underpinned by real substance
lingering coffee
lingering mouth presence
lingering richness, long-
lingering thoroughbred
lingers for ages
lingers for an impossibly long time
lingers for minutes, seemingly
lingers harmoniously
lingers in the throat like nectar
lingers in your mouth forever
lingers languidly
lingers like a nice dream
lingers on the palate for an eternity
lingers on the tongue for ages
lingers two minutes or more
lingers, has a grip that
lipsmacking
liqueur, coffee
liqueur, Grand Marnier-esque orange
liqueur, tarry blackberry
lithe and fruity
little
lived, short-
lively and polished
lively, none too
lively, surprisingly

loitering

long and as fresh as one could ever imagine, as
long and beguiling
long and piercing
long and slightly abrasive
long anise-tinged
long as an F-18 vapor trail, as
long as Pavarotti's high C, creamy
long taste that reverberates at least as
long as the swallow itself, only as
long at all, not
long barley-sugar
long blackberry
long carry
long carry, very
long cream fruit
long crystalline
long cymbal-crashing
long drawn out
long enough, not
long European-style
long honeyed
long long
long long blackberry

long lusty
long mouthquenching
long multiflavored
long multilayered
long on the palate, ever so
long palate, gloriously
long personality, exceptionally
long sassy fruit
long steely
long sultry
long time, lasts an exceedingly long
long toffee-filled
long voluptuous, extraordinarily
long, caressing-silky-
long, chewy and
long, chewy, ripe tannic
long, endlessly
long, ever so
long, exceedingly/exceptionally/ fabulously/fantastically/ formidably/gorgeously/ impossibly/incredibly/ prodigiously/staggeringly/ stunningly/stupendously/ terrifically/unbelievably/ whoppingly
long, excitingly
long, fantastically
long, gratifyingly
long, insatiably

long, lethally

long, lip-smackingly
long, long
long, majestically
long, mind-blowingly/ mind-bogglingly/ mind-numbingly
long, mouth-wateringly
long, nearly unendingly
long, not terribly
long, plump
long, rich...utterly luxurious and
long, rich-utterly luxurious-
long, ripe and
long, surprisingly
long, tannic and
long, very
long, very very very
long...complex
long...pure and supple
longer than you can hold your breath, lasts
longest and purist
longest in the business, one of the
long-focused fruit
long-lasting
long-lived
long-rich

long-spicy
lo-o-o-o-ng
loses it in the glass
lovely/loverly
luscious, utterly
lush, gorgeously
lusty
luxurious, utterly
magnificent
majestic
malty
mandarin
marmalade, dry
marmalade, orange
marmaladelike kick
marvelous
marzipan, faintly bitter
masculine
masked
massive
masterful/masterly
matty, slightly
mawkish, trifle
meaty
medium
mellow/mellowed
melon, Charentais
melony
memorable and cleansing
memories in the mouth, leaves symphonic
menthol
mentholated, slightly
metallic tweak
metallic, your basic
metallic...almost copperlike
methylated-spirity
miles, goes on for

Milk Duds

milk, condensed
mind-boggling
mineral piquancy
mineral, almond-pit
mineral, gripping
mineral...almost steely
mineral-driven, flinty
minerals, gripping
minerals, sleek
mint/minty
minute, lasts beyond a
minutes after the glass has been emptied, flavors lingers in the mouth with magnificent intensity...for even 10
minutes long
minutes or more, lingers 2
minutes pass, gets better and better as the

minutes, flavors seem to float in midair for

minutes, goes on for/lasts/runs on for

minutes, lasts a good two

minutes, seemingly lingers for

minutes, stays with you for four or five

minutes, wraps itself around your taste buds and doesn't let go for what seems like

moderate/moderate-ish

modest

monolithic

monster

monumental

morning, could last 'til

mouth-staining

mouthwatering

multidimensional

muscular

mushroom/mushroom note/ mushroomy

musk/musky

muted, little

nail, rusty

narrow

narrowing, slight

narrows out

nectar, orange

negligible

neutral

never-ending

nice

niggardly, bit

night, lasts all

noble

nonexistent

normal

notable

notable, not

nothing, big

noticeable

nougat and marzipan

Novocaine-like

nuanced/nuanced-filled

nuanced, sweet

nut skin, pleasing

nut, roasted

nutmeg and hazelnut

nuts in honey, crushed

nuttiness, light

nutty, nice and

oak paints broader strokes

oak shadings, pretty

oak undertow, almondy toasty

oak, gentle dry

oak, new

oak, nice lick of vanilla

oak, smoky

oak, wisp of smoky-vanilla

oak-chocolaty, sensuous

oak-laden

oak-toast

oaky-acid, good

oily and fiery

oily, pleasantly

oily, powerful

Old-World-style

olive, inky black

olive, touch of green

olive, varietally correct twist of

on and on and on, continues/goes

on and on, should go

onslaught, ferocious tannin

open-ended

opulent, rather too

orange, candied

orange, tart

orange-flavored/-infused

orange-perfumed, long clean

orchestrated, well

outstanding

overprolonged

PAI (Persistent Aromatic Intensity)

palate-coating, long

palate-saturating, real

palate-staining

peach kernel, stunning oily

peach, touch of

peach-themed

peachy, longish

pear, delicate essence of fresh

peas, English

penetrating

pepper, hot

pepper, tangy bell

pepper-filled, freshly cracked black

pepper-fruit

pepper-spice

peppers and Brussels sprouts, green bell

perfection, absolute

perfumed, well

perfunctory, slightly

persistence of scents, seemingly in exhaustible

persistence, aromatic

persistence, could have more

persistence, great

persistence, incredible

persistence, overall

persistence, subtle

persistency, good

persistent, awesomely

persistent, quite/very/extremely

persistent, scarcely

persistent, untiringly

persists almost magically on the palate

persuasive

petrol kick

petrol pucker

phenolic, slightly

phenolics, touch of oak

phenomenal

pie crust

pie, apple

pie, lemon meringue

pie, sweet cherry

piercing

pillowy

pinched and compressed

pineapple, roasted

Pinot, mature

piquant to sharp

plastic/plasticky

pleasant/pleasing

pleasurable

plum and truffle

plump

plums, spiced

pointed, slightly

poised

polished

ponderous

poor

Port or Banyuls, vintage

porty/portlike

positive

powerful

powerhouse

praiseworthy

precious

precise

pretty

pristine

profound

prolonged, stunningly

prolonged, wondrously

prominent/pronounced

pronounced alcohol nip

proper

protracted

prunes and meatiness

pulsating, richly

punch, packs a

punchless

punctuation, nice

puny

pure

purist, one of the

purposeful

quick and forgettable, surprisingly
quickly melts into your palate
quiet
quinine note, gin-and-tonic
quinine-infused, sultry
quit, just doesn't
quits, never
racy
radiant
rainwater
raisin, roasted
raisiny, very
rapier-like
rare
raspberry, tannic
raspberry-blueberry, long
raspberry-bramble
raw...spiky
realistic
reasonable
red, long
reduced
refined
refreshing
reliable
relishable
remarkable, utterly
remnant
resinous
resonant
resonates nicely
restrained, surprisingly
retreat, abbreviated
reverberates
rich
richness, full rip-roaring
richness, long-lingering
right, just
rigid, bit
rind, mature cheese
ripe, sweet and
rising
riveting, utterly
robust
rolling, smooth
rot, trace of
rough, little
rough, slightly
rough-hewn
roughness, chalky
rounded, well
rules supreme
rushed, tad
rustic
rusticity, touch of
sails on and on, just
salt, sea
salt/salty

salt-tinged
salty tang
satin/satiny
satisfying, completely/supremely
satsuma
savory, gently
scarce
scintillating
scour, tannic
scrappy, slightly
screwed-up
seashell-like, minerally
seconds or more, lasts a good 90
seconds, lasts a flawless 50 plus
seconds, lasts an awesome 60
seconds, lasts for over 75 plus
seductive
semibitterness, Italianate
sensation/sensational
sensual
sensuous, truly
Sercial-like, old
severe, rather
sexy
shadow
sharp/sharpish
sheepdog, Shetland
shells, snail
sherbet dip
sherbet-fresh
sherrylike
short and chocolaty
short, disappointingly
short, falls a little
short, pulls up a trifle
short, stops
short-lived
shrill
signature, long
signs off long and aromatic
signs off clean and fresh
signoff, crisp
signoff, lengthy
signoff, satisfying
silken
silken, roughly
silky-violety
simple, extremely
sinewy
singing
sinuses, seizes your
skank/skanky
skeletal
skimpy
skinny, slightly
slam dunk
slate that takes over, powerful
sledgehammer

sleek
slender
slick, bitter tannin
slick, tannic
slinky
slippery
slowly drifts into memory
smashing
smiling
smoke nip capping it off,
   pleasing cigar-
smoky beefy quality
smoky, delightfully
smoky-roasted
smooth
smudgy, slightly
snap, distinctive
snappy
snazzy
sneaky
soapy
soft and easygoing
soft and succulent
soft, cuddly
soil, long rich
solid, rock
soothing
sophisticated
soporific
so-so
soufflé, orange
soulful/has soul
sound
soupy, bit
sour edge
sour-creaminess
sparse
spectacular as it unfolds in waves
spice, bitter
spice, Christmas
spice, dashes of
spice, hefty whack of leathery
spice, kick of
spice, marvelous twist of
spice-filled, velvety
spices, intricately constructed of
   dusty brown
spices, oriental
spices, ton of
spicy-peppery
spirit, hot
spirity, slightly
splendid
spongy, slightly
squishy
starching
starchy and tannic

stay with you even as you drive out of the parking lot, will
stay, bred to
stayer
stayer, dyed-in-the-wool
stayer, not a long
staying power, doesn't have
staying power, great
staying power, has immense/lots of
stays with you for four or five minutes
steady
steam, picks up
steam, runs out of
steely-flinty
stellar
stems, curious crushed
sting, dry
stingy
stone, wet
stones roll in
stony, characteristic
stony, intriguingly
stop in its tracks, seems to
straightforward
straw
strawberry, earthy
strawberry, grilled
strawberry, pungent
strawberry-laden, wild
stretches out
strict
strong
structured, richly
stunning...lazy and insouciant
stupendous
sturdy

stuttering a bit

suave, richly
subdued
sublime
substantial
subtle
succulence, right degree of
succulent, engagingly
suede with emery edges, rough
sugar, caramelized
sugar, long barley-
sugar, powdered
sugar, residual
sugar, slight burnt
sugar, vanilla
suitable
summarizing
superb
superfruity
superlively
superlong

supple
supple and long, decadently
supple yet lively
suppressed
surging
sustained
sweep of acidity, clean
sweet almost candied
sweet and sexy, irresistibly
sweet and sour
sweet plus leather and iron
sweet, honey-
sweet-and-sour
sweet-edge(d)
sweet-hot
sweetness, awkward
sweetness, chewy
sweet-tart
swingeing
swoopy
syrup and coffee, maple
T & A, usual
taffy, saltwater
tail, bit of tannin on the
tail, bitter snap in the
tail, broadens/opens like a peacock's
tail, classic peacock's
tail, crisp
tail, explosive peacock's
tail, good
tail, grainy
tail, hardly any
tail, long
tail, persistent
tail, pervasive
tail, quickly vanishing
tail, thread of sweetness in the
tail, very quickly disappearing
tailing off
tail-less
tails away prematurely
tails off in a stately fashion
tails off rather abruptly
talented
tang, mouthwatering mineral
tang, nice
Tang, orange
tang, sweet-salty
tangy, sharp and
tangy-tart
tannic clout and power, considerable
tannic oak-imbued
tannic, pungent

tannic, sour...cheesy ...

tannic, youthfully
tannin lick

tannin-filled, super-ripe
tannin-free
tannins, chalky
tannins, feathery
tannins, fine filigreed
tannins, forbidding
tannins, green
tannins, hard
tannins, heaps of
tannins, hefty
tannins, leaking
tannins, leathery
tannins, little skin
tannins, near-perfect
tannins, powerful blast of
tannins, prickly
tannins, punchy
tannins, slightly green
tannins, slippery
tannins, slowly building
tannins, sueded
tannins, swoop of firm
tannins, tongue-dusting
tannins, wall-to-wall
tannins, wood
tannins, woodsy
tape measure
tapers off much too soon
tar, lick of
tarry, attractively
tart, bramble
tart, quite
tartness, Persian lime
tartness, snap of

Tasmanian, typically

tea, black
tea, earthy
tea, spiced
tea leaf-tinged
tea-laden, herbal
tenacious
tenuous
termination, fine
terra cotta
terrific, utterly
terse
textured, sumptuously
thick and viscous
thick, slightly
thickens slightly
thickens up somewhat, seems to
thin, bit
thins off
thirst-quenching, gorgeous
throaty
tight
tight and focused
tight as a drum, as

tightening-up
time, dies on its ass in no
tingling in the mouth, slight
tireless
toast and butter/buttered toast
toast, cinnamon
toast, warm
toastiness, graham cracker
toasty, itching to go
toasty, long
tobacco
Toblerone, white
toes, will curl your
toffee touch, nice
toffee, amazingly enjoyable
toffee, soft banana-split
toffee-coffee, smooth
Tokaji-like
tomato leaf
tongue, remains on the
tough and minerally, little
tough side, on the
tough, bit
toughens up slightly
trace
trails off
train, comes on like a freight
tranquil
treacle, lingering
tremendous, nothing short of
trip, weird
tripping over itself
tropical
true
truffle
truffley splendor
tumultuous
tuned, nicely/well
turbocharged, long
tweak, savory
twist, sharp
twisted

überdry

ultralong
ultrapolished
ultrasmooth
unashamed
unbalanced
unbelievable
unclean
uncomplicated
uncompromising
undemanding
underdeveloped
underpowered
undistinguished
unending, seemingly

unhurried
uninteresting
unintimidating
unique
unmeasurable
unpleasant
unreal
unremarkable
unsubstantial
untraceable, almost
upfront
upturned...almost spritzy
vanilla and bitter chocolate
vanilla milkshake
vanilla, deftest touch of
vanilla, frail
vanilla, light
vanilla, voluptuous
vanilla-dusted, sweetish
vanillaed without seeing wood
vanilla-oak, expansive
vanilla-violet
vanish, quick to
vanishing
vanishing point, almost no/
   without a
vanishing point...the flavors
   linger on forever, no
vapid
varnishy
velvet, crushed
velvet, dry
vibrant
vigorous
vinous
violated...Spackled or on fire, you
   shouldn't feel
violets
viscosity, mild
viscous...almost prunelike, quite
vital
vivacious, elegantly
Volnay-like
voluptuous, endlessly
voluptuous, sexy
walnut and bittersweet chocolate
walnut and raisin
walnuts

warm and hazy

warm, very
washed-out
watered/watery
wave, continuous
waxy
weak, little
weak, surprisingly
weird, little
whack, touch out of

whoo-ee
whopping
wild
wine/fruit gum
winey
winning
withering, rapidly
wishy-washy
wobbles fractionally
wonderful/wondrous
wood, burnt
wood, long burnt

woody-rough

Yquem-like
yummy
zesty fellow
zingy

Popularity breeds mediocrity.
Mary Ewing-Mulligan & Ed McCarthy

Quality means doing it right when no one is looking.
Henry Ford

Quality is never an accident; it is always the result of high intention, sincere effort, intelligent direction and skillful execution; it represents the wise choice of many alternatives.
William A. Foster

27. Quality

This is the longest, and, mercifully, the final category of wine tasting descriptors. It tries to capture the qualitative impressions by asking questions such as: "Is this stuff good or what?" or, "How could they bottle this swill in clear conscience?" We might also want to remember the label because the wine was so damn tasty; on the other hand, we might also want to forget we ever put this rotgut to our lips. So relax, dear reader, and dig out those descriptions that make sense to *your* eyes, *your* nose and *your* mouth. In plain English, *drink what you like* and *like what you drink*.

A1
A ^{2} (Aromatically Awesome)
A report card, straight-
aah
abnormal to recommend, too
abominable
above the rest, cork-and-shoulders
above, stands head-and-shoulders
abysmal
acceptability, trembling on the
 brink of
acceptable; just
acclaim, track record of critical
accomplished, most totally
aces
achievement, amazing/
 brilliant/rare
acrobat, taste equivalent of a
 Cirque du Soleil
act, class
addictive, disturbingly/wickedly
addictive, highly
addictive, mysteriously
addictive: you have been warned!

adequate, barely
adequate, more than
adore this wine, damn…I
aesthetic considerations, inspires
affront to wine drinkers
 everywhere, an
ages, destined for the
ages, not a wine for the
agreeable mouthful, most
agreeable, well beyond
ahead of its peers, way
alight, utterly failing to set the
 world
alive and kicking in the glass/
 on the palate
alive, most
all, has it
alluring, mysteriously
aloof
amaze a wine connoisseur, would
amazement, makes your jaw
 drop in
amazement, should have heads
 turning in

amazing, absolutely/quite/utterly
ambitious, overly
ambrosia on the planet, finest
ambrosia, pure
amiable, truly
and how!
angel peed on my tongue, like an
angel, kiss of an
angelic nose
angels singing, hear the
angst-ridden, least
animated but dignified
anodyne
anything for me, didn't do
A-OK
apart, a league
appalling
appeal and personality, loaded with
appeal, upfront
appealing, gloriously
appealing, uniquely
appetizing, ridiculously
approach with extreme caution

aristocrat, as uncompromising as an English
aristocrat, rather seedy
aristocratic, undeniably
arms, offers itself with supple open
aroma, dramatic
aroma, superb
aromas are like a welcome mat
aromas as sweet and erotic as a handbag full of lipstick and scents
aromas hits you between the eyes
aromas leap out of the glass to meet you
aromas practically defy description
aromas, almost palpable abundance of
aromas, attractive/excellent/nice/pleasant/superb/thrilling
aromas, captivatingly broad swath of
aromas, haunting/strange
aromas, heady
aromas, highly extroverted nearly ostentatious
aromas, plethora of celestial
aromas, smoldering
aromas, unusual wake-me-up
aromatherapy in a glass
aromatic and flavorsome, profoundly
aromatic and rich, dizzyingly
aromatic display, dazzlingly explosive
aromatic extravagance
aromatic fireworks, impressive
aromatic strength, stuporous
aromatic welcoming committee
aromatic you'll want to sniff this for hours, so
aromatic, endlessly
aromatic, deeply/extravagantly/floridly/gloriously/outrageously/sumptuously/wildly
aromatic, head-spinningly
aromatically irresistible
aromatics could fill a large room, awesome
aromatics, blatant
aromatics, compelling
aromatics, explosive/pyrotechnic
aromatics, incredibly forceful
arrogant but kind
art, high
art, a work of
art…it's a work of nature brought to life by the dedication of man: the purist expression possible of its soil, more than a work of

artifact in its makeup, plenty of winery
artful/artsy/arty
artistic from nose to throat, beautifully
artistic presence
artless
as it should be
ashamed of, absolutely nothing to be
ass, kick-/kicks
assembled, extremely well
assured, self-
astonishing, nothing less than
astounding, quite
astute
atrocious
attack on the taste buds, unashamed blistering
attack, aromatic
attack, clean/sound
attack, coarse
attack, fine/good
attack, full-bodied
attack, good clean
attack, intense/powerful
attack, invasive
attack, shocking
attention of the taster from first sip to last, demands the
attention, commands
attention, don't drink this unless you're paying
attention, grabs your
attention, repays close
attention, screaming for
attention-getting/-grabbing
attitude, melancholic rainy-day drizzle
attitude, plenty of
attractive in an austere idiosyncratic way, curiously
attractive, curiously
attractive, most/pretty
attractive, unquestionably
audacious
austere and rich, somewhere between
austerity only a Puritan could love
austerity, savory
authoritative, completely
authority, real air of
authority, without any
average for a normally boring wine, well above
average, barely/just/only
average, not your
average, way above

avoid at all costs
avoided unless desperate, better
avoiding, well worth
awe, sip it in
awesome, quite simply
awful, frankly/simply
awful, god-
awful, smells
awful, unspeakably
bacchanalian
bad but not good enough, not
bad thing, no
bad, appallingly/overwhelmingly
bad, exotically
bad, just plain/plain old
bad, not at all/not by any means/not half-
bad, shockingly/stupefying
bad, very very
baffling
bail out now
baleful
bam!
banal, anything but
banality oppresses you, its
bang on
bank, you can take it to the
banned, deserves to be
barbaric/barbarous
baronial in size and stature
barren, rather
base
baser…not finer…instincts, designed to appeal to one's
basic, doesn't really transcend the
batty
bawdy
be-all and end-all, the
bearing, aristocratic
bearing, needs to find its
beaten/beaten down
beatific
beautiful as a ballet dancer, as light and
beautiful in all respects
beautiful young wine from any-where that I have ever tasted, the most
beautiful, at its most bouncily
beautiful, beyond
beautiful, bloody
beautiful, breathtakingly/indescribably/insanely/ravishingly/spectacularly
beautiful, drop-dead
beautiful, ethereally shimmeringly
beautiful, hauntingly
beautiful, helplessly

beautiful, piercingly
beautiful, so outrageously
beautiful, tempestuously
beauty and inner structure, sense of outer
beauty and sheer voluptuousness, blows you away through the force of its
beauty to death, let's just enjoy this delicious tidbit without analyzing its
beauty, austere haughty
beauty, dark smoldering
beauty, extroverted
beauty, kaleidoscope of
beauty, real inside-track
beauty, seamless
beauty, sheer ripe-fruit
beauty, surreal
beauty...nobility and breed plus complexity and richness, pure
beckoning
bedazzling
bedecked
bedeviled
Beethoven in a mellow mood
beguiling with mood
beguiling, completely/quite/ totally/truly/utterly
behaved, well
bell-ringer
bells and whistles, has all the
bells, doesn't ring any
bells, will ring your vinous
belly, makes you want to put on Barry White and lap it off someone's
benchmark, important
best and most romantic seductive drink
best liquids we've ever tasted, one of the
best of the best
best on a starry night, at its absolute
best wines ever to touch my lips, one of the
best you'll find, among the
best, can duke it out with the world's
best, simply one of the world's
best, the absolute very
bet, sucker
better and bigger than most
better than good
better than this, wine can hardly get
bewitching

beyond, way/well
big deal
big in concept
big is happening here, something
big player
big shot, real
big...big...big—did I say big— flavors?
bigger than life
biggest end of town, from the
billing, gets star
billows out of the glass
blah, kind of
bland, far/mile from
bland, indifferently
blandness, lowest common- denominator
blaring, not
blasé
blast of flavors, sharp
blatant
bleak
blech
blessed, drinker feels
blessing, absolute
blessing, heaven-sent
blew me away, completely
blinder, real
bliss in a glass
bliss, pure/total/utter
bliss, silky luscious
bliss, transcendental
blithe/blithesome
blockbuster, not a hedonistic
blood of the grape, akin to drinking the
bloodlines, good
blown, full-
blowsy
blunted, all too
boastful/boasting
bodacious
boffo
bog standards, rises above
boisterous, overly
bold
bombastic
bonny, very
boom-boom
borderline
boring and obvious
boring stuff, offers more than the usual
boring, blandly
boring, ponderous and
born, well
bottled, well
bottom, has hit

bottom, needs a smack on the
bottomless
bottomless, leaves you wishing the bottle was
bouncy
bouquet is so tight it gives the impression of opacity
bouquet unraveled deliciously
bouquet, attractive
bouquet, big/plenty of/strong
bouquet, clean/neutral/no/ no identifiable
bouquet, attractive/delightful/ excellent/grand/nice/pleasant
bouquet, elusive
bouquet, exotic/haunting/strange
bouquet, explicit/identifiable
bouquet, glass
bouquet, knockout
bouquet, light
bouquet, persistent
bouquet, red-carpet
bouquet, rich blossoming
bouquet, riveting
bouquet, soaring
bouquet, switchback
bouquet, thought-provoking
bouquet, wary
bowled me over, just
brain, goes straight to the pleasure center of the
brain, nothing that would tax your
brain, sharpens the
brainer, no-
brash, almost carelessly
bravado, sheer
brave little wine
bravo
brazen
breath away, takes one's
breathtaking, simply
bred, extremely well
bred, poorly
breed and beauty, brimful of
breed as well as class, true
breed, best-of-
breed, fantastically full of
breed, of good
breed, pure
breeding really separates it from the pack
breeding, higher
breeding, lacks/no
breezy, fun-
brilliance like a diamond
brilliance, falls short of
brilliance, flawed
brilliance, odd flash of

brilliant effort
brilliant it brings tears to my eyes, so
brilliant through and through, totally
brilliant, jaw-droppingly
brilliant, just/simply
brilliant, none too
brilliant, right off the bat it's
brilliant, transcendently
brooding
brusque
brutality and grace, alliance of
brutish on first taste, little
bullet, silver
bullet-proof
bull's-eye, total/veritable
bull's-eye, hits the
bumps, gives me goose
bumptious
buoyant, expressively
burlesque of a wine
button, doesn't hit the hot
buzz, hedonistic
buzz, invigorating
cachet, centuries-old cajoling
caliber, exceptional
calibration, quieter subtler
call for the nose and palate, wake-up
calm/calming
cantankerous, downright
capable
capricious
captivating, totally/utterly
care, made with uncommon
carefree
careful
caress to a punch in the nose, for those who prefer a tender
caricature, descending into
caring
cautious
celebrated wine, single most
celebratory
celestial
censored, this wine should be
center, left of
cerebral aromas
cerebral complexity, positive
cerebral offering
cerebral or highbrow, nothing
cerebral or soulful appeal, has
cerebral, elegant but
cerebral, not
cerebral, simultaneously sensual and
cerebral, wonderfully

challenged, aromatically
challenging on the tongue
challenging, always
challenging, not terribly
champ/champion
chaotic
character can almost suck you over the event horizon, tannic charge and depth of
character if your teeth hold out, profound
character than most Hollywood movies, has more
character to speak of, no
character, abundant/bags of/ chock full of/ considerable/ crawling with/full of/huge/ loaded with/great/masses of/tons of/ tremendous
character, astonishing
character, breadth of
character, classical
character, crystalline
character, distinct/distinctive
character, drink-me-now
character, ethereal
character, expressive driven
character, fine/genuine/good/ outstanding/real/ serious/ superior
character, forbidding
character, in
character, indeterminate
character, lacks/no/out of/poor/ stripped of/without
character, little discernible
character, marked
character, memorable
character, modest
character, muddy
character, off-
character, precious secret
character, significant
character, smoke-crammed
character, smooth
character, stubborn streak to its
character, sultry
character, sweet-and-sour
character, unpalatable
character, unsullied
character, weird
character, well-formed
characteristic huskiness
characteristics difficult to identify
characterless
charisma compels you to return to your glass again and again
charm and silk, liquid

charm of a frigid smile
charm, cheery
charm, considerable
charm, decadent
charm, devoid of/lacks
charm, flirtatious
charm, has winning
charm, lacking any vestige of
charm, lacks compelling
charm, melting
charm, mysterious
charm, oozes devilish
charm, puppy-dog
charm, ravishing
charm, seductive/seductively charming
charm, subversive
charm, supple
charm, upfront
charm?, where's the
charm, yokel
charmer, no gay little
charmer, silky
charmer, specious
charmer, surface
charmer, tangy
charming as charming can be, as
charming, something less than
charming, utterly
charmless, rough and
charms, beautifully mannered
cheeky
cheerful/cheery
cheerless, relatively
cheery, exceedingly
cheesy
chef d'oeuvre
cherished
chill-out, ultimate palate
chills, gave me
chimerical
chip, blue-
chipper
chirpy
chiseled bouquet, precisely
chiseled, elegantly
choice, unlikely
choice/choicest
choose whom you share this with, carefully
chords, hits nearly all the right
chosen, well
churlish
civility, elegant
class act
class and nobility, utmost
class and power, small marvel of
class and refinement, indescribable

class from nose to throat, high-
class in a glass
class in the making, real
class is all about, what
class of its own, in a
class on your palate, stamps
class, all-
class, bags/lots of
class, best-in-/first-/true/
  unquestionable
class, complete wine of great
class, crystalline
class, defines harmony and
class, exceptional/pure/rare/sheer
class, extra
class, fantastic masterpiece of
  absolute first
class, great sense of
class, high-/highest/supreme-/
  top-/ultimate-
class, oozing with fruit and
class, underbelly of
classiest on the block
classiness and wit, pleasing
classy and fun at one and the same
  time
classy and sassy
classy as an old Bugatti automobile,
  as

classy beast
classy little number
classy stuff
classy, awesomely
classy, effortlessly
classy, supremely
clean and attractive like a well-
  produced record of American
  West Coast rock
clean and mean, quite
clean and tingly, how you feel
  when you just get out of the
  shower...
clean as a whistle, as/whistle-clean
clean innocuous effort, not a
  squeaky
clean, marvelously/remarkably/
  spotlessly/squeaky
clean, none-too-/not entirely
clean, piercingly
clean, plushy
clean, spotlessly
clean, totally
clean, very high-tech
clean: no sweaty armpits
clean-cut
cleaning false teeth, good for
cleanliness, rapier

cleanliness, striking
cleanly made
cleanness, mouthwash
clever stuff
climactic
cloddish/cloddy
close but no cigar
clueless, little
clumsiness, crude
clumsy in presentation, bit
clunker
clunky, little
cocky
cogent
colors, with flying
colossal/colossus
combat, made for
come-hither
comely
comfort, has deep
comfortable as old jeans, as
comfortable, very
comforting like a blazing fire
comfy, damned
commander-in-chief
commanding
commendable
communiqués from soil to air to
  nose, quiet
companionable
compelling juice
compelling, most/quite
compelling, not
competent, not a thriller but
complaisant

complete package
complete symmetrical wine
complete wine from start to finish
complete, aesthetically
complete, completely
complete, remarkably/totally/
  utterly/wonderfully
complete, satisfyingly
complimentary
comprehend, confusing to
comprehensible
compressed
conceived, beautifully
concessions, doesn't make any
condition, in good
condition, in perfect
condition, not out of
condition, way out of
confidence in a glass
confidence, inspires
confident
conflicted

confrontational, rather/somewhat
confused but it will be happy,
  your tongue might be
confusing wine to comprehend
congenial
connoisseur, for the
conscientious
consequence, not of great
conservative
considerate
consistency, epitome of
consistent, unerringly
consoling, curiously
constant...so true, so
consummate
contemplation, begs for
contemplation, deserves
contemplation, excellent
  companion for moments of
contemplative enjoyment,
  lesson in
contented
contradictions, study in
conundrum, cryptic
conversation at the dinner table,
  stops
conversation at the table, initiates
conversation flowing, gets the
conversation, constant source of
  thought-provoking
conversationalist, restrained
conviction, lacks both fruit and
convincing, unusually
convivial
cool, seriously/very
cooperative
cor blimey!
cordiality, pleasant
cork, don't bother pulling the
counterfeit
courageous
courteous
courtly
couth and civilized, marvelously
couth...civilized and polished of
  manner
coveted
covetous, ultimately
cow!, holy
cozy
cracker
crackerjack
cracking good
cracks a smile and winks at you
cracks in its veneer, shows some
crafted and sculpted, well

crafted with a Michelangelo-like
touch
crafted, artistically/beautifully/
impeccably/magnificently/
meticulously/skillfully/well
crafted, exceptionally well/
superwell
crafted, soulfully
crafted, thoughtfully
craftsmanship, sophisticated
crafty
crapoir?, *terroir* or
crappy
crass without class
crayon in the box, not the brightest
crazy, moonstruck
creation, amazing/stunning
creation, artistic/gorgeous
creation, cosmic
creative
creditable effort
creeps up on you stealthily
crème de la crème
crippling
criticism, beyond the powers of
measured
crown, worthy of a triple
cruddy
crude
cry on a rainy day in Aÿ, actually
made him
cuddly
cultivated, well
cultured
cultured plum-in-the-mouth
elocution, very
cumbersome/cumbrous
cunning
cure whatever ails you, one to
curio than a source of any great
pleasure, more interesting as a
curious
curmudgeonly
cursed
cut above
cut and zip, lacks
cut, clean-
cute
cuts above, many
cuvée, irresistible old-vine
cylinders, wasn't firing on all
cynical
dame, grande
dance, makes the taste buds
danced in my mouth
dancer, exquisite ballet
dancer, Polynesian
dances happily on your taste buds

dances on my tongue/palate
dances/dancing out of the glass
dandy, just
dandy, like candy...this is
dandy tossed in the mud, like a
dangerous stuff
dapper
dappled
daring
dark and exciting like a novel by
Umberto Eco
darting
dash and style, made with
dashing, unquestionably
daunting
dauntless
dazzler in every respect
dazzles without cheap aftereffects
dazzles, rarely
dazzling since birth
dazzling, simply/utterly
dead, brain-
deadly/deathly
deal, no big
deal, this is a very big
debonair
decadence and civility
decadence, brazen
decadence, liquid
decadence, pure unadulterated
decadence, sweet
decadent and clean, so
decadent attraction, near-
decadent but delicious
decadent edge
decadent mouthful, rich
decadent, absolutely/deliciously/
divinely/extremely/gloriously/
positively/truly
decadent, almost
decadent, just plain
decadent, so
decadent, warmly
deceitful
decency, masculine
decent, merely
deceptive
decisive
dedication can create wines like
these, only pure
defective
defects than delights, has more
defects, no noticeable
defects, void of
defiant
definition, good
definitive
deft

degenerate
delectable, utterly
deliberate, artistically/
artistic deliberateness
delicioso, devastatingly
delicioso, utterly
delicious from first sniff to last sip
delicious from start/first to finish
delicious glug-glug available, most
delicious it melts the heart, so
delicious it provokes nervous
giggles, so
delicious it's probably illegal in
25 states, so wickedly
delicious to new levels, has taken
the word
delicious you almost won't want to
swallow, so
delicious, absolutely/downright
delicious, audaciously
ingratiatingly
delicious, comprehensively/totally
delicious, deliriously
delicious, devilishly
delicious, drop-dead
delicious, ground-breakingly
delicious, gulpably
delicious, hugely/impossibly/
outrageously/ phenomenally/
screamingly/staggeringly/
stupefyingly/unabashedly/
unbelievably/unusually/utterly
delicious, immediately
delicious, juicily
delicious, madly/wildly
delicious, mouthfillingly
delicious, perfect-pitch
delicious, quintessentially
delicious, silkily
delicious, so far...so
delicious, speciously
delicious, straight-ahead
delicious, swooningly
delicious, utterly sinfully
delicious, wickedly
deliciously and softly, hits the taste
buds
deliciousness in it eluded analysis
deliciousness, cold explosion of
deliciousness, pure fun
deliciousness, towering
deliciousness, urgent
delight or disgust, wrapped in
layers of sensory
delight to drink by itself
delight to drink, absolutely
delight to taste I was seriously
tempted to swallow, such a

delight to the senses
delight to the taste buds
delight, earthly
delight, epicurean's
delight, genuine/sheer
delight, hedonistic/hedonist's
delight, ravishing
delight, triumphant peal of
delight, yummy
delighted to the point of hearing
 angels sing
delightful, wholly
delights, extraordinary ambrosially
 bawdy
delirious
delish/de-lish
deliver, doesn't quite
delivers the goods
deluxe
demand, much in
demanding
demands savoring
demands, makes no
demeanor, fine
demure
denatured
denominator, lowest-common
dependable, ever-
dependable, utterly

depraved but interesting

depth, out of its
describe, not a wine to
description, beyond/defies
deserving
designed, poorly
designed, well
desirable
desperate
detached
determined
detour, not worth a
devilish/diabolical
devilish and heavenly together
devil-may-care
devious, rather quite
diamond of a wine
diamond, real
diamond, rough/uncut
dicey
die drinking it, may I
die for, spicy come-hither wine to
die for, to happily
died in there, something curled up
 and
difficult
difficult to spit out
diffident and evasive, rather
dignified in a rustic way

diligently without pretensions or
 phoniness, performs
dimension in flavor, ultimate
dimension that evoked thoughts of
 religion and some sort of higher
 power, almost an extra
dimension, altogether in another
diplomatic
direct
direction, off in another
disagreeable, frankly
disappoint, doesn't/won't
disappointing, downright/frankly
disappointing, overall
disappointment, sorry
disarming, totally
discardable
disciplined
discombobulated
disconcerting
discourse, above rational
discreet...restrained...fine
discriminating
disgraceful

disgusting, truly

dishonest
dislike this mellow caressing wine,
 no one alive could
dislike, impossible to
dismal
disobedient
disoriented, bit
dispassionate
dispiriting
disposition, attractively sunny
disposition, zesty
distant
distinct personality
distinction and distinctiveness,
 huge
distinction, does not have much
distinction, eclectic
distinction, real
distinction, without any great
distinctive
distingué/distinguished
diva with exquisite refined features
diva, superannuated
diverse
divide, on the big side of the
divine!
divine, belongs in the world of the
divinity, pure
dodgy
dog talking, truly the
dog, real
dollars, tastes like a million
dominates any conversation

done, expertly/well
dorky
doughnut, bit of a
dour, rather
down, low-
down, never lets you
down, you just cannot put it
downward, great leap
DPIM (don't put in mouth)
drabness, infinite
draconian
drain, pour it down the
drainpipe, destined for the
drama and complexity
drama, deep intense emotional
drama, high
drama, lacks/needs some
dramatic
drawer, top-
dreadful, simply
dream about, to
dream of far-off places, makes you
dream to gulp down, a
dream, hedonism addict's/
 hedonist's
dream, purist's
dreamlike/dreamy
dreams, stuff of
dreams but of legends, the stuff not
 just made of
dreary example
dreary, astonishingly/extremely

dreck, total

dress up or dress down
dress, little black
dressed in Versace and a feather
 boa
dressed to the nines
dressed up to go out, all
drink it as much as you absorb it,
 you just don't
drink it, begs you to
drink me, says
drink this sitting down or risk
 your knees buckling
drink, deceptively easy to
drink, easy to/easy drinker/easy
 drinkin'/easy drinking/oh so
 easy to
drink, fit to
drink, hard to
drink, jolly good
drink, not fit/unfit to
drink, quality
drinkability, amazingly high
drinkability, real
drinkability, sheer
drinkability, wide band of

drinkable drop, fantastically
drinkable except on an icy night by a raging bonfire, hardly
drinkable, appealingly
drinkable, barely/hardly/just about
drinkable, beautifully
drinkable, eminently/terrifically/ utterly
drinkable, exuberantly/ shamelessly
drinkable, hugely/immensely/ terribly/very
drinkable, merely
drinkable, mouthwateringly
drinkable, oh-so-
drinkable, potentially
drinkable, really remarkably
drinkable, unstoppably
drinkable, well and truly
drinkable…but not likable
drinking fine/well
drinking gloriously
drinking, for uncritical uncomplicated
drinking, happy
drinking, much too easy
drinking, not worth
drinking, on-the-spot
drinking, worth
drinking…pouring on ice cream or dousing cakes, good for
drinks above its station
drollish

drool-inducing
drooped in the glass
dross
drum roll, please!
drunk, begs to be
dubious, extremely
dud, a
dud, no
dull around the edges
dull, deadly/deathly
dull, disconcertingly
dull, far from
dull, rather
dullness, jammy
dumb and then grinned like a fool for at least a half hour, I was immediately struck
dumbed down, bit
dump down the sink
dumpy and squashy, bit
dung, almost as rare as rocking-horse
dwell on, nothing to
dynamic

dynamics going on, very interesting
dynamite/dy-na-mite
eager to please
earnest
earth move, makes the
earth move, will never make the
earth won't move
earth-mover, will never be an
earth-shaking yet, nothing
easy sip, especially
easy to drink it could hurt you, so
easy to drink too much of, far too
easy to drink, all/almost too
easy to drink, dangerously/ disturbingly
easy to empty this bottle, all too
easy to get on with
easy, real
easy-drinkers, not one of your
easygoing wine, not an ebullient
ecstasy, could bring any deity to
ecstasy, could move one to
ecstasy, liquid
edge, hasn't lost its
edge, treads perilously close to the
edgy and rocky and steep and sparse
eerie
effete
effort, amazing/brilliant/ dazzling/glorious/heroic/ knockout/monumental/sterling
effort, more than creditable
effort, not a squeaky clean innocuous
effort, weak
effortless to drink
effulgent
effusive
egocentric
elaborate
élan, made with
élan, possesses
elastic taste

electric experience
electric wine with power…polish… subtlety and grace
electrifies every taste bud in your mouth
elegance and complexity, every facet of
elegance and delicacy, epitome of
elegance difficult to describe
elegance impossible to convey using the standard vocabulary of a wine taster

elegance in a thousand different ways, exudes
elegance meets mineral *terroir*, featherlight
elegance of a greyhound, body and
elegance personified, seductive
elegance vinified
elegance with primordial hedonism, melds suave
elegance, accomplished
elegance, admirably balances power and
elegance, airy
elegance, antithesis of
elegance, certain steely
elegance, charmingly gruff
elegance, classic example of power allied to
elegance, combines natural power and
elegance, cultivated
elegance, divine/sublime
elegance, easygoing
elegance, enchanting/ethereal/ surreal/uncanny
elegance, epitome of discreet perfumed
elegance, feathery
elegance, flashes of
elegance, gossamer-thin
elegance, great/quintessential/ towering
elegance, incomparable
elegance, masculine/muscular
elegance, minimalist
elegance, nascent
elegance, object lesson in
elegance, outspoken
elegance, pinpoint
elegance, sheer
elegance, silky/velvety
elegance, straight-backed
elegance, tableside
elegance, tattered
elegance, telltale
elegance, timeless
elegance, toasty
elegance, unbridled
elegance, underlying
elegance, unforced
elegance, voluptuous
elegant all around
elegant and complex with big muscles at rest
elegant and pretty
elegant and refined, supremely
elegant and sophisticated as an Italian sports car, as

elegant and sophisticated, colossally
elegant but cerebral
elegant in the extreme
elegant, indescribably
elegant, longingly
elegant, majestically
elegant, marvelously/ quintessentially/supremely/ utterly
elegant, powerful and muscular yet remarkably feminine and
elegant, seductively
elegant, svelt and
elegant, uncannily
elegant, uncommonly
elegiac
elevated
eloquent, not very
eloquent, strangely
elusive as a puff of smoke, as
elusive, unusual tastes prove
embattled
embodies everything great
embraceable
eminent
emotional
emphatic
empty
enchanting character
enchanting, totally/utterly
enchantress, wondrous
encompassing, all-
encountered, rarely
end, high-
end, top-
endearing
energizing rather than fatiguing
engaging, hugely
engaging, intellectually
engrossing
enigma, something of an
enigmatic, inexplicably
enjoy ourselves, still gives us sybarites a good excuse to
enjoy, flatteringly easy to
enjoy, sinfully easy to
enjoyable than this, can't get more
enjoyable the more you drink it, becomes less
enjoyable, consistently
enjoyable, disarmingly/easily
enjoyable, hedonistically
enjoyable, massively
enjoyable, smoothly
enlivened/enlivening
enriched
entertainer, great

entertainment on the tongue, provides great
enthralling, totally
enthusiasm, doesn't spark much
enthusiastic
enticing, strangely
entrancing
enveloping on the palate
enveloping, all-
ephemeral, both intense and
epic
epicurean
epitome
epochal
erratic
Escher drawings: elaborate... linear...intricate...precise... mathematical and captivating, like M.C.
essence of forbidden delight
essence of itself behind, leaves the
essence of life
essence of the grape, really the
essence than a wine, more of an
essence, pure
essence...it really delivers the goods, like an
essences, aromatic
essential
established
esteemed
etched, beautifully
eternal flavor
ethereal
euphoria, breeze of
euphoric bouquet
eureka!
evanescent...the grin without the cat
evasive
everything and more, has
everything but the kitchen sink
everything one would ever want in a wine, has
everything, has virtually
everything, just
everything, plenty of
everything, too much of
evil, blandly
evil, freakishly
evil, just plain
evil, savagely
evocative
exalted
examination, does not demand or merit microscopic
excellence, hallmark/standard of
excellence, par

excellent due to the sheer fabulosity of its flavors
excellent, most consistently/ uniformly
excels
exceptional all the way
excess, avoids
excited about, little/ nothing to be/get
excited, not one to get you
excitement on the tongue, some real
excitement, not exactly brimming over with
excitement, underpinning of almost vibrating
excitement, without any particular
excites deep-down senses
excites...intrigues and entices
exciting, none too/rather less
exciting, rarely
excruciating
execrable, thoroughly
executed, well
exemplary
exhilarating
exotically aromatic
expanding/expansive
expectations, doesn't meet/ not up to
expectations, exceeds
expectations, meets/up to
expectations, reeling with
expected, as
experience rather than a pleasure
experience, almost a religious
experience, enriching/ life-enhancing
experience, exceptional enological
experience, heady
experience, mind-boggling quasiorgasmic
experience, once-tried-never- forgotten
experience, quite an
experience, real
experience, superior
experience, unparalleled sensory
exploited, fully
exploited, not fully
exploring them, makes you want to spend time
expression, economical
expression, full/fullest/great/ marvelous/superior
expression, pure/purest
expression, wacky
expressive, explosively

expressive, extremely/fully/
  highly/immensely/
  massively/most
expressive, mind-bogglingly
expressive, remarkably
exquisite, simply
exquisiteness, subtle
extensive
extra, has that little
extraneous, nothing
extraordinary, quite
extrarich
extraspecial
extravagance, explosive aromatic
extravagance, sheer
extravagance, true
extreme
extroverted, little
exuberance in a bottle
exuberance, playful
exuberance, wild untamed
eye opener, real
eye, hits the bull's
eyebrows, won't raise too many
eyed, wild-
eyelids droop, doesn't make your
eye-opener
eye-popping
fabled
fables, the stuff of
fabulous in every way
fabulous mouthful
fabulous, fucking
fabulous, only
fabulous, this stuff is
façade, deceiving
face, hits you in the
face, not in-your-
face, quintessentially in-your-
face, will always keep a straight
facile
fair, only
fairies, visions of sugar-plum

fairy tale
fairy-dust scented
faith not required
false
falter, doesn't
falters
fantastic
fantastic and unforgettable
fascinating mouthful
fascinating, utterly
fashioned, beautifully
fastidious
fatal
fatiguing to drink
fault-free/no-fault

faultless, absolutely
faultless, almost/near/virtually
faults but no real merits either,
  no real
faults, no particular
faults, visible
faulty, quite/very
favorable
fearless, certainly not for the
feast, rich unctuous liquid
featureless, somewhat
feedback, lacks/no
feel to it, raw
feeling, natural
feet, swoops in and knocks
  you off your
fence a bit, sits on the
fervent
fetching little thing
fetching, totally
fettle, in fine
few and far between, one of the

fickle
fiendish
fiesta in a bottle
fills the mouth and blows the mind
fine and classic as they come, as
fine and dandy
fine and rustic, at once
fine by any standards
fine fine fine
fine indeed, very very
fine wine, of little interest to
  someone seeking a truly
fine, especially/unmistakably
fine, just plain
fine, quite/very
finely wrought
finesse and precision
finesse aplenty
finesse goes further than brawn
finesse not on the agenda
finesse of a horny hippopotamus,
  has all the
finesse rather than substance
finesse straight through, extreme
finesse than power, more
finesse, amazing/fabulous/
  remarkable/stunning/
  superlative/unbelievable
finesse, brilliant marriage of power
  and
finesse, defines
finesse, elements of
finesse, epitome of
finesse, evident
finesse, exhilarating sensation: all
finesse, filled with

finesse, fine lemony-oak
finesse, fireworks of
finesse, haunting mouthful of
finesse, incomparable
finesse, mineral/minerally
finesse, model/paragon of
finesse, not a study in
finesse, not overburdened with
finesse, paradigm of
finesse, pure
finesse, somewhat lacking in
finesse, supreme world-class
finesse, textbook example of
  intensity meets
finesse, uncommon
finesse, undeniable
finesse, unique
finesse, vanilla-coffee and black-
  fruit
finesse, vanillary
finessed, most
finesse-driven
finesse-filled
finest imaginable
finest wines I have ever put my lips
  to, one of the
finest wines in the world,
  absolutely ranks with the
finicky
fire, full of/on fire
fired up
firework display, gustatory
firework display, veritable
fireworks, aromatic
fireworks, boatload of hedonistic
fireworks, dazzling/impressive
  olfactory
fireworks, don't expect
first-rate, absolutely
flagrant
flagrant, never/not
flagship wine
flair, has
flamboyance, flashy
flamboyant, rather
flash and no substance, all
flash, lots of/flashy
flash/flashiness, no
flash-in-the-pan, only a
flash-in-the-pan...this, no
flashy, altogether too/rather
flashy, not too
flashy, not/nothing
flashy, verging on
flattened by filtration
flattering
flattish, rather
flaunts its wares

flavor activity, intensity
flavor authority, no shortage of
flavor authority, sound
flavor bomb
flavor one expects, not the
flavor profile, discreet
flavor profile, unusual
flavor, alive with
flavor, bottomless depth of
flavor, empty of
flavor, rainbow of
flavor, tightly wound beams of pinpoint
flavor, volcano of
flavored, broad-
flavored, coldly
flavored, deep-/deeply/full-/fuller/fully
flavored, emphatically
flavored, pure-
flavored, rich-/richly
flavored, slim-
flavorful, bewitchingly
flavorful, expansively
flavorful, explosively/intensely
flavorless
flavor-packed
flavors and aromas, unimpeded
flavors and character, stacks of
flavors are hard to read
flavors blooming at different times, various
flavors boogie around the glass
flavors bring tears to the eyes
flavors burst like stars across my palate and into my brain
flavors dance lightly to a tune
flavors freely, gives out its
flavors gallop across the palate
flavors in play, plenty of
flavors of frank breadth
flavors of heaven and earth
flavors on its sleeve, wearing all its
flavors pouring into my mouth, waterfall of
flavors rock the house
flavors rocket around the mouth
flavors run on and on
flavors shining like a hologram
flavors straight from an Eastern bazaar
flavors that are not easily forgotten, eye-opening
flavors will shock your taste buds, awesome
flavors you could ever wish for, all the
flavors, active

flavors, admirably pure
flavors, arpeggio of
flavors, bang of/exploded with/explosion of
flavors, bounty of opulent
flavors, cacophony of
flavors, candy shop of
flavors, chock-a-block with
flavors, clean uninhibited
flavors, come-and-get-me
flavors, crystalline
flavors, cubist pastiche of
flavors, cut-glass purity of
flavors, deep resounding
flavors, deep-set
flavors, delivers a boatload of
flavors, distinctive
flavors, doughnut of
flavors, dripping/packed with
flavors, earth-shaking
flavors, fathoms of
flavors, fleeting
flavors, floods the mouth with
flavors, full-on action painting of
flavors, globules/gobs/lots of
flavors, grandest most sumptuous
flavors, great blobs of
flavors, hard
flavors, hard-to-pin-down
flavors, has tenacity of/tenacious
flavors, heavy with
flavors, immediate
flavors, intoxicating purity of
flavors, in-your-face exotic
flavors, Joseph's coat of many
flavors, layer after layer of shimmering
flavors, lifted
flavors, look-at-me
flavors, massive black
flavors, massive/pronounced
flavors, middling
flavors, modulating
flavors, never-ending passion play of
flavors, no shortage of
flavors, panoply of sweet
flavors, parade of fresh
flavors, persistent stream of
flavors, piercing linear
flavors, plenty of all-up
flavors, plenty of driving
flavors, primal ancient
flavors, pulsing with
flavors, real wraparound rich
flavors, real-time
flavors, remarkably delicate pretty lacework of

flavors, resonates in
flavors, runs up and down the scales of
flavors, savage almost coarse throaty roar of
flavors, savory cascade of
flavors, sharp blast of
flavors, sharply drawn
flavors, sinister
flavors, slender weak-kneed
flavors, souk's worth of
flavors, starburst of
flavors, stuffed to the gills with wondrous
flavors, sun-kissed
flavors, supermarket of complex
flavors, swooping
flavors, tenacious
flavors, thrillingly vivid searching
flavors, throaty roar of
flavors, tight kernel of
flavors, uncanny range of
flavors, uncontaminated by extraneous
flavors, unique spectrum of
flavors, universe of
flavors, very good inner-mouth
flavors, warm authoritative
flavors, washed-out
flavors, weak-kneed
flavors...from spring blossoms to summer and autumn fruit to wintry mineral austerity, four
flavory in an obscure kind of way, very
flaw anywhere, nary/not a
flawed, brilliantly
flawed, deeply/quite
flawed, hopelessly
flawed, probably
flawed, seriously and hopelessly
flawless, rather quite
flawless, totally/virtually
flawlessly crafted
flaws, minor
flaws, noticeable
flesh, dissolves into your
flight, gossamer
flighty, charmingly
flimsy
flippant at times
flirtatious/flirty
floating, ethereally
floats and stings
flourishing
flow and line, ultrasmooth
flow, even
flowing

fluent, delightfully
flush, royal
fluttery
foolhardy/foolish
foolproof
footed, sure-
footloose and fancy-free
forbidden, bit
forbidding, almost
forbidding, not
foretaste, good/strong
foretaste, promising
forget it anytime soon,
  you aren't likely to
forget it, I will never
forget it/forget about it
forgettable, eminently/instantly/
  totally
forgiving
forgotten, not easily
forgotten, should perhaps best be
form, in perfect/top
formidable, truly
forthcoming, charmingly/
  deliciously
forthright
fortitude, amazing
forward, somewhat
four-square
fragile
fragrance and flavor, imbued with
  every possible
fragrance leaps from the glass
fragrance, inimitable
fragrance, pure crystalline
fragrances that can't wait, sort of
fragrances, dazzled by its
fragrances, extraordinary whoosh
  of
fragrances, glorious
fragrances, immediate belch of
fragrances, lacking
fragrances, surging
fragrances, tenuous
fragrant, coaxingly/enchantingly
fragrant, expansively
fragrant, explosively/piercingly/
  vividly/wildly
fragrant, very
frank
frankness, great aromatic
frankness, upfront
freakish
frenzied
fresh
friend, not an easy
friendless
friendly personality

friendly tail, wags a
friendly, barely/none too/not
  particularly
friendly, very
frightening
frills, no
frilly
frippery, no
frippery, pretty little
frisky
frivolity, gives the impression of
frivolous
frivolous, less
frivolous, not at all
frolicsome
frugal
frustrating
fuddled and wrapped up, rather
fulfilling, generously
full no-compromise mouthfiller
full of itself, very
fulsome verging on specious
fun and games, no indication of
fun as having your teeth drilled,
  as much
fun in the mouth
fun to drink, downright
fun, no
fun, quite
fun, sheer/wicked
fun, undeniable blast of
fun-filled/funny
furious
furtive
fuss all about?, what's the
fuss drop, no-
fuss-free
fussy
ga-ga, hedonists will go
gaiety, Dionysian
gaiety, natural
gaiety, winey
gallant dressed in white for a
  summer evening
gallant effort
game, at the top of its
garish about this subtle yet
  powerful giant, nothing
gauche
gaudy
gauntlet, runs the
gay
gay exhilarating effect
gear, in top
gear, stuck in second
gem, absolute/utter
gem, delightful
gem, little

gem, mind-bending/-blowing
gem, unexpected
genial/geniality
generosity, boundless
generosity, lacks
generous and difficult to get to
  know, less than
generous to a fault
generous, undeniably/
  unsparingly
generous, very
genius, bottle of winemaking
genius, statement of humankind's
  creative
genteel yet firm
gentle
ghastly
ghostly
giant of a wine
giddy
gift from Mother Nature
gift of the gods
gift that unwraps itself halfway
  across your tongue
gifted
giggle, makes you
gilt-edged
giving as some, not as
giving than most, more
glamorous
glass, I could climb into the
glasses off your head,
  will knock the
glib
gloomy affair, rather
glorious mouthful
glorious, absolutely
glory that has never been
  surpassed, a
gloss, classy
glossy
glow, delicate inner
glow, glorious
glows through the centuries
glugability, succulent
glug-glug
go to whoa, superb from
goals, kicking lots of
gobsmacked
God not by man, made by
God!, oh-my-
God, touched by
godawful
godlike
goes down easy
go-go, all set to
going nowhere
gold, liquid

gold, pot of
gold, pure
gold-plated
gone before you know it, a glass of
  this is
good account of itself, gave a
good as expected, as
good as it gets/they come, as
good but not tops, very
good drinking, straight-ahead
good drunk from a tankard,
  would be
good etc. (good, bad, etc.),
  when it's
good even if poured from a can,
  would taste
good for the kid in everyone
good in its way
good indeed
good intentions, has
good it makes you want to shout,
  so
good it must be illegal, so
good it's almost painful, so
good mouthfiller/mouthful
good on its own scale
good plus
good rich mouthfiller
good stuff
good thing, almost much too much
  of a
good things happening here, lots of
good to be true, almost/virtually
  too
good wine should be eye candy
good winecraft
good winemaking, all the signs of
good wines you can surf in to shore
  on
good you may just want to sink
  your nose into the glass, smells so
good, absurdly/astonishingly/
  breathtakingly/devilishly/
  exceedingly/incredibly/
  indescribably/phenomenally/
  ridiculously/sensationally/
  shockingly/staggeringly/
  stupendously/stupefyingly/
  terrifically/thunderingly/
  unquestionably
good, addictively
good, better than
good, blindingly/glitteringly
good, bloody
good, brutally
good, cracking
good, crazy
good, damn/darn

good, dangerously
good, freakishly
good, insanely over-the-top
good, jolly
good, just stupid
good, lipsmackingly
good, mouthfillingly
good, oh so
good, pretty darn
good, pretty/quite/rather
good, really really
good, seriously/very
good, simply unquestionably
good, startlingly
good, superlatively
good, surprisingly
good, thunderingly
good, too damn
good, very very very
good, write-home-about
goodie, a
goodies, packed with
goodish, barely
goodish, only
good-natured
goodness, pure delicious focused
goodness, sheer
goods, delivers the
good-time gal
good-to-be-true, too
goooood; any more left?, this is
goosebumps, generates
goosebumps, gives me/you
gorgeous drinking
gorgeous, absolutely
gorgeous. period.
gosh!, oh
grace and finesse that Baryshnikov
  would appreciate, offers a
grace and refinement, magical
grace, eases over the palate with a
  creamy
grace, ethereal
grace, flavor-laden explosion of
  power and
grace, gossamer
grace, infinite
grace, noble
grace, stoic
grace, uncommon
grace, understated
grace...power and generosity, rules
  with
graced the cup of Bacchus himself,
  could have
graceful enough to win the heart of
  a lady, powerful enough to fuel a
  musketeer and

graceful in every way
graceful, exquisitely
graceful, supremely/utterly
graceless, little
gracelessness, earnest
graces whatever, no saving
gracious
graciousness, feminine
grade at all checkpoints, makes the
grand
grand cru, puts the *grand* in
grand in all its dimensions
grand way to end a meal
grand, nothing
grand, regally
grandee
grandeur, frightening
grandeur, natural
grandeur, some
grandiose
grape, tastes like you're getting the
  whole
grapes grown outdoors?, how can
  anything like this be made from
gratification, delivers immense
gratification, enormous sensory
gratification, not for those looking
  for intellectual
gratification, satisfies my cravings
  for both corporeal and
  intellectual
gravitas, lacks
gravitas, real
great among greats, a
great but cannot manage even to be
  good, tries so hard to be
great by-the-glass pour
great shakes, no
great stuff
great to relish
great wine holds your attention
  and has more than you can say
  in words
great wine is no accident
great, devastatingly
great, embodies everything
great, just plain/merely
great, never
great, profoundly/unbelievably/
  unquestionably
great, truly/very
greater wine, it's not possible to
  make a
greatest red, possibly the
greatest wine on the planet
greatest wine we ever had
greatest wines ever made, one of
  the

greatest wines I've ever tasted,
  among the
greatest wines of all time,
  unquestionably one of the
greatest, the absolute
greatness of this wine, impossible
  to intellectualize away the
greatness, definition of
greatness, just misses
greatness, not destined for
greatness, rarified air of
greatness, sheer unequivocal
greatness, touched with
greats, in a pantheon of
greats, one of the all-time
greeting, last passionate
gregarious
grim
grin insanely, makes you
grinning from ear to ear,
  one sip will leave you
grisly
groan, disgusted
groomed, well
groovy, deeply
gross and vulgar
grotesque, just plain
grotesque, monstrous to the point
  of being

grotty

grouchy
grounding, plenty of chocolate and
grounding, serious
grows and grows on the palate
grows on you
grrrrreat!, tastes
grubby
grudging
gruff
gruff in character, little
gruff, somewhat
grumpy
grungy
grunty
guessing, keeps you
guileless/no guile
guiltless
gullible
gulpable, dangerously
gulpability, slippery
gulps, invites large
gulps, to be drunk in great
  refreshing
gusher/gushing
gusto, goes for the
gusto, lacks a little
guzzley
hailed

hallelujah!, will make you sing
hallmarked
hallucinatory
hand, needs a firm
handed, heavy-
handicapped
handsome
hapless
happiness, makes me cry with
happy wine, very
Harm", fulfils the Hippocratic oath
  of "Do No
harmful
harmless
harshness, charmless
hat, hold on to your
hated it; left most in the bottle
hating, not worth

haughty demeanor

haughty...almost arrogant
haunting and brilliant and subtle
  and thrilling and ancient on the
  planet, most
haunting aromas
haunting as a cello solo by
  Yo-Yo Ma, as
haunting edge
have, definite must-
havoc, delicious
hazardous to your health if drunk,
  may be
hazard, a health
head high, holds its
heads to turn, will unquestionably
  cause
heads, sure to turn
head-turner, hedonistic
head-turning, should prove to be
health, brimming with
  intoxicating
health, lovely
health, oozes ripeness and
health, so full of
healthy, surprisingly
heart, brilliant
heart, from the
heart, gladdens the
heart, good/has
heart, lots of
heartbreaking
hearted, big-
hearted, essentially good-
hearted, warm-/heartwarming
heartfelt
heartless
heart-on-sleeve, quickly evolving
heart-racing
heart-rending

hearts and flowers in either
  the smells or tastes, no
heart-stopping
heaven experience, kind of
  touching-
heaven in a glass
heaven is like, what
heaven, hedonistic
heaven, made in
heaven, pure/utter
heavenly experience
heavenly glass and the flat sludge
  that finished the bottle,
  incredible difference between
  the first
heavenly mouthful
heavenly voluptuous sensationally
  good wine
heavenly with so many tiny
  nuances that I could fill an entire
  page, so
heavenly, absolutely
heaven-sent
hectic, somewhat
hedonism in a bottle
hedonism incarnate
hedonism on the palate, blueprint
  for pure
hedonism, by-itself
hedonism, pure/refined
hedonism, restrained
hedonism: sensuality by numbers,
  disciplined
hedonistic and intellectual senses,
  satiates both the
hedonistic atmosphere
hedonistic drinking experience,
  quintessential
hedonistic experience far beyond
  the ordinary
hedonistic experience,
  extraordinary
hedonistic impression, makes one
  heck of a
hedonistic, entirely
hedonistic, joyfully
hedonists, not for
heightens all the senses
heights, dizzy Olympian
heights, hits giddy
heights, illustrious

heights, scales celestial

hellish
here nor there, neither
heroic
high notes, hits all the
high, sky
high, staggeringly/stunningly

high, wine tasting
highlights nor lowlights, has neither
highlights, no particular
highs, devoid of
history, sip of
histrionics, no
hit the nail on the head
hit, direct
ho-hum
hold its own among the world's best, will
hold on to your hat
holds barred, no
hole in the middle
hole, proverbial black
holistic
home-run of a wine, delightful delicious
homogeneous
honed, finely/nicely/well
honest as the day is long, as
honest natural wine with roots in the earth
honest, supremely/totally
honesty, rugged
honorable
hooch, lousy
hoorah/hooray/hurrah/hurray
hopeful
hopeless mess
horrible to taste, too
horrible. period.
horrid

horrid, dry...raw...

hot, red-
hot, white-
hottie, real
housebroken
hubba hubba
hug from the inside, a
hug, big
hug, wraps you in a great bear
hugs you, just
huge
human, deeply
humble
humbling experience for a wine drinker
humdinger
humor, engaging sense of
humored about it, nothing ill-
humored, good-
humorless
humorous
hurly-burly you can't ignore, barges in and creates a strident larger-than-life

hushed
hyper
hyper-rich
hypertrophied
hypnotic
hypocritical

icky, ineffably

idea, witty
ideal at any hour
ideas about itself, high
idyllic
ignore or resist, impossible to
illegal, probably
illuminating
illusory
illustrious
imaginary
imagination and fuels conversation, lubricates
imaginative
imbibation, rewarding
imitation, deserves
immemorial
immersion, total
immodest
immoral
immortal, almost
immutable
impact, explosive
impact, high
impact, quiet
impaired
impassioned
impeccability scale, always scores high on the
impeccable, technically
imperfect
imperfections, full of
imperial
imperious, austerely
imperious, quite
impersonal, touch
impertinence, blessed with saucy
impertinent
impish
implacable
impolite
imponderables, one of life's great
importance, a wine of
important
impossible to resist
impress and it does, out to
impression, dandyish first
impression, quite unforgettable
impressive and expressive, exceptionally
impressive aroma
impressive stuff, uncompromising

impressive, enormously/ imposingly/mightily/ powerfully/splendidly/very
improbable
improved
improvement likely, no
impudent
impulsive
inadequate
inane
incandescent
incisive, less
incisive, more
incoherent
incomparable
inconclusive
incongruous about it, something
inconsistent, fiendishly
inconsistent, stubbornly
incontestable
incorrect
incorrigible
incredible
indelible
indescribable
indestructible
indifferent
indignant
indiscreet
indistinct

indolence, voluptuous

indomitable, absolutely
indulgence, sheer
indulgent, positively
industrious
ineffable
inelegant
inept
inert
inexcusable
inexorable
inexpressive
inferior, just plain
infinite
infirm
inflict this on yourself, try not to
infuriating
ingenious
ingratiating, rather
inhospitable
inimitable, totally
innocent
innocuous final impression, somewhat
innocuous, extremely
inoffensive on all counts
inoffensive, pleasantly
inoffensiveness, overall

inscrutable
insensitive
insidious but good
insignificant
insinuating character
insipid
insipidity, sinks into
insolent
insouciance of great charm, brisk
insouciant, hugely
insouciant, superbly
inspiration, bolt of
inspirational, deeply
inspire any musketeer to heroic
  deeds, could
inspired winemaking
inspired, divinely
inspiring, awe-
instructive
insubstantial
insult, an/insulting
insuperable
intangible
integrity and intelligence, rare
integrity, oozing with
intellect rather than the stomach,
  appeals to the
intellect, constantly challenges the
intellect, engages the
intellect, fails to engage the
intellect, makes no demands on
  the
intellectual challenge
intellectual charm
intellectual gratification,
  not for those looking for
intellectual gratification, satisfies
  my cravings for both corporeal
  and
intellectual interest, of
intellectual meets the sensual,
  truly a wine where the
intellectual satisfaction,
  physical pleasure but not
intellectual senses, satiates both
  the hedonistic and
intellectual turn-on
intellectual yearnings, satiates the
  olfactory senses yet pleases the
  mind's
intellectual, rather
intellectual...slightly boring,
  slightly
intelligent, quite
intelligible
intentioned, well
interest, holds our

interesting and conversation-
  worthy
interesting and nourishing bits and
  bobs, full of
interesting glassful
interesting, altogether
interesting, fantastically
interesting, ve-e-e-ery
interlocked
interlude
intimidating on the palate
intimidating, almost
intolerable
intoxicating
intrepid
intricate
intrigue, full of/great
intriguing
introspection, demands some
  degree of
introspection, doesn't require
  much
introspective, deeply
intuitive
invaluable
inventive
invigorating rather than fatiguing
invigorating, thoroughly
invigorating, thrillingly
invincible
invites you to dinner
inviting, not terribly
inviting, smells
inviting, warmly
invulnerable
irksome
ironic
irrational
irresistible
irreverent
jacked up
jackpot, wins the
jarring
jaunty
jazzed palate, fully
jazzy
jejune
Jekyll and Hyde characteristics
jewel of the wine world, gorgeous
jewel, beautiful/wonderful
jewel, crown
jewel, elegant harmonious
jewel, exquisitely fashioned
jewel, little
jewel, perfect
jewel, unexpected
jiggy

joie de vivre, full of/pure
joie de vivre, lusty
joint, little out of
joker in the pack
jolly, not terribly
jolly-natured, gutsy
jovial
joy and enthusiasm
joy here, not a lot of
joy to drink, a
joy to taste, absolute
joy to experience
joy, bottled
joy, defies description for sheer
  hedonistic
joy, huge mouthful of
joy, jump for
joy, life-enhancing experience of
  pure
joy, pure/utter
joy, sensory
joy, simple/uncomplicated
joyful as this, young red wine is
  seldom as exuberantly
joyful workout, gives your tongue a
joyful, totally
joyless
joyride
jubilant
juice, great
juice, riveting
jumble at the moment,
  somewhat of a
jumbled, somewhat
jumps all over you
jumps out of the glass
jumpy
junk, industrial insipid
junk, sweet
junk, unrefreshing
kaleidoscopic
keeper, not a/not for keeping
keeper/keep this one/for keeping
key, all in a minor
key/keyed, low-
keyed than expected, lower-
KIA (Killed In Action)
kicker
kicks up its heels
kill for, to
killer
killing for, almost worth
kind/kindly
kinder...gentler
kinetic
kingly
kinky

klutz/klutzy
knees go weak, makes the
knockout stuff
knockout, simply a
knowing, all-
knowledgeable
labyrinthine
lacking
lackluster
laid-back
landmark
languid/languorous
lap it up
larger than life
laudable/laudatory
laughable
laughing/all laughter
laughs, not a barrel of
laurels, not one resting on its
lavish
laws of modern oenology, defies
lax
layer upon layer
lazy thing
leading
league of its own, in a
league, major
league, minor
leap out of the glass, seems to
leave it on the shelf
left field, straight out of
legend in liquid form
legend in the making, potential
legend, destined to be a
legend, seamless
legend, something of a
legend, the stuff of
legends, the stuff not just made
    of dreams but of
legs buckle, will make your
legitimate
leprechaun
less can mean more
less than the sum of its parts
letdown, big/full/total
letdown, partial
lethal
levitating experience to taste
liberal
libidinous
lick it off your lover
life-changing
life enhancer, true
life, bursting with
life, essence of
life, exudes
life, filled with
life, full of lust for

life, sparkles with
life-affirming
life-changing, practically
life-enhancing experience,
    fresh and
life-enhancing experience, lovely
life-fulfilling
lifeless, completely
lifted, cleverly
lifting, heavy
light and shade, lack of
light under a barrel, does not hide
lighthearted
likable, immediately/instantly
like it...the more you taste it,
    the more you
like, difficult/hard to
like, hard not to/much too easy to
like, lots to
lilting
lily in a mud pond
limbo, in
line, excellent
linear
lines are clean and well fitted
lionhearted
lipsmacking
little
liveliness, extra jolt of
lively convivial palate
lively dinner companion
living everchanging mystery-in-a-
    bottle
living up to princely expectations,
    not
loaded from the get-go
loaded with good stuff
loaded, fully
loathsome
loco
lode, delicious mother-
lofty
lofty aims, made with
logic, defies all
logical
lollapalooza
loner
long and wide as an American
    highway, as
lordly, bit
lose yourself in, to
loss for words, at a
lot in the glass
loud and upside down
loud, not
loutish
lovable, instantly
love it, just

love with, easy to fall in
love, easy to
love, hard to
lovely all around, just
lovely stuff
lovely, aggressively
lovely, really/unquestionably
lovely, sensationally
lover than a fighter, more of a
loyal
lucid
lucky
Lucy in the Sky with Diamonds
lugubrious
lullaby
lumbering, bit
lumpen
lurch, made my stomach
lurid
luscious and ethereal all at once
luscious as luscious can be, as
luscious can be ephemeral,
    amazing that anything this
luscious it could make grown men
    swoon, so
luscious, absolutely
luscious, decadently
luscious, delicately
luscious, overwhelmingly
luscious, rewardingly
lush and giving
lushness, wondrous
luxuriance of aromas
luxuriance, deliciously voluptuous
luxurious, totally
luxury in a bottle
luxury, conspiratorial
luxury, ephemeral
luxury, epitomizes
luxury, mouthful of
luxury, unabashed/unadulterated
lyrical
lyrical about, nothing much
    to wax
mad
maddening
made as a Swiss watch, as well
made, beautifully/perfectly/
    skillfully
made, cleanly
made, cleverly/cunningly
made, indifferently/poorly/
    sloppily
made, interestingly
made, looks just-
made, none too skillfully
made, phenomenally well
made, well/very well

magic in a bottle
magic, black
magic, completely fails to deliver the
magic, liquid voodoo
magic, missed out on the
magic, no
magic, sheer/total
magical moment
magical stuff
magical, absolutely
magical: has everything going for it
magisterial
magnanimous
magnetic
magnificence piled upon magnificence
magnificent by any standard
magnificent in its way
magnificent, just short of
magnificent, unabashedly
magnificent...with few equals
majestic, most
majesty of the Royal Oak
majesty, honeyed
majesty, marvel at its
majesty, power and
majesty, sheer/true
major
malicious
malodorous
mambo...polka...foxtrot and jitterbug too, can
mamma mia!
mangy
manifold
manipulative
mannered, gentle-
mannered, ill-
mannered, unusually well
manners, good
manufactured, poorly
manufactured, well
marginal
mark, up to the
marks, high
marred
marriage made in the heaven and hell of richness and decay, astonishing
marvel to the senses
marvelous, bloody
masochistic
masterful sense of craft
masterful, truly
masterpiece of freshness... drinkability and finesse, small
masterpiece without equal

masterpiece, ageless
masterpiece, authentic/true
masterpiece, in one word: a
masterpiece/masterwork, minor
masterpiece, New-World
masterpiece, rustic
masterpiece, symphonic
masterwork, majestic
matchless
matter-of-fact
meager
mean
mean, not
meandering
meaning/meant, well
measured
mediocre, decidedly
mediocre, irretrievably
mediocrity, descends rapidly into
meditate on, to
meditate, for people who like to
meditative
meditazione, vino da
megafabulous
megastunning
megawine in magnum
melancholy
mellifluous
mellow silhouette
mellowness, enveloping
mellowness, unforgettable
melodious
memorable drinking experience, truly
memorable, highly
memorable, not extremely
memorable, really quite
memories are made of this
memories long after it's gone, not a wine that will evoke fond
memories, heady mélange of
memory lane
memory of such a wine doesn't disappear
memory, etches deep in your
memory, treasured
menacing
mentality, made with a hedonist's
merciless
mercurial
merit, no/without
merit, of some
meritorious
merrily down the throat, flows
merry
mesmerized, get ready to be
mesmerizing
messy

meteor shower, soars like a
meteoric material, not
meticulous
mettlesome
microtreasure
middle, bit of grubbiness in the
middle, dead/flat in the
middle, lacks a/no
middling
middle-of-the-road stuff
mile, goes the extra
milestone of the history of wine, archeological
mind, blew/blows my/your
mind-bending
mind-blowing in a Methuselah
mind-blowing, absolutely/truly
mind-boggling
minded, broad-/fair-/open-
minded, simple-
mind-numbing
minds, for inquiring
miniclassic
minor
miracle continues
miracle of nature
miracle, a mystery or a
miracle, truly a
mirrors, no
mischief and abandon, full of
mischievous
misjudged
miss, a don't-
miss, a near-
missed, not to be/should not be
misses the mark by a long shot
misses, just
missing, nothing is
missing, something is
misunderstood
mixed up
m-m-m
moderate
moderation as a virtue
modest
modest and fine, extraordinarily
moist and tender
mollified
molten
momentous
monotonous
monstrous
monty, the full
monumental work of art
mood on course, puts one's
moody, bit
moonstruck

more you taste it the more you like it, the
more, brought me back for
more...please
moreish, compulsively
moreish, utterly
motion to your soul, brings
motionless
mouth does not live up to the promise of the nose, the
mouthful, good
mouthful, passable
moving
much to it, not
much to write home about, not
mucked about with too much
mucked-up, least
mucosa, ravishes the olfactory
muddled, completely
muddled, little/slightly
muddy characters

mumpish

murky...muffled and moderate
murmurings, subtle
music for the palate, easy-listening
music in a bottle, luscious
music of the grapes
musical
musical wine with perfect pitch
musings, thick honeyed
mustard, doesn't cut the
muster, does not pass
muster, easily passes
muted
Muzak for your palate
muzzy, slightly
mysteries...secrets and layers of promise, holds
mysterious, rather
mystery about it, faint/slight air/aura of
mystery and surprise, living wine of
mystery here, good measure of
mystery or a miracle, a
mystery, distant
mystery, shrouded in
mystic/mystical
mystique, pretty big
mythical mouthful, huge
mythical/mythic proportions, of
naïve
nasty
natty
nature, bounty of
nature, easygoing
natured, good-
naughtiness in a glass of pink

naughty, decadently rich and
naughty, extremely
ne plus ultra
near but not quite
neat
nebulous
neck out, certainly doesn't stick its
nectar of the gods
nectar, out-of-this-world ambrosial
needy
neoclassic
nerve and liquidity, fine
nerve, considerable/good
nervy
neutral/neutral character
nice 'n easy
nice, almost too
nice, really/thoroughly
nice enough
nicely done
nifty
night here...a bit of daylight might come as a welcome relief, plenty of
nightmare, absolute
nightmarish
nimble on the palate
nimble, surprisingly
nirvana, achieves
nirvana, pure
nirvana, vinous
nobility, bona fide/unimpeachable
nobility, brooding
nobility, liquid
nobility, not a member of
noble but regal, not just
noble relatives, has
noble wines, one of the most powerful of
noisome
noncerebral
nonchalance, amazing
nonchalant

nondescript

none, second to
nonpareil
nonsense, no-
nonsensical
nonserious
normal
normal and ordinary that I can't find any words to describe it, so
nose is so terrific that you taste it long before you drink it
nose out of the glass, you don't want to take your
nose, bottomless
nose, porous

nostalgic
notable, not
noteworthy
notes, hits all the right
notes, no discordant
notes, suavely mellifluous
nothing there
nothing to be ashamed of
nothing to dwell on
nothing to get excited about
nothing to write home about
nothing, big
notice what's in your glass, makes you sit up and
noticeable

notorious

nuanced, beautifully/marvelously
nuanced, delicately/lightly
nuanced, highly/supremely/very
nuances that my senses have experienced, filled with some of the most delicious
nuances, fracas of
nuances, intriguing
nuances, staggering range of
number one
number, edgy little
number, naughty cheeky little
number, rich toasty
oafish
obliging
oblique
oblivion, headed for
obnoxious
obscene, slightly
obsequious
obstinate
obstreperous
obtrusive
obtuse, wholly
obvious, much too
obvious, nothing about it is
oddball feeling, rather
odor, indefinite spineless
offense, couldn't possibly cause
offense, won't cause any
offensive...just uninspired, wasn't
offer and explore, much to
offer, little to
offering, modest
offering, seductive
off-flavor(s)/-odor(s)/smells/-taste(s)
off-song, strangely
oh-my-God/oh-my-god/omigosh
OK plus, just
OK, barely/no better than

olfactory senses yet pleases the mind's intellectual yearnings, satiates the
Olympic/Olympian
on, full-
one and only
one-off wine that inhabits a world of its own
one-off, perfect
one-off, thrilling
ooh and aah over, a wine to
ooh la la
oompah
oomph, little
open-minded
opinion, will divide
opportunistic
optimistic
opulence on a solid base
opulence, compelling
opulence, decadently overripe
opulence, exotic
opulence, hedonistic
opulence, layered
opulence, noteworthy
opulence, rare
opulence, scented
opulence, stewed
opulence, unbelievable/unreal
opulence, wonderful
opulent but depraved
opulent, exquisitely/incredibly
opulent, gently
opulent, most magnificently
opulent, obscenely
opulent, winningly
opus, expertly composed
order, of a high
ordinary, more than/out of the
ordinary, plain/pretty/quite
ordinary, supremely
ordinary, surprisingly
organized
organoleptic bandwidth, has wide
ostentatious
ostentatious it is impossible to ignore, so
ostentatious personality
otherworldly
OTT (over the top), not
out of sorts
out of this world, simply
out there, most
out there, so tantalizingly
outgoing
outlandish
out-of-body experience
out-of-bounds

out-of-doors inside, brings the
outrageous, stunningly
outspoken
outstanding and faultless in all departments: smell...taste and finish in the throat
outstanding as ever, simply as
outstanding by any measure
outstanding, absolutely/truly
outstanding, falls just short of being
over and above
over the top, almost/close to being
overachiever/overachieving
overambitious
overbearing and crude
overbearing, stops short of being
overbearing, unnecessarily
overblown, no way/not
overblown, way
overdelivers big time/in a big way
overdone, not/nothing
overdone, unnecessarily
overdrive, puts the olfactory senses on
overexplicit
overgroomed
overintellectualized
overlavish
overload most tasters' olfactory sensors, will
overloads the senses, really
overopulent
overprominent
over-refined
over-riding
overscented
overshadowed
over-the-top, nearly
over-the-top, way
overtones, strange
overwhelm you, doesn't aspire to
overwhelming, not
overwhelming...drawing saliva from every corner of the mouth, tiniest sip is
overworked
overwrought
oy!
pace, decidedly off the
pacesetting
package, a total/the complete
package, really smart
package, zesty
packed with goodies, stunningly well
packet, real surprise
painful, so good it's almost painful

painstaking
pajamas, the cat's
palace, palate is more of a
palatable, marginally
palate-whetting
palatial
palls
pampered
panache, full of
par excellence
par, below/under
paradise in a bottle
paradise, took me straight to
paradise, utter
paradoxical
paradoxicality: dryness with sensual fruitiness, achieves the apotheosis of
paramount
parody
passable mouthful
passable, more than
passion, has/passionate
pat, has it down
patchy
pathetic
patrician
pay dirt, hits
peace with itself, does not seem at
peachy/peachy-keen
peak, at its
pearl, absolute
peculiarities, hidden
pedestrian, rather
pedigree, ancient historical
pedigree, carefully groomed with generations of
pedigree, blue-chip/excellent/full of
pedigree, ritzy
pedigree, terrific
pedigreed
peerless
peeuueee!
peevish
penetrating
pensive
penultimate
peppy
perfect and symmetrical wine, the most
perfect drinking experience
perfect in every sense
perfect sweetness...body...flavors...tannin and acidity
perfect to get your appetite going
perfect weight...balance...texture and control

perfect wine be described?, how
    can such a
perfect wine, simply a
perfect, about as graceful as red
    wine ever gets...in a word...
perfect, almost/close to/near-/
    nearly/pretty well
perfect, elliptically
perfect, just/simply/utterly/
    virtually
perfect, less than
perfect, nigh on/well-nigh
perfect, not
perfect, picture-
perfect, quite some way beyond
perfect, smells and tastes
perfect...this is as perfect as wine
    can get, if a wine can ever be
perfection as one could ever expect,
    as close to
perfection, absolute/sheer
perfection, candidate for
perfection, close to/flirts with
perfection, excitingly close to
perfection, fully on its plateau of
perfection, God-given
perfection, height/peak of
perfection, judged to
perfection, liquid
perfection, nothing short of
perfection, poised
perfection, scratching at the door
    of
perfection, sheer unadulterated
perfection, silky

perfection, soulful

perfection...almost too good
perfection?, how can one describe
perfectly mature red imaginable:
    à point, most
perfectly, drinking
performance, classy
performance, show-stopping
performance, sterling
performance, very controlled
    polished
performer, big-time circus
performer, bonny
performer, uneven
perfume a room at twenty paces,
    able to
perfume and pleasure, all
perfume and silky texture seduce
    with poetry where other wines
    flash credit cards and gold chains,
    its
perfume and taste, overemphatic
perfume essence

perfume, arresting
perfume, divine/exquisite/
    fabulous/heavenly
perfume, drenched in
perfume, generous belt of
perfume, herbal minerally
perfume, inebriating /intoxicating
perfume, lovely inner-mouth
perfume, sensual
perfume, strangely elegant

perfume, sweet elusive

perfume...in bursts and towers of
    scents, innumerable drops of
perfumed, exotically
perfumed, exquisitely/gloriously/
    gorgeously/marvelously/richly
perfumed, gently/lightly/vaguely
perfumed, hauntingly
perfumed, headily/head-
    spinningly
perfumed, heavily/highly/
    immensely/ intensely/
    robustly/strongly
perfumed, most fragrantly
perfumed, outrageously
perfumes, knockout
perky
perplexing
persevering
persistent, smoothly
persists and crescendos
personable
personal
personality affair, big
personality and soul, plenty of
personality isn't for everyone,
    heavy ponderous
personality well defined
personality, alluring sexy
personality, bags/lashings of
personality, beaming with
personality, bit lacking in
personality, boisterous/exuberant/
    sparkling/supercharged/vibrant
personality, boldly assertive
personality, brims with/
    filled with/ full of/loaded
    with/plenty of
personality, butch
personality, devoid of any/no real
personality, distinct
personality, easy-to-understand
personality, fistful of chunky
personality, forward
personality, great/huge/outsized
personality, hasn't got much/
    lacking in/little
personality, impenetrable

personality, incisive
personality, in-your-face
personality, laserlike syrupy
personality, little discernible
personality, long on
personality, medium
personality, ostentatious
personality, plump-cheeked
    cherubic
personality, proud and willful
personality, severe
personality, sheer gutsy
personality, stripped-out
personality...poise and purpose,
    real
pertinacity, good
perverse
pesky thing
pessimistic
phantasmal/phantasmagoric/
    phantasmagorical/phantasmic
phenomenal
Phlegm '89, Château
picaresque/picturesque
picayune
pick of the litter
piece, conversation
piece, of a
pigswill
pillowy
pinnacle of its century
pinnacle, doesn't quite reach the
    absolute
pioneering
pips have been incorporated into
    the flavors, tastes as if the
pipsqueaky
piquant
pitch, higher/high-pitched
pitch, musical wine with perfect
pitched, beautifully/perfectly
pitched, deeply

pitiful

pits, the absolute/utter
pixieish
pizzazz, has
pizzazz, lacks a little
place, all over the
place, everything is in the right
place, not a hair out of
place, nothing is out of
placid
plaintive
plane all of its own, on a
plane than most, reaches a higher
planet as a wine, can represent the
planet, from another
play, very much in

playful, most
plays for keeps
pleasant rather than great
pleasant, just so darn
pleasant, minimally/quietly
pleasant, perfectly
please anyone the world over, would
please, eager-to-
please, simply made to
pleases at first sip
pleases the palate no end
pleasing, modestly
pleasing, not very
pleasing, utterly
pleasurable, extremely/immensely/very
pleasurable, immediately
pleasurable, most decadently
pleasurable, not
pleasure and leaves you with no food for thought--just like an American comedy, gives temporary
pleasure but not intellectual satisfaction, gives physical
pleasure button, will push your
pleasure center of the brain, goes straight to the
pleasure in a glass, pure
pleasure of the highest class, olfactory
pleasure to give, plenty of
pleasure without demanding a lot of thought, offers a lot of
pleasure, apex of wine-drinking
pleasure, delivers loads of decadent levels of
pleasure, delivers mounds of
pleasure, embodiment of flesh and
pleasure, hedonistic
pleasure, innocent
pleasure, long voyage through
pleasure, loud hedonic
pleasure, pure unadulterated drinking
pleasure, pure unalloyed wondrously luxurious
pleasure, real
pleasure, transcendent
pleasure, unbridled
pleasure, virtually charmless offerings devoid of
pleasure-giving
pleasure-inducing
pleasures aplenty
plodding

plonk, awful/ghastly/horrible/utter/vile
plonk, cheerful
plonk, everyday
plonk, generic
plonk, good glugging
plonk, high-octane
plonk, house
plonk, light quaffing
plonk, low-grade
plonk, most unmemorable bottles of
plonk, nondescript
plonk, orange-colored
plonk, overoaked
plonk, rock-bottom
plonk, rough-as-guts
plonk, unspeakably awful
plonk, watery
plonk, white
plot-lines, complicated
plus, big
plush
poetry, bottled/poetry in a bottle
poetry, pure
poignant
point, has a
point, to the
pointless
points from Robert Parker, zillion
points, I can't give more than 100
points, scored a kazillion
poise and finesse
poise of a ballet dancer, has
poise, bracing
poise, great/perfect
poise, vivid
poised, artfully/beautifully
poised, delicately/gracefully
poised, precociously
poised, stunningly
poised, well
poisonous but drinkable, not
pole-vaults out of the glass with Olympic precision, nose
polish, has a certain
polish, urbane
polished and elegant, very
polished but unpretentious, very
polished mouthful
polished to a high sheen
polished, highly/very/well
polished, none too
polished, spit-
polished, unexpectedly
polite, almost effortlessly
polite, excessively

pompous
ponder, not one to
ponderous
pongs, it doesn't just smell...it
pongy
pony, hardly a one-trick
pony, show
poor, piss-
pope, worthy of a
portrait, glorious
posh
positive from start to finish
positive, very
positives, racks up plenty of
possession of you, creeps up and takes
possibility, seems to defy
potion, rare
pour, fascinating
pour, poor
pours well
pouting
powerful...viscous...noble...endless...incredible
pragmatic
praise one could heap upon it, justly deserving about every
praiseworthy
precious stuff
precious, less
precise, extraordinarily
predictable, little too
predominant
preeminent
preferred
pregnant with possibilities
premier
premium
presence and weight, great
presence, formidable
presence, plenty of overall
presentable
prestigious
presumptuous
pretenses are left behind, all
pretension, classic lack of
pretentions, no
pretentious, boringly
prettiness, exhibits
pretty as the proprietor's wife, not as
pretty child with an upturned nose
pretty on the nose you'll want to smell the glass even after it's empty, so
prim, bit
primal fire, will light your

prince, pure and polished
princely
princess, ice
principled
pristine
privilege to drink
privileged
prize, unforgettable
prized, highly
prized, not likely to be
prodigal
prodigious
profile, bad/poor
profile, clear-cut
profile, fine/good
profile, high-
profile, low-
profligate
profound drinking experience
profound stuff
profound with panache
profound, most
profound, stupendously
profundity, deep brambly
progressive
prolific
prominent/pronounced
proper
prophet in a cave
prosaic, fairly
protean, almost
proud
provocative yet caressing
prowess

prrrrrfect!

prudent
prudent, quite
puckish
puerile
puffed up
pulsating...penetrating and pure
pulse race, will not make your
pulse racing, does not send/set the
pulses as you drink it
pulses race, makes
punishment, palate
pure and driven
pure as an alpine spring, as
pure, admirably
pure, extremely/frightfully/
    incredibly/totally
pure, sun-
pure, uncommonly/uncommon
    purity
pure...clean and serene it could
    enroll as a nun, so
purity, astonishing/dazzling/
    fabulous/remarkable/thrilling

purity, blinding
purity, excellent/exceptional/
    gorgeous/impeccable/lovely/
    superb/terrific
purity, extreme
purity, quite special
purity, seamless
purity, streamlined
purity...snap and pop
purpose, some seriousness of
purposeful
purring/purrs
puzzling, just so
qualified, exceedingly well
qualities, has the fewest bad
qualities, hidden
qualities, special
qualities, white wine with red wine
quality aspirations
quality is everywhere
quality is unquestionable, total
    commitment to
quality standards, redefines the
quality winemaking, high-
quality, anthem of intensity and
quality, beacon of
quality, come-to-me
quality, elusive diffuse
quality, first-
quality, *grand cru-*
quality, little better than cask
quality, on a plateau of
quality, oozes
quality, stunningly high-
quality-driven
qualityless
quarrelsome
queenly
quenched/quenches/quenching
questions, asks no
quiet
quiet, too
quintessential
quintessential nonwine:
    no bouquet...no fruit...
    no flavors...no finish
quotient, high pour-me-more
race, lots of
race, of good
race, wins the
racing, does not send the pulse
radar, comes in under the
radiant, unabashedly
radical
rainbow, on the right side of the
rakish

rambunctious

range, not a lot of

rank, high-/highest
rank, second-
ransom, king's
rapture, in a state of
rapture, pure
rapturous, less than
rara avis/rare bird
rare and eclectic
rare and elusive as hummingbird
    tears, as
rare and wonderful
rare beast
rarified, very
rate, first-
rate, second-
rational
rat's ass, not worth a
rats, use it to kill
raucous, almost/pretty

raunchy

rave reviews, gets
ravishes the olfactory mucosa
ravishing, utterly
raw or vulgar, not at all
read, pretty hard to
real
real mouthful
realistic
realm of the celestial, in the
reasonable
reassuring
recalcitrant
reckless
recommended, highly
recommended, not
record, phenomenal track
redemption, beyond
reference point, new
reference wine, a
refined and virile at once
refined, deliciously
refined, highly/terribly
refinement and elegance, acme/
    epitome/model of
refinement, compelling
    juxtaposition of muscle and
refinement, magical grace and
refinement, uncommon
refinement, subtle
refresh even the most jaded taste
    buds, will
refreshing
refreshment, pure
regal, positively
regality in a bottle
regarded, deserves to be more
    highly
regarded, well

register, upper
regrets, no-
regrettable
regular, unfailingly/unfailing
  regularity
reincarnation ever, best
relaxed, wonderfully
relaxing into a favorite chair, like
relentless
reliability, beacon of
reliable, always/ever-/usually
reliable, extremely/very
relishable/relished
remarkable but really a curio
remarkable in its way, quite
remarkable wines in the world,
  one of the most
remarkable, absolutely
remarkable, beyond just
remember, not a whole lot to
rendered, beautifully/elegantly
renowned but not unsullied,
  great diva...world
repellent
reposing
repressed, somewhat
repugnant
repulsive
reputation, legendary
resilient
resist, difficult/hard/tough to
resist, impossible to
resolute
resolved
resonance, retronasal
resonance, wonderful
resourceful
respectable/respected/respectful
responsible
restful, very
restless
restrained, strangely
restrained, very

restraint, Apollonian

restraint, appreciated
restraint, exercise in
restraint, unshowy
retiring
revelation/revelational/revelatory
reveling
revered
reverie, wafts you off into red-wine
revivifying
rewarding, endlessly
rewarding, more
rhapsodic/rhapsody
rhythmic

rich and concentrated that it takes
  one's breath away,
  so unbelievably
rich and delicious to the end
rich and flavorsome, opulently
rich and fruity it should be a
  controlled substance,
  so outrageously
rich and ripe, smells
rich and sensuous it's almost
  illegal, so
rich as blackberry sauce, as
rich as sin, as
rich decadent mouthful
rich enough for dessert, almost
rich in niceties, unbelievably
rich it almost goes overboard and
  turns itself inside out, so
rich it'll glue your gums together
  after the first sip, so
rich it might clog the arteries, so
rich it's almost its own food group,
  so
rich stuff, really

rich sweet beast

rich that one could almost spread it
  on toast, so
rich to drink, almost too
rich to the point of decadence,
  gloriously
rich toasty number
rich without losing focus
rich yet diaphanous/light
rich yet shy, mysteriously
rich you must drink it in teaspoon
  amounts, so
rich, astonishingly/astoundingly
rich, commandingly/imposingly
rich, decadently/seductively/
  sinfully/voluptuously
rich and naughty, decadently
rich, delightfully/exquisitely/
  splendidly
rich, deliriously/thrillingly
rich, explosively/extravagantly/
  hugely/impossibly/inordinately/
  intensely/lavishly/outrageously/
  phenomenally/resoundingly/
  staggeringly/stunningly/
  unbelievably/whoppingly
rich, fearlessly
rich, gloriously/majestically
rich, hypnotizingly/mesmerizingly
rich, magically/theatrically
rich, oh-so-
rich, oily-
rich, pastry-

rich, somewhere between austere
  and
rich, soulfully
rich, sweetly
rich, too
rich, uncommonly
rich, undeniably
rich, unnervingly
rich...heady and fruity that it
  would attract bees from the
  whole neighborhood, so dark...
rich...painfully so, immensely

rich...rich...rich

riches, embarrassment of
richness and complexity, lacks the
  ineffable sublimity of
richness and complexity, smoky-
  buttery-spicy
richness and concentration,
  epitome of
richness and extract, major-league
richness and generosity,
  playing-to-the-galleries
richness and vibrancy,
  fetching combination of
richness is definitely this wine's
  calling card
richness of essence
richness teased out by maturity
richness, almost earthy
richness, almost over-the-top
richness, almost syrupy
richness, astonishing aromatic
richness, awesome levels of
richness, blissful
richness, center-heavy
richness, chewy
richness, coagulated
richness, distinctive/rare/
  uncommon/unique/
  unparalleled/unreal
richness, enthralling
richness, enveloping
richness, explosive/volcanic
richness, farmyard animal
richness, great/mammoth/
  profound/stunning
richness, headspinning/
  mind-numbing
richness, heady perfume of
richness, jammy
richness, languorous/restrained
richness, liqueurlike
richness, lurking
richness, majestic
richness, memorable/
  unforgettable

richness, midpalate
richness, modicum of
richness, mouthfilling/
   palate-coating
richness, multifacited
richness, multilayered
richness, musky
richness, oodles of
richness, oriental
richness, reaching for
richness, restrained
richness, sensory
richness, singed
richness, soupy
richness, supersweet
richness, sweet berrylike
richness, true rock-solid
richness, ultimate
richness, unflashy creamy
richness, unparalleled
richness, waxy
thrilling ride or a wrong turn down
   Queens Boulevard
ride, bumpy
ride, fantastic
ride, far from a bumpy
ride, really fun
ride, regular roller-coaster
riff-raff
right as rain, as
right in the slot
right place, painted by a master
   with every stroke in the
right, all-
right, just
righteous
rigorous
riotous
rip-and-tear, fantastically good
ripper, absolute
ripper, right little
rip-snorter, overblown
rises above the herd
rises out of the glass with such force
   and density you might wonder
   how the bottle held the cork
risky, terribly
risqué
ritzy
riveting drinking
riveting, endlessly
roars, it doesn't warble or trill...it
   richly
rocks, flat out
rocks, this wine
rogue, untrustworthy
roguish, quite

roller coaster, bit/something of a
rolling
romance, instant
romantic, darkly/deeply
ropy
rotten flavors
round and complete that it's
   spheric, so absolutely
routine
royal
royalty, almost like being
   introduced to
rubbish, flavorless
rude, devilishly
rumba, your tongue will
rumbled uneasily in the glass
rumbustious
run, home
run-of-the-mill
ruthless
sable, like stroking a pelt of Russian
sacred
sad
safe, electrifyingly
sagacious, serene and
sagacity, measured
sailing close to the wind
sailing, smooth
salivate, makes you
salt-of-the-earth
sanguine
sapid
sardonic
sass, lots of
sassy, upfront and
satiating, totally
satiric/satirical
satisfaction, for those seeking
   immediate corporeal
satisfaction, total hedonistic
satisfactory
satisfies on many levels
satisfies the soul in that dark
   cavernous interior where few
   wines dare descend
satisfies, a thimbleful
satisfying on all counts
satisfying on the highest level
satisfying, completely/thoroughly/
   totally
satisfying, eye-closingly
satisfying, immensely
satisfying, not really
satisfying, primordially
satisfying, richly
satisfying, sensually immensely
saucy

savage and half-refined, half-
savage personality, nearly
savageness, underlying
savored after the meal just as the
   British sip port, to be
savors, pomp of sophisticated
savory coziness
savory edge
savory thrust
savory, lip-smackingly
savory, none too
savory-nutty-brambly
scarce, absurdly
scary
scattered
scent billowed into the room,
   dark sweet soul-deep
scent that the perfume-makers of
   Grasse might dream of creating,
   the most beautiful
scented, divinely/heavenly
scented, gorgeously/pleasantly
scented, heavily/very
scented, sterile-
scents, head-spinning/heady
scents, resinous rasping
scents, spellbinding
schizophrenic/schizophrenia,
   suffers from
scholarly
scintillating
scores high on both pleasure and
   cerebral meters
scrappy
scratch, really up to
scratch, simply not up to
scream, primal
screaming
screams from the glass in a
   reassuring rather than
   frightening manner
screams, really
screwed up, bit
scrummy
scrumptious, incredibly
scrumptious, seriously
scrumptious, wickedly
scrumptiousness, tongue-lashing
scrutiny, doesn't hold up to heavy
sculpted, perfectly
seamless in every respect
seamlessly interwoven, fruit and
   oak
sear, far from
seasick
secret
sedate

seductive
seductive glass of fun, wholly
seductive majestic wine drinking
    experience
seductive with spirit and breed
seemly
self-assured, phenomenally
self-confident, supremely
self-indulgence, pure
selfish
self-possessed
sensation, very enjoyable
sensational, simply
sensational...indescribably glorious
sensational...so excuse the
    verbose winespeak, simply
sensations, font of
sensations, irresistibly appetizing
    whirlwind of
senses as a bungee jump from
    Mount Cook, as thrilling a jolt
    to the
senses soar, makes your
senses unforgettably, seizes your
senses were numbed by this
    bombshell
senses, does not pierce the
senses, doesn't so much seduce
    you as launch a full-out
    perfumed assault on the
senses, thrill to the/sensory thrill
sensible
sensitive, very
sensory battle royal
sensory circuits into overdrive,
    pushes the
sensory energy
sensory experience that stays with
    one for life
sensory impact, overall
sentimental
serene
serenity, delicious
serious for its own good, too
serious mouthful
serious, menacingly
serious, not too
serious, very
seriousness, certain
seriousness, deep
serious-yet-fun mouthful
served, well
service, merits a church
serviceable
severe
shabby, not too
shabby-genteel
shaded

shadowy
shakes, no great
shaky
shameful
shameless
sheen, sophisticated
sheen, undeniably luxurious
shimmers, something about it
shine, continues to
shines from the get-go
shines like a beacon
shines through
shivers down your spine, sends
shock and thrill you,
    will alternately
shock wave of great and obvious
    authority
shock, in
shock, puts tasters used to insipid
    wines in catatonic
shone like a star
short, falls
show, best-in-
showcase/showpiece/showy
show-off
show-off, not a-
shows off a bit
show-stopper, real/undeniable
showy, not very
shrewd
shrill...more like a high note on a
    violin, not exactly
sick and twisted
sighted, far-
signature
significant
silly
simpering
sincere
sinful, decadently/shamelessly
sinful, just this side of
sing and dance, doesn't exactly
sing, continues to
sing, fails to
sing, just doesn't
singed
singer not the song, it's the
singing beautifully
singing from the rooftops, won't
    get you
sings a pretty song/tune
sings from/out in the glass
sings on key
sings on the palate
sings out in the glass
sinister, touch of the
sink into it, so come-hither you
sink into, wine you just want to

sip is like a glassful, each
sip, begging for another
sip, easy to
sip, hard not to take another
sip, pretty nice
sippable
sipping, hard to stop
sit up and take note, made me
sit up and notice, didn't make us
sitting up in our seats, had us
sizzling
skilled
slam dunk
slatternly
sleek character
sleek, pretty
sleeper of the vintage
sleepy
slick
slinky, decidedly
slop, pure
sloppy
slouch, no
slurpable, most
slurpy, totally
sly and difficult
small
small talk of wine, the
smashing drink
smashing effort
smells alone are worth the price
smells so good you might be
    tempted just to keep sniffing, this
smells, nuanced
smile on any wine lover's face,
    guaranteed to put a
smile on your face, not bestowing
    its broadest
smile on your face, will put a
smile to your face, brings a
smile, makes you
smile-inducing
smiles, glassful of
smiling
smokes, this one
snap, real
snappy
snazzy, not all that
snazzy, real
snazzy, sensationally
sneaks up on you rather than hits
    you over the head
sneaky
snobbish
snorter, rip-
snug
soars majestically from the glass
soars out of the glass

sociability, essence of
sociable, rather
society, high
socko
socks off, blew/knocked our
soft-soap you, doesn't
soggy
solemn
solid citizen
solid rather than sensational
solid, almost
solid, irreproachably
solitary
somber, downright
something else, really
song, off-
song, totally on-
sonorous
soothing than assertive, more
sophisticated treat
sophistication with deep
    soulfulness, combines
sophistication, steely
sorcery, pure
so-so
sought after, highly
soul in a very special way,
    touches my
soul wax embarrassingly poetic,
    makes the
soul, bypasses the brain to grab the
soul, has/soulful
soul, no/without
soul, real

soul, speaks to your
soul, ungarbled product of the
    earth that's good for the
soul, whole lot of
souled, dark-
soulful, quietly
soul-less, somewhat
soul-satisfying, truly
soul-stirring
sound as a bell, as
sound, perfectly
sour and squalid like bad breath
    on a good goose with bad teeth
sour, slightly
sovereign
space on a dark night,
    like staring into
space to move and spread its wings,
    needs
spark plug
spartan
speak for itself, just let it
speaks with polish and wry soft
    vowels

special in its own way
special, nothing very
special, simply makes life
special", stick your nose in this and
    it says "I'm extra/rather/really/
    truly/very
specious, rather
spectacular, unquestionably
speechless, can leave you utterly
speechless, I'm/leaves me
speechless, left an entire panel of
    tasters
spell in the book, weaves every

spellbinding
spiffy
spine-tingling
spirit, bright zippy
spirit, full of/generous in
spirit, has/real
spirit, independent
spirit, lifts your
spirit, livens up the
spirit, lovely inner
spirited, high-
spirited, much too high-
spiritual
spiritually purifying
spit, difficult to
spiteful
splashy
splendid, incredibly
splendor, pure
spoken appeal, softly
spontaneous
spoofalated/spoofulated
spooky
sporty
spot, hits the
spot-on, absolutely
spots, hits all the sweet
spotty
sprightly
spring in anyone's step, will put a
spunk, full of/spunk, has/spunky
squalid parts, slightly
square on the mark
square, tolerably
squaring the circle, something like
stable
staggering mouthful
staggering, quite
stale
stalwart
stand back
stand in the presence of this wine
stand, no one-night
"standard," the
standard, bog-

standard, gold
standard, just
standard, maintains the
standard, sets the
standard-bearer
standards, not up to the usual
standoffish, little
stands out of the crowd,
    immediately
stands tall
stanza, great opening
star billing, gets
star is born, a
star of the vintage
star quality
star, cellar
star, confident and stylish
star, shooting
star, sure to be a
star...more of a damp squib,
    less of a shooting
star-crossed
stark
starry
stars, five
stately
stately manners
statement, makes a
statesmanlike
stature, great/real
steadfast
steady, rock
stealth, gracious
steers the course while never
    overreaching its limits
stellar
stellar, never been anything
    less than
step about a simple refresher
sterile...insipid...wimpish
sterling
stern but relaxed
stern, rather
sticky...hearty...soulful
stimulating, hedonistically and
    intellectually
sting, venomous
stingy beyond belief
stingy with the goodies
stink bomb
stink-bomb smell, sulphury
    chemical
stinker, absolute

stinky rotten wine
stirring
stodgy, rather
stole the show, really
stolid

stopped everyone in their tracks
stouthearted
straggly
straight and narrow, on the
straight-ahead/straightforward
straining at the leash
strapped
strategic
strayed
streak, wild
streamlined
streetplonk
streetwalker
strength to strength, goes from
stress buster, ultimate
strewn, decadently
striking
stringent
stripes, earns its
struggling
strung, well
struts its stuff, really
stuck-up
stuff not just made of dreams but
    of legends, the
stuff, beautiful/great/super
stuff, cheerful
stuff, classy
stuff, crazy
stuff, dreamy
stuff, easy-peasy
stuff, filled with
stuff, four-star
stuff, frivolous
stuff, good
stuff, got the
stuff, happy to strut its
stuff, heady/lusty/snappy
stuff, heart-warming
stuff, mind-boggling
stuff, real/serious

stuff, really struts its

stuff, riveting
stuff, seriously good
stuff, shows its
stuff, stampin' stompin'
stuff, this is the
stuff, very cool
stuffy
stunned every nerve in the body
stunner, absolute/absolutely
    stunning
stunner, real
stunning, really quite
stunning, unexpectedly
stupefying
stupendous
stupid

suave elegant feel
suave juice, very
suave, amazingly
subdued
sublime and unworldly that it
    could create a stampede at
    auction, so incredibly
sublime experiences, one of life's
sublime, extravagantly exotic and
sublime, indescribably
sublime, quite/most/truly/utterly

sublime, verges on the

sublimity of richness and
    complexity, ineffable
subpar/substandard
substance, exquisite
subtle as a brass band, as
subtle as a 2x4 over the head, as
subtle, erotically
subtle, most
subtle, not very
subtle, satisfyingly
subtle...elegant and timelessly
    beautiful as a design by
    Valentino, as
subtlety is not in the game plan
subtlety over flamboyance,
    recognizes balance and
subtlety, bereft of/lacks/no
subtlety, does not lack
subtlety, few claims to
subtlety, immense
success, brilliant
successful, not blindingly
successful, very
succulence, biscuity
succulence, gorgeous
succulence, juicy
succulence, noteworthy
succulence, unapologetic
succulence, tangy
succulence, very toothsome
succulent fleshy mouthfiller
succulent, gloriously
succulent, improperly
succulent, seductively
succulently mouthfilling
sucks
suffusing
suggestive
suit mended...hair combed...
    but that's about it
suitable
sultry as a tango, as
sultry mouthful
sultry, languorously
sum of its parts, more than the
sumptuous

sumptuousness, conflicted
sunny
super, wild and
superappetizing
superaromatic
superb by any standards
superb in every way
superb, really
superb, unfailingly
superb...buy a case
superdelicate
superdelicious
super-duper
superexcellent
superexpressive
superficial, essentially
superfine
superfriendly
supergood
superimpressive
superior, clearly/obviously
superior, consistently
superior, morally
superiority, has the stamp of
superiority, unmistakable
superjuicy
superlative, absolutely
superlatives, almost beyond
superlush
supernacular
supernatural
superneutral
superopulent
superperfumed
superperky

superplonk, everyday

superplonk, summer
superpolished
superpremium
super-refined
super-rich
supersavory
superserious
supersleek
supersmart
superstar, deserved
superstar, true
superstuff
supersucculent
superwine
superyummy
supple
supreme
sure of itself, absolutely
sure of itself, unselfconsciously
sure thing
sure thing, no
surefooted

surging
surly
surpassing
surprise, delightful
surprise, great/major
surprise, interesting
surprise, nasty
surprises, no
surprising
surreal, uncomfortably
surreptitious
sustained/sustaining
swaggers/swaggering
swallowable
swanky
swath across the palate, cuts a wide
sweetie-pie
swell
swell of fragrance and flavors
swelling in the glass, positively
swill, barely drinkable
swill, ghastly insipid industrial
swill, picnic
swill, pretty good
swill, provincial
swill, southern
swill, swell
swill, ugly

swill, unimprovable

swill, utter
swinging
swirls and sashays lithely and
    elegantly
swoon, does not make me
swooning
sybaritic
symbol of the flower of civilization
synergistic
system barely contains it,
    the 100-point scoring
taboo
tacky, simply
tacky...tacky...tacky
tactful, too
tailored, well
taken for granted, not to be
talented, not terribly
talks well
tall/taller, stands
tame, elegantly
T'ang than Ming, more
tang, has/tangy
tango
tangy-steely
tantalizing
target squarely in the center,
    hits the
tarted-up and nowhere to go, all

tarted-up out of recognition
taste buds, will titillate your
taste marks, top
taste of heaven
taste this as much as eat it,
    you don't
taste treat
taste, almost bursting with
taste, each small sip explodes with
taste, may not be to everybody's
taste, paragon of good
taste, privilege to
taste, relaxed come-hither
taste, thud to the
taste, walks the right line down
    every
tasted to be believed, must be
tasteless
tastes all the time, new surprising
tastes better than it smells
tastes black
tastes pink
tastes purple
tastes red
tastes wise
tastes, contradictory
tastes, cut-glass
tastes, dark-cherry
tastes, densely packed with
tastes, great thick whack of
tastes, kindergarten
tastes, lovely blue-black
tastes, overly pronounced
tastes, pronounced surface
tastes, remarkable purity of
tastescape, glorious
tasting notes don't do it justice
tasting, off-
tasting this as it was made,
    someone was

tasty, lip-smackingly

tasty, so very
tasty, well beyond
tasty, wildly
tasty?...oh yes
tawdry
tea, not really my cup of
tears to the eyes, so good it brings
tears, almost reduced a good friend
    of mine to
teases the senses
teasing
technotasting
tedious
tedious, never
tedium, overwhelming sense of
temperament, plenty of
temperamental and unstable

temperamental artist
tempered, bad-/ill-
tempered, even-
tempered, finely/well
tempered, hot-
tempestuous
tempting to drain the glass, very
temptress, oily rich tropical
tenacious
tender
tense and expressive
tension, elemental
tension, fine racy
tension, romantic
terrible, absolutely
terrible, basically tastes
terrific, just plain
territory, straying into clumsy

terrorizing

testy
thanks, this is a wine one should
    drink on bended knee and with
    heartfelt and humble
theatrical
there, very
thesaurus has no superlatives
    enough to do it justice
thing, the real
think, one of those wines that
    causes you to stop and
thinking about what's in their
    mouth, will appeal to tasters who
    enjoy
thinking, clear-
thirst-quenching, devastatingly
thorough
thoroughbred, harmonious
thoughtful care, drink with
thoughtful, adult and
thoughtful, somewhat
thought-provoking
thrill to drink
thrill you, will alternately
    shock and
thrill, eye-spinning
thrill, fails to
thriller but not bad at all, not a
thrilling drinking, positively
thrilling to drink, undeniably
thrilling to smell...taste and drink
thrilling, not
thrilling, nothing overly
thrilling, remarkably
thrilling, truly
thrills, contrived
thrills, dirty
thrills, no cheap
through, shines

throws itself about, shamelessly
timbre, unmistakable
time moving across your palate, takes its
time, stood the test of
timeless
tingle your taste buds, apt to
tingler, taste bud
tip-top
tired, made my mouth
tiresome after a while, little
tiring on our palates, very
tiring to drink, might get a bit
titan/titanic
titillating
toast with this wine is reason in and of itself to get married, to
together from front to back, keeps itself
together, beautifully/cleverly/nicely/well put
toilet, the only red wine of Veedercrest I can swallow without looking for a
tolerable
tonality, high
tone, good
tone, pure
toned, extraordinarily high-
toned, low-
tones, makes you want to speak in hushed
tongue, pampers your

tongue-happy

tony
tooled, finely
toothsome
top class act from go to whoa
top flight, consistently
top of the line
top shape, in
top, at the
top, nearly over-the-
top, nothing over-the-
top, totally/very over-the-
top-class/-dog/-drawer/-end/-flight/-gear/-gun/-most/-notch/-shelf/-tier/-whack
top-flight, consistently
top-of-the-line/-pyramid/-range/-tree
topsy-turvy
touch, shows a master's
touching
touchy
tour de force, amazing/thrilling
tour-de-force, modern day

tour de force, stunningly pure winemaking
tousled
towering
towers majestically
traditional
traits to speak, no unpleasant
trampy

transcendent

transcendent pleasure
transcendent, far from
transcends it *terroir*, clearly
transfixed/transfixes
transparency, has
transportive
trash, utter
travesty, absolute/utter
treacherous
treasure, absolute
treasure, rare
treasured, dearly
treasures, greatest of vinous
treat to drink
treat, great
treat, heavenly
treat, indulgent
treat, luscious
treat, plush and fragrant
treat, rare/uncommon/unexpected
treat, real
treat!, what a
tremendous
trenchant
tricks, flavor-flaunting
tried-and-true
trifle
trifled with, not a wine to be
trimmer, real
triumphant effort
true
trumps, turned up
trustworthy
try, brave
trying, well worth
tune, sings a pretty
tuned, finely/nicely/well
turn down Queens Boulevard, thrilling ride or a wrong
turncoat
turned-in
turning a sow's ear into a silk purse, almost
turn-off, absolute
turn-on, intellectual
turn-on, total hedonistic
twist, pleasant
twisted, sick and
ugliest bottle in the history of wine

ugliest wine I have ever tasted
ugly sister
ugly, downright
ugly, just plain
ultimate
ultra everything
ultra, the
ultradelicious
ultradigestible
ultradistinctive
ultraelegant
ultraexpressive
ultrafine
ultrafragrant
ultragenerous
ultraneutral
ultrapremium
ultrarefined
ultrarich
ultrasophisticated
umami, mouthwatering with
umamilike definition, bright
unabashed
unacceptable, totally
unadorned, almost
unaffected
unafraid
unaired
unapologetic
unappealing
unappetizing
unassuming
unattractive
unattractive, not
unbeatable mouthful, almost
unbecoming
unbelievable
unblemished, almost
uncanny
uncelebrated
unchallenging
unchanged and unchanging

uncivilized

unclean
uncomfortable, downright
uncommon
uncomplicated
uncompromising
unconditional
unconventional
unconvincing
uncouth
uncowardly
uncultivated/uncultured
undaunted
undecided
undefined
undemanding

undemonstrative
underappreciated, tragically
underblown
underestimated
underhanded
underperformer/underperforming
underplayed
under-rated
under-regarded
understand, easy to
understand, hard to
understand, takes time to
understated, elegantly
understated, nicely
understatement, masterpiece in
   restrained
understood, easily
undersung
underwhelming, decidedly
underworked and jagged, distinctly
underworked, not
undescribable
undesirable/undesired
undiplomatic
undisciplined
undistinctive
undistinguished
undomesticated
undramatic
undreamed of
undrinkable, almost/verging on
undrinkable, revoltingly
undrinkable, totally/well-nigh
unearthly
unemotional
unenjoyable, absolutely
unenjoyed
unequaled/unequalable
unerring
unestablished
unethical
unexcelled
unexceptional
unexciting, seemed a little
unexpected
unextraordinary
unfavorable
unfit
unflattering
unflawed
unflinching
unforced
unforgettable, fantastic and
unforgettable edge
unforgettable tasting experience
unforgettable wine I've ever had,
   the most

unfriendly as tripping over in a
   patch of nettles, as
unfriendly, just plain
unfulfilled
unfussy
ungenerous/ungiving
ungenerous at the beginning,
   borderline
ungodly
ungracious
unimpeachable
unimportant
unimpressive
unimprovable
uninhibited
uninspired/uninspiring
unintellectual
unintelligent
uninteresting, dismally
uninteresting, plain
unintimidating
unique these days, virtually
unkempt
unlikable
unlimited
unlovable
unlucky
unmade, not
unmarked
unmatchable/unmatched
unmemorable
un-nerving
unobjectionable
unobnoxious
unobtrusive
unobvious
unpalatable
unparalleled
unpleasant but not charming
   either, not
unpleasant, aggressively
unpleasant, distinctly
unpleasant, far from
unpolished
unprecedented
unpredictable
unprepossessing
unpretentious, gloriously
unpretentious, technically
unputdownable
unqualified...period.
unreadable aromas
unreal
unrecommendable
unredeemable/unredeemed
unrefined
unregarded
unremarkable

unrepentant
unrivaled
unruliness, irresistible
unruly
unsatisfying
unsavory
unseemly
unshowy
unskillful
unsound
unspeakable
unspectacular
unstable
unstimulating
unsubtle
unsurpassable/unsurpassed
unswallowable
untamed
untidy
untouchable/untouched
untroubled
unvarnished
unvarying
unwavering
unwelcome
unwieldy
unwiney
unwraps itself halfway across your
   tongue, a gift that
up, very
up-and-coming
upbeat
upchucky
up-close and personal
upfront and obvious, not all
upfront appeal
uplifting as a springtime walk in a
   beech forest in bloom, as
uplifting, cheerily
upright
ups and downs, has its
upscale, rather
upswing, big
upswing, in an
uptight
up-to-snuff, well
urbane
urggh
usable/useful
usual
usual, not your
utmost
vacation on the island of sweet
   dreams
vacuity, watery
vacuous
vague
valiant

valid
value, devoid of any redeeming
   social
vapidness, intellectual
vaporous exclamation point
variable, infuriatingly
varies alarmingly
vaunted
venerable
vengeful
versatility, decent
verve, bright exciting
verve, shirt-collar grabbing
vest, plays it close to the
victorious
vile, grotty and
vile, particularly
villainous
vinification technique,
   has mastery of the
vinosity, bespoke
vinosity, great
vinous black hole in space
vinous embarrassment
vinous equivalent to potato chips...
   I bet you can't drink just one glass
vinous Lothario
violet, no shrinking
virtue out of nothing, clever
   winemaking has made a
virtues, easy
virtuosity
virtuous
visionary
vita in a glass, *la dolce*
vital
vital, snortingly
vitality of a flamenco dancer,
   all the
vitality, buzzing with
vivacity, lacks
vociferous
voice, distinctive
voiced, thin-
voluptuosity, homogeneous
vulgar
vulgarity and coarseness, touch of
wafting
waggish
wake-up call
walk-by wine, ultimate
wallop, upfront
warm and cuddly it's not
warmer, classic soul-
warmth and ripeness, beautiful
   impression of
weak effort
wealthy

wear this behind my ears, I could
weird
welcome, doesn't outstay its
welcoming
wet, at least it's
whew!
whimsical
whipped
whisper, seductive
whispers instead of shouts
whoa!
whole is better than its parts
wholesome, organically
whoopee!
whopper/whopping
whore of a wine
whore, nice
whore, vinous
whore, well-built garishly attired
wicked stuff
wicked, delightfully
wide/wide of the mark
wide-ranging
wild and unexpected
wild and woolly
wild one/thing
wild side, attractive
wild side, teetering on the
wild side, walk on the
wildfire, spreads like
wildness at its core, suggestion of
wildness, erotic
will, rangy strength of
willful
willing
willpower, has
wily
wimpish...subtle...innocuous
wimpy
winealicious
wine but an experience, not just a
wine made our socks roll
   up and down, not a single
wine making, good/intelligent
wine of heaven and earth
wine showing neither opulence
   nor restraint, incredibly
   well-poised
wine that shows the care that went
   into it, rich
wine to think about as you drink it
wine, dream/wine to dream about/
   wine that dreams are made of
wine, like drinking pills of
wine, love-em or leave-em
wine, not a smooth cuddly
wine, perfect grapes made into
   perfect

wine, quite a
wine, regal old
wine, superb old
Wine, The
wine, thin nothing
winemaking tricks, full kit of
winemaking, brilliant/intelligent
winemaking, clean/immaculate
winemaking, good
winemaking, pinnacle of
winemaking, ultrasophisticated
wings to take off and fly, just needs
   a couple of
winner as you'll find, as reliable a
winner, big
winner, everyone a
winner, hardly a
winner, mainstream
winner, potential prize
winner, warm-weather
winning, totally/utterly
wins you over bit by bit working an
   interesting spell
winsome
wire act, high-
wire, live
wise, tasted
wishy-washy
wistful
wit, dry
witty
withdrawn
without, a wine one can do
witted, dull-
witted, sharp-
wizardry, pure
wobbly, little
woeful
wonderful, don't share this
   anyone...it's too
wonderful, inestimably
wonderful, not
wonderful, truly
wonderful, wickedly
wonders, *mélange* of
wonders, one of life's true
wondrous, aromatically
words are inadequate at this level
words cannot do it justice
words, (so nearly perfect) it can't
   be described with
words, almost beyond
words, at a loss for
work of modern art, true
worked, beautifully
world apart, a
world renowned but not unsullied,
   like a great diva...

world, not of this
world, out of this
worshipful
worst of any wine tasted, absolute
worst wine in the world, possibly
   the
worthless
worthy of a pope
wow factor, definitely has the
wow!, just plain
wow!, oh
wows in any tasting...blind or
   otherwise, will elicit more
   than a few
wraps itself around you
wrath, must have been made from
   the grapes of
wretched, truly
write home about,
   not something to
wrought, well
x-rating, merits an
yachting set, will put you in the
yawnworthy, profoundly
yech!
yelp, delighted
yowza!
yucky, truly
yum factor, plenty of
yum fest
yummy, deliriously
yummy, wickedly
yummy...yummy...yes...Yes...YES!
zany but good
zeal, perfectionist
zeal, unapologetic
zealot's pride
zealous
zero, big
zesty
zilch
zillion points from Robert Parker
zing went my strings
zowie!
zymurgy, miracle of

The taste of wine is like
the sound of music:
limitlessly various.
Thomas Jefferson

From *Elemental Odes* (1954) by Pablo Neruda

[This highly emotional poem, by the great Chilean poet and Nobel laureate who died in 1973, may well be one of the finest literary expressions yet about this incredibly sensual, and sensuous, beverage.]

V. Ode to Wine

Wine color of day,
wine color of night,
wine with feet of purple
or topaz blood,
wine,
starry child
of the earth,
wine, smooth
as a golden sword,
smooth
as ruffled velvet,
wine spiral-shelled
and suspended,
amorous,
marine,
you've never been held in one glass,
in one song, in one man,
you are choral, gregarious,

and, at the least, mutual.
Sometimes
you feed on mortal
memories,
on your wave
we go from tomb to tomb,
stonecutter of icy graves,
and we weep
transitory tears,
but
your beautiful
spring dress
is different,
the blood rises to the branches,
the wind moves the day,
nothing remains
within your motionless soul.

Wine
stirs in the springtime,
joy grows like a plant,
walls, boulders,
crumble,
abysses close up,
song is born.
Oh, thou, jug of wine, in the desert
 with the woman I love,
said the old poet.
Let the pitcher of wine
add its kiss to the kiss of love.

My love, suddenly
your hip
is the full curve
of the wineglass,
your breast is the cluster,
your hair is the light of alcohol,
your nipples, the grapes,
your navel, a pure seal
stamped on the vessel of your belly,
and your love is the unquenchable
cascade of wine,
the light that illuminates my senses,
the earthly splendor of life.

But not only love,
the burning kiss
or the ignited heart,
you are, wine of life,
also
fellowship, transparency,
chorus of discipline,
abundance of flowers.

I like, on the table,
while people are talking,
the light of a bottle
of intelligent wine.
Let them drink it,
let them remember that in each
golden drop
or topaz goblet
or purple glass,
that autumn labored
till it filled the vessels with wine,
and let the simple man learn,
in the rituals of his trade,
to remember the earth and his
duties,
to propagate the canticle of the fruit.

[Wine] sloweth age, it strengtheneth youth, it helpeth digestion, it abandoneth melancholie, it relisheth the heart, it lighteneth the mind, it quickeneth the spirits, it keepeth and preserveth the head from whirling, the eyes from dazzling, the tongue from lisping, the mouth from snaffling, the teeth from chattering, and the throat from rattling; it keepeth the stomach from wambling, the heart from swelling, the hands from shivering, the sinews from shrinking, the veins from crumbling, the bones from aching, and the marrow from soaking.
Thirteenth-century manuscript

VI. Quantifiers (more or less)

Much of the language used by wine reviewers contains quantifiers running ahead of wine tasting descriptors. To picky prescriptive grammarians these esoterica are known as *partitive expressions* (no wonder we can't remember them). Many of these would be preceded by the indefinite articles *a* or *an*. If this is at all meaningful to you, and you write about wine professionally, please help yourself to the pages of goodies below; most of them are in all major dictionaries and all free for the taking. Now go forth and quantify.

abetted by
abounding/
   abounds
   in/with
absence of
abundance of/
   abundant
accent of
acre of
afterthought of
ahead of
airbrush of
all/all but
allotment of
allowance of
alludes to
almost/almost
   no
aloft with
amalgam of
amount(s) of
ample
amplified by
anchored by/
   with/anchors
appetizer of

arc of
armed with
aroma of
array of
aspect of
assault of/
   assaults
at bay
atom of
attack of
attenuated
attired in
attitude in
avalanche of
awash in/with
babble of
backbone of
backdrop of/to
background of
bag of
balanced with
bale of
band of
bang of
banquet of
barbed by/with
barely

barge (load) of
barrage of
barrel of
base of
baseline of
basin of
basket/
   basketful of
batch of
bathed in
beaker of
beam of
bebops with
bed of
begins with
beehive of
belt of
bestows
billows with
bin of
bit of/bitty
bite of
bites you with
blanket of
blanketed by/
   in/with

blast of
blasted by/with
blasting/blasts
   with
blaze of
blend of
blended with
blessed with
blindsided by
blizzard of
block of
blooms with
boasting/boasts
boatload of
bolstered by
bolt of
bomb of
bonanza of
boned with
boost of
boosted with
bordering on
bottle of
bounded by
boundless
bounteous

bountiful
bounty of
bouquet of
bowl/bowlful of
bowled over by
box of
boxed in by
brace of
braid of
braided with
brandishing/
   brandishes
brawl of
breath of
breeze of
brew of
brewed with
brimful of
brimming/
   brims with
brink of
bristling/bristles
   with
brook of
brush of

brushed by/
   with
bubbling with
bucket (load) of
buffers
bulge of
bulges with
bulk of
bump of
bunch of
bundle of
buoyant with
buoyed with
burden of
burdened by
buried by
buried in/under
burr of
burst of/
   bursting/
   bursts with
bushel of
buttressed by
buzz of
buzzing with
cacophony of

cake of
can of
cannonade of
cantata of
cap of
capped (off)
  by/with
caressed by/
  with
caress of
cargo of
carnival of
carpet of
carries
cart/cartload of
carton of
cascade of
cascades with
case of
cask of
cast of
cavalcade of
ceiling of
celebration of
cell of
cements
centers on
channels
charge of
charges out with
chiseled/
  chiseling
chime of/
  chimes (in)
  with
chip of
chock-a-block
chock-full of
choir of
chop of
chord of
chorus of
chunk of
circus of
clad with
clip of
cloaking
cloak of
cloaked in
clod of
close to
clump of
cluster of
clutch of
coalesces into
coated with
coaxed by
cocktail of

cocoon of
cocooned in/
  with
coddled by
collision of
colossus of
column of
comes on like
commingled/
  commingles
  with
complex of
complexed with
complicated by/
  with
concerto of
concoction of
conjoined with
conjures/
  conjuring up
connotation of
considerable
constellation of
contains
context of
contour of
copious
core of
cornering
corset of
cornucopia of
corpuscle of
couched in/with
counter of
countless
coupled/couples
  with
courtship of
crackle of/
  crackles/
  crackling with
cradle of
cradling
crammed with
crashing along-
  side
crash of
crate of
creek of
creep(s)
crescendo of
crest of
crumb of
crush of
cuddles
cue of
cup of
cushion of

cushioned by/
  with
cusp of
cut by/of
dab of
damps (down)
  with
dash of
deal of
dealing in/with
deals
deals in/with
dearth of
deficiency of
deficit of
degree of
delivers
deluge of
delves into
dense
deprived of
desert of
detectable/
  detects
detonates/
  detonation of
diddly
display of/
  displays
distillate of
dole of
doles out
dollop of
dosage of
dose of/dosed
  with
dot of
dotted with
doused in/with
douse of
dovetails with
downpour of
dram of
draped in/over/
  with
draw of
drenched
  in/with
drenching of
dressed in/
  dressed up
  with
dribble of
dribbling with
driblet of
drift of
drip/droplet of

dripping /drips
  in/of/with
drizzle of
drizzled with
drop/droplet of
duet of
dusting of
dustup of
earthquake of
eases into
echo of
edge of
edged with
edifice of
effusive in
element of
embarrassment
  of
embellished
  by/with
embroidered
  by/with
emerges
encapsulated by
encapsulates
encased by/with
enchanted/
  enchants by/
  with
endless
endowed/
  endows with
energized by/
  with
enriched with
enrobed in/with
enrobes
enveloped by/
  in/with
envelopes
epidemic of
epitome of
eschews
essence of
etched by/with
ever-so-slight
excluding/
  excludes
exhibiting/
  exhibits
explodes with/
  explosion of
expressed by/
  with
expression of
extensive
exudes
eyelash of

faint
fair amount of
fanfare of
fans out into/
  with
farm of
feast of
festival of
few
fidget of
field of
fiesta of
filigree of
filigreed with
filing of
filled (out) with
filling of
fistful of
flagon of
flare of
flashes
flashing with
flash of
flask of
flatters with
flaunting of
flaunts
fleck of
flecked with
fleshes out with
flick/flicker of
flirtation of
flirts with
flits from
flits in and out
floats
flood of
flooded with
flooding/floods
floor of
flotilla of
flourish of
flush of
flushed with
flute of
flutter of
flyspeck of
foil to
folding into
folds in
forays into
force of
forest of
foretells
fount (ain) of
fraction
fraction of
fragment of

framed by/with
frames
framing
frisson of
frizzle of
front-loaded
  with
full of
fully
fuses
fusion of
gaggle of
galaxy of
gallon of
gangs up on
garden of
gargantuan
garland of
ghost of
gill of
girded with
girdle of
gift of
glance of
glancing blow of
glass of
glaze of
gleam of
glides into/over
glimmer of
glint of
glistens with
glob/globule of
glut of
gob/gobbet/
  gobful of
gold mine of
goliath of
grain/granule of
great
greets/greets
  you with
grind of
grip of/gripping
grounded by
growth of
guided by
gush of/gushes/
  gushes with
gust of
hair of
hammered
  together
  from/with
hand of
hangs on to
hardly any
harvest of

haze of
heap of/heaped with
hearth of
heath of
heaving with
heavy with
hefty
held together by/with
helluva lot of
helping of
hemmed in by
hews to
hiding under
high/highly
hill of
hint of/hinting with
hit of
hits you with
hit-and-run by
hits the groove with
hive of
horde of
host of
hovers over
huge
hums with

hunk of

hurricane of
idea of
illusion of
imbedded
imbued with
imbues
immeasurable
imparting/imparts
incalculable
indulges with
indulgence of
inflection of
influenced by/with
infused with/infusion of
in need of
insinuates
instilling/instills
integrated into
interlacing of
interplay of
intertwined with/intertwines

interwoven with
in the context of
intimation of
inundated by/with
inundation of
iota of
issue(s) of
jab of
jagged
jammed with
jar of
jazzed up by/with

jigger of

jolt of
jostles
jot of
juggles
jumble of
jumps (on you) with
just
keg of
kernel of
kettle of
kick of/kicks into
kicks off with
kicks out with
kicks you with
kind of
kiss of/kissed by/with
laced with/lacing of
laden with
lake of
landslide of
lash/lashing of
lather of
lathered/lathered up with
launches with
lavished/lavishes with
layer of/layered with
leading/leads into
leaks
leavening of
legion of
lens of
lets rip a
level of

leviathan of
lick of/licked with
lies like
lift of
lilt of
limitless
limit of
line of
lion's share of
litany of
liter of
little (bit of)
load of/loaded with
loaf/loaves of
long
lorry/lorryload of
lot of/lotta/lots/lotsa
lousy with
low
lurking/lurks beneath/in/under
lump of
lunges
maelstrom of
majority of
mammoth
manifests
market of
marriage of
married to/with/marries
mash of
mass of
matches wits with

maze of

meadow of
measly
measureless
measure of
medley of
meeting of
meets
mélange of
melded by/to/with
melding/melds
meld of
melody of
memories of
mere/merely
meshed with
meshing

mess of
mild
milligram of
milliliter of
mingled with
minim/minimum of
minority of
mint of
mirrors
mish-mash of
mite/mite of
mix of
mixture of
mobbed by/with
modicum of
molecule of
monolith of
monster of

moonstruck by

moor of
more/more of
more than
morsel of
mosaic of
most (of)
mostly all
mote of
mother/motherload of
mound of
mountain of
mounting from
mouth/mouthful of
muddle of
mug of
multitude of
muscle of
myriad of
narrow
narrow band of
near/nearly
nearest thing to
negligible
nerve of
nest of
nestled in
nibble of
nip of
nose of
notch of
note of
not quite
nucleus of
nudge of

nudging into
nugget of
numberless
number of
nutshell of
ocean of
ode to
offset by
onslaught of
on the brink of
on the heels of
on the cusp of
oodles of
ooze of/oozes/oozes with/oozing with
opens with
opulence of
orgy of
oscillates between
ounce of
outbreak of
outburst of
overcoat of
overdelivers
overdose of
overflowing/overflows with
overlay of/overlays
overly
over-rides the
pack/package/packet of
packed with
packs in
pail of
palate of
pandemic of
pangs of
panoply of
parade of/parades
parcel of
paring of
part/particle of
passel of

pastiche of

patina of
paucity of
pebble of
peck of
peek of
peeks out with
peep of
pennyweight of

peppered with
perceptible
perfect
pervades
picture of
piece of
piled with
pile of
pillow of
pinch of
ping of
pings with
pint of
piqued by/with
pirouette of
pitcher of
pitches of

pittance of

pixel of
plane/planeload of
plastered with
plaster of
plate of
plentiful
plenty of
plethora of
plowed under with
plows ahead with
plummy with
plumped us with
plumped with
pocket of
point of
poke of
pokes through with
polish of
polished by/with
pond of
pongs with
pool of
pop of
pops/popping with
popping with
porridge of
portion of
pot/potful of
potpourri of
pound of
powder keg of
powered by/powers with

precious little
preponderance
   of
pretty
primal blast of
proffers
profuse
profusion of
prolonged
propelled
   by/with
puddle of
pulsing with
pumped (up)
   by/with
pumped with
pumps
pumps out
punch of
punched with
punchbowl of
purrs along with
pushes
push of
pyrotechnic of
quantity of
quantum of
quart of
quicksand of
quite
quorum of
quota of
racked by/with
raft of
rammed with
rasher of
rather
ration of
ravishes with
reading of
ream of
recalls
redolent of
reeked of/
   reeking with/
   reeks of
reels in
regales with
reigns over/with
reined in by
reins in
reminds you of
reminiscent of
replete with
resembles
reservoir of
resolves to
resonates/

resonating
   with
reveals
ribbon of
richness of
rides with
riding over
rife with
riff of
rill of
rimmed by/
   with
ring of
rings out with
riot of
ripple of/
   ripples/
   rippling with
ripping/rips
   along with
river of
roar of
roars with
robe of
roll of
rolls into
room of
roots it in/to
rope of
rounded out
   with
row of
rub of
ruckus of
rules (with)
runneth over
   with
runs with
rush of
sack/sackful/
   sackload of
salted with
sample of
sandstorm of
saturated by/
   with
scads of
scant
scent of
scintilla of
scoop of
score of
scour of
scrap of
scrapbin of
scrape of
scratch of
scream of

screams with
screeching with
scrim of
scuffed by
sea of
seam of
seared onto
section of
seduced/seduces
   by/with
seed of
seeps into
segment of
segues into
semitrailer load
   of
sends up
serves up
serving of
set against
sewn together
   by
sexed up with
shade of
shaded with
shading of
shadowed by
shadow of
shake of
shard of
shaft of
share of
shaving of
sheath of
sheathed in
sheet of
shifts into
shimmies
shipload of
shitload of
shiver of
shock of
shop of
short
shortage of
shortfall of
shot of
shot through
   with
shotglass of
shovel of
showcases
shower of
shows
shred of
shrouded in
sidelight of
sideswiped by

sidles in with
sigh of
signs off with
singing/sings
   (out) with
sip of
sirocco of
sits above/below
sizzle of
sizzles with
skates between
skates with
skein of
skimp of
skimpy
skinch of
skips along with
skosh of
slab of
slap of
slash of
slate of
slathered with
slathering of
slew of
slice of
slightly
slides into
slip of
slither of
sliver of
slop of
slosh of
slug of
sluice of
slung together
   with
slurp of
slurry of
smack(s) of
smattering of
smear of
smell of
smidge/smidgen
   of
smolders with
smoothed out
   with
smorgasbord of
smothered by/
   with
smothers with
smudge of
snap of
snatch of
sneaking in
sneaking
   through with

spectrum of
splash of
snick of
sniff of
snip/snippet of
snoot(ful) of
snort of
softened by/
   with
solo
some
somewhat
song of
soup of
soupçon/soupçon
   of
source of
sourced with
spadeful of
spanning
spans
spark of
sparked with
sparks
spate of
speck of
speckled with
spews
spike of
spiked with
spine of
splashed with
splash of
splays into
splinter of
spoon of
sporting
sports
spot of
spreading
spring of
springboard of
sprinkle of
sprinkled with
spritzed with
squeezed
squeeze of
squirt of
stab of
stack of/stacked
   with
stain of
stained with
stall of
starburst of
startles with
starts with
stint of

stints on
stitch of
stitched with
stock of
stocked with
stocks
store/storehouse
   of
storm of
straddling
straddles the
   line with
strain of
strand of
strapped across
strapped with
strays/straying
   into
streak of/
   streaked with
stream of
streamer of
strewn with
striking
strikes
string of
strip of
stripe of
stroke of
struts its
studded with
stuffed with
stupendous
submerged/
   submerges by/
   under/with
subtle
suggestion of
subdued by
substantial
sunburst of
sun-crazed with
supplied with
supported by/
   with
supply of
surf of
surge of
surplus of
surrounded by/
   with
surrounds
suspicion of
svelte with
swaddled in
swagger of
swallow of
swamped by

swamping
swamps the
swarm of
swarms out
swash of
swat of
swatch of
swath of
swathed in
sweep of
swell/swelling
  of/swelling
  into
swimming in/
  with
swings into
swipe of
swirled with
swirl into/of
swish of
swoosh of
symphony of
tablespoon of
tad
tang of
tangle of
tank of
tankard of
tanker/
  tankerload of
taste of
taut with
teacup of
tease/teasing of
teases out
teaspoon of
teeming/teems
  with
teeny-weeny
teetering on
tempered by/
  with
tethered by/
  with
thick with
thimble of
thought of
thread of
threaded
  (through)
  with
throbbing/
  throbs with
throw of
thrust of
thumping with
thunderstorm of
thwack of

tickle of/with
tidal wave of
tide of
tiers of
tilt at
tilts toward
tin of
tincture of
tinge of/tinged
  with
tingle of/tingles
  with
tint of
tinted with
tiny
tipple of
titan of
tittle of
toast of
tome of
ton/tonne of
tonnage of
tone of
top of
tops it with
tornado of
torrent of
tosses up
tossing out
totally
touch/touch of/
  touched by
tower of
trace/tracing of
trades
trail of
transitions
  (in)to/
transitioning
  (in)to
treasure of
treasure trove of
trembler of
triangulates
trickle of
trifle of
trimmed in/
  with
trough of
trove of
trowel of
truck/truckload
  of
trumpeting of
trumpets
tsunami of
tub of
tucked into

tucker-bag/
  -box of
tuft of
tug of
tumble of
turn of
turning to
twang of
tweak of
twig of
twinge of
twist (of)
twitch of
ultralong
ultrastrong
uncountable
uncounted
undercuts
  by/with
underblast of
undercurrent of
undergirding of
undergirds
underlay of
underlaid with
underlined by/
  with
underlining of
underpinned
  by/with/
  underpinning
  of/underpins
underscored by/
  with
undertow of
unending
unfolds
unfurls
unfurls with
unleashed/
  unleashes/
  unleashing
unscored by/
  with
unstained by
upheld by/
  upholds
uplift of/
  uplifted by
upswell of
ushers in
veers into/
  toward
veiled by/with
veil of
vein of
veneer of

verges/verging
  on
very
vibrates/
  vibrating with
volcano of
volume of
voluminous
vortex of
wad of
waft of/wafts
  (into)
waggle of
wagon/
  wagonload of
walled (off) by
wall of
wallow of/
  wallows in
wallpapering of
wallop of
warp of
wars with
wash of
washed by
washes over
waterfall of
wave of
wealth of
weave of
weaves along
  with
weaves into
weaves together
web of
wedge of
wee (bit) of
well/wellspring
  of
welter of
whack of/
  wacked by
whale of
wheelbarrow of
whiff of
whip of
whiplash of
whirl of
whirlpool of
whirlwind of
whisk of
whisker of
whisper of
whit of
whole range of
whopper of
whoosh of
wings of

wink of
wire of
wisp of
wodge of
woof of
world of
wound (up)
  with
woven with
wrapped/wraps
  (up) in/with
wrapping of
wraps around
yard of
zephyr of
zest of
zing of
zings through
zings with
zip of

I really don't want my favourite subject [wine] to be ridiculed. There is a problem when these people [Jilly Goolden and Oz Clarke] list all the flavours and aromas they think they have detected. It then gets on to the label of the bottle and what you are looking at appears to be a recipe for fruit salad.... That is not what wine is like. It is not appley or black-curranty. People don't sniff a rose and say, "Oh, yes, pineapple, cucumber." It smells like a rose—and a bottle of wine smells like wine. Too much of this borrowing of terms to describe wine really doesn't help.
Hugh Johnson

VII. Bibliographic Resources
Important* Works (The Best of the Best)
* Important in the context of wine tasting descriptors.

Amerine, Maynard A., and Edward B. Roessler. *Wines: Their Sensory Evaluation*, 2nd ed. New York: Freeman, 1983. A towering, exhaustive opus on wine tasting by two renowned enologists from the University of California at Davis. One of a handful of landmark books that every serious wine lover should own.

Atkins, Susy. *Wine Wisdom: A Complete Wine-Tasting Course*. London: Quadrille, 2005. A well-organized introduction to all the major grapes and the wine made from them. Good how-to stuff for beginning tasters.

Baldy, Marian W. *The University Wine Course*, 3rd ed. South San Francisco: Wine Appreciation Guild, 1997. As thorough a college course in wine evaluation as one could wish for, by an American wine scholar.

Basset, Gérard. *The Wine Experience: A New Method Which Will Revolutionise the Practice and Art of Wine Tasting*. London: Kyle Cathie, 2000. Acclaimed as the finest nose in Europe, this French Master of Wine and Master Sommelier has produced a very comprehensive book on tasting wine.

Best, Richard. *The Frugal Oenophile's Lexicon of Wine Tasting Terms*, 2nd ed. Oakville, Ontario: Chester, 2003. An ingenious, well-fleshed collection of over 650 terms by a Canadian lover of wine and its language.

Broadbent, Michael. *Michael Broadbent's Vintage Wines*. London: Little Brown/Christies, 2002. Other than Broadbent and his buddy, Hugh Johnson, below, there are few people alive who could claim "Fifty Years of Tasting Three Centuries of Wines"! By any standard a stupendous effort from an international standard himself in wine appreciation. Broadbent, a British living legend and claret connoisseur, has distilled his half-century of wine evaluation into a colossal, tightly packed 560-page work. An amazing and amusing peek into an ever-so-comfortable world of important wine events with his beloved wife, Daphne, friends and fellow wine professionals.

--------. *Michael Broadbent's Winetasting*, 9th ed. London: Mitchell Beazley, 2003. Another of the few definitive volumes in the field. Broadbent's much-updated classic reflects a hypersensitive palate, immense vocabulary and irrepressible wit with an encyclopedic memory. A perfect amalgam from this well-seasoned British wine writer and master wine auctioneer.

Casamayor, Pierre. *How to Taste Wine*. London: Cassell, 2002. A really very fine, authoritative and handsome effort by a skillful and prolific French authority on wine tasting.

Clarke, Oz. *Oz Clarke's Winetasting*. London: Z-Publishing/Webster's International, 2001. A teeny-tiny pocket introduction to wine tasting from yet another articulate British wine authority with a renowned palate and a publishing empire to promote it.

Croft, Nicolle. *Winetasting*. London: Ryland Peters & Small, 2002. Another nice introduction for beginners to the many pleasures of the grape.

De Long, Steve and Deborah. *De Long's Wine Grape Varietal Table*, rev. ed. New York: De Long, 2004. Quite an impressive poster-sized guide to all the important wine grapes of the world.

Elder, Jim. "Varietal Features as Revealed by the Analysis of Online Wine Reviews." *www.ncf.ca/jim/wine*. [8/20/2001]. A mind-bogglingly long compilation of wine tasting terms from *Wine Spectator* reviews by a Canadian sommelier whose love of wine and language is of the highest order.

Fischer, John R. *The Evaluation of Wine: A Comprehensive Guide to the Art of Wine Tasting*. Lincoln NE: Writers Club, 2001. An extensive but useful self-publishing effort by a noted Nebraskan wine lover.

Gasnier, Vincent. *A Taste for Wine: 20 Key Tastings to Unlock Your Personal Wine Style*. New York: DK, 2006. More eye-candy from DK, the hyperillustrated publisher that believes words just aren't enough. This time, a paperback with 95 color photos of the photogenic author as he takes us by the hand through his garden of wine knowledge. Looks like a wine superstar in the making.

----------. *Drinks: Enjoying, Choosing, Storing, Serving and Appreciating Wines, Beers, Cocktails, Spirits, Aperitifs, Liqueurs and Ciders*. New York: DK, 2005. A very comprehensive survey of everything potable with alcohol, by the young but accomplished French Master Sommelier, above. As usual, DK has provided a masterful work of information for wine book lovers.

Gawel, Richard. *Wine Aroma Dictionary*. Kings Park, Australia: Recognose, 2003. An extensive overview of the aromas and tastes of wine by an Australian sensory expert.

Gawel, Richard, A. Oberholster and Leigh Francis. "A 'Mouth-Feel Wheel': Terminology for Communicating the Mouth-Feel Characteristics of Red Wine." *Australian Journal of Grape and Wine Research*, 6/2000, 203-207. A focused Australian take on Ann Noble's *Wine Aroma Wheel*, below.

Gluck, Malcolm. *The Sensational Liquid: A Guide to Wine Tasting*. London: Hodder & Stoughton, 2000. In an idiosyncratically designed and written book, this prolific London wine guru lectures us on his view of vinous art and science. A strange but attractive essay on wine.

Goode, Jamie. "Senses and Sensibilities: Synaesthesia and Wine Description." *The World of Fine Wine*, 9/2005, 86-91. Synesthesia (American spelling) is the bizarre stimulation of one sense by another, such as tasting "red," or hearing "sweet." It's a fascinating article on the figurative language of wine description.

Green, Glen. *Essential Wine Tasting Guide*. Alexandria, NSW, Australia: Vinum Vitae, 2000. Another of those ingenious Z-Card shirt-pocket foldups, this time featuring an amazing collection of descriptive wine terms from an Australian enthusiast.

Hawkins, Anthony. "Glossary of Wine-Tasting Terminology." *www.stratsplace.com/hawkins/winetaste*. [7/1/2001]. Eighteen packed pages of some of the best definitions in the business. An outstanding effort.

Henderson, J. Patrick and Dellie Rex. *About Wine*. Clifton Park NY: Thomson Delmar, 2007. A big new soup-to-nuts, or rather, Albariño-to-Zinfandel, textbooklike tome for those in the wine service part of the industry. Quite a nice, thorough effort full of many little nuggets of information.

Herbst, Ron, and Sharon Tyler Herbst. *The New Wine Lover's Companion*, 2nd ed. Hauppauge NY: Barron's, 2003. A popular and dependable collection of close to 4,000 general wine definitions. Mrs. Herbst also produces the even more popular *Food Lover's Companion*.

Hills, Phillip. *Appreciating Wine: The Flavour of Wine Explained*. Glasgow: HarperCollins, 2004. A sometimes overly scholarly attempt at explaining how we smell and taste wine by the Scottish founder of the Scotch Malt Whisky Society.

Hunt, Alex. "The Foundations of Flavour." *The World of Fine Wine*, 8/2005, 74-77. A fresh new look at how we describe wine from an up-and-coming young Master of Wine from Oxford.

------. "The Foundations of Quality." *The World of Fine Wine*, 10/2006, 84-87. More insightful analysis of the essence of quality in wine by the same young scholar, above.

------. "The Foundations of Structure and Texture." *The World of Fine Wine*, 9/2005, 82-85. A continuation of Hunt's examination of tasting terms, and a fine academic job it is, too.

Jackson, Ronald S. *Wine Tasting: A Professional Handbook*. London: Academic, 2002. A chart- and graph-heavy academic but well-organized work by a distinguished Canadian enologist.

Jefferies, Brian. "Wine Tasting: Adventures with some of the finer things in life!" *www.torbwine.com*. [12/10/2004]. Another amazingly long exposition of wine tasting techniques and definitions by an Australian enthusiast. Is there no end of them, or are all Australians born to love and write about wine?

Johnson, Hugh. *Hugh Johnson: A Life Uncorked*. Berkeley and Los Angeles: University of California, 2005. Like his friend and fellow wine traveler, Michael Broadbent (above), Johnson opens his heart and memory to fifty years of wine tasting and writing. This is an important book, full of strong opinions, detailed trips and experiences, and, altogether, a show of grape-love of the highest standard. What a long and successful life Johnson has had as a wine merchant, wine writer, wine critic and all-around nice guy.

Joseph, Robert. *The Ultimate Encyclopedia of Wine*. London: Carlton, 1999. An international wine authority, Joseph has produced an excellent but nowhere near ultimate overview for the serious wine drinker.

Juhlin, Richard. *4000 Champagnes*. Paris: Flammarion, 2004. As definitive an *oeuvre* on the French bubbly as ever published, by a world-class Swedish expert. Both Juhlin and Tom Stevenson (below) have noses and palates to die for, and both are at the very top of their game.

Kolpan, Steven, Brian H. Smith and Michael A. Weiss. *Exploring Wine*, 2nd ed. New York: Wiley, 2002. Three of the best and brightest of the famed Culinary Institute of America (the other CIA), in historic Hyde Park, New York. A very major guide to everything you wanted to know about wine, and then some.

Kincaid, Les. "Wine Vocabulary." *www.leskincaid.com/wine* [2/26/2002]. A really good long list of wine descriptors by an active American wine writer and broadcaster.

Laithwaites "Taste Prompter." *The Sunday Times Wine Club London Vintage Festival 2006*. London: Sunday Times, 2006. A handsomely illustrated full-color page showing lots of wine descriptors as if laid out in a classic European herb garden format. Pity we don't know the author of this charming page.

Lehrer, Adrienne. *Wine and Conversation*, 2nd ed. New York: Oxford, 2009. A major revision of a pioneering treatise on the intersection of wine and language by a distinguished American linguist who knows the inventive and perplexing language surrounding fermented grape juice. A very fine scholarly effort.

Lenoir, Jean. *Le Nez du Vin, 2006*. A pioneering spirit in the difficult art and science of identifying wine aromas by a creative French genius. His many little vials of different smells help us to understand wine in all its complex guises.

MacNeil, Karen. *The Wine Bible*. New York: Workman, 2001. To many wine lovers, indeed it is. An encyclopedic, knowledgeable and witty book by the American pro who runs the Napa CIA wine program.

McGee, Harold, and Daniel Patterson. "Talk Dirt to Me." *New York Times Style Magazine*, May 6, 2007, 76-79, 96. A very important put-down of the whole *terroir* craze that has winemakers the world over drawing lines in the sand about the controversial concept of tasting "place" in wine.

Meades, Jonathan. "Vintage Hyperbole, If I'm Not Mistaken." *www.timesonline.co.uk*. [4/30/2005]. A humorous yet serious peek at over-the-top wine descriptors corrupting our language, as observed by the recognized food and architectural critic with *The Times of London*.

Michelsen, Clive S. *Tasting & Grading Wine*. Linhamn, Sweden: JAC, 2005. Newly published in English, this is an amazing but almost excessive analysis of the science of wine tasting and sensory evaluation, by a Swedish expert who understands wine grapes and their destiny.

Noble, Ann C. *Wine Aroma Wheel*. Davis CA: Department of Viticulture and Enology, University of California, 1984. Retired in 2002, professor emerita Noble and her former band of enthusiastic enophiliacs created this trail-blazing mother of all wine wheels. The first and still one of the most successful.

Parker Jr., Robert M. *The World's Greatest Wine Estates: A Modern Perspective*. New York: Simon & Schuster, 2005. Yet another definitive tome from the prolific Mr. Parker, who here lavishes his close and experienced attention on 175 of the world's most accomplished wine producers. An updated and more focused review of the best of the best from the most influential living wine evaluator.

Parker, Jr., Robert M., with Pierre-Antoine Rovani. *Parker's Wine Buyer's Guide*, 6th ed. New York: Simon & Schuster, 2002. The biggest Parker yet at 1635 pages. A mind-boggling directory of the world's great and near-great wines, vineyards and their vintners, as only the Parker team can deliver. A masterpiece of scholarship (and record-keeping).

Peynaud, Émile. *Knowing and Making Wine*, trans. Alan Spencer. New York: Wiley 1984. A very highly technical treatise on the chemistry of why wines look, smell and taste as they do. His follow-up book, below, expands on the tasting front and is a true classic.

--------. *The Taste of Wine: The Art and Science of Wine Appreciation*, 2nd ed., trans. Michael Schuster. New York: Wiley, 1996. As major a lifetime summary on wine tasting as you're likely to find. Peynaud's astonishing contributions to the making of fine wine, not to mention his contribution to the great literature of wine and its language, have inspired enologists, vintners and wine lovers everywhere.

Priewe, Jens. *Wine: From Grape to Glass*, 3rd ed. New York: Abbeville, 2006. A really comprehensive look at the grape from bud-break to swallow, by a European well versed in all aspects of viticulture, viniculture and wine appreciation.

Ridgway, Judy. *The Wine-Tasting Class: Expertise in 12 Tastings*. New York: Clarkson Potter, 1996. A fine, colorful inauguration into what we taste in wine and why, by the English author of over fifty books.

Robinson, Jancis. *How to Taste: A Guide to Enjoying Win*, rev. ed. New York: Simon & Schuster, 2008. The great Jancis describing the whys and hows of wine tasting. A fine work, newly revised, from the complete wine pro.

----------. *Jancis Robinson's Wine Tasting Workbook*. London: Conran/Octopus, 2000. A wonderful introduction to this artful science by the prolific English Master of Wine and major force in wine circles.

Robinson, Jancis, ed. *The Oxford Companion to Wine*, 3rd ed. Oxford: Oxford University, 2006. Here's another big one for your groaning reference shelf, from one of the best and brightest of the British wine experts. In matters of wine, if Jancis doesn't know about it, it probably isn't worth knowing.

Schildknecht, David. "The Face of Wine." *The World of Fine Wine*, 14/2006, 126-131. An academic but stimulating examination of how we recognize wine. Another deep look into the secrets of the grape, by a well-known British expert, who's also knowledgeable about German wines.

Schultz, Julian. "A Discussion of Wine Tasting Terms in Illustration and Parody." *www.oxfordwineroom.com* [8/22/2001]. Mr. Schultz places a light touch on an endlessly fascinating subject in a cute but still informative way.

Schuster, Michael. *Essential Winetasting*. London: Mitchell Beazley, 2000. A well-rounded presentation of this flavorful beverage by the same British expert who translated Peynaud's French classic, above.

Searle, Ronald. *The Illustrated Winespeak: Ronald Searle's Wicked World of Winetasting*. London: Souvenir, 1983. The very one and the very only. The sharpest eye and the funniest book in all winedom.

Sharp, Andrew. *Winetaster's Secrets: A Step-by-Step Guide to the Joy of Winetasting*, rev. ed. Toronto: Warwick, 2005. A highly respected Canadian authority who certainly knows what grapes could become.

Shesgreen, Sean. "Wet Dogs and Gushing Oranges: Winespeak for a New Millennium." *Chronicle Review of Higher Education*. 3/7/2003, 59/26, B15. A hilarious yet penetrating look at the current state of wine tasting language from an English professor at a university in middle America. His was the recent rant on the Internet that drew countless yeas and boos, depending on one's view of winespeak.

Simon, Joanna. *Discovering Wine: A Refreshingly Unfussy Beginner's Guide to Finding, Tasting, Judging, Storing, Serving, Cellaring and, Most of All, Discovering Wine*, rev. ed. New York: Fireside, 2003. Quite a nice introduction to wine in all its glory by a well-known British writer.

Simon, Pat. *Wine-Tasters' Logic*. London: Faber and Faber, 2000. Another British Master of Wine whose effort here is knowledgeable if a bit academic.

Smith, Barry C., ed. *Questions of Taste: The Philosophy of Wine*. Oxford: Signal, 2007. Ten important new articles by some big names on the subject of wine, how we look at it and how we value it in today's society. A major new work of serious wine drinking analysis.

Sonnenfeld, Albert. "The Languages of Wine." *Wine, Food and the Arts: Works Gathered by The American Institute of Wine & Food*, vol. 1, 91-95. San Francisco: American Institute of Wine & Food, 1996. A retired college professor French literature and working food writer, Sonnenfeld has penned a poetic piece on wine's many languages.

Spence, Godfrey. *Teach Yourself Wine Tasting*. London: Hodder & Stoughton, 2003. A very nicely organized little book for the serious beginner by an English wine lecturer.

Spurrier, Steven and Michel Dovaz. *Académie du Vin Wine Course*, 2nd ed. New York: Macmillan, 1990. A well-rounded course in wine and its appreciation in a fine collaboration by two experts: one English and one French.

Stevenson, Tom. *The New Sotheby's Wine Encyclopedia*, 4th ed. rev. New York: DK, 2007. A truly comprehensive overview of wine in all its aspects and complexities by a prolific British expert, renowned as an authority on Alsatian wines, as well as Champagne and other fizzies from around the world. Amazing.

-------. *World Encyclopedia of Champagne and Sparkling Wine*, rev ed. South San Francisco: Wine Appreciation Guild, 2003. Another excellent study of the most important sparkling wines by an acknowledged expert in the field. He and Richard Juhlin (above) are probably the top fizzy noses and palates today.

Suárez-Toste, Ernesto. "Metaphor inside the wine cellar: On the ubiquity of Personification Schemas in Winespeak." n.d. A Spanish professor takes a curiously academic look at metaphor in wine descriptors.

Sumner, Greg. "Silly Tasting Notes Generator." *www.gmon.tech/stng* [3/1/2001]. An ingenious exercise in creating ridiculous wine tasting reviews by a gifted Seattle enthusiast who borrowed selected terms from *Wine Spectator* reviews and rearranges them into an absurd but hilarious word game.

Tudor, Anthony. "Tudor's Faint Praise." *www.ryerson.ca/~dtudor/faintpraise* [4/21/2007]. Yet another very funny but still useful collection of wine-related material from the omnivorous mind of a Canadian ex-professor of journalism.

Vaynerchuk, Gary. *Gary Vaynerchuk's 101 Wines Guaranteed to Inspire, Delight, and Bring Thunder to Your World*. New York: Rodale, 2008. An amusing look at current wines by a new-age wine writer, critic and blogger whose popularity is in direct proportion to his colorfully amusing wine descriptions.

Wine Enthusiast Magazine Essential Buying Guide 2008. Philadelphia: Running, 2008. Fifteen hundred and eighty four pages of wall-to-wall wine reviews from recent pages, as sniffed and sloshed by seven of its contributors. A good but heavy all-around reference for those who don't keep their monthly copies. A fine doorstop if you tire of it.

Wine Spectator's Ultimate Guide to Buying Wine, 8th ed. Philadelphia: Running, 2004. One thousand and four pages from *Wine Enthusiast's* bigger brother, this tome is reminiscent of an old Sears, Roebuck catalog at its height. Useful but exhausting to hold and plow through.

Yarrow, Alder. *Vinography Aroma Card*. Vinography.com. 11.19.2007. Another one of those cute little shirt-pocket-sized cards with listings of common wine aromas.

Young, Alan. *Making Sense of Wine: A Study in Sensory Perception*, 5th ed. South San Francisco: Wine Appreciation Guild, 2009. A very revision of a very good, important book by a highly respected Australian expert.

Zraly, Kevin. *Windows on the World Complete Wine Course*, 2008 ed. New York: Sterling, 2007. Zraly is one of finest American wine experts and teachers, having started his famous wine course back in 1976 while working as the cellar master (in the sky) of Windows on the World. His has been a remarkable success story both before and after the World Trade Center disaster. Teach and write on, Mr. Z.

Notable* Works *(The Best of the Rest)*
*Other really good stuff containing wine tasting descriptors.

Ainsworth, Jim. *Red Wine Guide: A Complete Introduction to Choosing Red Wines*, rev. ed. by Simon Woods. London: Mitchell Beazley, 2002.

------- .*White Wine Guide: A Complete Introduction to Choosing White Wine*, rev. ed. by Simon Woods. London: Mitchell Beazley, 2002.

Allen, Max. *Red and White*, rev. ed. South San Francisco: Wine Appreciation Guild, 2001.

-------. *Sniff, Swirl & Slurp: How to Get More Pleasure Out of Every Glass of Wine*. London: Mitchell Beazley, 2002.

Amey, Ralph. *Wines of Baja California: Touring and Tasting Mexico's Undiscovered Treasures*. South San Francisco: Wine Appreciation Guild, 2003.

Amorose, Michael A. *A Catalog of California Wines*, 6th ed. San Francisco: Arthur Young, 1989.

Anderson, Burton. *Burton Anderson's Best Italian Wines*. London: Little, Brown/Websters, 2001.

Arkell, Julie. *Wine: A Comprehensive Guide to Drinking and Appreciating Wine*. London: New Holland, 2003.

Asher, Gerald. *Vineyard Tales: Reflections on Wine*. San Francisco: Chronicle, 1996.

Aspler, Tony. *Tony Aspler's Wine Lover's Companion*. Toronto: McGraw-Hill Ryerson, 1991.

Atkin, Tim, forward to *Hachette Vins de Pays: A Buyer's Guide to the Best French Country Wines*. London: Hachette/Mitchell Beazley, 2003.

Atkins, Susy. *Girls' Guide to Wine*. London: Mitchell Beazley, 2002.

Atkins, Susy, and Dave Broom. *Drink*. Minocqua WI: Willow Creek, 2001.

Ausmus, William A. *Wines & Wineries of California's Central Coast*. Berkeley and Los Angeles: University of California, 2008.

Baldy, Marian W. *Wine Appreciation Through the Senses: A Practical Guide for Winetasters*. Rochester: American Wine Society, 1997.

Balik, Allen R., and Virginia B. Morris. *Guide to Choosing, Serving and Enjoying Wine*. New York: Lightbulb, 2000.

Bamforth, Charles. *Grape vs. Grain*. .New York: Cambridge University, 2008.

Bastianich, Joseph, and David Lynch. *Vino Italiano Buying Guide: The Ultimate Quick Reference to the Great Wines of Italy*. New York: Clarkson Potter, 2004.

-------. *Vino Italiano: The Regional Wines of Italy*. New York: Clarkson Potter, 2002.

Beckett, Fiona. *Wine by Style: A Practical Guide to Choosing Wine by Flavour, Body, and Colour*. London: Mitchell Beazley, 2007.

-------. *Wine Uncorked*. Minocqua WI: Willow Creek, 1999.

Beckett, Neil, gen. ed. *1001 Wines You Must Try Before You Die*. New York: Universe, 2008.

Behrendt, Axel and Bibiana. *Cognac*. New York: Abbeville, 1997.

-------. *Grappa*. New York: Abbeville, 1999.

Bernstein, Leonard S. *The Official Guide to Wine Snobbery*, 2nd ed. New York: Barricade, 2003.

Besch, Andy, with Ellen Kaye. *The Wine Guy: Everything You Want to Know About Buying & Enjoying Wine From Someone Who Sells It*. New York: William Morrow, 2005.

Bespaloff, Alexis. *The New Frank Schoonmaker Encyclopedia of Wine*. New York: William Morrow, 1988.

Blackburn, Ian, and Allison Levine. *The Learning Annex Presents The Pleasure of Wine: The Smarter Approach to the World of Wine*. New York: Wiley, 2005.

Blue, Anthony Dias. *Anthony Dias Blue's Pocket Guide to Wine 2006*. New York: Simon & Schuster, 2005.

-------. *The Complete Book of Spirits: A Guide to Their History, Production, and Enjoyment*. New York: Harper-Collins, 2004.

Brenner, Leslie. *Fear of Wine*. New York: Bantam, 1995.

Budd, Jim. *Appreciating Fine Wines: The New Accessible Guide to the Subtleties of the World's Finest Wines*. New York: Todtri, 2001.

Cadiau, Paul. *LexiVin/LexiWine*, 5th ed. Pernand-Vergelesses, France: Les Publications de Catherine et Paul Cadiau, 2005.

Caillard, Andrew. *The Rewards of Patience: A Definitive Guide to Cellaring and Enjoying Penfolds Wines*, 5th ed. Magill, South Australia: Penfolds, 2004.

Caillard, Andrew, and Stewart Langton. *Langton's Australian Fine Wine Guide*, 5th ed. Double Bay, New South Wales, Australia: Media 21, 2002.

Callec, Christian. *Wine Encyclopædia*. Lisse, The Netherlands: Rebo, 1999.

Cassidy, Chip. *Chip Cassidy's Wine Travels*. Coral Gables FL: Crown Wine and Spirits, 2001.

Cernilli, Daniele, and GiGi Piumatti, eds. *Italian Wines 2008*. New York: Gambero Rosso/Slow Food, 2008.

Champagne Notebook. Épernay, France. Comité Interprofessionnel du Vin de Champagne (Champagne Trade Association), 1996.

Chapleau, Marc. *Let's Talk Wine*. Montreal: XYZ, 2004.

Charters, Steve. *Wine and Society: The Social and Cultural Context of a Drink*. Oxford: Elsevier, 2006.

Clark, Corbet. *American Wines of the Northwest: A Guide to the Wines of Oregon, Washington and Idaho*. New York: William Morrow, 1989.

Clarke, Oz. *Oz Clark's Bordeaux: The Wines, The Vineyards, The Winemakers*. London: Harcourt/Webster's, 2006.

-------. *Oz Clarke's New Essential Wine Book: An Indispensable Guide to the Wines of the World*. New York: Simon & Schuster, 2005.

-------. *Oz Clarke's Pocket Wine Guide 2008*. London: Harcourt/Websters, 2007.

Clarke, Oz, and Margaret Rand. *Oz Clarke's Grapes and Wines: The Definitive Guide to the World's Great Grapes and the Wines They Make*. London: Websters, 2007.

Clarke, Oz, and Steven Spurrier. *Clarke & Spurrier's Fine Wine Guide. A Connoisseur's Bible*, rev. ed. New York: Harcourt, 2001.

Coates, Clive. *Grand Vins: The Finest Châteaux of Bordeaux and Their Wines*. Berkeley and Los Angeles: University of California, 1995.

-------. *The Wines of Bordeaux*. Berkeley and Los Angeles: University of California, 2004.

-------. *The Wines of Burgundy*. Berkeley and Los Angeles: University of California, 2008.

Cohen, Jon. "Jabberwiney," *Slate*, January 20, 2000.

Collin, Simon. *Dictionary of Wine*. London: Bloomsbury, 2005.

Colman, Tyler. *Wine Politics: How Governments, Environmentalists, Mobsters and Critics Influence the Wines We Drink*. Berkeley and Los Angeles: University of California, 2008

Cordon Bleu Wine Essentials: Professional Secrets to Buying, Storing, Serving and Drinking Wine. New York: Wiley, 2001.

Cox, Jeff. *Cellaring Wine: Managing Your Wine Collection ... to Perfection*. North Adams MA: Storey, 2003.

D'Agata, Ian. *The Ecco Guide to the Best Wines of Italy*. New York: HarperCollins, 2008.

DeBord, Matthew. *The New York Book of Wine*. New York: Universe/Rizzoli, 2003.

DeLissio, Joseph. *The River Café Wine Primer*. New York: Little Brown, 2000.

Difford, Simon, ed. *Sauce Guide to Drinks & Drinking*. London: Sauce, 2001.

Dominé, André. *Wine*, rev. ed. Königswinter, Germany: Ullmann, 2008.

Dovaz, Michel. *Fine Wines: The Best Vintages of the 20th Century*. New York: Assouline, 2000.

Doyle, Brian. *The Grail*. Corvallis OR: Oregon State, 2006.

DuBose, Fred, and Evan Spingarn with Nancy Maniscalco. *The Ultimate Wine Lover's Guide 2006*. New York: Sterling, 2005.

Dunkling, Leslie. *The Guinness Drinking Companion*. Guilford CT: Lyons, 2002.

Durac, Jack. *A Matter of Taste: Wine and Wine-Tasting*. Magnum, 1979.

-------. *Wines and the Art of Tasting*. New York: Dutton, 1974.

Durkin, Andrew, and John Cousins. *Teach Yourself Wine Appreciation*. Chicago: NTC, 1995.

Edwards, Michael. *Red Wine Companion*. Buffalo: Firefly, 1998.
-------. *The Champagne Companion: The Authoritative Connoisseur's Guide*. Buffalo: Firefly, 1999.

Ejbich, Konrad. *A Pocket Guide to Ontario Wines, Wineries, Vineyards & Wines*. Toronto: McClelland & Stewart, 2005.

Elkjer, Thom, ed. *Adventures in Wine: True Stories of Vineyards and Vintages Around the World*. San Francisco: Travelers' Tales, 2002.

Ensrud, Barbara. *Wine with Food: A Guide to Entertaining Through the Seasons.* New York: Congdon & Weed, 1984.

Ewing-Mulligan, Mary, and Ed McCarthy. *Wine for Dummies,* 4th ed. Wiley: Hoboken NJ, 2006.

--------. *Wine Style: Using Your Senses to Explore and Enjoy Wine.* New York: Wiley, 2005.

Fallis, Catherine, and Robert M. Cohen. *Great Boutique Wines You Can Buy Online.* San Francisco: Silverback, 2006.

Fanet, Jacques. *Great Wine Terroirs.* Berkeley and Los Angeles: University of California, 2004.

Feiring, Alice. *The Battle for Wine and Love or How I Saved the World from Parkerization..* Orlando: Harcourt, 2008.

Finigan, Robert. *Robert Finigan's Essentials of Wine: A Guide to Discovering the World's Most Pleasing Wines.* New York: Knopf, 1987.

Fischer, Christina. *DuMont's Lexicon of Wine.* Lisse, The Netherlands: Rebo, 2004.

Forest, Louis. *Wine Album.* New York: Metropolitan Museum of Art, 1982.

Francisco, Cathleen. *Pinot Noir: A Reference Guide to California and Oregon Pinot Noir.* Sonoma: Wine Key, n.d.

--------. *Zinfandel: A Reference Guide to California Zinfandel.* South San Francisco: Wine Appreciation Guild, 2001.

Friedrich, Jacqueline. *The Wines of France: The Essential Guide for Savvy Shoppers.* Berkeley: Ten Speed, 2006.

Gabler, James M., Bryce C. Rankine and Kevin Starr. *Wine Into Words: A History and Bibliography of Wine Books in the English Language,* 2nd ed. Baltimore: Bacchus, 2004.

Gaiter, Dorothy J., and John Brecher. *The Wall Street Journal Guide to Wine,* 2nd ed. New York: Broadway, 2002.

--------. *Weekend Journal: Adventures in Wine.* New York: Wall Street Journal, 1998.

--------. *Wine for Every Day and Every Occasion.* New York: Morrow, 2004.

Galet, Pierre. *Grape Varieties.* London: Cassell, 2002.

Geiss, Lisbet. *The Gay Language of Wine: Expressions Used in Wine Terminology.* Neustadt, West Germany, n.d.

George, Rosemary. *Lateral Wine Tasting Guide: Expand Your Wine-Drinking Horizons,* rev. ed. London: Bloomsbury, 1992.

Gianotti, Peter M. *A Guide to Long Island Wine Country.* Melville NY: Newsday, 2001.

Giglio, Anthony. *Food & Wine Wine Guide 2009.* New York: AMEX, 2008

Gillette, Paul. *Wine Tasting Handbook.* Los Angeles: Camaro, 1988.

Givton, Albert. *Carte Blanche: A Quarter Century of Wine Tasting Diaries and Cellar Notes: 1974-1999.* Turnagain, 1999.

Glatre, Eric. *Champagne Guide.* New York: Abbeville, 1999.

Gluck, Malcolm. *Malcolm Gluck's Brave New World.* London: Mitchell Beazley, 2006.

--------. *Streetplonk 2001: Gluck's Guide to Wine Shops.* London. Hodder & Stoughton, 2000.

--------. *Summer Superplonk 1999.* London: Hodder & Stoughton, 1999.

--------. *Superplonk 2004: The Top 1000.* London: Collins, 2003.

-------. *Why Water Just Won't Do*. London: Little Books, 2003.

Goldstein, Evan. *Perfect Pairings*. Berkeley and Los Angeles: University of California, 2006.

Goldstein, Robin. *The Wine Trials: A Fearless Critic Book*. Austin TX: Fearless Critic, 2008.

Goode, Jamie. *The Science of Wine: From Vine to Glass*. Berkeley and Los Angeles: University of California, 2005.

The Good Taste of Wine. Waukesha WI: NCL Graphic Specialties, 1999.

Goolden, Jilly. *The Taste of Wine*. London: BBC, 1990.

Gottfried, John and Patricia. *A Wine Tasting Course: The Practical Way to Know and Enjoy Wine*. New York: David McKay, 1978.

Grahm, Randall. "The Phenomenology of Terroir: A Meditation." *The World of Fine Wine*, 13/2006, 102-107.

Gregutt, Paul. *Washington Wines and Wineries: The Essential Guide*. Berkeley and Los Angeles: University of California, 2007.

Grudzinski, Ted. *Winequest: The Wine Dictionary*. Bay Shore NY: Winequest, 1985.

Guy, Patricia. *Wines of Italy/Il Gusto Italiano del Vino*. Windsor CT: Tide-Mark, 2003.

Haddad, Laura Holmes. *Anything But Chardonnay: a guide to the other grapes*. New York: Stewart, Tabori & Chang, 2008.

Haeger, John Winthrop. *North American Pinot Noir*. Berkeley and Los Angeles: University of California, 2004.

-------. *Pacific Pinot Noir: A Comprehensive Guide for Consumers and Connoisseurs*. Berkeley and Los Angeles: University of California, 2008.

Halley, Ned. *Best Wine Buys in the High Street 2003*. London: Foulsham, 2003.

-------. *Ned Halley's Supermarket Wine Report 2004*. London: Foulsham, 2004.

Halliday, James. *Australia & New Zealand Wine Companion*, 2000 ed. Sydney: HarperCollins, 1999.

-------. *Classic Wines of Australia and New Zealand*, 3rd ed. Sydney: HarperCollins, 2002.

-------. *James Halliday's Australian Wine Companion*, 2004 ed. Sydney: HarperCollins, 2003.

Halliday, James, and Hugh Johnson. *The Art and Science of Wine*. Buffalo NY: Firefly, 2007.

Hammond, Carolyn. *1000 Best Wine Secrets*. Naperville Il: Sourcebooks, 2006.

Hannum, Hurst, and Robert S. Blumberg. *The Fine Wines of California*. Garden City NY: Doubleday, 1971.

Harding, Graham. *A Wine Miscellany: A Jaunt Through the Whimsical World of Wine*. New York: Potter, 2005.

Harrington, Robert J. *Food and Wine Pairing: A Sensory Experience*. Hoboken NJ: Wiley, 2008.

Hazen, Victor. *Italian Wine*. New York: Knopf, 1982.

Hinkle, Richard Paul. *Good Wine: The New Basics*. San Francisco: Silverback, 2005.

Hooke, Huon. *Words on Wine*. Sydney: SMH, 1997.

Immer-Robinson, Andrea. *Great Wine Made Simple: Straight Talk from a Master Sommelier*, rev. ed. New York: Broadway, 2005.

Ivey, Jamie. *Extremely Pale Rosé: A Very French Adventure*. New York: St. Martin's, 2006.

Jefford, Andrew. *Wine Tastes, Wine Styles*. London: Ryland Peters & Small, 2000.
----------. *Choosing Wine*. London: Ryland Peters & Small, 2003.

--------. *Andrew Jefford's Wine Course*. London: Ryland Peters & Small, 2008.

Johnnes, Daniel, with Michael Stephenson. *Daniel Johnnes's Top 200 Wines: An Expert's Guide to Maximum Enjoyment for Your Dollar*, 2004 ed. New York: Penguin, 2003.

Johnson, Hugh. *Hugh Johnson's Wine Companion: The Encyclopedia of Wines, Vineyards & Winemakers*, rev. ed. London: Mitchell Beazley, 2003.

Johnson, Hugh, and Jancis Robinson. *The World Atlas of Wine*, 6th ed. London: Mitchell Beazley, 2007.

Johnson, Linda. *The Wine Collector's Handbook*. Guilford CT: Lyons, 1997.

Johnson-Bell, Linda. *Pairing Wine and Food*. Short Hills NJ: Burford, 1999.

Jones, Andrew. *Wine Talk: A Vintage Collection of Facts and Legends for Wine Lovers*. London: Judy Piatkus, 1997.

Joseph, Robert. *Good Wine Guide 2004*. New York: DK, 2003.

--------. *The Sunday Telegraph: Wine Appreciation Collection/The Wine Appreciation Guide/The Wine Tasting Record*. London: Carleton, 2000.

--------. *Wine Buyers' Guide 2006*. London: Mitchell Beazley, 2006.

Joy, Rupert. "Terroir: The Truth." *Decanter*, 7/2007, 42-51.

Juhlin, Richard. *2000 Champagnes*. M.T. Train/Scala, 1999.

Jukes, Matthew. *Wine: Everything You Ever Wanted to Know About Wine But Were Afraid to Ask*. London: Hodder Headline, 1999.

--------. *The Wine List 2007: The Top 250 Wines of the Year*. London: Headline, 2006.

Kamp, David, and David Lynch. *The Wine Snob's Dictionary: An Essential Lexicon of Oenological Knowledge*. New York: Broadway, 2008.

Keevil, Susan, consultant. *Wines of the World*. New York: DK, 2004.

Keevil, Susan, with Susy Atkins. *The Which? Wine Guide 2003*. London: Which?, 2002.

Kime, Giles. *Secrets of Wine: Know Your Cab from Your Merlot—Without the Terroir*. New York: Penguin, 2007.

King, Alice. *Fabulous Fizz: Choosing Champagne and Sparkling Wine for Every Occasion*. London: Ryland Peters & Small, 1999.

Kinssies, Richard. *The Art of Wine Tasting: An Illustration Guidebook*. Bellevue WA: Becker&Mayer, 2004.

Kolpan, Steven, Brian H. Smith and Michael A. Weiss. *WineWise: Your Complete Guide to Understanding, Selecting, and Enjoying Wine*. Hoboken NJ: Wiley, 2008.

Kramer, Matt. *Making Sense of Wine*, rev. ed. Philadelphia: Running, 2004.

--------. *Matt Kramer's Making Sense of Italian Wine*. Philadelphia: Running, 2006.

Kyte-Powell, Ralph, and Huon Hooke. *The Penguin Good Australian Wine Guide 2007*. Victoria: Penguin, 2006.

Lake, Max. *The Flavour of Wine: A Qualitative Approach for the Serious Wine Taster*. Brisbane: Jacaranda, 1969.

Laube, James. *Wine Spectator's California Wine*, 2nd ed. New York: Wine Spectator, 1999.

Laverick, Charles, ed. *The Beverage Testing Institute's Buying Guide to Wine*. New York: Sterling, 1999.

Le Lacheur, Paul. *The International Language of Wine*. Stepney, South Australia: Axiom, 2001.

Lembeck, Harriet. *Grossman's Cyclopedia: The Concise Guide to Wines, Beers and Spirits*. Philadelphia: Running, 2002.

Liger-Belair, Gérard. *Uncorked: The Science of Champagne*. Princeton: Princeton University, 2004.

Lipinski, Robert A. and Kathie. *The Complete Beverage Dictionary*. New York: Wiley, 1997.

Livingstone-Learmonth, John. *The Wines of the Northern Rhône*. Berkeley and Los Angeles: University of California, 2005.

Lord, Tony. *Dictionary of French Wines*. New York: Sterling, 2002.

Lynch, Kermit. *Inspiring Thirst: Vintage Selections from the Kermit Lynch Wine Brochure*. Berkeley: Ten Speed, 2004.

MacLean, Natalie. *Red, White and Drunk All Over: A Wine-Soaked Journey From Grape to Glass*. New York: Bloomsbury, 2006.

MacDonogh, Giles. *Portuguese Table Wines*. London: Grub Street, 2001.

March, James, James Halliday, et al. *The Winemaker's Essential Phrasebook*. London: Mitchell Beazley, 2004.

Marcus, Irving H. *How to Test and Improve Your Wine Judging Ability*, 2nd ed. Berkeley: Wine Publications, 1984.

May, Peter F. *Marilyn Merlot and the Naked Grape: Odd Wines from Around the World*. Philadelphia: Quirk, 2006.

Mayberry, Robert W. *Wines of the Rhône Valley: A Guide to Origins*. Totowa NJ: Rowman & Littlefield, 1987.

Mayson, Richard. *Port and the Douro*, rev. ed. London: Mitchell Beazley, 2004.

--------. *Portugal's Wines & Wine Makers: Port, Madeira & Regional Wines*, rev. ed. South San Francisco: Wine Appreciation Guild, 1997.

--------. *The Wines and Vineyards of Portugal*. London: Mitchell Beazley, 2003.

McCoy, Elin. *The Emperor of Wine: The Rise of Robert M. Parker, Jr. and the Reign of American Taste*. New York: Ecco, 2005.

McInerney, Jay. *A Hedonist in the Cellar: Adventures in Wine*. New York: Knopf, 2006.

--------. *Bacchus & Me: Adventures in the Wine Cellar*. New York: Vintage, 2002.

Meyer, Justin. *Plain Talk About Fine Wine*. Santa Barbara CA: Capra, 1989.

Middles, Mick. *Wine: Pocket Reference Book*. London: Parragon, 2001.

Miller, Gloria Bley. *The Glory of Wine*. New York: Ibrod, 2001.

Mingo, Jack. *Wannabe Guide to Wine*. Berkeley: RDR, 1995.

Mitchell, Brian and Evan. *Drinking Your Own Words*. Sydney: Inmediaares, 2007.

Montalbetti, Catherine, ed. *The Hachette Guide to French Wines 2005: The Definitive Guide to Over 9,000 of the Best Wines of France*. London: Mitchell Beazley, 2004.

Moore, Greg. *The Wine Chronicles: Writing Your Own Fine Wine Book*. Philadelphia: Running, 2002.

Morgan, Jeff. *Rosé: A Guide to the World's Most Versatile Wine*. San Francisco: Chronicle, 2005.

Morrell, Peter. *I'm in the Wine Store, Now What!?* New York: Silver Lining, 2000.

Morris, Roger. *The Genie in the Bottle: Unraveling the Myths About Wine*. New York: A&W, 1981.

Moser, Peter. *The Ultimate Austrian Wine Guide*. Klosterneuberg, Austria: Falstaff, 2004.

Muir, Augustus, ed. *How to Choose and Enjoy Wine*. New York: Bonanza/Brown, 1972.

Murphy, Dan. *A Guide to Wine Tasting*. South Melbourne: Macmillan, 1977.

Murphy, Linda. "Here, kitty kitty. Wine critics love cat pee, but hate wet dog. We explain why." *SFGate.com*. [3/24/2005].

Muscatine, Doris, Maynard A. Amerine, Bob Thompson, eds. *The University of California/Sotheby Book of California Wine*. Berkeley and Los Angeles: University of California, and London: Sotheby, 1984.

Nelson, James. *The Poor Person's Guide to Great Cheap Wines*. New York: McGraw-Hill, 1977.

Nickles, Jane A. *WineSpeak 101*. Charleston: BookSurge, 2006.

Nicklès, Sara. ed. *Wine Memories: Great Writers on the Pleasures of Wine*. San Francisco: Chronicle, 2000.

Nowak, Barbara, and Beverly Wichman. *Saucy Sisters' Guide to Wine: What Every Girl Should Know Before She Uncorks*. New York: New American, 2004.

Oldman, Mark. *Oldman's Guide to Outsmarting Wine*. New York: Penguin, 2004.

Oliver, Jeremy. *The Australian Wine Annual 2007*, 10th ed. Victoria: Jeremy Oliver, 2006.

Olney, Richard. *Romanée-Conti: The World's Most Fabled Wine*. New York: Rizzoli, 1995.

Osborne, Lawrence. *The Accidental Connoisseur: An Irreverent Journey Through the Wine World*. New York: North Point, 2004.

Page, Susan, ed. *Wine Encyclopedia*. San Diego: Portable, 2002.

Parker, Jr., Robert M. *Bordeaux: A Consumer's Guide to the World's Finest Wines*, 4th ed. New York: Simon & Schuster, 2003.

--------. *Wines of the Rhône Valley*, rev. ed. New York: Simon & Schuster, 1997.

Peñín, José. *Peñín Guide to Spanish Wine 2009*, trans. Antonio Casado. Madrid: Grupo Peñín, 2008.

Perdue, Andy. *The Northwest Wine Guide: A Buyer's Handbook*. Seattle: Sequatchie, 2003.

Peterson, James. *Sweet Wines: A Guide to the World's Best with Recipes*. New York: Stewart, Tabori & Chang, 2002.

Pitcher, Steve. *Wine*. Lincolnwood IL: New Seasons, 2002.

Pratt, James Norwood, with Jacques DeCaso. *The Wine Bibber's Bible*, 2nd ed. New York: Macmillan, 1982.

Prial, Frank J. *Decantations*. New York: St. Martin's/Griffin, 2001.

--------. *Wine Talk*. New York: Times, 1978.

Price, Freddy. *Riesling Renaissance*. London: Mitchell Beazley, 2004.

Price, Pamela Vandyke. *The Taste of Wine*. New York: Random House, 1975.

Priewe, Jens. *Wine: A Practical Guide to Enjoying Your Selection*. New York: Abbeville, 2001.

Puisais, J., R. L. Chabanon, et al. *Initiation Into the Art of Wine Tasting*. Madison WI: Interpublish, 1974.

Rankine, Bryce. *Tasting and Enjoying Wine: A Guide to Wine Evaluation for Australia and New Zealand*. Wine, 2001.

Rapp, Alyssa. *Guide to Wine: Around the World in 80 Sips*. Avon MA: Adams, 2008.

Reichl, Ruth, ed. *History in a Glass: Sixty Years of Wine Writing from Gourmet*. New York: Modern, 2006.

Robards, Terry. *California Wine Label Album*. New York: Workman, 1986.

Roberts, Darryl, Stewart Dorman, et al. *The Wine X Magazine Guide to X-Rated Wines*. New York: Three Rivers, 2000.

Robinson, Andrea. *Andrea Robinson's 2007 Wine Buying Guide for Everyone*. New York: Broadway, 2007.

Robinson, Jancis. *Jancis Robinson's Concise Wine Companion*. Oxford: Oxford University, 2001.

--------. *Jancis Robinson's Wine Course*, 2nd ed. New York: Abbeville, 2003.

--------. *Tasting Pleasure: Confessions of a Wine Lover*. New York: Viking, 1997.

--------. *Vines, Grapes and Wines: The Wine Drinker's Guide to Grape Varieties*, rev. ed. London: Mitchell Beazley, 1992.

Robinson, Jancis, ed. *The Oxford Companion to Wine*, 3rd ed. Oxford: Oxford University, 2006.

Roby, Norman S., and Charles E. Olken. *The Connoisseurs' Handbook of the Wines of California and the Pacific Northwest*, 4th ed. New York: Knopf, 1999.

Rogov, Daniel. *Rogov's Guide to Israeli Wines: 2008*. New Milford CT: Toby, 2008.

Rosen, Jennifer "Chotzi". *The Cork Jester's Guide to Wine: An Entertaining Companion to Tasting It, Ordering It, and Enjoying It*. Cincinnati: Clerisy, 2006.

--------. *Waiter, There's a Horse in My Wine*. Denver: Dauphin, 2004.

Rowe, David. *Collins Gem Wine Dictionary*. Glascow: HarperCollins, 2000.

Saker, John. *How To Drink a Glass of Wine*. Wellington: Awa, 2005.

Sbrocco, Leslie. *Wine for Women*. New York: William Morrow, 2003.

Schuster, Michael. *The Simon & Schuster Beginner's Guide to Understanding Wine*. New York: Simon & Schuster, 1989.

Sendzik, Walter, and Christopher Waters. *Vines: Buyer's Guide to Canadian Wine*, 2nd ed. North Vancouver: Whitecap, 2002.

Sherman, Chris. *The Buzz on Wine*. New York: Lebhar-Friedman, 2000.

Simon, Alain. *How to Taste and Recognise Single Grape Wines*. Paris: Fitway, 2004.

Sims, Fiona. *Guide to Wine: An Introduction for Beginners*. Bath UK: Parragon, 2003.

Skinner, Matt. *The Juice 2007: 100 Wines You Should be Drinking*. London: Mitchell Beazley, 2006.

--------. *Thirsty Work: Love Wine Drink Better*. London: Octopus, 2005.

Smith, Barry C. "Is a Sip Worth a Thousand Words?" *The World of Fine Wine*. No. 21, 2008; 114-119.

Smith, Brian H. *The Sommelier's Guide to Wine: A Primer for Selecting, Serving & Savoring Wine*. New York: Black Dog & Leventhal, 2003.

Sommers, Brian J. The *Geography of Wine: How Landscapes, Cultures, Terroir and the Weather Make a Good Drop*. New York: Penguin, 2008

Spence, Godfrey. *The Port Companion: A Connoisseur's Guide*. New York: Macmillan, 1997.

--------. *White Wine Companion*. Buffalo NY: Firefly, 1998.

Steinberger, Mike. "Cherries, Berries, Asphalt, and Jam," *Slate*, June 15, 2007.

Stevenson, Tom. *The Millennium Champagne & Sparkling Wine Guide*. London: DK, 1998.

--------. *Tom Stevenson's Champagne & Sparkling Wine Guide*, 4th ed. South San Francisco: Wine Appreciation Guild, 2002.

--------. *Wine Report 2009*. New York: DK, 2008.

St. Pierre, Brian. *Wine Deck*. San Francisco: Chronicle, 2003.

Suckling, James. *Vintage Port: The Wine Spectator's Ultimate Guide for Consumers, Collectors and Investors*. San Francisco: Wine Spectator, 1990.

Sutcliffe, Serena. *Champagne: The History and Character of the World's Most Celebrated Wine*. London: Mitchell Beazley, 1988.

--------. *The Wine Handbook: For the Discriminating Wine Lover*. New York: Fireside, 1982.

--------. *The Wine Access Buyer's Guide: The World's Best Wines and Where to Find Them*. New York: Sterling, 2006.

Teague, Lettie. *Educating Peter: How I Taught a Famous Movie Critic the Difference Between Cabernet and Merlot, or How Anybody Can Become an (Almost) Instant Wine Expert*. New York: Scribner, 2007.

Terni, Antonio, ed. *Guide to South American Vineyards, Wineries & Wines*. Buenos Aires: Austral Spectator, 2003.

Thompson, Bob. *Notes on a California Cellarbook: Reflections on Memorable Wines*. New York: WilliamMorrow, 1988.

Tross-Deamer, Elizabeth. *Wine for the Super Beginner*. Mercer Island WA: ETD, 1990.

Waller, James. *Drink´·ol·o·gy Wine: A Guide to the Grape*. New York: Stewart, Tabori & Chang, 2005.

Walton, Stuart. *The Complete Guide to Wine and Wine Drinking*. London: Southwater, 2004.

Wasserman, Sheldon and Pauline. *Sparkling Wine*. Piscataway NJ: New Century, 1984.

Waugh, Alec. *In Praise of Wine and Certain Noble Spirits*. New York: Morrow, 1959.

Waugh, Auberon. *Waugh on Wine*. London: Fourth Estate, 1986.

Wesson, Joshua. *Wine & Food: A New Look at Flavor*. New York: Free, 2007.

Williams, Vic. *The Penguin New Zealand Wine Guide 2003*. Auckland: Penguin, 2003.

Williamson, Philip, and David Moore. *Wine Behind the Label 2008: The Ultimate Guide to the World's Leading Wine Providers and their Wine*. London: BTL, 2007.

Witte, Bert. *You're a Real Wine Lover When ...* South San Francisco: Wine Appreciation Guild, 2002.

Woods, Simon. *I Don't Know Much About Wine, But I Know What I Like*. London: Mitchell Beazley, 2003.

Ziraldo, Donald, and Karl Kaiser. *Icewine: Extreme Winemaking*. Toronto: Key Porter, 2007.

Zyl, Philip van, ed. *John Platter South African Wines 2007*. Hermanus, South Africa: JohnPlatter, 2006.

Special* Works
*Exceptional other resources.

Ackerman, Diane. *A Natural History of the Senses*. New York: Random House, 1990.

Ackerman, Jennifer. *Sex Sleep Eat Drink Dream: A Day in the Life of Your Body*. New York: Houghton Mifflin, 2007.

Allen, Stewart Lee. *In the Devil's Garden: A Sinful History of Forbidden Food*. New York: Ballantine, 2002.

Baroshuk, Linda, and Jacques Pépin. "An education in taste: A conversation with Linda Bartoshuk, an expert on the physiology of taste, and Jacques Pépin, celebrity chef and cookbook author, explores the many facets of taste." *Yale Medicine*. Spring 1999.

Civille, Gail Lance and Brenda G. Lyon, eds. *Aroma and Flavor Lexicon for Sensory Evaluation: Terms, Definitions, References and Examples*. West Conshohocken PA: American Society for Testing and Materials (ASTM), 1996.

Gawel, Richard. "Challenging the Tongue Taste Map." *www.aromadictionary.com* [November 1, 2006].

Gilbert, Avery. *What the Nose Knows: The Science of Scent in Everyday Life*. New York: Crown 2008.

Glaser, Gabrielle. *The Nose: A Profile of Sex, Beauty, and Survival*. New York: Atria, 2002.

Herz, Rachel. *The Scent of Desire*. New York: HarperCollins, 2007.

Masumoto, David Mas. *Four Seasons in Five Senses: Things Worth Savoring*. New York: Norton, 2003.

Máté, Ferenc. *A Vineyard in Tuscany: a wine lover's dream*. New York: Norton, 2007.

McGee, Harold. *On Food and Cooking: The Science and Lore of the Kitchen*, rev. ed. New York: Scribner, 2004.

Morrot, Gil, Frédéric Brochet and Denis Dubourdieu. "The Colors of Odors," *Brain and Language*, 10. no. 2: 309-320.

Pelletier, Cathy. "Beyond the Tongue Map: Evaluating Taste and Smell Perception." *ASHA Leader*. October 22, 2002.

Shepherd, Gordon M. "Smell images and flavour system in the human brain." *Nature*. November 15, 2006, 316-321.

This, Hervé. *Kitchen Mysteries: Revealing the Science of Cooking*. New York: Columbia University, 2007.

----------. *Molecular Gastronomy: Exploring the Science of Flavor*. New York: Columbia University, 2006.

Turin, Luca. *The Secret of Scent: Adventures in Perfume and the Science of Smell*. New York: HarperCollins, 2006.

Wallenstein, Gene. *The Pleasure Instinct*. Hoboken NJ: Wiley, 2009.

Periodicals

Arizona Republic
Art of Eating
Better Homes & Gardens
Bon Appétit
Boston Globe
Boston Phoenix
Canadian Business
Chicago Tribune
color and aroma
Connoisseur's Guide to
   California Wine
Contra Costa Times
Cuisine
Cuizine
Daily Telegraph
Dan Berger's Vintage
   Experience
Decanter
Detroit Free Press
Detroit News
Donna Hay
Drinks
East Valley Tribune
Edinburgh Evening News
Eurovin News
Fine Champagne
Fine Wine
Fogwell's Guides
Food and Drink Weekly
Food & Wine
Forbes
Friends of Wine

Gambero Rosso
Gilbert & Gaillard Wine
Gloucester Daily Times
Gourmet
Gourmet Traveller Wine
Guardian
Home Winemaster
Houston Chronicle
Imbibe
Independent
Intermezzo
International Wine
   Cellar
Just Drinks
London Evening Standard
London Times
Los Angeles Times
Manchester Guardian
Market Watch
Mercury News
Miami Herald
Monterey Herald
Nashville City Paper
Nation's Restaurant
   News
Nature
New Scientist
New Statesman
New York
New York Inquirer
New York Post
New York Times

Oregonian
Oregon Wine Press
Quarterly Review of
   Wines
Pittsburgh Tribune-Review
Portland Press Herald
President's Choice
Restaurants & Institutions
San Antonio Express-News
San Francisco Chronicle
Santa Cruz Sentinel
Sauce
Saveur
Seattle Post-Intelligencer
Seattle Times
Smart Wine
Sommelier International
Sommelier Journal
Sonoma Valley
Spokane Spokesman Review
Star-Gazette
Statesman Journal
St. Petersburg Times
Sunday Times
Sunset
Swirl Wine News
Sydney Morning Herald
Tastings
Tidings
Time-Picayune
Toronto Star
Touring & Tasting

USA Today
U.S. News & World Report
Wall Street Journal
Washington CEO
Wine
Wine Access
Wine Advocate
Wine & Dine
Wine & Spirits
Wine & Vines
Wine Business Monthly
Wine Country Cuisine
Wine Country Living
Wine Enthusiast
Wine Institute
Wine Maker
Wine News
Wine Pocket List
Wine Press Northwest
WineS
Wines
Wine Spectator
WineState
Wine X
World of Fine Wine

Websites and Blogsites

aboutwines.com
affairsofthevine.com
aiwf.org
alcoholicreviews.com
allieddomecq.com
americansommelier.org
americanwinesociety.org
andys-scribblings.co.uk
azcentral.com
aoweb.com
aromadictionary.com
auswine.com.au
awineryreview.com
basicjuice.blogs.com
bbr.com
bcawa.ca
beekmanwine.com
bestcellars.com
beveragebusiness.com

beverageworld.com
bipin.com
blmwine.com
bluewine.com
bobcampbell.com.nz
Bordeaux.com
boston.com
brentwoodwine.com
britannica.com
brownderby.com
bu.edu/lifelong/wine
burgundy-report.com
burghound.com
callawaycoastal.com
canadianbusiness.com
celebrationcellars.com
cellarbration.com
cellartastings.com/en/wine
champagne-online.net

cheapwinereviews.com
cheftalkcafe.com
chiantinet.com
chiantinet.it
chocolateloveswine.com
ciachef.edu
citypages.com
city.reuters.com
clifty.com/wine
clive-coates.com
cockburns-usa.com
colorandaroma.com
completewinegeek.com
copia.org
corksavvy.com
courtofmastersommeliers.org
creativeloafing.com
cressis.com
ctwineclub.com

cuisine.co.nz
cultureandwine.
   blogspot.com
damngoodwine.com
decanter.com
delongwine.com
detnews.com
deutschweine.de
drink-pink.com
drvino.com
duboeuf.com
duerowines.com
eastvalleytribune.com
edhwm.com
egullet.com
elitewine.com
encyclowine.org
enologix.com
enologyinternational.com

epicurious.com
erobertparker.com
ewineasia.com
ewineplanet.com
fermentation.typepad.com
finewinecentral.
    blogspot.com
finewinediary.com
finewinemag.com
finewinepress.com
fizzbuzz.com
flavornet.com
flavourpress.co.uk
flavurence.com
flicksforfun.com
fogwells.com
foodandwine.com
foodandwineaccess.com
forbes.com
forkncork.com
frenchculinary.com
frenchways.com
frenchwineexplorers.com
frugal-wine.com
funwithwine.com
gallosonoma.com
gamberorosso.it
gangofpour.com
geerwade.com
geocities.com
gilroydispatch.com
goodgrape.typepad.com
grape.org
grapeescape.co.uk
guamdiner.com
guardian.co.uk
gust-aroma.com
harpers-wine.com
hellerestate.com
hillsboroughwine.com
homewinemaker.com
hospicedurhone.org
houstonchronicle.com
ifs.tu-darmstadt.de
ifwtwa.org
ihc.ca/wine
imperator-wine.de
inniskillin.com
internetwineguide.com
internationalwinecellar.com
intowine.com
itre.cis.upenn.edu/~mly/
    languagelog
ivenus.com
i-winereview.com
jacobscreek.com.au
jancisrobinson.com
just-drinks.com
kalincellars.com
kamiljuices.com
kj.com

klwine.com
languagehat.com
learnaboutwine.com
learnwine.com
learn2.com
leskincaid.com
lewrockwell.com
mainecoastnow.com
makescentsofwine.com
manchesteronline.co.uk
manischewitzwine.com
masters-of-wine.org
mastersommeliers.org
memphisflyer.com
mercurynews.com
metaphor.uj.es
metawines.com
miami.com
montereyherald.com
mynrma.com.au
my-wine.blogspot.com
napawinetrader.com/blog
nature.com
nataliemaclean.com
natdecants.com
newhousenews.com
newscientist.com
ninemsn.com.au/
    gourmettraveller
nola.com
nomerlot.com
novusvinum.com
nyinquirer.com
nysaes.cornell.edu
nzwine.co.nz
observer.guardian.co.uk
oddbins.com
onwine.com.au
oregonlive.com
oregonwines.com
oxfordwineroom.com
ozclarke.com
pittsburghlive.com
platteronline.com
platterwineguide.com
popswine.com
portugal-info.net
pressherald.com
princeofpinot.com
punch.co.uk
purists.com
qitaly.it
ranchozabaco.com
rarewineco.com
rickspicks.com
ronnweigand.com
ryerson.ca/~dtudor/
    wine
sallys-place.com
santacruzsentinel.com
savoreachglass.com

sbwines.com
scotsman.com
scrugy.com
seattletimes.com
sensoryspectrum.com
seriouseats.com
sfgate.com
shpl.org/winelib
skurnikwines.com
slate.msn.com
slowfood.com
smh.com.au
sommelierjournal.com
sonomalibrary.com/wine
snooth.com
spittoon.biz
stargazettenews.com
statesmanjournal.com
store.morrellwine.com
straight.com
stratsplace.com
stratsplace.com/hawkins/
    winetaste
stratsplace.com/rogov
stratsplace.com/wine
stltoday.com
superplonk.com
s-wine.com/swine2
sydneymorningherald.com
tablewine.com
taproom.com
tasquacellars.com.au
taste-in.com
tasteoftx.com
tastersguild.com
tastersguildny.com
tasting-australia.com.au
tastings.com
tasting-wine.com
telegraph.co.uk
terroir-france.com
theage.com.au
thejosephreport.com
thenoseofwine.com
thephoenix.com
thepour.blogs.nytimes.com
thestar.com
theunion.com
thewinedoctor.com
thewinedudes.com
thewinekey.com
thewineman.com
thewineportal.com
thewineroom.com
tidingsmag.com
timeforwine.com
tizwine.com
tonyaspler.com
torbwine.com
travelenvoy.com
tropix.net/wine

turningleaf.com
tv.winelibrary.com
ukwinereport.com
usatoday.com
valleyvineyards.com
vinbladet.dk
vinchotzi.com
vines.org
vino.com
vinocellar.com
vinography.com
vinsouth.com
vine2wine.com
vineswinger.com
vintagecellars.com.au
vintageschool.com
virginwines.com
washingtonceo.com
washingtonpost.com
washingtonstate.
    wineclub.com
wein-plus.com
wholefoodsmarket.com
wikipedia.org
windowswineschool.com
wine.com
wine.co.za
wine.about.com
wineaccess.com
wineaccess.com/expert/
    tanzer
wineaccess.com/expert/
    connoisseurs/about
wineandhospitality
    network.com
wineadvocate.com
wineangels.com
wineanorak.com
wineappreciation.com
winebarrels.com
wine.blogs.com/winewhys
wine-by-benito.blogspot.com
winebork.com
winebrats.org
winebroker.com
winebusiness.com
winecask.blogspot.com
winecast.net
winecrimes.com
wineeducation.com
wineeducators.com
wineenthusiast.com
winefornewbies.com
wine.gurus.com
winehorizon.com
wineinstitute.org
wineint.com
wineintelligence.com
wine-journal.com
winelabels.org
winelearningcenter.com

winelibrary.com
winelibrarytv.com
wine-lines.com
winelove.org
wineloverspage.com
wineloverspage.com/
    randysworld
winemafia.net
winemag.com
winemag.co.za
winemakermag.com
winemakersemporium.com
winematch.com
winemega.com
winemessenger.com
winenews.it
wineoffensive.com/blog
wineonline.ca
wineonline.ie

wineonline.net
wineonline.co.uk
wineontheweb.com
wineout.com
wine-pages.com
wine-people.com
wineperspective.com
winepocketlist.com
wineprofessor.com
winepros.com.au
winepros.org
winerant.com
winereviewonline.com
wineroom.com
wines.com
winesandvines.com
wine-school.com
winesenz.co.nz
wine-searcher.com

wineserver.ucdavis.edu
wset.co.uk
winesimple.com
wine-site.com
wineskinny.com
wineskool.com
winesocieties.com
winespeak.com
winespectator.com
winespectatorschool.com
winestate.com.au
winetasting.com
winetastingguide.com
winetech.com
wine-tours-france.com
wine.tradeworlds.com
winetrail.com
winetutors.co.uk
wineweb.com

winewriters.org
winewriting.com
winexwired.com
winezap.com
winezone.com.au
winezone.it
wired.com
wordlab.com
worldcooperage.com
worldsofwine.com
wset.co.uk
yakshaya.com
zinfandel.org

People*
*Other than the authors listed above.

Geoff Adams
Nick Alabaster
Adrienne Asher-Gepford
Eric Asimov
Christine Austin
Kent Bach
Mitzi Baker
Jan Baldwin
Robert Lawrence Balzer
John Barker
Andrew Barr
Andrew Barrow
Richard Baudains
James Beard
Dan Berger
Karen Berman
Sally Bernstein
Sandy Block
Bob Blumer
Brenda Boblitt
Michael Bonadies
David Borzo
Gerald Boyd
George H. Boynton
Gail Bradney
Steve Broadhead
Frédéric Brochet
Stephen Brook
Gary Brown
Christopher Buckley
Kathleen Buckley
Edwin Bühler
Chandler Burr
Rod Byers
Rosario Caballero

Salvatore Calabrese
Tom Cannavan
Randy Caparoso
Tina Caputo
John Geoffrey Carr
Bruce Cass
Toby Cecchini
Anne Chalfant
Jules Chauvet
Chelle Christy
Joan Cirillo
Bill Clapperton
Jon Cohen
Kate Colemen
Brian Cooper
David Cox
Heidi Haughy Cusick
Joe Czerwinski
Roald Dahl
Bill Daley
Robert Daley
Laurie Daniel
Wilson Daniels
David Darlington
Marlena de Blasi
Teresa de Cuadra
Karen De Coster
Roy Andries de Groot
Mike DeNike
David Derbyshire
Dave De Simone
Thierry Dessauve
Marq de Villiers
Betsy Devine
João Roque Dias

Marc Dornan
Denis Dubourdieu
David Downie
Michael Durphy
Taylor Eason
Richard Eccleston
Manfred Eggers
Richard Ehrlich
Eric Englund
Florence Fabricant
S.S. Fair
Giles Fallowfield
Patrick W. Fegan
Kate Fiduccia
Martin Field
Alice S. Fiering
Edward Finstein
Janet Fletcher
Colin Ford
Peter Forrestal
Christopher Foulkes
Aaron M. Frank
Eunice Fried
Doug Frost
Griffith Frost
Janice Fuhrman
Alan Fulmer
Betty Fussell
Rusty Gaffney
Fred Galacar
Robin Garr
John Gauntner
Richard Geoffroy
David Gibbons
Caroline Gilby

Ben Giliberti
Matt Girard
Gillian Glover
Willie Gluckstern
Nia Godsmark
Adam Gopnik
Jurgen Gothe
Constance Gray
W. Blake Gray
Michael Green
Gail Greene
Lauriann Greene
John Griffin
Lisa Shara Hall
Sally Hammond
Gilian Handelman
Tom Hansen
Anthony Hanson
Jim Harrison
Nathaniel Hawthorne
James Hayes
Mervyn L. Hecht
Steve Heimoff
Tony Hendra
Geoff Henricks
Amanda Hesser
Mort Hochstein
Brian Hoffer
David Holzganz
Anthony Hopkins
Maria Ibald
Jeff Isbrandtsen
Thor Iverson
Harry Ives
Tim James

Mark Johnson
Linda Johnson-Bell
N.P. Jolly
Richard Jones
Chris Kassel
John Keats
Carole Kelleher
Christina Kelly
Leslie Kelly
Steve Kirwan
Chris Kissack
Linda Kulman
Malcolm Kushner
Joyce LaFray
Adair Lara
Monica Larner
Greg Laslo
Matthew Latkiewicz
Harry Lawless
James Lawther
Cliff & Cheryl Lede
Maurice P. Lee
Terry Lee
Allison Levine
Rick Lewis
Mark Liberman
Alexis Lichine
Audra Ligumsky
August Lind
Angela Lloyd
Michael Lonsford
Jordan Mackay
Jane MacQuitty
Norman Mailer
Michal Majchrzak
Per-Henrik Mansson
Kim Marcus
Thomas E. Maresca
Dewey Markham
Peter Marks
Don & Betty Martin
Andrew Masterson
Thomas Matthews
Robert Mayfield
Peter Mayle
Jeanne McGill
Dave McIntyre
Malcolm McLaren
Tom McNamee
James McQuillen
Stephen Meuse
Fern Michaels
Bryan Miller
Henry Miller
Warren Miller
Robert D. Millman
James Molesworth
H. Montanile
Victoria Moore
Dara Moskowitz
G.H. Mowbray

Rebecca Murray
Stephen Mutkoski
Richard Nalley
Charles Neal
Richard Neill
William Nesto
William Neuman
Remington Noble
Leslie Norris
Zena Olijnyk
Steven Olson
Richard O'Neill
Roger Ormon
P.J. O'Rourke
Dennis Overstreet
Giampoalo Pacini
Ronald S. Page
Jim Painter
Michael Palij
Alexander J. Pandell
David Parker
Nick Passmore
Tim Patterson
Helen Pearson
Neil Pendock
David Peppercorn
Richard G. Peterson
François Peyraud
Jim Pfiffer
Andrew Plotkin
Mark Steven Pope
Jeni Port
Kimberley Porteous
Raymond Postgate
Jacqueline L. Quillen
John Radford
Tim Radford
Dante Ramos
James Randerson
Johnathan Ray
Stephen Reiss
Norman Remington
Jason Rennie
Jonathan Reynolds
Michelle Richmond
Maria Polushkin Robbins
Anthony Rose
Bob Ross
Jordan Ross
Peter Ruhrberg
Erica Sagon
E. Sammlung
Bruce Sanderson
Michael Schachner
Anne Schamberg
Robert Schoolsky
Frank Schoonmaker
John Schreiner
Roger Scruton
Dru Sefton
Raquel Segovia

William J. Sharp
David Shaw
Lisa Shea
Randy Sheahan
Felicia Sherbert
Peter M.F. Sichel
Sandra Silfven
Andre Simon
Patrick & Dee Sindt
Clark Smith
William Sokolin
Jean-Pierre Sollin
Ralph Steadman
Harvey Steiman
Joel Stein
Michael Stephenson
Jessica Stillman
Gordon Stimmell
John Stimpfig
Paul Strang
Art & Betsy Stratemeyer
Ernesto Suárez-Toste
Laurel Sumner
Jock Sutherland
Peter Svans
Richard Swearinger
Fred Tasker
Jennifer Taylor
Gerard Ternois
Alan Thomas
Sally Thomason
Ch'ng Poh Tiong
Darnya Tobey
Erika Trafton
Calvin Trillin
Dean Tudor
James Turnbull
Willy Van Cammeren
Tim Vandergrift
Victor Van Keuren
John Vankat
Richard P. Vine
S. Irene Virbila
Roger Voss
Ann & Larry Walker
John F. Walker
Shelagh Wallace
Joseph Ward
Harry Waugh
Ronn Weigand
Christopher Weir
Ernie Whalley
Paul White
Tim White
Robert Whitley
Glenn Whitney
Leslie Williams
Daniel M. Winger
Brendan Wood
Sean Wood
Heidi Yorkshire

Stephen Yafa
Man Young
H.W. Yoxall
Amy Zavatto

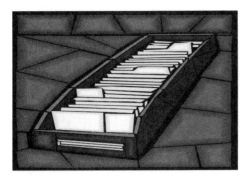

There is more rubbish talked about wine and wine tasting than anything else.
André Launay

I was convinced forty years ago and the conviction remains to this day—that in wine tasting and wine talk there is an enormous amount of humbug.
Thomas George Shaw

VIII. Keyword Index

No respectable nonfiction book should be published without a decent index that directs readers to pages where they can find popular entries of interest. So be it.

(The end. Whew!)